The Vintage Motorcyclists' Workshop

by Radco

ISBN 0 85429 472 4

A FOULIS Motorcycling Book

First published October 1986,
reprinted March 1987,
September 1987 and June 1991

Published by:
Haynes Publishing Group
Sparkford, Nr. Yeovil, Somerset
BA22 7JJ, England

Haynes Publications Inc.
861 Lawrence Drive, Newbury Park,
California 91320, USA

British Library Cataloguing in Publication Data
RADCO
The vintage motorcyclists' workshop.
1. Motorcycles—Maintenance and repair
—Amateurs' manuals
1. Title
629.28'775
ISBN 0-85429-472-4

Library of Congress catalog card number
86-82145

Editor: Jeff Clew
Page layout: Mike King
Printed in England by J.H. Haynes & Co. Ltd.

Dedication

John Masterman's workshop was sometimes a scooped-out sand dune in the desert or the shade of a tree in Italy, Africa or Turkey. Yet somehow he kept "Old Faithful", his venerable 588 cc ohv Norton, going for over half a million miles of globe-trotting.
His incredibly scruffy machine bore evidence of "temporary" repairs (eg. a screw-jack wedged between the cylinder head and frame tube) for over fifty years. This book is dedicated to the memory of John and "Old Faithful", two of England's true gentlemen — it must not be forgotten that motorcycles are meant to be ridden.

Contents

"They say 'the war may last three years or more ..." were Graham Walker's words on 20th September 1939, when this splendid pen-and-ink drawing appeared in "The Green 'Un". Note the black-out precautions, gas mask and ARP sign on the door. Alas, many enthusiasts were never to see their workshops again ...

Introduction

SOME books on vehicle restoration commence with tempting layout drawings of "The Ideal Workshop". This is usually a double-glazed, centrally-heated edifice complete with brazing hearth and tiled inspection pit. This book contains no such illustration.

The author, whilst an engineer by profession, is a restorer of thirty five years experience and as such recognises that the average motorcyclist has to make do with what he has got. This usually means an ordinary garage, garden shed or spare bedroom

Obviously some tools are needed to undertake a rebuild and it is anticipated that the reader will probably possess such essentials as a vice and spanners. By attempting most aspects of the renovation himself, the restorer will be less dependent on outside suppliers and will thus save money. He will also gain much pleasure and experience.

Some of the best restorations are done in tiny workshops with perhaps the aid of an ancient lathe (man's most useful machine tool!) and a few hand tools. The writer's first rebuild project was completed in a wooden hen shed by the light of acetylene gas — there was no electricity supply so all holes were drilled by hand and all machining carried out on a tiny treadle-lathe!

This is a book about practical restoration work. It does not pretend to be a reference source on general workshop practice, although the reader will find many hints and tips on such matters. Every aspect of the work described herein has been carried out at some time or other by the writer, so the book is based on first-hand experience. Some processes, such as saddlery and wheelbuilding, had to be learned the hard way — there were no library books to consult, or experts willing to pass on their skills.

A cautionary note for beginners. Patience is a quality the budding restorer will need in abundance! There are no short cuts. Restoration work can be tedious, back-breaking and expensive at times. For reasons such as these, many bikes remain in pieces once the initial enthusiasm has worn off. The beginner is well advised to select a simple machine for his first rebuild and steer clear of exotica. Matchless Silver Hawks, early camshaft Square Fours, Mk 8 KTT Velocettes and Plus 90 Douglases are all delightful machines in their own way but are best left to the expert restorer.

Fortunately some restorers stay the course to sample the pleasures of riding a veteran, vintage, or classic motorcycle in the company of like souls. The *Vintage Motor Cycle Club* can now boast of some 5,000 members, many of whom have rebuilt several machines. All the hard work involved in transforming a useless conglomeration of scrap metal into a living showpiece will be forgotten when the bike is taken out for a trial spin.

RADCO
1985

Acknowledgements

FIRST and foremost my thanks are due to Ian Young, Editor of the Official Journal of the *Vintage Motor Cycle Club,* for his encouragement throughout my long-running *Vintage Workshop* series in the magazine. Members seemed to like the meanderings of *Radco,* many suggesting that the information should be collated in book form some day. It was Jeff Clew who was to bring the idea into fruition, providing much professional advice throughout the preparation of the manuscript.

Without whose help this work would not have been possible is a well-worn expression, but truly applicable to Richard Platt, VMCC Photographic Librarian. As always, nothing was too much trouble for Richard. Les Taverner, whose own instructive articles appeared in the *VMCC Journal,* was kind enough to allow me to use excerpts from his writings, and also provide photos to accompany them. Help was also generously given by Barry Jones of the Panther Owners' Club, Stan Thorpe of the Morgan Three Wheeler Club, and Tom Wess of the Scott Owners Club.

Of the firms who were kind enough to give permission for their material to be used, special mention must be made of Triumph Motorcycles (Coventry) Ltd and L.F. Harris (Rushden) Ltd. Other companies deserving my thanks are TRW Valves Ltd., Thomas Mercer Ltd., Naerok Ltd., Wipac Ltd., I.M.I.-Amal Ltd., Hepworth & Grandage Ltd., L.S.Starrett & Co. Ltd., James Niell Tools of Sheffield, Carl Zeiss Jena Ltd., A.E. Autoparts, and also Stan Greenway of Dynic Sales.

Last but not least, my appreciation also goes to all those private enthusiasts and friends who have either lent workshop manuals or provided some vital shred of information.

RADCO

Chapter 1

Screwthreads For The Vintagent

Cycle threads and other screwforms. Taps, dies, chasers, with random notes on materials for the restorer. Heat treatment explained.

WHEN dismantling a motorcycle prior to restoration always keep nuts, bolts and other fasteners for future reference, no matter how rusty or damaged they might be. It helps to slip a bolt back in its rightful place so you know where it belongs, or failing that to label each special nut and bolt with its location on the machine. *Front wheel nut, LH side or gearbox mainshaft locking nut,* for example. Such items are easily lost and when you come to make a replacement you might wonder what size hexagons it had, or how many threads per inch, or whether it was hardened etc.

Motorcycle manufacturers followed the example of early bicycle makers in choosing weird and wonderful thread sizes for certain applications. Just to quote one example, most cycle and motorcycle crank cotters are threaded 17/64 in x 26 tpi. It is also hard to imagine why any designer would want to specify 7/32 in diameter screws when he had a choice of either 3/16 in or 1/4 in. Such *in-between sizes,* as engineers are apt to call them, crop up periodically on vintage machines so it's as well to be conversant with the various screwthread systems in use.

Cycle Engineers' Institute (CEI) thread.

Prior to 1902, when the CEI thread was formulated, cycle and motorcycle manufacturers used a motley variety of screwforms. Some makers stuck to the old Whitworth (BSW) system and those who imported their engines from France or Belgium adopted the metric system of the period. It is therefore possible on some pioneer motorcycles to find both metric and Imperial screw sizes. Other manufacturers could not make up their minds and instituted a thread form of their own.

It is generally assumed that all cycle threads are of 26 tpi (26 threads per inch). Whilst this is true of the common sizes, ie. 1/4 in diameter to 3/4 diameter, a glance at the tables will reveal the use of 40, 32, 24 and even 56 tpi threads. Indeed, 20 tpi is a pitch sometimes encountered, although when the CEI thread was superseded by the similar BSC (British Standard Cycle) thread, the use of the 20 tpi series was frowned upon.

CEI and BSC threaded screws were to all intents and purposes confined in their usage to the cycle and motorcycle industries, although the odd motor car manufacturer was known to slip one in when it suited his purpose. Cycle threads have two basic advantages over their Whitworth contemporaries; a fine pitch means that nuts are less likely to vibrate loose and the relatively large core diameter results in greater shear strength.

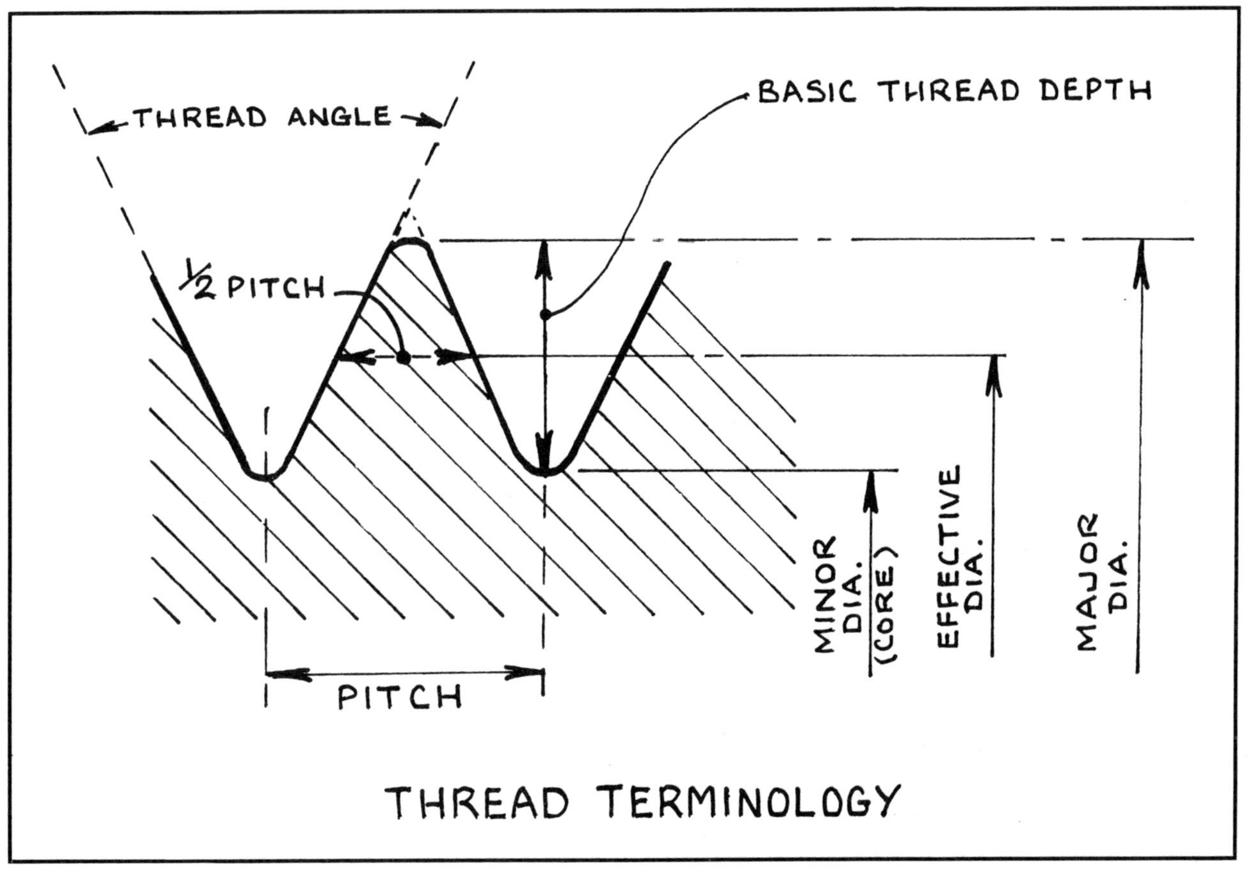

CYCLE ENGINEERS' INSTITUTE THREAD

60° ANGLE THREAD, ROUNDED AT TOP AND BOTTOM

DIA.	THREADS PER in.	WIRE GAUGE	CORE DIA.	APPLICATIONS
0·056	62	17	0.0388	SPOKES
0.064	62	16	0.0468	"
0.072	62	15	0.0598	"
0.080	62	14	0.0628	"
0.092	56	13	0.0729	"
0.104	44	12	0.0798	"
0.125	40	—	0.0984	SMALL SCREWS
0.154	40	—	0.1274	CHAIN COUPLINGS
0.175	32	—	0.1417	
0.1875	32	—	0.1542	CHAIN ADJUSTERS, MISC. SCREWS
0.250	26	—	0.2091	CRANK COTTERS
0.266	26	—	—	—
0.281	26	—	—	—
0.3125	26	—	0.2715	FRONT WHEEL SPINDLES, HEAD PINS, SADDLE STEM BOLTS ETC.
0.375	26	—	0.3341	REAR WHEEL SPINDLES.
0.5625	20	—	0.498	PEDAL PINS R.H AND L.H.
0.9675	30	—	0.932	STEERING COLUMNS
1.000	26	—	0.959	" "
1.290	24	—	1.2456	HUB LOCK-RINGS, L.H.
1.370	24	—	1.3256	HUB CHAIN WHEELS
1.4375	24	—	1.393	HUBS, L.H.
1.500	24	—	1.4556	CHAIN WHEELS

British Standard Cycle thread (BSC)

This thread is identical in thread form to the CEI system which it replaced. All taps and dies currently available conform to the BSC system although there is ever-increasing pressure on the few remaining British cycle manufacturers to adopt the metric system.

The reader would be well advised to purchase a set of cycle thread (BSC) taps and dies while they are still available. Generally such sets include the following sizes:-

1/4 in. x 26 tpi	(3 taps and one die)
5/16 in. x 26 tpi	(3 taps and one die)
3/18 in. x 26 tpi	(3 taps and one die)
7/16 in. x 26 tpi	(3 taps and one die)
1/2 in. x 26 tpi	(3 taps and one die)

Three taps for each diameter comprise a taper, second, and plug tap. At the time of writing most of the odd sizes are available, such as 1.290 x 24 tpi left hand (for sprocket locking rings), and certain 20 tpi tools. Obviously, with falling demand, this situation cannot continue indefinitely.

Spark plug threads

Recommended by the British Standards Institution for sparking plug threads, the following tables apply to most vintage motorcycles:-

SPARKING PLUG THREADS

THE STANDARD SPARKING PLUG THREAD ADOPTED BY MOST MOTORCYCLE MAKERS WAS IN ACCORDANCE WITH THE SYSTEME INTERNATIONAL (SI) EXCEPT THAT THE PITCH DIFFERS :-

14 mm PLUG THREAD = 1.25 mm PITCH
18 mm " " = 1.50 mm PITCH

PLUG SIZE	PITCH	FULL DIA.		EFFECTIVE DIA.		CORE DIA.	
		PLUG	TAPPED HOLE	PLUG	TAPPED HOLE	PLUG	TAPPED HOLE
14 mm	1.25	13.977	14.125	13.035 TO 13.165	13.188 TO 13.278	12.250	12.390
18 mm	1.50	17.950 TO 17.750	18.337 TO 18.162	16.976 TO 16.776	17.201 TO 17.026	15.839 TO 15.639	16.226 TO 16.051

(ALL DIMENSIONS IN mm)

NOTE :-
THE FOLLOWING SIZES ARE OCCASIONALLY ENCOUNTERED :
7/8 in AMERICAN THREAD (A.L.A.M.)
1/2 in GAS TAPER (LODGE TYPE AF)
12 mm, 10mm (LODGE TYPES C12/C10 CL10)
3/8 in x 24 TPI MODEL PLUGS

BRITISH STANDARD CYCLE THREAD

FORMERLY KNOWN AS THE CEI THREAD, THE FORM IS IDENTICAL (60° ANGLE)

DIA.	THREADS PER in.	PITCH	THREAD DEPTH	DIAMETERS FULL	EFFECTIVE	CORE
1/8	40	.025	.0133	.125	.1117	.0984
5/32	32	.03125	.0166	.1563	.1397	.1231
3/16	32	.03125	.0166	.1875	.1709	.1543
7/32	26	.03846	.0205	.2188	.1983	.1778
1/4	"	"	"	.250	.2295	.2090
9/32	"	"	"	.2813	.2608	.2403
5/16	"	"	"	.3125	.2920	.2715
3/8	"	"	"	.375	.3545	.3340
7/16	"	"	"	.4375	.4170	.3965
1/2	"	"	"	.500	.4795	.4590
9/16	"	"	"	.5625	.5420	.5215
5/8	"	"	"	.625	.6045	.5840
11/16	"	"	"	.6875	.6670	.6465
3/4	"	"	"	.750	.7295	.7090

SPECIAL SIZES

DIA.	THREADS PER in.	PITCH	APPLICATION
17/64	26	.03846	BICYCLE AND MOTOR CYCLE COTTERS
7/8	24	.04167	SMALL STEERING COLUMNS
31/32	30	.03333	STEERING COLUMNS (CYCLE)
1.000	24	.04167	" " "
1 1/8	26	.03846	STEERING COLUMNS (MOTOR CYCLE)
1.290	24 L.H.	.04167	REAR HUB/SPROCKET LOCK RINGS
1.370	24	.04167	BOTTOM BRACKETS L.H. AND R.H. THREAD
1.450	26	.03846	" " "
1 9/16	24 L.H.	.04167	SPROCKET CENTRES
1 5/8	24	.04167	" "

BSW THREAD THREAD ANGLE 55°

DIA. in	TPI	PITCH (in)	CORE (in)	TAPPING DRILL	CLEARANCE DRILL
3/16	24	.04167	.1341	3.7mm	4.9mm
7/32	24	.04167	.1654	4.5mm	5.7mm
1/4	20	.05000	.1860	5.1mm	6.5mm
5/16	18	.05556	.2413	6.5mm	8.1 mm
3/8	16	.0625	.2950	5/16 in	9.7mm
7/16	14	.07143	.3461	9.3mm	11.3mm
1/2	12	.08333	.3932	10.5mm	13.0mm
9/16	12	.08333	.4557	12.1mm	37/64 in
5/8	11	.09091	.5086	13.5mm	41/64 in
11/16	11	.09091	.5711	19/32 in	45/64 in
3/4	10	.1000	.6220	41/64 in	49/64 in
13/16	10	.1000	.6844	18 mm	53/64 in
7/8	9	.11111	.7328	19.25mm	57/64 in
1	8	.1250	.8400	22mm	1 1/64 in

TAPPING DRILLS FOR CYCLE THREAD

SIZE	T.P.I.	DIA.	TAPPING DRILLS SIZE	TAPPING DRILLS DIA.	
17 swg	62	.056	61	.0390	EARLY 'CUT' SPOKES (ie. NOT ROLLED)
16 "	62	.064	3/64 in	.0469	
15 "	62	.072	54	.0550	
14 "	62	.080	52	.0635	
13 "	56	.092	49	.0730	
12 "	44	.104	46	.0810	
1/8 in	40	.125	39	.0995	
.154 in	40	.154	30	.1285	
.175 in	32	.175	27	.1417	
3/16 in	32	.185	5/32 in	.1562	
1/4 in	26	.250	No.3	.2130	5.5mm
.266 in	26	.266	No.1	.2280	5.75mm
.281 in	26	.281	Letter D	.2460	6.25mm
5/16 in	26	.3125	" J	.2770	7.0mm
3/8 in	26	.375	" R	.3390	8.7mm
9/16 in	20	.562	33/64 in	.5156	
1 in	26	1.000	31/32 in	.9687	
1.290 in	24	1.290	1 1/4 in	1.2500	
1.370 in	24	1.370	1 21/64 in	1.3281	
1 7/16 in	24	1.4375	1 13/32 in	1.4062	
1 1/2 in	24	1.500	1 15/32 in	1.4687	

(5.5mm – 8.7mm: APPROX. METRIC EQUIVALENTS)

British Standard Whitworth (BSW)

BSW threads are likely to be found in crankcases and other aluminium components. Sometimes BSW nuts and bolts were used for minor applications such as mudguard stay bolts, saddle mountings and acetylene lamp fittings. It is not good practice to thread engine bolts BSW as the nuts are almost certain to vibrate loose.

Together with BSF components the Whitworth thread, first formulated in 1841 by Joseph Whitworth, is gradually being phased out. Non-preferred threads are what the suppliers call them these days and it is anticipated that the metric system will eventually apply to all threaded fasteners.

British Standard Fine (BSF)

First introduced in 1908, the BSF series of threads complements the BSW range and is used when finer pitches are required. Popular with motorcycle manufacturers.

It is worth noting that the 3/16 BSF size can be confused with 2BA, having the same diameter. The pitches are different and so screws are not interchangeable. This point is worth remembering when overhauling electrical fittings and accessories.

BSF THREAD. THREAD ANGLE 55°

DIA. in	TPI	PITCH(in)	CORE(in)	TAPPING DRILL	CLEARANCE DRILL
3/16	32	.03125	.1475	No. 23 OR 4mm	4.9mm
7/32	28	.03571	.1730	No. 15 OR 4.6mm	5.7mm
1/4	26	.03846	.2008	No. 4 OR 13/64in	6.5mm
9/32	26	.03846	.2320	B OR 6mm	7.5mm
5/16	22	.04545	.2543	G OR 6.8mm	8.1mm
3/8	20	.0500	.3110	O OR 8.3mm	9.7mm
7/16	18	.05556	.3663	3/8in	11.3mm
1/2	16	.0625	.4200	27/64in OR 11mm	13.0mm
9/16	16	.0625	.4825	31/64in OR 12.5mm	37/64in
5/8	14	.07143	.5336	35/64in OR 14mm	41/64in
11/16	14	.07143	.5961	39/64in OR 15.5mm	45/64in
3/4	12	.08333	.6432	21/32in OR 16.75mm	49/64in
13/16	12	.08333	.7057	23/32in OR 18.25mm	53/64in
7/8	11	.09091	.7586	25/32in OR 19.85mm	57/64in
1	10	.1000	.8720	57/64in OR 22.75mm	1 1/64in

British Association (BA) threads

Many small screws on motorcycle fittings are of BA type. This thread series has been with us for a long time — it was originally formulated in 1884 and standardised in 1903. Although screws as tiny as .013 in. in diameter (23 BA) were mentioned in the original tables it is most unlikely that these will be encountered. Most motorcyclists will be familiar with 2BA and 4BA screws, which are often found in electrical components. Some "tin" primary chaincases are fastened together with a myriad of small BA screws.

BA THREAD. THREAD ANGLE 47½°

BA No.	PITCH(in)	BASIC MAJOR DIA.(in)	CORE DIA.(in)	TAPPING DRILL	CLEARANCE DRILL
0	.0394	.2362	.1890	5.1mm	6.1mm
1	.0354	.2087	.1661	4.5mm	5.4mm
2	.0319	.1850	.1468	4.0mm	4.8mm
3	.0287	.1614	.1268	3.4mm	4.2mm
4	.0260	.1417	.1106	3.0mm	3.7mm
5	.0232	.1260	.0980	2.65mm	3.3mm
6	.0209	.1102	.0850	2.3mm	2.9mm
7	.0189	.0984	.0756	2.05mm	2.6mm
8	.0169	.0866	.0661	1.8mm	2.25mm

Notes:-
THE BA SERIES CONTINUES DOWN TO No.16 (.0266in) DIAMETER BUT IT IS UNLIKELY THE SMALLER SIZES WILL BE ENCOUNTERED.
No.'O'BA IS, FOR PRACTICAL PURPOSES, INTERCHANGEABLE WITH 6mm, ALTHOUGH THREAD ANGLES DIFFER.

Foreign threads

It is not generally realised that several metric thread systems existed at one time. Owners of early continental machines may find screws which do not correspond with the modern ISO metric system.

In the early days (1898) the Zurich Congress standardised a thread system which came to be known as the International System but this did not deter other countries from adopting their own variations on the theme. Thus we had the French Series Metric Thread, which had screws under 3

UNF (COMMON SIZES) THREAD ANGLE 60°

DIA. (in)	TPI	BASIC DIA. (in)	CORE (in)	TAPPING DRILL	CLEARANCE DRILL
No.8	36	.1640	.1299	9/64in	4.3mm
1/4	28	.2500	.2062	5.5mm	6.5mm
5/16	24	.3125	.2614	6.9mm	8.1mm
3/8	24	.3750	.3239	8.5mm	9.7mm
7/16	20	.4375	.3762	9.9mm	11.3mm
1/2	20	.5000	.4387	11.5mm	13mm
9/16	18	.5625	.4943	12.9mm	37/64in
5/8	18	.6250	.5568	14.5mm	41/64in
3/4	16	.7500	.6733	11/16in	49/64in
7/8	14	.8750	.7874	.804in	57/64in
1	12	1.0000	.8978	23.25mm	1 1/64in

mm of both 50 degrees and 60 degrees thread angle, Metric Fine Thread (German and Swiss) and French Fine Thread.

All this may sound confusing. However, suffice it to say that most of these strange threaded fasteners can be replaced with modern metric bolts. In some cases it may be necessary to run a tap through the original threaded object to accept a modern bolt. There may be a slight difference in pitches but this is of little consequence.

American threads

The National Coarse and National Fine series of threads were standardised in 1918 at a USA Congress Commission, so amalgamating the traditions of the American Society of Mechanical Engineers (ASME) and the Society of Automotive Engineers (SAE).

Today, American standard threads are called the UNC and UNF series (refer to table). They are rarely found on British or continental machines but are of course encountered on motorcycles made in the country of origin.

UNC (COMMON SIZES) THREAD ANGLE 60°

DIA. (in)	TPI	BASIC DIA. (in)	CORE (in)	TAPPING DRILL	CLEARANCE DRILL
No8	32	.1640	.1257	3.5mm	4.3mm
1/4	20	.2500	.1887	5.2mm	6.5mm
5/16	18	.3125	.2443	6.6mm	8.1mm
3/8	16	.3750	.2983	8.0mm	9.7mm
7/16	14	.4375	.3499	9.4mm	11.3mm
1/2	13	.5000	.4056	10.8mm	13mm
9/16	12	.5625	.4603	12.2mm	37/64 in
5/8	11	.6250	.5135	13.5mm	41/64 in
3/4	10	.7500	.6273	16.5mm	49/64 in
7/8	9	.8750	.7387	49/64 in	57/64 in
1	8	1.0000	.8466	22.5mm	1 1/64 in

Taps and dies, and how to use them

Sooner or later in the restoration programme there will be holes to tap out or rods to die down and it is appreciated that not all readers will be familiar with the use of simple hand threading tools. Excessive force is the beginner's bugbear — it's obvious that a tap must be extremely hard to cut into steel; unfortunately it is also very brittle. It takes a little while (and a few broken taps) to learn how much pressure to apply to a tap wrench.

As we have seen, a set of taps consists of a taper, second, and plug. Many fitters miss out the second stage. In order to tap a hole it is of course necessary to drill it out to the correct tapping size; reference to the thread tables will indicate drill sizes. To ensure centrality it is best to start off with a small drill and work up to the tapping size; the hole must finish up

A set of thread gauges will enable the restorer to determine the pitch of wierd and wonderful screwthreads beloved of motorcycle manufacturers in the vintage period! *(Photo: Neill Tools Ltd.)*

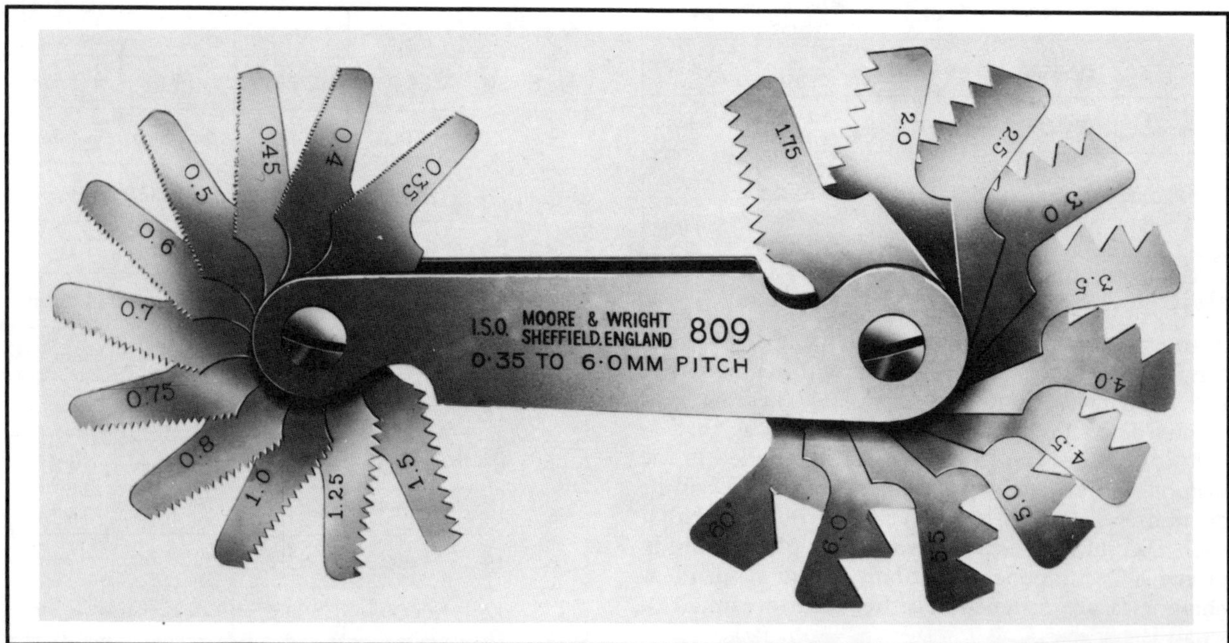

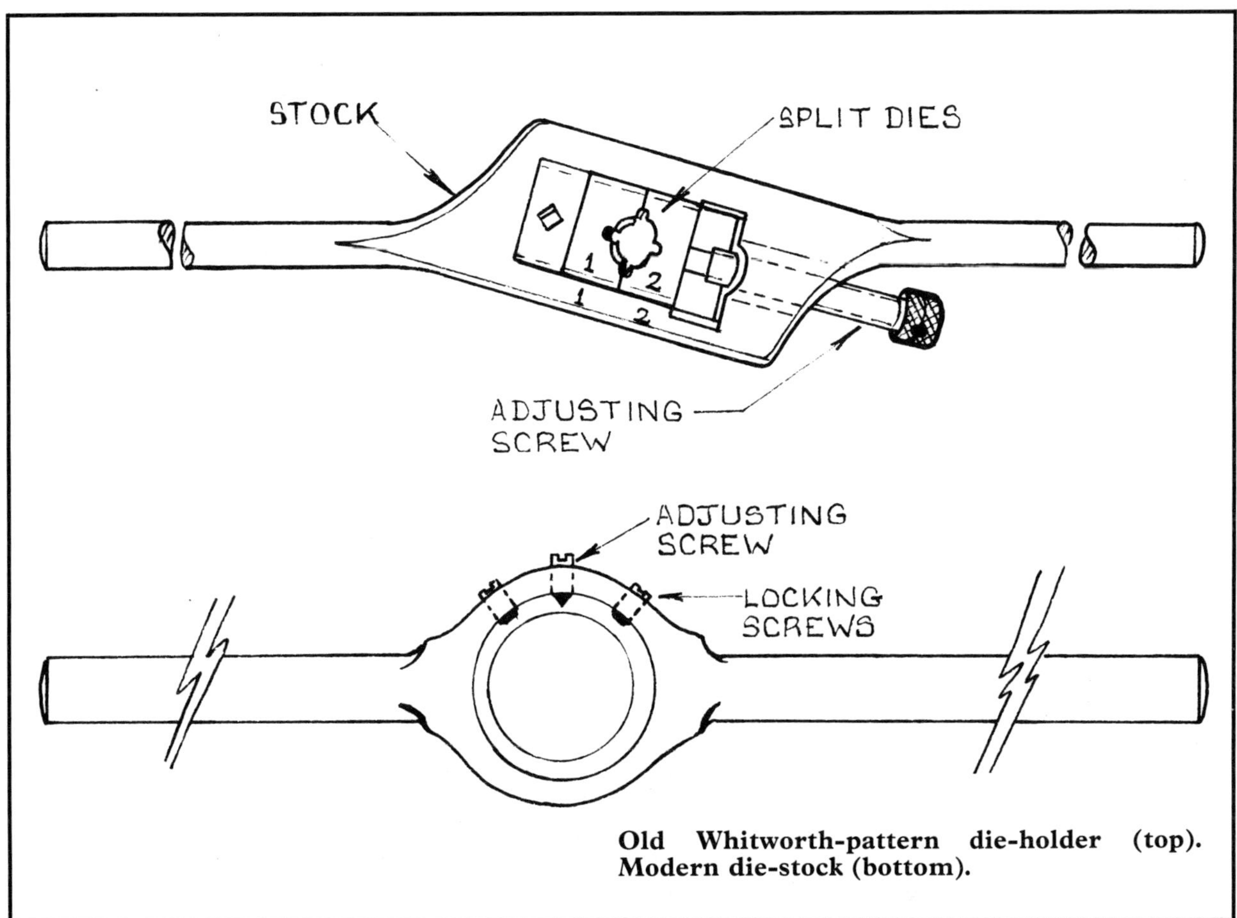

Old Whitworth-pattern die-holder (top). Modern die-stock (bottom).

at right angles to the surface — not always easy to achieve with an electric hand drill.

Commence tapping with the first, or taper, tap. Make sure the tap is quite vertical and apply some cutting oil; paraffin is fine for aluminium, cutting compound or engine oil for steel, and nothing at all when working on cast iron or brass. Enter the tap a couple of turns or so and then ease it back about half a turn. Throughout the operation the tap must be eased-back regularly — continuous rotation in the forward direction only will clog-up the flutes, resulting in a broken tap. Avoid undue pressure at all costs. Keep checking to see that the tap is going through square (verify with an engineers' set-square if necessary).

If you are dealing with a blind hole, the taper tap will soon bottom, in which case a second-tap will cut a little more thread, followed by the plug-tap. Swarf will collect in the bottom of the hole so this must be blown out at regular intervals (if you don't possess an airline, a good blower can be made out of an old horn bulb with an Amal carburettor needle-jet in the end).

It may be found that the resultant thread is rough, with perhaps two or three missing threads. This is usually caused by lack of lubricant, coupled with impatience, but may be due to a damaged tap.

Broken taps

Sooner or later you will find yourself with a tap which has sheared off flush with the surface. If you are lucky it might shift with light blows from a pin-punch, but this procedure is fraught with danger. An awful mess can be made of the surrounding metal, especially if it's an aluminium crankcase.

Soak the broken piece in easing oil. Make a small tool with two prongs on the end to engage the tap flutes — some insensitive individuals use a pair of dividers — and see if it moves. Try warming the surrounding metal. Unfortunately there is no magical solution to the catastrophe, although in certain circumstances it may be possible to heat and soften the fragment, whereupon it can be drilled and extracted in the normal way. Occasionally a hole drilled in from the opposite direction will allow access to the broken piece.

When all else fails, the spark erosion process will remove a broken tap or stud without affecting the surrounding area in any way. Well-equipped toolmaking establishments possess the necessary equipment and are quite used to correcting fitters' mistakes. The component in question must be completely stripped and cleaned before seeking professional help.

Broken studs

Studs, being relatively soft are much easier to deal with. Most engineering text books advise the use of stud extractors, those corkscrew-like devices with left-handed spiral flutes, to remove broken studs. Maybe writers of such literature have never worked on vintage motorcycles — when a cylinder head stud breaks, the remaining piece is firmly seized in its hole. Otherwise it would not have snapped in the first place! There may be those who disagree, but to this writer at least the use of slender (and brittle) stud extractors is courting disaster. Generally it is much safer to drill out the stud and re-tap the hole.

To drill through the centre of a broken stud requires skill and patience. Centre-pop the stud in its exact centre — examine the pop-mark with an eyeglass to be certain — and start drilling with a small drill (say, 3/32 in). When the drill has entered a fraction, check progress and budge the drill over a little if the hole is not truly central. Gradually open out the hole until the correct tapping-size is reached. If the hole has been accurately drilled, the tap will (if you're lucky) bring out the remaining thread in the form of a thin cylinder.

If the stud hole is damaged in any way, a stepped-stud can be inserted. The hole is tapped one size larger (eg 3/8 BSF instead of 5/16 BSF) and a double-diameter stud screwed tightly home. Mild steel is not good enough; all studs (stepped or otherwise) used on motorcycles should be made from high tensile material. Allen screws can be machined down and made into special studs, when required.

Sound studs should never be removed with pliers or mole-grips. The correct method is to thread two nuts on, lock them together, and withdraw the stud by applying spanner pressure to the lower nut. Stud replacement is, of course, a reversal of the procedure, adding a drop of Loctite *Stud-Lock* to the thread.

Dies

Most hand dies these days are of the round button type. Many years ago amateur mechanics and clockmakers used die-plates, or screw-plates, which consisted of a row of threaded holes in a flat hardened steel plate. Two handles were provided on the plate, enabling a range of threads from 1/8 in to 3/8 in diameter to be cut. More often than not the thread, which could be Whitworth or some other strange form, was ripped off, as this type of die was non-adjustable.

Another old type of stock and die, which still has its adherents, is the fully-adjustable Whitworth pattern. The stock is fitted with two-piece dies working in V-slides, the movable half being adjusted by means of a thumb screw. A big advantage with this type of die is that the thread can be cut in stages, unlike the modern button die which screws a rod in one or two passes.

A die is handled in similar fashion to a tap, insofar as it needs to be backed-off frequently to prevent clogging. Except on brass and cast-iron a lubricant (and plenty of it) must be used to ensure clean threads. This is most important in the case of stainless and silver steel, comparatively hard metals to deal with. Worn dies are a nuisance, requiring much effort and screeching like a stuck pig — either discard them or have the cutting edges reground by a toolmaker. Do not attempt to contract a die beyond its capabilities by forcing the adjustment screws too far in as it will in all probability break in two. A good die should see about four or five years intermittent use.

Nuts and bolts

Due to rising demand new cycle thread fasteners are now being made by specialists who advertise regularly in the monthly "classic" magazines. Usually finished in bright zinc there is no way of telling whether the material used is mild steel or high-tensile steel. The latter should always be used in areas of high stress, such as cylinder head or base mountings, selecting a steel grade of at least EN8. Obviously some engines are more highly stressed than others — what is satisfactory for a slow-revving side valve motor might not fit the bill in a dope-guzzling V-twin.

From the authenticity angle it would be undesirable to use *Nyloc* nuts on vintage machines although they would not look out of place on a post-1958 bike. The fact that nylon-inserted nuts had been available for twenty or more years before motorcycle manufacturers finally adopted them would indicate that the nuts were too expensive or the aforesaid manufacturers were slow to appreciate their advantages.

In the veteran and vintage era fasteners were generally finished in black or nickel. Black nuts and bolts were either chemically-blacked or japanned, which in practise meant a quick dip in paint followed by stoving. Pre-war (ie post vintage) fasteners were also blacked, cadmium-plated or chromed (not as often as some concours entrants seem to believe!). War Department bikes invariably featured cadmium plating, although this was usually daubed over with olive-drab or khaki during overhauls. Post-war bright zinc began to appear, although nuts and bolts on cheap machines were

Opposite page: Another wartime illustration from *Motor Cycling*. Workshop tidyness is just as important now! The wooden object (top right) is a chock for slipping under the crankcase. Some of the BSA gaskets would appear to be circa 1935, although the timing cover and sump gaskets will be familiar to owners of Val Page-designed 'B' and 'M' group models.

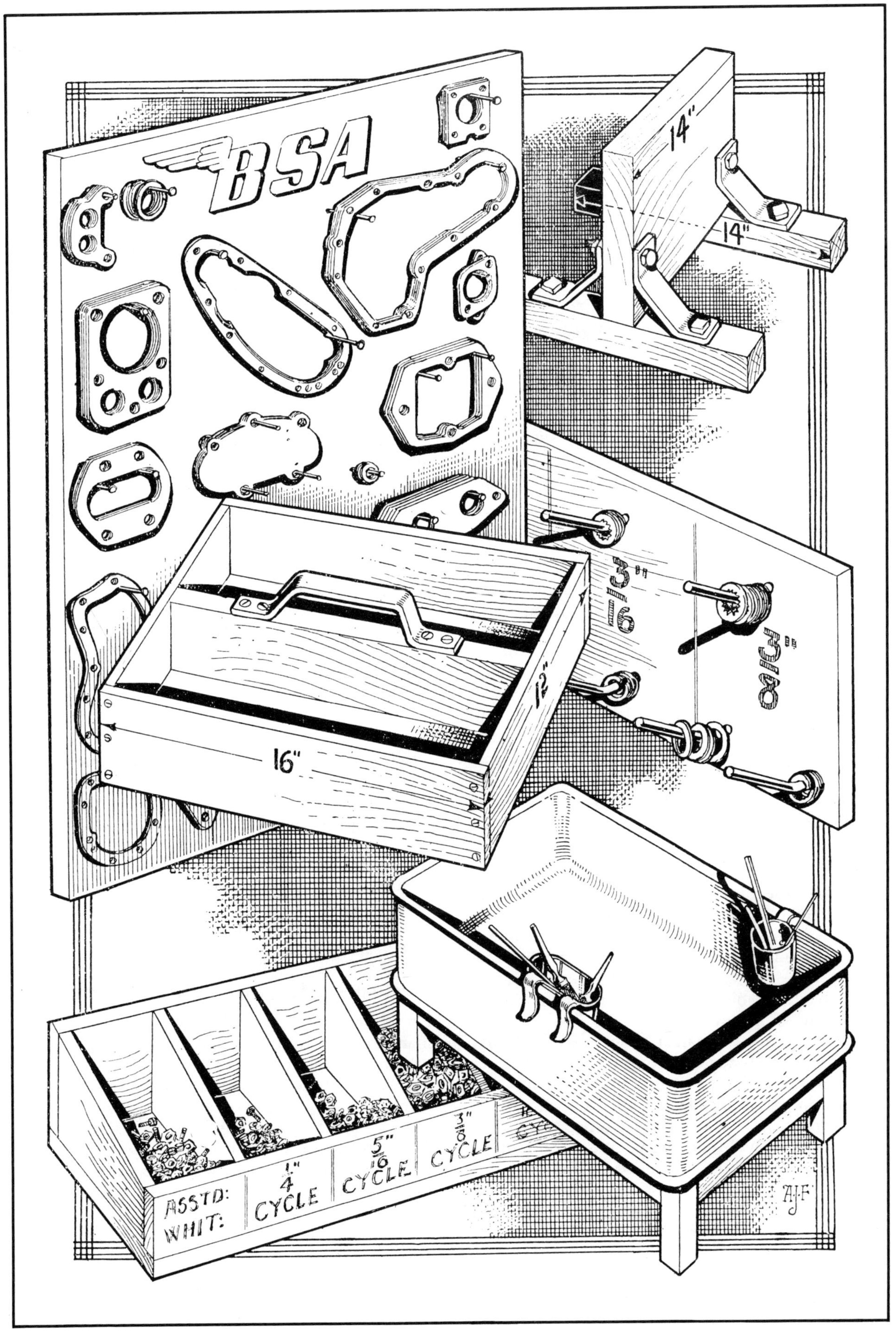
BSA
14"
14"
3/16"
3/8"
12"
16"
ASSTD: WHIT:
1/4" CYCLE
5/16" CYCLE
3/8" CYCLE
AJF

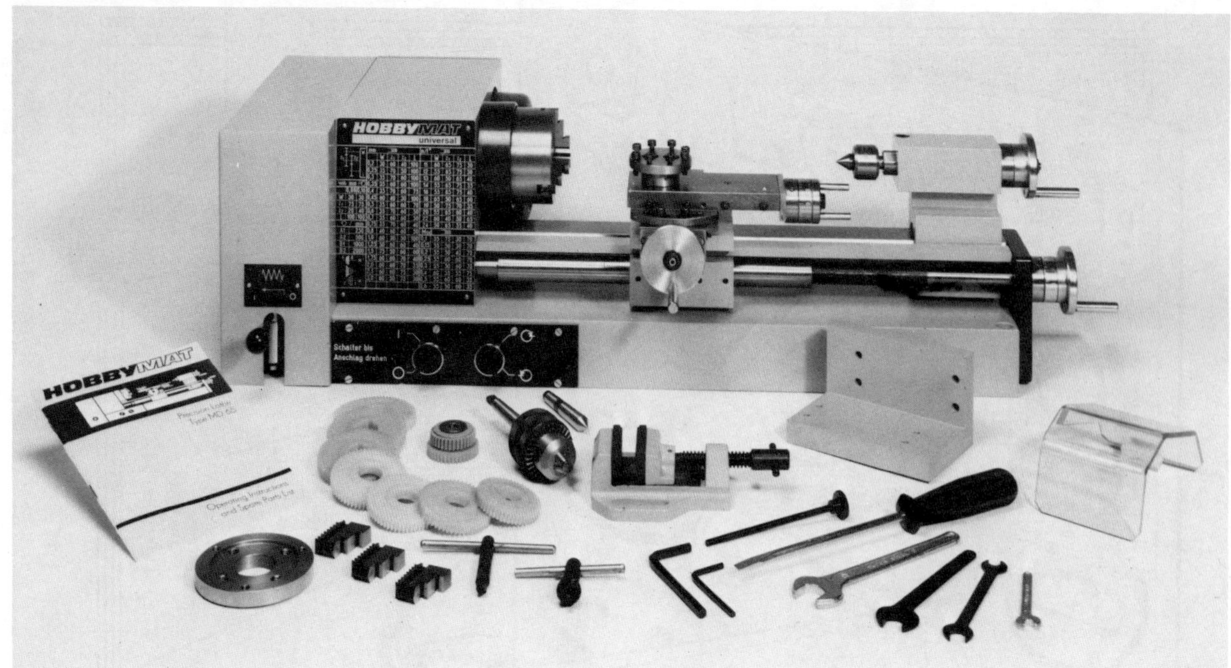

The MD65 Hobbymat by Carl Zeiss Jena Ltd. Ideal for the small workshop, this lathe comes complete with screw-cutting gear and a host of accessories. Restorers who have bought lathes wonder how they ever did without them. ***(Photo: Carl Zeiss Jena Ltd.)***

often black, as before. Some makers could just about afford to chrome their small parts, although the nickel shortage in 1952 meant a few economies in that year.

Purists may quibble at the idea, but stainless steel is an excellent material for most threaded parts and will look just like nickel when highly polished. An 18/8 grade is satisfactory. If bought-out stainless hexagon-headed bolts are fitted to a vintage machine, the manufacturer's lettering or trade mark should be polished out otherwise it will catch the eye of eager concours judges.

Metals for the restorer

One advantage the professional engineer has over his amateur counterpart is the ready supply of raw materials at his fingertips. He is usually able to beg or borrow odd scraps of steel, or seek advice on specifications. What of the amateur? How does he lay his hands on bits and pieces, and the necessary information to go with them?

There are many amateur machinists who may possess the rudimentary equipment to produce parts for their bikes, but finding out about steel specifications is a problem if the said enthusiasts work in a bank, or behind an office desk. The following notes will therefore be of interest to these souls, even if they do not intend to undertake the work themselves.

Steel comes in various shapes and sizes as everyone knows, but there is also a vast selection of compositions to suit special applications. Choose the wrong one and you could be in trouble. A fork spindle, for example, would not last long if made out of mild steel or silver steel. Closely allied to the selection of suitable raw material is the question of heat treatment, which will be discussed in brief later.

Specialist dealers in alloy steels are usually helpful people but they cannot be expected to roll out the red carpet for someone who wants a couple of inches of tool steel. Most amateurs resort to scrounging from pals in the engineering business but even in this event some knowledge of steel specifications is handy.

Steel specs. The BS970 range

For reasons best known to themselves the British Standards Institution concocted a new coding system for steels in recent years. A six-digit number was alloted to various grades, thus replacing the familiar EN system. For example, EN16 became BS970 Part 2. 1970: 605M36. The new system, whilst being of interest to college students and desk-bound metallurgists, was promptly ignored by practical engineers who still use the EN coding to this day.

Thus the following lists omit the six-digit system. Only materials of interest to vintagents are included as a complete run-down of the BS970 range would fill several books.

Many of the grades listed are available to special

composition and certain types will be supplied in a heat-treated condition, if requested. In either case the basic EN number is suffixed by a letter (eg. EN16T).

Above: The Hobbymat with milling attachment. A luxury for the small workshop, enabling the amateur to machine all sorts of replica parts. ***(Photo: Carl Zeiss Jena Ltd.)***

EN1A & EN1B. Low-carbon steel for light-duty. Low strength of approx 23 tons tensile. Used for lightly-stressed parts.

EN3B. A mild steel for general engineering. Low tensile, approx. 28/30 tons. Good machineability, welds well. For making lightly-stressed shafts, bolts etc. from bright bar.

EN8. A useful 40 carbon steel of reasonable strength. (35 tons tensile, or 45-55 when in the heat-treated condition.) Suitable for spindles, studs, bolts. Harden at 830° – 860°C. Quench in oil. Temper at 550° – 660°C. Can also be nitrocarburised.

EN9. 45 tons/sq.in. minimum tensile strength as normalised. Wear-resisting. Suitable for some gears, ideal for sprockets. Heat treatment: harden at 810° – 840°C. Quench in oil. Temper between 550° – 660 °C. Sprockets can be flame-hardened on the teeth only.

EN16. A manganese-molybdenum steel. Tough (55 tons tensile) and shock-resistant. Good for fork spindles, wheel spindles, shafts of various kinds, high-tensile studs, bolts.

Below: A perfect choice for motorcycle restoration work, the Naerok Model SSB 5MK geared head lathe complete with 1 hp motor and chuck. A 10 in swing, 18 in between centres, facility is ample for most work and the headstock is 1$^1/_8$ in bore — a very desirable feature. ***(Photo: Naerok Ltd.)***

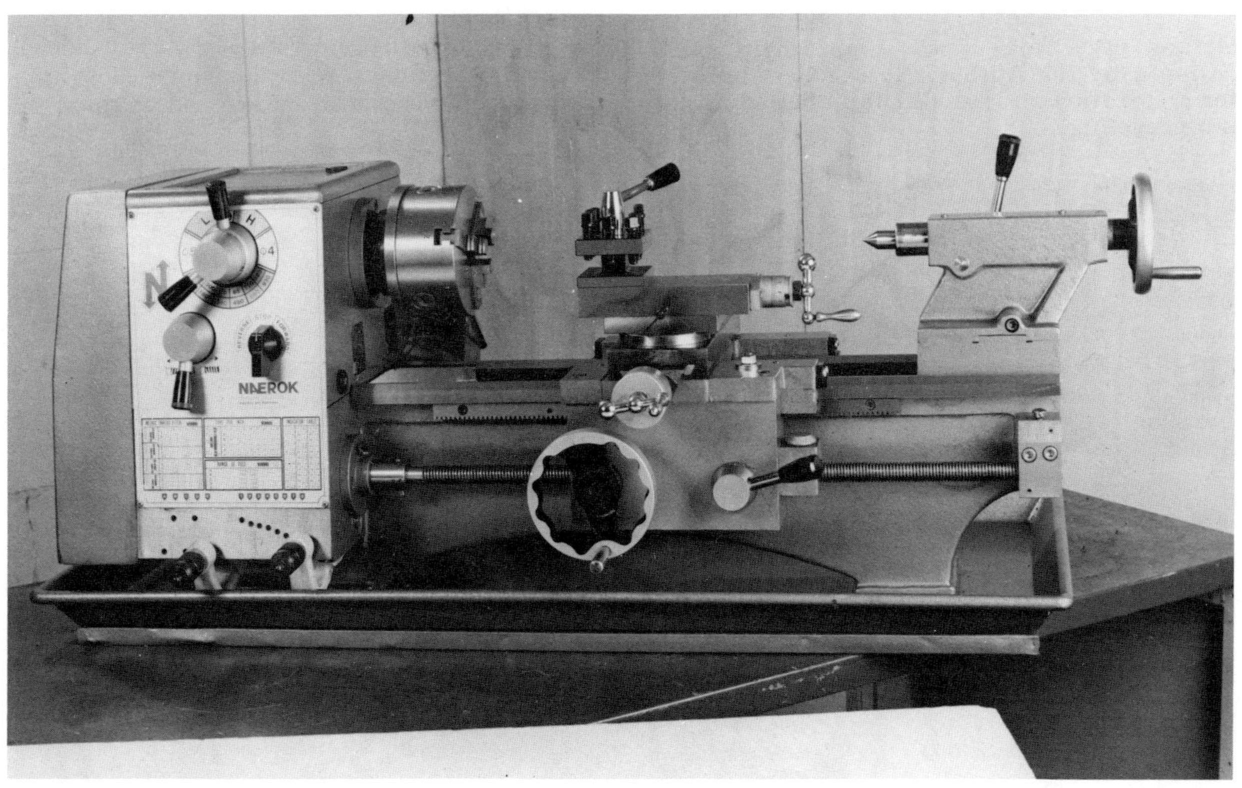

EN24. Very popular with toolmakers, this nickel-chromium molybdenum steel is readily available and is suitable for shafts, spindles, connecting rods, gearwheels and hardened bushes. Harden at 820° – 850°C and quench in oil. Temper at 660°C maximum. Good resistance to wear and shock-loadings. 55/65 tons tensile at least (more with suitable heat-treatment).

EN31. This is ball race steel, used for making ball and roller race components. Great resistance to wear when hardened. Harden at 800°C – 840°C. Quench in water or oil. Temper (if necessary) at 130°C to 180°C.

EN32. Carbon case-hardening steel. High core strength and very hard surface when heat-treated. Suitable for gears and cams etc. Carburise 900° – 930°C, harden at 760° – 780°C. Quench in water.

EN36. A nickel-chromium case-hardening steel. Perfect choice for gearwheels. Also good for camshafts, cams, cam follower rollers and other engine parts subject to wear. Can be heat-treated by various means or case-hardened. Carburise at 880° – 930°C. Refine at 850° – 880°C (cool in air, water or oil), harden at 760°C – 780°C and quench in oil. Temper in oil at 150° – 200°C.

EN40B. Chromium-molybdenum nitriding steel. When nitrided is very resistant to wear and has a good core strength.

EN45 & 46. Used for car springs etc.

EN49 & 50. Valve-spring steel.

EN51 to 55. Suitable for valves; generally EN51 would be for inlets although some reasonably cool-running engines have exhaust valves made from this material. EN52 is used for inlet and exhaust valves on touring engines (also EN53).

EN54. A heavy duty nickel-chromium tungsten steel for valves, as is EN55, which is more resistant to leaded-petrol in its natural form. (KE965 valves for racing were, in fact EN54).

EN57. A stainless steel with good corrosion resistance.

EN58AN, 58B, and 58J. All stainless steels with various compositions. All very expensive. Useful for bright parts such as nuts and bolts, brackets etc. When polished most stainless steels will pass for nickel-plated items and are therefore handy for reproducing 'new' vintage parts such as brake and clutch levers.

Silver steel. Available in rods, and ground to exact size (mild steels are usually up to .002 in undersize on nominal diameter). Silver steel is a very handy material for making various spindles. Not recommended however for girder fork spindles due to its brittle nature. Punches and small lathe tools can be made from this material. Harden to cherry red, quench in water or oil, and temper to a straw colour.

Aluminium. Ordinary aluminium is very soft and is therefore not much use to the motorcyclist. Most forms are in fact **alloys,** such as *Dural* (a trade name). Duralumin, to give it its full title, is a relatively hard and tough aluminium alloy with a composition of 3.5 to 4.5% copper, 0.4 to 0.7% manganese, 0.4 to 0.7% magnesium and the remainder aluminium. To all intents and purposes HE30, HP30 and HT30 aluminium alloys are the modern equivalents.

Y Alloys, originally developed by the National Physical Laboratories, were aluminium alloys with the addition of copper, nickel and magnesium.

Details of a 1924 250cc Lightweight BSA restored by the Author. An excellent subject for restoration and suitable for a newcomer to motorcycling.

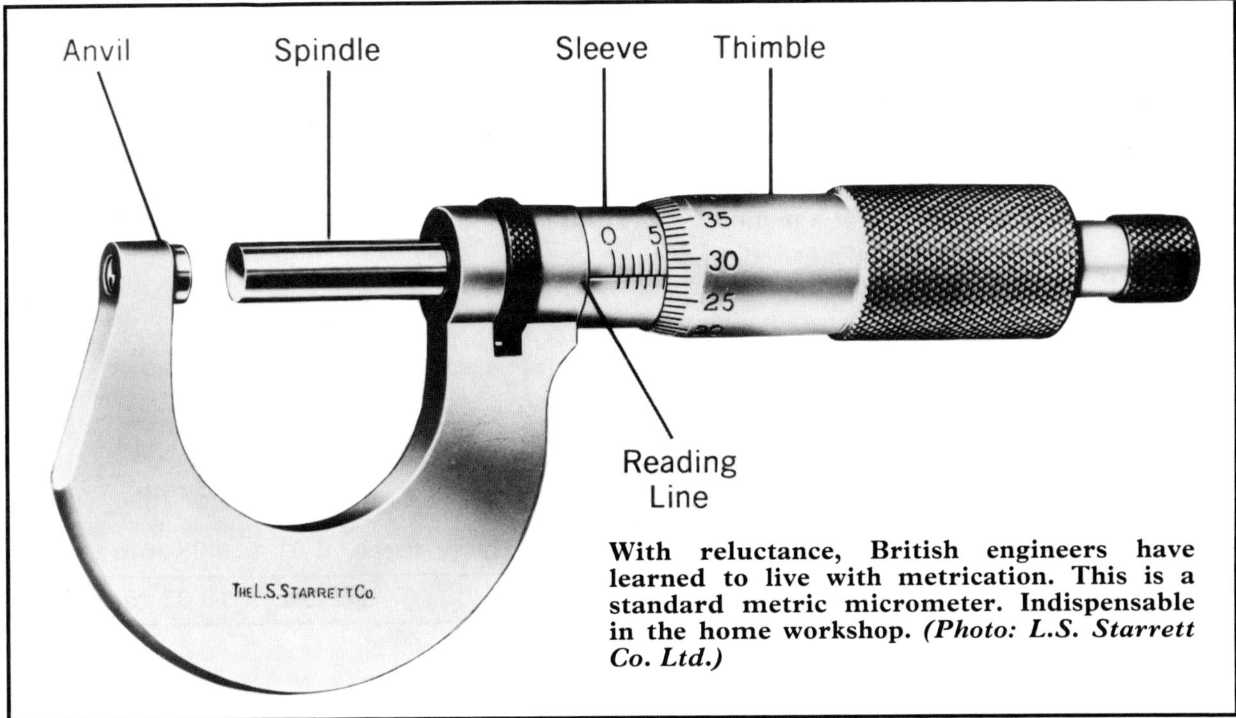

With reluctance, British engineers have learned to live with metrication. This is a standard metric micrometer. Indispensable in the home workshop. *(Photo: L.S. Starrett Co. Ltd.)*

Retaining strength at high temperature, the material was a natural choice for pistons and cylinders. R.R. Alloys were so named after Rolls Royce, their creators. RR50 was suitable for castings and grades RR53 and 59 were used in pistons, heads, cylinders etc. The production of R.R. Alloys was eventually undertaken by High Duty Alloys Ltd – hence the trade name *Hiduminium*.

Elektron is a magnesium alloy chiefly remembered for gearbox shells and crankcases (eg. 1938 M24 Gold Star BSA) on sporting machines. Lightness is its main characteristic, although inflammability is another feature to be considered. Fortunately Elektron's ability to ignite is not in the same league as photographic magnesium flash ribbon – if it were, then there would be few machine shops surviving in the Birmingham area!

Bearing metals

Gunmetal is an alloy of 85/92% copper and tin. An admirable plain bearing material, as is leaded phosphor bronze and white metal. Babbitt metal was an example of the latter, consisting of 80% tin, 10% copper and 10% antimony.

Although not metals, *Tufnol* and *Nylatron GSM* are useful materials for dry bearings or gears. The former is a bonded resinous substance laminated under high pressure with cloth interlayers. *Nylatron GSM* is a black nylon filled with, among other ingredients, molybdenum, which makes it ideal for non-lubricated bushes such as those found in vintage spring frames and leaf-sprung saddles.

Heat-treatment processes

All steels consist of iron with small percentages of carbon and various other elements. It is the amount of carbon and the nature of elements which decides the type of heat treatment necessary. Mild steel contains from .05 to .20% carbon. It cannot be hardened by heating and quenching (as with silver steel) but can be given a hard outer case by the simple process of case-hardening. This is the only form of heat treatment practicable in the home workshop.

Case-hardening with Kasenite

A large blowlamp or propane torch is necessary, together with a tin of *Kasenite* (from tool merchants) and a temporary hearth of fire bricks to conserve heat.

Warm up the part to red-hot and roll it around in *Kasenite* powder, maintaining heat. The part requiring hardening should be well covered with powder. The longer it is heated, the greater the case depth. Some cams were hardened to a depth of .030 to .050 in but this would take hours – .010 to .015 in is ample for small spindles etc.

When the part is well cooked plunge it in cold water. Oil is sometimes recommended but most people use water. The outer skin should now be impervious to a file. The function of the Kasenite carburising powder is to soak into the top metal layer so producing a high-carbon skin. A relatively soft core remains an advantage as we don't want the component to snap in two.

HOW TO READ A MICROMETER

METRIC

Reading in hundredths of a millimetre (0.01 mm).

1 First note the whole number of mm divisions on the sleeve (Major divisions – below datum line)

2 Then observe whether there is a half mm visible (minor divisions above datum line)

3 Finally read the line on the thimble coinciding with the datum line. This gives hundredths of a mm.

Ten × 1·0 = 10·0 mm

One × 0·5 = 0·5 mm

Thirty-three × 0·01 = 0·33 mm

TOTAL = 10·83 mm

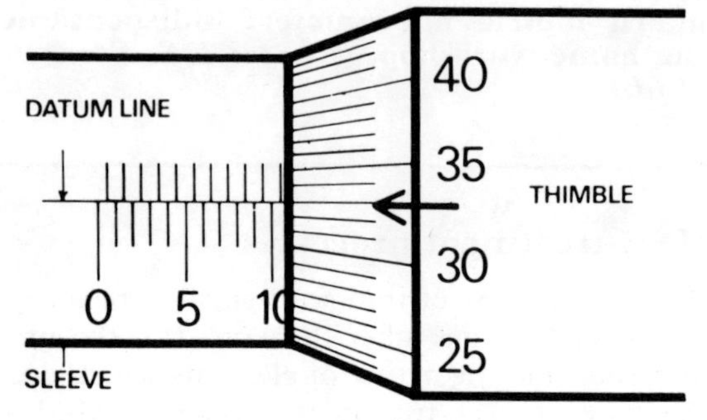

Many British engineers (the Author included) were reluctant to adopt the metric system but it must be said that it makes workshop calculations much easier.

In Victorian days components were case-hardened in boxes stuffed with bits of leather, horn or charcoal, and it's amazing how hard they managed to make things by such wizardry. Ordinary sugar can be used in an emergency providing the part is small (eg. a pushrod end); this vintage hint might come in useful when a replacement is needed out in the Bush.

Professional heat-treatment

Most large cities harbour at least one heat-treatment specialist – the English Midlands area abounds with them.

Having selected a suitable material for a particular application the amateur machinist will need an elementary knowledge of available heat treatment processes to enable him to discuss problems with the professional.

When a part is delivered to a heat-treatment shop it must be clearly labelled with the type of heat treatment expected and the nature of the material itself (eg. EN24). The specialist may suggest a better process than the one you thought of, but he can't guess what material you have used!

Distortion

It is an unfortunate fact that most heat-treatment processes distort the component to some degree. Certain processes create more problems than others. To be on the safe side a grinding allowance should always be left to allow for this distortion; generally .005 to .010 in on small spindles is sufficient.

Cyanide hardening. Another case-hardening process in which parts are heated in molten sodium cyanide. For obvious reasons the amateur is unable to attempt this, or any other sophisticated heat-treatment process. Parts after treatment are much cleaner with very little surface scaling.

Nitriding is a special process carried out on crankshafts, gudgeon pins, gears and camshafts. A high resistance to wear is imparted on the surface skin. Parts are heated in airtight containers with the introduction of dry ammonia for a period of twenty hours or more. Distortion is minimal (EN40B is suitable for nitriding).

Carburising is simply a common heat-treatment term denoting the way in which carbon is transferred to the top layer of metal. The carburising medium can be solid, gaseous or liquid.

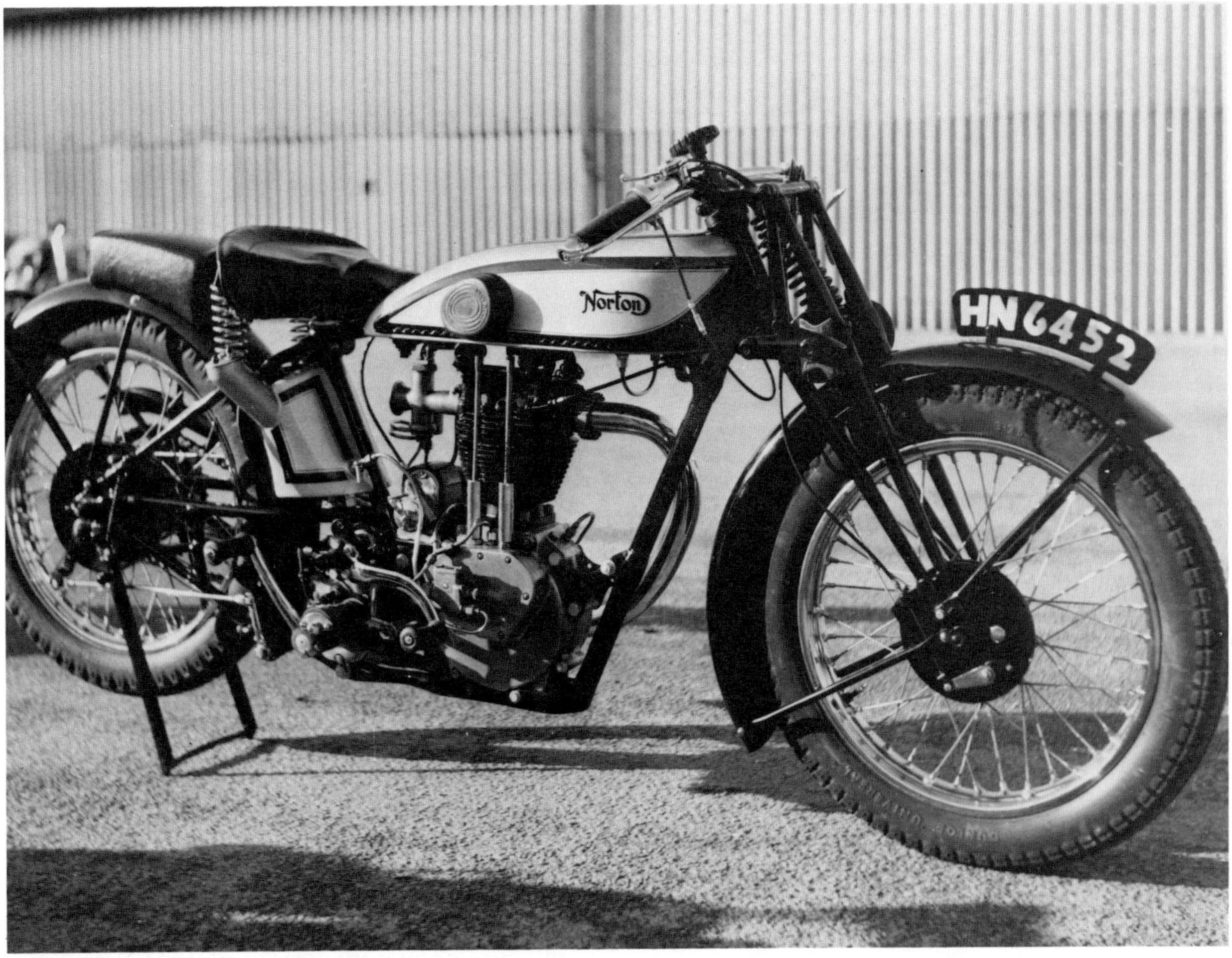

Above: A cradle-frame 490cc ES2 Norton with enclosed pushrod return springs, of 1928/9. The Sturmey-Archer gearbox has an external 'hit or miss' foot gearchange stop mechanism. A well-restored machine but perhaps a little too much chrome.

Normalising. More or less the same as annealing, in which steel is heated above the transformation range and cooled slowly.
Pre-heating. Can be applied to a component, such as a cast-iron cylinder block, before welding, to minimise the chance of distortion. Also carried out on certain tool steels prior to heat-treatment proper.
Quenching. Rapid cooling in water, oil or gas.
Soaking. Prolonged heating, as in a carburising process.
Stress relieving. Components are oven-heated at a high temperature for some considerable time in order to relieve internal stresses induced by welding or forging. Steel billets sometimes require stabilisation before machining.
Flame-hardening. As the title suggests, this is a heat-treatment process in which the metal surface is heated by an intense flame, after which the component is quenched. Used commercially for

Below: A close-up of the Norton's valve gear. The rockers run on rollers held in special cages and are grease lubricated. After a prolonged mileage the rocker spindles indent, causing excess play. A conversion to plain bearings (a la AJS) is worth considering under the circumstances.

gears and sprockets. Only certain steels (eg. EN9) can be treated thus.
Induction hardening. Controlled hardening of a

Above: Without doubt one of the most coveted of all vintage motorcycles, the 1927 Model 90 Sunbeam is fast, reliable and very sporting.

steel held within a coil through which a current of high frequency is passed. The steel is then quenched, usually in oil, or by means of a water spray. Distortion is relatively low. Steels with a medium or high carbon content are suitable; alloy steels must be chosen with care due to the danger of surface stress and cracking.

Tempering. The process of reheating a steel after hardening, followed by quenching or gradual cooling.

Vacuum hardening. A very sophisticated process in which certain high grade steels (eg. Carr's 69S, EN30B, EN40C, EN57, BA2, BD2, BD3 and some hotwork steels) are hardened throughout. Absolute minimal distortion and no surface scaling.

Acquiring the metal

As stated earlier, steel stockholders may be unwilling to supply odd scraps of metal, although a personal visit sometimes works wonders! There are other avenues the restorer can explore, the first of which is the motorcar scrapyard. Old car parts can be recycled (no pun intended) so long as the matter

Below: A Super-Sports model, the 1927 348cc TT Model 80. Ideal for all kinds of events and reasonably straight-forward to restore – but beware of 'chewed' gear pinions.

An ideal beginner's project, the 1949 Competition BSA Bantam. Features which distinguish it from the standard roadster are: raised footrests, an exhaust pipe with an upswept end, a different front mudguard, a raised saddle and knobbly tyres. The gearing was lowered also but the engine remained standard.

is approached sensibly.

Diesel engine head-studs make excellent engine bolts and spindles. Half-shafts are made from extremely tough material — they have to be — thus many replacement shafts and spindles can be turned from scrap ones. Car gearbox main and layshafts, when annealed, also provide good raw material. The list is endless.

It may be argued by metallurgists that the use of scrap car materials is a haphazard method insofar as the amateur may be unaware of the basic composition. This is very true, but so long as no chances are taken with such parts as girder fork spindles, steering columns and brake components he should not go far wrong. The amateur mechanic may take heart from the fact that many prototype components in the motorcycle and general engineering industries were made by the method outlined.

Tool steels are obtainable in small quantities from suppliers listed in the *Model Engineer* magazine. Last but not least is the time-honoured scrounging method! Most toolmaking establishments have bins of offcuts lying around, just waiting for the vintage enthusiast. It's well worth nipping down to your local toolmakers with a pleading expression — it costs nothing to ask.

Chapter 2

The Cycle Parts

Wheels, brakes, forks etc

Wheel rebuilding

VERY few people attempt re-spoking or truing of wheel rims, considering the task a mystical art quite beyond the amateur. Rebuilding a wheel is surprisingly simple and requires very little in the way of workshop equipment, so why not have a go? You may not be able to do the job as quickly as a professional but there is no reason why you should not achieve a fair degree of accuracy. The whole operation is well within the capabilities of the novice but requires some thought and a fair degree of patience.

Measure the offset

Before stripping a wheel it is most important to measure the amount the rim is offset from the hub centre-line. Usually rims are set over to one side, either to allow for transmission chains, belts, brake mechanisms. Some front rims, on stirrup-braked veterans for instance, are central in relation to their hubs, but it is well to adopt the golden rule of always measuring rim displacement before dismantling. This also applies if you intend to have the wheel built by an expert.

It does not matter how you actually measure the offset so long as you note the results of your findings. A simple sketch is handy, showing the relationship of the rim to hub; you can either place a straight-edge across the rim and measure up to the outer bearing cone, or hold the straight-edge against the cone and measure the gap between straight-edge and rim (see sketch). Some rims were very deeply offset by as much as two inches. Yet another way of determining the hub-to-rim relationship is to push a rod through the valve hole and, sighting-up the rod vertically, mark where it touches the hub. This method depends on how good your judgement is and whether or not you intend to paint the hub afterwards.

Try to unscrew at least two spokes intact, one from each side of the wheel, and measure their lengths. Retain them as patterns, noting the wire gauge and type of finish (eg. cadmium, nickel or black enamel.) Almost all replacement spokes nowadays are described as rustless, being plated with a thin flash of zinc or cadmium, and are acceptable left as they are by most restorers. Many vintage and pre-war machines had black spokes (enamelled) and nickel-plated brass nipples; concours enthusiasts will find it necessary to reproduce this finish by painting each spoke individually either before or after rebuilding. To paint spokes black they must first of all be de-greased to remove the protective oil and then lightly etched with wet-and-dry emery. Neglecting this procedure will mean that

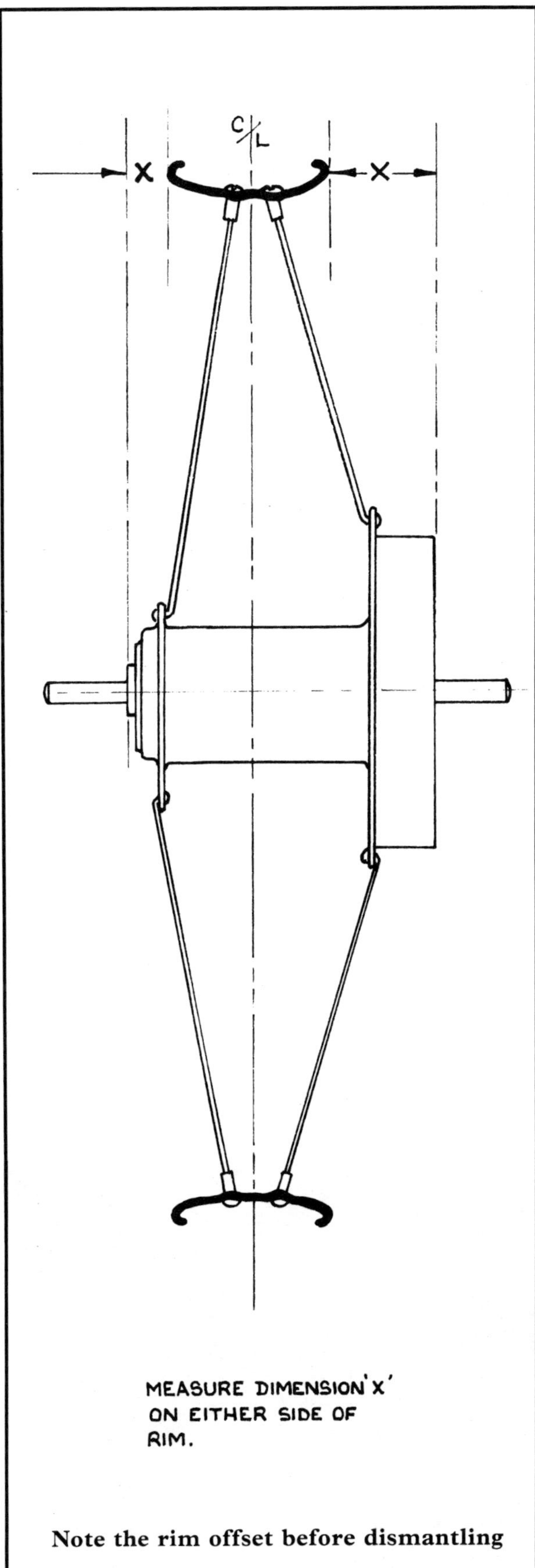

Note the rim offset before dismantling

the paint will flake off at some future date.

One useful tip for painting spokes (prior to wheel-building) is to hang them under a garage roof beam so you can spray them all in one go with an aerosol. Fix a bar magnet underneath the beam, fit old nipples on the spokes and attach them, hanging downwards, to the magnet. Spray on one coat of etch primer and two of colour.

To return to wheel dismantling; rusty spokes will usually be seized in position and it is a waste of time attempting to unscrew the nipples. Making sure you have all the relevant details, cut the spokes out with a junior hacksaw (this plays havoc with the blades) or a large pair of wire-cutters. Ex-WD wire-cutters of the folding type make short work of this task.

Rebuilding the Hub

Bent spindles and worn bearings must, of course, be renewed, otherwise it will be virtually impossible to true the rim. Cup and cone bearings are usually pitted or badly grooved and must be replaced. There are a few specialists willing to undertake the manufacture of new cups and cones but expert machinists will be able to make them.

One of the case-hardening steels, such as EN31, 32 or 36, should be selected for cups and cones. If grinding facilities are not available it should be possible to fine-turn the profiles and finish off with emery cloth wrapped around a bar or similar object. After heat-treatment the parts will need further cleaning-up with emery; to save much hand-refinishing, one of the clean heat-treatment processes, such as cyanide-hardening, is advantageous. An even better solution would be to make the cups and cones out of Carr's 69s, or a similar material, and have them vacuum-hardened. This process will leave the new parts bright and shiny, requiring no further work. Distortion is also eliminated (see Chapter 1, ref. heat-treatment).

Ball and taper-roller races present no problem as replacements are easily obtained. Although bearing suppliers will hate the suggestion, try to get the new bearings off an engineering pal as he will be able to secure a sixty per cent discount with trade references. Ball races should always be drifted-out by their outer races if you intend using them again. Belting them out by the inner races could result in the bearing tracks being indented. These remarks of course apply when fitting new races.

Enterprising individuals might like to consider modifying their vintage cup-and-cone hubs to accept ball races. This conversion has been done on many occasions and is quite a good idea — nobody will know you have cheated as the modification is indistinguishable from the outside. Usually there will be a ball race of a suitable size to fit the hub, even if a simple machining operation is called for. A new spindle can be made from EN16, threaded 26tpi at the ends. Right-hand threads will suffice

The importance of measuring wheel offset was amply demonstrated during the rebuild of a 1924 PV-Bradshaw. No more than 1/8 in lateral displacement error could be tolerated due to the proximity of various tubes and fitments associated with the maker's spring frame.

A nice little ABC. One can sympathise with riders who fit wired-on tyres to early machines such as this: after all, the ABC was modern in most other respects. It had a four-speed gearbox, rear springing and electric lights in 1921.

when ball races are fitted. The very worst choice of material you could possibly make for wheel spindles is silver steel. Attractive though it may be for its ground finish, such a choice could land you on your ear when it snaps like carrot. Except for heavy and high-powered racing machines, most common grades of stainless steel will perform well as wheel-spindle material.

New bearing balls can be found at most bicycle shops. Don't make the mistake of trying to fit too many in a cup-and-cone bearing. There is sometimes almost enough room for another one but in fact most bearing balls are quite loosely spaced. About half a ball-diameter will be left when all the other balls are in juxtaposition. Pack the bearing well with grease and assemble any felt seals which may be present. It might be necessary to put a spacing washer over the cone on the brake drum side to stop the backplate from rubbing. Sometimes it will be found that the brake shoes rub on the inner face of the drum and the same cure will suffice.

Adjust cup-and-cone bearings so that there is just perceptible shake, bearing in mind that the clearances will close-up when the wheel spindles are tightened. Final adjustment must be made when the wheel is in situ. Screwing up the cones until they are hard up against the balls will quickly ruin the bearing tracks in service, so allow about 1/16 in shake at the wheel rim.

Making a wheel-building jig

Professional wheel-builders generally use a universal jig which is able to cope with wheels of the cup-and-cone type (fixed spindles) and modern wheels with knock-out spindles. Wheels minus spindles can be mounted between centres by means of adjustable conically-ended screws which engage in the bearing inners. Such jigs are often substantial cast-iron affairs in the form of a giant pair of fork legs.

Amateurs who may only wish to build two or three pairs of wheels can make do with a temporary jig. By far the simplest set-up consists of two pieces of 2 x 2 in timber, each 2 ft long, screwed to the bench front. Notch the end of each piece and screw

The rear brake arrangement on a 1913 Scott. The instruction book said "put a drop of oil between pad and drum"!

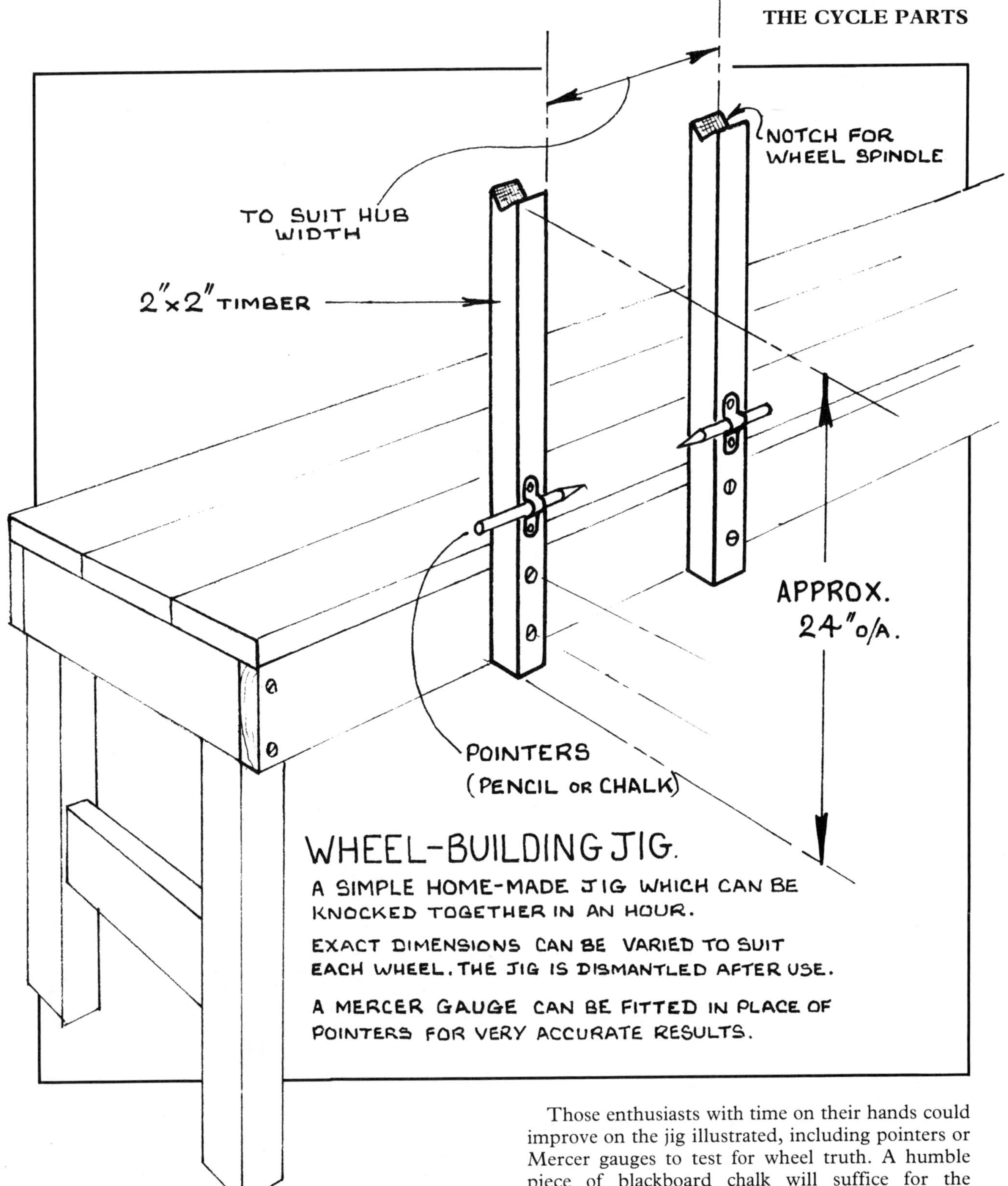

them to the side of the bench with spacing to suit your hub. Rest a bar of metal across both notches when screwing the second leg to the bench to ensure the wheel spindle will be horizontal. This crude jig is perfectly adequate for most wheels, and different widths of hubs can be accommodated by the simple expedient of shifting the legs apart and re-screwing them to the bench.

Those enthusiasts with time on their hands could improve on the jig illustrated, including pointers or Mercer gauges to test for wheel truth. A humble piece of blackboard chalk will suffice for the less-enthusiastic. The general idea is to place the wheel in the jig with the spindle sitting in the notches — it is not necessary to clamp it in position. By spinning the rim slowly, any deflection can be noted by means of the pointer, gauge or whatever. When the deflection is observed, it can be marked with chalk and gradually corrected until the rim is running dead true (to within 1/16 in), as discussed later in this Chapter.

Rims and spokes

Rims which are badly dented, rusty or cracked should be replaced. If a rim has a certain amount of rust-pitting it can be re-used (if it is to be painted) so long as the rust is not severe enough to weaken it. Chrome rims are generally uneconomical to replate.

Beaded-edge rims are often damaged by running over kerbs, especially when tyres are under-inflated. Examine the rim where the tyre beads seat to see that the rolled edges are not dented; if they are, the dents can be levered out or hammered into shape with a metal wedge. Fortunately most sizes of beaded-edge rims are available again through specialists advertising in the *VMCC Journal* and the "classic" monthlies.

Wired rims are also freely available, although some of the larger diameters (20 and 21 inch) are becoming scarcer as the years go by. Unplated rims are hard to come by, so if a chrome rim is to be painted it must be shot-blasted or etched with emery cloth to enable the paint to stick. Those chrome rims with painted centre strips create problems for the restorer; modern chrome rims are polished all over so it is necessary to mask-off the outer portions and shot-blast the centres before painting.

Apply an etch primer before the final coat. Hand-painting complete wheels is a frightful job; if a wheel is to be finished all over in black much time can be saved by having it powder coated. It may not give a concours finish but is suitable for cheap lightweights, trials machines, and most everyday riders will be happy with the results. Powder coating will **not** fill in pit-marks, nor will ordinary stove-enamelling, so the time-honoured method of filling and rubbing-down will have to be resorted to if pitting is present. Obviously it is easier to do such work before the wheel is spoked up.

Spokes should be obtained to exact wire gauge and length. These days all spokes have rolled threads as standard, although some wheel specialists still have the old type of cut-thread dies for certain applications. Butt-ended spokes are those which are thickened up near the head for extra strength. Professional wheel-builders are understandably reluctant to sell spokes separately so don't be surprised if they refuse. Apart from the satisfaction of having done the job yourself, the other advantage of building your own wheels is that you can do the hub repairing and painting at your convenience.

Spoking patterns

Hopefully you should have noted the spoking pattern before you stripped down the wheels. If you didn't, not to worry. Most motorcycle wheels are built to the two-cross or three-cross configuration; all this means is that an outermost spoke crosses either two or three spokes beneath it. Before proceeding with the awe-inspiring task of lacing-up,

ROLLED THREAD SPOKES

			BASIC DIAMETERS			
SWG	INCHES	TPI	THREAD DEPTH	FULL	EFF.	CORE
16	.064	56	.0095	.0735	.064	.0545
15	.072	56	.0095	.0815	.072	.0625
14	.080	56	.0095	.0895	.080	.0705
13	.092	56	.0095	.1015	.092	.0825
12	.104	56	.0095	.1135	.104	.0945
11	.116	44	.0121	.1281	.116	.1039
10	.128	40	.0133	.1413	.128	.1147
9	.144	40	.0133	.1573	.144	.1307
8	.160	32	.0166	.1766	.160	.1434

let us consider for a moment the basic principle of a spoked wheel.

Before the turn of the century bicycle wheels featured spokes which radiated fan-wise from their hubs. In early examples spokes were screwed directly in the hubs, the swaged heads being at the rim ends. This was true radial spoking. If a motorcycle wheel was spoked thus the hub would

Rudge employed an unusual spoking configuration, with the rim holes offset on the brake side. This arrangement was intended to cope with brake loading. (The Rudge braking system was unusually effective for the period.)

almost certainly part company with the rim under braking.

Today all wheels are spoked tangentially, each spoke having an opposite member on the other side of the hub. By means of this arrangement loads are shared and braking forces absorbed. Consequently the wheel is very much stronger.

Lacing the wheel

Some hubs are blessed with keyhole-shaped holes — if yours has, you're in luck, as these are so much easier to assemble. Hubs with plain holes must be loosely assembled away from the truing jig, which in most crowded workshops means doing the job on the floor.

The first step is to run a drill through all spoke holes in painted components. Lay the rim on a sheet to protect enamelled or plated surfaces; if you prefer, it can be placed on blocks to allow for the hub width.

Now comes the awkward bit. Grasping the hub vertically in the left hand, pop all the spokes through the holes on either side. Start with the lower flange first, noting that each alternate spoke goes through the opposite way to its neighbour. Put the first one in downwards, the next one upwards, and so on. The inside spokes will, of course, need fanning-out to stop them dropping back through the holes. Deal with the upper flange likewise, threading all spokes through from alternate sides. You are then left with what appears to be an impossible, tangled, festoon of spokes and hub in your hand!

The beginner may well ask why he cannot build the wheel one-spoke-at-a-time in the truing jig. On those hubs with keyhole-slotted flanges this may be possible, but common round-holed flanges present more of a problem. It will be found that all the spokes on one side of the hub can be fitted and laced into the rim easily enough, but when you start on the opposite flange you can't get the spokes in because those previously fitted are in the way. In passing it should be mentioned that bending spokes when fitting single replacements is **not** recommendedd as this seriously weakens them.

Place the hub, with spokes, central to the wheel rim, resting on the floor or bench. We will now deal with the lower flange first. Arrange the spokes

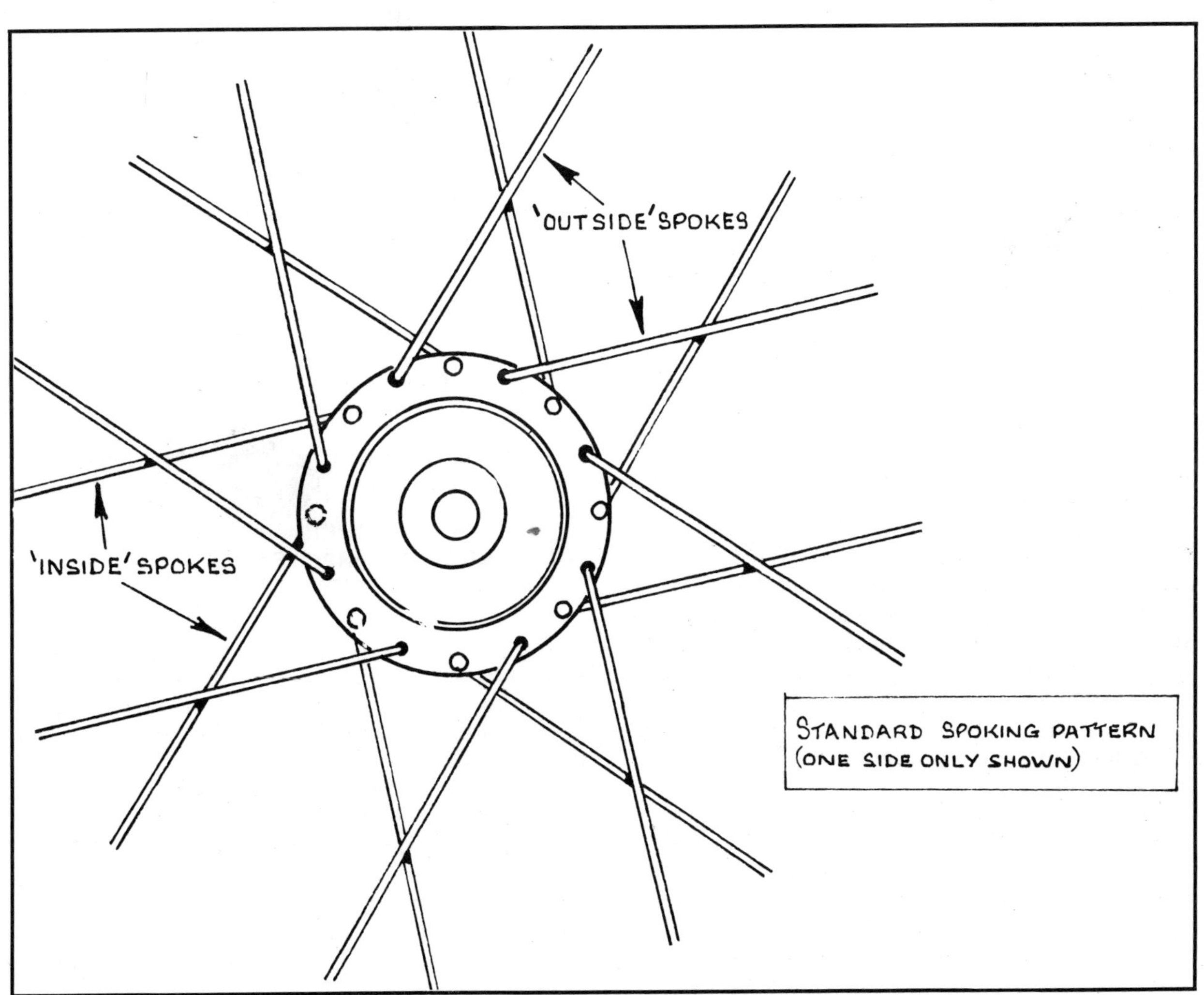

STANDARD SPOKING PATTERN (ONE SIDE ONLY SHOWN)

approximately tangential to the hub, noting that the outer ones go in the opposite direction to the inners. A glance at a built-up wheel will indicate the basic configuration.

Look closely at the rim and you will see that the spoke hole dimples point in different directions. Connect up one outer (ie. lower) spoke with the rim dimple in line and on the same side as the spoke. Screw the nipple on a few turns. Fix the next-but-one spoke, which will be another outer, in its appropriate rim hole. Proceed around the flange, connecting up all the outer spokes tangentially and the wheel will begin to take shape.

Still dealing with the same flange, lace-up all the inner spokes on that side noting that these go in the opposite direction; again, look at a complete wheel to get the basic idea. Now you should have one hub flange spoked loosely, still sitting on the floor or bench top.

The opposite flange, ie the one nearest to you, can now be dealt with in exactly the same fashion as the first, carefully checking that spokes and dimples are in line. In some ways the second flange is easier to lace as there are fewer rim holes to choose from. During this whole operation (which takes far longer to describe than do) care must be exercised to avoid scratching the rim — always attach a nipple as soon as the spoke is inserted.

Final truing

Do up all the nipples finger-tight and fix the wheel in your wooden jig. You will probably find it revolves like a cam and wobbles from side to side. The wheel must now be checked and adjusted for:-

1 Offset
2 Radial run-out (eccentricity)
3 Lateral truth (side to side movement)
4 Spoke tension

Dealing with point 1, the amount of offset should be within half an inch of your noted dimension even **before** adjustment, providing the spokes are of the correct length. If the rim is too far over to the left, tighten up all the spokes on the right-hand side. Try to avoid screwing up the nipples rock-tight at this stage. Spoke keys are available at cycle shops or you could cut a small spanner out of 3/16 in ms plate to suit (magneto spanners are too thin and will destroy the nipple hexagons). Don't be too bothered about rim centrality or offset at this juncture as minor corrections can be made during final truing. Aim for an accuracy of about 1/4 in either way for the time being.

Eccentricity (point 2) can now be checked. Fix a simple pointer to the jig and observe radial run-out as the wheel slowly revolves. This can be corrected quite easily; pause for a few moments to study the basic construction of the wheel before deciding which spokes to tighten. Let's assume your pointer is fixed underneath the rim. As you rotate the wheel there will of course be a high spot and a low. When the rim is at its lowest point, tighten the nipples in the top of the rim and slacken the lower ones to pull the rim in an upwards direction.

It will be necessary to repeat this procedure several times, adjusting the spokes a little at a time until any error is eliminated. You may find the rim "kicks" at one point, where it is welded, but nothing can be done about this; an overall accuracy of approximately 1/8 in total run-out is good enough for most roadsters. Racing enthusiasts could aim for 1/16 in (or less).

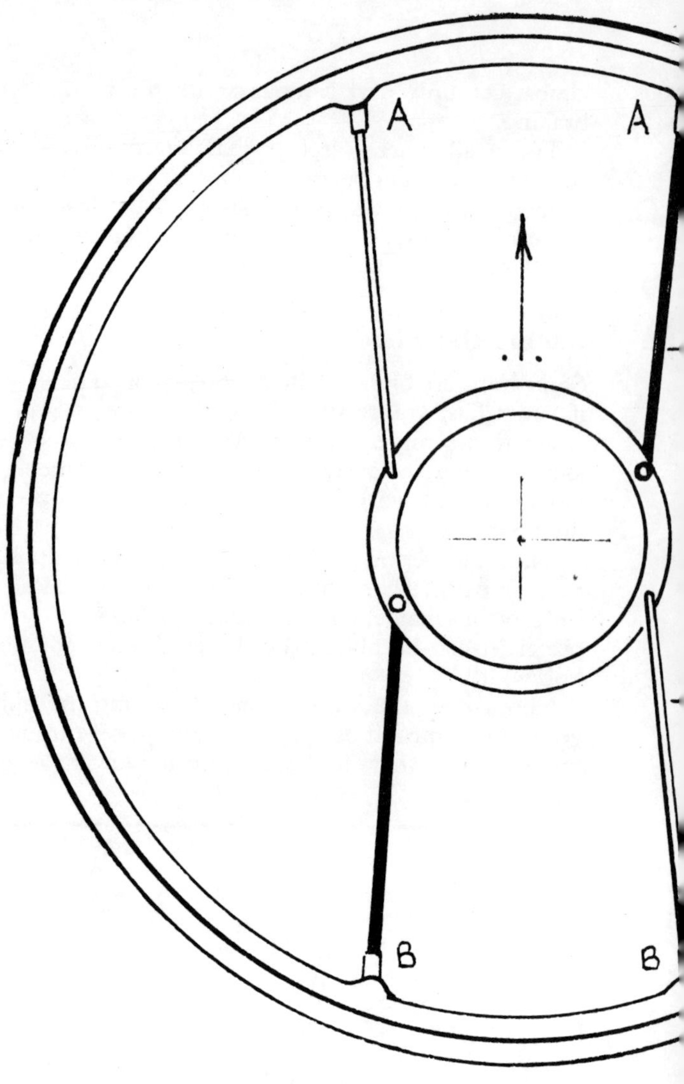

SKETCH SHOWING PRINCIPLE OF A SPOKED WHEEL
TO MOVE THE HUB IN THE DIRECTION SHOWN :→
TIGHTEN NIPPLES 'A'
SLACKEN NIPPLES 'B'

Considering points 3 and 4 together, side-to-side movement and spoke tension, these are the adjustments which seem to perplex most beginners. Study the spoke layout yet again. Fix your pointer, or chalk, to one side of the rim and rotate the wheel. Assuming you are stood in front of it and the rim wobbles over to the right, tighten up the left-hand side spokes only — ie those opposite to the deflection. A little at a time is the rule to adopt. You will find the rim will pull over quite easily.

Rotate the rim again, holding the chalk against one edge. With luck your first correction will have helped the situation somewhat and the wheel is now running truer. Go round all the spokes and do up the nipples a little more. Repeat the operation several times, making minor corrections to each side until you get the rim running dead true (to within $^1/_{32}$ in or so) and offset correctly.

Ideally, all the spokes should finish up equally-tensioned; when tapped with a screwdriver they should ring. A dull lifeless clack will indicate a loose spoke. Keen types using a dial (Mercer) gauge will note how flexible a rim is. Just a quarter of a turn on a spoke nipple is enough to send the needle haywire.

When you are satisfied with your efforts all that remains is to trim all spoke threads to length. These can be chopped off with a junior hacksaw and ground flush. Finish off with a rim-tape. If you can't get one, a few turns of black PVC electricians' tape will suffice (not sticky insulating tape).

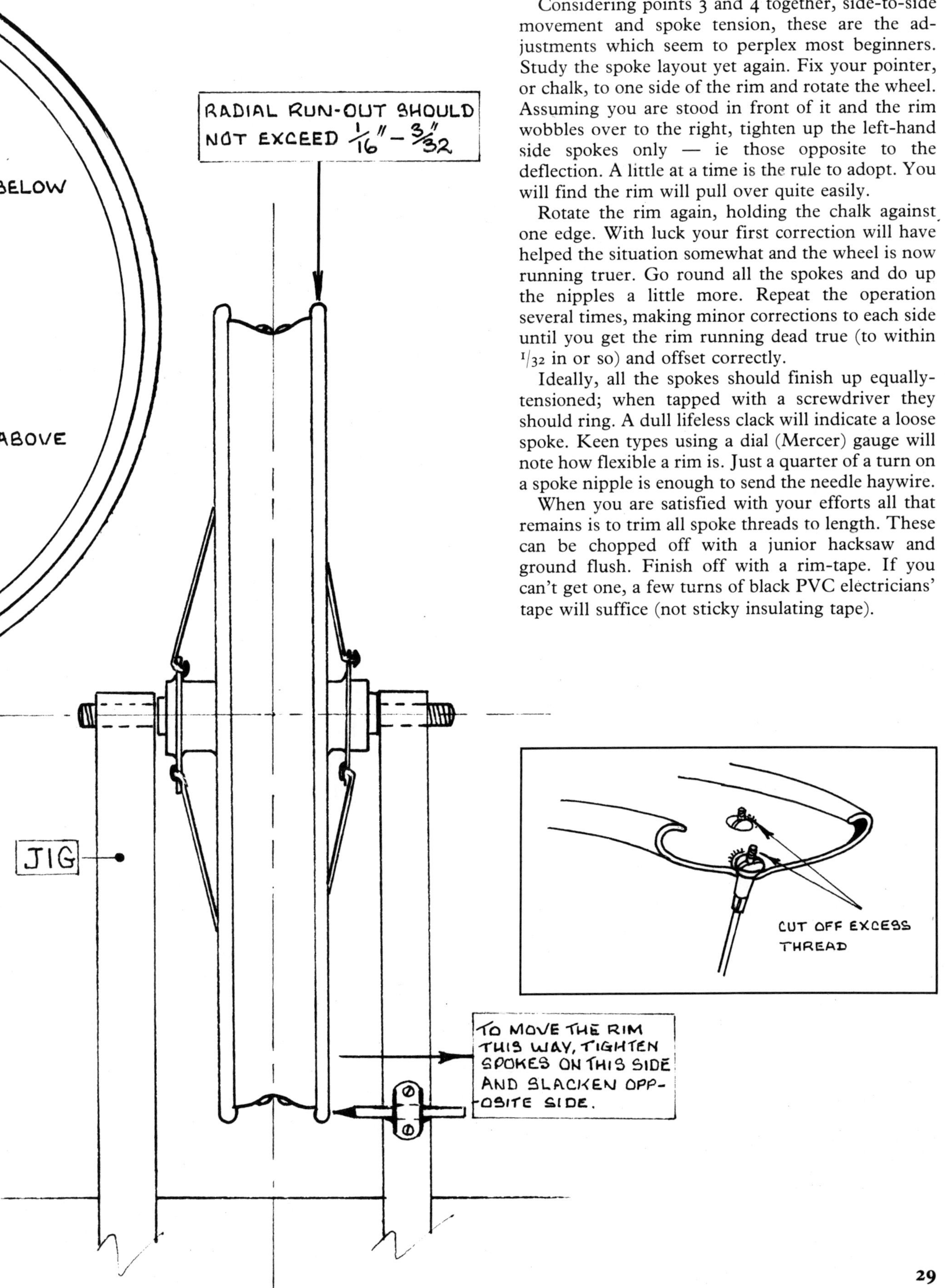

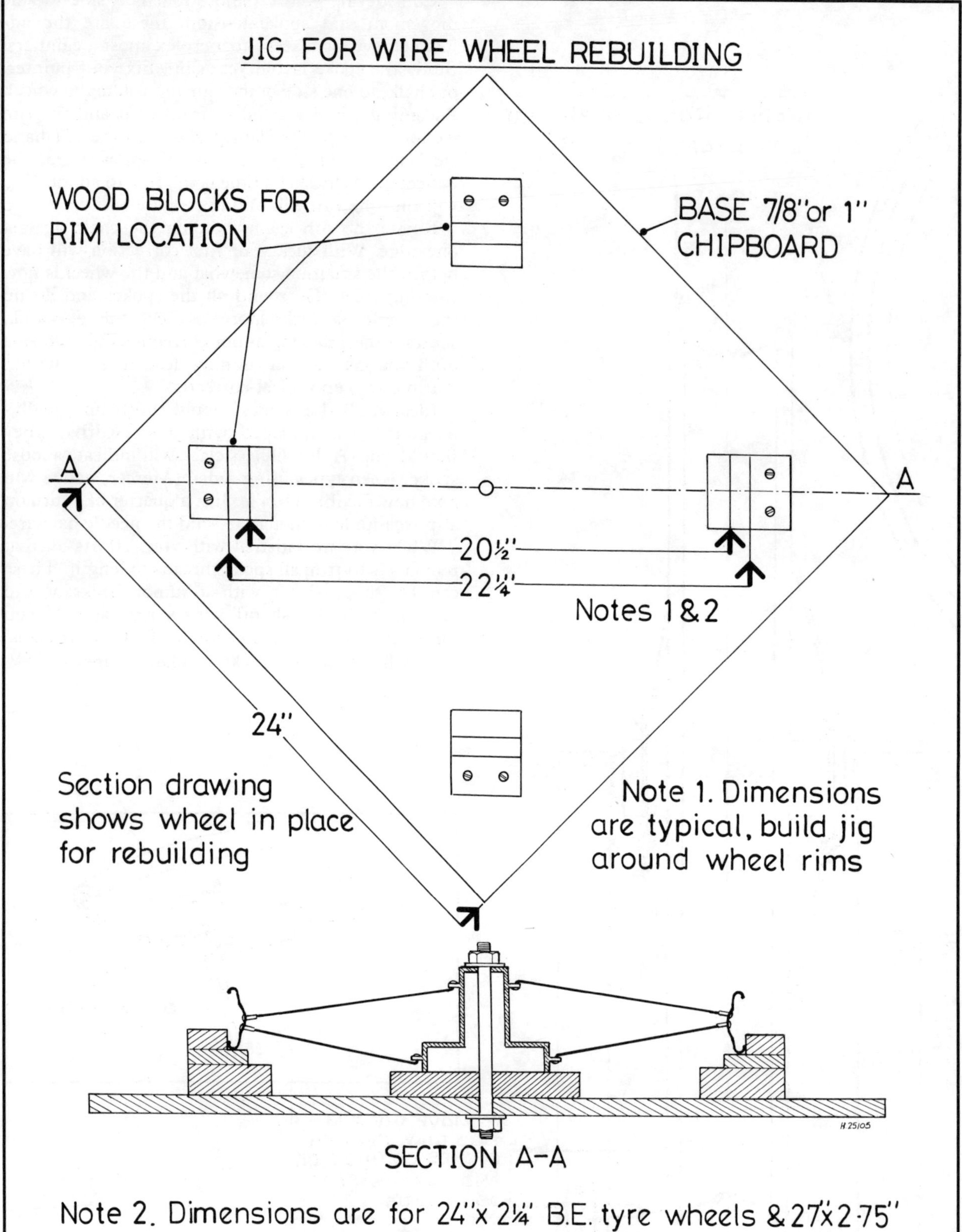

The Taverner wheel-building jig.

The Taverner Jig

The following wheel-building method appeared in the *VMCC Journal* (March 1984). The system, evolved by Les Taverner, is quite unique and will appeal to beginners because of its remarkable simplicity.

The Taverner Jig is easy to make — a few pieces of blockboard and a nail or two are the only materials required.

"The usual advice to the restorer detemined to rebuild his own wheels is to loosely assemble spokes, hub and rims — spokes having previously been cut to correct length — tighten up and correct eccentricity and lateral run-out by alternate tightening and loosening of spoke nipples. Fine for the expert, but very frustrating for the novice with the possibility eventually of a visit to the expert to 'please true this up for me'.

The majority of wheels from restoration projects run reasonably true even though the spokes are deeply rusted. And so it was on my 1927 350 cc AJS. Rims, hubs and spokes were deeply rusted and obviously needed to be dismantled for restoration. But a check revealed that there was less than $^1/_8$ in run-out on both wheels. Surely then, thought I, if a jig was built around the old wheels then the restored hub and rim and new spokes could be rebuilt to match the original accuracy. The drawing shows the jig and a typical wheel hub and rim in place.

Materials required for the jig are: $^3/_4$ in or 1 in chipboard 24 inches square which must be absolutely flat and a strip of softwood from which to cut the steps, nails and screws. The dimensions on the drawing are for a 21 inch wire wheel (27 x 2.75 tyre) and a beaded edge wheel for a 24 x $2^1/_4$ tyre. Thus the jig as shown is suitable for two wheel sizes.

Method:- Select the wheel with the deepest offset and adjust its bearing for no play. It won't matter if the bearings are adjusted a bit tight for the purpose of setting up the exercise. Determine and note the rim run-out. If $^1/_8$ in or less, all is well. If this figure is exceeded be prepared to do some final adjustments when the rebuilt wheel is removed from the jig.

Drill a hole in the centre of the chipboard to take the wheel spindle. A good fit is essential. Set the wheel in place with the widest hub area down. If this is the brake drum so much the better. The AJS design helps here for the brake drum spoke rim is set in from the drum. It matters not, however, if the spoke heads rest on the base, but make sure none is sticking out proud.

Set the wheel in place and determine the thickness of wood needed to set the wheel rim

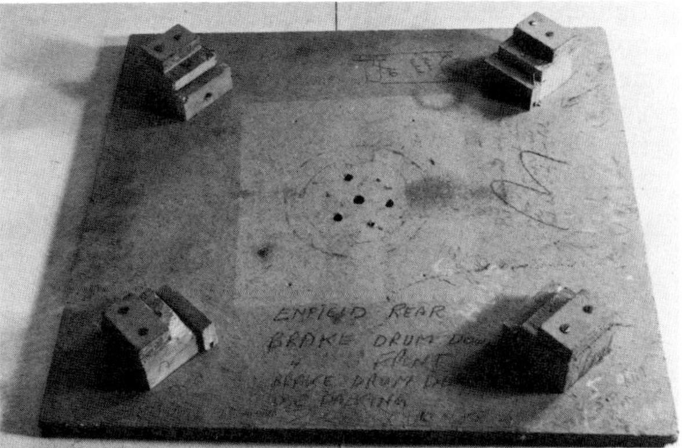

Photo of the Taverner wheel-building jig, an ingenious solution to the problem of how to achieve correct offset and concentricity. *(Photo: L. Taverner.)*

on to the first step. Prepare the wood, cut it into four pieces, and fix in position as shown on the drawing. The wheel should now sit snugly in place with no perceptible rock. Prepare four more pieces of wood and fix these against the wheel rim thus setting the wheel accurately in both planes. Remove the wheel for dismantling. The blocks are nailed initially but finally fixed with long screws through to the baseboard. This ensures that no movement is possible during the wheel rebuilding process. It helps to fix the rim positively by temporary clamps screwed to the step blocks.

Before dismantling the wheel make detailed sketches of the lacing pattern, taking particular note of spoke head positions.

The old spokes will almost certainly be beyond redemption and so new spokes of correct gauge and length with ends threaded, plus nipples, will be needed. It may be possible to unscrew the nipples from the old spokes but this is most unlikely on a veteran or vintage machine. And so the old spokes must be cut free and here great care must be exercised to ensure that the exact length of spokes is recorded. Spokes are supplied rustless (cadmium plated) black or nickel. I note recently stainless steel spokes have appeared. Stainless steel when polished is, I find, indistinguishable from nickel.

With hub and rim restored (or new rims) and spokes complete with nipples to hand, rebuilding can start. The initial lacing up is done loosely away from the jig. The wheel is then put in place ready for final spoke tightening. Fix the temporary clamps to lock the rim securely. Now screw the nipples up gradually working from one point to its opposite number at 180°, then at 45° to that pair and so on. Ignore initially those hidden by the jig steps. Final tensioning is done by tightening and then plucking the spokes and noting the ping and tightening again as necessary, using the 180° method. When all available spokes give an equal ping note, ease the clamps, slide the wheel round a bit, and tighten the few previously hidden spokes.

The wheel is now removed from the jig and checked for run-out which should not exceed the previously recorded figure. A little correction may be done to reduce run-out but beware; it is easy to make matters worse. If this happens, loosen the nipples, return the wheel to the jig and repeat the exercise.

Finally, remove by filing the protruding spoke ends from inside the rim.

Although the method is based on having a good wheel as the basis for jig construction it may also be used to assemble a wheel from an originally separate hub and rim. This entails accurate jig construction from measurement paying particular attention to hub location in relation to the rim and spoke length.

For the second wheel of the set put the wheel in place and if necessary fix packing of appropriate thickness under the hub.

Wheels rebuilt by the method described are still sound and true after several years of hard use ..."

Beaded-edge tyres

Removal and replacement of Dunlop, and most European, beaded-edge covers presents no problem. Due to the semi-elastic nature of the beads hardly any effort is required to stretch them over the rims, in fact most beaded-edge tyres can be fitted without levers.

Not so with some far-eastern tyres. Cheng Shin (CS) beaded-edge covers are particularly difficult to fit for the first time so the following hints might prove useful:-

1 Remove moulding flash from both beads with a very sharp knife
2 Warm the cover either in hot sunlight or in an airing cupboard
3 Fit one bead (ie on one side of the rim only)
4 Leave the tyre for a few days
5 Warm it up again and fit the other bead

Considerable muscle-power is needed to stretch the beads of CS tyres, so to avoid damage to a repainted rim it is advisable to have a dummy run on an unrestored rim. A good idea is to fit both covers to old rims at the outset of the restoration schedule so that the beads will be pre-stretched when the time comes. It has even been suggested in the past that Cheng Shin BE tyres can be pre-stretched on an expanding device made out of an old car rim cut in half. By jacking out the rim halves and leaving the tyre in a warm place, it is supposed to expand sufficiently to facilitate fitting. Indeed, one enthusiast claims to have expanded a 26 in tyre to fit a 28 in rim by this method! Tyre manufacturers would be horrified at the suggestion, therefore the reader is warned that any such experiments are at his own risk.

Tyre fitting in general is made so much easier if the beads are smeared with tyre soap solution or dusted with French Chalk. Dunlops can be fitted by hand but CS tyres will require the assistance of tyre levers; to prevent damage to paintwork wedge a slip of card underneath the lever when forcing the bead over the rim clench.

RECOMMENDED RIM/TYRE SIZES

TYRE	RIM	O/A DIA	O/A WIDTH
2.75 x 21	WM1 x 21	27.37	2.86
	WM2 x 21	27.38	2.86
300 x 21	WM1 x 21	27.70	3.12
	WM2 x 21	27.85	3.15
300 x 20	WM1 x 20	26.70	3.12
	WM2 x 20	26.90	3.15
300 x 19	WM1 x 19	25.70	3.12
	WM2 x 19	25.90	3.15
325 x 19	WM2 x 19	26.47	3.53
	WM3 x 19	26.54	3.58
350 x 19	WM2 x 19	26.90	3.80
	WM3 x 19	26.95	3.85
400 x 19	WM3 x 19	27.90	4.30
400 x 18	WM3 x 18	26.90	4.30

INFLATION TABLE (MOTOR CYCLE TYRES)

TYRE SIZE	INFLATION PRESSURE (PSI) 16	18	20	22	24	27	30	33	36	40
WIRED EDGE	MAX. LOAD IN LBS. PER TYRE									
2.375 in	120	140	160	175	185	200	235			
2.75 in	140	160	180	195	215	240	275			
3.00 in	160	180	190	200	240	290	330	360		
3.25 in	200	240	280	320	350	390	430			
3.50 in	280	320	350	370	400	440	480	500		
4.00 in	360	400	430	450	490	500				
BEADED-EDGE										
2 in						130	150	170	180	
2¼ in					110	160	200	220	240	
2½ in/65mm					150	200	240	280	320	
3 in/80mm					230	290	320	360	390	440

ENGINEERING STD. COMMITTEE RIM SECTIONS C/D/G/H

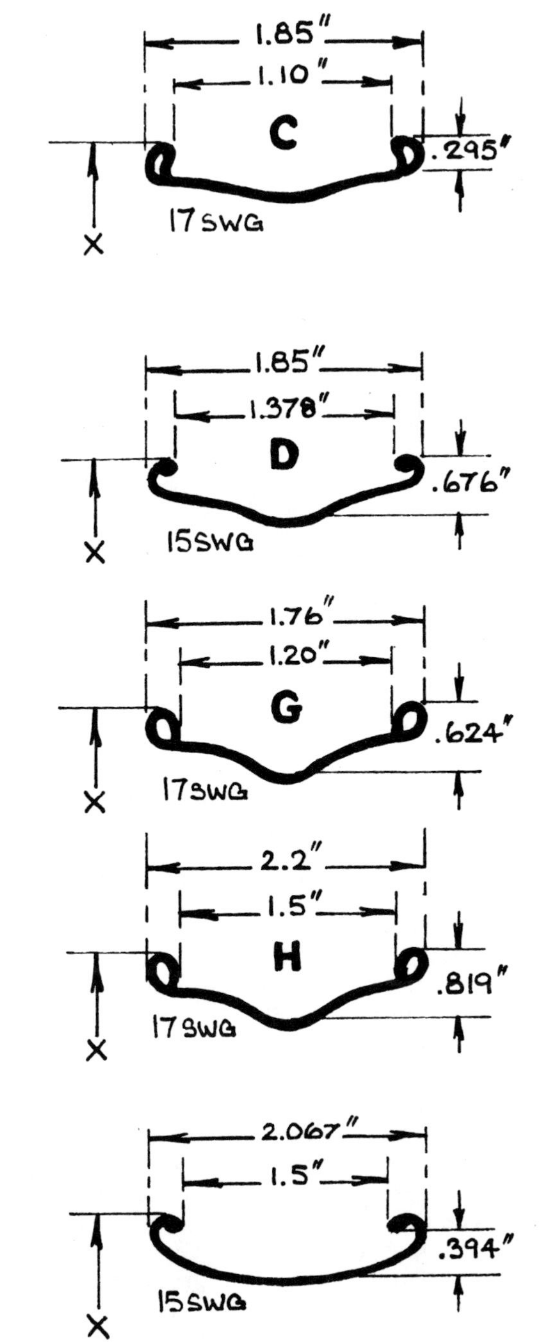

RIM No.	TYRE SIZES	CIRCUMF. (DIM. X)
C 1	24 x 2	64.125
C 2	26 x 2	71.3125
C 3	28 x 2	77.375
D 1	24 x 2¼ 24 x 2⅜ 24 x 2½	64.174
D 2	26 x 2¼ 26 x 2⅜ 26 x 2½	71.261
D 3	28 x 2¼ 28 x 2⅜	77.364
G 1	22 x 2	56.5
G 2	24 x 2	62.875
G 3	26 x 2	69.125
G 4	28 x 2	75.375
H 1	26 x 2¼	69.125
H 2	26 x 2½	66.0
LIGHT SECTION 65 mm RIM FOR 650 x 75 mm BE TYRES		

Old beaded-edge tyres are prone to cracking and must be replaced, if only to satisfy the MOT Examiner. Under-inflated BE covers will warm-up and chafe through the beads in no time; worse still, as any old rider will confirm, they can fly off the rims with disastrous consequences. So check tyre pressures frequently. Higher pressures are required with beaded-edge tyres than for wired types (refer to table).

Wired-edge tyres

Most motorcyclists are familiar with these, and yet the fitting of wired tyres still seems to cause problems. As with beaded-edge covers, a smear of lubricant on the beads works wonders and many wired covers will go on without levers. Always start opposite the valve when fitting and around the valve when removing.

To fit a wired-on cover smear both beads with tyre soap and ease one side of the tyre into position. Fit the tube, making sure it isn't twisted (a frequent occurrence). Place the wheel on the floor, preferably with a piece of old carpet underneath to prevent scratching. Starting opposite the valve, tread the bead over the rim by working round it with feet akimbo, Charlie Chaplin–fashion. A good stout pair of boots help enormously.

When you have got to about the half-way mark see that the bead has gone down into the well of the rim; this is important as it makes the remaining portion easier to fit. With luck you might be able to complete the operation with foot pressure alone; if not, use a small lever for the last bit near the valve. At this point you are quite likely to nip the tube — we have all been guilty of this misdemeanor at one time or other — so exercise due caution.

Inflate the tyre partially and bounce it up and down a few times to seat the beads. The fitting line around the tyre walls should be equidistant from the rims. In stubborn cases, when a tyre refuses to seat centrally, almost deflate the tube and push the motorcycle a few yards. With luck it will then seat squarely. Try blowing it up suddenly with a high-pressure airline to about 50 psi — sometimes this surprises a tyre into re-seating. (Don't forget to reduce the pressure to the recommended figure!)

Rear "handbrake" block and cable on a 1924 lightweight 250 cc BSA. Two brakes operate on the rear wheel, the second (footbrake) block being behind the silencer. This system provides surprisingly good results, except in wet weather. The BSA company won a famous court case in the 1920s when they proved to the satisfaction of the judiciary that their 'round tank' models had, in fact, two independently-operating brakes. If the case had gone against BSA, thousands of machines would have been affected.

Brakes

Vintage brake blocks

To their credit, The Vintage Motor Cycle Club has in recent years inaugurated a Brake Block Scheme to meet the demands of vintage machine owners with primitive brakes. A synthetic rubber-based material with no fibre content is offered to Club members in sizes to enable the following to be made:-

a A set of stirrup brake blocks
b A dummy belt-rim brake block

The material is sold per cubic inch and the onus of deciding suitability rests entirely with the customer; for this reason the material is classed as a *retarding medium*. Blocks can be fashioned out of the product with the aid of simple hand tools such as files, rasps and *Surform* blades.

Enthusiasts in far-off corners of the globe might like to try making their dummy belt rim blocks out of wood. After all, stagecoaches and railway carriages used to be braked by means of wooden blocks and surprisingly enough, this material has fairly good stopping powers.

Opinion is sharply divided among hard veteran riders as to which is the best type of wood to use; some say poplar and others swear by beech. I make my blocks out of the latter and find they last at least a couple of season's riding.

The blocks are fashioned by hand and "veed" to fit the belt rim; you can make enough blocks for twenty years' riding in one session. With a touch of black paint they look quite authentic and actually work much better than some original vulcanite-hard replacements found at autojumbles. Slots or grooves, to fit brake levers, can be made in the back of the blocks with a milling cutter — an ordinary twist drill reground with an almost flat business-end is a good substitute.

Check that the block seats squarely in the belt rim; apply the brake hard and slacken off the adjustment or clamping screws a touch to let the block align itself. Tighten up the screws. Rub some chalk on the working faces of the block, apply the brake gently and rotate the wheel by hand. If all the block braking area is contacted all is well; if not, a few minutes work with a file and emery paper will take off any high spots. This technique applies also to front stirrup brake blocks, which can be improved by careful alignment and bedding-in.

Most dummy belt rim brakes do not perform well in wet weather — there is usually an appreciable time lag before they dry-out. Skilful riding will compensate for this shortcoming. Fortunately in dry weather such brakes are usually quite effective, indeed there are some belt rim brakes which will lock the rear wheel at the slightest provocation.

Internal expanding brakes — a personal experience

Back brakes never seem to give me much cause for concern, perhaps because the application of a hefty DR boot overcomes design shortcomings. Front brakes are a different matter. I'm sure everyone recognises the symptoms of a spongy front anchor — you can pull the lever up to the handlebar with little effect whilst the bike can be pushed forward in pre-MOT constabulary fashion. When I was a hard-up apprentice I remember being stopped three times in one week by the local bobby, who applied such a rudimentary test to my 350 cc Levis; after the third attempt to make my brake work he said wearily, *I'll have to see your dad about this.* Over a pint in the local he advised my father to fix my brakes, otherwise he *would not be responsible for the consequences* if his sergeant was to catch me. Needless to say, the brake was attended to and I was allowed to continue my daily commuting unhampered by the law. What you might call a case of community-police relationship in today's jargon — unfortunately things have changed and the Ministry of Transport Test has put an end to such escapades!

Spongy brakes, such as those on the Levis of long ago, can be quite mystifying and difficult to correct. In such cases I usually run down my check list of possible faults, which goes something like this:-

1 Grease on linings
2 Brake not centralised (braking on one shoe only)
3 Bad relining (air gap between shoe and lining)
4 Oval drum
5 Wrong grade of friction material
6 Wear in cam pivot
7 Brake cable too weak for the size of brake

It is most unlikely for a single brake to display all the faults listed — usually the snag can be traced to just one malady, as the following experience will serve to illustrate:-

A recently-restored machine had been road-tested and the front brake was disappointing in its performance. The brake should have worked well as new bonded linings had been fitted by the previous owner, ruling out any possibility of air-gaps between linings and shoes.

The linings were checked — no oil or grease on them. They showed evidence of good contact all the way round so that was not the problem. The general brake geometry was checked, including the cable strength (this point is mentioned as occasionally some feeble brake cables tend to wilt under pressure. Heavier cables usually cure this problem of course, although such stern measures should be considered as a last resort).

Eventually, having checked everything else on the list, including girder fork spindles (sloppiness can cause erratic brake behaviour) the friction material was closely examined. The linings had a high percentage of metal in them, more suitable for a Leyland bus than a vintage motor bicycle! This material, albeit brand new, was chiselled off and replaced by some non-metallic woven *Ferodo*. It was much thicker than standard, which suited me fine as

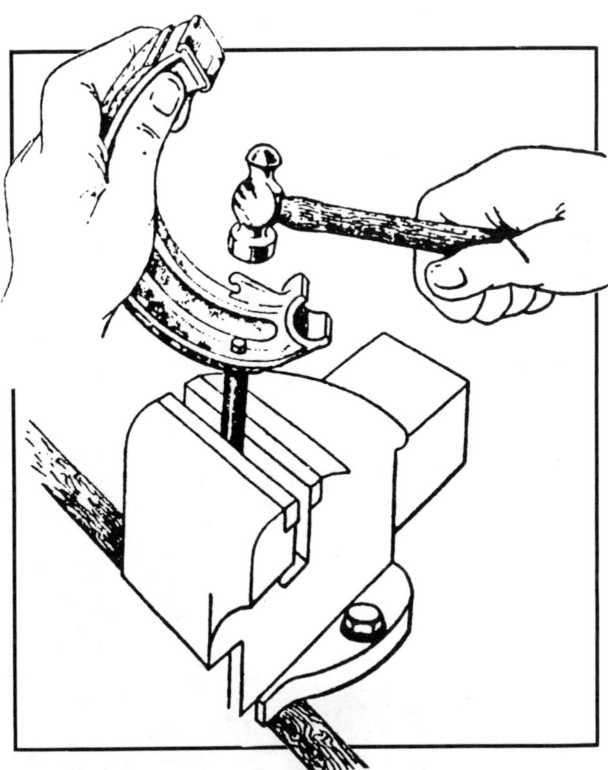

When riveting on new linings it is best to start in the middle and work outwards. There should be no gap between lining and shoe. A punch of the same diameter as the rivet head is placed in the vice as shown and the rivet neatly hammered over. All rivet heads must be below the lining surface.

it enabled me to skim down the diameter in the lathe, racing style.

I made up an arbour for the backplate and mounted the brake assembly in the chuck, making sure it ran true to start with, and machined the linings to a truly circular form.

With the wheel reassembled, a short road test confirmed that what had once been an indifferent brake was now a really good stopper, completely transformed by the softer linings. Readers with tiny "tobacco tin" front brakes might be interested in the above experiences (which occurred with the author's early 'big-port' AJS) as quite often small brakes can be made to work surprisingly well with a change in friction material.

Those contemplating vintage racing would do well to consult a brake specialist with regard to their application, particularly if very fast work is envisaged. So many factors have to be taken into account — type of front forks (girder, telescopic or leading-link), brake drum material, weights and speeds involved etc etc. On vintage (pre-1930) racers a conversion to dual front brakes is worth contemplating if the forks are strong enough to resist bending (early unbraced Scott forks will certainly bend with non-standard brakes). Sometimes a longer brake torque arm, attached towards the top of the girder blade, helps prevent bending.

Whatever the type of brake, do check the brake plate anchorage from time to time. It is not unknown for anchor bolts to shear, with alarming consequences; when this happens the whole brake plate revolves and locks up the wheel as effectively as a stick pushed through the spokes. Not a pleasant experience when travelling at 70 mph!

Making inverted levers

For those readers with limited machining facilities, ie a lathe, the manufacture of inverted levers should present no problem. Clutch and brake levers of this type have not been available commercially for many years and, for some strange reason, they are invariably missing when an early machine turns up.

I make mine out of brass castings and can vouch for their strength. First step is to make two wooden patterns, one for the lug and one for the lever. The patterns should be slightly oversize to allow for machining; about 1/8 in thicker on the lever and 1/8 in "all round" on lug dimensions should be

A newly-rebuilt Grand Prix Triumph arrives at the Belle Vue Show, the largest event of its kind in the world for classic bikes. It is equipped with the famous (or infamous!) spring hub.

sufficient. If you can, borrow a sample lever and copy this. If you are making levers for yourself you might as well adjust the reach (dimension x in the sketch) to suit your own hand-spread. Most commercial levers were originally made for a universal-sized hand; riders with small hands often had difficulty in manipulating inverted levers, many lady riders being quite unable to cope with the reach required.

Enlist the aid of a friendly foundryman and get two sets of castings run off in brass. Even if you have to pay for them it should not cost more than three or four pounds for the material. No core boxes or complicated moulds are used.

The machining operations are both simple and rewarding. Start by chucking the lug in the four-jaw and machine the spigot truly circular to suit your handlebar end. Bore out the inside of the lug, leaving about a 1/8 in wall thickness. Follow suit with the other lug; all subsequent operations can be done in the three-jaw self-centering chuck. Gripping on the spigots, clean-up the outer ends of both lugs. Unless a milling machine is part of the workshop equipment, all other surfaces of the lug will have to be filed, but this does not take long.

Mark out and slot the lugs (where the levers fit) using either a hacksaw, or a milling cutter fixed in the lathe chuck. If the latter method is decided upon, the lug can be fixed to the cross-slide. Finish off the slots with a file, if necessary. Touch up all sharp edges with a smooth file and polish all visible surfaces until they shine like gold, ready for nickel plating.

Carefully file the levers to shape — this is a time-consuming operation but most satisfying if done properly. Try to make the levers a nice close fit in the lugs and smooth-off all surfaces with strip emery. It helps to have an original lever on hand so you know what to aim for. Polish lever blades on a buffing mop if you have one, or finish by hand with smooth emery and metal polish.

Assemble the levers into their lugs and drill and tap for the pivot screws. A nice touch is to make the lugs right and left-handed by ensuring that the pivot screw heads are on the uppermost sides. Cheese-head screws look best. If you don't have this type in the screw box you can always make them by turning down hexagon-head screws and slotting the heads. 1/4 BSF is a handy size, although there is no reason why 1/4 UNF or 6 mm should not be used. Thin locknuts should be fitted on the underside.

When the screws are tightened and the locknuts done up, the levers should move without binding, but not flap up and down. If you are restoring old levers, the pivot screw holes invariably need bushing, or welding-up and re-drilling. Oval screw holes give rise to a surprising amount of lost motion in a brake or clutch control. Turn up cable stops (see sketch) from brass bar and make these a push fit in the lugs.

All that remains to be done is to give all the parts a final clean and polish, and send them off to the

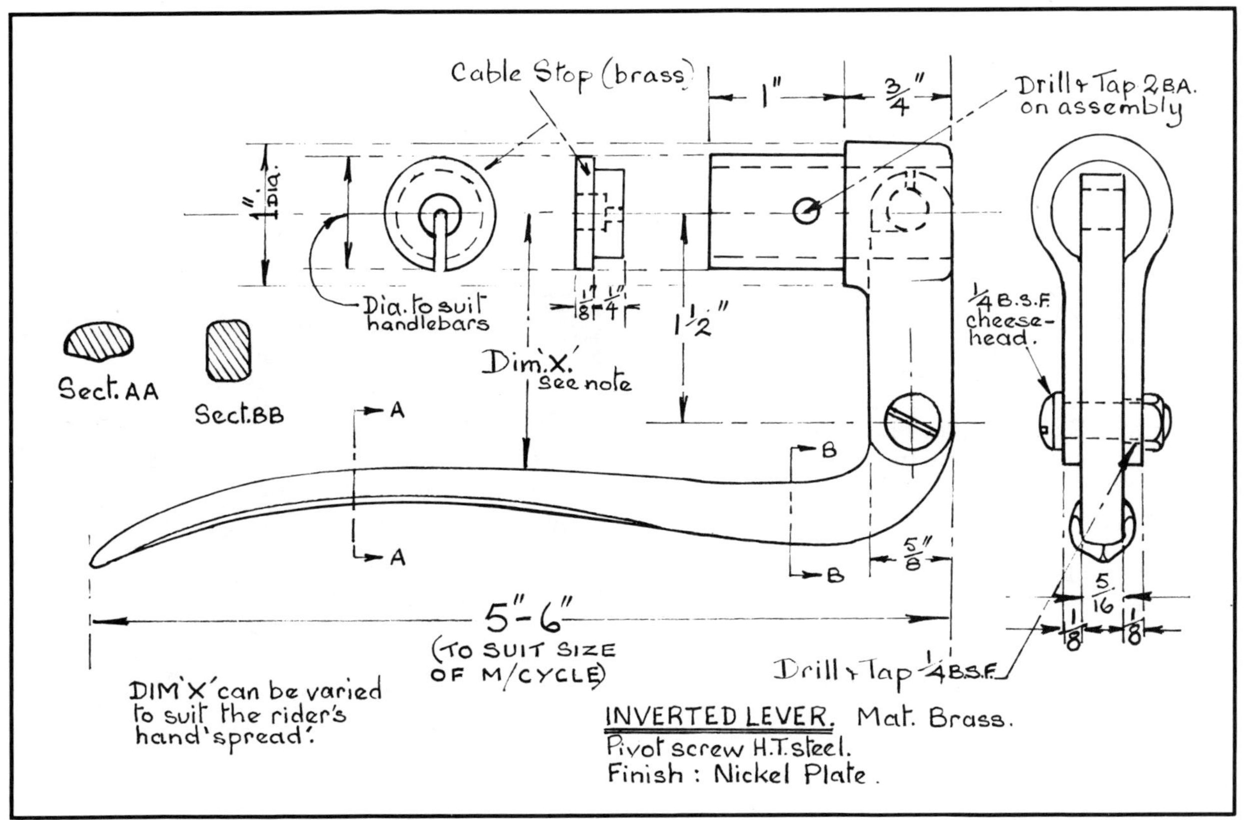

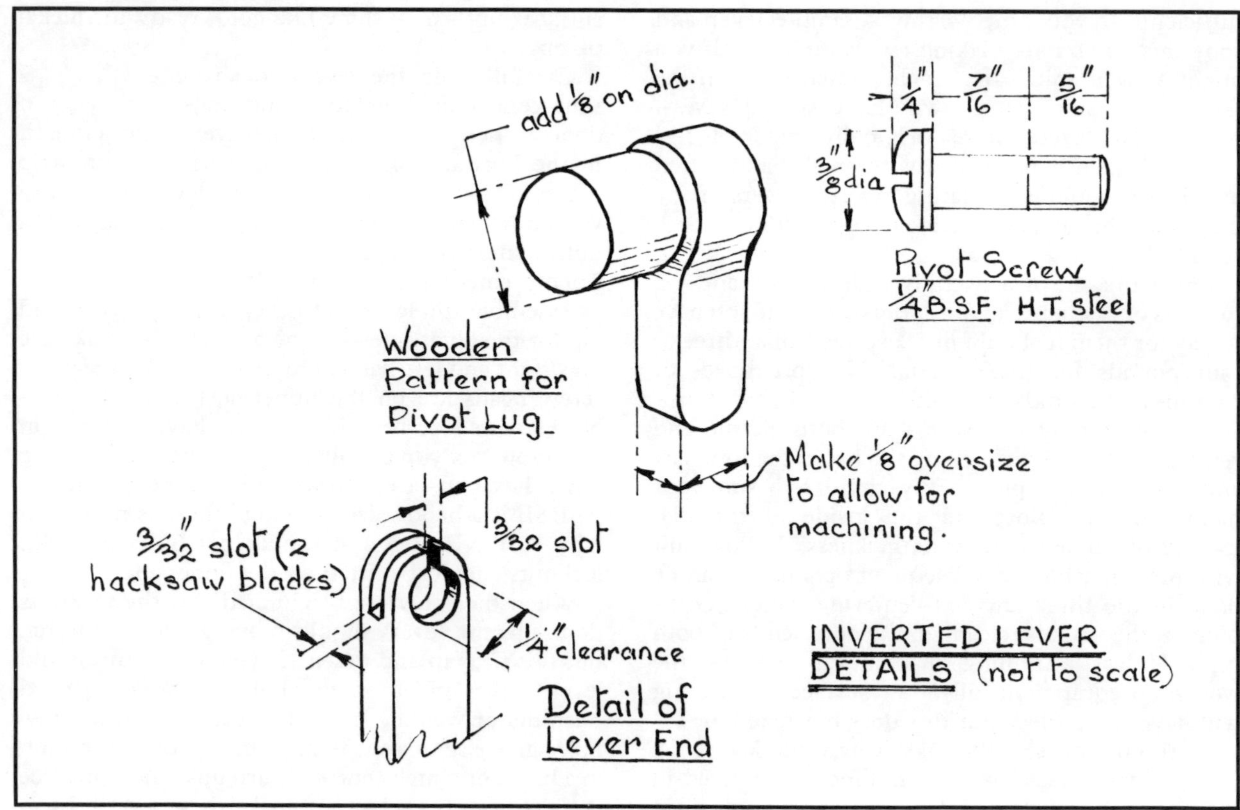

platers. The drawing shows an average-sized lever of 5 in to 6 in long but you can always vary this dimension to suit your machine. Adjust control cables so there is a minimum of free movement — approximately 1/8 in in the case of a clutch lever and about 1/4 in for a brake.

When inverted levers are fitted, this means that cables have to pass through the handlebars. Sometimes they exit through a central hole, and sometimes through a hole on either side of the bar. If both cables pass through one hole this should be well-radiused and of sufficiently large diameter to prevent kinking. Individual cable holes can be drilled at an angle and all sharp edges touched up with a riffler file. When the handlebars are turned on full lock, make sure the cables are still free — you might find the front brake pulls on, or the clutch will not free. Re-routing the cables will usually cure this snag, together with careful adjustment.

The front forks

Telescopic forks should be checked for straightness and wear in the bushes; the method of dismantling will vary in accordance with the make of machine so it is best to consult the appropriate workshop manual. Usually they are held in the bottom yokes by pinch bolts and to the top yokes by a simple tapered joint or plain flange arrangement. Slight misalignment of the front wheel can be corrected by slackening the various pinch-bolts and yanking the handlebars in the appropriate direction. With the machine on its stand, the front wheel is held between the legs (pushbike fashion) whilst the handlebars are turned. Tighten up all pinch-bolts and check alignment once again.

Providing the damage is not too severe, bent fork legs can be straightened in an hydraulic press with

The leaf spring front forks fitted to a 1926 BMW twin.

Two veteran fork assemblies. Left, a 1912 3½ hp P & M and right, Stauffer lubricated spindles on a 1914 Matchless.

the aid of vee-blocks. Legs which are kinked or twisted more than four or five degrees are best discarded as further bending could weaken them. The tubes can be tested for straightness on rollers, using a clock gauge, or in a lathe. A rough check can be made by rolling them along a surface plate, or sheet of plate glass.

Worn legs can be reclaimed by hard-chrome deposition (a different proposition than ordinary flash chrome) or metal spraying. Both processes should be done by a specialist, who will usually grind the tubes after treatment; alternatively the grinding can be farmed-out to a light engineering concern. If it is decided to patch-repair legs by the metal-spraying process the affected areas will have to be etched, either by coarse turning or shot-blasting. The new metal is sprayed on molten as the leg revolves, the remaining unworn portion being masked off. As with hard-chroming, the leg will require grinding afterwards to a superfine finish.

New bushes can be made from phospor-bronze bar. Bearing stockists sell a material known as *Encon;* this is simply cored phosphor bronze in conventional tube form and it saves much boring. It is ideal for making fork bushes and can be obtained in a variety of sizes. Bushes should naturally be a good sliding fit with no excess clearance.

Some lightweight machines were fitted with undamped teles and these often had *Tufnol* fork bushes. This material is excellent for bushes which receive spasmodic lubrication; however it is difficult to obtain by those outside the engineering industry. Replacements could be made from *Nylatron GSM,* plain nylon bar, or sintered bronze as a temporary measure.

New wheel spindles should be made from good high-tensile material, preferably EN16. Light-weight machines may only require EN8 but it is best not to take chances. On many telescopics the wheel spindle is clamped on one side by a pinch-bolt; ensure that the hole where the spindle passes through is not oval and closely inspect the lug for cracks. Fractures in this area are quite common.

Always fit new seals during reassembly. Some makers, just to be awkward, used non-standard seals with their own catalogue numbers. There is no option in such cases but to buy the recommended replacements, which is precisely what the makers intended. Have a look at the various letters and numbers around the seals, and with luck you might find they correspond with standard *Gaco* or *Weston* references. Bearing stockists will help if you are able to quote the housing bore and leg diameter.

Unobtainable head races can be made out of EN31, case-hardened and ground. If you have access to the vacuum-hardening process through engineering contacts (toolmakers can often help) make the races from one of the steels recommended in Chapter 1. As previously mentioned, it should be possible to finish the races completely before heat-treatment as there is little or no distortion with vacuum-hardening.

When new head races have been fitted, always re-check the adjustment after a hundred miles or so as they tend to settle and bed-in. Races which are left slack will indent very quickly. Races which are too tight give rise to an unpleasant wallowing when on the straight. So try and get them just right; tighten-up the top nut on the steering head until resistance is felt and then slack-off 1/4 of a turn. The forks and wheel assembly should flop over from one side to the other under their own weight when the machine is propped up at the front end.

Steering dampers

A machine with good steering characteristics should not need a steering damper. Be that as it may, if a damper is fitted examine the friction discs as they tend to wear to wafer thickness. Discs used to be made from wood — indeed, this traditional raw material is excellent for the purpose (poplar or beech) but can absorb moisture in the wet. Wooden discs have been known to swell and stiffen-up the steering, requiring the adjusting knob to be slackened a turn or so.

New discs can be manufactured from *Ferodo* sheet, turned in the lathe. Whilst the fabrication of a couple of discs is not likely to cause death from asbestosis, it is always good policy to wear a mask when handling brake and clutch lining material. Light engineering firms use items known as *Morse torque limiters,* which are very much like friction dampers in principle; discs from these can often be adapted for use in steering dampers.

Girder fork maintenance

Girder blades should be checked for twist, as viewed from above, and bending as viewed from the front and side elevations. Due to accidents, or sidecar hauling, girder forks are very prone to misaligment, especially on heavier machines. When a 500 cc bike is dropped at high speed there's a lot of momentum to arrest, and if the immovable object is a stone wall or high kerb you have problems.

Insert mandrels into the fork spindle holes and wheel spindle lugs. The mandrels should be straight and clean. Silver steel rod, which is exactly to size, is ideal for the purpose but failing that, bright mild steel bar will suffice. Length of the mandrels should be about 14 to 18 inches. A length of screwed rod, with nuts and washers, will do for the wheel spindle-lug mandrel.

Exacting persons will like to make up a jig consisting of two straight edges, upon which the girder fork unit can be placed. Any lateral twist is easily spotted by the amount of daylight under each mandrel end. Those with good eyesight will be able to detect misalignment without the aid of jigs by sighting along the forks with the mandrels in position.

Minor twists and bends can be corrected by bending the blades cold with rods (not the checking mandrels!) shoved through pivot holes. Due to the springy nature of fork tubing the blades may have to be twisted beyond the amount of misalignment and then brought back to true. Severely bent blades present a problem which is best dealt with by one of the few surviving girder fork specialists. New tubes may be required — an extremely difficult task for the amateur.

Early Druid forks (side-spring type) were made from relatively thin-walled tube so watch out for excessive rust-pitting in the blades. Filling-in the pit-marks with body filler may disguise them but will not increase the strength of the fork so it is advisable to look for a set of replacement fork blades, difficult though that may be. Examine the blades and steering-head tube for hairline cracks as it is not unknown for forks to snap in two in service — an alarming experience indeed.

It is almost certain that the fork spindles will be worn so new ones should be made from a good high tensile steel. EN16 bar is ideal, ground or fine-turned to size. Due to its brittle nature, silver steel is

Left: A very popular fork assembly, the lightweight side-spring Druid, seen here on a 1920 New Hudson. Druid fork members of this period are of relatively thin gauge material and should be closely-examined for serious rust pitting. Above: The heavyweight Brampton front fork, correctly finished with black-enamelled springs and nickel-plated nuts. Also visible are authentic screw-down lubricators.

not recommended. The threads should be screw-cut for accuracy; if a lathe is not available, great care should be taken to avoid drunken threads when using a hand die-stock.

Fork bushes

Unbushed forks are a headache to restorers; sometimes it is possible to get away with oversize spindles in reamed holes if enough metal is present. This method is usually only practicable on veteran and early vintage machines with plain holes in the fork links. Occasionally, enough meat in the fork cross tubes will allow an increase in spindle size from, say 3/8 in to 7/16 in diameter. Obviously such a modification should be approached with caution, such factors as wall thickness and fork link section being taken into account.

Thin walled bronze bushes can be inserted into spindle holes to restore them to size, but here again there must be sufficient wall thickness to allow for boring and reaming. With bushed forks, the old bushes can be pressed out, or drilled out if obstinate, and replaced with new ones machined from phosphor bronze. This operation is not quite as easy as it sounds.

Before pressing in the new bushes, clean up the holes by taking a very light cut through with an expanding reamer. Bore the bushes to size, ie a sliding-fit on the spindles, and finish off the OD to a .001 to .0015 inch interference fit (no more, as the bushes might collapse under pressure). Press in the bushes using a long piece of stud-iron and flanged washers to locate in the bores; it is better to draw

Front and rear ends of a 1951 Moto Guzzi Falcone. Guzzis were first produced in 1921 at Mandello del Lario, the Falcone model surviving up to the 1970s. The adjustable friction damper on the rear pivoting fork system was a Guzzi hallmark for generations.

bushes in by this method, rather than knock them in, because of their fragile nature. When in position the bores will have closed-in a fraction and will need reaming-out. The correct tool for this operation is a double-ended reamer with a pilot spigot — not easy to come by. With luck an expanding reamer will do the job if light cuts are taken, or a special "D" shaped reamer can be made from silver steel to line-ream both bushes in one go.

Another method is to make bushes a hand push-fit and *Loctite* them in. Clean out the fork holes with primer and fit with *Loctite Retainer*. Make up a fitting mandrel, or use the new fork spindle, and push in the bushes from each side. If the bushes were pre-reamed before assembly no further reaming should be necessary. For this method to be successful the bush-holes in the forks must be fairly true to start with. If they are not, clean them out with a long-series drill or reamer, removing as little metal as possible.

BSA machines from the early 1920s onwards featured an unusual design of fork link. The spindles were integral with the links, and long draw bolts held both sides together. Tightening-up these draw bolts, or tie rods, takes up any side-play and the forged hollow spindles will last for years if well greased. Unfortunately ride-to-work motorcyclists were liable to neglect routine lubrication, consequently fork spindles and bushes often had to run dry. Repairing BSA links is more difficult than others, but the following method is one solution to the problem.

BSA link repair

Usually it is the integral spindle spigots which wear most. Saw them off flush with the links, or side plates. Machine new spigots from high-tensile steel (EN16 or 24), bore and thread where required. Bore out the link plate holes to suit the new spigots, making sure the spigots are a neat slide fit in the holes, and braze or silver solder the assembly. Clean up excess brazing material and file lubrication flats on the spigots (this can be done before assembly, if preferred).

It is imperative that all spigots should be parallel and in line with their opposite partners. Naturally they should all be the same distance apart, ie the centres should be exactly uniform on each pair of links. For these reasons it is essential to bore out the link plates in pairs and to braze in the spigots using a jig-plate (a dummy side-link made from bright mild steel flat bar). An alternative method of ensuring spigot parallelism is to assemble a LH and RH pair of links, complete with draw-bolts, and braze-up each side in situ. Be careful not to braze the draw-bolts also.

New phosphor-bronze bushes can be fitted to the forks, or if you are not worried about making the issue non-standard, the existing bushes can be reamed out and oversize spigots made to suit.

In the case of lightweight BSAs (250 cc models of the vintage and immediate post-vintage period) the new spigots can be made a medium press-fit and *Loctited* in position. Parallelism is thus assured, and providing the draw-bolts are kept in adjustment there should be no fear of the spigots working loose. Even if they did work loose no great calamity would ensue as it would of course be impossible for them to come out altogether. This repair is perfectly satisfactory and will last for a long period; with heavyweight BSAs of 500 cc and above, the brazing method outlined previously is perhaps more durable.

Fork spindle lubrication

Most veteran and early vintage fork spindles were oil-lubricated by means of cycle-type flip-top oilers. A light oil, such as that sold for pushbikes at

Heavyweight BSA girder forks on this nicely-restored 1939 1000 cc vee twin sidecar outfit. Usually, these models led an ignominious career, hauling window cleaners' floats and tradesmens' box sidecars. A shame, for they were beautifully made, luxurious mounts. The tank finish, correct for 1939, is semi-matt silver on chrome.

Halfords branches, is satisfactory for these early oilers. Heavy engine oil takes too long to penetrate the microscopic oil hole, admirable though it may be in other respects.

A few early machines were fitted with miniature screw-down *Stauffer* grease cups which, on account of their small proportions, were not very effective. Fill them regularly and **use** them often.

By far the best spindle lubricant is graphited grease, applied through a *Tecalemit* grease nipple. However, it must be remembered that even grease does not retain its properties indefinitely so apply the grease gun three or four times in a season's riding. Once a fortnight is not too often if the bike is ridden daily.

Spring frames

A sloppy back-end, whether of the early leaf-sprung type or later plunger pattern, should not be tolerated under any circumstances. Dodgy handling will certainly be the result of excessive play in sprung frames; usually this manifests itself in a queasy feeling when the bike is cornered, like a semi-

Above and below: The Grand Prix Triumph engine, developed from the wartime AAPP (airborne auxiliary power plant) motor. This unit (or rather the distinctive square cylinder barrel) first came into the limelight when Ernie Lyons won the 1946 Manx Grand Prix, the engine of his machine having an AAPP cylinder head and block mounted on a T100 bottom end. Ernie's bike also featured a spring hub, an Edward Turner brainchild.

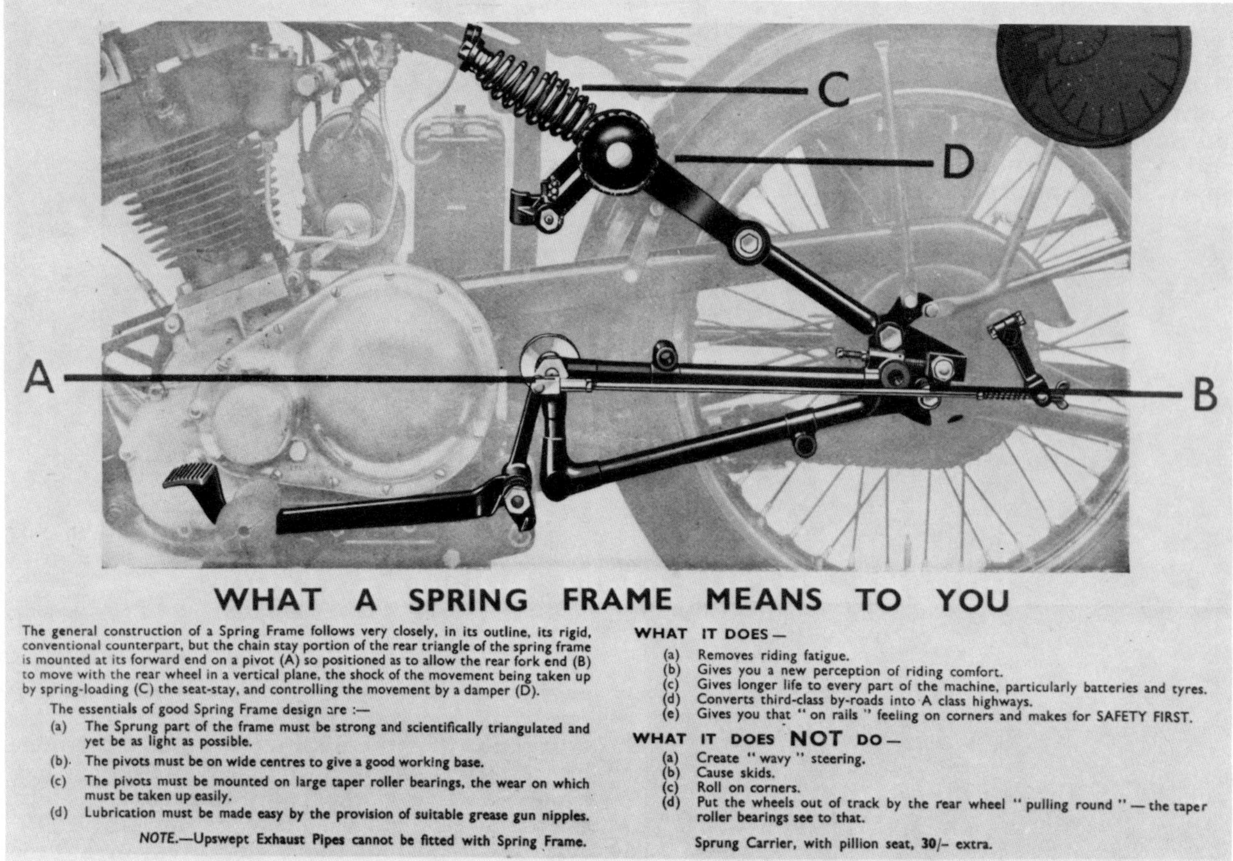

WHAT A SPRING FRAME MEANS TO YOU

The general construction of a Spring Frame follows very closely, in its outline, its rigid, conventional counterpart, but the chain stay portion of the rear triangle of the spring frame is mounted at its forward end on a pivot (A) so positioned as to allow the rear fork end (B) to move with the rear wheel in a vertical plane, the shock of the movement being taken up by spring-loading (C) the seat-stay, and controlling the movement by a damper (D).

The essentials of good Spring Frame design are :—

(a) The Sprung part of the frame must be strong and scientifically triangulated and yet be as light as possible.
(b). The pivots must be on wide centres to give a good working base.
(c) The pivots must be mounted on large taper roller bearings, the wear on which must be taken up easily.
(d) Lubrication must be made easy by the provision of suitable grease gun nipples.

NOTE.—Upswept Exhaust Pipes cannot be fitted with Spring Frame.

WHAT IT DOES—

(a) Removes riding fatigue.
(b) Gives you a new perception of riding comfort.
(c) Gives longer life to every part of the machine, particularly batteries and tyres.
(d) Converts third-class by-roads into A class highways.
(e) Gives you that "on rails" feeling on corners and makes for SAFETY FIRST.

WHAT IT DOES NOT DO—

(a) Create "wavy" steering.
(b) Cause skids.
(c) Roll on corners.
(d) Put the wheels out of track by the rear wheel "pulling round"—the taper roller bearings see to that.

Sprung Carrier, with pillion seat, 30/– extra.

What modern motorcyclists would call a "mono-shock" system, the 1937 New Imperial spring frame.

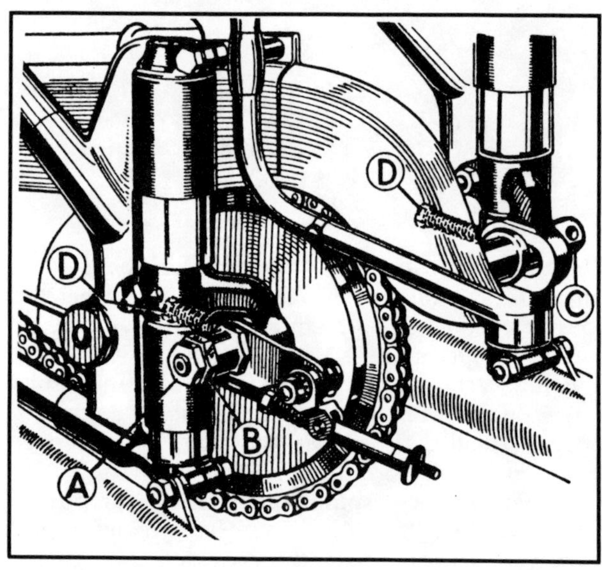

Typical BSA plunger rear suspension units and rear hub as fitted to the A7, A10, B31 and B33 models.
A — knock out spindle nut (R.H. thread)
B — wheel securing sleeve nut (R.H. thread)
C — knock out spindle
D — wheel adjuster screws (spring-loaded)

deflated rear tyre. Plungers suffer badly from excessive bush wear, giving rise to the theory that all plunger systems promote bad handling — a fallacy of course, the problem not being bad design but bad maintenance.

Recourse to the manufacturer's workshop manual will indicate the correct procedure for dismantling and reassembly. If this information is not available, do proceed with caution as plunger springs can fly out with tremendous force. Usually some form of spring compressor fashioned from threaded rod will prevent catastrophies.

Originally many plunger centre-posts were hard-chromed and ground, an expensive process to repeat should they be worn. If the machine is rarely used, plain ground high-tensile or stainless steel is a cheaper alternative.

Examine the QD hub bolt holes for elongation and rectify by welding up and re-drilling. Wire-up the bolts on assembly (whether or not this was originally done) to prevent loss.

Triumph spring hub

Dismantling the infamous spring-hub is not a job

for the faint-hearted and should **not** be carried out without access to special tools. The plunger guide box springs require a special compressor, as illustrated, although the ingenious amateur could fabricate his own version.

Brake anchor plate

Place the wheel on the bench, brake side up. Prise off the anchor lever and remove the two split collars. Withdraw the dust excluder centre sleeve and sliding portion. Remove the dust cover. Lift the brake anchor plate and cast-iron ring.

Slipper roller

The roller should rotate freely with up to .002 in clearance each side. After checking remove the slipper roller.

End plate

Remove the securing nuts and withdraw the end plate. A special tool was available for this task but a normal 3-leg puller, with the feet ground thin, should suffice. Check and make a note of any aluminium shims beneath the plate.

Plunger guide box

Withdraw the assembly from the hub. Undo the four outside bolts and unscrew the two middle bolts a little to enable the cases to be parted about 3/8 in using the jig, tension the springs. Remove the last two bolts and part the cases.

Release spring pressure gradually. Withdraw the springs from the plunger guide.

Slipper pads

Check for wear, which usually occurs on the thrust

Above: Mark I Triumph spring hub and below, the jig for compressing plunger guide box springs (Courtesy Triumph Motorcycles (Coventry) Ltd.)

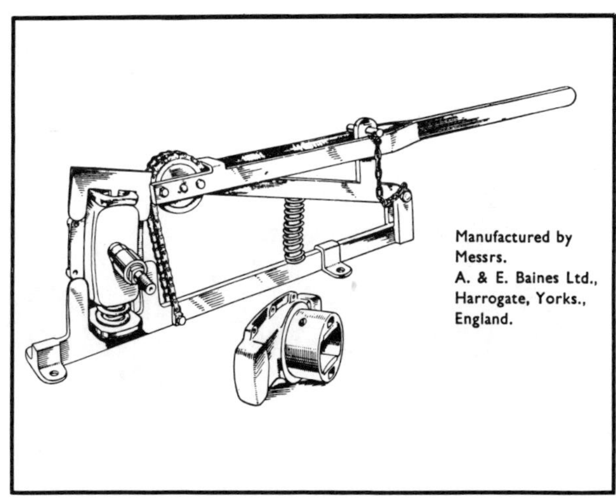

side only (front pad on the chain side and rear pad opposite). To remove, unscrew the two screws holding the pad.

Reassembly points

If the steel slipper pads were removed or replaced with new parts it will be necessary to assemble the plunger box less springs, plates and rubbers. Check that the roller to slipper pad clearance is 0.002 in each side as mentioned. Adjust with aluminium shims. When the pads are in position, tighten up the screws.

Springs

Take the case apart again and fit the springs, using the special jig. The springs should be lightly greased and the spring curvature should of course conform with the guide shape. Don't forget the rubber buffers.

Grease and fit the casings, release the jig and remove the assembly. Fill with lubricant through the casing gap, tap the cases together and fit and tighten the nuts and bolts. The top rear and bottom front should be from high-tensile material.

Reassemble the rest of the hub, replacing bearings where necessary. Replace any shims which were removed.

Final inspection

Before painting anything it is advisable to do a temporary rebuild to make sure everything fits together. Now is the time to find out if those replica parts fit, and if the wheels are in line. Make all the mudguard stays at this stage, not when the guards are stove-enamelled.

Check that engine bolts slide into place without having to spring the frame with a crowbar. Have another look for frame cracks or faulty brazing.

Chapter 3

ENGINE WORK: The Top Half

Inspection; Checking piston and ring wear. Machining pistons. Valves, guides, seats. Timing checks.

Dismantling and preliminary inspection

THE dismantling process will be made much easier if all nuts, bolts, locking rings and valve stems are given a good dose of easing oil a week or so before the task commences. If there is much cylinder bore rust, pour a copious amount of easing oil or diesel fuel down the plug hole.

In my opinion it is a waste of time trying to make a long-dormant engine run without a preliminary inspection. The temptation to hear it run must be resisted, difficult though this may be. Apart from bore rust (more of which later) all other working parts are probably as dry as a bone. There may even be internal damage, such as a loose crankpin, which will only be made worse with a test run. So, forget about temporary lash-ups, have patience, and wait until the motor is completely rebuilt. A well-built engine should start first or second kick — providing it was a sound design to start with.

Usually the best procedure is to leave the mainshaft (sprocket) nut in position at the outset; this can be firmly gripped with a ring or socket spanner if the piston is rusted-up. Take off the timing cover and note the timing marks on the cam wheels. Some timing cover screws can be very difficult to budge; an old tip is to give the screwdriver handle a sharp clout with a mallet before attempting to turn it. This often loosens the screw like magic; it need hardly be said that the screwdriver blade must be properly ground and the full width of the screw slot. An impact screwdriver will do the same thing — as you wallop the driver the blade twists against a cam.

Screws which will **not** shift by normal means can be drilled out. This is not as difficult as it may sound — if a hole is drilled truly central (start off with a 1/16 in drill) to a depth not exceeding that of the screw head, a sharp twist with the screwdriver will usually shear the head off. The remaining screw shank can be dealt with later. Attempting to remove an immovable cheesehead screw with a hammer and punch invariably ends in the surrounding aluminium being severely damaged.

Check the timing

Back to the timing marks. Almost every manufacturer marked their cams in some way or other so they could be replaced in the same relationship. Usually a series of dots and lines engraved in the cam-wheel faces will be found; there are variations on the theme but the method will be obvious on inspection. A few makers ground-off the corners of mating gear teeth; you might find, for instance, one

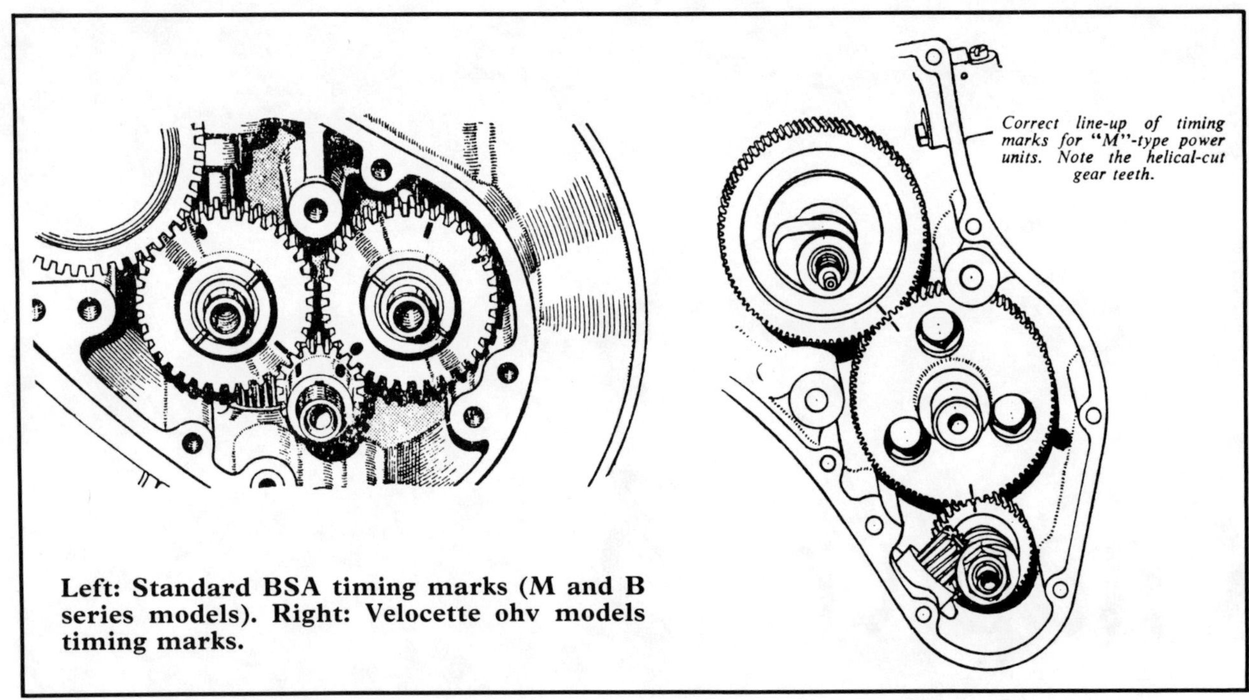

Left: Standard BSA timing marks (M and B series models). Right: Velocette ohv models timing marks.

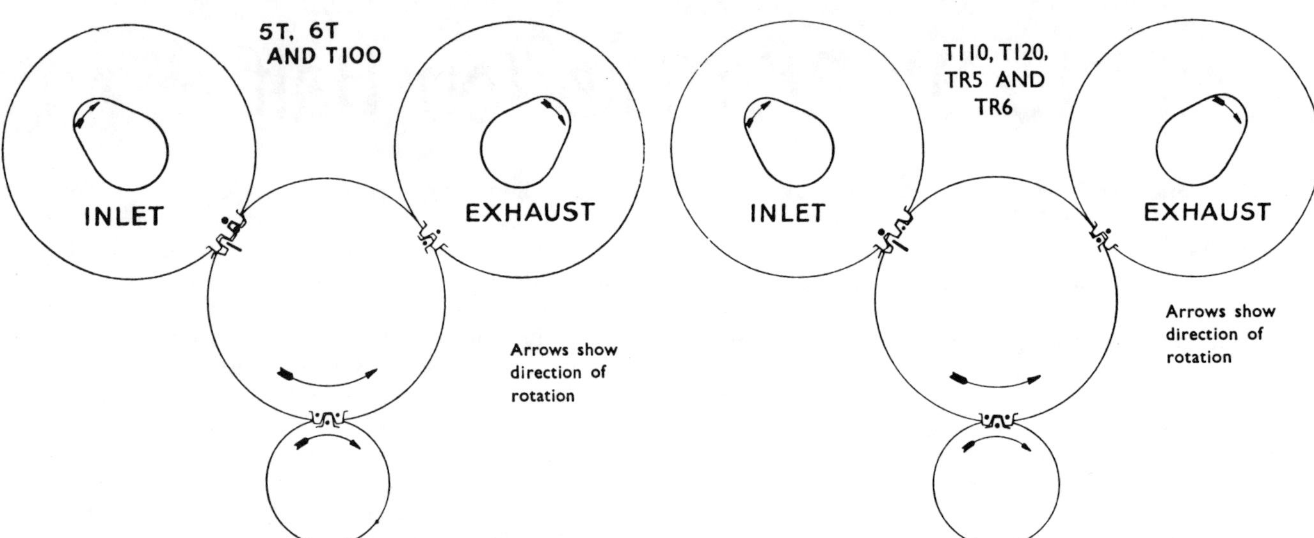

Triumph twins timing marks *(Courtesy Triumph Motorcycles (Coventry) Ltd.)*

nicked tooth on the half-time pinion (that's the gear attached to the end of the crankshaft) and two ground teeth on an adjacent cam-wheel. Obviously in this case the half-time pinion marked tooth fits in between the two marked cam teeth.

If in doubt (some pioneer engine manufacturers didn't mark their cams at all!) it is a good idea to paint some marks on yourself so that the timing wheels can be replaced correctly. Even so, an early engine of unknown quantity should have its timing checked on assembly, marks or no marks. To jump ahead a little, if the engine is of a rare make and valve timing figures are not available, the restorer will have to resort to average timing figures. It is a fact that engines of any given period (and of similar design to their contemporaries) will have roughly similar valve timing characteristics. For example, veteran engines (ie pre 1914) had their inlets opening either **on** top dead centre or no more than five degrees before. In the 1920s inlets opened perhaps five to ten degrees before TDC and gradually crept up to twenty to twenty five degrees before in the post-war years.

The foregoing rule of thumb of course applies to touring motors, racing engines being a different kettle of fish and subject to vast variations in timing figures. Still considering your unknown quantity motor, a good tip is to compare its timing to a

VALVE AND IGNITION TIMINGS FOR 1932–48 J.A.P. ENGINES

Pre-war engines continued for 1947–8 indicated thus: (1947–8)

TYPE OF ENGINE (See also pp. 59, 74-5, 142-3)	INLET Opens Before T.D.C.	INLET Closes After B.D.C.	EXHAUST Opens Before B.D.C.	EXHAUST Closes After T.D.C.	Ignition Advance Before T.D.C.
150 c.c. S.V. Standard	15°	50°	50°	20°	35°
175 c.c. S.V. Standard (1947)					
200 c.c. ,, ,,					
250 c.c. ,, ,, (1947–8)					
300 c.c. ,, ,,	15°	50°	50°	20°	40°
350 c.c. ,, ,,					
350 c.c. S.V. Special					
350 c.c. ,, ,, Sports (1947)					
*350 c.c. ,, ,, ,, D.S.	23°	63°	65°	25°	40°
†350 c.c. ,, ,, ,, D.S.	25°	60°	65°	20°	40°
500 c.c. S.V. Standard (1947)					
550 c.c. ,, ,,					
600 c.c. ,, ,,					
600 c.c. S.V. (1947–8)					
600 c.c. ,, Sports	16°	65°	65°	25°	40°
500 c.c. ,, ,,					
500 c.c. ,, W/C					
600 c.c. ,, ,,					
680 c.c. S.V. Standard Twin	18°	45°	60°	25°	40°
750 c.c. ,, ,, ,, (1947)					
1100 c.c. S.V. W/C 60° Twin					
1100 c.c. ,, A/C ,, ,, (1947–8)	16°	65°	65°	25°	38°
1323 c.c. ,, ,, ,, ,, (1947–8)					
1100 c.c. O.H.V. W/C ,, ,,					
980 c.c.S.V. Twin	17°	65°	65°	25°	45°
175 c.c. O.H.V. Standard					
200 c.c. ,, ,,	27°	67°	67°	27°	45°
250 c.c. ,, ,, (1947)					
*350 c.c. O.H.V. Standard (1947)	23°	63°	65°	25°	45°
*350 c.c. ,, Special					
*500 c.c. O.H.V. Standard (1947)	22°	62°	65°	25°	40°
*500 c.c. ,, Sports					
*600 c.c. ,, Standard	22°	62°	65°	25°	45°
†350 c.c. ,, Standard	28°	55°	60°	20°	45°
†350 c.c. ,, Special					
†500 c.c ,, Standard	16°	65°	65°	25°	40°
†600 c.c. ,, ,,	16°	65°	65°	25°	45°
680 c.c. O.H.V. Std. Twin	23°	63°	65°	25°	45°
*1000 c.c. O.H.V. Std. Twin	25°	66°	65°	23°	45°
*175 c.c. O.H.V. Racing	27°	67°	67°	27°	45°
*250 c.c. O.H.V. Racing	27°	67°	67°	27°	45°
†1000 c.c. O.H.V. Std. Twin	15°	60°	63°	23°	45°
†175 c.c. O.H.V. Racing	38°	68°	63°	22°	45°
†250 c.c. O.H.V. Racing	24°	55°	62°	25°	45°
350 c.c. O.H.V. Racing (1947–8)					
500 c.c. ,, ,,	45°	65°	70°	35°	42°
500, 350 c.c. Speedway (1947–8)					
*1000 c.c. O.H.V. Racing Twin	25°	66°	65°	23°	45°
†1000 c.c. O.H.V. Racing Twin	15°	60°	63°	23°	45°
*8/75 h.p. Touring	15°	65°	65°	25°	45°
8/80 h.p. Racing (1947–8)	45°	65°	70°	35°	42°L/C 38°H/C

* These timings are applicable to 1935–7 engines only
† These apply to 1932–4 engines

contemporary JAP engine of similar design characteristics. JAPs made almost every conceivable type of engine throughout their history, so there's bound to be one similar to yours. For example, if you have an ancient, perhaps foreign, make of 1000 cc side valve V-twin, then its valve-timing characteristics are probably in line with those of a JAP of the same capacity and era. At the worst you will only be a tooth out in your experiments.

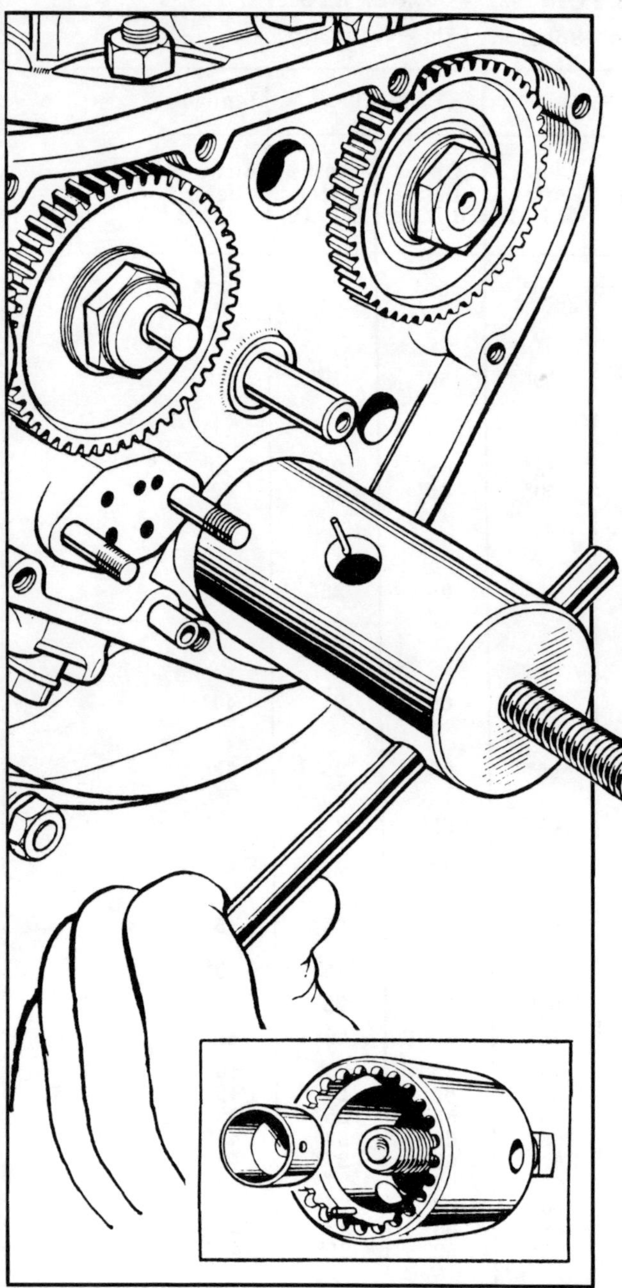

The use of special extractors is often vital for withdrawing 'half time' pinions and camwheels. Shown here are standard Triumph extractors *(Courtesy Triumph Motorcycles (Coventry) Ltd.)*

Cam removal

Undo the half-time pinion nut. Almost certainly this will be a left-hand thread. A good-fitting socket spanner or ring spanner, together with a thump from a copper hammer, will slacken the nut easily. Half-time pinions are best drawn off with an extractor, either a sprocket puller (it may be necessary to grind the feet thinner to fit behind the gear) or a specially-made two-legged extractor. Sometimes two tyre levers will prise out the pinion, but great care must be exercised not to damage the aluminium timing chest. On single-cylinder engines the half-time pinion is nearly always a parallel fit, keywayed of course, and generally not very tight. Note which way round the pinion goes — there may be a spigot on one side only.

Triumph parallel-twin camwheels are pulled off with extractor D178 and replaced with tool No. D182. These wheels are pressed quite tightly on their shafts, which have three keyways to facilitate precise timing. Some makes, Rudge for example, have taper-fitting half-time pinions with no key — this method also enables the timing to be set exactly — and JAP pinions have a number of keyways for the same reason. Whatever the system, remember to mark the settings with dabs of paint if you are not familiar with the marque.

Once the cams, wheels, pinion and cam-followers are removed, and the timing chest is empty, dismantling of the top-half can begin. Every engine is, of course, different, so we will have to confine our remarks to general things to watch out for.

Head bolts on side valve engines should always be undone a bit at a time, working from the middle outwards. This releases the stresses evenly. Easing oil helps as these bolts are usually rusted in place (when replacing head bolts use *Copaslip* to ease the problem at a later date). Aluminium alloy sv heads are prone to warping, so treat them with care, even when undoing the bolts. The importance of using tightly-fitting box-spanners, or sockets, cannot be stressed too highly. If the correct size of socket seems a little slack due to the bolt hexagon being eaten by rust, try tapping on a metric or A/F socket. This dodge often works, although it doesn't do your sockets any good!

Ohv heads are usually easier to get off, their bolts not being subject to quite the same amount of heat as sidevalve heads. Do be careful to avoid chipping the cooling fins, especially on those heads where the bolt enters from below. Label the pushrods inlet and exhaust if they are of different lengths.

AJS 'big-port' heads were held on in a delightfully simple manner by an inverted U-bolt stirrup (up to 1925) and by a two-bolt strap in the later vintage period. In all such designs it is important to slacken each side progressively, a little at a time, and to tighten up in a similar fashion. BSA heads on B group ohv models all have four through-bolts securely fastened in the crankcase. It is not recommended to remove these bolts unless replacements are required; the head should be released by means of the hexagonal portions half-way up. Gold Star heads have extra short bolts in between the through-bolts — don't forget the one inside the pushrod tunnel!

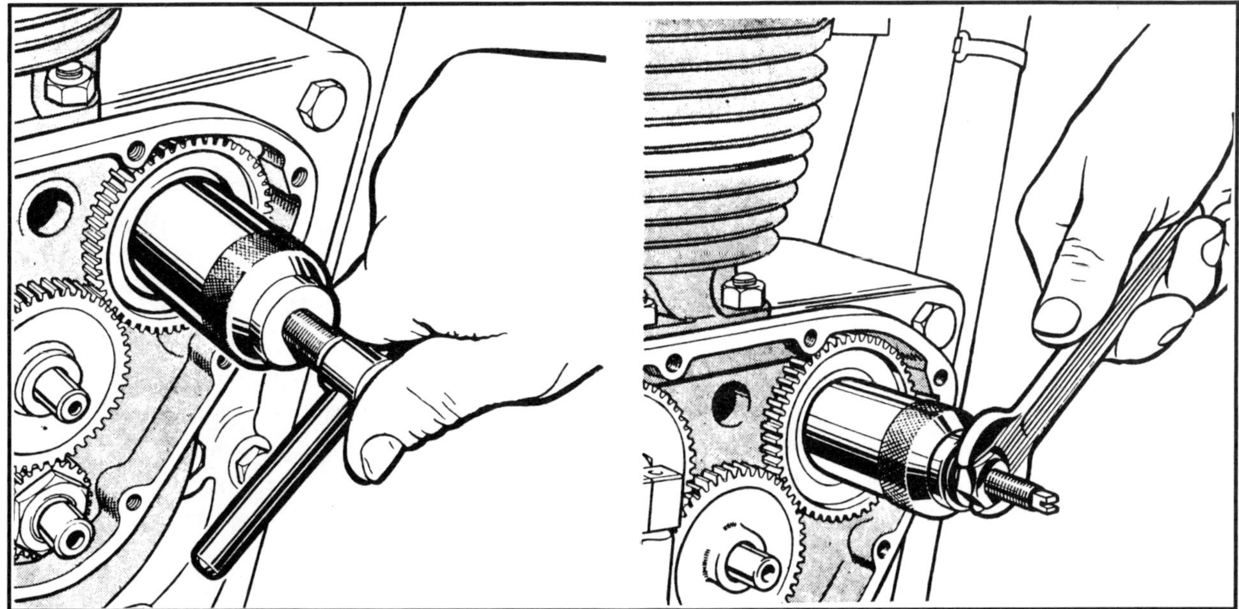

Above left: Removing a camwheel ***(Courtesy Triumph Motorcycles (Coventry) Ltd.)***

Above right: Replacing a camwheel ***(Courtesy Triumph Motorcycles (Coventry) Ltd.)***

Tight valve caps

Vintage side valve engines of the non-detachable head variety were fitted with hexagonal valve-caps, usually of brass but occasionally steel. These caps are often wedged firmly in place.

The correct tool for dealing with valve caps is a flat ring spanner, stamped from steel plate approximately 3/16 or 1/4 in thick. On no account should an adjustable wrench be used. Nor should it be necessary to resort to a hammer and chisel, as was often done in the vintage period.

You can make a flat valve-cap spanner from 1/4 in thick steel plate, laboriously filing out the hexagonal hole, or modify a telescopic fork top-nut tool to suit. It should fit the valve-cap snugly.

First of all try tapping the end of the spanner with a copper-headed hammer. If the cap shows no sign of shifting, try warming-up the cylinder barrel; drop some dry ice, or cubes of fridge ice in the valve-cap hollow and try again. The idea is to try and expand the head thread, at the same time keeping the cap as cool as possible.

The foregoing procedure is of course ruled out where solid or fir-cone caps are concerned. A tip when dealing with the latter is to fabricate a thick ring spanner from mild steel plate, in the normal manner, but to line the hexagonal portions with red fibre or *Tufnol*. This should be bonded on with *Araldite* and touched up afterwards with a file to achieve a close fit. Alloy fir-cone hexagons are thus protected during removal — concours enthusiasts take note!

When the cap budges a fraction, anoint it with easing-oil and continue working it backwards and forwards. If all else fails it will unfortunately be necessary to drill it out; drill a line of holes across the cap and complete the job with a cold chisel, taking care not to damage the head threads. Thankfully such a course of action is very rare.

It will be apparent that valve-cap removal is best carried out before the cylinder barrel is detached from the bottom half. When you come to replace the caps, clean their threads thoroughly with a chaser and make sure the caps do not project into the combustion chamber. If they do, turn a bit off in the lathe. Projecting threads will cause pre-ignition and, ultimately, removal problems due to carbon build-up.

Cap Repairs

Chewed up cap hexagons are easily renewed by the following method:-

1 Machine off the chewed hexagons in the lathe.
2 Turn a recess approximately 1/4 in deep in the cap face.
3 Purchase, from a pipe-fitters' merchants, a brass hexagonal fitting of about the right size "across flats". You will not be interested in the threaded portion as this will be cut off anyway. A blanking plug would be ideal.
4 Cut off the threaded part from the brass fitting and machine a spigot on one face of the hexagonal bit. This spigot should be an easy fit in the recess you have just turned in the valve cap.
5 Silver-solder the two parts together (see sketch).

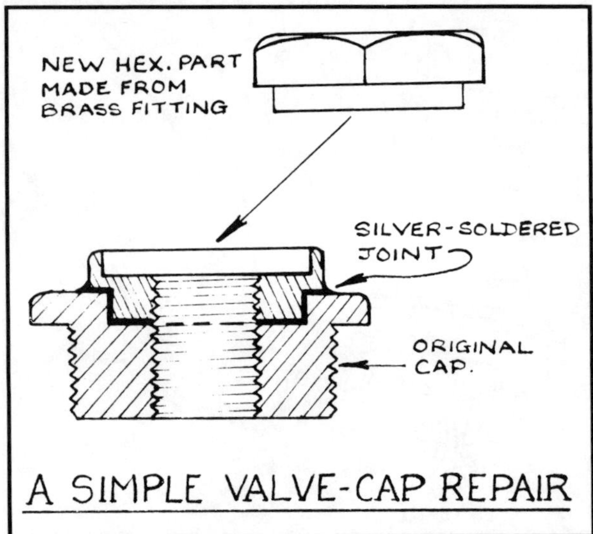

6 Finish off the cap in the lathe, running an 18 mm tap through the spark plug hole if necessary. A double-ended (18/14 mm) spark-plug tap is a good investment for such jobs.

The above repair will last indefinitely and when polished and nickel-plated the cap will be indistinguishable from the original. There is of course no danger of the silver-solder melting as it would be almost impossible to make the cap turn cherry-red in normal use; if it does then there's something seriously wrong with the timing!

A 1908 Minerva cylinder barrel 'as found'. Surprisingly, dismantling revealed the perfect piston shown below. Such early cast iron pistons should be handled with extreme care. Wide piston rings are irreplaceable. *(Photos: L. Taverner.)*

Stuck Piston

Pistons have a habit of becoming firmly wedged in bores when the machine has lain unused for years. This happens when the plug is permanently removed, or the head left off, but on odd occasions moisture can creep in when the valves are left open. Rust takes time to form but eventually the piston will seize firmly as it if were welded in the barrel. Two-strokes are prime culprits.

As mentioned previously, easing-oil poured into the barrel and left to soak in for a week or two will help. Fit a hefty spanner to the mainshaft nut and apply gentle pressure in a clockwise direction. If there is no sign of movement give the spanner a rap with the palm of your hand. Try easing it in the opposite direction, although this usually results in the nut slackening off.

With luck, a slight movement may be detected. If so, pour some more easing-oil in and wait for another day. Gradually work the mainshaft clockwise and anti-clockwise, a fraction at a time, until the piston has loosened. Don't belt away at the spanner as you could bend a slender connecting rod.

Maybe, after all your attempts, the piston is still wedged. Try heating-up the barrel with a blowlamp. This sometimes softens solidified oil and

other combustion products around the piston rings. Tackle the mainshaft nut again. If this does not produce results, drastic action is called for. With the aid of a baulk of timber try a few judicious blows on the piston crown. The slightest movement will mean that the battle is almost won. Don't be too worried about the piston rings as they will probably be useless anyway.

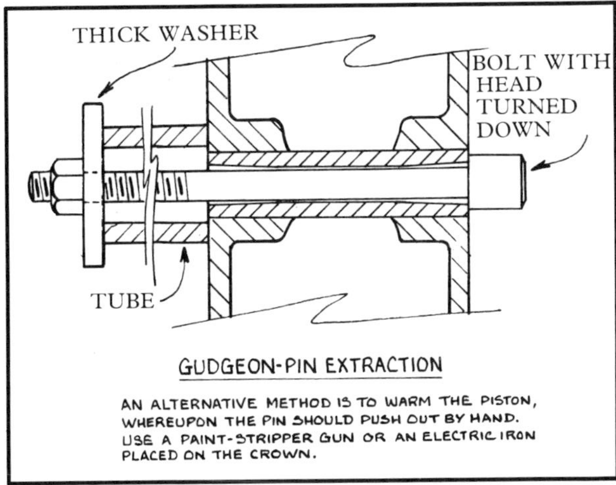

GUDGEON-PIN EXTRACTION

AN ALTERNATIVE METHOD IS TO WARM THE PISTON, WHEREUPON THE PIN SHOULD PUSH OUT BY HAND. USE A PAINT-STRIPPER GUN OR AN ELECTRIC IRON PLACED ON THE CROWN.

Checking bore wear

How much wear is permissible in a cylinder bore? There are many differing views on this subject, but when all is said and done it all depends how the engine performs. If it starts first kick, runs smoothly and pulls well up hills I would not even bother looking inside. There may be .008 in (eight thou.) ovality — so what? If the machine is just used for the odd rally or two it will still be thumping along in another ten years' time with hardly any increase in clearance. The oil regulator may have to be opened up another notch or two, but oil is relatively cheap especially if you use a straight SAE50!

It might be thought that the foregoing remarks are an encouragement to neglect vintage machinery; that is not intentional. It is a fact that we all get slightly paranoid over precise clearance figures when dealing with elderly engines. I know I have, and I've lived to regret it. I can think of several occasions when I have had barrels rebored, nicely seasoned barrels, because the wear exceeded the makers' recommended tolerances by a few thou and then I have had to endure a running-in period stretching over a few years. With the old piston clearances I could thrash the bike up hills, give it the gun when late for a rally time-check, and not worry about it overheating on a summer's day.

Side valve barrels in particular take a long time to mature due to their assymmetrical shapes. What else

RECOMMENDED HEPOLITE PISTON CLEARANCES

THE FOLLOWING CLEARANCES ARE IN THOUSANDTHS PER INCH OF CYLINDER DIAMETER FOR AIR-COOLED ENGINES

	BOTTOM OF SKIRT	TOP OF SKIRT	LAND 4TH	3RD	2ND	1ST
HEPOLITE						
SOLID SKIRT	.0015	.0025	.004	.004	.006	.007
SPLIT SKIRT	.0010	.0015	.004	.004	.006	.007
T-SLOT	.00125	.00175	.004	.004	.006	.007
2-STROKE	.0015	.0025	.004	.004	.006	.007
HEPLEX						
SOLID SKIRT	.0015	.00225	.0028	.0028	.0032	.0042
W TYPE	.0010	.0015	.008	.008	.008	.008
T-SLOT	.0010	.0015	.0028	.0028	.0032	.0042
2-STROKE	.0015	.00225	.0028	.0028	.0032	.0042
CAST-IRON	.001	.0015	.0045	.0045	.0045	.0045

NOTE: ALL HEPOLITE ALLOY PISTONS ARE OVAL FORM-GROUND. CLEARANCES SHOULD THEREFORE BE MEASURED AT RIGHT-ANGLES TO THE GUDGEON-PIN AXIS, WHICH IS USUALLY FROM 'FRONT TO BACK' ON A SINGLE-CYLINDER MOTORCYCLE PISTON.
TYPICAL OVALITY IS .002/.003 in AT THE SKIRT BOTTOM AND .007/.011 AT THE SKIRT TOP (ON PISTONS UP TO 3½ in DIA)

This Ariel arrived with the North Lancs Motor Club contingent for their 1985 Belle Vue Show stand. Listed in the programme as a 1935 350cc Ariel Red Hunter, Radco's camera lens shows the inscription RH500 on the timing cover! Be that as it may, the Red Hunter was an outstanding sports machine in pre-war days and much easier to overhaul than most so-called "thoroughbreds".

can be expected with a huge lump of metal on one side (the valve chest) and scanty finning on the other? The moral of all this is that one should think twice before reboring a well-seasoned cylinder.

To return to the original question, permissible wear, let's first of all consider standard piston clearances. If you have the maker's recommended clearances to hand that's all well and good. If the barrel is worn over ten thou above these sizes it's on the way out. However, with pre- 1930 and early post vintage engines it is often the case that no figures are available.

For vintage-type alloy pistons the following clearances are good average figures (four-stroke motors):-

Top land	.006 in	
2nd land	.005 in	
3rd land	.0045 in	Per inch of
Top of skirt	.003 in	bore diameter
Bottom of skirt	.0025 in	

It is assumed that iron barrels are under discussion; the above figures are suitable for vintage alloy pistons of such grades as Y-alloy or RR53B.

A typical early piston material was an aluminium alloy 2L8, consisting of approximately 11 to 13% copper and the remainder aluminium. This material was about 50% stronger than pure aluminium. Another material was 3L11, with 6 to 8% copper, 1% tin, and aluminium.

With these types of alloys racing clearances are preferable even in standard vintage motors, which generally have small cooling fins and odd-shaped barrels. It is a mistake to have ultra-close clearances when fitting an autojumble piston of unknown composition.

RECOMMENDED PISTON CLEARANCES FOR POPULAR POST-WAR MODELS (CLEARANCES IN INCHES)

MAKE	MODELS	PISTON TOP LAND	PISTON SKIRT TOP	PISTON SKIRT BOTTOM	RINGS GAP	RINGS VERTICAL CLEARANCE
ARIEL	347cc NG NH	.020/.023	.007/.009	.003/.005	.011/.015	.003/.006
	497cc VG VH	.019/.022	.0065/.0085	.005/.007	.014/.018	.003/.006
	498cc TWIN	.0198/.0223	.0048/.0063	.0028/.0043	.009/.015	.0015/.0035
	997cc FOUR (ALLOY ENGINE)	.020/.023	.003/.005	.001/.003	.009/.015	.0015/.0035
AMC	347cc 16M AJS / 347cc G3L	.031±.0005	.011±.0005	.001±.0005	.006/.009	.002
	498cc 18 AJS / 498cc G80	.0355 "	.0015 "	.001 "	.006/.009	.002
	498cc 20 AJS / 498cc G.9 TWIN	.015	.015	.001	.006/.009	.002
	7R	.024	.010	.009	.015	.003
BSA	249cc C10 C11	.0125	.0065	.005	.008	.002
	348cc B31/32	.011	.0065	.004	.008/.012	.003
	348cc B32 GS TRIALS/TOURING	.010/.012	.0045/.006	.003/.004	.008/.012	.002/.004 (COMP.)
	B32 GS RACING	.010/.012	.0045/.006	.003/.004	.008/.012	.001/.003
	499cc B33/34	.016	.0065	.004	.008/.012	.003
	499cc B34 GS TRIALS/TOURING	.013/.015	.0045/.006	.0033/.004	.008/.012	.002/.004 (COMP)
	B34 GS RACING	.013/.015	.005/.007	.0025/.0045	.008/.012	"
	496cc M20 / 591cc M21	.0275	.0095	.005	.008/.012	.003
	495cc A7	.0135	.006	.003	.010/.015	.002
	646cc A10	.0133/.0163	.0018/.0038	.0011/.0031	.008/.013	.001/.003
DOUGLAS Mk III & SPORTS	350cc 1948/9	.013	.007	.0045	.007/.011	.002

MAKE	MODELS	PISTON TOP LAND	PISTON SKIRT TOP	PISTON SKIRT BOTTOM	RINGS GAP	RINGS VERTICAL CLEARANCE
NORTON	348cc 40	.027/.029	.012/.013	.007/.008	.015/.020 COMP. .008 SCRAPER	.002 "
	348cc 40M / 490cc 30M	"	.014/.015	.008/.009	.020/.025 COMP. .008 SCRAPER	" "
	490cc 30	"	.009/.010	.006/.007	.015/.020 COMP. .008 SCRAPER	" "
	490cc ES2 18.16H	"	.006/.0065	.004/.0055	.012/.016 COMP. .005 SCRAPER	" "
	596cc		.0065/.0075	.0045/.0055	AS ES2	"
PANTHER	248cc 65	.010/.012	.0035/.0041	.003/.0035	.010/.015	.002
	348cc 75	.013/.014	.005	.0043	.011/.016	.001 COMP. .002 SCRAPER
	490cc 80	.021/.0225	.0036/.0041	.0036/.0041	.010	.001
	598cc 100	"	"	"	"	"
ROYAL-ENFIELD	346cc G	.030	.005	.0025	.005/.009	.001/.003 COMP. .002/.004 SCRAPER
	346cc BULLET	SOLID SKIRT .031	.006	.0035	.008/.012	AS ABOVE
		SPLIT SKIRT .020	.005	.003	"	AS ABOVE
	496cc TWIN	SOLID SKIRT .030	.0055	.0035	"	AS ABOVE
		SPLIT SKIRT .020	.0035	.0022	"	AS ABOVE
SUNBEAM	497cc S7, S8	.0137/.0107	.0047/.0065	.0047/.0065	.004/.008	.0017/.0037 SCRAPER .0015/.0035 COMP.

Cast iron pistons require clearances of about one third those of aluminium alloy pistons; approximately .0005 in to .001 in per inch of piston diameter is about right. Cast iron pistons seem to last indefinitely, although they are of course very fragile. It is easy to knock a piece out of the skirt if the piston is allowed to cant over suddenly onto the connecting rod when dismantling. (Providing a crack has not developed, a small chunk missing out of the skirt will not make much difference to its lasting qualities.)

Hiduminium, Y-alloys, and the RR grades of aluminium came along later and were a great improvement so far as their strength at high temperatures was concerned. For post-war engines using *Hepolite Alloy* and *Heplex Alloy* pistons refer to table on page 53.

MAKE	MODELS	PISTON TOP LAND	PISTON SKIRT TOP	PISTON SKIRT BOTTOM	RINGS GAP	RINGS VERTICAL CLEARANCE
TRIUMPH	349cc 3T	.012/.015	.0045/.005	.0025	.010/.014	.001/.003 COMP. .0015/.0025 SCRAPER
	498cc 5T / T100	.012/.015	.006/.0065	.004/.0045	"	"
	TROPHY	"	"	"	"	"
	T'BIRD	"	"	"	"	"
VELOCETTE	348cc KTT	.0145/.0165	.0095/.0115	.0065/.0085	COMP. .012 SCR. .030	.0015/.0025
	248cc MOV / 349cc MAC	.0125/.014	.007/.0085	.0045/.006	COMP. .010 SCR. .012	.0015/.0025 .0025/.0045
	495cc MSS	.0178/.0185	.0092/.0105	.0052/.0065	COMP. .018 SCR. .016	.0008/.0028 .002/.004
VINCENT	499cc COMET / 998cc RAPIDE SHADOW	.020	.007	.004	TOURING: .016/.020 RACING: .025/.035	.001/.002 COMP. .003/.005 SCRAPER

Above left: This Moto Guzzi engine, with its 'exhaust over inlet' valve arrangement, is most probably that of a 498cc GTS model made in 1937/8.

Above right: A rare bird. One of the few Horex machines in British hands. Horex was the first German marque to get into production with a relatively large bike (the 350cc Regina) after the war. They later made Sachs-engined lightweights. The machine pictured is a 1949 model owned by David Trent.

Below: The engine unit of a Redwing 90 Panther of 1936. P & Ms are often thought of as sidecar-hauling plodders, whereas in fact they were deceptively fast and handled well solo. Panther restorers are strongly advised to join the Panther Owners Club, which has a comprehensive technical library catering for all models. ***(Photo: Panther Owners Club.)***

Measuring piston clearance

There are two basic ways of measuring the fit of a piston in its cylinder, with internal and external micrometers and with feeler gauges. In both cases the piston clearance should be measured at right angles to the gudgeon-pin axis as most aluminium alloy pistons are form-ground oval.

Most amateurs will employ the second method, a set of feelers being much cheaper than inside and outside mikes. To obtain an accurate figure the piston rings should be removed, the cylinder washed-out, and the measurement taken from the bottom of the bore. It is better to use three or four thin feelers together than one thick blade, which would not conform to the piston curvature. Narrow feelers could be cut out of standard-width blades.

It will be found that most cylinder wear occurs towards the top of the bore. A well-worn barrel will display a ridge at the upper extremity of piston travel. Very badly-worn pistons are barrel-shaped with bright areas at the top and bottom where piston rock has taken place — such a piston should be discarded. Frequent piston ring breakage indicates that the piston is at the end of its life and a rebore is called for. A quick and simple check for bore wear can be made with a piston ring inserted at various points up the bore. The ring should be square in the cylinder — push it up the bore using the piston as a guide. The gap will gradually increase, reaching a maximum about 1½ to 2 in below the top in a worn cylinder. Feelers can be used to measure the variation in gap, but usually it can be seen with the naked eye.

Recommended piston ring gaps are usually stated on the packet or box that they come in, but the following figures are average:-

Air-cooled Racing Engines	At least .005 in per inch of bore
Standard engines	At least .003 in per inch of bore

If gaps exceed ten thou per inch of bore, new rings are called for.

Side clearances (on engines up to 4 in bore) should be .0015 in to .0035 in on four strokes, and .003 in to .005 in in the case of two strokes.

Rusty bores

A small amount of surface rust in a cylinder bore is no cause for concern. The rust can be removed by applying *Jenolite,* or a similar rust-remover, and vigorously scrubbing with wire wool. Minute rust-pits will be left but these are of little consequence; in fact oil will be retained by the pits, actually assisting lubrication at the top end.

A home-made cylinder lap

Bores which are slightly marked can be cleaned-up with a lapping tool made from an old piston of the appropriate diameter.

Cut the piston in half. Make a dummy connecting rod from wood (an old hammer shaft will do) and fit a handle to the bottom end. Slip two short springs over the gudgeon-pin inside the piston halves and you have a very efficient hand lap.

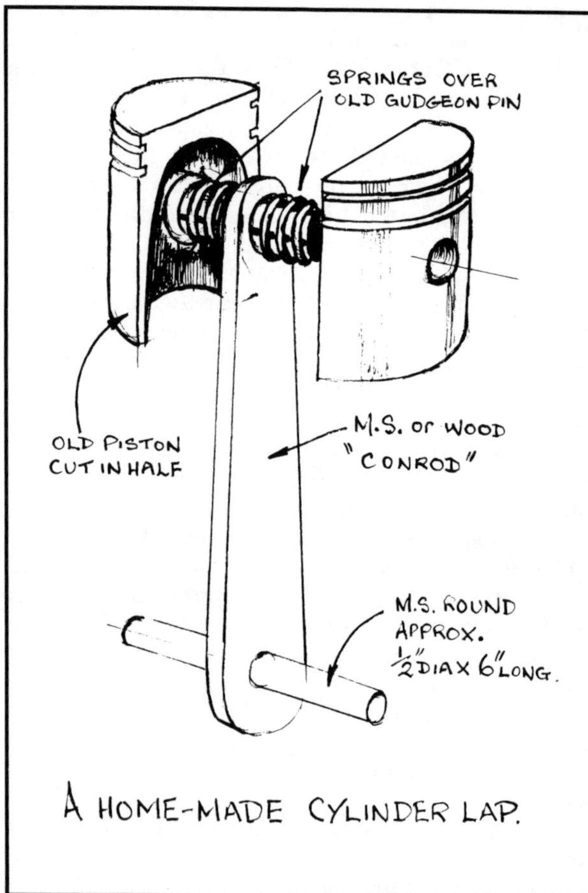

A HOME-MADE CYLINDER LAP.

Work the lap up and down the bore in a twisting motion, with grinding paste and paraffin as the lapping medium. Follow up with metal polish.

If a largish lathe is available the barrel can be firmly mounted on a faceplate and the lapping tool pushed in and out as the lathe revolves. This will soon clean up the bore without removing a significant amount of metal.

Grooved bores

An omitted gudgeon-pin circlip will inevitably result in tramlines being worn up the cylinder bore. A **slight** amount of scoring does not mean that the cylinder is scrap, or that a rebore is required; probably no difference in compression will be noticed if the groove is only three or four thou deep. If, however, the groove is about ten to fifteen thou in depth something will have to be done about it, or the compression will suffer and the engine will use oil in copious amounts.

The easiest way of dealing with a very deep groove is, of course, to rebore the cylinder, or bore and sleeve it. On certain vintage engines this may not be possible for one reason or another. A skilful welder can build-up the groove with bronze or cast-iron; the barrel should be pre-heated and cooled slowly afterwards. It will of course be necessary to bore out the cylinder a fraction to clean-up the repair. Less hazardous, from the point of view of distortion, is the metal-spraying process in which metal is deposited in the groove and machined-off afterwards.

Some years ago there were firms who specialised in filling-in grooved bores, but it is not known if these exist today. As a matter of interest these were the *Lawrence, Bulldog* and *Eagle* processes, all originating in America and all variations on the same theme. A dovetail slot was machined in the score and a metal filler (special alloy) fused into the slot. The cylinder was then skimmed out just sufficiently to clean-up. Such a repair was carried out on cylinders which would not stand a re-sleeve, or on large blocks where the cost of replacement would be prohibitive.

Two-stroke cylinders **must** be rebored or scrapped if scoring is very deep or crankcase compression will be lost. A rebored two stroke must be run-in carefully to avoid seizure; due to apertures cut in the cylinder walls unequal expansion occurs within the bore and it takes quite some time for the piston to settle down. It is a fallacy however to drive the machine at 30 mph for 1000 miles and then belt the daylights out of it. The engine must be given work to do; an occasional burst up to three-quarters throttle, followed by a short easing-off period will do it good.

The perfectionist's way of running-in a two stroke is to give the engine a short burst of revs (almost to maximum) after fifty miles or so and then dismantle

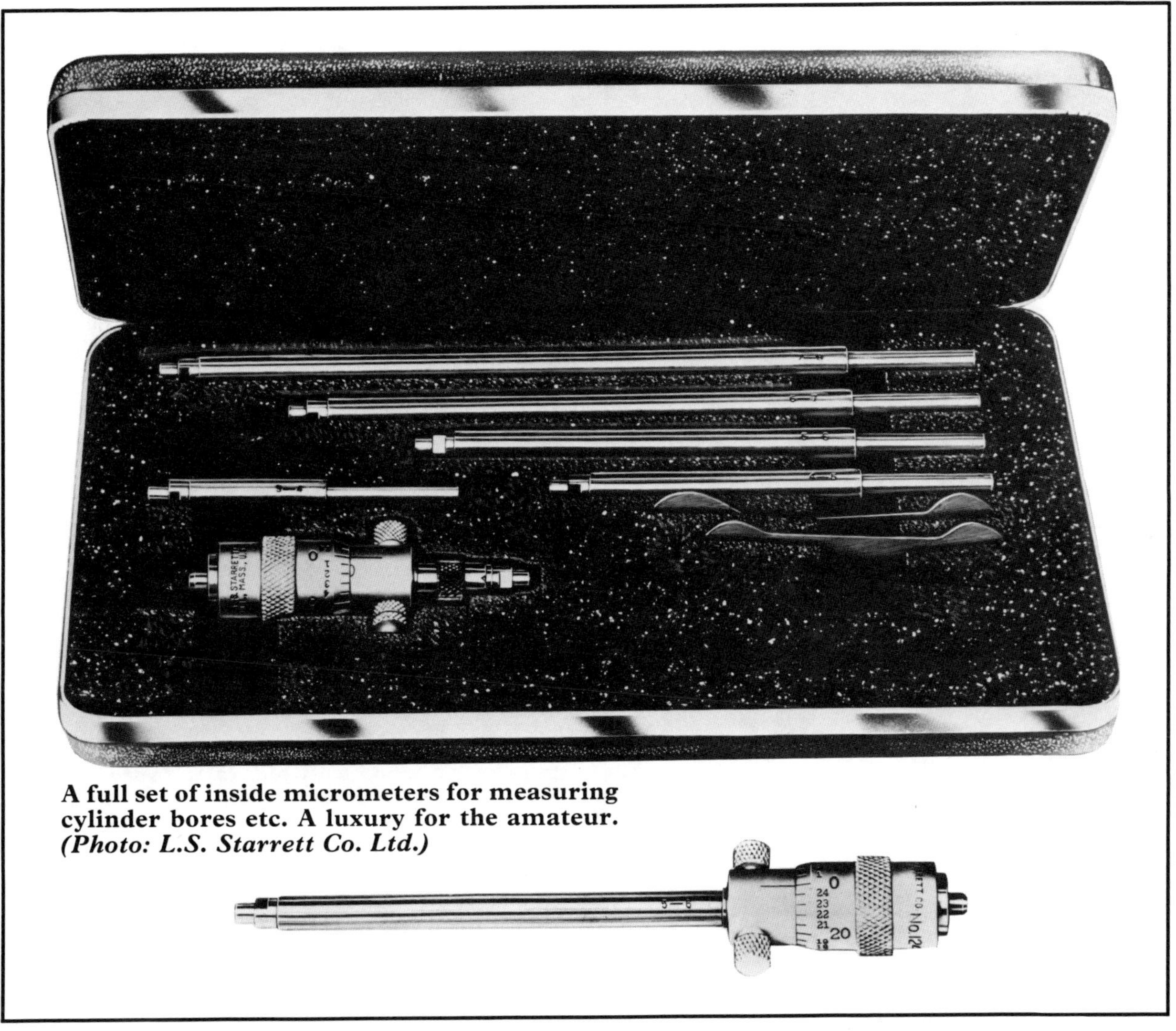

A full set of inside micrometers for measuring cylinder bores etc. A luxury for the amateur. ***(Photo: L.S. Starrett Co. Ltd.)***

the cylinder. High-spots, or very bright patches, are then removed with a fine file. The process is repeated, with a final light lapping-in with metal polish. It may be necessary to strip the top half several times before even contact is achieved, and it must be said that a trained eye is needed to distinguish between normal and excessive contact.

Excess wear

To summarise the situation regarding cylinder bore wear the following examples can be quoted.

According to tests carried out on motor car engines thirty-odd years ago it was noted that cast-iron cylinders showed an average wear of .001 in per 2,000 to 3,000 miles of running. Nitrided cast-iron liners gave from 7,000 to 10,000 miles for the same amount of wear.

It was observed that the greatest amount of wear occurred, as might be expected, in the first few thousand miles and once the engine had settled down, the rate of wear was much less.

A typical worn-out cylinder, considered ready for boring, displayed .015 in wear near the top of the bore and only .003 in wear at the bottom. This was with a bore of 85 mm.

On smaller motorcycle cylinders of around 70 mm bore, permissible wear would be no greater than .010 in.

Two-stroke clearances

Two-stroke piston skirt clearance should be .0015 to .002 in per inch of diameter and rings should be in good condition. A new set of rings will often rejuvenate a tired two-stroke engine but it is as well to check the crankcase compression sealing arrangement if bad starting occurs. Early two-strokes, and this includes millions of Villiers engines, relied on the long phosphor-bronze main bearings to retain crankcase compression. These bushes should be in good condition — fortunately their life is remarkably long — and no up-and-down play is permissible. A fair degree of end-play can be tolerated in a plain-bearing crankshaft, .020 in not being uncommon.

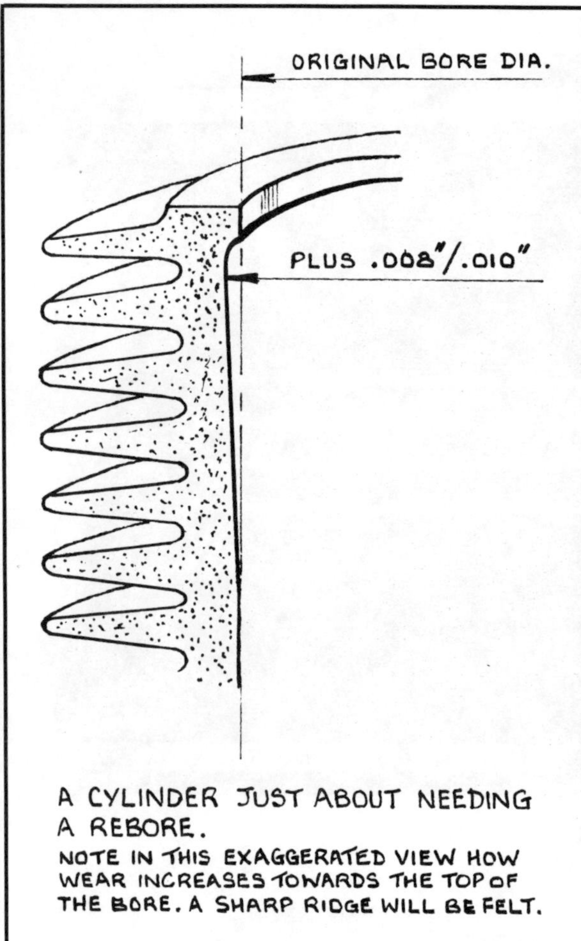

A selection of shots for vee-twin fans. Above: 1927 998cc sv JAP fitted to a Morgan Aero owned by John Minns. Opposite page: a 1933 ohv JAP of 1100cc fitted to a three-speed Morgan owned by Albert Harper. Below Some say the Blackburne was the best Morgan power-unit. The Author would not disagree – this is his Type KMC 1096cc engine fitted to an Aero model of 1926.

Reboring

Oversize pistons were generally available in .010, .020, .030, .040, and .060 in sizes. Some thought should be given to cylinder barrel strength before boring out to .060 in (or .080 in, a size occasionally encountered). Those barrels with through-bolts holding down both head and barrel will generally stand a greater degree of boring-out.

It is not unknown for a barrel to part company with its flange after excessive boring or sleeving. As so many factors are involved — compression ratio, stroke, height of cylinder, method of cylinder fixing, spigot dimensions etc. — it is difficult to state a minimum cylinder wall thickness. If in doubt, take the barrel along to an established expert in the field of vintage tuning. An unwritten rule in engineering is what **looks** right **is** right and the expert eye will assess cylinder wall strength at a glance.

Owners of thoroughbred machinery such as Vincents, Rudges, Velos and the like are of course well-served with respect to spares. One-make clubs, thanks to a band of hard-working (and generally unpaid) officials usually have a good stock of pistons, rings and valves. The position is very different however if the motorcycle in question is a rare model, or a very early example from a long-deceased manufacturer.

Substitute Pistons

It really is amazing just what turns up at autojumbles these days. Pistons, valves, liners and a whole variety of new parts for early machines make their appearance from time to time as yet another old-established dealer's premises is combed through. With much diligent searching, and a degree of luck, it is possible to locate new pistons and rings for quite early machines but there's no reason for despair if the exact replacment cannot be found.

Certain makes of engines need specially designed pistons — there is no substitute for a Scott piston, or a stepped Dunelt — but for almost every four-stroke engine there will be an alternative type amongst the millions produced by *Hepolite* (Hepworth & Grandage Ltd.) since the year dot. Possession of an old Hepolite catalogue will enable the restorer to check salient features of a whole variety of pistons, from Austin to Wolseley in the car world and AJS to Zundapp in the motorcycle category, and select one which suits his purpose. *Hepolite* catalogues can sometimes be scrounged or borrowed from dealers, or the enthusiast can take his piston along to one of the major suppliers.

When searching for a substitute piston the restorer must be armed with all the relevant

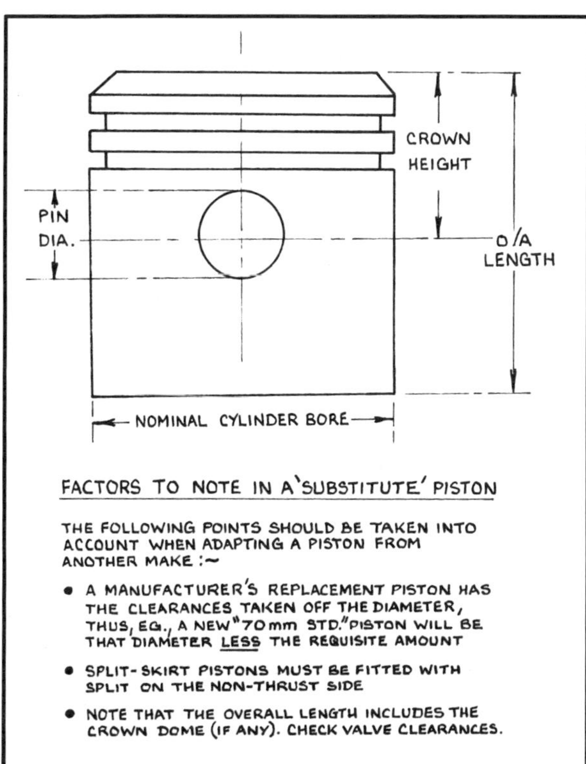

information. There is a number of important dimensions to note, as follows:-

1 Bore
2 Amount of oversize required
3 Piston crown height (ie distance from the gudgeon-pin centre to the top of the crown. In a domed piston, this **includes** the dome.
4 Gudgeon-pin diameter.
5 Overall length.

Dealing with the above points in order, obviously the bore is of importance and is closely linked with item 2, the amount of oversize. For example if the cylinder in question is of 63 mm bore plus .020 in oversize, and is worn, it might be found that a standard 64 mm piston off another make of machine will fit the bill. There is always the alternative of finding a substitute which is satisfactory in other respects but too large in diameter by 2 mm or so; in this case the cylinder can be bored out by 1 mm and the piston diameter turned down the appropriate amount, bearing in mind correct clearances.

Crown height is naturally critical, although on most early engines it is quite permissible to increase the compression ratio a small amount. Early side-valve engines of the 1920s had ratios in the region of 4.5 to 1 and will stand an increase to at least $5^1/_2$ to 1 on modern fuels. Ohv machines of the late twenties and throughout the 1930s had relatively low ratios of around 5.75 or 6 to 1 and a moderate increase in crown height will produce a general increase in performance with no ill effects.

The main criterion is not to overdo things on a

standard road-going engine; many vintage motors with poor combustion chamber design and weak cylinder barrels will not withstand compression ratio increases to modern standards. On an iron-engined pre '39 roadster it's best to play safe and go no higher than 6.5 to 1, with a maximum of (say) 7.5 to 1 on a sports ohv machine. The position with racing engines is, of course, entirely different and outside the scope of this book.

If a piston of increased crown height is substituted it is essential to check that the valves do not foul it on full lift. This can be easily verified by sticking some plasticine on the piston crown and turning the engine over by hand. The amount by which the valves miss the piston will be readily observed; a clearance of 1/16 in between valve head and piston should be adequate.

On sv engines the question of piston crown clearance must of course be considered; generally vintage engines will withstand a 1/8 increase in crown height with no problems ensuing. Aluminium pistons can be substituted for cast-iron if genuine replacements cannot be found. Rebalancing is seldom required; in fact many engines have been known to run smoother on aluminium pistons **without** re-balancing!

Gudgeon-pin diameter (point 4) on the replacement piston must either be exactly the same, or (as a last resort) no more than 1/16 in larger. If the latter is the case the old little-end bush will have to be machined out to suit the increased pin diameter. Providing that the bush is bored-out in situ, in the connecting rod, a wall thickness of 1/32 in is adequate. For example, there is not much difference between 22 mm and 7/8 in therefore a conversion from one size to the other should not present any problems.

With regard to point 5, overall height, surprisingly this is the least important of all measurements on a 4-stroke piston. Providing that the crown height is within limits, a shorter skirt length can be tolerated. The difference in length should not upset balance too much in a touring engine. Obviously a long piston is easily shortened in the lathe; most of the excess metal can be sawn off with a junior hacksaw, finishing off with a facing tool. Parting-off the unwanted portion in a light-duty amateurs' lathe is a hazardous operation due to tool flexure and lack of rigidity.

Machining pistons

On odd occasions pistons have to be modified, or new ones turned from blanks, so the following notes will be of interest to amateur machinists.

Before machining a split-skirt piston some means must be found of bridging the split, otherwise the skirt will move about under tool pressure. A fillet of *Araldite* in the slit, or a small bridge of aluminium weld will suffice.

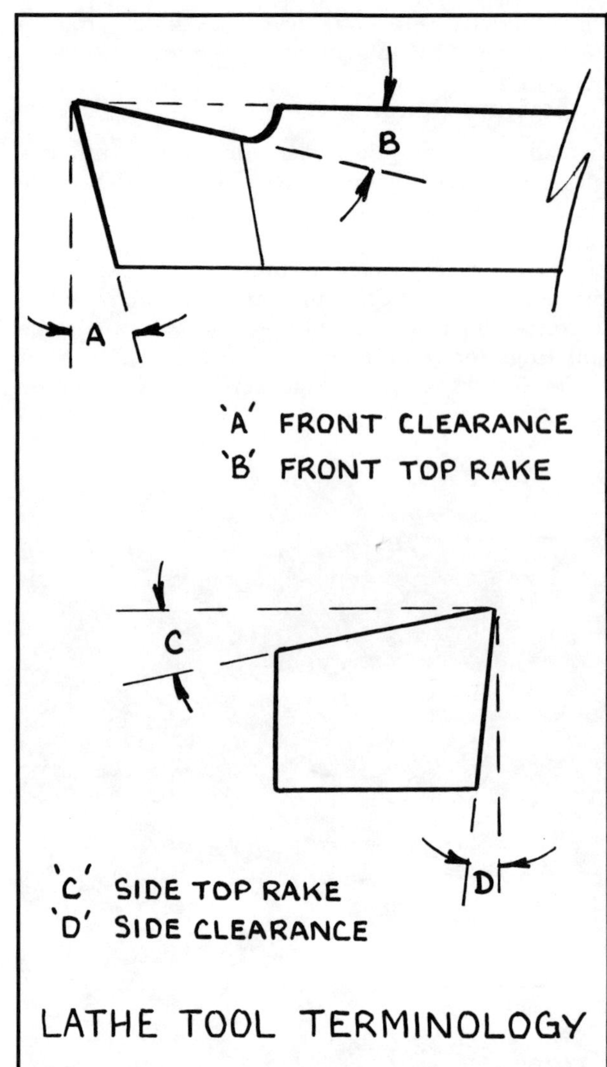

LATHE TOOL TERMINOLOGY

Tools should have very keen cutting edges, with a clearance angle of 20° and a top rake of 30° to 40°. Aluminium alloy should be finished at approximately 600 to 800 ft per minute. Roughing cuts are taken at a lower speed. Many amateurs' lathes have but three speeds, without back gears, each ratio being obtained by shifting the belt over to another pulley. With such old lathes it is Hobson's Choice as to which is the most suitable speed — the operator will have little alternative but to make all preparatory cuts on the lowest speed (ie the large diameter headstock pulley) and finish on the fastest the lathe is capable of achieving. If the final finish is not as good as it was hoped, the piston can be lapped in the barrel with metal polish. Under no circumstances should emery cloth be used to polish-up the piston as abrasive particles will embed themselves in the soft metal.

A delightful metal to machine, requiring no lubricant, cast iron should be turned at a much lower speed. Sixty feet per minute is about right, which will mean approximate lathe revs of around

115 rpm for a 2 in diameter piston and 76 rpm for a 3 in one. The best advice that can be given, when machining any kind of metal, is to experiment on a scrap piece first and when you find the tool angle and speed which suit you best, stick to them. Lathe text books quote all sorts of complicated formulae for calculating cutting tool angles; such information may be vital to the repetition machinist but is of academic interest to the amateur turner with a fifty year-old lathe and a motley assortment of lathe tools. In the world of amateur turning one man's lathe tool may not suit another, so the novice is advised to use the text book approach as a starting point and modify rake and clearance angles to suit himself. Better still, a demonstation on cutting speed and feed by a skilled turner or model engineer will save hours of experimentation.

A suitable lubricant for machining aluminium alloy is paraffin (and plenty of it). Not many amateurs have the luxury of an automatic lubricant feed on their lathes but it is a simple matter to rig-up a drip-feed from a container mounted above the chuck. A *Swarfega* tin with an oil-tap and a length of 3/16 in copper pipe soldered in the bottom will suffice. Many turners make do with a jam jar and an old paint brush.

Aluminium should be drilled at high speed — eg. approx. 2000/2,400 rpm for a 1/4 in drill — with paraffin as a lubricant. Special cutting oil is also available. Single-cut files do not clog as easily as double-cuts (immersion in caustic will clean-up a badly-clogged file).

A trial cut

Most parallel-skirt pistons have a recess, or register, bored inside the bottom (or open) end. If not, the first operation will be to grip the piston lightly at the top end in a 4-jaw chuck. Centralise the piston with a dial gauge and bore the recess to a depth of about 3/16 in, or whatever the piston casting allows. Only light cuts should be taken to avoid springing the piston out of the chuck.

The best way to hold a piston when turning the outside diameter is by means of a spigot held in the lathe chuck, this spigot fitting into the skirt recess. It is not good practice to expand the chuck jaws to fit inside the piston as it may well be distorted, especially when a 3-jaw chuck is used.

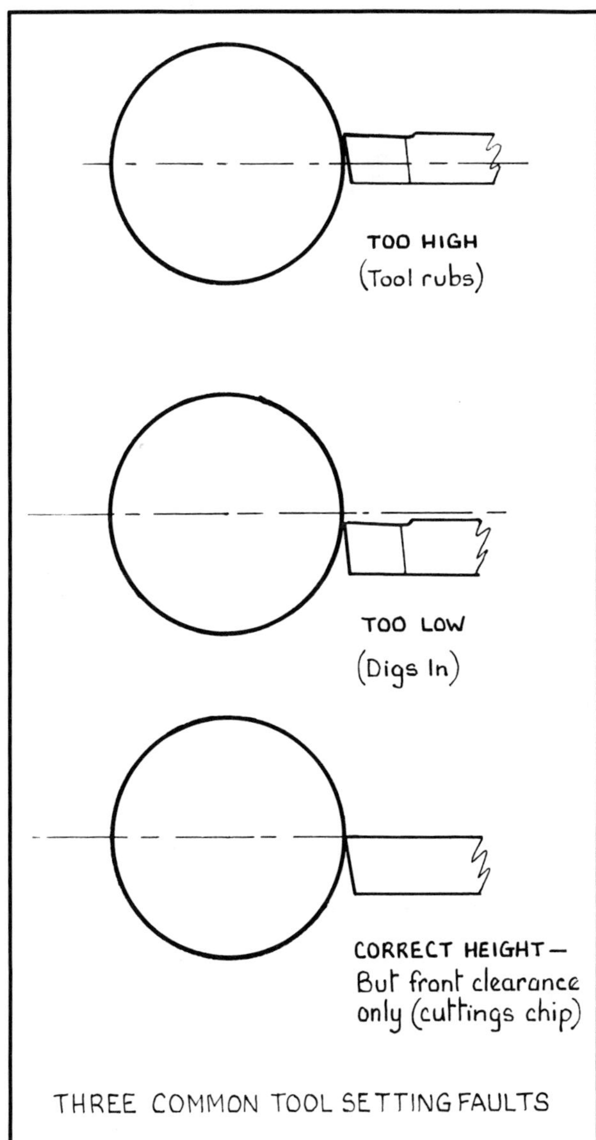

THREE COMMON TOOL SETTING FAULTS

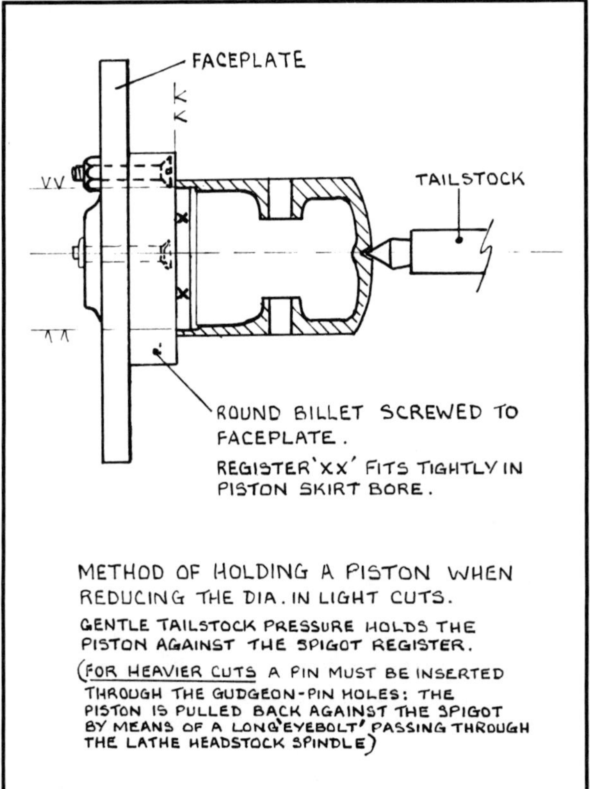

METHOD OF HOLDING A PISTON WHEN REDUCING THE DIA. IN LIGHT CUTS.
GENTLE TAILSTOCK PRESSURE HOLDS THE PISTON AGAINST THE SPIGOT REGISTER.
(FOR HEAVIER CUTS A PIN MUST BE INSERTED THROUGH THE GUDGEON-PIN HOLES: THE PISTON IS PULLED BACK AGAINST THE SPIGOT BY MEANS OF A LONG 'EYEBOLT' PASSING THROUGH THE LATHE HEADSTOCK SPINDLE)

Mount a piece of aluminium or steel bar in the lathe chuck and machine a parallel spigot on it to suit the skirt bore. The chunk of round bar should be about 1/4 in larger in diameter than the piston to start with. Aim for a nice push-on fit.

Press the piston on to the spigot and then rotate the lathe to see if it is running true. It **should** be spot-on, but if it isn't, any eccentricity can be corrected by readjusting the four chuck jaws. Centre the piston crown with a Slocombe (centre) drill and bring up the tailstock centre.

Light tailstock pressure will be sufficient to hold the piston against the spigot and if only light cuts are taken there will be no danger of the piston slipping on its register. Apply a drop of oil to the tailstock centre, if it is the old non-rotating type, and check the adjustment from time to time.

Take a light cut along the entire length of the piston. If the lathe appears to be turning tapered (as old hands would say) set-over the tailstock to compensate. This adjustment may not be necessary if the amount of taper is very small and running in the right direction. It will be recalled that most so-called parallel skirt pistons are in fact larger at the bottom of the skirt than the top (reference to the Hepolite figures will reveal a difference of .001 in per inch diameter of piston). Many old lathes will give this amount of taper without any help from the operator!

Finish turning

The amateur lathe turner has one advantage over his professional counterpart — time is no object, so he can make a number of light cuts rather than a couple of roughing cuts. After each pass the diameter should be checked with a micrometer at both ends of the piston. Adjust the amount of taper, if necessary.

Using plenty of paraffin, the final cut should have a depth of only a thousandth of an inch or so. Lathe speed should be fairly fast and tool traverse speed low. Primitive lathes with no automatic feed need care in handling — if you stop halfway along a cut to adjust your grip the finish will be impaired at that point. Chatter, in the form of wavy lines on the piston, is caused by excessive lathe speed combined with tool flexure.

Reduce the land diameters in accordance with the recommended *Hepolite* figures. The groove depths may also need deepening; this can be accomplished with a parting tool ground to shape. Very light cuts must be taken to avoid the possibility of the tool digging-in, with disastrous consequences.

Chamfer the groove edges lightly with a smooth file. This assists ring lubrication and may prevent the rings from becoming jammed in the event of a mild seizure.

A fine-turned finish is normally good enough for immediate use, although pistons were originally ground to a micro-fine standard. To reduce friction, the piston can be lapped-in with metal polish.

Top: The first Matchless-Morgan appeared in 1933, albeit in side valve guise. This is the ohv MX4 990cc engine of later years, renowned for its smooth running and gentlemanly characteristics. Once owned by Alan Whitehead of Belle Vue Show fame. Opposite page: And what have we here? An odd beast indeed! This is the HRD-powered Morgan campaigned so successfully over many years by Harold Pass. It is shown here in its latest format with twin Amal Concentric carburettors. An interesting hybrid that has seen action on most tracks in the UK and is also regularly rallied.

Temporarily fit the connecting rod and gudgeon pin and work the piston (minus rings) up and down the cylinder in a twisting motion. *Brasso*, or a similar mild abrasive polish, is used in copious amounts. **Never** use emery paste.

The piston sides below the gudgeon pin hole can be relieved manually with a smooth flat file, care being exercised to blend-in the relief. Skilled lathe operators can accomplish this task by setting-over the piston and turning each side individually. Two thou per side is ample. Again, the relief should be blended into the thrust face by hand.

In practice, some engines seem to run quite happily with truly cylindrical pistons. Examination of the piston after a trial running period will indicate any high spots requiring attention.

It should be mentioned, for the benefit of beginners, that pistons should never be clamped up directly in a vice. Not even with soft-jaws. Surprisingly little pressure is needed to permanently distort the skirt; when shifting high-spots with a smooth single-cut file the piston should be held in the palm of your hand. You can if you like rest the piston **on top** of a partly-opened vice which has had some rag draped across the jaws for protection. Cast iron pistons may not distort so readily, but are as brittle as eggshells. (Always wrap them in rag when cylinders are removed to prevent damage on cylinder base studs).

Ring troubles

Early engines with wide piston rings are a problem when replacements are needed. If the piston is sound in every other respect two thin rings can be fitted in one groove. This may necessitate the groove being widened with a thin parting-off tool.

When fitting a new ring to an old piston check that there is sufficient radial depth for the ring to enter fully in its groove. Any carbon must be scraped out (a piece of old piston ring set in a wooden handle makes a good scraper). Roll the new ring round the groove; if it is tight it will have to be thinned-down. To reduce the thickness, lay a piece of emery paper on some plate glass and carefully rub the ring on it, employing a sort of rotary movement.

A SIMPLE "MOD." TO AN EARLY PISTON WHEN WIDE RINGS ARE NOT AVAILABLE THE GROOVE IS SKIMMED OUT AND TWO THIN RINGS FITTED.

Keep shifting the position of your fingers on the ring. A better way is to cut a flat groove in a wooden block and use this to apply the pressure. An even better way is to get someone to take a lick off the ring with a magnetic surface grinder. Every toolmaking shop has one. Usually very little metal has to be removed; the finished side clearance between ring and piston groove should be about .0015 in to .002 in in the case of compression rings and roughly double this for oil-control scrapers.

Two-stroke rings are pegged to prevent rotation; new pegs can be made from stainless steel screws fixed firmly in the piston with *Loctite Retainer*. Drill and tap the piston an appropriate BA size for the groove width and screw the peg in tightly, cutting off the screw head and finishing with a square needle file.

Rings from another make of machine can be used; for example 225 cc Villiers rings, which fit a 63 mm bore and are $3/32$ in deep, will go straight on a 250 cc lightweight (Round-tank) BSA piston with due attention to the gaps. No matter how old the piston, it is almost certain that suitable rings can be found by consulting a *Hepolite* catalogue. Continual ring breakage can indicate that the engine needs a re-bore or that the ring grooves have widened, so causing ring-flutter. In either case the remedy is obvious.

A skilled engine fitter can remove and replace rings with his fingers alone. The novice is not advised to attempt this as he is liable to have problems. An old and well-tried method of removing and replacing rings is the three-strip dodge, whereby three thin strips of metal are placed around the piston and the rings slid over them into their grooves. When the rings are in place they are rotated until the gaps are spaced at 120° to each other (in the case of a three-ringed piston).

Ridge removal

A worn cylinder will display a distinct ridge at the top end, at the limit of piston ring travel. Usually this ridge can be felt with the finger nail. If a different piston has been fitted, or a cylinder base compression plate removed, the ridge must be

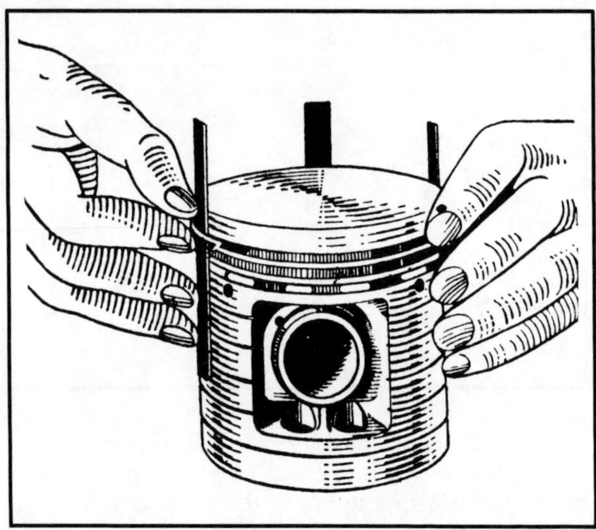

Method of removing and replacing piston rings using three thin strips of metal.

eradicated or ring breakage will occur. In the good old days when there were proper motor engineers (as opposed to parts-fitters) various machine tools existed for removing the unworn cylinder ridge. Such a tool was the *Hall Cylinder Ridge Remover* by Morris Ingram Ltd, of London. It was a hand-operated cutter, with three expanding rollers acting as guides against the cylinder wall. Turned by a ratchet mechanism, the cutters stopped cutting when the ridge was removed, making it impossible to go any further into the wall. Most of these tools have disappeared so the amateur has to make do with a sharp hand-scraper. After scraping away most of the ridge it can be finished off by means of an abrasive flap-wheel mounted in an electric drill.

Boring a gudgeon pin hole

When machining a piston from solid, the skirt recess, skirt bottom face, and piston outside diameter should first be turned as described.

The gudgeon pin hole centre is then carefully marked off with a scribing block. Bolt an angle-plate to the lathe faceplate and mount the piston as shown in the illustration. Juggle the angle-plate and piston around until the gudgeon-pin hole centre is truly aligned and tighten-up.

Start the hole with a centre-drill and then bore it out with a succession of drills, followed by a sharp boring tool. An expanding reamer may be used to take out the final thou or so, but it is sometimes difficult to avoid chatter by this means. A hand-scraper may be used instead, trying the fit of the gudgeon pin as the final stages are reached.

The following gudgeon pin fits are recommended:-

1 **Drop through**
Cast iron pistons where the pin is anchored in the connecting rod (ie. early engines). Clearance, approx. .00055 in. The pin will fall through both holes under its own weight. CAUTION:- Some early pistons (eg. Triumph Model H) have pins which fit from one side only and are thus marked. A push-fit is occasionally employed.

2 **Thumb push**
Where the piston is in aluminium alloy and the pin is secured with circlips or is located by end-buttons. Fit is transitional, ie size-for-size. The pin cannot be pushed through either boss with a finger but is not so tight that it cannot be pushed through a boss with the thumb.

Missing end-buttons should be made from brass, phosphor bronze or aluminium and should be a press fit in the pin. Ends should be radiused and polished. The radius should be slightly less than that of the cylinder bore.

3 **Hand push**
Aluminium-alloy pistons and cast-iron, with circlip fastening. Interference .0001 in. Tighter than a thumb push but can be forced through with the palm.

4 **Light tap**
Used frequently in two-strokes and other air-cooled engines. Interference approx .0002 in. Can be fitted and removed by warming up the piston with scalding-hot rags, or with a paint-stripper gun. (Never attempt to belt the pin out of an unsupported piston).

Having bored out one gudgeon pin boss you can, if the piston is of small diameter, follow through and bore the second boss in one setting. There is a danger however that the second hole may not end up

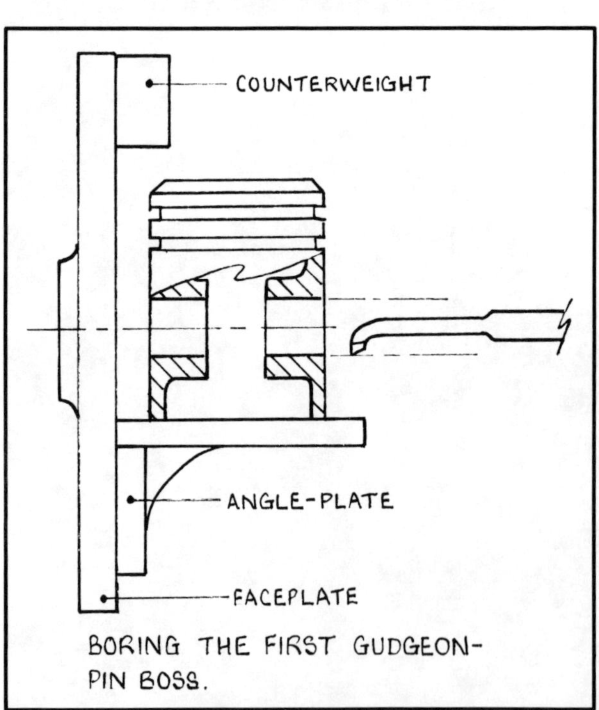

BORING THE FIRST GUDGEON-PIN BOSS.

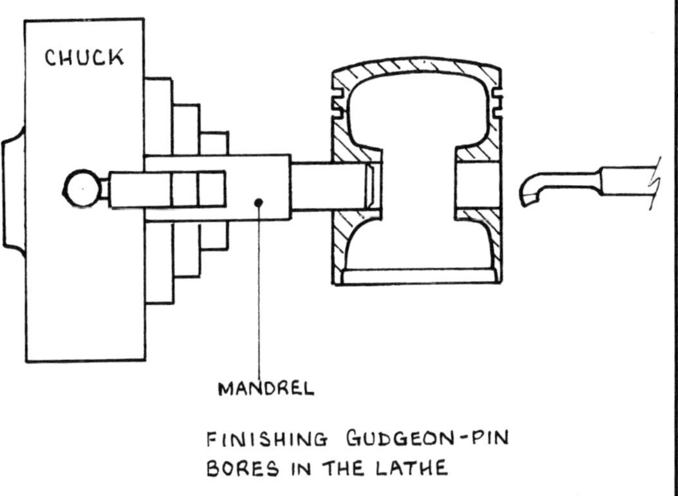

FINISHING GUDGEON-PIN BORES IN THE LATHE

An excerpt from the 1960 Hepolite catalogue showing various types of gudgeon pins. Types RC1 and SC1 are common to all makes of motorcycle pistons and type FF will be found on many vintage engines. Veteran enthusiasts will be familiar with types AP1 and 2. *(Courtesy Hepworth and Grandage Ltd.)*

GUDGEON PIN ABBREVIATIONS

GUDGEON PIN SPECIFICATIONS

Hepolite Gudgeon Pins are made from special steels selected for the nature of the work for which they are intended.

The following steels are employed in the manufacture of Hepolite Gudgeon Pins for various purposes :—

Grade HG.500.
A Plain Carbon Case Hardening steel (conforming to Air Board Specification 2S. 14). Specially heat treated to give maximum strength and fatigue life. Used for the majority of Gudgeon Pins for all normal types of internal combustion engine.

Grade HG.503.
Chrome Vanadium steel. This steel is found to be most satisfactory for the making of highly stressed Gudgeon Pins of small diameter for Motor Cycles.

Grade HG.504.
This steel contains nickel and chromium in quantity, which makes it most suitable for Special Diesel Engine Gudgeon Pins.

Grade HG.507.
This steel contains slightly greater quantities of nickel and chromium than HG.504 and in special cases is used for Gudgeon Pins in Aircraft Engines and Racing types of Automobile and Motor Cycle Engines.

GUDGEON PIN ABBREVIATIONS

RC Type Denotes Fully Floating Pin retained by Wire Circlips.
SWC Type Denotes Fully Floating Pin retained by Square Wire Circlips.
SC Type Denotes Fully Floating Pin retained by Seeger Circlips.
FF Type Denotes Fully Floating Pin fitted with Aluminium or Brass End Pads.
AC Type Denotes Pin anchored in Con-Rod by Bolt or Circlip.
TP Type Denotes Pin anchored in Con-Rod by a Taper Pin.
AP Type Denotes anchored in Piston by a Set Screw.
RR Type Denotes Pin retained by Steel or Cast Iron Retaining Ring.

NOTE.—The letter "A" after the gudgeon pin reference number denotes the pin is retained by circlips.
The letters " B ", " C ", " D " or " E," after the gudgeon pin reference number denotes the pin is fitted with Aluminium or Brass End Pads.
The length quoted in this Catalogue for Gudgeon Pins fitted with Aluminium or Brass End Pads is not the Overall Length, but the length of the Pin only, excluding End Pads. Overall length equals Standard Cylinder diameter minus ·5%.
Gudgeon Pins anchored with a Taper Pin through the connecting rods have a centre portion only left soft. This facilitates the sizing of the Taper Pin hole with Gudgeon Pin in position in the connecting rod, as invariably oversize Taper Pins are necessary, due to wear.

TYPES OF GUDGEON PIN FASTENINGS

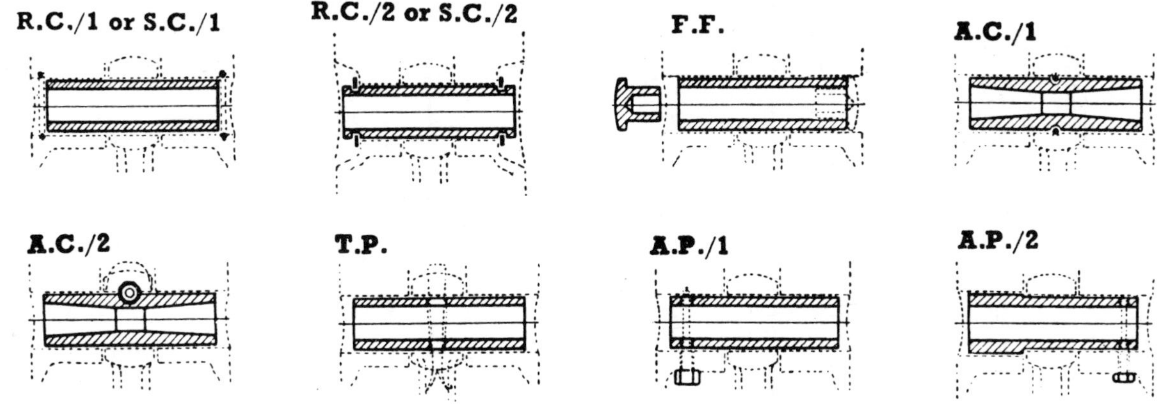

the same size as the first due to tool flexure on the amateurs' lathe. In addition, you can't see what is happening as you proceed up the far hole and there is no easy way of measuring its diameter.

A simple method of boring the opposite boss accurately is to mount a piece of steel bar in the 3-jaw chuck and turn a mandrel diameter to suit the hole you have just bored. The piston is pushed on to the mandrel and the opposite boss is bored out in line. By this means both holes are in the same plane and you can't go wrong.

Circlip grooves can be machined at the same time as the bores are finished. This will entail grinding-up a special tool to suit the circlip, which will either

This most useful table of Tranco valve dimensions can be consulted when selecting substitute valves. ***(Courtesy TRW Valves Ltd.)***

VALVES

VALVE No.	ENGLISH				METRIC				HEAD STYLE	STEM END	MAKE
	HEAD DIA.	STEM DIA.	STEM LENGTH	OVERALL LENGTH	HEAD DIA.	STEM DIA.	STEM LENGTH	OVERALL LENGTH			
4000	1 3/4	11/32	4 3/16	4 19/64	44.4	8.73	106.3	109.2	ST	RG	J.A.P.
4001	1 41/64	11/32	4 5/32	4 19/64	41.6	8.73	105.6	109.2	ST	RG	,,
4003	1 11/16	3/8	4	4 5/32	42.8	9.53	101.6	105.6	ST	TG	P. & M.
4007	1 1/2	3/8	3 15/16	4 1/16	38.1	9.53	100.0	103.2	ST	2NG	A.J.S., MATCHLESS
4010	1 19/32	3/8	3 15/16	4 1/16	40.5	9.53	100.0	103.2	ST	2NG	,, ,,
4012	1 5/8	11/32	4 55/64	5 1/64	41.3	8.73	123.4	127.4	D	TG	NORTON
4017	1 9/32	5/16	3 29/64	3 37/64	32.5	7.94	87.7	90.9	ST	PG	B.S.A.
4027	1 5/8	11/32	5 13/32	5 9/16	41.3	8.73	137.3	141.3	F	PG	HARLEY DAVIDSON
4028	1 15/16	3/8	6 5/64	6 9/32	49.2	9.53	154.4	159.5	ST	PG	,, ,,
4030	1 3/4	3/8	3 7/16	3 19/32	44.5	9.53	87.3	91.3	ST	PG	,, ,,
4031	1 3/4	3/8	3 9/16	3 19/32	44.5	9.53	90.5	91.3	ST	PG	,, ,,
4034	2	3/8	4 63/64	5 1/8	50.8	9.53	126.6	130.2	F	NG	INDIAN
4035	2	3/8	4 63/64	5 17/64	50.8	9.53	126.6	133.7	D	NG	
4054	1 9/16	5/16	3 37/64	3 11/16	39.7	7.94	90.9	93.6	ST	PG	ARIEL
4055	1 23/32	11/32	3 63/64	4 3/32	43.7	8.73	101.2	104.0	ST	PG	,,
4056	1 23/32	3/8	3 63/64	4 3/32	43.7	9.53	101.2	104.0	ST	PG	,,
4121	1 3/8	3/8	3 53/64	3 15/16	34.9	9.53	97.2	100.0	ST	TG	P. & M.
4169	1 23/32	5/16	4 19/64	4 33/64	43.6	7.94	109.1	114.7	D	PG	ARIEL
4171	1 7/16	5/16	4 11/64	4 9/32	36.5	7.94	105.9	108.7	ST	NG	VELOCETTE
4175	1 1/2	11/32	3 11/16	3 53/64	38.1	8.73	93.6	97.2	ST	TG	ROYAL ENFIELD
4183	1 9/16	11/32	3 37/64	3 45/64	39.7	8.73	91.0	94.2	ST	PG	ARIEL
4190	1 1/8	5/16	3 15/32	3 35/64	28.6	7.94	88.1	90.1	ST	PG	TRIUMPH
4191	1 1/8	5/16	3 15/32	3 35/64	28.6	7.94	88.1	90.1	ST	PG	,,
4220	1 3/8	5/16	3 31/32	4 5/64	34.9	7.94	100.8	103.6	F	PG	B.S.A.
4221	1 5/16	5/16	3 31/32	4 3/32	33.3	7.94	100.8	104.0	F	PG	,,
4222	1 47/64	.354	5 33/64	5 43/64	44.0	9.0	140.1	144.1	F	PG	,,
4223	1 5/8	.354	5 1/2	5 43/64	41.3	9.0	139.7	144.1	F	PG	,,
4228	1 17/32	5/16	3 23/32	3 53/64	38.9	7.94	94.5	97.2	ST	PG	,,
4229	1 31/64	.354	3 23/32	3 27/32	37.7	9.0	94.5	97.6	T	PG	,,
4313	1 9/16	3/8	4 7/32	4 21/64	39.7	9.53	107.1	109.9	ST	NG	VELOCETTE
4320	1 5/16	5/16	3 25/32	3 55/64	33.3	7.94	96.0	98.0	ST	PG	TRIUMPH
4321	1 5/16	5/16	3 25/32	3 55/64	33.3	7.94	96.0	98.0	ST	PG	,,
4324	1 21/32	.354	3 11/16	3 53/64	42.0	9.0	93.6	97.2	ST	PG	B.S.A.
4325	1 19/32	3/8	3 11/16	3 27/32	40.5	9.53	93.6	97.6	ST	PG	,,
4330	1 25/32	11/32	4 17/32	4 5/8	45.2	8.73	115.1	117.5	ST	PG/T	NORTON
4331	1 47/64	3/8	4 1/2	4 19/32	44.0	9.53	114.3	116.7	F	PG/T	,,
4333	1 5/16	5/16	3 17/32	3 5/8	33.3	7.94	89.7	92.1	ST	PG	ARIEL
4334	1 1/4	5/16	3 33/64	3 5/8	31.8	7.94	89.3	92.1	F	PG	,,
4350	1 11/16	3/8	3 15/16	4 1/16	42.9	9.53	100.0	103.2	ST	2NG	A.J.S., MATCHLESS
4351	1 19/32	3/8	4 3/16	4 5/16	40.5	9.53	106.3	109.5	ST	2NG	A.J.S.
4352	1 1/2	3/8	4 9/64	4 17/64	38.1	9.53	105.2	108.3	ST	2NG	,,
4353	1 7/32	5/16	3 3/8	3 29/64	31.0	7.94	85.7	87.7	F	PG	ARIEL
4354	1 3/32	5/16	3 3/8	3 15/32	27.8	7.94	85.7	88.1	F	PG	,,
4357	1 25/64	9/32	4 3/64	4 5/32	35.3	7.14	102.8	105.6	ST	PG	A.J.S., MATCHLESS
4358	1 19/64	5/16	4 1/64	4 1/8	33.0	7.94	102.0	104.8	ST	PG	,, ,,
4362	1 7/16	5/16	4 1/16	4 5/32	36.5	7.94	103.2	105.6	F	PG	SUNBEAM
4363	1 5/16	5/16	4 1/16	4 3/16	33.3	7.94	103.2	106.4	F	PG	,,
4364	1 3/4	3/8	3 43/64	3 13/16	44.5	9.53	93.3	96.8	ST	PG	HARLEY DAVIDSON
4365	1 3/4	3/8	3 43/64	3 27/32	44.5	9.53	93.3	97.6	F	PG	,, ,,
4368	1 1/4	11/32	4	4 5/32	31.7	8.73	101.6	105.6	ST	TG	ROYAL ENFIELD
4371	1 47/64	3/8	4 13/64	4 19/64	44.0	9.53	106.7	109.4	ST	TG	NORTON
4373	1 3/8	5/16	3 27/32	3 15/16	35.0	7.94	97.6	100.0	F	PG	,,
4374	1 7/16	5/16	3 11/16	3 49/64	36.5	7.94	93.6	95.6	ST	PG	TRIUMPH
4375	1 7/16	5/16	3 11/16	3 25/32	36.5	7.94	93.6	96.0	ST	PG	,,
4382	1 11/16	5/16	4 9/32	4 3/8	42.9	7.94	108.7	111.1	ST	NG	VELOCETTE
4386	1 1/2	11/32	3 11/16	3 25/32	38.1	8.73	93.6	96.0	ST	TG	ROYAL ENFIELD
4387	1 3/8	11/32	3 11/16	3 25/32	35.0	8.73	93.6	96.0	ST	TG	,, ,,
4388	1 19/32	5/16	4 19/64	4 33/64	40.5	7.94	109.1	114.7	D	TG	ARIEL
4389	1 53/64	11/32	4 3/16	4 5/16	46.4	8.73	106.3	109.5	ST	RG	J.A.P.
4400	7/8	7/32	3 27/64	3 33/64	22.2	5.56	86.9	88.9	F	PG	VELOCETTE

Motor Cycle Section

GUIDES

Guide No.	Overall Length	Type	Bore Diam.	Fit Diam.	Make
5000B	2 1/64	P	5/16	9/16	VELOCETTE
5002B	2	P	3/8	9/16	,,
5005B	1 31/32	1 7/32	5/16	1/2	TRIUMPH
5006B	2 1/4	1 1/2	5/16	1/2	,,
5008B	43	P	7	13.1	B.M.W.
5012	42	P/R	7.9	13.1	N.S.U.
5013	43	P/R	9	17.1	,,
5014	2 5/64	1 9/32	3/8	41/64	HARLEY-DAVIDSON
5015	2 5/64	1 9/32	3/8	41/64	,, ,,
6042	2 3/8	1 1/2	5/16	5/8	ARIEL
6046	2 3/16	1 3/16	11/32	5/8	,,
6048	2 1/8	1 1/4	5/16	5/8	,,
6270	2 5/32	1 5/8	3/8	5/8	NORTON
6300	2 3/16	1 5/16	11/32	5/8	ARIEL
6305	2 23/32	1 9/16	11/32	41/64	NORTON
6366	1 3/4	1 1/4	5/16	9/16	B.S.A.
6367	2 7/16	1 7/16	3/8	5/8	ARIEL
6406B	1 15/32	P	7/32	3/8	VELOCETTE
6407B	1 11/16	P	7/32	3/8	,,
6408	3 7/32	1 15/16	3/8	19/32	HARLEY-DAVIDSON
6409	1 7/8	P	9/32	1/2	NORTON
6416	2 1/4	1 3/8	3/8	5/8	P. & M.
6417	2 1/4	1 17/32	3/8	5/8	,,
6419	1 13/16	1 3/8	11/32	5/8	ROYAL ENFIELD
6427B	2	1 3/8	3/8	9/16	VELOCETTE
6428B	2	1 3/8	5/16	9/16	,,
6430	2 1/4	1 13/16	9	9/16	B.S.A.
6431	2 7/32	1 15/32	5/16	1/2	TRIUMPH
6434	2 27/32	1 3/4	11/32	41/64	NORTON
6435	2 1/64	1 17/64	5/16	1/2	TRIUMPH
6436	2 3/8	P	3/8	5/8	A.J.S.
6437	1 7/8	P	5/16	9/16	B.S.A.
6438	2 1/8	P	5/16	9/16	,,
6439	2 1/4	1 13/16	5/16	9/16	,,
6441	2 3/32	1 23/32	23/64	5/8	,,
6442	2 1/8	1 3/4	3/8	5/8	,,
6443	3 1/4	P	9	5/8	,,
6444	3 7/16	P	9	5/8	,,
6449	2 11/16	1 3/8	11/32	9/16	HARLEY-DAVIDSON
6453	2 1/8	1 7/16	5/16	1/2	TRIUMPH
6455	2 5/32	1 7/16	5/16	1/2	ARIEL
6455B	2 5/32	1 7/16	5/16	1/2	,,
6457B	2	P	5/16	1/2	,,
6458B	2	1 3/8	11/32	11/16	J.A.P.
6459B	2 13/32	1 3/4	11/32	11/16	,,
6460	2 1/8	1 5/8	9	5/8	B.S.A.
6463	2 5/16	P	9/32	5/8	A.J.S., MATCHLESS
6464	2 1/2	P	5/16	5/8	,, ,,
6465	2 1/8	1 7/16	5/16	1/2	NORTON
6468	2 1/4	1 11/16	5/16	9/16	B.S.A.
6469	2 1/4	1 11/16	9	9/16	,,
6471	2 1/8	1 5/8	3/8	5/8	,,
6472	1 49/64	P	5/16	1/2	TRIUMPH
6473	2 3/8	P/R	3/8	5/8	A.J.S., MATCHLESS
6474	2 7/16	P	3/8	5/8	,, ,,
6475B	1 27/32	1 7/16	11/32	5/8	ROYAL ENFIELD
6476B	2 5/16	1 5/8	11/32	5/8	,, ,,
6477	2 13/32	2	5/16	9/16	SUNBEAM
6478	2	P	7/32	3/8	VELOCETTE
6481	3 7/32	2	3/8	5/8	INDIAN
6482B	1 21/32	1 9/64	5/16	9/16	ARIEL
6483B	2 1/16	1 3/8	11/32	5/8	ROYAL ENFIELD
6484	2 1/16	1 5/8	11/32	5/8	,, ,,
6484B	2 1/16	1 5/8	11/32	5/8	,, ,,
6489	2 3/32	1 11/32	5/16	9/16	B.S.A.
6489B	2 3/32	1 11/32	5/16	9/16	,,
6490B	1 7/8	1 13/32	5/16	1/2	ARIEL
6492B	2 5/32	1 3/16	11/32	5/8	,,
6493B	2 13/32	1 7/16	3/8	5/8	,,
6494B	2 5/16	1 17/32	5/16	5/8	,,
6495B	2 5/16	1 17/32	5/16	5/8	,,
6496	2 3/8	P/R	3/8	5/8	A.J.S., MATCHLESS
6497	2 1/16	P/R	3/8	5/8	,, ,,
6498	2 5/16	P	9/32	5/8	,, ,,
6499	1 15/16	P	5/16	5/8	,, ,,
6499L	1 15/16	P	11/32	5/8	,, ,,
6510B	2 1/16	1 3/8	11/32	5/8	ROYAL ENFIELD
6512B	2 1/8	1 3/4	5/16	5/8	B.S.A.
6513B	1 13/16	1 7/16	9	5/8	,,
6514	1 23/32	1 21/64	9/32	7/16	B.S.A., TRIUMPH
6515B	2 1/16	1 5/8	11/32	5/8	ROYAL ENFIELD
6516	2 1/32	P/R	5/16	5/8	A.J.S., MATCHLESS
6517	2 1/32	P/R	3/8	5/8	,, ,,
6521	1 55/64	1 3/16	5/16	1/2	B.S.A.
6522B	2 1/32	1 11/16	11/32	5/8	ROYAL ENFIELD
6523	2 25/64	P	5/16	5/8	A.J.S., MATCHLESS
6524	2 9/64	P	9/32	5/8	,, ,,
6525	2	P	5/16	5/8	,, ,,
6526	2 21/64	P/R	5/16	5/8	,, ,,
6527	2	1 7/32	5/16	1/2	B.S.A.
6603	2 11/64	1 29/64	.380	9/16	HARLEY-DAVIDSON
6616B	2 5/32	1 5/8	3/8	5/8	NORTON

The Tranco valve guide list showing sizes for the more popular makes of motorcycle. *(Courtesy TRW Valves Ltd.)*

be a round-wire type or the *Anderton* pattern with ears. In the latter case, consult an *Anderton* catalogue for the recommended circlip groove width and depth. (Bearing stockists will advise).

Repairing chipped fins

Welding facilities are not always available, in which case a neat cosmetic repair can be made with Araldite, bonding the broken piece in place. Epoxy-resin should withstand the temperatures involved and the bodge will not be noticed when the cylinder is blacked.

Perfectionists will prefer welding. Although it is possible to arc-weld a cast iron fin back on, most people prefer the braze-welding process employing oxy-acetylene. By this method the parent metals are not melted. Aluminium fins are best fixed by argon or helium-shield welding; daunting though it may sound it is often necessary to break off adjacent fins to get at a deeply recessed fracture.

Valves and valve replacements

The question of valve replacement will be dealt with in greater detail than normal in the following pages — most period handbooks dismiss the subject with the casual statement "And now grind-in the valves"!

No matter how obscure the make or type of engine replacement valves should be no problem. Out of all the millions of valves made for more modern vehicles, and this includes tractors and lorries, there is bound to be something suitable for your vintage motor. I never waste time searching for the correct valves for a vintage or veteran engine; even if they could be found, the chances are the metal would be of a relatively inferior grade. A few late vintage manufacturers, such as AJS and Blackburne, made valves from decent material (usually marked "KE") and as a general rule post WWII valves are of good quality.

In the pioneer period valves gave an awful lot of trouble and a rider was well advised to carry a spare exhaust valve and cotter on any lengthy journey. Seats would burn out quickly and, worse still, heads were known to drop off due to poor materials and overheated engines. Today things are different, insofar as the cheapest car and bike engines are expected to do at least sixty thousand miles without valve replacement. Many do twice this mileage of course; sixty years ago most engines would have gone through several sets of valves and guides (and bores) in this period. So why bother looking for original valves?

At the time of writing the position regarding valve replacement for machines of the 1950 to 1960 period is quite favourable, most specialist dealers carrying large stocks. How long this situation will continue is open to question as more and more machines remain as static exhibits in private collections. Obviously valve manufacturers cannot be expected to run off large batches of little-used valves and guides. There will probably always be a demand for replacement valves for popular vertical twins such as Triumph, BSA and Norton; owners of Vincents, Velocettes, Rudges, and those immortal Inter and Manx Nortons are well catered for by specialist spares organisations.

A *Tranco* Valves catalogue is a most useful acquisition as it containes complete dimensional details of thousands of valves for cars, bikes and tractors. *Tranco* valves, guides and springs (manufactured by TRW Valves Ltd., Woden Rd West, Wednesbury, W. Midlands, England) are of excellent quality, being standard replacements during the original period of manufacture of most British motorcycles. Many motor engineers have *Tranco* catalogues and can be persuaded to let you have a browse through the lists for a suitable valve or guide.

Make a sketch

Assuming you have a pair of valves to replace, the first thing to do is to make a simple drawing of them. Make a note of the exact head diameter, stem diameter, stem length and overall length. These are the most important features but the supplier will also want to know the head style (eg. if it's a tulip or flat head) and stem-end details (eg. cotter slot or taper-groove). Obviously you are not going to find a valve that will fit straight in. You will have to be satisfied with one that is perhaps too long, or one with a larger diameter head.

I always aim for a valve with the correct-size stem diameter, with the right-size head if possible, and a long enough stem so it can be cut down and whatever cotter details required machined into it. As mentioned previously, a lathe is a handy machine tool and no valve modifications can be done without one. Of course such jobs can be farmed-out to engineering firms but the cost is prohibitive and it is usually difficult to find someone interested enough to listen to your specific instructions.

If you are going to the trouble of making new valves for your vintage engine, you might as well make them out of good stuff right from the start. Even veteran side valve engines will benefit from having their exhaust valves made from KE965, *Jessop's* G2 or a similar austenitic steel. In the case of racing machines it is imperative to use such materials. On the other hand a few vintage motors (water-cooled ones in particular) are cool-running and seem quite happy with modern inlet valve material used in the exhaust position. Fortunately metallurgy has progressed since the 1920s and modern inlets are often as good as vintage exhausts. BSA M20/21 exhaust valves were made out of excellent material (they had to be!) and are useful replacements for many vintage engines with minor modifications.

Valve materials

The following are various types of valve materials specified by *Tranco*:-

Type	
NS	Nickel Steel. An alloy steel suitable for inlet valves
NC	Nickel-Chromium-Molybdenum (EN24). A hard-wearing and superior alloy steel for inlet valves.
SC	Silicon-Chromium (Silchrome 1) (EN52). Suitable for petrol and diesel engine valves and for exhaust valves in some diesel engines.
XB	Chromium-Nickel-Silicon (EN59). A quality exhaust valve steel which has good resistance to high temperature scaling and corrosion.
KE	High Nickel-Chromium-Tungsten (EN54/KE965). A high alloy austenitic steel for exhaust valves.
TF	High Chromium-Manganese Austenitic Steel (21-4N). An exhaust valve steel with increased hot strength and corrosion resistance.

YEAR AND MODELS	VALVE NUMBER MAKER'S REF.	VALVE NUMBER INLET	VALVE NUMBER EXHAUST	GUIDE NUMBER MAKER'S REF.	GUIDE NUMBER INLET	GUIDE NUMBER EXHAUST
A.J.S.						
1958/60 14 (O.H.V.).	042032 042033	**4469** –	– **4470**	042068 042069	**6498** –	– **6499**
1960/64 14, 14CS and Scrambler. **1962/64** 14CSR.	042032 042868	**4469** –	– **4524**	042068 042869	**6498** –	– **6499L**
1937/48 16, 16M (O.H.V.)	STD676 STD677	**4010** –	– **4007**	014510 39-12E-148 STD660	**6436** –	– **6436**
1949/53 16, 16M, 16MC, 16MCS.	013985 013986	**4351** –	– **4352**	014510	**6436** –	– **6436**
1954/55 16M, 16MC, 16MCS, 16MS.	013985 013986	**4351** –	– **4352**	021184 021185	**6473** –	– **6474**
1956/57 16, 16M, 16MC, 16MS.	013985 013986 018103	**4351** –	– **4352**	014510 022208	**6436** –	– **6496**
1957/59 16MC, 16MS, 16MCS.	013985 013986	**4351** –	– **4352**	014510 023370	**6436** –	– **6497**
1959/64 16C.	013985 013986 018103	**4351** –	– **4352**	014510 022208	**6436** –	– **6496**
1959/64 16CS (O.H.V.).	024525 013986 023367	**4515** –	– **4352**	024359 024519	**6516** –	– **6517**
1962/64 16, 16S, (O.H.V.)	024525 013986 023367	**4515** –	– **4352**	026030 024519	**6526** –	– **6517**

A page from the Tranco catalogue listing valves and guides against specific makes and models. *(Courtesy TRW Valves Ltd.)*

N80A Nickel-Chromium-Cobalt. A steel developed especially for use at high temperatures where there are strict limitations on maximum creep under high stress.

BM Bi-metal. Consisting of an austenitic head and NS or NC stem.

SAS Special Armoured Seat. On this valve the seat area is faced with special alloy which was developed to increase the service life of exhaust valves and gives exceptional resistance to hot corrosion and scaling.

SS *Stellite* Seat.

ST *Stellite* Tappet End.

Choosing a valve

First of all look down the catalogue lists for a valve with the correct stem diameter. If yours happens to be 5/16 or 3/8 in, you are in luck as these are the most common sizes. Some manufacturers (JAP, Royal Enfield and Ariel for instance) were fond of 11/32 dia. stems, and BSA were alone in preferring 9 mm (.354 in). This latter size is useful however, as worn 11/32 guides can be reamed out to accept them. (Owners of 1925 Model P Triumphs may care to note this fact, as these engines did not have detachable guides until 1926).

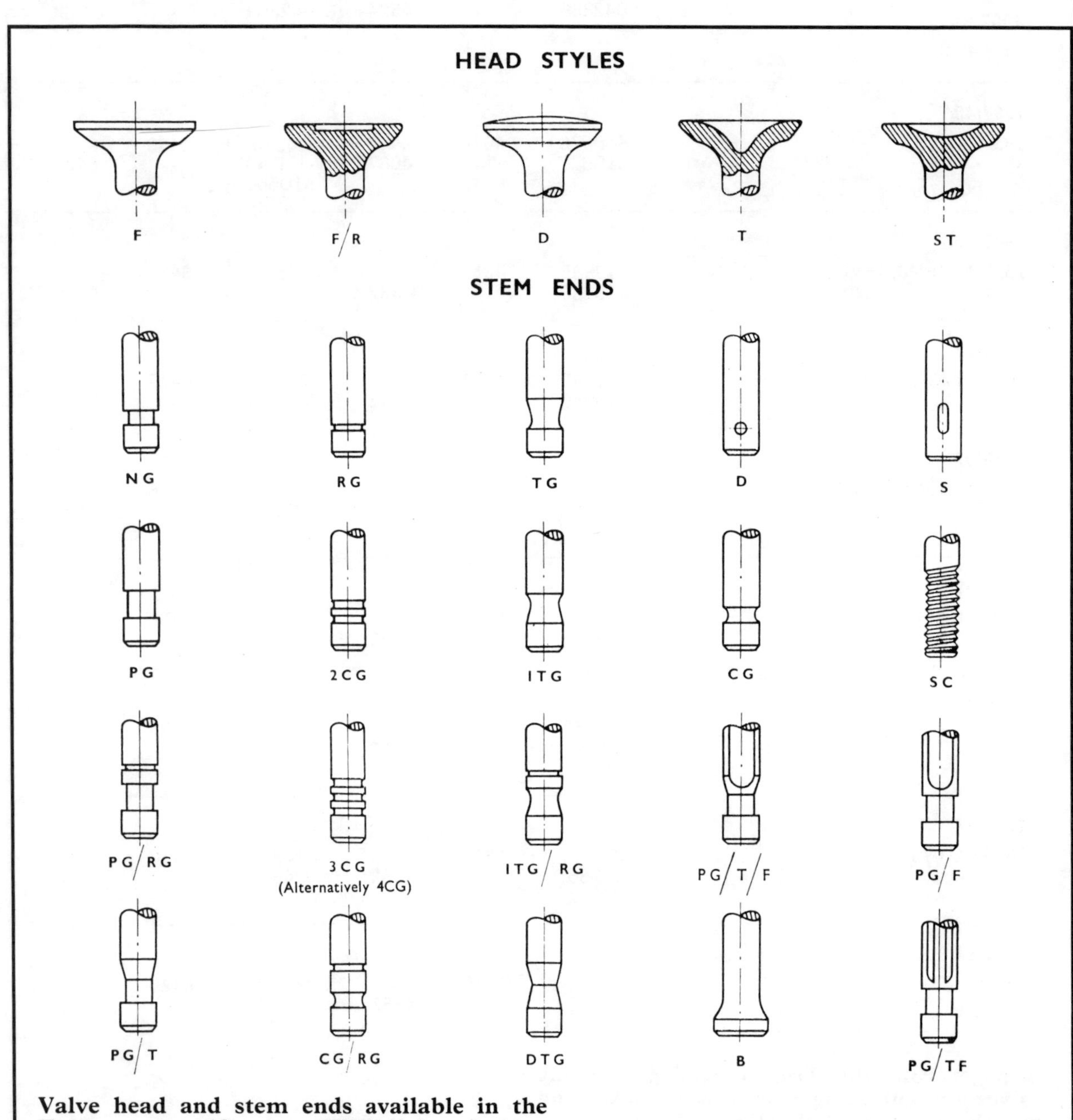

Valve head and stem ends available in the Tranco range. *(Courtesy TRW Valves Ltd.)*

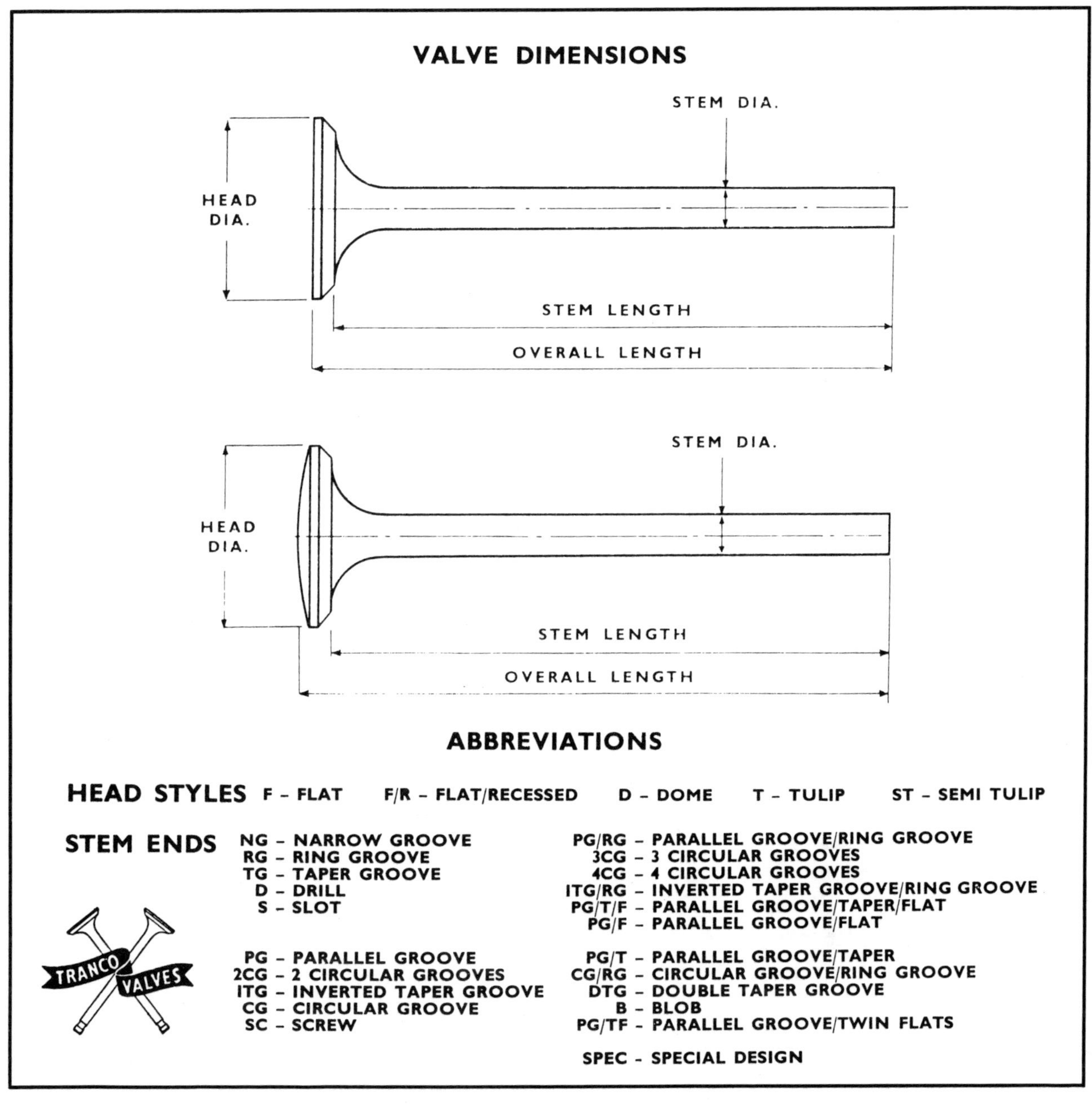

How to measure valve dimensions and the Tranco abbreviations used. *(Courtesy TRW Valves Ltd.)*

An example

Looking down the *Tranco* measurements you may find several valves with the same size head and stem, so choose the longest one you can find to be on the safe side. Let's quote an example; we will assume for a few moments you are restoring an early Werner engine of about 1904. This will have an exhaust valve with a 32 mm diameter head, a stem diameter of 8.5 mm and an overall length of 106 mm. The head is slightly domed and slotted (to take a screwdriver) and the stem has a 1/16 in wide cotter slot, but these are mere details for the moment. A half-hour's perusal of the catalogue will give a short list of a few car and lorry valves having 8.5 mm stems.

Gradually the list will be narrowed down to two or three contenders until we find — what's this? One valve with the correct stem diameter AND a 32 mm head? Not only this, but the overall length is 129.3 mm which is amply long for modifications. The valve listed is No. 2177 for a Morris Commercial and cross-reference to the main *Tranco* index indicates that our friend 2177 is an exhaust valve fitted to types LC, PV, LCS, Morris Commercial of 1938 and 1953. With such a long production run there's a good chance it is still available, and if not autojumble stalls should be stacked high with them!

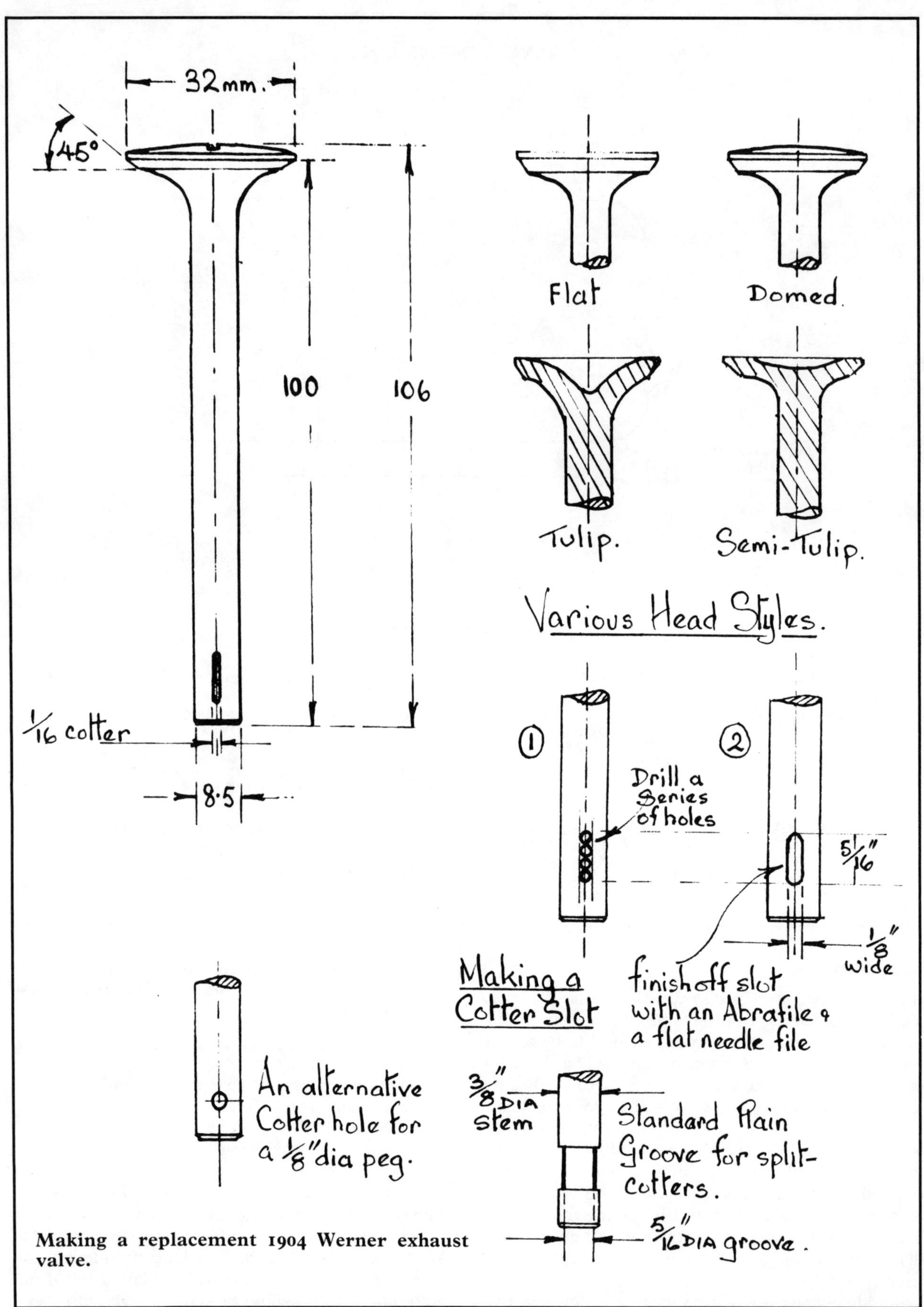

Making a replacement 1904 Werner exhaust valve.

Modifying the valve

In the case of our Tranco-Morris-Werner valve all we have to do is shorten the stem in a lathe and machine a cotter slot in it. Cutting a sixteenth-width slot in a valve stem is difficult without the proper tackle but a 1/8 in slot is easy, and a 3/8 stem (or even 5/16) will not be weakened unduly with a wider slot. Providing, that is, the valve springs are relatively docile. In the case of early ohv designs with flat-cotter valves it would be wise to adhere to the original slot widths, or better still modify them to accept taper cotter caps of more modern type.

To make a 1/8 in wide slot, drill a series of holes 3/32 in diameter dead in-line in the appropriate place. Use V-blocks when drilling to get all the holes vertical. Join them up by hand with an *Abrafile*, which is a thin round sawblade fixed in a hacksaw frame. Finish off the slot with a thin flat file. The slot ends are best left round (as drilled) as square-ends could promote fatigue fractures. After lapping-in the valve the usual way the job is done and the 1904 Werner is equipped with a better valve than it's ever had in its lifetime!

The foregoing case is a hypothetical example as there can't be many readers about to undertake the renovation of such an early engine. However, the same procedure holds good for any elderly motor. If the valve had been the more usual vintage or post-vintage type with taper-cotters it would have been an easy task to turn a groove in the stem with a parting tool to accept them.

Split cotters

New split taper cotters can be made from silver-steel by the following method:

1. Turn the exact taper on the tip of the silver steel rod.
2. Lap the taper into the existing valve spring cap with fine grinding paste.
3. Bore out the middle of the cotter to suit the valve stem groove diameter.
4. Part-off to length.
5. Split the cotters with a junior hacksaw and dress-off the edges with a small smooth file
6. Try the cotters, valve and valve-spring cap together and examine the mating parts with an eyeglass; the cotters should fit into the valve-spring cap snugly.

Where ordinary touring engines are concerned it is unnecessary to harden cotters. Side-valve engines with floppy valve springs can be fitted with valves having simple round-peg cotter pins of 1/8 in diameter. Stainless steel rod is a good material for these. Flat cotter-pins can also be made from stainless steel; a number can be cut from sheet (1/16 or 1/8 in thick) in one session — all edges should be radiused.

New valve spring caps are easily made on a lathe. Mild steel is quite adequate for touring ohv and side-valve motors, with EN8 as an alternative for racing engines. Dural spring caps are of course suitable for touring and competition engines alike, although it may be advisable to beef-up the dimensions in some cases. A suitable aluminium alloy is HE30.

Machining the head diameter

Say you were unable to find a valve with the exact head dimensions. Not to worry. Choose one with a larger head and machine it down to suit your valve seat, or if the difference is small open out the valve seat to suit. Vintage racing enthusiasts will wish to follow the latter course anyway.

If you have a precision lathe simply fix the stem in an accurate collet, centre the head to support it and turn down the diameter with a sharp tool. Machine the face to 45 degrees (or 30 degrees in rare cases) and lap-in the valve in the usual manner. If your lathe has seen better days it is advisable to hold the stem in a four-jaw chuck and clock the head so that

Two handy home-made gadgets for holding cylinder heads when working in a vice.

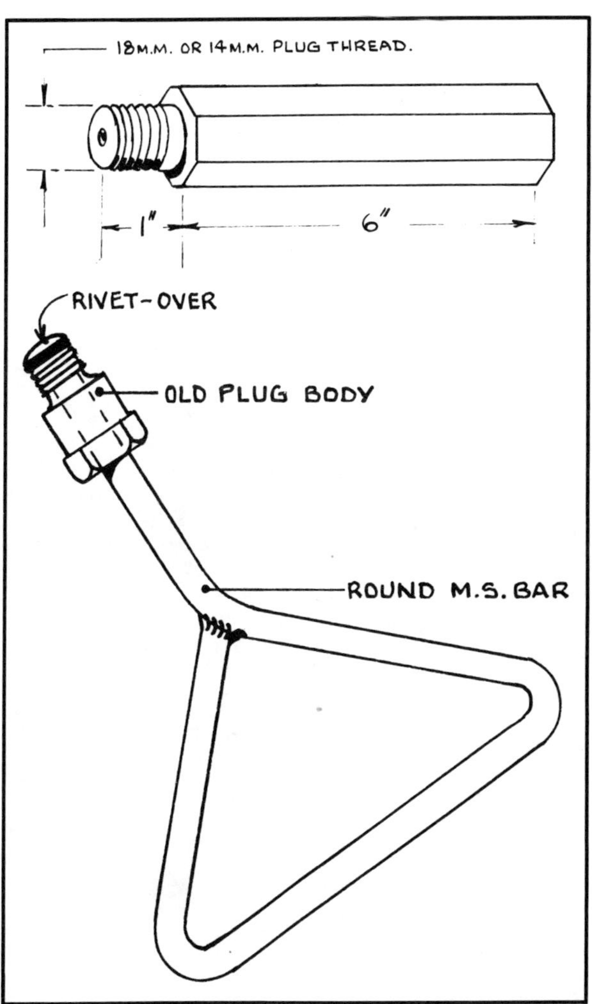

it is running perfectly concentric before machining commences. This point is mentioned as old, worn, three-jaw chucks are not usually accurate enough for valve-face machining.

Just a word about machining exhaust valve material. As any experienced turner will confirm, austenitic steel is not the easiest of material to machine. A sharp tool (tipped if possible) should be used and should not be allowed to skid on the surface of the metal. If it does, the steel may instantly work-harden and resist further machining. An ear-splitting screech will inform the lathe operator that things are not going too well. A deeper cut under the outer skin usually suffices.

Finishing of the valve face is made so much easier if a tool-post grinder is available, but most amateur turners do not possess such luxuries. The face is fine-turned at 45 degrees and then finished with emery cloth tacked to a flat piece of wood. Grinding-in with valve-grinding paste (thin) will complete the job, although it does no harm to check the seating with a smear of engineers' blue.

Other alternatives

If you come across a spare valve which is ideal in every other respect except that the stem diameter is too big, it should be remembered that this can be reduced to suit your guide. Turning down a stem in an ordinary amateur's lathe is an uphill task; this is a job for a grinder (tool-post or proper grinding machine) so the job will have to be sub-contracted in most cases. Whoever does it, make sure the stem is blended well in to the head as any step would obviously cause severe weakness.

New guides can be made to suit different stem diameters of course; if this plan of action is decided upon bear in mind that other makes of car or motorcycle valve guides can often be adapted. Otherwise turn new ones from close-grained or spun cast-iron bar; suitable material is obtained from an old motorcar cast-iron camshaft — machine-off the lobes and you are left with a bar of jolly good stuff for valve and tappet guides.

More recent ohv engines, particularly those with alloy heads, had phosphor-bronze valve guides and these are quite easy to make. This material would be ill-advised for exposed vintage (un-lubricated) guides. Cast iron, with its peculiar self-lubricating qualities, cannot be equalled for the latter.

Valve seat attention

Many years ago the ritual of grinding in the valves was a regular Sunday morning task, just like mowing the lawn or washing the car. Valves were much easier to get at and the operation was understood by laymen. Consequently seats became badly sunk over a long period — sometimes as much as 3/16 in below their original level. To restore status quo the seats must be built up again with weld or inserts.

A competent welder will have no difficulty in building up worn seats by means of oxy-acetylene welding (pre-heating the barrel or head and allowing it to cool slowly afterwards). If a hard-facing alloy of a 3½% nickel steel or *Stellite* is used, ordinary hand cutters may prove ineffective. In this

Opposite page: A page from the 1960 Hepolite catalogue relating to valve seat inserts. *(Courtesy Hepworth and Grandage Ltd.)*

The old and the new. Below left: A 1926 500cc sv BMW owned by Geoff Green. Below right: A restored 1956 'R' Series BMW.

VALVE SEAT INSERTS

SELECTING A SUITABLE INSERT

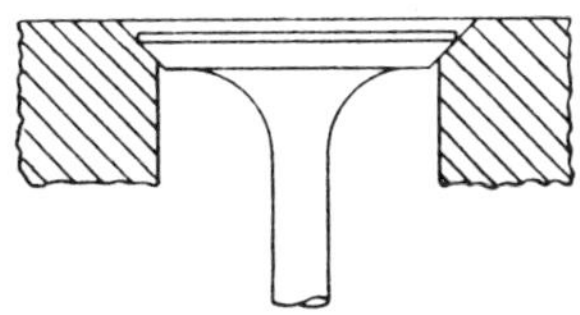

1. *Poor Valve Seat*

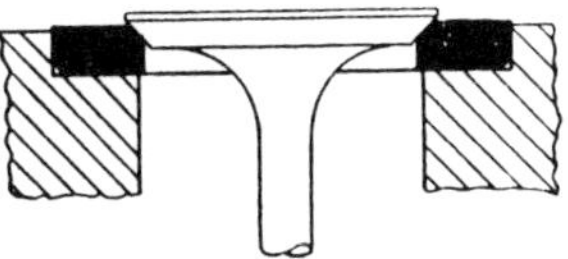

2. *Good Valve Seat after fitting Insert*

When valve seats become badly burnt or worn resulting in abnormally wide seating faces when reground (see sketch 1) they should be reclaimed by installing inserts. Some engines are fitted with inserts as original equipment, and replacements can be ordered by checking the dimensions, but the majority have the seat machined into the parent metal of the cylinder block or head. For these a suitable insert can be chosen from the diametral lists (opposite) if the following points are checked.

(1) The inside diameter 'A' of the insert should be slightly larger than the smaller diameter of the seating face on the valve head. (see sketch opposite).

(2) The outside diameter 'B' should be small enough to allow for sufficient metal between it and adjacent inserts, stud holes or water passages, otherwise the insert may work loose or distort.

(3) The depth 'C' will depend on the cylinder or cylinder head sections and care should be taken to ensure these are adequate.

MACHINING THE RECESS

A special cutting tool, which has a pilot bar locating in the valve guide, should be used for machining the recess. The cutter should be set to cut to the nominal diameter, shown in column 'B' of the diametral list, working to a tolerance of $^{+\cdot005''}_{-\cdot0005''}$ and *not* to the actual diameter of the insert. Hepolite Valve Seat Inserts are provided with the correct interference allowance over and above the nominal diameter shown. In machining the recess make sure that a sharp corner is left so that the insert can be pressed right home. To assist in this respect all inserts have a small bevel on one outer edge and should always be fitted with this to the bottom of the recess. (see sketch 2.)

FITTING INSTRUCTIONS

Make sure the recess and insert are clean and free from burrs. Coat the insert with 'Pressoline' or similar lubricant and press or draw into position. If possible the cylinder block or head should be heated and the insert cooled to facilitate this operation. Finally, machine or grind the seating face locating from the valve guide.

ALUMINIUM CYLINDER HEADS

High expansion inserts are necessary for use in aluminium alloy heads and the Austenitic type to specification HG.205 should be used. They should not be forcibly fit as they will tear the alloy but the head should be heated and the insert frozen to enable them to be assembled with only light pressure. After fitting, the seats can be cut in the normal way. Inserts in this material are not listed but quotations will be furnished on request.

RENEWING OLD VALVE SEAT INSERTS

If an old insert is found to be loose or is badly burned resulting in an abnormally wide seat after being ground, it should be replaced. To remove the insert, a puller designed for the purpose is desirable but, if this is not available, removal may be affected as follows.

Drill two holes in the insert 180° apart, not exceeding the width of the insert in depth, using a drill slightly less than the radial thickness of the insert. A small chisel may then be used to cut the sections of metal between the holes and the edges of the insert which will then be in two pieces and may be easily prised out. When drilling and cutting care must be taken not to damage the sides or bottom of the recesses in the head or block.

Remove all rough edges or burrs from around the outer edges of the recess and make sure that the bottom face is free from dirt. Measure the diameter of the recess and compare this with the outside diameter of the new insert. The interference fit should be .004" to .006", but if the counterbore has worn so that the fit is easier than this, oversize inserts should be used. Hepolite inserts are supplied + .003" oversize for this purpose. Should this not be sufficiently oversize special inserts will have to be made to the size specified.

CLEANLINESS

After cutting recesses, fitting and grinding or lapping valve seats, it is imperative that all swarf and grinding dust be removed from the valves, seats and ports. Should any of this material find its way into the cylinders destructive wear will rapidly ensue.

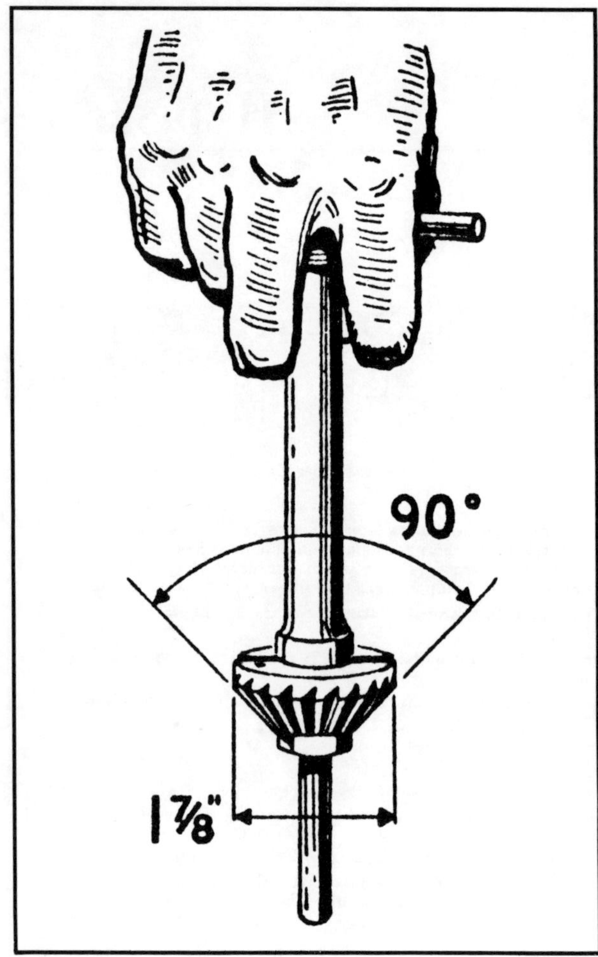

A common valve seat cutter. A set usually comprises large and small cutters, with a selection of arbors to suit 5/16, 9/32, 3/8 and 11/32 in valve guide bores.

case seat grinding stones will be required, even if it means hiring the appropriate equipment.

Inserts are available at various motor factors and the procedure for removal and replacement is as recommended by Hepworth & Grandage Ltd.*

Aluminium heads require inserts with a fair degree of interference, otherwise they will loosen at high temperatures. Some rings (eg. BSA M24 Gold Star etc.) were screwed-in and are difficult to replace; if the head thread is badly damaged there is little alternative but to build up the recess with aluminium-alloy weld and machine it out to suit a parallel insert.

Although difficult to find these days, aluminium bronze (wrought) is an excellent material for exhaust seat inserts with an interference fit of .003 to .004 in per inch diameter. Austenitic cast-iron inserts are suitable for the inlet side, with a similar interference, these recommendations being for aluminium heads.

Iron heads are less of a problem as seat inserts expand at more-or-less the same rate as the parent metal. An interference of around 1 to 1½ thou per inch diameter should be adequate. Inserts should never be forced in cold as this is the quickest way of ruining the recess. As far as the amateur is concerned, the easiest method is to stick the insert rings in the freezer and the head in the oven. Only a modest amount of heat is required — the rings should slip into the recesses without force. The job needs to be done quickly, using a fitting mandrel, or you may jam the inserts half-way.

Cracks

Cracked heads should be treated with caution if a weld repair is contemplated. Think twice before welding an irreplaceable head or barrel as it's all too easy to make a small crack much larger! Indeed, you may find yourself — to use welders' vernacular — chasing the crack all over the place. Tiny cracks are best left alone in early cylinder heads; if the crack does not appear to be causing any problems **and does not show any sign of developing** it is better to learn to live with it. Cracks in water-cooled heads, external or internal, can often be repaired by the time-honoured cold stitching method.

Water jacket repairs

Scott barrels were wont to crack in a horizontal line half-way down the block at the rear, and most V-twin heads and barrels crack almost as soon as they are bolted to the front end of a Morgan.

To stitch-repair a water jacket no preparation is required (as with welded repairs). Find out exactly where the crack commences and drill and tap a ¼ BSF thread into the jacket. Die-down the tip of a ¼ in diameter copper rod and screw it tightly into the hole, with a touch of *Loctite* or jointing-compound on the end.

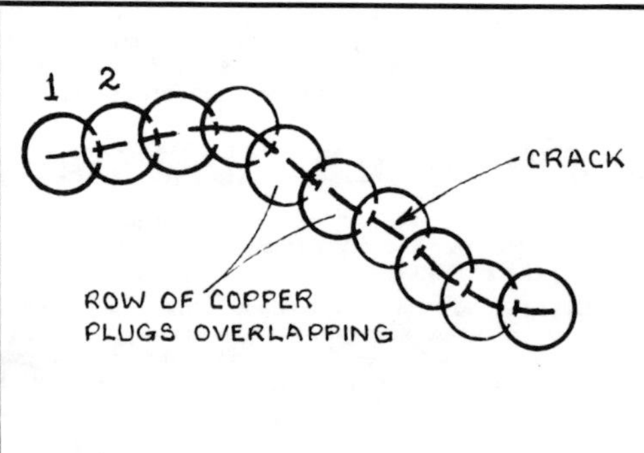

*See Hepworth & Grandage Information Sheet

Cut off, leaving the plug 1/32 in proud. Drill and tap another hole, but this time overlapping the first plug by about 1/4 of the diameter. Screw in another plug. Work along the crack in this manner, taking care to finish beyond the other extremity so there's no danger of it spreading in the future.

You should now have a neat row of copper plugs which can then be lightly peened over with a ball-peine hammer. Finish-off with a file and emery. The repair is a joy to behold if done nicely — the author's Morgan-Blackburne barrels and heads were repaired thus and have not leaked in twenty-five years.

Welding experts may point out that most metals can be welded or brazed successfully with modern rods — so why bother with an archaic method dating back to James Watt? In answer to this contention, the aforementioned snag (that of further cracks developing) should be considered and there is also the risk of distortion in welding.

Internal cracks can sometimes be repaired by stitching although it may be necessary to use smaller diameter plugs. I once managed to repair a crack inside a water-cooled head which ran from the sparking plug hole right across the exhaust valve seat. First of all an 18 mm to 14 mm adaptor was tightly screwed into the plug hole. Up as far as the valve seat the stitching was accomplished with the usual copper plugs; across the seat face I screwed-in wrought iron plugs and recut the seat with a hand cutter. The repair was completely successful in this instance but naturally it would be unwise to guarantee similar results on a highly-tuned racing engine. Nevertheless this dodge also worked on a very expensive alloy Jaguar engine (using dural plugs) and is mentioned for the benefit of readers in remote areas without recourse to welding expertise.

Tappets and pushrods

Tappet guides usually suffer little wear, even on exposed side-valve mechanisms. If only for the sake of oil retention they should be checked and renewed if necessary. Screw-in guides are often tightly fitted so removal is easier if the crankcase is warmed first; providing no side-loading is present the old guides can be bored-out and bushed with phosphor-bronze. Otherwise cast-iron is an excellent material.

Ball-ended tappet rods, which bear up against cam-followers can be made from silver steel heated to cherry red and plunged in oil. The threaded portion should be left soft. For tappets which act directly on cams, without the benefit of followers, a case-hardening steel is essential. If expert heat-treatment facilities are on hand it is worth considering EN8 (a material cheaper and easier to obtain than EN32) hardened by the *Beta* process. This imparts a very tough outer case.

Pushrods are not too difficult to make, either from HT30 aluminium tube (*Dural*) or thin-walled steel tube. Although some pushrod end-fittings are pinned as standard, this should not be necessary if the fitting is made a tight fit and fixed with *Loctite Retainer*. New cup-ends should be manufactured from a case-hardening steel, the internal radius being as near as possible to that of the pushrod ends. One way of forming an internal cup is to bore and shape the socket to the approximate radius using a specially ground drill or hand-held tool; the fitting is then heated-up to bright red and a bearing ball (3/8 in dia. or other appropriate size) is tapped into the cup. A hearty clout from a hammer and punch will do the trick. The hole for the pushrod tube is then machined in the opposite end. A final polish

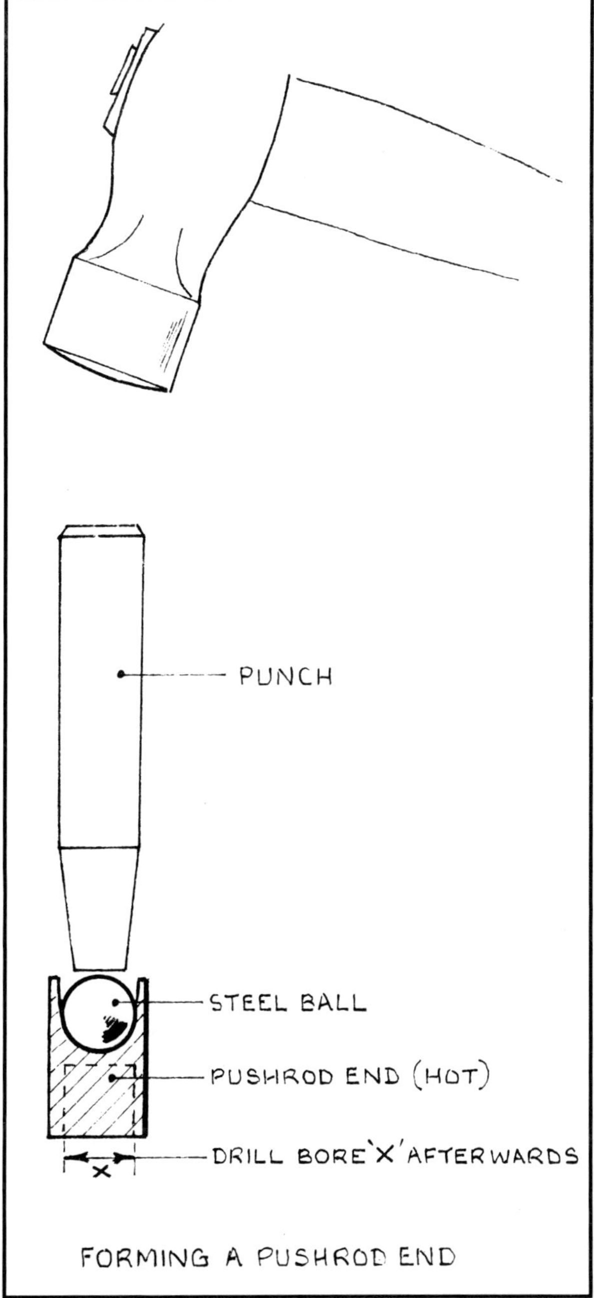

FORMING A PUSHROD END

with emery and the fitting can then be heat-treated in the normal way.

Valve springs and cams

No advantage whatsoever is to be gained from beefing-up floppy valve springs on early side valve engines. Nor should ohv springs be made stronger than standard, except perhaps for racing, as premature cam wear may well occur. In the case of highly-tuned vintage ohv motors it sometimes pays to feed oil directly onto the cam follower heels via external copper pipes and unions; Castrol R is highly recommended for such applications. An extra sight-feed hand pump, or a double delivery Pilgrim mechanical pump off a twin cylinder engine, can be arranged to supply the positive feed.

Post-vintage and classic engines do not normally suffer from oil starvation in their cam-chests, therefore cams and followers lead a relatively easy life. JAP roller followers are prone to wear and occasionally cease to revolve, in which case flats are worn on the periphery. The best material for rollers is EN31 ball-race steel or vacuum-hardened Carrs' 69s (which hardens right through); failing this one of the other case-hardening steels will suffice, such as EN32 or EN36. New roller pins should have a good core strength, therefore heat-treated EN24 or a nitriding steel such as EN40B should be used.

Valve springs should be checked for length against new spares — if they are tired to the extent of a 1/8 in settlement they should be discarded. Spring makers will want to know the following details if new springs have to be made for a rare motor:-

1 Outside diameter
2 Wire diameter (gauge)
3 Free length (this is the total length)
4 Number of active coils

Conical Springs

Conical springs can be made, although this is a fairly expensive procedure requiring a specially-made mandrel. Many vintage side-valve springs were conical, eg AJS, BSA, some Sunbeam, and a few ohv springs (as in the early 'big-port' AJS and some Blackburnes) but in most cases later parallel springs can be substituted without dire effects. The change will necessitate new spring caps, turned from *Dural* or steel.

Hairpin springs

Hairpin valve springs present special problems and should be carefully checked for wear. This occurs on the straight lengths of wire contacted by the spring retainer; failure will take place where the straight piece starts to bend into the coil so these areas should be examined closely for flaws. Springs should always be renewed in pairs.

Coil springs

If new coil-springs have been fitted to a vintage motor it is advisable to check that they do not become coil-bound at full lift. The valve spring cap must also be clear of the valve guide end by at least 1/16 in; problems in this department can occur if non-standard valves or valve-guides are fitted.

Hardened valve stem end-caps can be made from silver-steel heated to cherry-red and quenched in oil. This material is normally adequate for touring engines but if rapid wear persists a set in case-hardening steel may be required. Check that the end caps do not foul the valve cotters, as sometimes happens when the projecting portion of stem above the spring cap is too short.

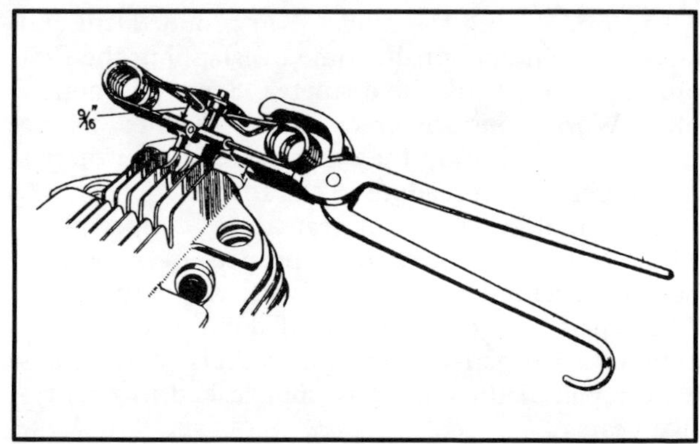

Fitting a hairpin valve spring to the cylinder head of an International Norton. After fitting the valves and springs there should be a gap of 1/2 to 9/16 in between the upper side of the valve spring collar and the underside of the spring.

This photo of a 1947 International Norton was taken after a hard 100 mile run in foul weather. The engine looks remarkably oil-tight!

Rocker geometry

A valve stem which is too long, or has been fitted with thick hardened end-caps when these were not part of the original specification, will cause undue wear in the stem and guide. It will be observed when the valve commences to open that a side thrust is imparted to the stem by the rocker arm. The remedy is obvious — shorten the valve stem or fit a thinner end-cap. There is no fixed rule about which engines need valve stem-end caps and which don't; spring strength, valve material, engine rpm, and lubrication are just some of the factors involved.

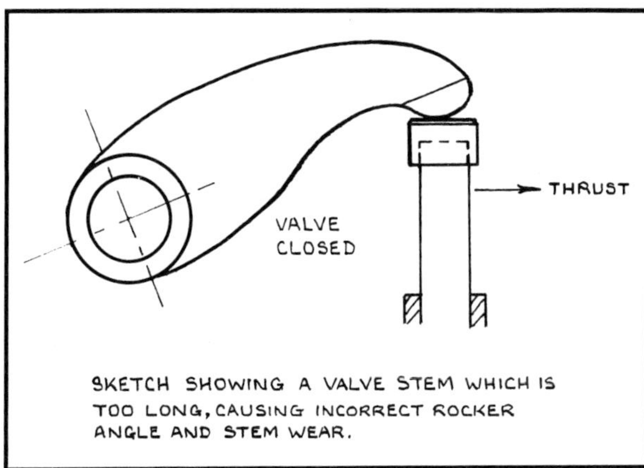

SKETCH SHOWING A VALVE STEM WHICH IS TOO LONG, CAUSING INCORRECT ROCKER ANGLE AND STEM WEAR.

A mystifying snag is when end-caps persistently fly off and vanish into thin air. If the malady occurs at peak revs it is quite likely that valve float is the culprit, coupled with excessive tappet clearance. Stronger valve springs or a restrained twistgrip hand may be the answer. Also, as described, examine the rocker arm geometry to ensure that the caps are not actually tipping when the valves begin to open.

Rocker arm bearings

It is open to question whether needle roller bearing rocker arms are a good thing. True, there is very little friction involved with this type of bearing, but after a great mileage the needles tend to wear grooves in the bearing surfaces due to limited radial movement. Early Model 18 Nortons suffer thus.

If the bearing surfaces are wide enough, it is worth considering phosphor-bronze bushes as replacements; they should have grease or oil distribution channels cut in by hand and should be lubricated regularly if the rockers are exposed to the elements. Plain bushes last a surprisingly long time.

Worn rocker heels, or tips, can be built up with a hard-facing material such as *Stellite*. The built-up surface should be correctly radiused and well polished.

With ordinary touring engines there is no advantage to be gained in drastically lightening rocker arms, although a little polishing will certainly do no harm and may in fact ward off the possibility of fatigue fracture. Deep marks, file cuts and nicks should be cleaned up for this reason but unless racing is envisaged there is no need for a mirror finish.

The rockers must pivot freely on their spindles after everything is bolted up; it may be necessary to skim a thou-or-two off a spacing washer to achieve this situation. On some machines, ohv B Group BSAs for example, rocker end-float is taken care of by double-coil spring washers; under normal roadgoing conditions there is no advantage in replacing these with plain distance pieces. The amount of friction provided by such spring washers is so small that no discernible difference will be noticed by their absence, at least not until the last morsel of power is required for sprint events.

Valve clearances must be closely observed, sticking rigidly to the manufacturer's recommendations. Certain ohv machines, such as KTT and KSS Velocettes, AMC twins and late Gold Star BSAs, have eccentric rocker-spindle adjustment for valve clearance setting. In such designs it is important to note that the rockers contact the valve stems centrally — some spindles are marked with arrows to indicate correct positioning.

If the correct clearance figures are unknown, a

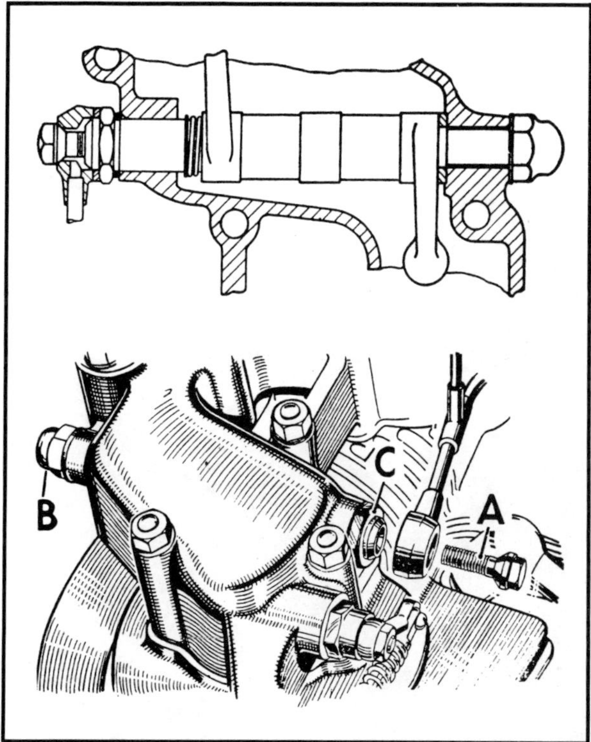

The BSA Gold Star eccentric rocker spindle assembly. To adjust the tappets, remove the oil feed bolt A, slacken the acorn nut B, then rotate spindle C until the correct tappet clearance is achieved. Check the clearance after locking oil feed bolt and acorn nut.

situation which might occur with an early engine, it is better to err on the excess side and make readjustments after the engine has run a while. With a veteran or vintage side valve engine you will not go far wrong if the exhaust valve and inlet clearances are set at .012 in and .010 in respectively. At least this will be more accurate than the thickness of a visiting card, as the old instruction books would advise! Unknown ohv clearances are more of a problem, as some increase when the engine is hot whereas others decrease. As a starting figure, try .010 in on the exhaust and .008 in on the inlet side; check as soon as the engine is thoroughly warmed-up and readjust as necessary. When the motor is hot it should be possible to rotate the pushrods or tappets easily; a few motors achieve a delightful state of equilibrium by requiring almost zero clearance hot or cold — probably more by accident than design.

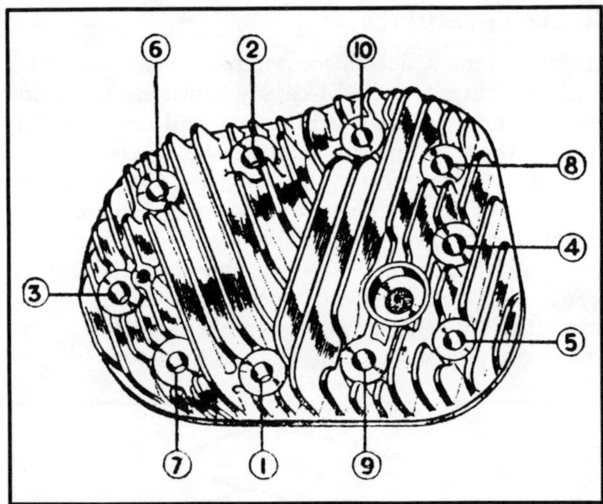

Cylinder heads must always be tightened evenly. This is the correct sequence for a side valve M20/M21 BSA.

Head joints

Unless the makers advise to the contrary, gasket cement should not be required on a copper-asbestos joint. A light smear of grease will suffice.

Plain gasket-less joints should be ground-in by hand with valve grinding paste. On the double-spigot type, in which the narrow barrel spigot fits in the head recess, coarse paste should be applied to the broad mating face and fine paste to the spigot. The head is then rotated back and forth by hand until good contact is noted round both faces. It will be necessary to lift the head from time to time, wash off the paste and observe progress. A little oil mixed in with the paste will help. By this method a sound gas-tight joint is achieved, with slightly more pressure on the narrow spigot than the broad flange. Again, no gasket cement should be necessary.

If copper-asbestos gaskets are not available, replacements can be made from solid copper. To anneal the copper, heat the gasket until it is bright red and drop it (edge-on) into a bucket of water.

Left: A 1956 DBD34 BSA Gold Star in restored condition. Departures from standard are the Allen screws around the timing cover and the finned tappet cover, the former being a much better proposition than the original cheese-head variety. The finned cover was a 'go faster' goodie of the period, sold by various Goldie specialists. Almost every Goldie restored today is to Clubmans' specification, a formula that makes the machine intractable on the road. It seems to have been forgotten that touring cams, footrests, handlebars, and a wide ratio gearbox were available for normal road use.

Opposite page left: An example of just what can be accomplished by a skilled pair of hands. The radiator on this 1929 Scott was fabricated by enthusiast Jim Baxter, of the Lark Lane Museum, Liverpool. Another book would be needed to describe this daunting task!

Opposite page right: A Minerva cylinder of the type shown earlier, in restored condition. Due to a design weakness the cylinder casting cracked between the inlet and the exhaust valve caps. Restorer Les Taverner's simple solution was the annealed copper plate spanning both cap holes. *(Photo: L. Taverner.)*

THE VAST RESOURCES OF THE FAMOUS ENFIELD WORKS

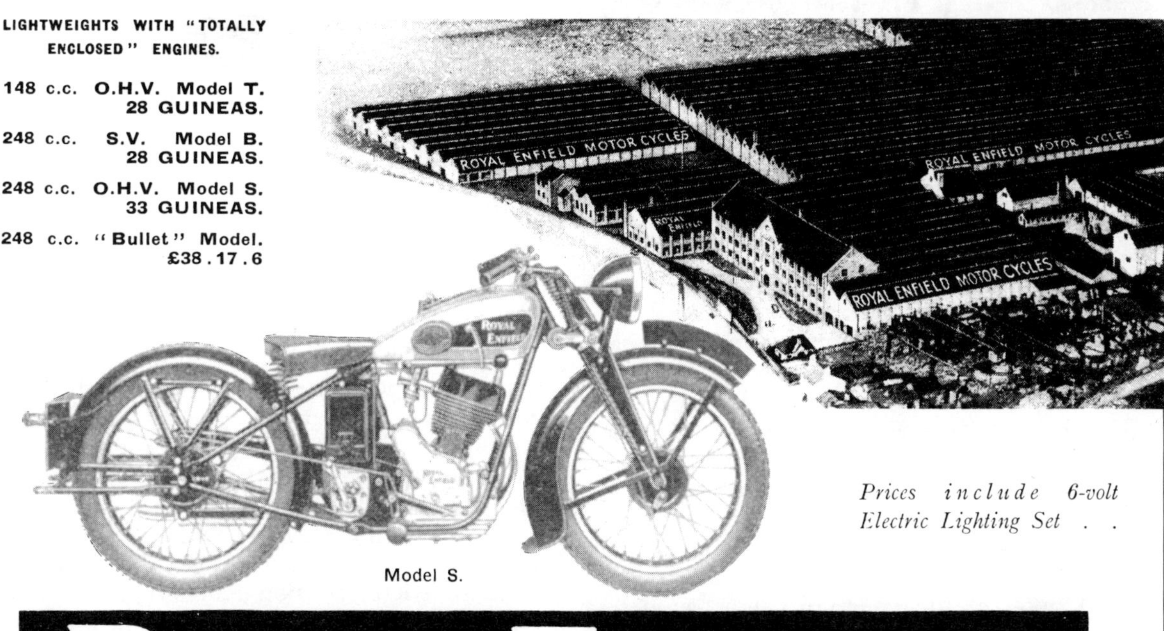

ROYAL ENFIELD

enable you to buy the best at the lowest possible price

Chapter 4

ENGINE WORK: The Bottom Half

Flywheels, Con-rods, Crankcases, Bearings & Bushes. Lubrication

---

Parting the Cases

THE writer's old engineering teacher, who spent his formative years repairing WD Scotts in the Kaiser War, was fond of saying "A judicious tap is one aimed with calculated deliverance". Never was the saying more true than when crankcases are parted. Once the bolts are removed, pause before reaching for any sort of hammer. Untold damage can be caused by belting away at the end of a crankshaft (especially a long and slender one such as a BSA Bantam generator-side mainshaft). Many people resort to screwdrivers wedged between crankcase flanges, a destructive act for which the culprits should be hung, drawn and quartered.

A little heat (boiling water or **gentle** application of blowlamp) works wonders. Once the cases are warmed up then is the time to pick up a hammer — hide-faced by choice, or copper if a few light blows can be risked on the mainshaft drive-end.

Main bearings

Early engines had phosphor-bronze mains and these very rarely gave trouble. Engine speed was much lower and compression ratios modest therefore the life of bronze main bushes was commendable. Up-and-down shake in mainshafts is easily detected — anything more than two thou or so is excessive and new bushes must be made. Particular attention must be paid to two-stroke main bushes (Villiers etc), which rely on a close running-fit to retain crankcase compression. End play is relatively unimportant.

Both bushes should be machined with the bores undersize by approximately .005 in and line-reamed, or bored, finally in situ. It must be possible to insert a test mandrel (eg. a silver-steel bar) through both bushes with ease when the crankcase halves are assembled. Line-boring can be accomplished in the amateurs' lathe, although this often involves a little ingenuity in mounting the crankcase to the top slide. A 3/4 in boring-bar mounted between centres will do the job, the crankcase being fed slowly backwards and forwards on successive cuts. The bush bores must be checked after each cut as it is all too easy to exceed the required size. If the bushes are left a fraction undersize, ie. slightly tight on the shaft, final lapping-in with metal polish will ensure a good running fit. Lubrication channels can be cut (before line-boring) by hand with a specially-made punch.

Ball and roller mains are usually made an interference fit in the crankcase halves. To remove a race from a blind hole warm-up the crankcase in boiling water, or in the oven, and strike it face downwards on the bench. With luck the bearing

One way of doing a job when your lathe swing is insufficient to mount the item on a faceplate. This veteran Minerva crankcase is having its main bearing bored by means of a milling attachment mounted on the end of a Myford ML7 lathe bed. *(Photo: L. Taverner.)*

should drop out. In some cases there is no alternative but to drill two diametrically-opposed 1/8 in diameter holes from the other side of the crankcase wall to coincide with the bearing outer ring. A pin-punch will then remove the race and the two holes can be plugged with aluminium rod.

The bearing should be examined for shake and roughness. A tiny piece of grit can give a false impression so wash the bearing in paraffin, spinning the outer ring in the process. If roughness is detected, examine the balls and bearing tracks with an eye-glass. Any pitting, however slight, means that a replacement is needed.

Bearing creep

There are several ways of dealing with bearings which have lost their interference fits in housings or on shafts. Creep, as the annoying habit is termed, is when a bearing outer-ring has rotated in its housing, or an inner-ring has spun on the shaft. If the situation is allowed to continue for any length of time it is obvious that both housing and shaft will wear considerably. Loctite *Bearing Fit* will restore the fit of an outer ring in a crankcase housing, providing that slackness does not exceed .002 in to .003 in (the makers claim a maximum gap of .006 in but it's best to play safe). A slack inner-ring is a different problem; *Loctite* will help to prevent further creep if little wear is evident, but future dismantling may be difficult if the mainshaft was originally intended to be a slide-fit.

A worn mainshaft is best corrected by metal spraying or copper-plating the affected area. The former is the easiest solution as very little prepara-

Possibly the earliest Triumph to survive with the maker's own engine. This is a 1905 model; previously Triumphs were equipped with JAP, Fafnir or Minerva engines. The engine was designed by Charles Hathaway at Maurice Schulte's instigation. Ixion tested an early model at the then incredible distance of 200 miles a day but unfortunately struck trouble in the form of rapid cylinder wear. Worse still, the tandem front down tubes broke. However, within a couple of years improvements were made and Triumph gained a reputation for reliability seldom equalled by any other make.

tion is required; the surface must be roughened in the vicinity of the worn area to provide a key for the sprayed-on metal. Usually a rough 26 tpi thread machined in the appropriate spot will satisfy the metal-sprayers. The surface should be ground true afterwards. A metal-sprayed finish looks slightly porous when examined under an eyeglass but this is nothing to worry about. (In fact, a sprayed shaft running direct in a bronze bush may last longer than an un-treated shaft due to the oil retention qualities of the porous surface). Surprisingly enough a roughened base-surface does **not** promote fatigue fractures as may be imagined — motorcar crankshafts are often built up thus.

Copper-plating of worn surfaces is quite practical but it is sometimes difficult to stop-off the untreated areas. Bearing rings can be built up this way, the tracks being masked with special varnish prior to plating. Commercial platers hate this kind of work as it is time-consuming. Copper will key better if the worn area is shot-blasted — for obvious reasons a complete ball race is impossible to handle and not really worth the trouble!

Badly worn crankcase housings should be bushed with bronze or stainless steel. This is not an easy task, calling for a large lathe and accurate machining. A 1/8 in wall-thickness bush is adequate but if there is not much metal to spare in the crankcase boss you might get away with 1/16 in. The insert should have an interference fit of about .002 in per inch of diameter and should drop into place with the crankcase heated to 200°C. As the insert will close-up on cooling, final machining is required. Bear in mind that the bearing itself will need to be an interference fit so the finished insert bore should be approximately .001 in per inch smaller than the bearing diameter.

If there is any doubt about the strength of the surrounding metal in the crankcase boss the insert can be made a size-for-size fit, *Loctite Retainer* providing the bond.

Bearing fits

Some knowledge of tolerance and bearing fits will be of assistance to the restorer, if only to enable him to talk the same language as bearing suppliers.

Ball and roller bearings are made to four ranges of tolerances, identified by the one, two, three and four dot system. In actual fact the marking consists of a series of polished rings, usually found in the vicinity of the maker's name on the outer ring face. Thus we have 0, 00, 000 and 0000 types, the significance of which is outlined by *Hoffmanns* as follows:-

O FIT "These bearings have the smallest amount of diametrical clearance. They should only be used where freedom from all shake is required in the assembled bearing and there is no possibility of the initial diametral clearances being eliminated by external causes. Therefore, special attention must be given to the seating dimensions, as the expansion of the inner ring, or contraction of the outer ring, may cause tight bearings. In this respect a one dot bearing should not be used unless recommended by us, when we will be pleased to specify seating fits".

OO FIT "This grade of diametral clearance is intended for use where only one ring is made an interference fit and there is no appreciable loss of clearance due to temperature differences. Ball journal bearings for general engineering applications are usually of this clearance".

OOO FIT "This grade of diametral clearance should be used when both rings of a bearing are made an interference fit, or when only one ring is an interference fit but there is likely to be some loss of clearance due to temperature differences. It is the grade normally employed for roller journal bearings on general engineering applications, but there is an increased tendency towards the use of two dot bearings. It is also the grade normally used for ball journal bearings that

A 1924 Matador-Bradshaw, fitted with a 350cc oil-cooled Bradshaw engine, Burman gearbox and Sports AMAC carburettor. The engine packed a tremendous punch for one of its size.

take axial loading, but for some purposes even 0000 fit bearings may be required.

0000 FIT "Where there will be some loss of clearance due to temperature differences and both rings must be an interference fit, this is the grade of diametral clearance to adopt. One example of its use is in bearings for traction motors. Customers should always consult us before ordering bearings with this grade of diametral clearance".

To summarise the situation, grade 00 is the most likely choice for main bearings and general motorcycle use, with the possibility of grade 000 for those applications where there is a likelihood of the bearing closing-up due to temperature variation. More often than not main bearings are a sliding, or light-push, fit on the mainshaft and an interference fit in the crankcase. Obviously if a heavy interference fit was applied in both these areas the engine would be difficult to take apart.

Standard shaft and housing limits are laid down by the bearing manufacturers (refer to tables) and due attention should be paid to these when new parts have to be made. Whilst a ground finish is recommended for mainshaft bearing registers the amateur turner can generally make do with a fine-turned finish, touched-up with emery cloth if necessary. An ideal material for new mainshafts would be EN16T, which has a very high tensile strength, but a veteran or early vintage engine would be quite happy with EN8.

Bearings should never be belted into housings with blows on the inner rings as this would cause indentation and subsequent failure. If heat cannot be applied to the housing (as with rear wheel hubs for example) the bearing should be tapped in by the outer ring, with a piece of tube machined to size. Better still, the race can be pressed or drawn in with continuous force.

End-play

In some designs end-play in the crankshaft assembly is eliminated by clamping one side against the main bearings; for example, in all Gold Star, B and M series BSAs, tightening of the mainshaft cush-drive ring nut will lock the crankshaft shoulder against the bearing assembly. Between the inner and outer bearings is a distance piece which must be within tolerance on the length. Other makes, such as AJS and Matchless of the post-war period, have a variation on this theme with spacing washers between the drive-side bearings. In all similar designs it is essential to replace any spacers or shims in the same position from whence they came.

Centrality of the connecting rod, or rods, in the crankcase mouth should be checked. With singles it is an easy matter to observe whether the little-end lies central with the split line of the crankcases. It may be necessary to move the crankshaft assembly over to one side by rearranging the shims. If there does not appear to be any end-play whatsoever and the crankshaft is a little tight, a tap with a copper hammer on both ends of the shaft may seat the bearings and free it off. Two light taps are sufficient, not heavy blows — if the assembly is still stiff to turn then a shim must be removed or a small skim taken off the flywheel/bearing abutment. This is all assuming that the flywheel assembly is correctly aligned and the mainshafts are not running out.

Overhead camshaft engines with bevel gear drive to the upstairs department must receive special attention. Cammy Nortons have virtually nil end-float; the crankshaft is located positively by the timing side ball race and any errors in centrality are corrected by adjustment of shim widths between the bearing and flywheel boss. In the Velocette design the flywheel assembly is nipped (pre-loaded) to the tune of two thou when cold. In all such configurations end-play should be checked again when the bevels are in situ and with everything tightened up.

Vintage side valve and pushrod ohv motors can usually tolerate a certain amount of end-float; where the flywheels are located end-wise by a pair of ball races or plain bronze bushes, about .010 in to .012 in play is normal. In very basic designs end-play can be considerably more than this — some crude two-

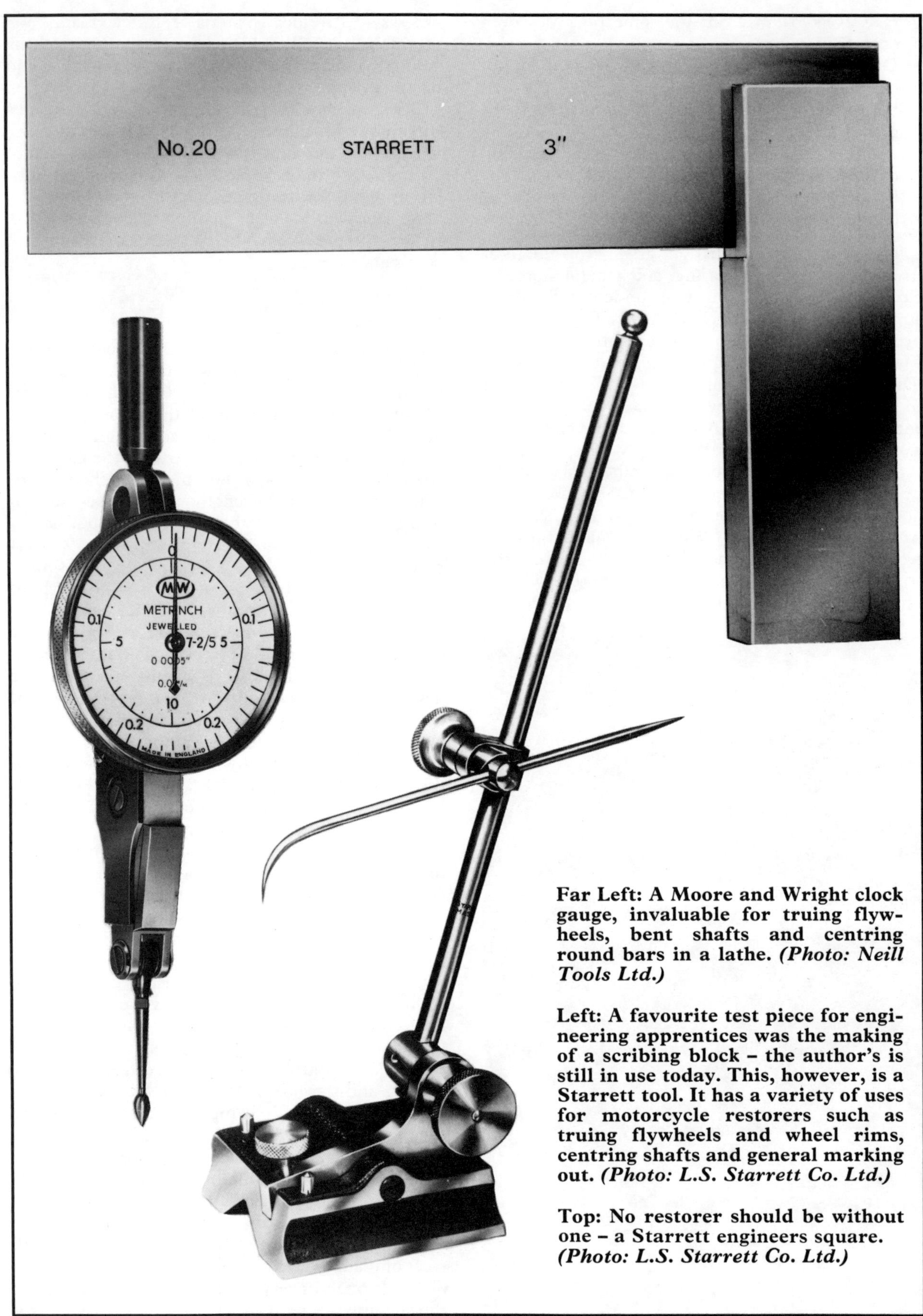

Far Left: A Moore and Wright clock gauge, invaluable for truing flywheels, bent shafts and centring round bars in a lathe. *(Photo: Neill Tools Ltd.)*

Left: A favourite test piece for engineering apprentices was the making of a scribing block – the author's is still in use today. This, however, is a Starrett tool. It has a variety of uses for motorcycle restorers such as truing flywheels and wheel rims, centring shafts and general marking out. *(Photo: L.S. Starrett Co. Ltd.)*

Top: No restorer should be without one – a Starrett engineers square. *(Photo: L.S. Starrett Co. Ltd.)*

strokes run quite happily with up to .020 in float.

As a general rule shim washers should not be placed between two components when one is rotating relative to the other. Therefore excessive end-float in a plain-bushed crank assembly should be rectified by inserting shims behind the bearing flanges and not between the flywheel and bush face. The situation with roller or ball bearing mains is, of course, entirely different, when it is quite in order to position shims between the flywheel cheek and bearing. In this case the two components are **relatively** stationary. Occasionally, end-float is adjusted by placing a large disc shim between the bearing outer and the crankcase recess, which also aids oil retention to a small degree.

Big-end wear

How much wear is permissible in a roller bearing big-end? Well, the answer to this is virtually none, bearing in mind that any roller bearing must have **some** internal clearance for the oil to get round. When making a preliminary survey, with the flywheel assembly in situ, there should be no excessive vertical movement of the rod when grasped with the fingers. For accurate readings the big-end should be washed in paraffin.

Excessive wear is easily distinguished by a distinctly audible click as the rod is eased up and down. If movement is there but can only **just** be felt, it may be that the crank still has more life left in it. A trained eye is needed to differentiate between permissible and excess wear; in terms of measurement, any movement in the region of .005 in means that the crank should be stripped and inspected.

On rare occasions a new set of rollers may take up a **slight** amount of wear providing the bearing tracks are in good condition. The old rollers should be inspected for pitting under a magnifying glass and measured for size with a micrometer. If they appear to be sound but .001 undersize then in all probability a new set will take up the slight discrepancy. It is however useless fitting new rollers if the crankpin or connecting rod eye display ovality, as may well be the case in a well-used engine.

At one time oversize b.e. rollers were available for repair jobs but supplies have dried up and the repairer may be faced with the manufacture of a new batch. A vacuum-hardening or ball-race steel must be chosen and a high degree of surface finish achieved. The crankpin and rod eye must be ground to accommodate the new rollers; very little metal is removed otherwise it is possible to break through the case hardened skin. This form of repair is sometimes carried out on obsolete units for which spares are unobtainable, or when it is desired to retain the original components for other reasons. The restorer must do his sums to determine roller diameters, not forgetting working clearances. If the rod is stiff to turn on assembly the connecting rod eye should be lapped-out a touch with a lead or wooden lap. A lap is simply a mandrel, machined from either of the materials mentioned to the con-rod eye diameter and smeared with emery powder and oil. Rotated in the lathe at a slowish speed, the lap will skim out a hand-held connecting rod the required amount. The rod should be held square-on and slowly moved backwards and forwards. On no account should grinding paste be introduced into a big-end bearing assembly in an attempt to free it off — obvious, maybe, but some have tried!

Flywheel dismantling & inspection

Anyone with a weak constitution is recommended NOT to attempt big-end renewal. Crankpin nuts are done-up very hard indeed and considerable strength is needed to deal with them, which is just one reason why there have been so few female motor-cycle mechanics throughout history. A JAP instruction book shows a fitter wielding a gigantic spanner at least three feet long, so the poor amateur is up against it when faced with an obstinate crankpin nut.

Ordinary cranked ring spanners are not much use as they tend to slip-off, taking half the restorer's knuckles away in the bargain. The best tool is a hefty socket with a 1 in diameter bar welded to it. The bar should be at least 18 in long and, if preferred, the tool can be welded-up as a 'T' wrench. (Unless you are lucky, a standard socket-set wrench is not man enough for the job). The socket must be close-fitting and have the last 1/8 in ground off the open-end to remove internal chamfering. Crankpin nuts are thin so you want to avoid slippage at all costs.

The factory method of holding flywheels was to clamp them by their rims in a fixture known as a flywheel bolster. This was a large floor-mounted

BEFORE DISMANTLING THE FLYWHEELS SCRIBE A LINE ACROSS THE RIMS TO FACILITATE REASSEMBLY. (THE LINE SHOULD BE APPROX. 90° FROM THE BIG-END.)

adjustable device, very solidly-made from cast-iron. Another method was to grip one flywheel in a large lathe chuck whilst attending to the crankpin nut.

The average amateur mechanic will have to make do with a stout bench vice and a pair of aluminium soft-jaws. Many four-stroke flywheels have large holes drilled right through both cheeks and if this is the case the mainshaft can be clamped vertically in the vice with a steel bar dropped through the holes as a stop. Another way is to grip one crankpin nut in the vice, not a very satisfactory method if the nut is partially recessed.

When you have recovered from the effort of removing one nut, bump the adjacent flywheel rim on the workbench top. A good solid thump on the rim about 90° from the crankpin will generally slew one wheel relative to the other. Once the taper is broken, the battle is over. If the wheel refuses to budge it may have to be helped on its way with a hydraulic press. The oft-illustrated ruse of jacking-out the flywheels by means of nuts and bolts is rarely successful — usually the threads strip long before there is any sign of movement — but it's worth a try.

A hydraulic press is essential to deal with parallel-fit or shallow-taper pins. The main criterion is to ensure that the pin is pressed out and replaced dead square to the flywheel. Those pins with expander-plugs driven in their ends on assembly are a nuisance as the flywheel holes are often swaged out when the pins are removed.

At one time crankpins with oversize spigots (in increments of .001 in diameter) were available to compensate for enlarged flywheel pin-holes. Apart from a few makes, the supply of these has almost dried up so it may be necessary to acquire a standard crankpin and build-up the ends a fraction. An interference of approximately .001 in should be aimed for.

If the amateur restorer harbours any doubts about his own engineering capabilities he would be well advised to contact *Alpha Bearings* of Dudley, West Midlands. This old-established concern will service any big-end, including obsolete vintage models. A standard *Alpha* modification on con-rods, in which the rollers run direct, is to bore-out the eyes and insert hardened steel bushes. V twin Ducati rods are typical examples requiring this treatment.

Replaceable big-end eyes should be manufactured from ball-race steel (EN31) heat-treated and ground to size. When pressing the sleeves into the con-rod eyes it is of paramount importance to ensure that they go in square. Unless contraction has been taken into account when manufacturing the sleeves it will be necessary to finish-grind the bores after assembly. An alternative material is Carr's 69s, or any of the other BD2 steels mentioned in Chapter 1, vacuum-hardened right through. Occasionally

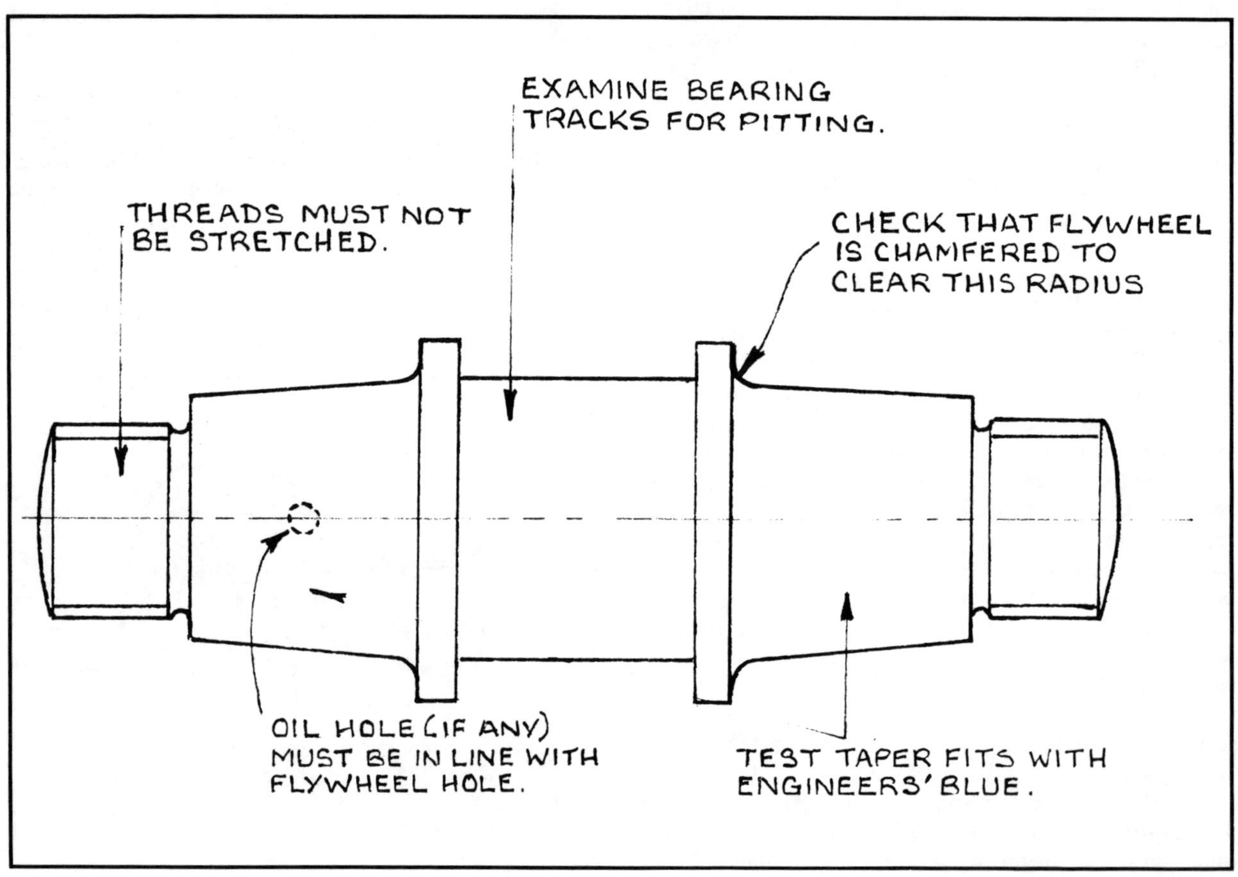

needle-roller outer shells can be modified to fit connecting rods, in fact small Villiers big-ends can be converted to needle roller bearings simply by pressing an *Ina* outer shell into the connecting rod and a standard *Ina* inner ring onto the crankpin. This conversion is worth considering for other small engines, consulting *Ina* or *Torrington* bearing catalogues for the appropriate bearing assemblies, but it is open to question whether large four-stroke singles should be modified thus.

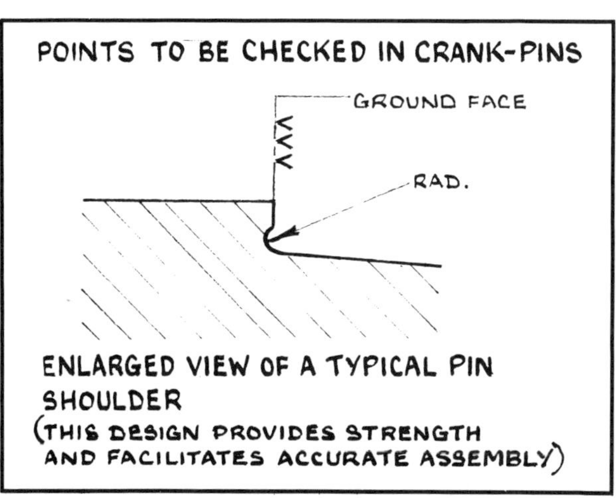

An unusual "big port" AJS – unusual insofar as its registration is 1925 when, according to factory records, no big-port was made! In this year the exhaust tract was of more modest dimensions. Believed to have been ordered for racing, an earlier (circa 1924) TTB3 Sports engine is fitted, complete with AMAC carburettor. The frame and cycle parts are to 1925 specifications (note the seat tube, which terminates in between the gearbox studs).

Drive-side view of the AJS engine. Note the stirrup arrangement for holding down the cylinder head and barrel. This enables the head to be removed in five to ten minutes. This machine was restored by the Author, who did the plating, paintwork, saddlery and wheel building in his modest workshop.

The AJS oil pump shown here on a late vintage M10 ohc model is mounted externally.

New crankpins

New crankpins should be manufactured from a steel possessing good core strength; for obvious reasons ballrace steel or one of the vacuum-hardening steels previously mentioned would be unsuitable if hardened right through. A 3½ per cent nickel-chrome case-hardening steel is advisable, carburised and hardened (refer to Chapter 1). The threaded portions must be left soft by copper-plating prior to heat-treatment. The amateur is unlikely to possess the necessary grinding facilities or heat-treatment equipment but there is no reason why he could not rough-turn the pins, leaving approximately .012 in on diameter for grinding. This work will have to be farmed-out together with a sketch showing the desired finished diameters and tolerances, (aim for a bearing diameter tolerance of plus zero, minus two tenths of a thou).

Fatigue fractures in shouldered crankpins generally occur across the end of the shoulder (at the reduction in diameter). At this point a radius should be left, if necessary chamfering the entry to the flywheel hole to clear this radius.

Even manufacturers' genuine replacement crankpins of the taper-fit variety should be checked for correct fitting in the flywheels. A smear of engineers' blue on the tapers will verify this point. Hand-lapping will correct minor discrepancies in taper, but don't overdo it or the pin may enter too far in its hole. In many designs the pin is pulled up against its shoulder by final crankpin nut tightening; usually the gap between the shoulder and flywheel before final tightening should be in the order of .008 to .012 in. If the pin shoulder immediately touches when the tapers are engaged by hand, it means that the fit is too loose and the tapers will need building-up. This can be done with metal-spray or nickel-plate. In either event the tapers should be ground between-centres in the lathe and lapped into the flywheels. Fine emery paste and oil should be used, checking progress with engineers' blue as mentioned.

Crankpin nuts should be replaced if there is any sign of thread distortion. Mild steel is not really strong enough, so use EN8 for vintage touring engines and EN16 for more potent machinery. Old nuts can be re-used if in good condition but it is a good idea to check them for squareness on the mating faces. Screw the nuts onto the crankpin with the flat faces outwards and skim them, with the pin mounted between-centres in the lathe.

Plain crankpins, ie those without shoulders, may enter further into flywheels which have experienced two or three big-end renewals. Connecting rod side clearance must be checked in such cases. If the rod is nipped, a light skim off the big-end eye-face may rectify matters, the rod being fixed to a magnetic surface grinder table (check that there is sufficient bearing roller end-clearance to permit reduction in width). Some manufacturers (eg. JAP) supplied pins in various lengths for such eventualities.

Checking the con-rod

Never **assume** that a connecting rod is straight! Even if it looks true the big-end eye might be cocked-over due to bad workmanship.

The best way (indeed the only way) of checking a con-rod in all planes is to make closely-fitting mandrels for the small-end and big-end eyes. A silver steel bar usually suffices for the top-end mandrel and double-diameter bar can be turned for the big-end bush.

If a lathe is part of the workshop equipment there is no need to make up two straightedges, as con-rod alignment can be checked simply by placing the mandrels across the lathe bed. Failing this, two flat mild steel bars placed on a piece of ground glass will provide temporary straight edges. Any twist will be seen immediately. Measurements taken from mandrel to mandrel (see illustration) on either side of the rod will highlight bends, if any.

A twist is easily corrected — a good yank in the appropriate direction, with a bar through the gudgeon pin hole, will do the trick. Rods are usually very springy, so it will be necessary to twist the top-end beyond the true position a fraction and then ease it back.

A bent rod can be straightened cold in the bench vice. By placing strips of metal strategically on either side of the rod, gentle vice pressure will re-align it. Again, the natural springiness will necessitate over-correcting and easing-back.

Rod side-play, between the flywheels, is relatively

It makes a change to see a bike in nice, usuable condition. This 1933 Ariel Red Hunter was photographed after the annual Buxton Rally, a tough event that takes in the hills of Derbyshire.

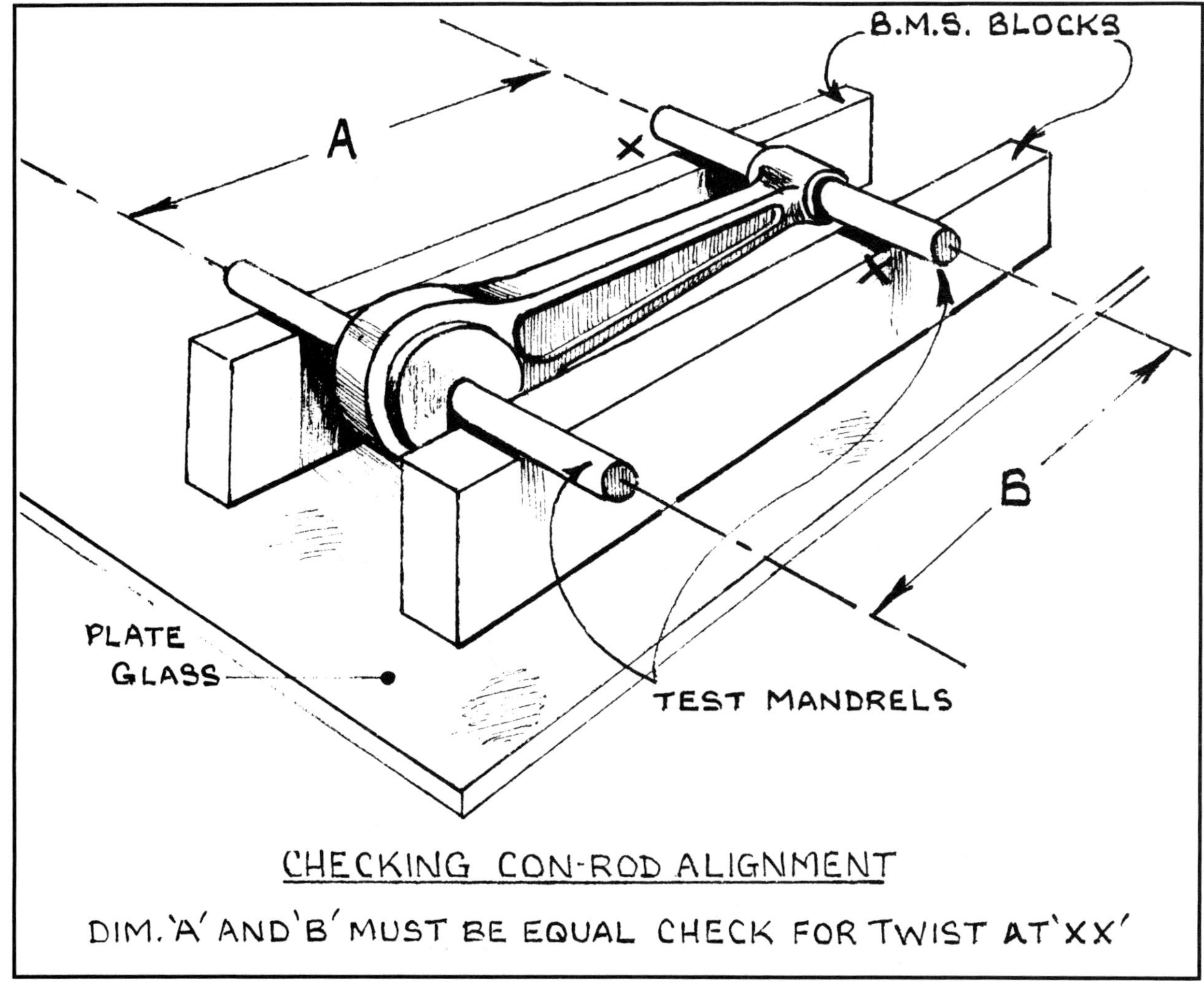

CHECKING CON-ROD ALIGNMENT

DIM. 'A' AND 'B' MUST BE EQUAL CHECK FOR TWIST AT 'XX'

unimportant. Sometimes grooves are scurfed out of the flywheel inside faces through the rod running over; if the grooves are very deep the affected area can be faced and the play taken up with bronze washers riveted in position. A few manufacturers fitted hardened steel washers as standard. Total side-clearance can be .010 in to .020 in.

Plain big-ends

Practically all parallel twins employ plain bearings, mostly of the shell pattern (as in motor car bottom ends). It is important that the crankpins are perfectly round and within manufacturers' tolerances before new shells are fitted. If the pins are found to be oval they must be reground by a reputable crankshaft reconditioner, to makers' standards. Some "cowboy" crank-grinders are not too fussy over tolerances and fillet radii so it pays to shop around.

Thin-wall shells must be fitted with extreme care. All mating faces should be scrupulously clean and the locating nibs should fit exactly into their recesses. **Under no circumstances** should a renewable shell be scraped to ease-off a tight bearing, and it need hardly be said that any abrasive compound introduced into the assembly will quickly ruin the bearing surfaces. White metal holds abrasive particles tenaciously and no amount of washing will get rid of them.

On the subject of abrasives it should be mentioned that crankshaft oilways harbour an incredible amount of grit. Sludge traps should be cleaned out before fitting new shells, making sure every scrap of dirt is forced out with a high-pressure paraffin jet. After a prolonged mileage the dirt solidifies like concrete and nothing short of a twist-drill will shift it. Makes one wonder how the oil ever managed to find its way to the bearings!

White metal bearings

Some early engines have split white-metalled or bronze bearings and a small amount of play can be taken up by relieving the cap faces. Firstly the crankpin must be checked for ovality. Take a number of micrometer readings around the journal. Any variation in excess of .003 in must be reduced to an acceptable level, say .001 in. The text-book method of correcting ovality is to have the shaft reground but the skilled engineer can get reasonable results with emery tape, checking progress with engineers' blue. A lap smeared with emery will achieve the same results.

Usually a gentle rub, face down, on a sheet of plate glass smeared with emery will remove sufficient metal from the bearing cap. It is vital that the abutment faces are kept dead square. The bearing surfaces must now be scraped-in.

Hand-scraping

Remove all traces of emery, smear the crankpin with marking blue and bolt up the connecting rod. In all probability it will be too tight, displaying excessive contact in the middle of each white metal bearing surface in rod and cap. These areas need paring away with a keen-edged bearing scraper.

Scraping is an art, requiring much skill and practice. The scraper must be meticulously maintained and **not** used for decarbonising. White metal is quite soft. Not much pressure is needed to remove a microscopically thin silver. If the novice is a little wary he should get an experienced man to show him how to hold the scraper and how much metal to remove.

The rod should be lightly assembled again and tested for high spots. Eventually, after a few scraping sessions and trial assemblies the bearing should show even contact over its entire surface. Do not fit the rod too tight - it should be capable of falling under its own weight. Sometimes a light tap on the bearing cap with a copper hammer may ease a marginally tight bearing.

Always fit new big-end bolts and nuts. The consequences of a sheared bolt are disastrous so it is just not worth trying to reclaim the old ones. Torque-up to the maker's recommended figures and replace any locking devices under the nuts.

Re-metalling is an expensive business and not many firms with the necessary equipment, or knowledge, survive. However, perusal of monthly vintage and classic car magazines should provide a few addresses.

Flywheel alignment

A simple home-made wooden jig can be fabricated as shown in the sketch. Alternatively the crank assembly can be fixed between-centres in a large lathe — take care not to apply too much tailstock pressure as this could deflect the shafts and give a false reading.

The crankpin should be pressed, or bolted-up,

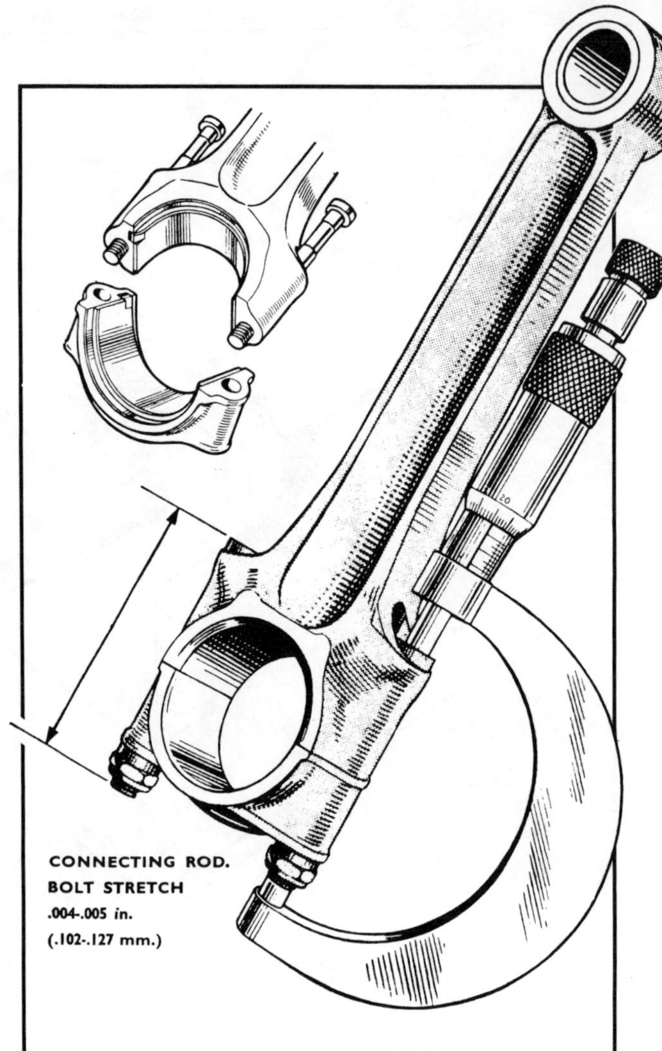

Above: Connecting rod bolts should always be checked for stretch. This is the Triumph method; to be safe it is better to fit new bolts during a major overhaul, especially if vintage racing is contemplated. *(Photo: Triumph Motorcycles (Coventry) Ltd.)*

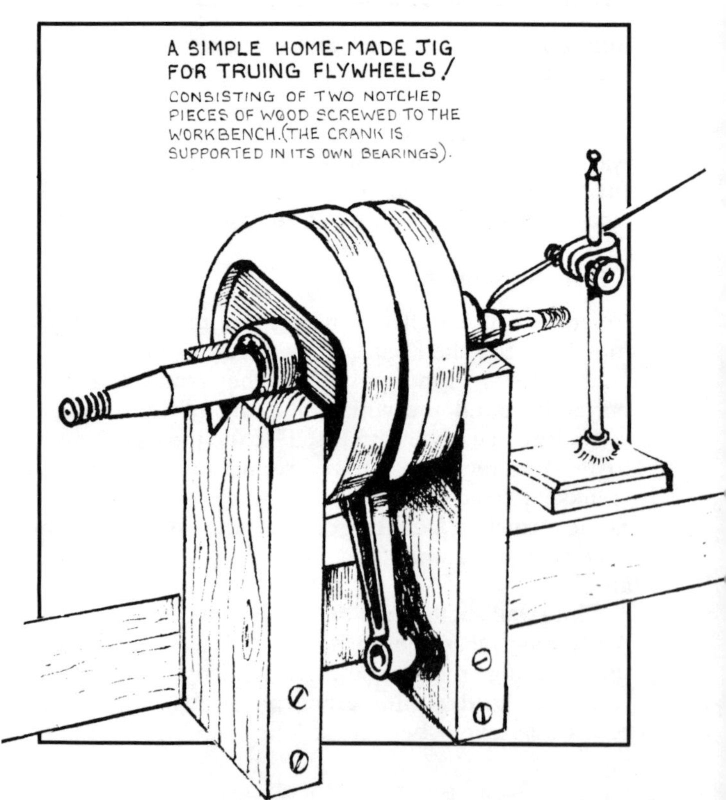

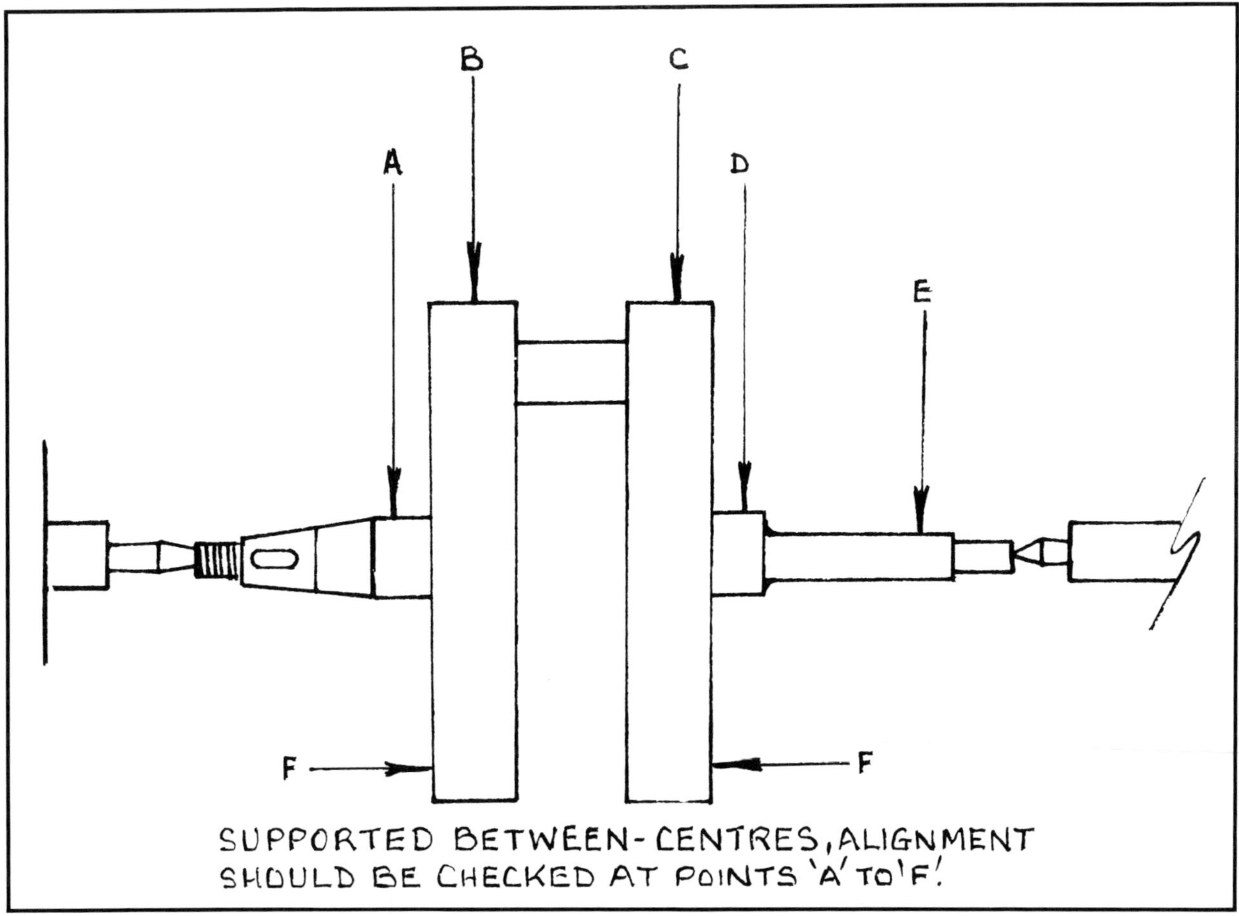

firmly to one flywheel. If there is an oil-hole in the tapered portion this is the side to fit first. Assemble the rollers with thick engine oil (not grease) and fit the con-rod. If the rod has to be screwed on, the roller assembly is too tight and the big-end eye will have to be lapped-out as previously mentioned. Fit the other flywheel and tighten the nut about three quarters tight, ensuring that any scribed marks on the rims are opposite each other.

With the aid of a Mercer dial gauge any discrepancies in alignment will be noted; if a clock gauge is not available, a reasonable degree of accuracy can be achieved with the usual type of bench scribing block, as illustrated in the sketch. Radial run-out of one wheel to the other can be corrected by bumping the flywheel rim (at a point roughly 90 degrees from the crankpin) on the bench. A well-aimed clout with a copper hammer will have the same effect. The object is to get both mainshafts dead in line.

It may be that the shafts are revolving in skipping-rope fashion, in other words both are high in the same place. Excess tailstock pressure can cause this but if the error is in the assembly, remedial action must be taken. Barbaric though it may seem, the usual method is to nip the rims in the vice, deflecting the shafts in the right direction. Not much pressure is needed to correct matters, so don't overdo it. This course of action is a little risky when dealing with slender pins or thin iron wheels — careful hand scraping in the crankpin hole or on the adjacent flywheel face may correct the error.

One form of error which is impossible to correct by normal methods arises when odd flywheels are paired. A minute difference in crankpin centre height will mean that one wheel and shaft will always be high in relation to their partners. Unless the engine is extremely rare it is easier to acquire a spare flywheel assembly as the repair is frightfully complicated and expensive.

When a tolerable degree of accuracy has been achieved the crankpin nut can be finally tightened. Always re-check afterwards. It would be gratifying to arrive at a zero error situation in which the gauge needle remains resolutely on "o" as the shafts are rotated. Unfortunately this rarely happens due to various factors and one has to live with a certain amount of run-out. The most important thing to remember is that both bearing registers must run true relative to each other. A **total** discrepancy of .0015 in to .0025 in is within reason. If one shaft is long and slender and carries a flywheel generator on the end it is advisable to get this shaft aligned as accurately as possible. (BSA Bantam generator-side mainshafts will soon chew-up their *Oilite* outrigger bushes if not accurately aligned).

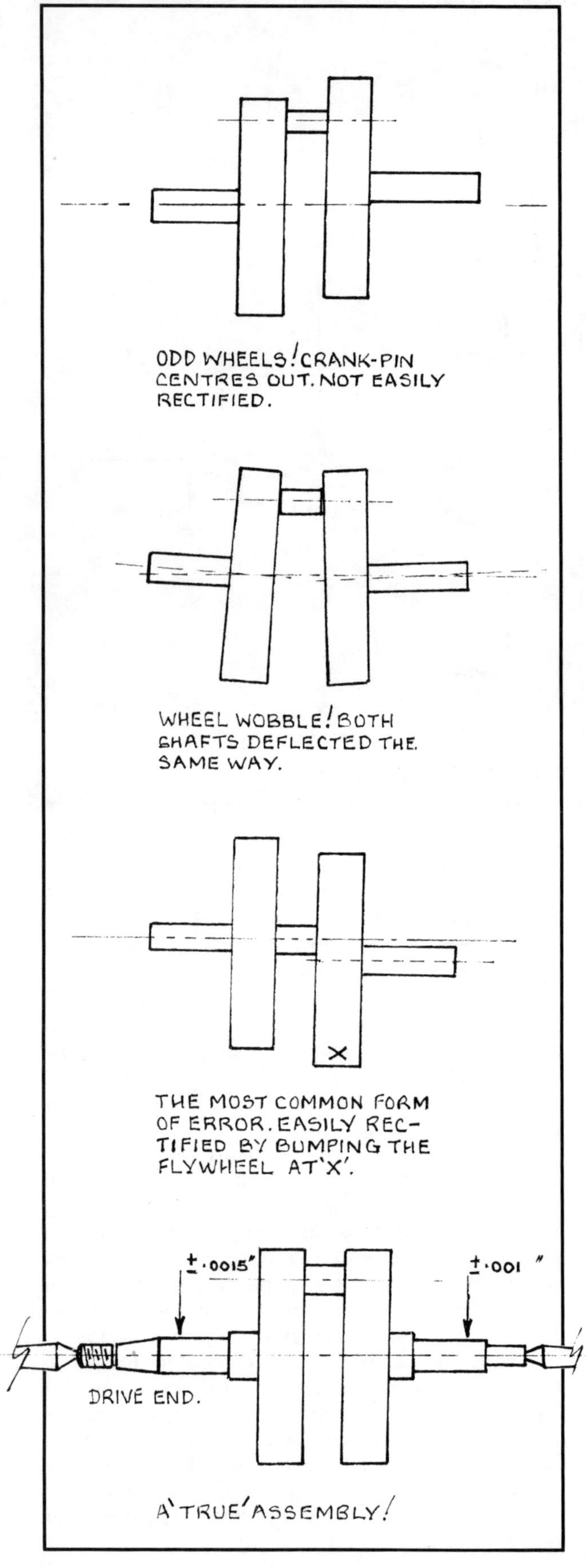

If both shafts are true, a certain amount of wheel wobble can be tolerated — side movement can be up to .005 in (repeat, **IF** the shafts are in line). I recall one flywheel which wobbled sideways as much as .0075 in (seven and half thou) and yet the engine ran as smooth as silk. However, the mainshafts were spot-on!

Final assembly points

Camshaft bushes are normally phospor bronze or cast iron and should be renewed if worn more than .005 in. End-play is not quite as critical, except where there is a danger of entanglement with the valve lifter mechanism or an adjacent cam follower. New bushes should have a side clearance of .003 to .005 in with a diametrical clearance of .0015 to .002 in. Where possible, the bushes should be turned .002 in under-size and line-reamed in situ, after which the cams should spin easily. End float is adjusted by the insertion of shims behind the bush flanges.

Worn cams

Worn cams are best dealt with by specialists in this field. A small amount of pitting on the flanks is nothing to grumble about but peak wear will only get worse if not attended to. Once the case-hardened skin is worn through, rapid deterioration will follow. Experts in this kind of work can build-up the worn surfaces and grind afterwards — even if the amateur has good welding facilities he may find it difficult to re-profile the cams to the maker's figures.

A little discrepancy between the manufacturer's timing figures and those actually recorded with a timing disc is quite normal and nothing to worry about. A difference of five degrees one way or the other is of little consequence in a touring engine. One 1000 cc V twin motor overhauled by the writer had an astounding performance and yet the inlet valves opened at 20 degrees and 17 degrees before TDC on front and rear cylinders respectively, compared with the makers' figure of 25 degrees. This is just one example, quoted as a crumb of comfort for those experiencing the same problem.

Vintage racing enthusiasts will naturally expect more favourable figures than those quoted above, so another set of cams should be acquired to remove nagging doubts. Quite often cams from a later model will fit; for example late model Gold Star touring cams will fit straight in a 1939 M24 GS (but not the 1938 Goldie, which had cams running directly in the timing cover) and in tuned B31 and B33 models of any year. Vintage AJS cams are freely interchangeable (ohv & sv).

Worn followers

Worn followers can be ground by hand but care

must be taken to finish the curved feet parallel to the pivot axis. If the wear is excessive, the surfaces can be built up with *Stellite*, re-profiled, and highly-polished afterwards. No advantage will be gained by lightening the followers in touring engines but there is a lot to be said for polishing-out deep nicks and forging flaws. When a follower breaks it is usually where there is an abrupt change in section, or coincident with a file-cut.

Before uniting the top half with the bottom end, it is just as well to check the crankcase mouth for flatness. It may be found there is a step where one crankcase half joins the other. Slackening the crankcase bolts and juggling the two halves about may eliminate the problem but if it doesn't it may be necessary to re-machine the face. Mercifully this does not occur very often but should be checked nevertheless, especially when two odd halves are united. A thicker cylinder base gasket is **NOT** the answer. If the snag is not eliminated, the barrel will never seat properly and, worse still, a broken flange could follow.

All that remains is to smear the piston and rings with oil and bolt-up the barrel. Red non-setting *Hermatite* or *Osotite* are the best gasket cements for cylinder base flanges as there is thus no need to rush the job. Many people prefer grease-smeared gaskets; certainly if the mating faces are in excellent condition there is no need for cement. Timing covers are best sealed with one of the modern gasket-less RTV (room-temperature-vulcanising) cements, applying the cement to one face and a light smear of oil to the other so the joint can be broken when adjustments are required.

Oil-sealing arrangements in timing cases left a lot to be desired in pre-war days. It is worth considering replacing a magneto spindle felt seal with a modern *Weston* or *Gaco* garter seal. The modification may mean a recess has to be machined inside the timing case but it is well worth the trouble, and will not be noticed by casual observers. With regard to oilseals in general, it is good practice to smear oil (preferably laced with molybdenum disulphide) on the shaft during assembly. A dry oilseal will not last long.

One final point. A rebuilt motor, minus pushrods and sparking plug, should be reasonably easy to turn by hand. If it isn't, something is wrong. A rebored engine will be only marginally stiffer; so, if you have to use an enormous ring spanner to force the engine round it would be advisable to investigate. The problem is not likely to go away. Number one suspect must be the piston not lying square and central in the bore.

Cockeyed piston

A tight piston, bearing heavily over to one side, can be verified by removing the rings and applying a light smear of marker blue in the bore. It must be borne in mind that the piston has to touch somewhere, therefore it is necessary to distinguish between normal and excessive contact. A rough check for a tilted piston can be made by holding an engineers' square up to the piston skirt, with the crankcase mouth as a datum. Allowances must be made for con-rod sideplay and tilt but this check should show up any major problems. If the piston appears to be lying out-of-square, or to one side, the problem is almost certainly due to one of the following:-

1. Bent connecting rod, verified by placing a mandrel through the little-end and taking measurements on either side. (Usually the misalignment can be spotted by eye).
2. An uneven crankcase mouth joint, as mentioned previously.
3. The small-end bush being bored out-of-true. (Not as rare as might be thought — I've found this snag on three occasions!).
4. If the piston has been got-at by a previous owner, or is of unknown origin, it is just as well to check that the gudgeon pin holes are in perfect alignment. It may be that the holes have been re-bushed out-of-square to the gudgeon pin axis. (Mercifully this is a very rare occurrence only encountered on modified pistons — new *Hepolites* can be fitted with complete confidence).

Any of the above snags **should** have been spotted long before the assembly stage. Whilst the subject of tuning for speed is beyond the scope of this book it should be mentioned that the elimination of wasteful frictional forces is half the battle; this philosophy holds good for the most humble touring engine. A motorcycle appears to go through three distinct stages in its life — the formative years when performance is not fully realised, followed by a lengthy period when all experiments have been completed and everything runs smoothly. Then comes a glorious but short-lived episode when the motor is almost, but not quite, worn out and goes like the clappers. (Homo sapiens also?)

Lubrication matters

It is generally agreed that a straight oil of SAE 50 or 40 is a suitable diet for vintage motors with drip-feed lubrication, with perhaps a change to SAE 30 in arctic conditions. The novice may ask "How much oil should I give may engine?" My usual advice is to adjust the drip-feed until a faint smoky haze is observed at the exhaust tailpipe, with a distinct puff when opening up. The golden rule is to err on the generous side; try one drip every two seconds to start with and cut down a few notches if you leave a smokescreen. Fortunately, most vintage engines are quite tolerant over excessive lubrication, as are their owners.

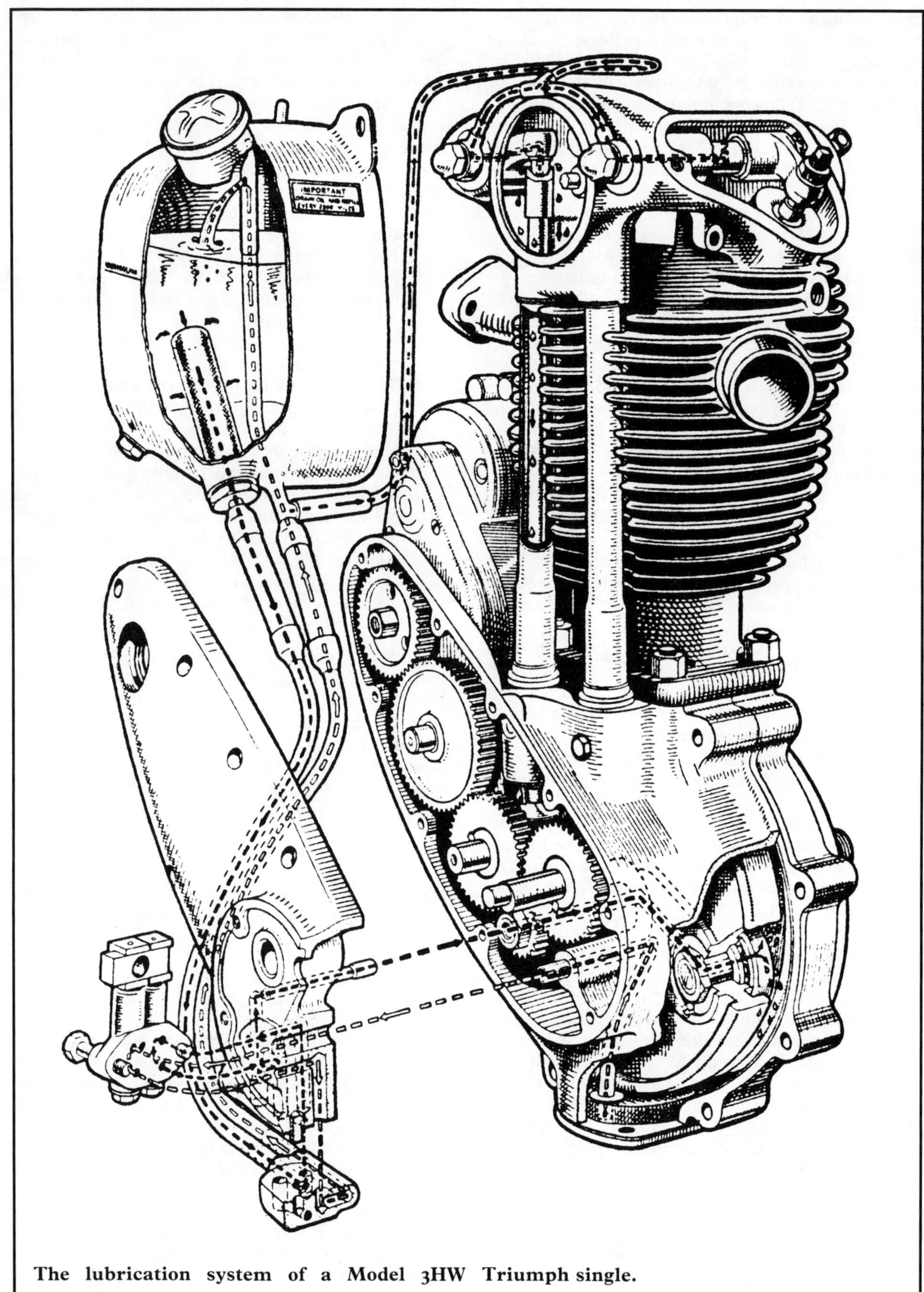

The lubrication system of a Model 3HW Triumph single.

Most parallel twins of the postwar years will run quite happily on a multigrade 20-50 oil, although it is wise to consult makers' recommendations for high-performance engines.

Modern technology has eliminated most of the problems associated with R type racing oils so it is worth considering a changeover for vintage competition events. R oils withstand extreme pressures and are therefore ideally suited to tuned air-cooled units. The following procedure for changing from a normal mineral oil to R grade is that recommended by Castrol:-

1 Drain the mineral oil when warm and re-fill with *Castrol Solvent Flushing Oil.*
2 Run the engine (not under load) at a fast idling speed for a quarter of an hour or so with an occasional burst of revs.
3 Drain the flushing oil while still warm and if it is dirty it is advisable to repeat the flushing process.
4 Re-fill with Castrol R.

The procedure when changing back from vegetable to mineral oil is of course similar. Removal of varnish-like deposits on the engine is best accomplished with a mixture of meths and benzole, applied with a stiff brush. Baked-on R can be lifted from exhaust systems by the careful application of paint stripper *(Nitromors)*.

Monograde oils are available from Ernest Newton Ltd., Holt St., Birmingham B74BB, who also supply R grades. Other companies supplying monogrades (also multigrades and gear oils in most cases) are:-

Dalton & Co. Ltd., Silkolene Oil Refinery, Belper, Derbyshire, DE5 1WF.
Filtrate Ltd., P.O. Box 67, Kidacre St., Leeds LS1 1LS.
Valvoline Oil Co. Ltd., Dock Rd., Birkenhead, Merseyside L41 1DR.
G.B. Lubricants Ltd., Albany Rd., Gateshead, Tyne & Wear, NE8 3BP.
Meteor Oil Co. Ltd., Tinsley St., Great Bridge, Staff, DY4 7LG.
R.L. Morris & Sons Ltd., Wellington St., Salford, Manchester. M3 6LJ.
Star Lubricants Ltd., Pipewellgate, Gateshead, Tyne & Wear.

(Note:- It may be necessary in certain cases to go through a distributor for small quantities — any of the companies mentioned will advise).

Hand oil pumps

The most common hand-pump fitted during the vintage period was the so-called semi-automatic type by Best and Lloyd, distinguishable by its adjustable sight feed. Considering the number of pumps produced, workmanship was excellent, consequently maintenance is seldom required. Apart from a leather washer, like the one in a common water tap, there is nothing else to wear out.

There were two variations of the popular Best and Lloyd; one had a cylindrical sight glass and the other a bowl. In each case the plunger was of a standard type, with minor differences in length for shallow or deep petrol tanks. Operation is simple — the plunger is depressed to charge the barrel and it rises against spring pressure to discharge the oil through the regulator.

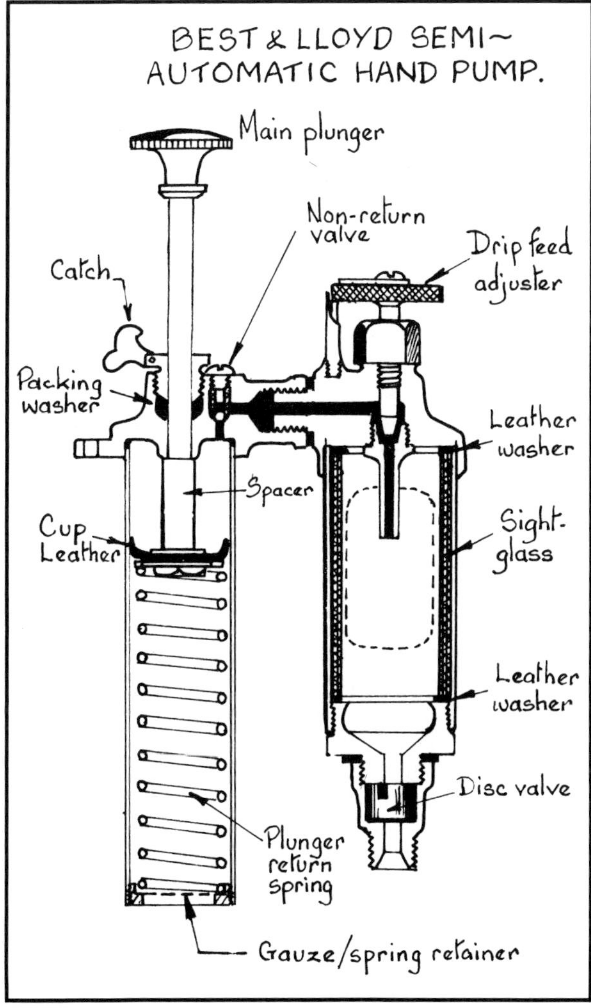

Pump renovation

Separate the drip-feed body from the pump barrel (RH thread), noting that there should be a fibre washer between the two portions. Grip the plunger rod, using vice soft jaws, and unscrew the plunger knob (1/4 BSW thread). Remove the threaded gauze holder from the plunger barrel base, take out the spring and withdraw the plunger.

Unscrew the top gland nut and carefully withdraw the packing washers — these will be either cork or leather — and retain them for future use if undamaged. There will be found a small screw (cheesehead) on top of the plunger barrel; unscrew this carefully to reveal a spring and ball non-return valve.

In the case of the bowl-type sight feed, unscrew

the rim with a leather strap wrench and retain the leather sealing washer. There should also be leather washers above and below sight glasses in the cylindrical pattern. New washers are easily made from 1/16 in thick leather.

Remove the drip adjuster spindle, together with the union nut and sealing washer. The knurled adjuster knob should have a graduated disc (either aluminium or celluloid) and a small aluminium pointer, held on by a small round-headed screw. Take these off, as they would be ruined in the nickel-plating process (aluminium is soluble in caustic, as many restorers know to their cost). Apart from appearance considerations, loss of the graduated disc is no catastrophe as they are quite useless — most riders adjust their pumps not by graduations but by the number of drips per minute.

Quite often plunger rods get bent, usually when ill-fitted handlebar-mounted acetylene generators clout them on full lock. The rods are brass, 1/4 diameter, and easily straightened in a lathe or drill. If the plunger knob is missing a new one can be turned from brass bar. Unless a friendly engraver can be recruited it's rather difficult to reproduce the trademark on top of the knob, but few people would notice anyway. Machining a new gauze holder should present no problem to the amateur machinist. Plunger return springs can be made from piano wire; this material is available at model shops (for making model aeroplane sprung undercarriages) and can be procured in various standard wire gauges (swg). Stainless steel wire is even better if available.

With a little patience new leather cup washers can be reproduced; this will entail the use of a lathe to make a simple male/female mould out of aluminium. Soak the leather in water for a day, press it into the mould and leave it to dry out. With a wad punch make the centre hole — this is easily made from a piece of tube sharpened at the end. Soak the washer in oil to make it pliable and reassembly the plunger.

In the common type of Best and Lloyd hand pump the cup faces uppermost. There should be a flat steel washer (brass in some models) on either side of the leather. The reader might be able to save himself some work if there is a good ironmonger in the district; selections of cup washers are often available at such establishments.

Replating

Later in this book the reader will be advised to purchase and set-up a home electroplating kit. Oil pump bits are easily lost by commercial platers; even if they don't lose them they can't be bothered with masking-off threads and some have the annoying habit of polishing-off makers' trademarks so beloved of us vintagents. So, unless the reader has been fortunate enough to have located a reliable electroplater, it is as well to nickel the pump parts within the confines of the home workshop.

After plating, bowl sight chambers should be painted white inside. Clockmakers will make new glasses, or one can be cut from 1/8 in thick Perspex. Cylindrical sight glasses present more of a problem if they are cracked or missing altogether; laboratory suppliers and gauge makers can make them, given a pattern or drawing. The back of the glass opposite the window can be painted white to make the oil drips more visible — original glasses had the white moulded in.

When replacing cylindrical sight glasses great care should be taken not to overtighten the base nut otherwise you may have another cracked glass on your hands!

Reassemble the pump plunger in the barrel and tighten the top gland nut (the one with the catch) just sufficient to prevent oil leaks. It is uncessary to force the nut right home, just enough pressure to compress the packing washer slightly is all that is required. New packing washers can be made from leather or cork, well oiled. (In a dire emergency a couple of turns of leather bootlace will provide a good enough seal to get the machine home).

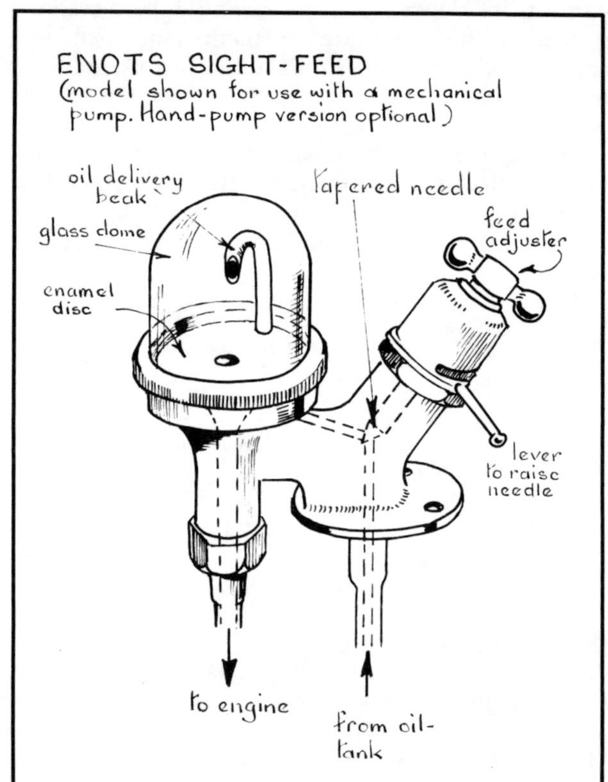

Replace the drip-feed adjuster. In the case of Best & Lloyd pumps the adjuster business-end does **not** have a sharp point — just in case you think yours is blunt! *Enots* (Benton and Stone) regulator screws **are** pointed.

New graduated drip-feed indicator discs can be made from white plastic (cut from an aerosol container lid) hand engraved to match the original.

This is not as difficult as it sounds. The circles can be etched with a pair of dividers and the divisions marked off with a scriber. A hand engraving tool for the numbers is made quite easily from a square, or triangular (three-square as old engineers would say) needle file ground to a lozenge-shaped point. Any clockmaker worth his salt will show you how to make one in five minutes flat. The new plastic dial will look exactly like a vintage celluloid original, especially when the graduations are filled with wax (an oily thumb is usually good enough).

Tank mountings

When the Best & Lloyd pump is finally assembled, all that remains is to fix it to the tank top by means of the three screws. More often than not these screw threads are stripped but they will tap-out to 2BA to accept cheese-headed screws. There should be a gasket between the pump and tank flanges, but don't make it too thick or you might distort the pump flange when the screws are tightened. Apply gasket cement to the joint and the job is done.

Although most of the foregoing instructions are directed at Best and Lloyd products they apply equally to *Enots* and most other hand-pumps of the vintage period. AJS pumps are just another variation on the B & L design, except that on some models the drip-feed sight glass was dispensed with. Instead of feeding the engine with small doses of oil the Ajay pump dispenses one great dollop every few miles, providing the rider remembers to press the plunger. With such non-automatic pumps, and this includes most pioneer lubricators, it is usually recommended to give half a pump at more regular intervals. Triumphs fitted non-automatic pumps well into the vintage period but the system was reliable, simple and remarkably effective.

Some vintage bikes are blessed with both mechanical and hand oil pumps, as on Model 18 Nortons, late SD Triumphs and racing AJS machines, to name but three. Occasionally the hand pump was cable-operated, to be applied by hand or foot. In such cases the hand pump, when it dispenses oil to approximately the same region of the crankcase, can be regarded as an auxiliary pump to be used under arduous conditions. Under normal circumstances the mechanical pump should supply all the engine's requirements, the hand pump being activated before climbing a steep hill or when *going for a blind* (to use a vintage expression)

Riders in the early days liked to have some say in the matter where lubrication was concerned. Mechanical pumps did not exactly take the motorcycling world by storm. Even when reliable fully-automatic pumps were fitted, riders still demanded sight glasses somewhere in the system so they could SEE the oil being delivered. This situation led to manufacturers, BSA for example, fitting systems whereby the oil was led by gravity from the tank to an engine-driven oil pump, back up again to a tank-mounted sight glass, and then all the way down again to the crankcase. Not content with this, a hand-pump was included for good measure. At least it kept copper pipe manufacturers in business!

Mechanical pumps

Fitted to many machines in the mid to late twenties, the Best and Lloyd mechanical oil pump was a fairly reliable device. Regrettably, the bodies were cast in zinc-based alloy (monkey-metal, as it's known in the engineering trade) which suffered in the hands of ham-fisted owners. Broken bodies and stripped threads were quite common.

Mazak base-metal is virtually impossible to weld or solder; it **has** been done with special techniques but the success rate is not very high on vintage metal. The snag is that there is no second chance — the pump body or whatever is usually rendered (literally) scrap in the attempt.

Repairs can sometimes be made with *Devcon* epoxy-resin but the zinc-alloy is usually too thin for the bodge to be successful.

(Rudge enthusiast and VMCC Member D. McMahon* has come to the rescue of all those stricken with pump problems. Not only can he supply beautifully-machined B & L bodies cast in high-grade aluminium alloy but repair can be executed on all makes of hand and mechanical pumps. An admirable service, worth bearing in mind.

As per the Best & Lloyd, the Pilgrim pump is worm-driven and suffers from similar problems, namely bodgery on the part of the owner. Both types are adjustable but the temptation to fiddle should be resisted; once a satisfactory rate of flow is achieved the pump should be left well alone. The best approach is to use the same oil viscosity (SAE 40 or 50) throughout the summer; any swapping of oil grades will play havoc with the pump setting.

Remember that an over-lubricated engine is preferable to a seized one, so set the pump on the generous side to begin with. A faint oily haze should be noted at the exhaust outlet. Two-strokes with mechanical or drip-feed lubrication like a lot of oil — try one drip (per cylinder) every couple of seconds initially and cut down a notch or so if you can't see the road behind.

Most vintage petroil-lubricated two-strokes prefer a 16:1 mixture; later models with ball-bearing mains generally run on 20:1 or even 25:1 in the case of some post-war machines. The manufacturer's instruction book should be consulted if in doubt. If straight oils are used it is preferable to make up the mixture in a separate container; if this is not possible the petrol tap should be turned off before introducing the oil direct into the tank. Shake the bike thoroughly before starting up. When laying-up a bike for any length of time run the mixture out of

* 1-3 Northey Road, Foleshill, Coventry CV6 5NF.

the float chamber to avoid gummy deposits. An oiled-up carburettor is a nuisance and nothing short of jet removal and cleaning will clear the problem.

Many motorcycle manufacturers made their own mechanical pumps and fortunately for us most were fairly reliable. Humbers, in the vintage period, fitted a neat little pump on the timing cover of their machines; although they claimed it as their own make it bore a striking resemblance to a contemporary Rotherham, also made in Coventry as it so happens. BSA relied on a simple worm pump for their lightweights; this was driven off the exhaust

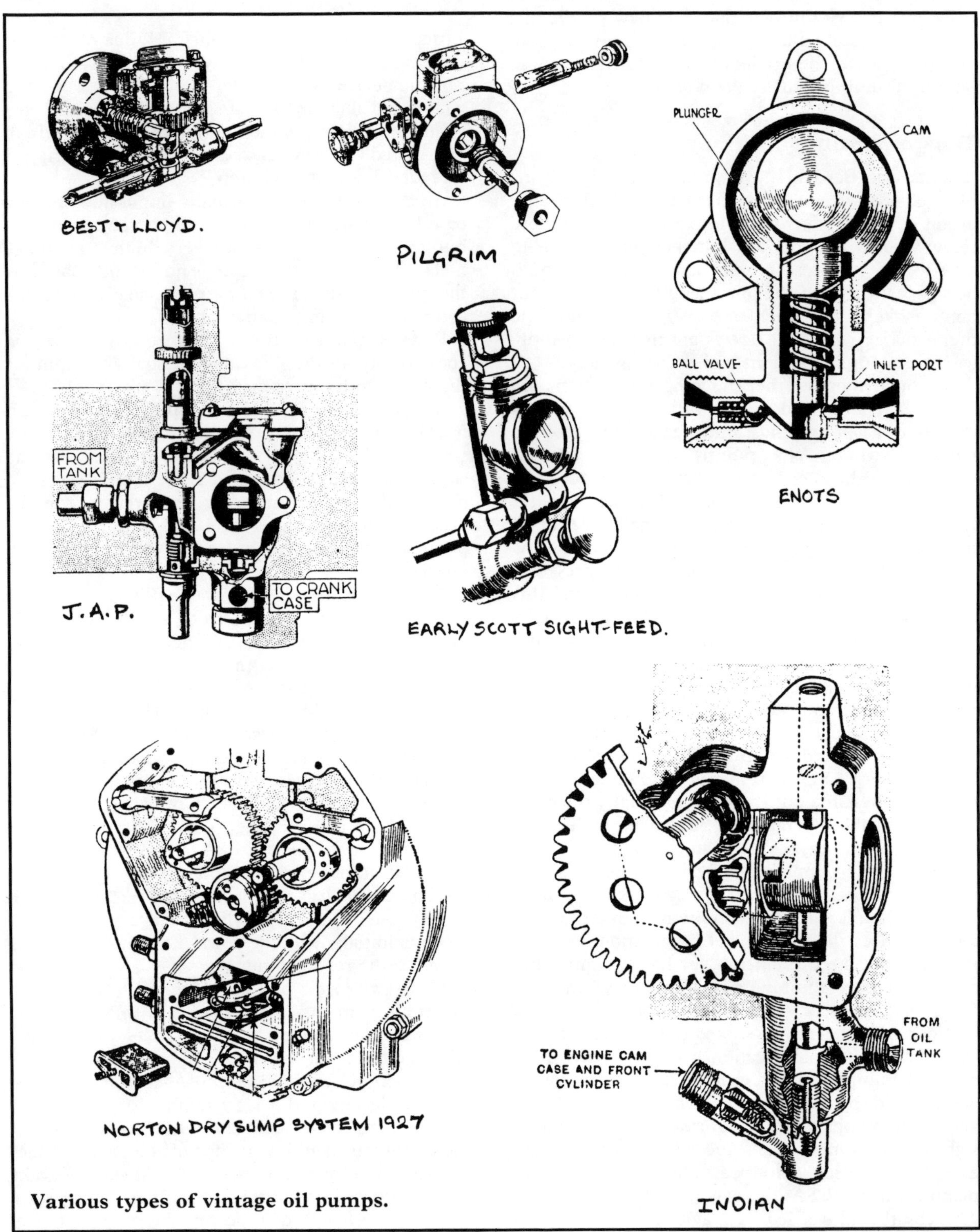

Various types of vintage oil pumps.

cam and gave very little trouble. The only faults likely to be encountered are excessive end-float in the worm (screw in the end-cap a little) or a perished worm sealing washer which leaks oil direct into the timing chest. (By the way, if anyone has cause to remove one of these pumps from a pre-1927 'round-tank' model the body is a press-fit in the timing chest, not screwed as might be thought).

In 1925 AJS machines were fitted with dreadful mechanical pumps, stamped on the flanges 2¾ and 7 h.p. for the 350 cc and 799 cc models respectively. These flat pancake pumps are best forgotten, being made out of poor materials (the large internal gear was in *Mazak* alloy with about the same tensile strength as a *Ryvita* cracker). Either convert the bike back to hand-pump lubrication or fit a Pilgrim — don't be too bothered about originality as all but one of the new range of AJS models introduced at Olympia in October 1926 were fitted with Pilgrims as standard. (The one exception was the cheapest 2¾ h.p. side-valve which relied on the well-proven hand-pump). It was at the same show that the new 3½ hp (500 cc) AJS side-valve model first saw the light of day and this had a Pilgrim mechancial pump driven off the exhaust cam.

Gear pumps

Double-gear pumps, as fitted by Velocette, BSA, and a host of other manufacturers before and after the war, generally give good service. There is not much to go wrong with this type of pump; usually a complete malfunction is caused by a piece of fluff blocking one of the oil-ways or jamming the ball valve (where fitted).

If the engine suffers a disastrous blow-up it is essential to remove the oil pump and clean it out thoroughly. Metal particles have a habit of making straight for pumps and chewing up teeth. A broken-up piston, or a main bearing spinning in its housing, results in millions of aluminium particles dispersing with remarkable rapidity throughout the engine.

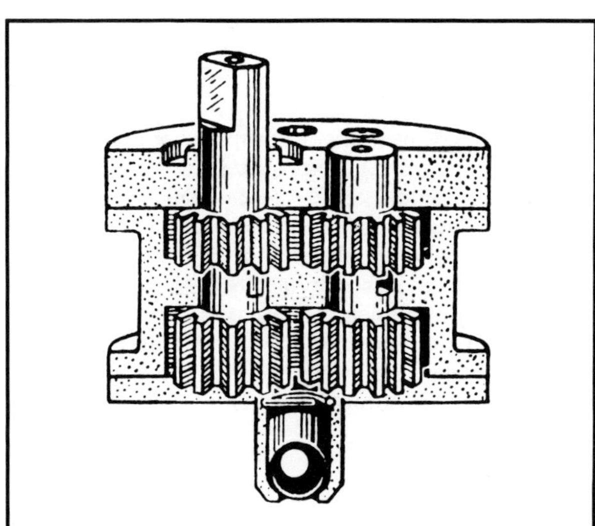

Cross sectional view of a typical double gear oil pump.

A seized oil-pump is a rare misfortune, indeed one may wonder how such a snag can ever occur. Nevertheless gear pumps occasionally tighten-up due to an accumulation of combustion by-products — hard black varnish or sludge.

The pump should be dismantled, cleaned, and the gear spindle ends lightly polished with fine emery cloth. After this treatment the gears should revolve quite easily when the main input shaft is turned by hand.

There should be little or no end-play between the gears and pump casing. If the detachable end-cover is grooved it can be rubbed-down on a piece of fine emery paper held on the workshop surface-plate. The paper gasket will provide all the clearance necessary; in most designs this amounts to .001 to .002 in. Where thin fibre or paper gaskets are fitted between the pump body and crankcase the use of gasket cement is not advisable as the oil passages could be blocked when the base screws are tightened.

Plunger pumps

The double-piston reciprocating type of pump (as fitted to Triumph twins etc) has a long life. The only problem likely to be encountered is failure of the non-return valve balls to seat; in this event the body

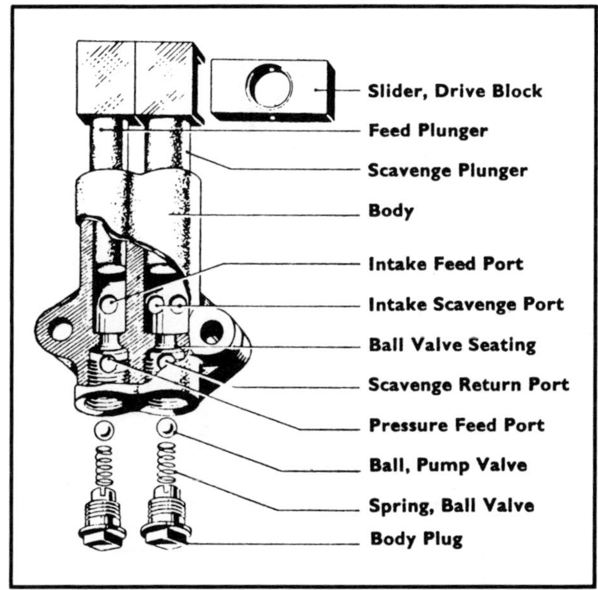

The Triumph plunger-type oil pump. The slider block should always be checked for wear. Points to be wary of are blocked oilways due to small fragments of rubber flaking from the oil pipes when end fittings are replaced or dirt on the ball seatings.

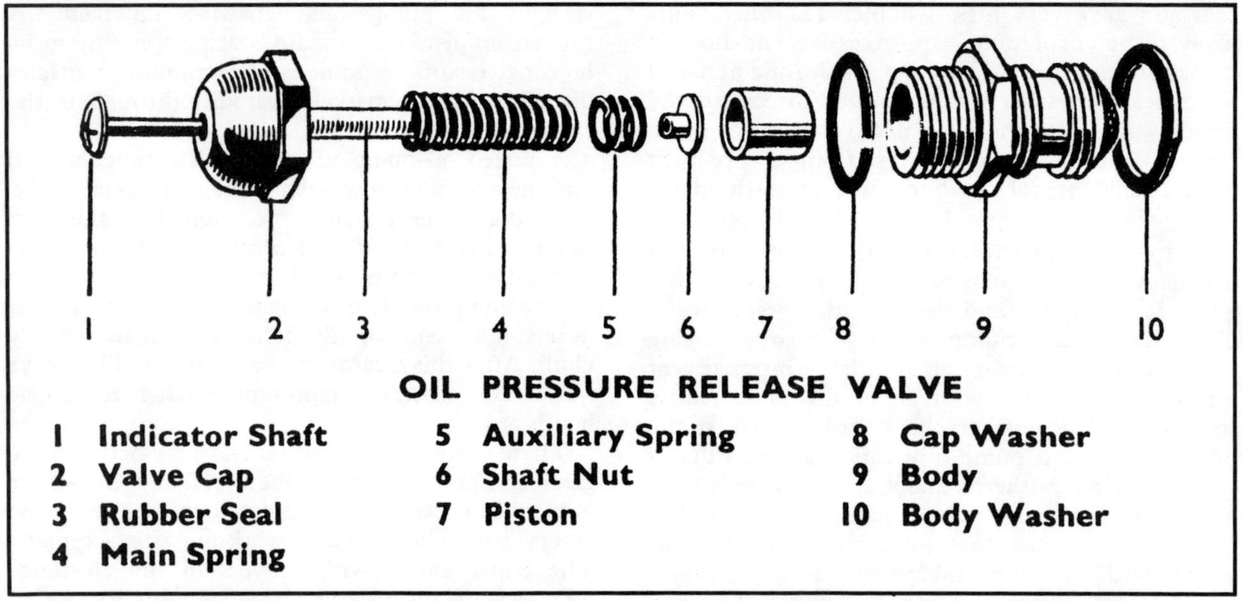

Above: Periodic cleaning of the oil pressure release valve will prevent sticking. It is imperative to use correct replacement springs. ***(Courtesy Triumph Motorcycles (Coventry) Ltd.)***

Below: Oil feed to the big ends on a Triumph twin. As with all vertical twins the oilways should be cleaned when a major overhaul is undertaken. ***(Courtesy Triumph Motorcycles (Coventry) Ltd.)***

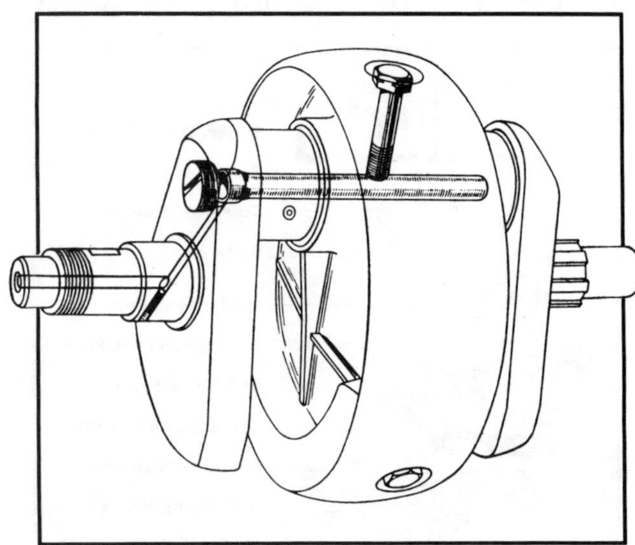

plugs, springs and balls should be removed and washed in petrol. It may be found that a piece of fluff or dirt has found its way in. When assembling the balls a light tap with a brass drift will re-seat them in their pockets.

As the pistons are constantly surrounded by oil it is unlikely that they will be seriously worn. The drive block slider, or trunnion as it is sometimes called, should be examined for wear and replaced if necessary.

The feed plunger is the smaller diameter piston which pumps oil from the tank (through a filter) to the timing side mainshaft and thus to the big-ends. In the case of Triumph engines a release valve and button indicator is fitted in this line — it is not uncommon for particles of dirt to upset the function of this valve also. Remove and wash in petrol.

Oil tanks must be thoroughly washed internally with petrol to shift all the black gunge which accumulates therein. A few nuts and bolts shaken around inside will help remove hard deposits. Several washes may be required before the tank is fit for service. The maker's recommended oil level, usually marked by a transfer on the tank exterior ($1^1/_2$ ins below the filler cap on most Triumphs), must be observed. Over-filling may result in excessive venting into the primary chaincase. The tank vent pipe must be kept clear or excess pressure could build up in the tank, so causing faulty scavenging.

Another type of plunger pump is that in which the piston rotates and reciprocates (Vincents, some Matchless models etc). The small peg which engages in the plunger cam should be inspected for wear or damage, as should the worm drive teeth. Damage can be caused by a blockage in the feed or scavenge pipes, which throws a loading on the gear teeth. Wear can occur on the pump spindle ends or in the housings, but most problems associated with this design of pump stem from ham-fistedness during assembly.

The JAP rotary pressure-release valve

Due to incorrect information in many reference books the timing of the JAP rotary breather has given rise to headaches and excessive oil consump-

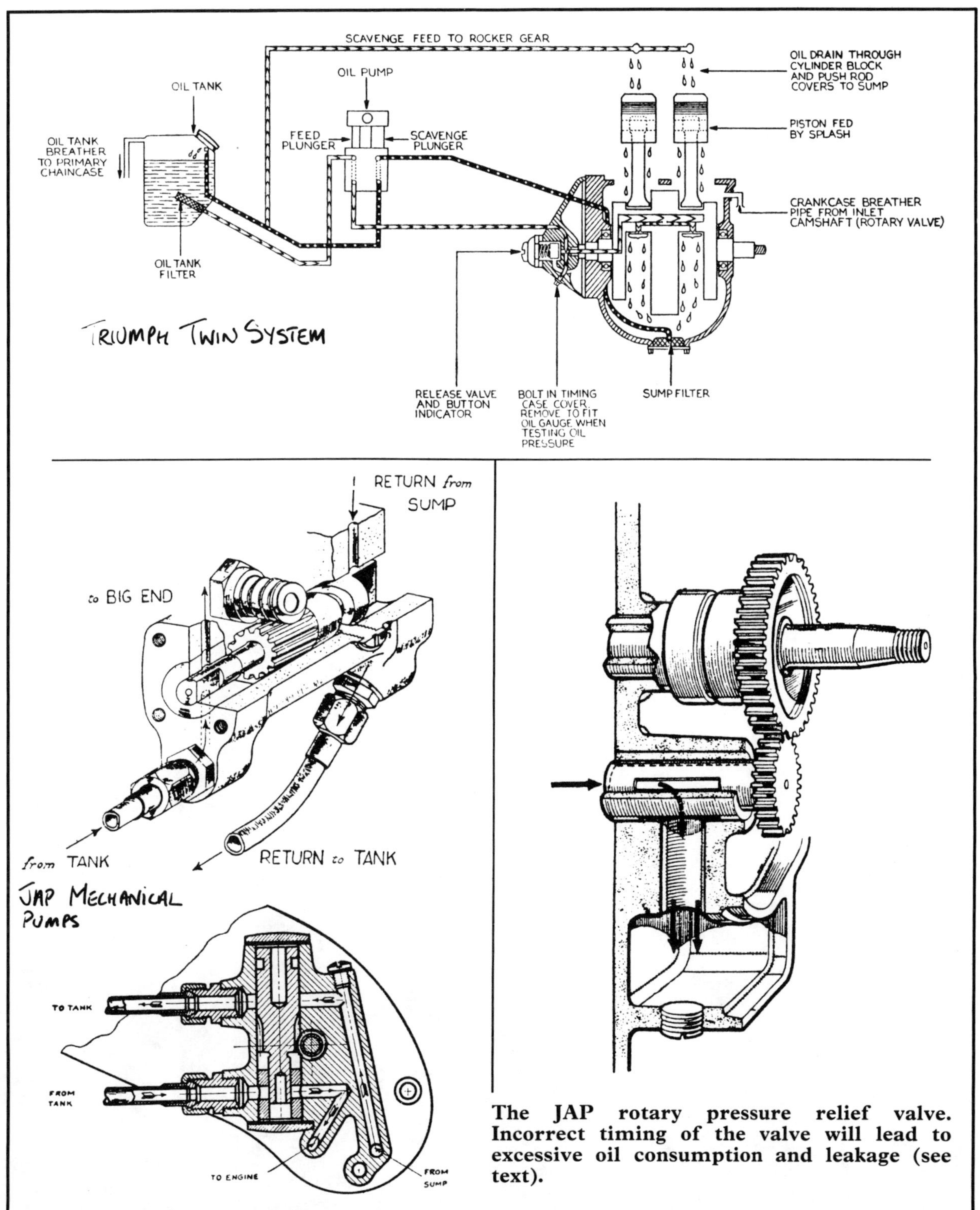

The JAP rotary pressure relief valve. Incorrect timing of the valve will lead to excessive oil consumption and leakage (see text).

tion over the years. The problem is related to V twin engines.

Thanks to the research of Messrs. Alker and Brassington of the Morgan Three Wheeler Club it has been discovered that timing figures in *The Book of the JAP* and similar publications have been wrong all along. The usual figure quoted for the opening point of the pressure relief valve is 65° before BDC on the front, passenger, side cylinder. This in fact results in excess crankcase pressure, not vacuum.

The 1933 edition of the JAP *Engine Reference Book* gives the **correct** method of timing the valve:-

"the rotary valve is timed so that the slot has just passed the oil-box opening when the front piston is at bottom dead centre". This is in essence an opening point of 90° before BDC on a 50-degree V Twin and 95° on a 60-degree motor.

The books which refer to the 65° degree opening position make the mistake of assuming that there is only one pressure rise per revolution of the crank and valve in twin-cylinder engines; this figure is correct for singles only.

Two shots to delight Morgan enthusiasts. Top: John Lindop (left) with the ex-Clive Lones Brooklands Morgan. This picture was taken in the 1950's just after Lindop, a noted Morgan expert, had rebuilt the beast. Bottom: The racing JAP engine of the Lones Morgan. This three-wheeler has two speeds – fast and very fast. Lones raced using a variety of JAP engine from 346cc to 1100cc, the small single propelling the Morgan to a new Hour Record for the 350cc class of 66.68mph in 1929.

Chapter 5

Transmission

Belts, gearboxes, clutches (with a few notes of interest to Scott owners)

Belt drive

THE newcomer to veteran motor bicycles may be surprised to learn that a well-maintained belt drive will not break at the drop of a hat. Nor should it slip, except perhaps in wet weather. Riding a single-speeder along a country lane is sheer delight — no clashing chains or howling gears. Just the steady click-click of a belt fastener to accompany the rustle of exposed valves, a truly relaxing experience — until the next hill is encountered!

Actually, a well tuned 3½ hp fixed-ratio machine should climb most main road gradients with ease. In the right hands single-speeders have climbed Sunrising, Edge Hill and Berriedale, vintage test-hills of repute. Back in the pioneering days of 1908–1910 when countershaft gears began to catch on, hard riders looked upon these as a form of cheating. Diehard single-speed enthusiasts would spend their Sundays roaming hilly districts, looking for new heights to conquer. The non-stop climb of a newly-discovered hill was something to talk about in the pub that evening. Alas, those golden days are gone forever, replaced by the frantic urge to get to a destination in the shortest time possible with never a thought for the scenery en route.

Brammer belts

Most people these days fit Brammer link-belting, the original type of rubber and canvas belting being hard to find. It is not generally realised that modern V-belts of the endless type, even if they could be cut and joined with fasteners, are not usually made to the same angle as vintage belting. In the veteran and vintage period V-pulley grooves had an angle of 28 degrees. Modern belting is made to a 40 degree angle, but fortunately for us Brammer still make the 28 degree type in link-belting.

In practice, modern V-pulleys do not have a constant 40 degree **pulley** angle, although this is the included angle of the **belt section**. The reason for this is simple. When a V-belt bends round a pulley the top surface is subject to tensile forces and the bottom section to compression. Hence the belt narrows slightly at the top, and the bottom portion squeezes outwards. This results in the belt section included angle being reduced. Pulley V-grooves are machined to compensate for this distortion; it naturally follows that the smaller the pulley, the greater the correction.

Brammer V-link belt is available from power transmission stockists in the following grades:-

160 (Orange) Wedgelink. Oil and heat-resistant and absorbs most power of the three grades.
100 (Red) Similar to the above, but an intermediate grade

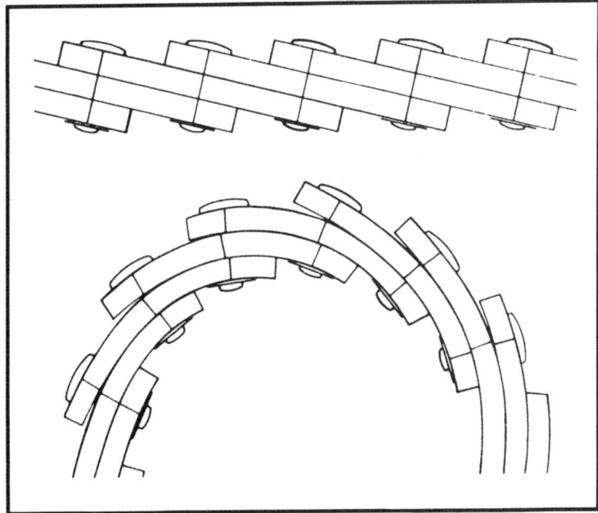

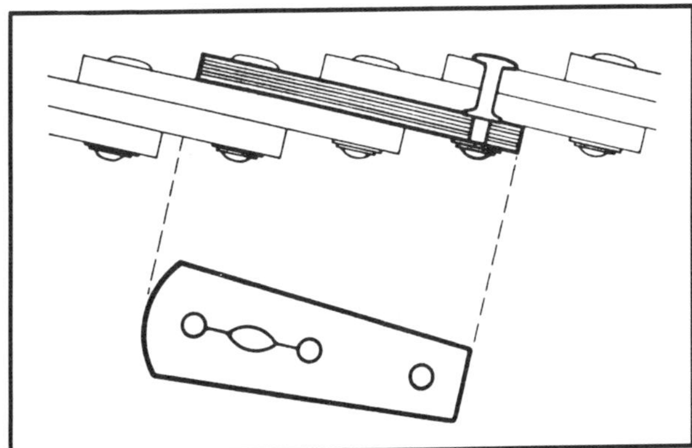

Above left: Sketch showing the basic construction of a Brammer V-link belt. *(Courtesy Brammer Transmissions Ltd.)*

Above right: The link belt is easily shortened by removing one or two links. *(Courtesy Brammer Transmissions Ltd.)*

Below: The most sporting of all single-speed belt drive motorcycles, the BRS Norton.

---

80 Standard (Black) Suitable for most veterans. In addition to the above, Brammer Ltd. have introduced a new immensely strong and durable belt called *NU-T-LINK* made from a polyurethane and polyester compound. Resistance to shock loading is said to be improved and a new type of fastener has been incorporated to make removal easier.

Pulley wear

Pulleys should be checked for grooving or accidental damage. If sufficient metal is present, the grooves can be skimmed out or built-up with metal spray and re-machined. The belt should not bottom in the V-groove or all wedging action will be lost.

Rear wheel belt rims should run concentric to within 1/8 in or so, out of consideration for the brake mechanism more than the belt. A brake shoe (especially a leading-action type) can grab with remarkable ferocity on an eccentric rim.

The drive belt should be adjusted with moderate tension — not so tight as to resemble a double-bass string. No hard-and-fast figures can be given as belt section and centre distances must be taken into account. An established belt-drive enthusiast will

check your settings by feel alone. Belt dressing is unnecessary on most V-belts, in fact manufacturers do not advise the use of resinous compounds on modern belts.

Chain drives

Avoid those chains which do not have dimples in the pin-ends as they are difficult to break with the normal link extractor. There are many foreign chains on the market these days, some of dubious quality and some with non-standard pin diameters. If possible, use only *Mk 10 Renolds* motorcycle chain (or *Renolds-Coventry* chain on some early machines and autocycles).

Reference to the diagrams will indicate the method of shortening or lengthening a chain. A spring-link is the weakest component in the chain, so the fewer the better. For safety's sake replace spring-links annually and always carry a spare one in the toolbox.

To test a chain for wear, lay it along the garage floor and carefully pull each end outwards. Renolds state, "As a general rule, the useful life of a chain is terminated, and the chain should be replaced, when the percentage extension reaches 2 per cent". The average person will be able to judge excessive wear without any complicated measurements so long as he bears in mind that even new links display **some** movement (there has to be a small amount of clearance between pins and bushes to make room for the lubricant).

It is a waste of time fitting new chains to worn sprockets. If the teeth are hooked the sprockets should be replaced at the same time otherwise the chain will soon wear out again. Apart from this, it is difficult to tension a chain correctly on worn sprockets due to more than one tight-spot.

SUPPLEMENTARY LIST OF COMMON MOTORCYCLE CHAINS

CHAIN No. (RENOLDS)	PITCH	ROLLER DIA.	WIDTH BETWEEN INNER-PLATES	SPROCKET TOOTH THICKNESS (NOM.)	BREAKING LOAD (lb.)
	DIMENSIONS IN INCHES				
110 037	.375	.250	.155	.141	2000
110 038	.375	.250	.225	.210	2000
110 044	.500	.335	.205	.189	4000
110 046	.500	.335	.305	.285	4000
*112 045	.500	.305	.192	.176	3000
*112 046	.500	.305	.250	.232	3000
110 054	.625	.400	.255	.237	5000
110 056	.625	.400	.380	.356	5000
110 066	.750	.475	.460	.433	6500
114 038 (DUPLEX)	.375	.250	.225	.210	4000

* COVENTRY SIZES AS USED ON SOME LIGHTWEIGHTS AND EARLY MACHINES. (EASILY CONFUSED WITH RENOLD MK10 SIZES BUT NOT INTERCHANGEABLE)

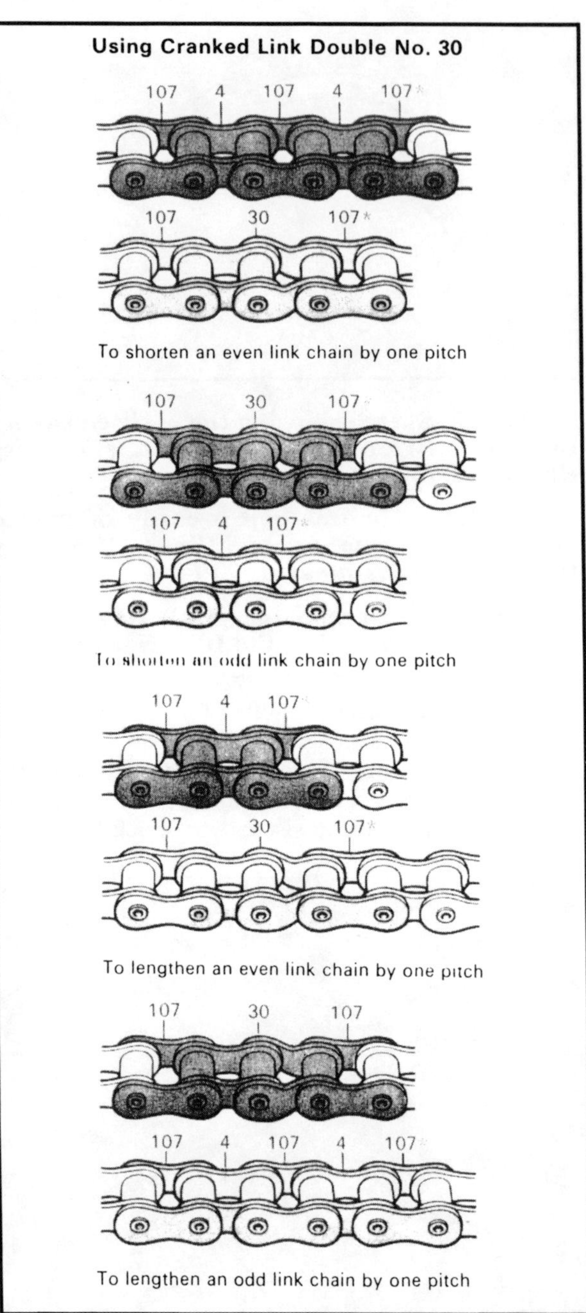

To shorten an even link chain by one pitch

To shorten an odd link chain by one pitch

To lengthen an even link chain by one pitch

To lengthen an odd link chain by one pitch

These drawings from the Renold catalogue show various ways of altering chain length. In each pair of illustrations the dark-shaded portions are removed, to be replaced by the components immediately below. Item 4 is a standard link and 107 an outer riveted link. Motorcyclists will prefer a spring link to No 107, but the number of spring links in a chain should be kept to a minimum. *(Courtesy Renold Ltd.)*

This page from a Renolds catalogue illustrates the variety of sizes and fittings available. Chain No. 110038 is sometimes found on lightweight primary drives. Nos 110046 and 110056 are also motorcycle sizes, whilst Morgan enthusiasts will be familiar with type 110066 (3/4 pitch). *(Courtesy Renold Ltd.)*

ROLLER CHAINS - B.S.

SIMPLE

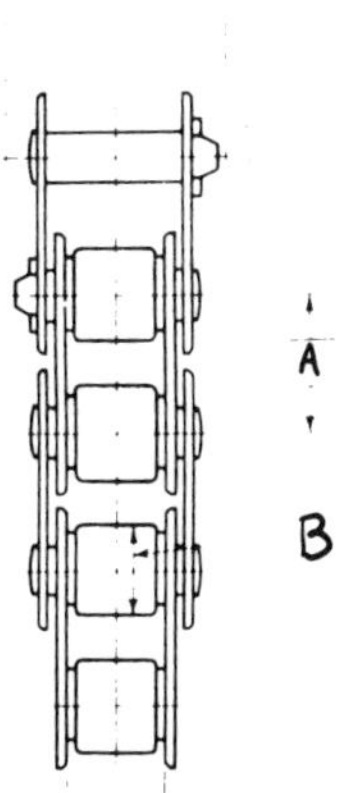

Chain No.	Pitch A in.	Pitch A mm	Roller diameter B in.	Roller diameter B mm	Between inner plates C in.	Between inner plates C mm	Chain track D in.	Nominal bearing area sq. in.	Breaking load lb.	Weight lb./ft.
110 500	·315	*8·00*	·197	*5·00*	·118	*3·0*	·45	·017	1,000	·11
110 038	·375	*9·53*	·250	*6·35*	·225	*5·7*	·65	·044	2,000	·26
111 044	·5	*12·70*	·305	*7·75*	·130	*3·3*	·52	·037	2,000	·204
111 046	·5	*12·70*	·305	*7·75*	·192	*4·9*	·60	·047	2,000	·234
110 046	·5	*12·70*	·335	*8·51*	·305	*7·8*	·85	·078	4,000	·46
110 056	·625	*15·88*	·400	*10·16*	·380	*9·7*	·95	·104	5,000	·57
110 066	·75	*19·05*	·475	*12·07*	·460	*11·7*	1·05	·138	6,500	·78
110 088	1·0	*25·40*	·625	*15·88*	·670	*17·0*	1·62	·32	10,000	1·82
110 106	1·25	*31·75*	·75	*19·05*	·770	*19·6*	1·86	·45	14,500	2·49
110 127	1·5	*38·10*	1·00	*25·40*	1·00	*25·4*	2·76	·85	24,000	4·50
110 147	1·75	*44·45*	1·10	*27·94*	1·22	*31·0*	3·22	1·14	29,000	5·55
110 166	2·0	*50·80*	1·15	*29·21*	1·22	*31·0*	3·28	1·25	38,000	6·20
110 206	2·5	*63·50*	1·55	*39·37*	1·50	*38·1*	4·00	1·97	60,000	10·40
110 245	3·0	*76·20*	1·90	*48·26*	1·80	*45·7*	4·90	3·19	90,000	16·60
110 281	3·5	*88·90*	2·125	*53·98*	2·10	*53·3*	5·60	4·32	130,000	22·30
110 325‡	4·0	*101·60*	2·50	*63·50*	2·40	*61·0*	6·10	5·62	160,000	32·00
110 366	4·5	*114·30*	2·85	*72·39*	2·70	*68·6*	7·10	7·15	225,000	40·00

SPARE PARTS

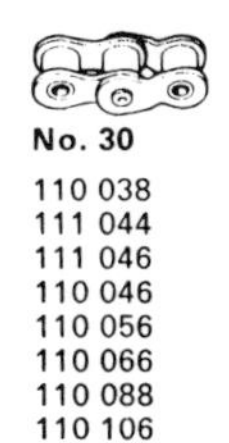
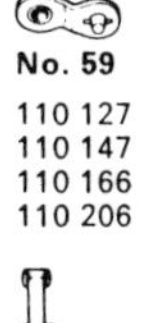
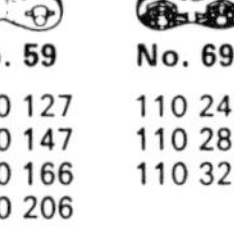

No. 4

No. 107 Available for all chains

No. 11 110 127, 110 147, 110 166, 110 206

No. 26 110 500, 110 038, 111 044, 111 046, 110 046, 110 056, 110 066, 110 088, 110 106

No. 30 110 038, 111 044, 111 046, 110 046, 110 056, 110 066, 110 088, 110 106

No. 59 110 127, 110 147, 110 166, 110 206

No. 118 Used with No. 59

No. 69 110 245, 110 281, 110 325

No. 50‡ 110 366

No. 111 110 245, 110 281, 110 325

No. 112 110 245

No. 108 Used with No. 112

No. 211 110 127, 110 147, 110 166, 110 206

‡ *Similar to No. 69 joint except split pins replaced by tab washers.*

Chain lubrication

For long-term protection against wear there is little to beat the time-honoured method of immersing the chain in a molten bath of graphite grease. The chain should be washed in paraffin and dried before soaking in the grease. Flat tins of chain lubricant are convenient to use as the containers can be popped right on a hot plate. For obvious reasons the process should be carried out within the confines of the workshop! One prominent sidecar racer missed an important leg of the British Sidecar Championship because he dropped an entire tin of molten lubricant — chain and all — on the living room carpet. Restoration of domestic bliss meant the purchase of a new carpet, which left the racer minus funds, hence no race. So be warned!

Chain adjustment

It should be borne in mind that spring frames, and plunger types in particular, promote a wide variation in chain tension from full load to rebound positions. The machine should therefore be checked for chain free-play when on the centre stand, and when loaded with a passenger.

It is necessary to ensure that no tight-spot remains after adjustment by rotating the rear wheel a complete revolution in both situations. Depending on the exact frame geometry, some chains tighten on full load and others slacken.

Replacement sprockets

Obsolete sprockets can be made or re-toothed using standard pinions and plate-wheels from firms such as Renolds and T.D. Cross and Morse Ltd. Originally, most sprockets were heat-treated but mild steel will suffice on a restored machine which only sees occasional use.

In cases where the original centre is splined, or is otherwise too complicated to machine from scratch, a new ring of teeth can be made and welded on. A radial depth of at least 1/4 in below the tooth bottom should be allowed. Full circumferential welds are not always necessary; unless appearance is a criterion three or four 1/2 in stitch-welds on either side of a gearbox sprocket will suffice. It is preferable to leave the welds proud for strength.

Those without welding facilities might consider riveting as an alternative. A rebate is turned on the old hub, and a corresponding recess in the toothed ring. The two components are then riveted together, using 3/16 in or 1/4 in diameter domed-head steel rivets. For this type of repair to be a success the rivet holes must be reamed out exactly to the rivet diameter.

Chainwheels can be repaired in similar fashion. If one is made from a platewheel blank all bolt-holes should be reamed as above. High-tensile steel bolts with *Nyloc* nuts or shakeproof washers are essential. Adding lightness, in the form of segmental-shaped cut-outs is a tedious job in the absence of a milling machine. The best solution is to drill a series of small holes around the shape and join them up with a hacksaw, finishing off with files. It is almost inevitable that as soon as the sprocket is finished a brand new one will turn up at the next autojumble! (It happens to us all.)

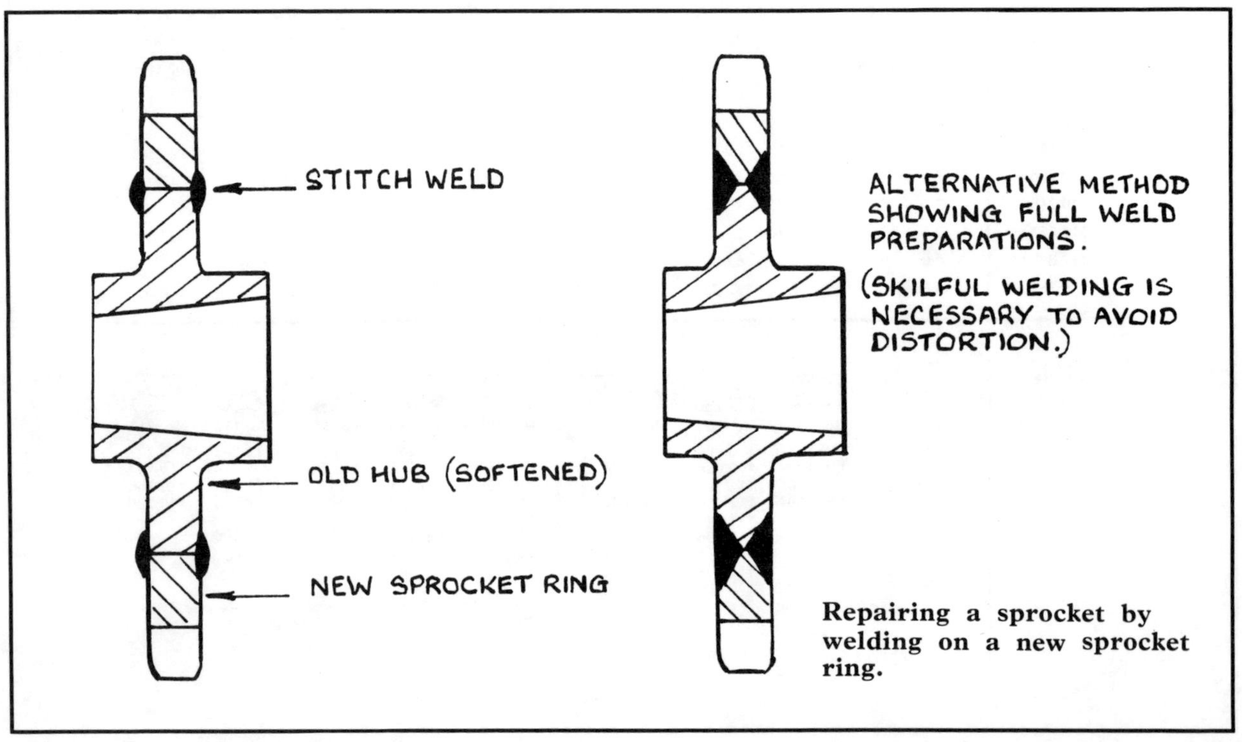

Repairing a sprocket by welding on a new sprocket ring.

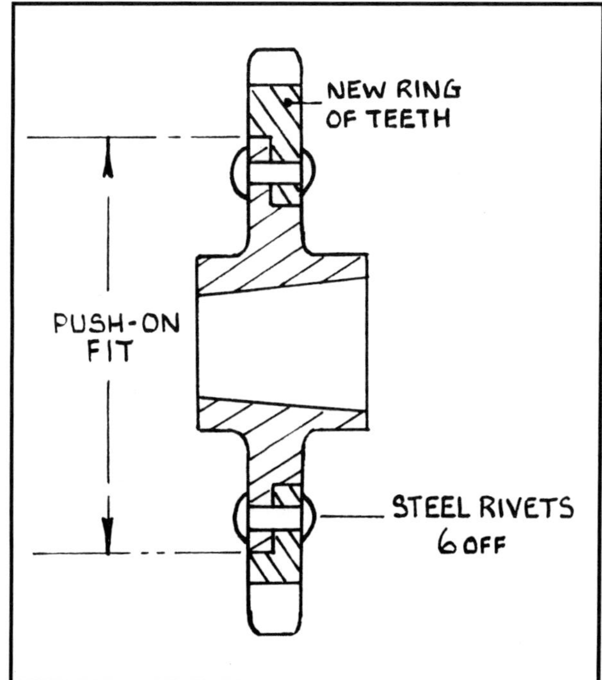

FOUR-SPEED BURMAN RECOMMENDATIONS

USE A SOFT GREASE. TOP-UP EVERY 1500 MILES.
SUITABLE LUBRICANTS :-

SHELL RETINAX CD
MOBILGREASE No 2
PRICE'S ENERGREASE C3
ESSO GREASE

Note :- The above grades are as specified Prewar. Most modern 'medium' greases are satisfactory, with the occasional addition of an eggcupful of thick oil. (Later Burmans were oil-lubricated)

FOUR-SPEED ALBION OIL-LUBRICATED BOXES

TOP-UP EVERY 500 MILES APPROX.
SUITABLE LUBRICANTS :-

MOBILOIL	BB
CASTROL	XXL
SHELL	X-100 (SAE 50)
ENERGOL	SAE 40
REGENT	SAE 50

Note :- For all practical purposes a modern Straight SAE 50 is suitable.

Above: Repairing a sprocket when welding facilities are not available.

Right: Lubrication instructions for two popular pre-war gearboxes.

Gearbox lubrication

Grease lubrication in certain pre-war boxes (Albion, Burman etc.) is reasonably effective, only falling short under very high speed conditions or when the lubricant level is allowed to drop below that recommended. Tests on industrial gearboxes have shown that at high speed the pinions tend to run in fresh air, having cut a trough for themselves. Full lubrication is resumed when the machine is stopped for a while and then re-started.

A small amount of heavy oil introduced into a grease-lubricated box will ensure that the lubricant keeps on the move and gets flung up as far as the mainshaft pinion bush. About a 1/8 pint of SAE90 gear oil poured through the filler aperture once or twice in a season's riding is sufficient.

Oil-lubricated boxes of vintage and pre-war origins often had sketchy oil sealing arrangements (eg. a reverse-thread groove on the final drive sprocket) which promoted oil leaks, especially when the machine is stationary and leaned over to the left-hand side. Many old boxes will benefit from the substitution of a thicker grade of oil (SAE 90 or even 140). Trouble may be experienced in the depths of winter, when the machine will be difficult to kick over, so a reversion to the original 40 grade may be necessary in these circumstances. In the early 1950s oil-sealing arrangements were improved with the general adoption of *Weston* or *Gaco* garter seals.

A molybdenum or graphited additive is not advisable when the chaincase shares the same lubricant as the gearbox, due to the possibility of clutch slip.

After a prolonged mileage there is bound to be a small amount of swarf floating about in any gearbox, but this should not give rise for concern unless the oil drains out looking like gold paint. In such an event the box must be stripped and examined for disintegrating thrust washers or a badly worn top gear pinion/mainshaft bush.

Inspection

The beginner attempting his first gearbox overhaul need have no fears about reassembling the gear clusters correctly providing he tackles the job systematically, noting where the various parts fit. Vintage boxes were generally of the true "crash" type with sliding pinions; being rather "agricultural" they are easy to dismantle but also suffer the most wear. Constant-mesh gearboxes of the post-vintage and post-war eras give very little trouble considering the amount of abuse they have to endure.

Clutch removal invariably requires the use of an extractor to draw the body off — never try to prise it free with levers. Removal of the chainwheel and clutch drum is usually accompanied by a shower of

The starting mechanism of a 1913 Humber.

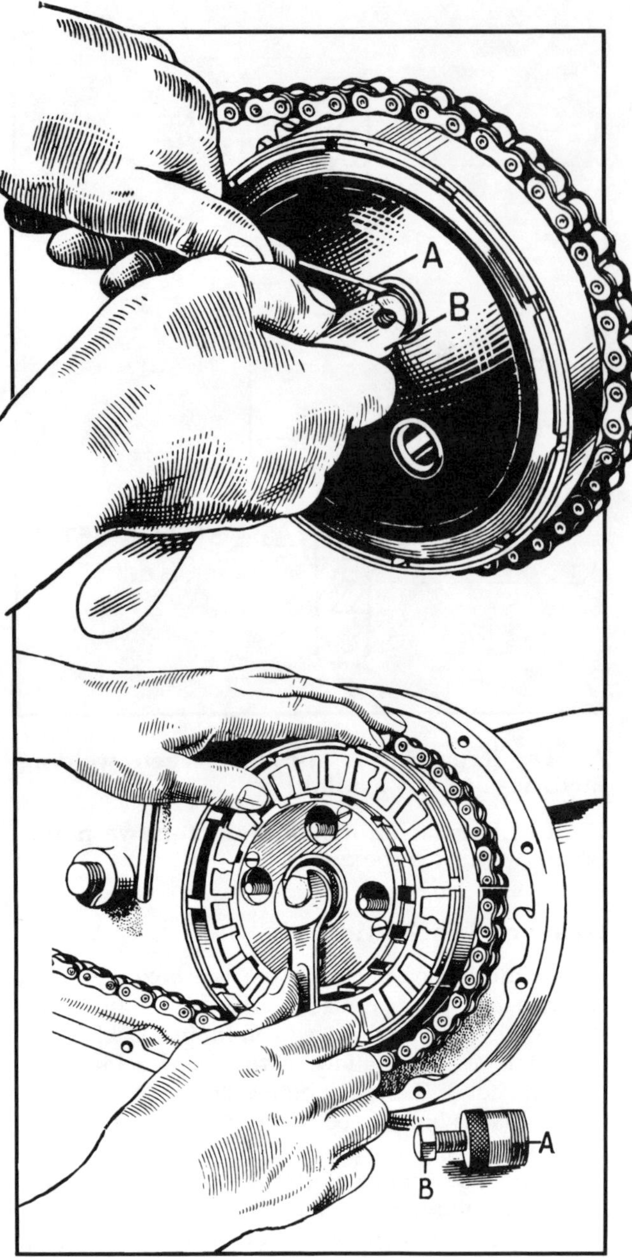

The Triumph clutch is typical of most British clutches as far as the dismantling procedure is concerned. First the springs and retaining nuts are removed (left above) by releasing the spring pressure with a screwdriver to disengage the nut-retaining 'pips'. Draw off the clutch centre with the correct extractor A. (below). Screw B should be made from a high tensile material such as EN8. *(Courtesy Triumph Motorcycles (Coventry) Ltd.)*

rollers over the bench — a squirt of thick oil in the race beforehand will limit the area of scatter. It is advisable to count the number of rollers (if of the uncaged variety) and store them carefully for future use. The condition of the bearing tracks should be noted. Fortunately wear is usually very slight and a small amount of pitting can be tolerated (bearing in mind that the race only revolves for a brief period during clutch withdrawal). As a last resort the tracks can be ground and oversize rollers (or balls) fitted. If the machine is rarely used, hardened silver steel rollers will last for a while until a set in EN31 ball-race steel can be made.

Checking pawls

The gearbox proper can now be tackled. If the gearchange mechanism is in the form of a separate external box, or an internal positive-stop unit (as on BSA M and B boxes) this should be removed without disturbing the threaded clevis ends.

Almost every type of positive-stop mechanism depends on some form of ratchet and pawl action and all suffer from the same problems. Stellite is a good material for building up worn pawls, which can then be filed by hand and left un-hardened. Weak selector springs cause uncertain gear-changing and should be replaced if stretching occurs. Springs and pawls are still available for most post-war gearboxes and there seems to be no shortage of gearbox innards at autojumbles.

Removing the clusters

Those readers unaccustomed to gear configurations should sit down and spend half an hour looking at the gear assembly, once the end-plate is removed. If the manufacturer's manual is not available sketches should be made, showing where the thrust washer (if any) fits and which way round certain pinions go on their shafts.

In most cases mainshaft and layshaft assemblies

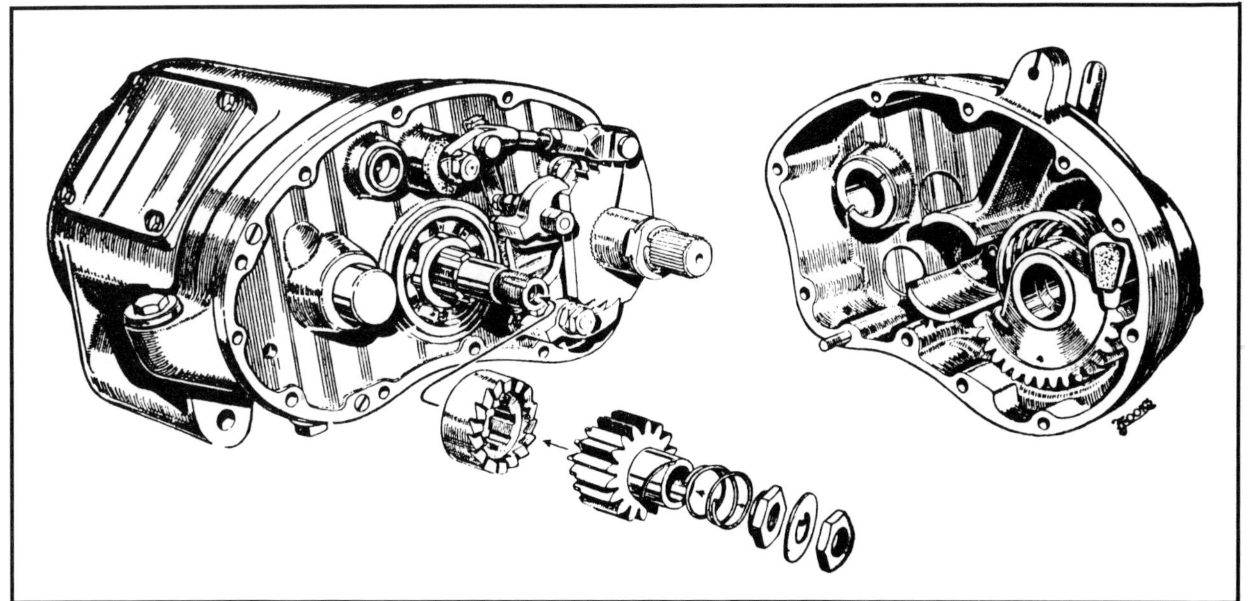

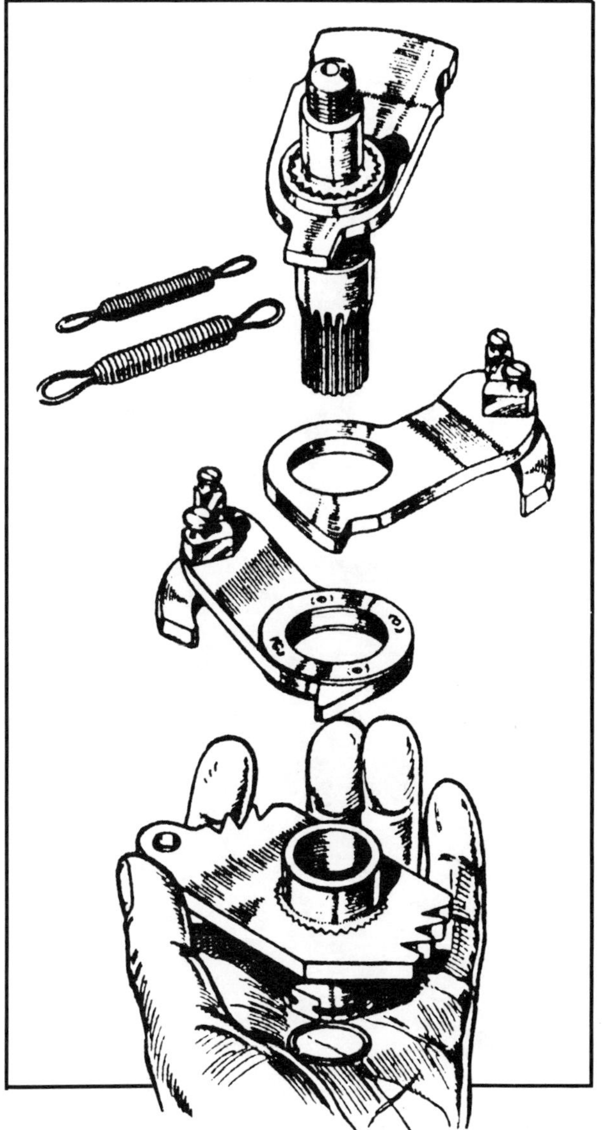

Component parts of the BSA positive stop unit. Usually it need not be removed from the gearbox inner cover and dismantled unless one of the pawl return springs has broken — an uncommon happening.

can be withdrawn as a pair, complete with one or both selector forks. There is no general rule, all boxes being different, but the main idea is to keep all the gears together for the time being. A certain amount of juggling is involved but eventually both gear shaft assemblies can be extracted, leaving the top gear pinion in situ. Lay the clusters on a piece of newspaper on the bench.

The selector forks should be inspected for wear on their operating faces. Such wear gives rise to lost motion during gear-changing and can, in severe cases, cause dogs to jump out under load. If another pair of forks cannot be obtained, the worn faces should be built up with a hard-facing welding rod and machined to size. Polish the thrust sides with emery cloth.

Pinion bushes

Top gear pinion bushes are subject to peculiar variations in speed and loading; due to their location, high up in the gearbox, they receive only spasdomic lubrication and also suffer from an ingress of road dirt. Wear rate is relatively high in these bushes, particularly on trials machines. New bushes are easily made from solid or cored bronze bar reamed to a running clearance of about .002 in. Wear up to .005 in is acceptable.

Removal of worn layshaft bushes is reasonably straightforward. The quickest method is to tap a thread in the bush and draw it out with a bolt. Phosphor bronze has a fairly high coefficient of

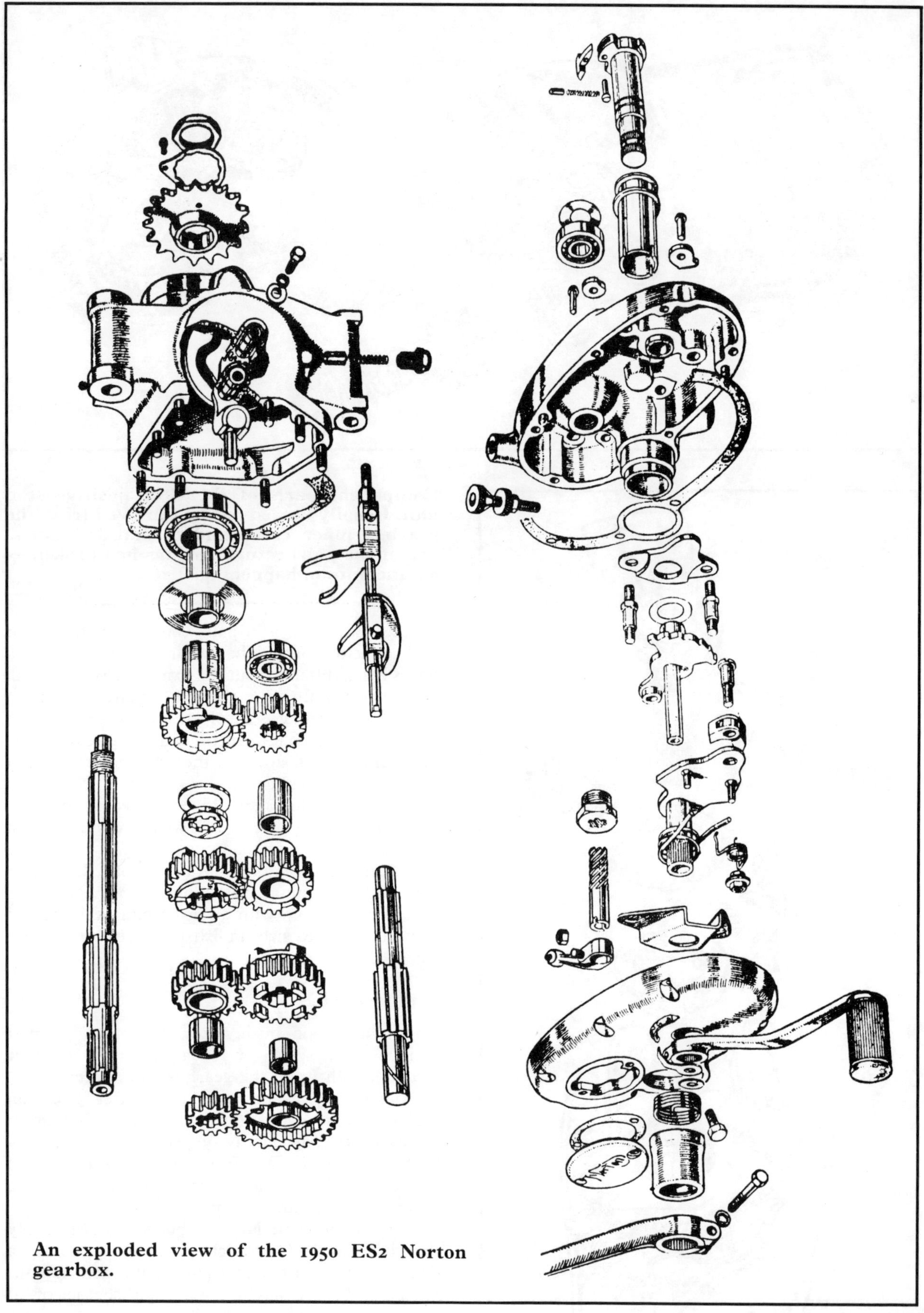

An exploded view of the 1950 ES2 Norton gearbox.

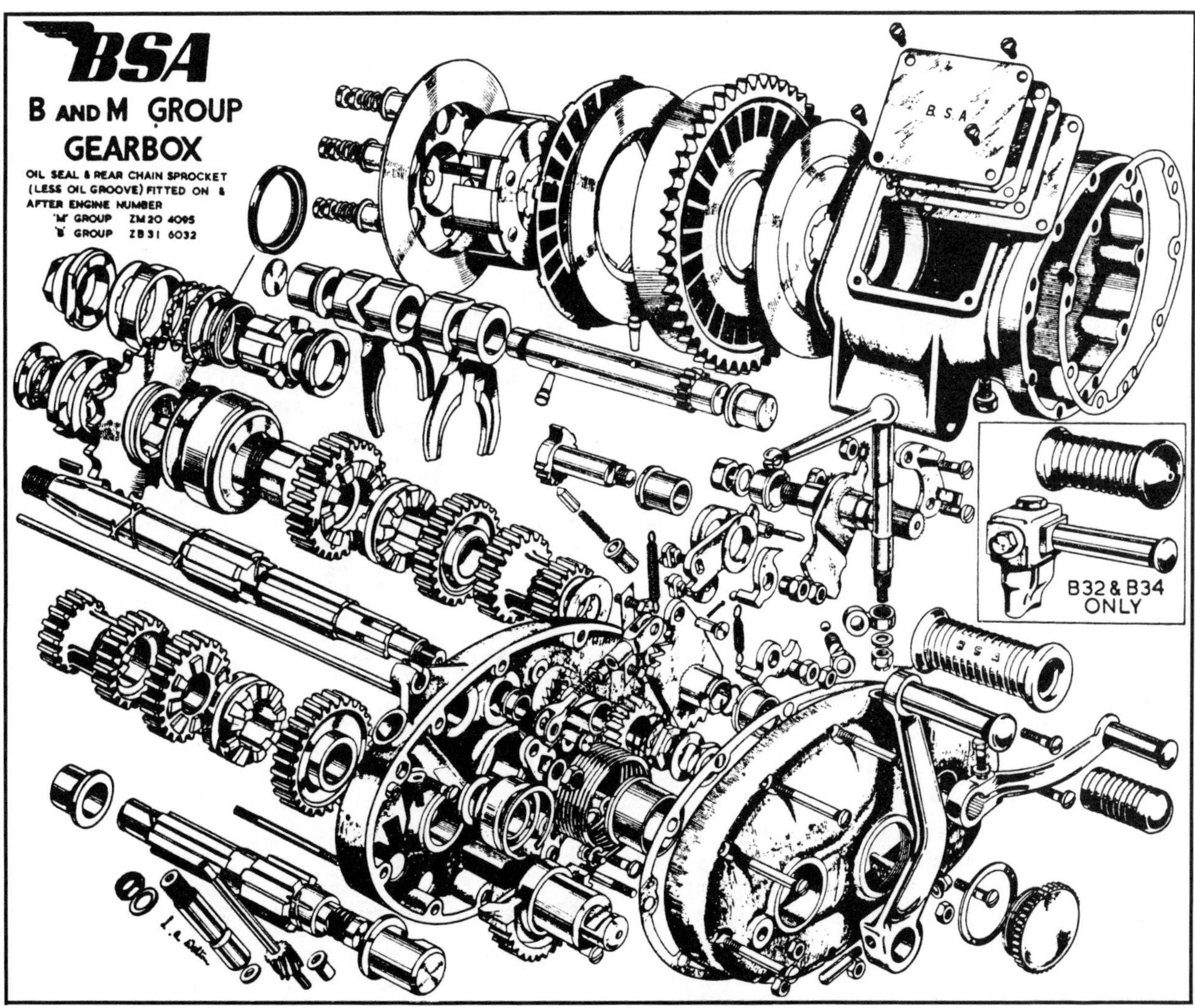

The nigh indestructable BSA 'M' and 'B' series gearbox shown in detail. Note the main oilseal, fitted after engine Nos ZM20 4095 (M20/21) and ZB31 6032 (B Group). Previous to this, oil retention was by means of a reverse thread on the drive sprocket.

expansion so the usual method of extracting ball journals (by heating up the alloy case and jarring them out) is not always successful with bushes.

Ball and roller bearings should be closely examined for shake and pitting, although gearbox bearings will tolerate slightly more play than their engine counterparts. Never thump new bearings in cold — this is the quickest way of ruining the housings. The correct method is to warm the case in boiling water and the races should drop in by hand. Some manufacturers (eg. AJS in the vintage period) adopted a belt-and-braces attitude by swaging over the aluminium surrounding the bearings but this should not be necessary if correct tolerances are observed. If there is any doubt as to journal security, use *Loctite Bearing Fit*.

A trial assembly

A trial assembly of layshaft and mainshaft is advised when new bushes and bearings have been fitted. Both shafts should spin quite easily with a minimum of end-float. As mentioned earlier, shims should not be placed between two rotating components and preferably not between a revolving shaft and fixed bush. The best place to insert a shim is **behind** the bush flange to pack it further out from the casing.

Worn dogs

Whilst gearboxes may differ in design their problems remain the same. Chewed-up dogs, causing the machine to jump out of gear when under load, is a very common snag. Over a long period of time (shorter, if the rider is heavy-booted) dogs become rounded and eventually slip at the slightest provocation. The corners can be built up with Stellite, or a similar hard-facing welding rod, and dressed to shape again. This repair is extremely successful when spares are not available. Many dogs were dovetailed to some degree; if so the angle should be

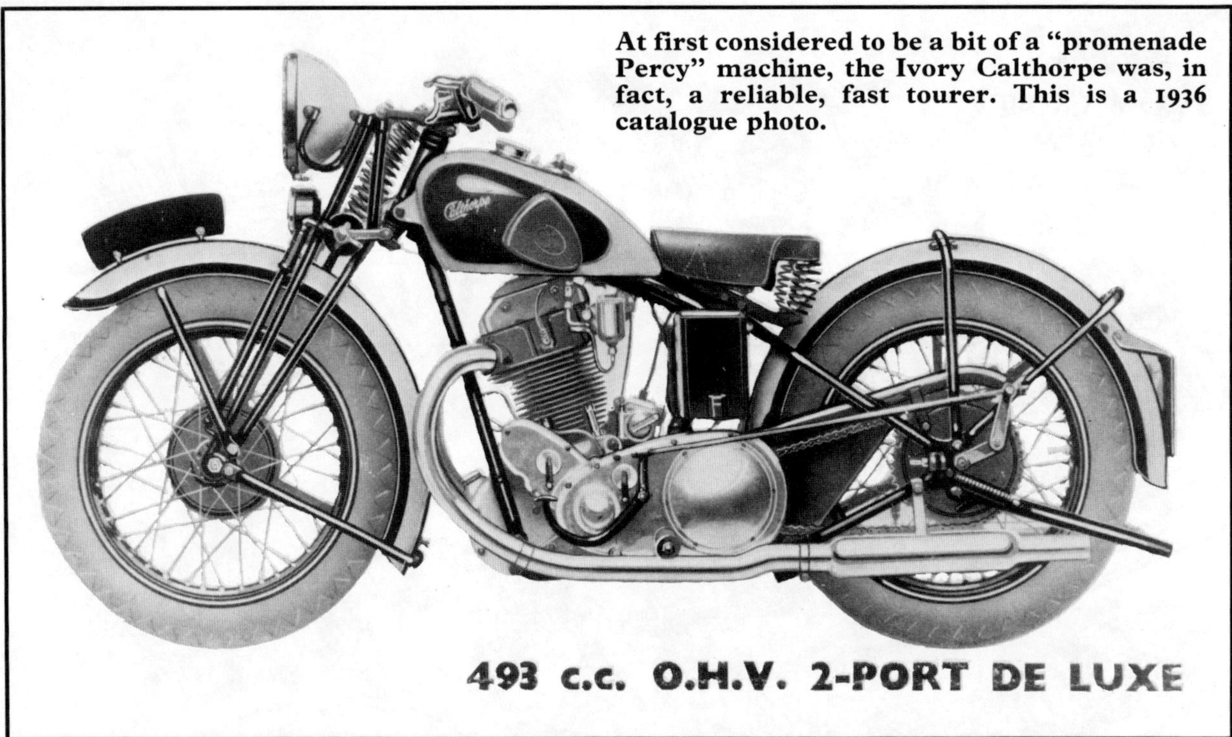

At first considered to be a bit of a "promenade Percy" machine, the Ivory Calthorpe was, in fact, a reliable, fast tourer. This is a 1936 catalogue photo.

maintained (but not overdone, which could make pinion withdrawal difficult).

Premature dental decay — the gearbox pinion variety — was rampant in the vintage period. "Crash" boxes, ie the type with sliding pinions, suffered terribly at the hands of laymen. Sixty years ago a village bystander would be entertained by the clip-clop of horses hooves and the graunching cacophony of missed gearchanges. A.J.S., Sunbeam, and Humber gearboxes were no worse than others of the mid-vintage period but the condition of their second-gear pinions sometimes has to be seen to be believed!

AMC-Norton modifications

AMC-Norton boxes, used on a wide variety of models, sometimes suffer from layshaft bearing wear. At one end of the layshaft is a ball bearing, housed inside the shell. When this breaks up, the layshaft flops about under load and rubs against the adjacent output bearing; occasionally troubles ensue in the kickstart mechanism when the bike is under way.

Originally, Norton boxes had roller bearings in this position, a much more satisfactory arrangement. Due to a number of complaints, Nortons eventually cottoned-on and recommended replacement of the later ball races with roller bearings of the old type.

If your AMC box is giving trouble, the replacement roller race is Norton part number 067710. A better (cheaper!) solution is to purchase it from a bearing supplier. In this case the SKF number is NJ203, or an equivalent FAG or R&M, with a C3 (three dot) fit.

Hand-change rod adjustment

When a vintage gearbox is replaced in the frame, or when there has been any significant alteration of its position due to chain tensioning, the operating rod must be re-adjusted. This is most important with the old type of sliding-pinion box. An inspection cover on the gearbox top helps, but failing this the gear engagement positions must be felt by hand.

Slack-off the rod clevis nuts and detach the bottom end of the rod from the gearbox arm. Grasp the arm and feel for the middle gear position (assuming we are dealing with a 3-speed box). It will be possible to detect when the middle pinion and gear begin to mesh, and further movement of the operating arm will indicate the point at which the sliding pinion leaves its partner. The mid-position should obviously be coincident with the middle gear notch in the gate, so the operating rod can then be adjusted to length and coupled up to the gearbox arm.

Whilst making these adjustments the rear wheel should be slowly revolved by hand. Providing the middle gear position is correct, low and high should also be right but it is as well to check. Adjust if necessary. After bottom or top gear dogs begin to engage there should be sufficient follow through movement of the hand lever before it hits the end of the gate.

The smaller capacity Ivory model was sold at a reduced price by Messrs. Pride and Clark Ltd (£35 compared to the manufacturer's listed £44 18s).

Clutches

"The clutch is a very important part of a modern motorcycle, since it enables the rider to glide away from rest with the engine running just like a car." So said a vintage instruction book. We all know better. The word glide is not the term I would use for some clutch actions! Slip and drag perhaps would be more common and there were some veteran multi-plate clutches which would grab with such ferocity the rider's hat was thrown off.

We sometimes forget that motorcycles, especially utility models, were ridden by laymen with no mechanical knowledge. Clutches were abused in traffic and when hill climbing. Most riders of the veteran and vintage eras hated having to change gear and would often slip their clutches instead. A good top-gear performance was a major selling point in any model; combination drivers would generally hang on to top for as long as possible when ascending a steep hill. A change-down was a momentous decision, not to be treated lightly.

No wonder then, that most vintage clutches need re-lining. New corks can often be found at autojumbles but if the reader is in difficulty the following method of clutch cork manufacture will be of interest (devised by Les Taverner, creator of the wheel jig described earlier).

Procure a number of corks from a home-brew shop. Some corks are more crumbly than others, so select the best. Make a tubular cutter, as shown in the photograph, from thin-walled tube, with the end sharpened to a knife edge.

The cutter works best when rotated in a lathe with

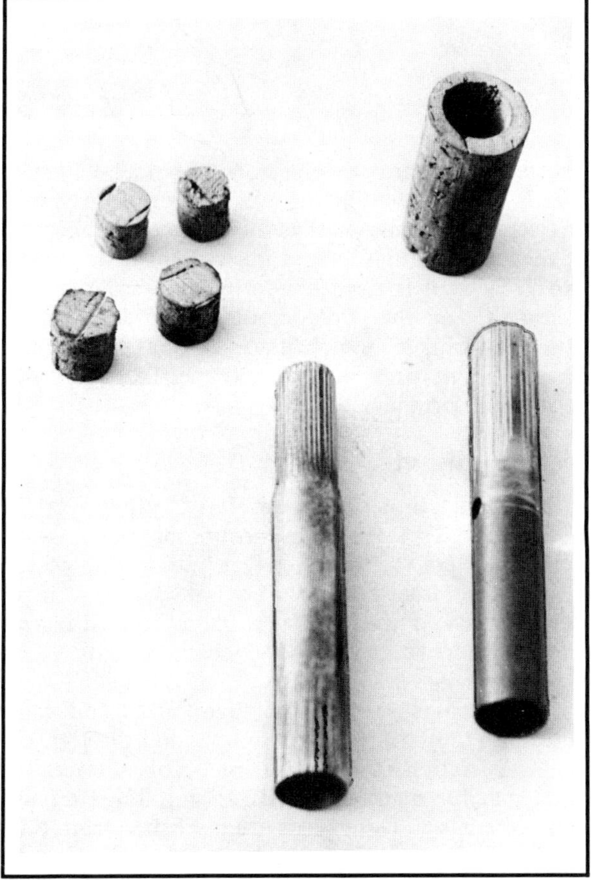

Cutting tools made from thin wall tubing. The clutch inserts are made from wine bottle corks. ***(Photo: L. Taverner.)***

Cutting out the corks on a lathe. ***(Photo: L. Taverner.)***

the cork fed into it. The cork should be pushed gently inwards, stopping just before the cutter breaks through and mashes the operator's fingers. It is then removed and sliced up with a Stanley knife. No great skill is needed, the only important point being that all the corks should protrude an equal amount from the clutch plate. A final finish on a sheet of glasspaper held over the surface plate will face the inserts level.

Ferodo inserts

It is difficult to lay down a definite ruling over the amount of permissible wear in Ferodo-type inserts, but in general a projection (on either side of the plate) of at least 1/32 in is advisable, or 1/16 in in certain cases. This does not apply to bonded inserts of more recent times, some of which are only 1/64 in thick when new.

Ferodo rings, as fitted to many BSA and early Triumph clutches can still be obtained through the VMCC friction material scheme. This service, for Vintage Club members, is administered by (unpaid) club officials and stock lists are published from time to time in the Club's Journal.

Burred slots

The slots in a clutch body wear ragged after a while,

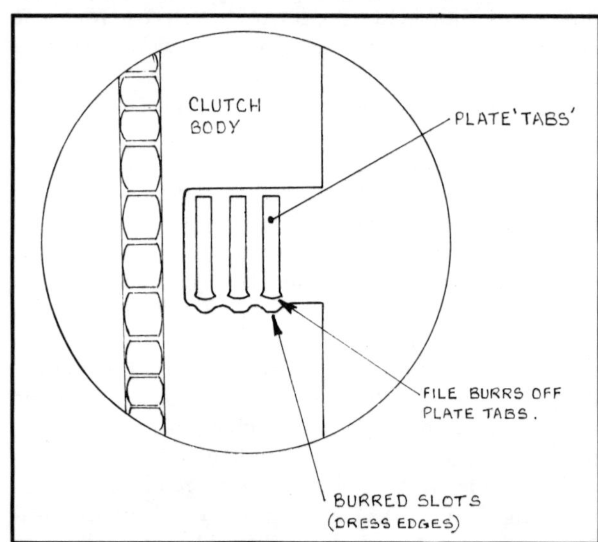

Burred clutch plates and drum.

resulting in uncertain clutch withdrawal as the plate tabs foul the burrs. Dressing the slot edges with a flat file will rectify matters and the slightly wider slot-width will not make any difference to the clutch action.

Plain steel plates should be examined for buckling. When a clutch overheats, plates are apt to turn bright blue and warp considerably; the bent plates should either be discarded or flattened so that no daylight can be seen between them and a surface plate. Tongues should be dressed with a file. Rusty plates are none the worse when cleaned up with a rotary wire brush; in this respect glazed plates may perform better (albeit temporarily) when scuffed with a wire brush or emery cloth.

Clutch springs rarely need replacing, but beware of packing washers which may have been inserted by a previous owner in a desperate attempt to obtain more grip. Supplementing spring strength by this means should only be considered a last-resort measure (for competitions use etc.) as there is a distinct possibility of the springs becoming coil-bound before complete clutch withdrawal.

The P. & M. PANTHETTE
Price £50.

Slipping clutches

A clutch which persistently slips under load is a thorough nuisance. The problem is almost certainly due to one of the following:

1 Incorrect spring adjustment (ie spring adjustment nuts too far out). The remedy is obvious, but make sure all the nuts are screwed in an equal amount.
2 Worn inserts or burnt corks.
3 Oily inserts, or clutch discs, in a dry clutch. Discs can be washed in petrol and then boiled in household detergent to remove oil. In bad cases it may be necessary to replace the inserts or discs.
4 Cable adjustment wrong. Re-adjust with detectable free play at the handlebar lever.
5 Insufficient number of clutch plates. A rare snag, but it has been known! (only likely to be encountered on autojumble clutches).

Dragging clutches

Almost as annoying as a slipping clutch, one that drags causes difficult gearchanging and creeping at traffic lights etc. Check the following points:

1 Uneven spring adjustment in multi-spring

Two more Cleckheaton masterpieces. Left: The rare and complex 250cc Panthette with a transverse v-twin, unit-construction power unit designed by Granville Bradshaw. *(Photo: Panther Owners Club.)* Below: A good subject for restoration, the 1937 Model 85 350cc Redwing. *(Photo: Panther Owners Club.)*

clutches causing the plates to cock-over on withdrawal. By far the most common cause.
2 On a single-spring clutch, end of spring not square. Grind flat.
3 Incorrect cable adjustment. Too much free play.
4 Worn clutch pushrod not allowing the clutch to withdraw sufficiently. Adjust pushrod lever (on the gearbox) by means of a grub screw and locknut (or centre screw in clutch pressure plate). Or make a longer pushrod from silver steel rod hardened at the ends. An increase in length of 1/8 in is often sufficient.
5 Wrong grade of oil in chaincase (ie too thick).
6 Coil-bound pressure springs. Caused by fitting wrong springs or packing-out the old ones with thick distance pieces.
7 Insufficient travel of handlebar lever; ie wrong lever fitted or lever bent inwards as a result of an accident.

Velocette clutches

Apart from variations in lining material and the number of plates included, the Velocette clutch design remained the same from 1929 onwards (in this year the internal bell crank and hinged thrust cup made their appearance).

Cork inserts were fitted on two-stroke models, certain early ohc machines (around 1925) and on most MOV and MAC models up to 1940. A few MACs had neoprene-inserted plates in 1939 and 1940 but many of these were altered back to cork during overhauls. All K models (except early units mentioned), MAF and MAC clutches from 1940 had *Ferodo* inserts, as did the larger M models.

The important point to remember regarding Velocette clutches in general is to adjust them *exactly* in accordance with the manufacturer's instruction book. They will then give good service. Over the years much unfair criticism has been levelled at this excellent design, mostly emanating from owners with a penchant for fiddling!

Clutch cable adjustment

One sure sign of good workmanship is a smooth and light clutch action. Levers which almost need two hands to depress them, and release with a jerky action, make riding a chore. First of all adjust the clutch withdrawal lever on the gearbox so that it assumes a correct angle in relation to the pushrod (see sketches). Then adjust the cable until there is about 1/8 in free play at the handlebar end. Check again after fifty miles or so if a new cable has been fitted.

Clutch cables should be well-lubricated with a graphited oil. A cable-oiler ought to be part of every motorcyclist's workshop equipment; most gadgets

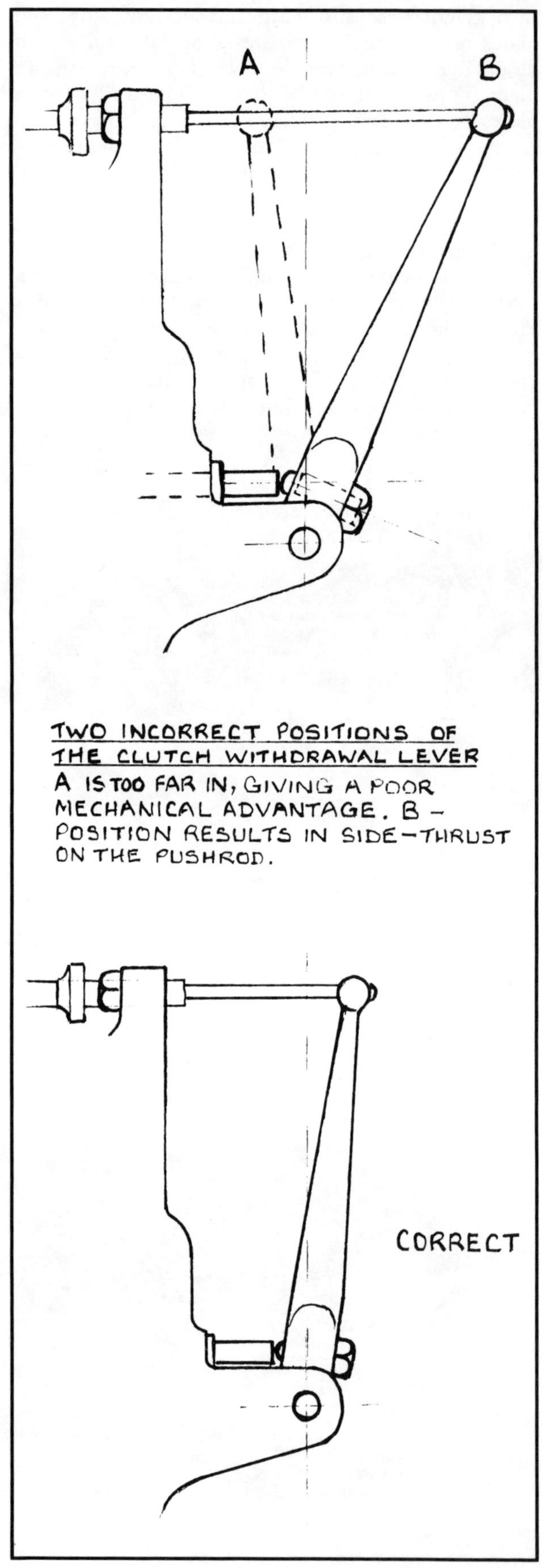

consist of a little oil reservoir which clamps onto the cable end by means of a screwed compression fitting, with an attachment at the other end to make a tyre pump connector. With a few strokes of a bike pump, oil is forced throughout the cable.

A stiff clutch action can usually be transformed simply by re-routing the cable, avoiding sharp bends. Experiment with different cable layouts and only restrain the cable with clips where there is danger of it becoming trapped by the fork spring or burnt on the exhaust system.

Nylon-lined cables impart a silky smoothness to a clutch action. Car accessory shops usually have a selection (originally intended as accelerator cables), the outers being suitable for medium-sized clutch cables on vintage machines. Generally the inners are of a braided type unsuitable for motorcycle controls

Right and below: Scott maestro George Reed at the age of 85 with the two-speed 532cc model he bought new in 1919. He always rode to events, generally in plus-fours, and his Scott rarely let him down. The Author remembers old George falling asleep whilst watching the Senior TT in 1957, unimpressed by a field which included the unforgettable Bob McIntyre (Gilera), Surtees and Massetti on MVs and Hartle and King on Nortons. "They are too noisy for me," was Mr. Reed's comment on waking up.

but these can be discarded in favour of Bowden wire. There is no need for the conventional lubrication procedure with nylon-lined cables, although a drop of oil on the exposed inner wire and barrel nipple will do no harm.

Taper-fit clutches

Care should be taken over the initial fitting of the clutch to the gearbox mainshaft. Frequently the tapered mating surfaces will be found to be scored due to the clutch centre coming loose on some previous occasion — almost certainly the result of bad fitting.

Lightly dress any burrs in the vicinity of the keyways and lap the centre to the mainshaft with fine grinding paste (very little grinding is required, so don't overdo it). Check the fit with engineers' blue, ignoring any light score-marks remaining so long as there is overall contact. When the key is fitted, make sure it does not stand too proud, so preventing the tapers from fully engaging.

A nicely-restored early two-speed Scott — not a task for beginners! The registration number appears to date from a later period than the 1912 year of manufacture.

Scrunching

A reminder about starting off from cold! Some clutches have a dreadful habit of sticking when the bike is parked overnight. To avoid a loud and damaging scrunch (a new word for the Oxford Dictionary and handy for Scrabble) when engaging bottom gear it's good practice to withdraw the clutch lever and ease the kickstart over a couple of times.

A simple procedure on hand-change machines is to slip the lever into second, withdraw the clutch, and paddle the bike forward a yard.

The Scott two-speed gear

The dismantling and reassembly of the Scott gear unit is fairly well covered in the Scott Handbook, copies of which are not hard to find. Even without an instruction manual the average mechanic could strip down a two-speed gear in a few minutes, the construction being so simple.

Generally speaking, the Scott gear is a masterpiece of engineering; light, beautifully made and extremely efficient. There are, however, a few problems which can develop over a long period of use. Constant attention to lubrication of the bearings and chains will help matters; one sound

idea is to rig-up a drip-feed to both primary chains, or a Y-piece in the gear oil-feed so that lubricant can be directed at will to the chains. With two chains running on fixed centres it is difficult to achieve equal tension in both over a long period, especially when one drive chain is freewheeling for most of the time. Therefore one chain suffers more wear than its neighbour.

In most well-worn gear units there will be found a pronounced tight-spot when chain adjustment is attempted. The tight spots on high and low chains will be in different places, which only makes adjustment more tricky! Some compromise must be made, but an over-tight chain must be avoided at all costs as this plays havoc with the hub bearings. An old dodge was to make the low gear chain up from two lengths, with two split-links, the major portion of which could be used in the high gear sprockets periodically. The basic idea was to spread the load, and wear rate, equally between both chains. Not many owners can be bothered with such a scheme so the next best thing is to remove the chains frequently and soak them in graphite grease.

The ultimate answer to two-speed chain problems is to renew all the sprockets. This means engine sprockets, gear chain wheels and magneto sprocket. (The question of correct chain tension cannot be stressed too highly as it is this factor more than any other which influences the life of the gear bearings.)

Cups and cones

New cups and cones should be made from EN31 case-hardening steel and the bearings adjusted with minimum shake. Some Scott specialist repairers are able to supply these parts ready-made, along with many other parts that are now almost impossible to obtain from the usual sources.

Drum bearing wear

Most gear drums wear in their bores, developing scored tracks where the caged balls run. The late Tom Ward, an old craftsman and devotee of the two-speed Scott, (who worked with Alfred Scott himself in the early days) repaired drums by broaching out the cages to take rollers. This was a very satisfactory solution to the problem which other Scott specialists can undertake.

In one of my *Vintage Workshop* articles for the Vintage Motor Cycle Club Journal, I raised the question of hub bearing wear, wondering if anyone had considered caged needle-roller bearings as an alternative. A Scott enthusiast of long-standing, advised that such a conversion had indeed been attempted, and what is more was the subject of an article in *Yowl*, the Scott Owners' Club Journal. The engineer concerned was a Mr. Ernie Scott (no relation to Alfred) and for the benefit of two-speeder enthusiasts his words are reproduced in full:

Notes on modifications to the Scott two-speed gear

"For some time I have studied the remains of a two-speed gear in my spares box. It was in a very sorry state and was unusable in that condition. I therefore decided to try to reclaim the gear, updating where possible bearing surfaces etc. The bulk of the wear was, of course, on the centre hubs where the bracelet bearings run — the inevitable tracking. This hub had tracked very badly, probably to a depth of 3 or 4 thou, and so had the thrust races which normally contain a collection of 9/32 in balls and a retaining ring, and of course the cups and cones were also well worn — these however did not prove quite as difficult to find at various autojumbles. Reading through back numbers of *Yowl* I found a couple of articles by Mr. Fox and George Reeves on modifications to the two-speed gear and the more I read them the more sense it was making — the stumbling block was still the bracelet bearings. Some careful measuring was done and the problem was taken to my friendly bearing merchant. He was, of course, somewhat surprised to know that bracelet bearings were still in use in these gears, and said 'Caged roller races'.

A search through his records and suppliers' books produced a needle roller bearing tolerably close to the sizes I had taken in. They were, I think NK47/20 type. A pair of these were ordered and in due course arrived. In the meantime I had discussed my proposed mods with people more knowledgeable than me, engineering-wise and two-speeder wise. Both schools of experts came to the same conclusion — they didn't see why not. Anyway, I had nothing to lose; the gear could not be used as it was, and that was for sure!

The new needle roller races proved to be slightly under-sized when fitting them into the gearwheels and also under-sized to go onto the hub — this was not overmuch a problem as I rather wanted to grind out the score marks on the hub. A shim ring about 2 thou thick was all that was needed to make these bearings a press fit into the gear wheels, and as the depth of these bearings was just under the depth of the old brass bracelet bearings, fairly careful fitting was required to centralise the new bearings in the gear wheels. Careful and tedious grinding of the hub removed the score marks and eventually produced an easy-running fit for the roller races. Most bits of the two-speed gear seemed hard right through, which was useful. So far so good.

The thrust races were renewed by another proprietary bearing consisting of two

> hardened rings and a set of balls contained in a steel or brass carrier* — so to get the correct, as original, thickness with good flat running surfaces was reasonably simple."

(*The caged bearing referred to by Mr. Scott was probably an EW7/8, as mentioned in the earlier researches by Messrs. Reeves and Fox.) Mr. Scott concluded his article by saying:

> "On completion I was pleasantly surprised to find a nice easy action of the gear with gear engagement by hand pressure on the end of the shaft and smooth wobble-free running otherwise. The other modification was to change the low gearwheel to one of 42 teeth . . . to give even tension on both chains and gear alignment correct in the frame."

So there it is . . . the foregoing modifications sound well worthwhile and should eliminate most of the problems associated with the ingenious Scott two-speed gear. Gone are the days when one could selectively assemble the best gear parts from an assortment of spares. It is now a case of making do with worn parts, building-up expanding hub rings until they are a close fit in the gear hubs and renewing sprockets where possible.

A well-tuned two-speed gear should engage with light pressure; the adjustment preferred by many Scott riders is that where low has to be held by light heel pressure, releasing when the heel is lifted. This makes life easier in traffic. There should be no excess pedal movement between low and high positions, high gear being positively engaged by a gentle tap on the pedal. Paraffin is recommended as a lubricant on the quick-thread selector scroll.

Adverts for modern two-stroke machines sometimes extol the virtues of a five-speed gearbox — it is regrettable that today's manufacturers are incapable of producing an engine which is flexible enough to require but **two** gears . . .

Chapter 6

Carburation

Servicing carburettors. Tuning various types. (Amac, Amal, B & B, Binks, BSA, Triumph, Senspray, Schebler, Bowden, SU.)

Air leaks

IT is no use proceeding with carburettor adjustments until all potential sources of air leaks have been eliminated. Worn valve guides and stems are the chief culprits on vintage motors where the working parts get coated with road dust and receive little, if any, lubrication. The amount of unwelcome air that can be sucked up past a worn inlet stem is akin to drilling a small hole in the induction pipe, and we all know what effect that would have on carburation!

Once the valves and guides have been attended to, the next point to watch out for is a leaking induction pipe joint. Clip-fitting carburettors, especially vintage brass-bodied types, do not give much trouble in this department, but if the stub is worn it can always be metal-sprayed or electroplated to bring it back to size. Whatever method of metal deposition is employed, the stub will need machining to a truly cylindrical form to fit the carburettor tightly. With zinc-based alloy bodies watch out for cracks around the clip spigot. Flange-fitting carburettors are apt to admit unwelcome air around the joints; a rough check for leaks can be made by smearing oil or soapy water around the offending flange when the engine is running. A bowed flange is the inevitable outcome of an excessively thick gasket combined with brute force. It is not unknown for there to be 1/16 in daylight in the middle.

A bent flange can be restored to normality by rubbing it face-down on a sheet of emery paper, held on a surface plate or sheet glass. Finish off with fine grinding paste and paraffin, on plate glass, washing thoroughly afterwards.

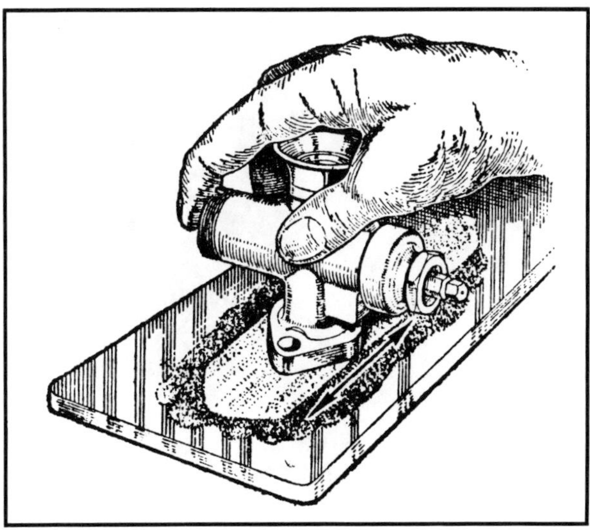

Rubbing down a carburettor flange to rectify a bowed joint flange.

V twin manifold joints must be carefully checked for air-tightness — some manufacturer's couplings left a lot to be desired and can only be made airtight when bound with insulating tape. Our predecessors had to rely on such all-purpose unguents as gold size and boiled fish glue, but today we are fortunate in having a selection of flexible sealants at our disposal. If you don't fancy the manifold looking like a mummified elbow, the nuts and conical joints etc. can be coated with a fuelproof cement on assembly. Room Temperature Vulcanising (or RTV for short) cement seems to be ideal for this purpose. Both the *Hermatite* and *Loctite* concerns make such a product.

Having achieved an airtight induction system, the carburettor itself can be tuned for speed and economy. Air-cleaners should be left in place during trials as their removal could lead to false readings.

Commencing with the AMAC, arguably the most popular vintage instrument, various old and not-so-old carburettors will come under discussion in this chapter. Irrespective of the make, by far the most likely snag on a newly-restored machine is dirt in the fuel system; a wise precaution against blocked jets and flooding float chambers is to coat the inside of the petrol tank with *Petseal* or a similar product. Fuel tank sealants are two-pack resinous liquids which form a skin on the inside of the tank, sealing small holes and damping down rust flakes.

The AMAC carburettor

The initials AMAC stand for the Aston Motor Accessories Co., this business being absorbed into Amalgamated Carburettors Limited (or Amal for short) in 1928. Other companies involved in the merger were Brown and Barlow and Binks. Many of the earlier Amac features were carried on into the

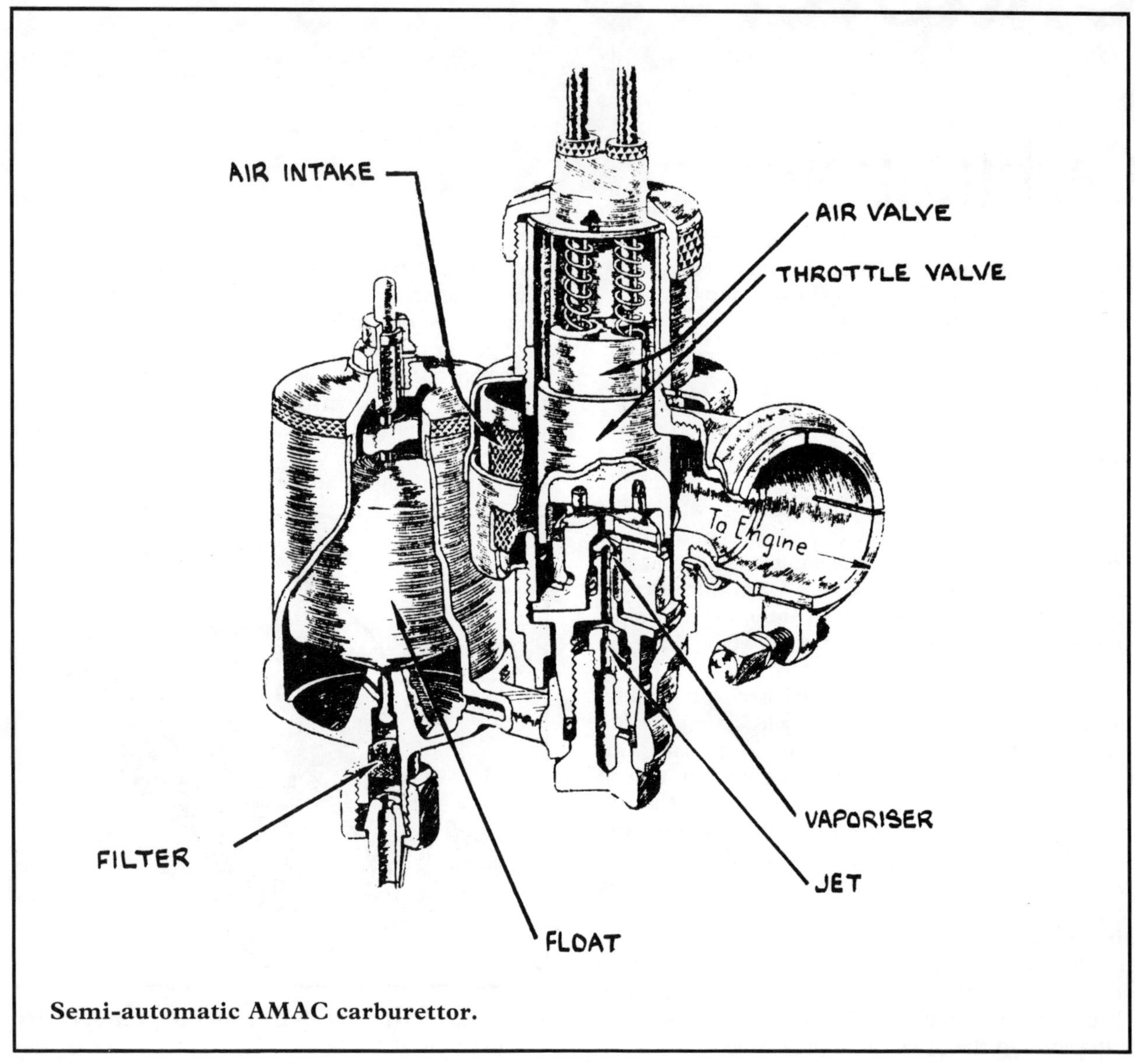

Semi-automatic AMAC carburettor.

Above: A rare 1928 AKD (Abingdon King Dick) fitted with a magnificent Sports AMAC carburettor. Now better known for spanners, AKD made a variety of machines throughout the vintage era. Their insignia depicted a bulldog said to have been inspired by a local schoolmaster's hound which answered to the name of "King Dick".

Below: This photo of the Author's 2 3/4hp AJS shows the Sports Model AMAC carburettor. Later "big ports" had Binks carburettors, the change taking place during 1925.

Amal design, but one significant difference between the two is that the common vintage Amac has no mixture needle.

Not everyone is familiar with the performance and handling characteristics of two-lever Amac carburettors; those riders brought up on modern Amals generally complain of a multitude of flat spots the first time they ride a vintage machine. This is understandable, as old-timers looked upon the skilful control of a carburettor as a kind of art-form, and the mastery of such an achievement to be proud of.

Although the needleless Amac requires a lot more skill to handle correctly, there are bonuses. A well-adjusted Amac in intelligent hands will result in excellent fuel consumption figures and there is a lot of pleasure to be gained in deciding for yourself what sort of mixture your engine needs.

The main difference, as far as the rider is concerned, lies with the use of the air control. As everyone knows, once you have started your post-vintage engine you can open the air lever wide and forget about it for the rest of the day. Not so with a vintage Amac. The sequence of mixture control with the latter is as follows:-

1. **Starting** — Air lever shut, throttle lever 1/4 to 1/3 open.
2. **Slow running** — Air lever almost closed; throttle lever just open.
3. **Normal cruising** — Air lever fully open; throttle lever open as necessary.

A Lightweight AMAC carburettor fitted to a 1924 "round tank" BSA. Note the neatly-coiled petrol pipe, bent per original catalogue illustrations, in this restored example.

4. **Hill climbing** — Air lever closed slightly (approx. 1/4); throttle lever open as necessary. Adjust to suit.
5. **Flat-out running** — It may be necessary to close the air lever slightly whilst fully opening the throttle.

If all the above sounds complicated, ask any vintage rider and he will probably say you will soon get used to it! Just remember that most early carbs were not automatic in their action and the rider must do the compensating.

Float level

Although Amac and Amal floats are slightly different in design (needle diameters, tapers and clips vary) the principle of level adjustment remains the same. With some of the smaller Amacs, such as those fitted to 2 1/4 hp machines, the mixing chamber can be removed, leaving the float chamber and mixing chamber base with jet in situ.

The fuel level can be adjusted by moving the float up and down the needle a bit at a time, until the level is observed to be just a fraction below the tip of the jet. You will have to top-up the chamber every time you make an adjustment and then wait until the level has stabilised. If the level cannot be readily observed due to the mixing chamber design, it will all be a matter of trial and error; raise the float a little until the carb overflows readily and then drop it gradually until you get it right.

The carburettor will, of course, flood when the tickler is depressed but it should not drip when the machine has been stationary for a while. If it does, then either the level is too high or the needle wants lapping-in with metal polish. Don't worry too much if the carburettor appears to shred a few drops of petrol when on the move; in moderation this is to be expected as the float needle gets jogged off its seat occasionally on bumpy roads.

A badly-grooved needle taper will never seat properly. Machine-off the tapered piece in a lathe, turn a new conical bit from brass rod (drilled to suit the needle) and silver-solder it in position. Lap-in the new needle seating with metal polish. For punctured floats, refer to the section on Amals.

When the optimum level is reached, the needle can be marked and a new notch made, if necessary. The makers would have been horrified at the suggestion, but these days so many carburettors are made up from autojumble parts, and some Amac float chambers form bad marriages with their mixing chamber partners due to minor differences in design.

Jet sizes

The main jet acts merely as a metering device and does not play any part in vaporising the mixture. The sprayer is, in the most common Amac models, a row of small holes drilled in the mixing chamber base. This vaporiser is detachable, being held in place by the large union nut at the base of the chamber. After many years' service the small holes get blocked with carbon and need cleaning out; it is no use drilling out the holes in order to get more speed, as some vintage home-tuners were known to do. If you do this the vaporising efficiency will be adversely affected, so leave well alone. When replacing the sprayer block don't forget the thin fibre washer which fits between it and the base nut.

A post-vintage Amal carburettor sticks out like a sore thumb on an otherwise desirable Sports sv Sunbeam. Such a conversion will no doubt improve handleability for everyday use but it does not necessarily result in better fuel economy.

Check that the main jet number is about right for the engine capacity and type (ie sv tourer or ohv sports) and try out the machine on a level road in average climatic conditions. When running flat-out the size of the jet is about right when the engine runs happily with the air lever closed a fraction (about 1/6th to 1/4 closed). The reason for this apparently strange state of affairs is that you then have a little more air lever travel in reserve for varying weather conditions. An engine will generally consume less petrol on hot days and more in cold weather.

At normal speeds, however, the air lever should be fully open. If the engine pops and spits and the

AMAC JET SIZES (1925) 4-STROKES		10 HY SPORTING.			15 HYDM			25 HYDM			30 HYDM		
		JET	VALVE	CHOKE	JET	VALVE	CHOKE	JET	VALVE	CHOKE	JET	VALVE	CHOKE
TWINS	1000 cc	36	3	1⅛"	29	2	⅞"	32	3	⅞"	–	–	–
	750 cc	—	—	—	28	2	⅞"	31	3	⅞"	–	—	—
	500 cc	—	—	—	—	—	—	27	2	¾"	27	4	¾"
	350 cc	—	—	—	—	—	—	26	2	⅝"	28	3	19/32"
SINGLES	600 cc	38	3	1⅛"	32	2	1"	30	3	⅞"	–	—	—
	500 cc	36	3	1⅛"	31	2	1"	—	—	—	—	—	—
	350 cc	—	—	—	—	—	—	28	2	¾"	30	5	¾"
	150 cc	—	—	—	—	—	—	—	—	—	24	3	19/32"

ENGINE	SIZE (C C)	CARB. TYPE	JET
VILLIERS	150 175 250 350	30 HXDM 25 " 25 " 15 "	24 27 27 30
LEVIS	211 211 247	30 HY SPORTS 25 HYDM "	24 26 27
VELOCETTE	2¼ HP	25 HXDM	27
SCOTT	TWIN	15 HY SPORTS	31
A Z A	150	30 HXDM	24
RADCO	211	25 HYDM	28
O.K.	2¼ HP	25 HXDM	26
ENFIELD	2¼ HP	25 HXDM	28
CONNAUGHT	2½ HP 3½ HP	25 HYDM 15 HXDM	28 29

AMAC recommendations for two-strokes.

JET EQUIVALENTS

B+B LATE AMAL BINKS AND AMAL (1BA)	AMAC ¼BSF	OLD BINKS + PRE-29 AMAL BINKS 2BA	DIA. (IN)
15		0	
20		1	
25	16	2	
30	18	3	
35	19	4	
40	20		
45	21		
50	22		
55	23	5	.026
60	24		.027
65	25	6	.028
70	27	7	.029
75	28		.030
80	29	8	.031
85			
90	30	9	.032
95	31		
100	32	11	.034
110	33	12	.035
120	35	13	.037
130	36	14	.038
140	38	15	.040
150	39	16	.041
160	40	17	.043
170	41	18	.044
180	43	20	.045
190			
200	45	21	.048

air lever has to be closed more than is normally necessary, this is a sure sign of weakness (try a larger jet). At low engine speeds it will be found that the air lever has to be closed right down until is almost shut to achieve an even tick-over. This is a normal feature of Amac carbs and nothing to worry about.

Amac jets have a different numbering system to their Amal counterparts, but in either case the larger the number the more fuel will be metered. Amac jets are not easily obtained nowadays, so if a change of jet size is called for you will have to do a little improvisation. There are two alternative courses of action:-

a Alter the Amac jet holder to take a pre-Monobloc Amal jet.

b Modify some Amal jets to fit the existing Amac jet holder. If you adopt the first course of action the jet holder thread should be tapped out to take a small brass adapter which is threaded internally 1 BA to suit Amal jets. This adapter, in the form of a bush threaded inside and out can be *Araldited* or soft-soldered in place.

The second option involves a cunning piece of lathe work. What you will need to do is to machine the thread off the Amal jet, leaving a plain spigot. Onto the spigot silver-solder a small piece of 1/4 in BSF thread (bored out to fit over the spigot). The modified jet will then fit the Amac jet holder. A number of Amal jets can be modified thus, enabling experiments to be made.

Both of these schemes are preferable to making

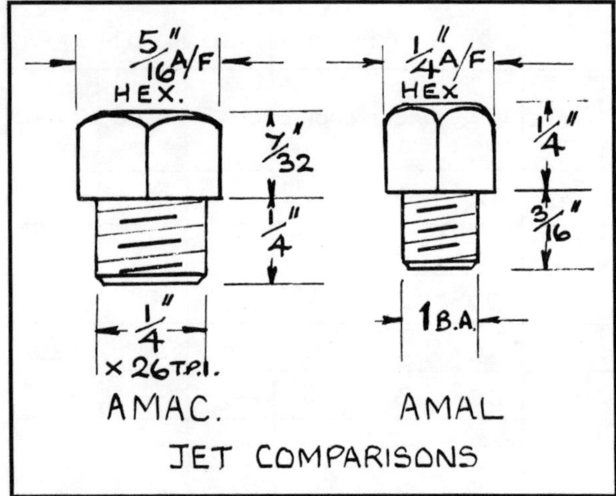

new Amac jets from scratch as the tiny holes are awkward to drill cleanly. Without properly calibrated and marked jets tuning is a rather hit-and-miss operation — there are enough problems to overcome in the normal sequence of events.

Throttle slides

As with modern carburettors, mixture strength at lower speeds is partly controlled by the throttle slide, or "valve" as Messrs. Amac would say. From closed to half throttle the valve cutaway governs mixture strength, the standard valve being a No 2. If the mixture is too rich (very rarely the case) a No 3 valve can be fitted or the cutaway filed carefully. Before modifying the slide remember that it is not so easy to put metal back on if you have made a mistake.

If the mixture is too weak when the machine is accelerating, ie. the carb spits back on opening the throttle lever, it may be necessary to fit a slide with a smaller cutaway. This is rarely necessary with a standard Amac as the trouble is usually caused by some other factor, such as an undersize main jet or incorrect manipulation of throttle and air levers.

Worn slides

A badly-worn throttle valve will play havoc with mixture strength, sometimes causing the engine revs to increase quite independent of the rider's action. There are various ways of tackling the problem, the method of repair depending on the amount of wear present.

To take the worst case, where the mixing chamber bore is worn tapered and the slide is shaped like a beer barrel; all that can be done in this instance is to mount the body in a 4-jaw chuck and bore out the chamber parallel. A new slide is then made from brass bar to a close running-fit in the chamber.

If however the wear is only slight and the mixing chamber is in good shape, the old slide can be built-up with silver solder and machined (or even carefully hand-filed) back to size. Soft solder is not much use for this job as it will wear through in no time. Most of the wear takes place at the bottom rear edge of the slide so this is the area needing most attention.

Spotted over thirty years ago in the Isle of Man, this beautiful Sunbeam features a Type HY Sporting AMAC carburettor and a Best and Lloyd mechanical oil pump. "A gentleman's motorcycle" as Titch Allen once said. Probably a 1925 600cc Model, usually seen in sidecar guise.

Re-sleeving a slide

If the reader is building up an autojumble special, ie an Amac or B & B carburettor from various odd parts, he might like to try a repair I have done many times. To reclaim a barrel-shaped slide, re-sleeve it with a thin-walled bush. It's quicker than making a new one from scratch.

The old slide is machined on the outside diameter until it is again round and parallel. It can be reduced in diameter by approximately 3/32 in (this measurement is not important) to accept a thin sleeve, turned from brass, to restore it to the correct outside diameter. The sleeve is soft soldered on to the old slide and skimmed in the lathe until it is a good fit in the mixing chamber. The cutaway can be filed to the same depth as before and any slots cut out also.

I sometimes make the thin-walled sleeves from *Oilite* (or *Lubrook)* sintered bronze bushes. These are obtainable from most bearing stockists. Many vintage mixing chambers are either 1 in or 1 1/8 in bore and *Oilites* are made with these outside diameters (the clearances work out just right). Incidentally, for the benefit of Doubting Thomases, you **can** soft-solder oil-impregnated bushes quite easily, strange as it may seem. Ordinary tinman's solder and flux will make a perfect joint. In service the solder will not melt — if your engine gets that hot there's something seriously wrong with it!

Final adjustments

Cables must be correctly adjusted and well-oiled for smooth operation. Just one more thing to add — take time adjusting the friction devices on the throttle and air levers. Each lever must work independently of its neighbour. It can be quite irritating when the air lever keeps vibrating shut, or if it has to be readjusted every time the throttle lever is moved.

B & B carburettors

Made by Brown and Barlow, these carburettors were fitted to many machines throughout the vintage era. Various models were made but as far as tuning is concerned, they can be divided into two groups, needle and needleless. Checks should be made for air leaks, as mentioned earlier, and it is as well to cast an eye over the float chamber base for signs of petrol seepage. Occasionally the outlet piece cracks around the joint line; this can be silver-soldered before the crack spreads.

The float level should be checked in the same manner as with Amacs; fuel level is set 3/16 in below the jet tip (although this looks higher due to capillary action). Some B & Bs had small fine-gauze filters beneath the petrol union and over a period of time these tend to clog. As on any other fuel system a main filter should be fitted, preferably to the petrol tap fitting inside the tank. In the case of a rebuilt machine it's a good idea to fit an external modern filter for the first 100 miles or so to trap rust particles.

Main jet (restrictor)

This is removed from below by unscrewing the mixing chamber base screw. The jet size should be such that the air lever can be opened fully at high speed with maximum throttle. A warm day should be chosen (difficult in Britain!) but if the test is carried out in winter it may be necessary to fit a slightly smaller jet when summer comes along.

The following size jets are recommended by the manufacturers for common (1923 type) single-jet semi-automatic B & Bs:

TYPE BOD	
Single-cylinder engines (solo)	.032 in
Single-cylinder engines (sidecar)	.034 in
Twins 6 hp	.028 in – .030 in
Twins 8 hp	.032 in – .034 in
TYPE LOD	
Twins up to 75 mm bore	.028 in – .030 in
Single-cylinder engines, lightwt.	.026 in – .030 in
TYPE TOD	
Two strokes	.028 in – .030 in

If the inlet dust cap is removed, larger jets may be required.

When starting from cold, close the air lever fully and open the throttle approximately one quarter. The air lever may need closing down a fraction when climbing hills or for slow running (carbs without pilot-jet adjustment).

Needle adjustment

Semi-automatic variable jet models (ie those with needles) are relatively easy to tune and perform in a similar fashion to Amals. Raising the needle will richen the mixture. Standard settings are as follows:

500 cc singles	1 13/16 in	
650 cc – 1000 cc twins	1 29/32 in	Types BSV, BSV Long
Lightweights	1 15/16 in	LSV Long and Short
Scotts	1 13/16 – 1 15/16	

The needle length is measured from the slide recess to the needle tip. At the risk of high fuel consumption the needle can be raised to give almost fully automatic action; normally it is necessary to compensate for weak mixture when coming off the pilot jet by closing the air lever momentarily. The needle is secured by a grub screw, situated in a recess in the side of the throttle valve. Jet sizes used in conjunction with the needle lengths quoted are as follows:

500 cc singles	.045 in	
650 – 770 cc twins	.050 in	
770 – 1000 cc twins	.055 in	BSV and LSV
Lightweights	.032 in – .036 in	
Scotts	.042 in	

The pilot jet is adjusted in the following manner: 1 Screw the adjuster in as far as it will go. 2 Start the engine and open the air lever 1/4. 3 Unscrew the knurled adjuster gradually until the engine fires regularly and slowly with the throttle lever nearly closed. The engine will not run with the throttle closed completely (on the pilot jet alone). Unscrewing the adjuster weakens the pilot mixture; it may be necessary to readjust the setting every time the

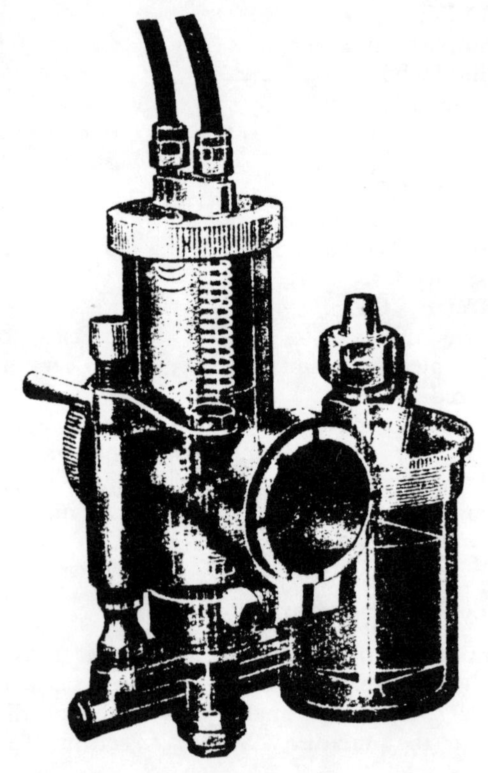

B&B CARBURETTOR B 9 V
WITH PILOT DEVICE

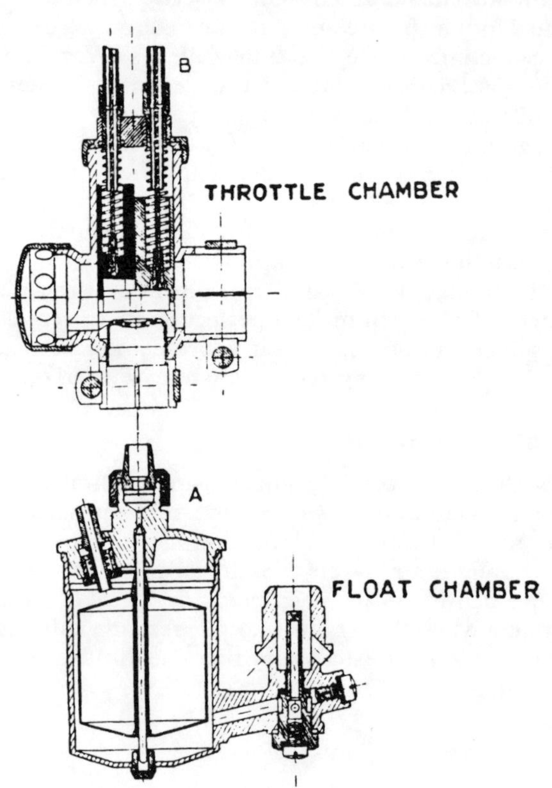

TWO-STROKE B & B

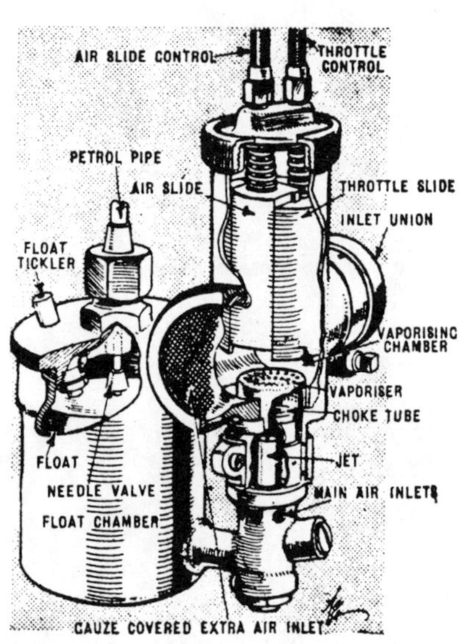

STANDARD 2-LEVER B+B

SPORTS MODEL B&B

Different types of B & B carburettor.

throttle lever is closed further until satisfactory slow-running is achieved.

Easy-start lever

Some B & B carburettors had an easy-starting device in the form of a lever on the side of the mixing chamber. The lever positions are (a) facing the engine: pilot not working (b) facing outwards: easy starting only (c) facing the intake: pilot working. To start from cold set the throttle lever open slightly, close the air lever and move the pilot lever to the "easy-starting" position. This temporarily cuts off the adjustable air supply. When the engine is running, move the pilot lever to the "pilot working" position, where it can remain for normal running. (Quite why the "pilot not working" position was included in the design remains a mystery; a contemporary report says "it is provided for those who prefer to dispense with a slow running device"!)

Sports model B & Bs of the mid-vintage period were distinguished by their flared intakes (similar to Amal bell-mouths) and adjustable pilot-jets. Needles were fitted, so giving an almost fully automatic action. The general construction was much simpler than earlier models and usually they give little trouble. Worn throttle valves should be attended to (refer to the section on Amacs) and the gauze vaporiser disc in the mixing-chamber hose should be cleaned occasionally. Some carburettors perform happily without these gauzes.

Early needleless B & B models, ie. the usual type of semi-automatic two-lever carburettor with air and throttle valves, function in much the same way as the popular Amacs of similar vintage. The two-stroke B & B model also has no needle and the rider must compensate for varying conditions by adjustment of the air lever. If the jet size is correct, full air can be used at high speeds on a warm day. The air lever will need to be shut down a little for slow-running and hill climbing and closed altogether for cold starts.

Dust caps with ten holes were normally fitted but alternative 12 or 14-hole caps were available for engines blessed with more urge than normal. If either of the latter is fitted, the jet size must be increased accordingly. Those experiencing mixture problems (popping-back etc.) with an autojumble carb may find they have a mis-match of intake cap and jet.

Binks two-jet carburettors

Made by C. Binks (1920) Ltd., the Binks two-jet model was a remarkably simple and effective

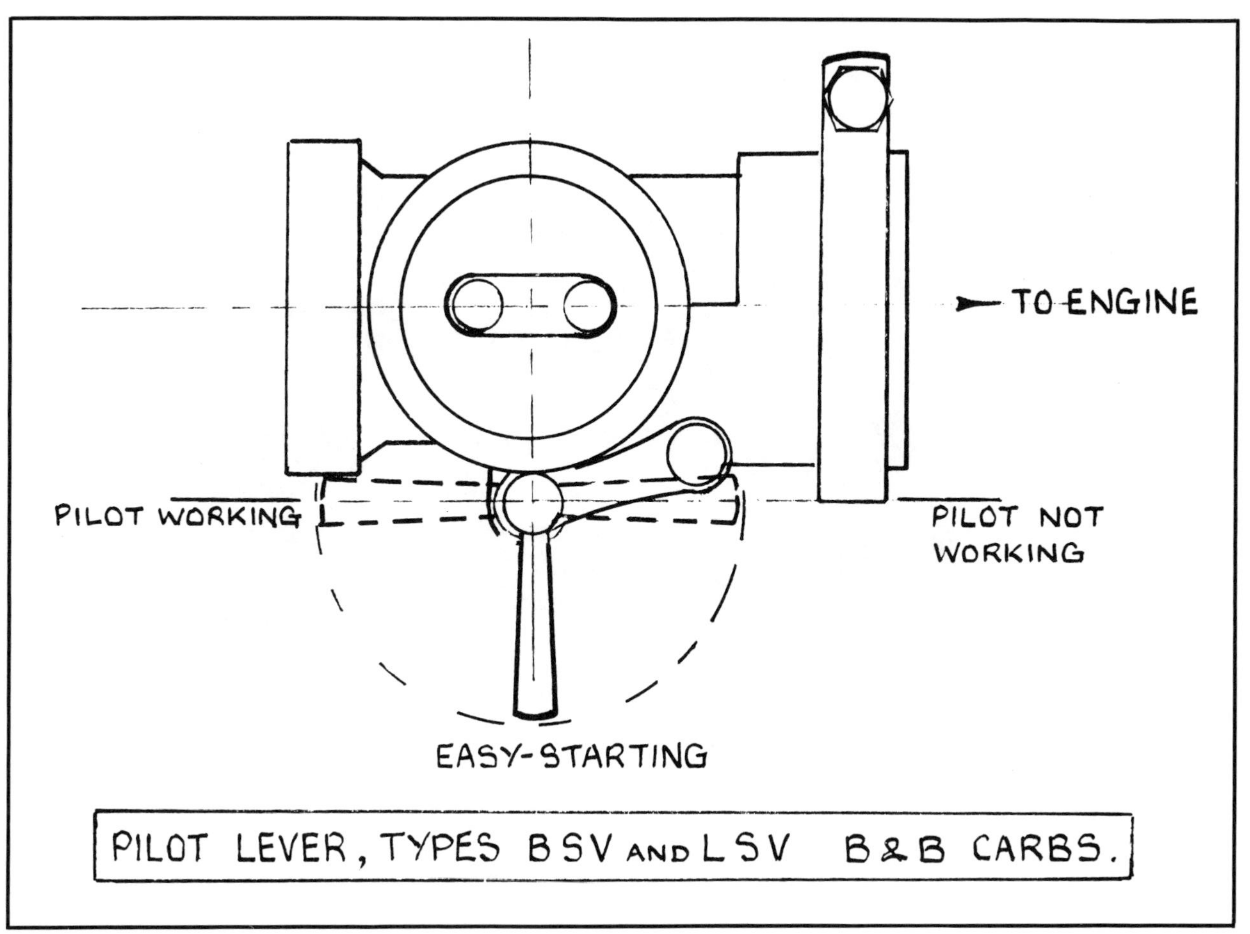

PILOT LEVER, TYPES BSV AND LSV B&B CARBS.

carburettor. Control of the instrument is as follows:-

1. **Starting.** Open the throttle lever a fraction to raise the valve about 1/8 in, or until the air is heard to swish through when the engine is turned. Lower the air valve over the main jet. Flood the carburettor and kick over.
2. **Normal running.** Air valve approximately three-quarters open; the acceleration should be good, without hesitation.
3. **Slow running.** Air shutter closed about halfway.
4. **Fast running.** Almost fully open air, or wide open when flat-out on a warm day.

Two jets are fixed in the mixing chamber base; the main jet is the higher (and larger of course) of the two. By means of the throttle valve action, suction on the main jet is controlled. Closing the throttle reduces the suction, at the same time increasing pilot jet suction. As in most carburettors, the air plunger is the one nearest the air intake (the longer main jet is situated beneath this plunger in the case of the Binks).

Both jets can be removed with a special key (made from an extended clock-key) once the large square or hexagon adaptor is undone from the base. This fitting contains a filter which should be cleaned periodically.

The following jet sizes are recommended:-

Engine	Choke dia.	Pilot	Main
250 cc	11/16 or 3/4	0	5
four-stroke			
350 cc	3/4 or 13/16	1	6

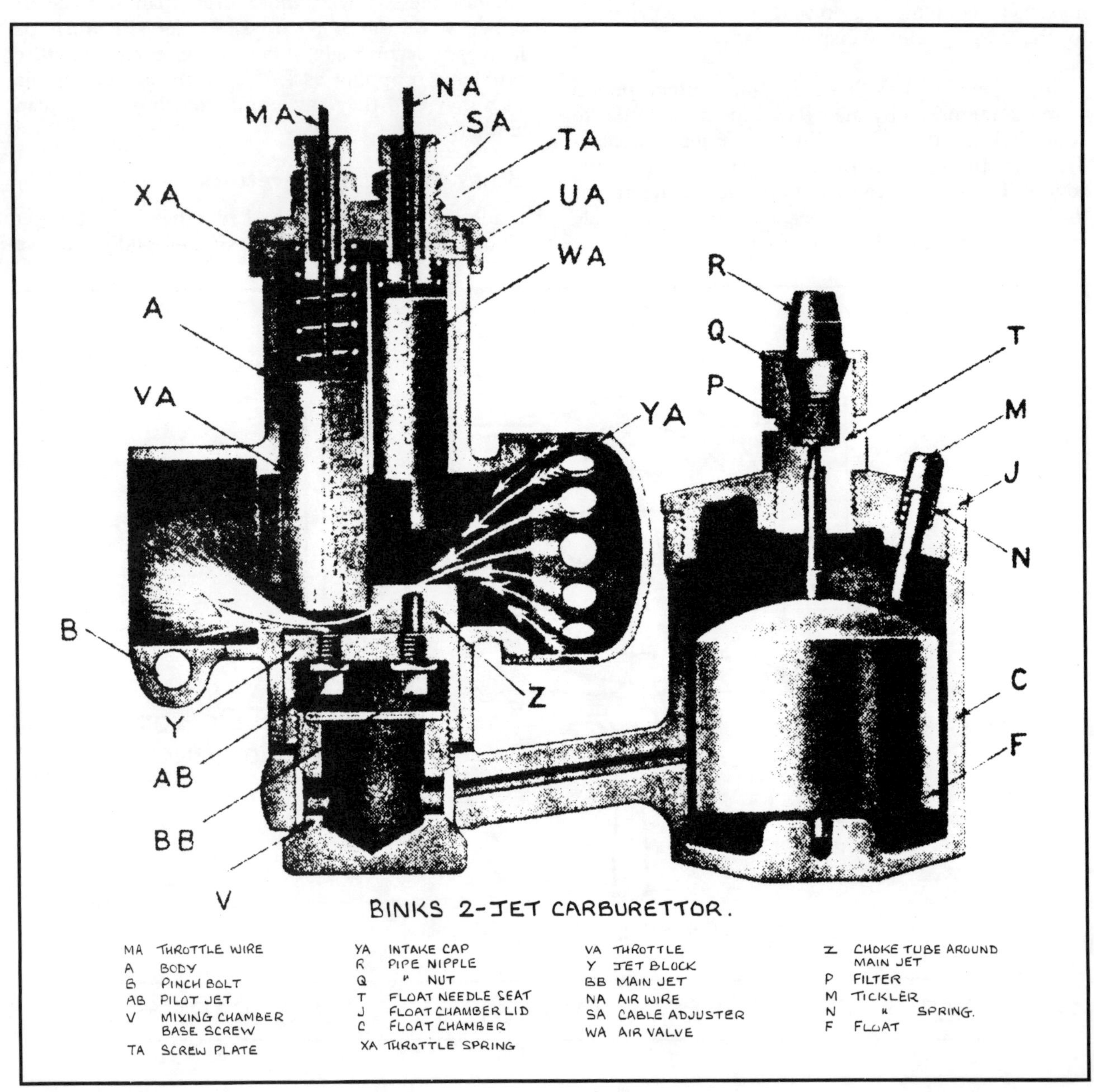

BINKS 2-JET CARBURETTOR.

MA THROTTLE WIRE
A BODY
B PINCH BOLT
AB PILOT JET
V MIXING CHAMBER BASE SCREW
TA SCREW PLATE
YA INTAKE CAP
R PIPE NIPPLE
Q " NUT
T FLOAT NEEDLE SEAT
J FLOAT CHAMBER LID
C FLOAT CHAMBER
XA THROTTLE SPRING
VA THROTTLE
Y JET BLOCK
BB MAIN JET
NA AIR WIRE
SA CABLE ADJUSTER
WA AIR VALVE
Z CHOKE TUBE AROUND MAIN JET
P FILTER
M TICKLER
N " SPRING.
F FLOAT

four-stroke			
500/600 cc four-stroke	1 in	2	8
350 cc twins	11/16 or 3/4	1	5
500/750 cc twins	13/16	2	6
800/1000 cc twins	1 in	2	8
100/200 cc two-strokes	11/16 or 3/4	0	5
200/300 cc two-strokes	3/4	1	6
300/350 cc two-strokes	1 in	1	8
Scotts*		3*	12*

*Note: The above Scott jet sizes are as quoted in *The Book of the Scott*. The official Amal-Binks leaflet 367 gives jets 3 and 11, so either combination could be used. An early Binks recommendation of pilot 1 and main 7 for Scotts is probably in respect of early 532 cc Tourers.

Careful selection of main and pilot jets will ensure a clean pick-up throughout the rev range. If there are signs of spitting-back at moderately high revs, and the air lever has to be closed down more than the usual amount, a larger main jet may be required. A plug reading will indicate mixture strength, although the situation is not quite so cut-and-dried with vintage instruments such as the Binks. An intelligent rider will be able to determine mixture strength by the sound and feel of an engine. Skilful manipulation of air and throttle levers is essential to get the best out of the engine, both from the economy and performance points of view. Insensitive owners would be well advised to fit a modern automatic Amal, twistgrip-controlled, and have done with it!

Although there should be no need for fuel level adjustments, float height is easily altered in the normal manner. Screw-in Binks models (AJS pattern etc.) must be vertically aligned. A float chamber which is canted slightly will naturally upset the fuel level (a fact which can be used to advantage when level experiments are being carried out). The petrol level is set approximately 1/4 in below the top of the jet plate.

Faults likely to be encountered are:

1 **Flooding.** Dirt under the float needle. Punctured float. Bent needle. The remedy is obvious in all cases.

2 **Engine refuses to run slowly.** Check the ignition system first, especially if bad starting is experienced. Look for air leaks in the system (poor flange joint or screwed-end, worn guides etc.) The pilot jet may be too small.

3 **Low power output,** accompanied by general weakness after the pilot jet stage — fit a larger main jet.

4 **Spitting-back** when the throttle is opened gradually can usually be cured by closing the air lever slightly. If not, check the fuel level. Clean the main jet and try the next larger size.

If the trouble still persists in spite of the engine giving good power on the main jet and running slowly on the pilot, this is an indication of the main being slightly out of phase with the pilot. In other words the main jet is coming in too late. Try shortening the main jet by 1/16 in. Binks at one time supplied special main jets with little perforations in the side to counteract this problem. The idea of the small holes was to leak a small amount of petrol to the mixture in the transitional stage between pilot and main. These jets are now unobtainable so the best way to solve the problem is to close the air lever to compensate, as mentioned.

5 **Misfiring** at low speeds, or four-stroking in two-strokes. Pilot jet too large.

A Binks carburettor and a rounded edge petrol tank date this 799cc AJS twin as 1925/6.

Binks 3-jet carburettors

Identified by its double-barrel configuration, the Binks 3-jet model was a clever, if somewhat expensive, way of achieving an almost completely automatic action.

The throttle valve contains dampers for closing the jets and two choke tubes which come into play

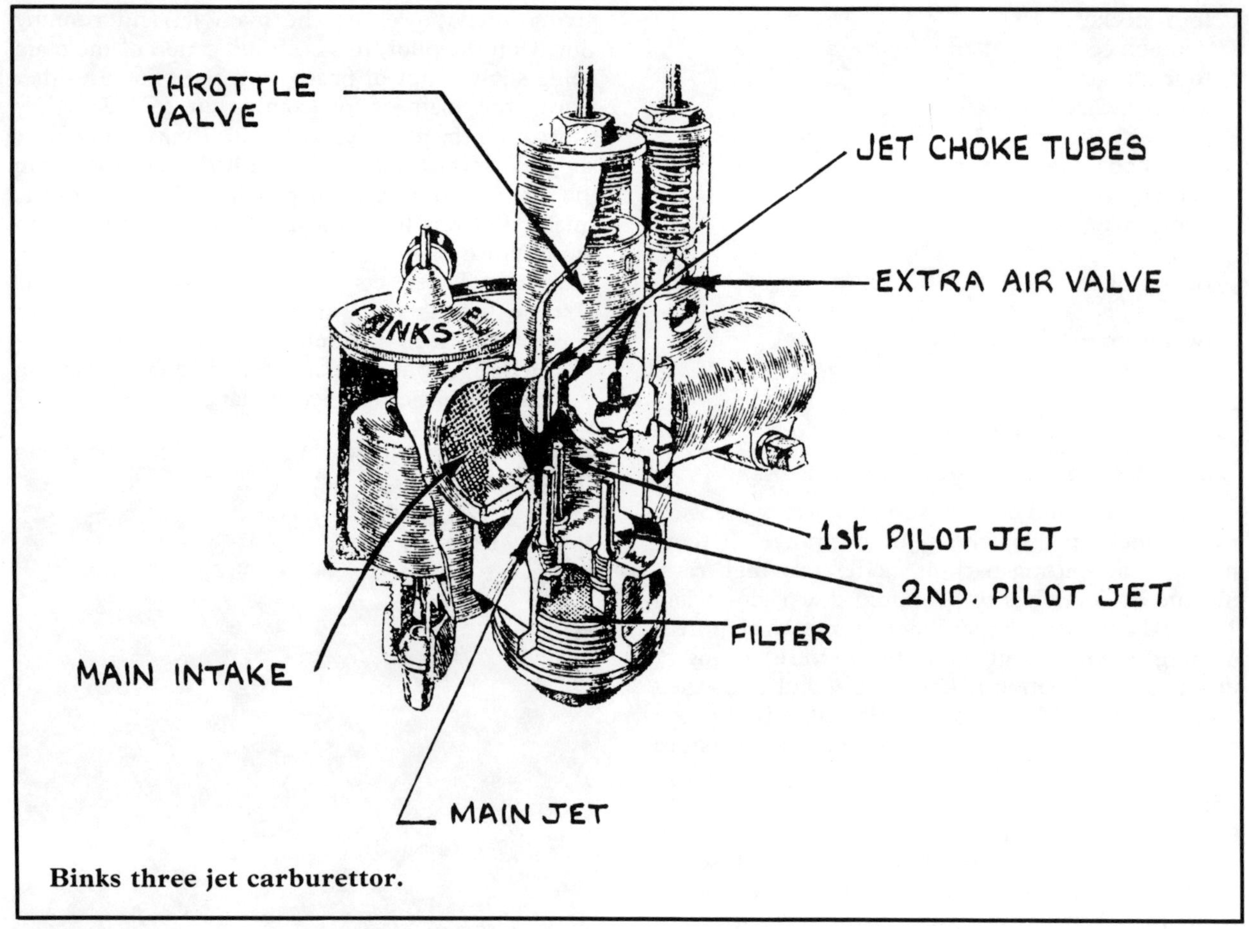

Binks three jet carburettor.

progressively. As the throttle is opened the small (first) pilot jet opens. The second jet and choke tube are then opened, followed finally by the main jet. The idea is so simple, it's a wonder other carburettor manufacturers did not follow suit (simple but expensive?)

As can be imagined, carburation will be haywire if wrong-sized jets are used in any of the three positions. Fortunately, due to the progressive action, it is easy to isolate the guilty jet. Symptoms of weakness are spitting or popping-back, and richness gives rise to lumpy running. New jets are practically unobtainable, although they sometimes turn up at autojumbles amongst oddment boxes. A skilled model engineer would have no difficulty machining new jets from brass rod; fine holes dictate a very fast lathe speed so the ideal machine is a watchmakers' or instrument lathe. One dodge worth remembering, when a jet has to be reduced in size, is to fill the hole with soft solder and re-drill it a size or two smaller. Messrs Binks of Eccles would not have condoned such experiments but the hint may help someone in trouble.

Air valve

On the side of the air tube will be found (on some models) a shutter valve; this should be closed for starting. The air valve itself is used for fine mixture adjustment, and when descending long hills the throttle is closed and the air valve opened. The makers claimed this feature "makes for economy and rapid cooling", although it must be said that long hills seemed to have vanished from the landscape since the vintage days. (What *has* happened to them . . . have they all been flattened out?)

The BSA variable-jet semi-automatic carburettor

Fitted to large capacity BSA twins in the early 1920s, the twin-barrel rotary valve BSA carburettor was a well-made device but complicated to repair if badly worn.

The design consisted of two tubular valves with a variable jet needle, manually-operated by a knurled screw mid-way between. When both valves are open, the intake system is a smooth venturi with no obstruction, apart from the needle.

For starting, the knurled jet adjuster should be open threequarter of a turn. The air lever is closed, or almost closed, and the throttle opened about 1/3rd. On most BSA machines the levers open outwards.

Maximum economy is achieved when the jet adjuster is so set that the air lever cannot be opened

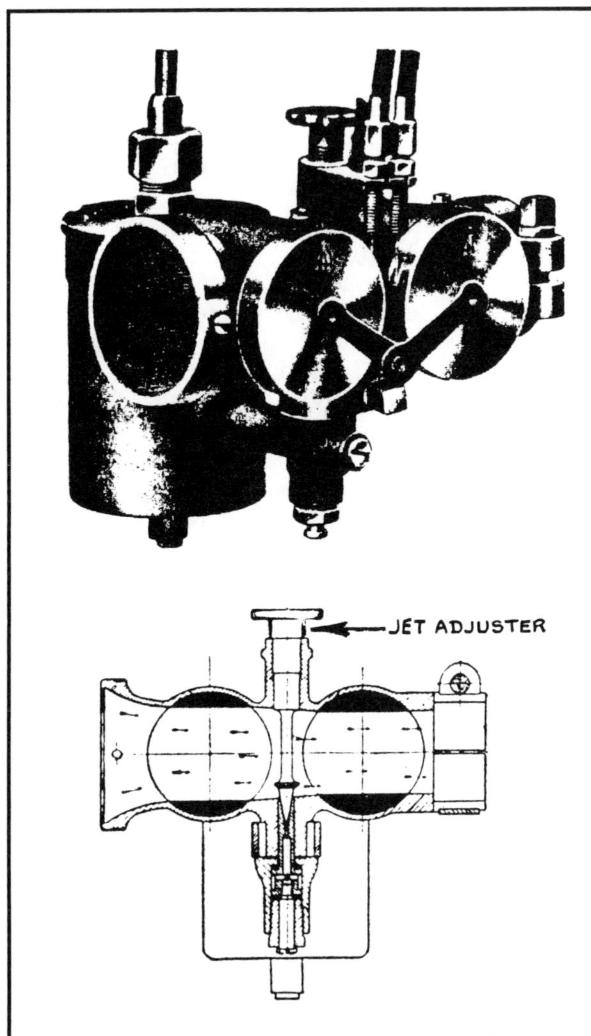

The BSA carburettor. Note the variable jet screw in between the barrels.

wider than the throttle lever without slowing down the engine.

For normal running the jet screw would be opened about one to one and a quarter turns, the air lever being adjusted accordingly.

For scorching or hill-climbing the adjuster can be opened-up, which richens the mixture and allows the air lever to be opened fully.

To summarise the situation, just bear in mind that any adjustment of the variable jet will require alteration of the air lever position. One can strive for economy or performance — the vintage family combination driver would almost certainly have plumped for the former.

Float level

To test for fuel level take out the stop screw from the end of the platform. Turn on the petrol and place your finger over the hole. Wait until the petrol has risen to its full height. Remove your finger and let the petrol flow out — repeat this a couple of times and observe the level. If more than $^{1}/_{8}$ in from the jet tip, raise the level by screwing up the float spindle nut. If less than $^{1}/_{8}$ in below, screw the nut down a fraction. Check the level again.

Foreign matter under the float needle will cause flooding; sometimes a thump with a piece of wood on the float chamber will temporarily cure this. If not, and the trouble persists, remove the float chamber top and clean out the guide hole, needle valve and seating. Lap the seating in, with metal polish if necessary.

Cable adjustment

Adjust throttle and air cables on the carburettor until there is no free play. This is very important in the case of the BSA carburettor. Sticking rotary valves should be cleaned — it pays to add a small quantity of *Redex* to the petrol to ensure smooth valve action.

The Senspray carburettor, 1920 pattern

Manufactured by Chas. H. Pugh, Ltd., this simple carburettor works, as the title suggests, on the scent-spray principle, with an elementary venturi

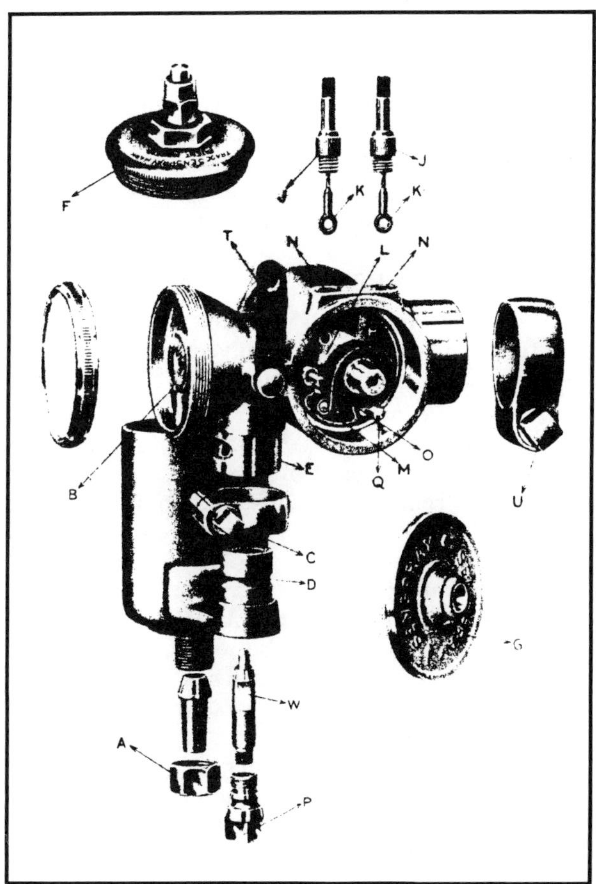

Top: An exploded view of the Senspray carburettor from the makers' catalogue.

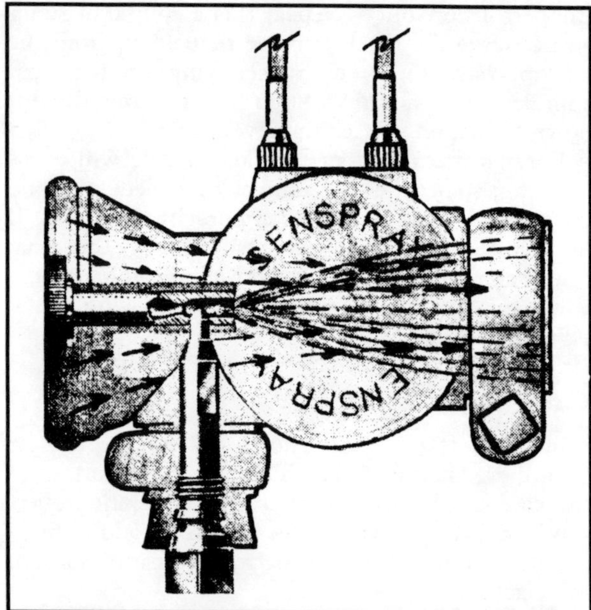

Ghost view showing the scent spray principle. principle.

and jet arrangement. It was fitted to many vintage machines, notably Rudge.

The throttle valve opens and closes throttle and air openings in conjunction, the air valve being included for fine adjustment of mixture. At small throttle openings there is a correspondingly small air passage and some air will enter by means of the vaporiser damper holes. The more the throttle is opened, the larger the air passage becomes, therefore less air comes through the damper holes. The damper holes are capable of fine adjustment.

Vaporiser settings

The carburettor can be, in effect, converted to a sensitive, semi-automatic or fully automatic type by adjusting the vaporiser settings:

1 **Sensitive position** — turn the vaporiser to the position marked *LESS*. In this mode the carburettor is used by the intelligent rider to give excellent fuel consumption figures; the usual air lever juggling is required to keep the engine on song.
2 **Semi-automatic** — turn the vaporiser a notch at a time towards *MORE*. Each notch progressively richens the mixture. Eventually a position will be found when the air can be opened fully except for slow running and hill-climbing. The carburettor then responds like any other semi-automatic type (Amac etc).
3 **Automatic** — turn up the vaporiser further towards *MORE*. This gives a rich mixture, enabling the air lever to be left open all the time, except for starting. A useful position for beginners to vintage motorcycling, but rather extravagant on petrol.

With a normal touring jet fitted, the air will need shutting down slightly when going flat-out, or when climbing steep hills. A completely automatic action can be obtained, if the vaporiser is already turned up to maximum, by fitting a larger jet. Naturally this results in an increase in fuel consumption at touring speeds also.

To remove a main jet, unscrew the square-headed mixing chamber bottom bolt; the jet is screwed into this fitting in the normal way.

In order to dismantle the throttle and air valve assembly, close both handlebar levers fully. Release the spring clip and detach the mixing chamber cap (the one marked Senspray). Lift the cable eyelets off their studs and unscrew the cable fittings. The complete rotary valve and air control may be removed — don't attempt to detach the clockwork spring (unless it is broken) as the valve mechanism will withdraw with this in place.

Clean the barrel and valves and replace the throttle unit complete, slipping the coil spring leg over the middle peg. New springs are rarely needed but if the old one is badly rusted a clockmaker should be able to make a replacement to pattern.

When the vaporiser screw is removed completely for renovation take care not to lose the pawl spring, which usually flies out across the workshop!

General maintenance

Cast an eye over the cable-ends occasionally, just above the eyelets, as these are known to fray over a long period. Do not oil the valves. A smear of light grease or vaseline on the spindle bearings is recommended and an occasional squirt of *WD40* on the spring and cable eyelets will ensure smooth action.

Float level adjustment is basically similar to that of any other vintage carburettor. Note: when removing the float chamber it is essential to extract the clip screw (square-headed) completely as this engages in a notch in the mixing chamber base spigot. Fuel level should be correct if the float clip is engaged with the needle groove. If the carburettor drips petrol continuously check for grit on the needle valve seatings or a punctured float. A new float can be made up from "foreign" parts, although it will be necessary to experiment with fuel level adjustments again.

Triumph carburettors

The double-barrelled Triumph carburettor hardly changed over a very long period of time. Very simple, easy to work on, and highly efficient, it was fitted to all Triumph models made during the early veteran period right up to the mid 1920s. Fuel consumption figures of between 90 and 110 mpg were quite commonplace on $3\frac{1}{2}$ hp (500 cc) machines — indeed, in a recent fuel economy test at

Mallory Park one veteran Triumph averaged around 300 mpg in skilled hands!

Of the semi-automatic two-lever type, the Triumph carburettor is probably one of the least sensitive of all vintage instruments. Often the air lever can be opened almost fully after starting and left in that position for normal running.

Above: An early Triumph carburettor.

Below: The Triumph carburettor in section.

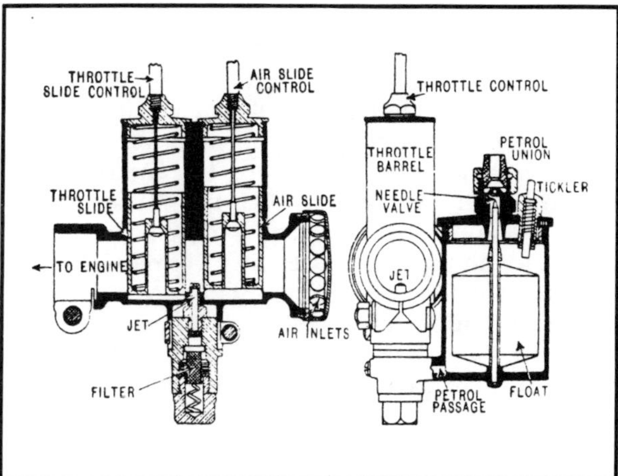

Float level

The correct fuel level is just below the jet tip. On the Triumph carburettor this is easily checked as the float chamber can be readily detached with jet assembly in situ.

Main jet mods.

"The manufacturers do not advise users to alter jet sizes, as the standard size supplied gives the best all-round result"; so states the vintage Triumph instruction book. What the manufacturers did not bargain for is their carburettors being built up out of a collection of autojumble parts! Jets are seldom of "standard size".

The Triumph main jet is quite unlike the jets used in Amal or Amac touring carburettors, having a long slender spout. Experiments can be carried out

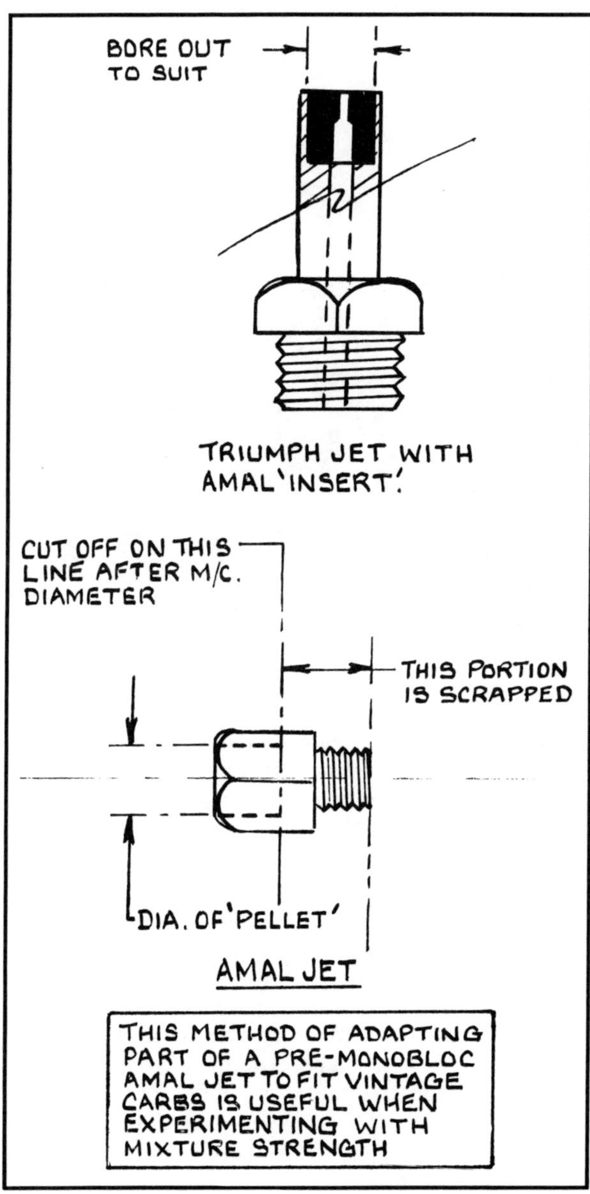

Offside view of the AJS power unit. Unusually, this machine is being ridden solo. Most were coupled to the manufacturer's own luxurious sidecars, a sizeable number of which have survived.

by boring out a spare jet to accept short inserts made from Amal pre-monobloc jets. For convenience we shall term these inserts jet pellets. First of all, acquire a selection of Amal jets with numbers from 80 to 110. Fix the threaded portions in a 3 jaw lathe-chuck (or collet) and machine off the hexagons down to a plain diameter, as shown in the sketch. Part off to about 1/8 in to 3/16 in long. The resultant articles, or jet pellets, can be soft-soldered into the end of the Triumph main jet which has been bored to suit.

Mixture strength can be altered by unsoldering the pellet and inserting another one, perhaps a couple of sizes different. Of course it will be necessary to mark the pellets in some way with the Amal designation (eg. 85 or 90). The insert should be flush with the Triumph jet tip. As a starting point, try an Amal size 100 and work downwards. It may be found that a 494 cc engine will require a size 85 or 90, and a 550 cc motor about 100.

New Triumph jets can be turned complete, if preferred, from brass rod. This is fairly straightforward but there are two small problems to overcome — screwcutting the small thread, and drilling the jet holes accurately. The latter is difficult to accomplish in the home workshop (and then there is the matter of calibration).

The jet insert, or pellet, idea is simple and can be used for any make of vintage carburettor when replacements are unobtainable.

Schebler automatic carburettors

Made in the USA and familiar to owners of American machines of the vintage era, the Schebler was an advanced design, quite unlike British instruments in its operation.

Starting

Pull out the knurled air button and give one-quarter of a turn. This locks the air valve closed. Release the button after starting.

Intermediate adjustment

See that the air valve is seated. Open the knurled needle screw (the inclined adjustment on the side of the body) about three turns. Gradually turn it to the right until the engine spits or misses and then open it again a fraction. The engine should begin to run smoothly with the throttle opened slightly (approx 1/4).

Slow-running

Close the throttle and open the slow-running air screw; this is situated on the opposite side of the body to the inclined-needle-screw and is horizontal. Turn the slow speed cam-adjusting screw to the left until the engine spits or misses and then enrichen it a touch by turning the screw to the right again. Further adjustment to the slow-running screw may be necessary.

High speed adjustment

Open the throttle and make adjustments to the graduated pointer marked 1, 2, 3. Moving the indicator towards 1 cuts down the flow of fuel. Adjust until the engine runs smoothly without back-firing.

If the mixture is still too weak at high speed with the pointer on 3, increase the tension on the air-valve spring. The valve should be closed when making all adjustments.

Fuel level

The float level should be 19/32 in from the top of the float bowl when the needle is seated.

Clean out the bowl periodically. Flooding is usually caused by dirt lodged under the needle valve.

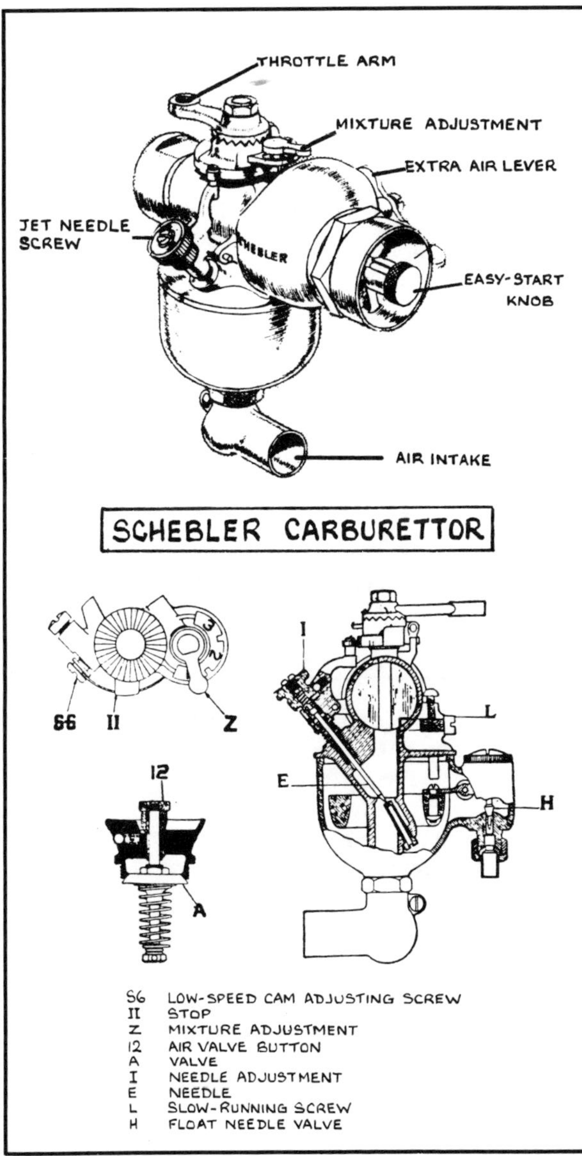

On vintage BSAs the throttle and air levers usually opened outwards (away from the rider). This photograph shows the correct combined brake and carburettor controls on a 1924 2¼hp BSA Lightweight. Note the metal-sheathed "Bowden-Silver" brake cable, as fitted to various BSAs during this period. The outer fabric covering was wound with German silver wire.

Bowden carburettors

Comparatively rare, the Bowden carburettor was fitted to some pre-war machines as standard (AJW etc.) and was also available as a proprietary fitting. Private owners claimed an increase in performance

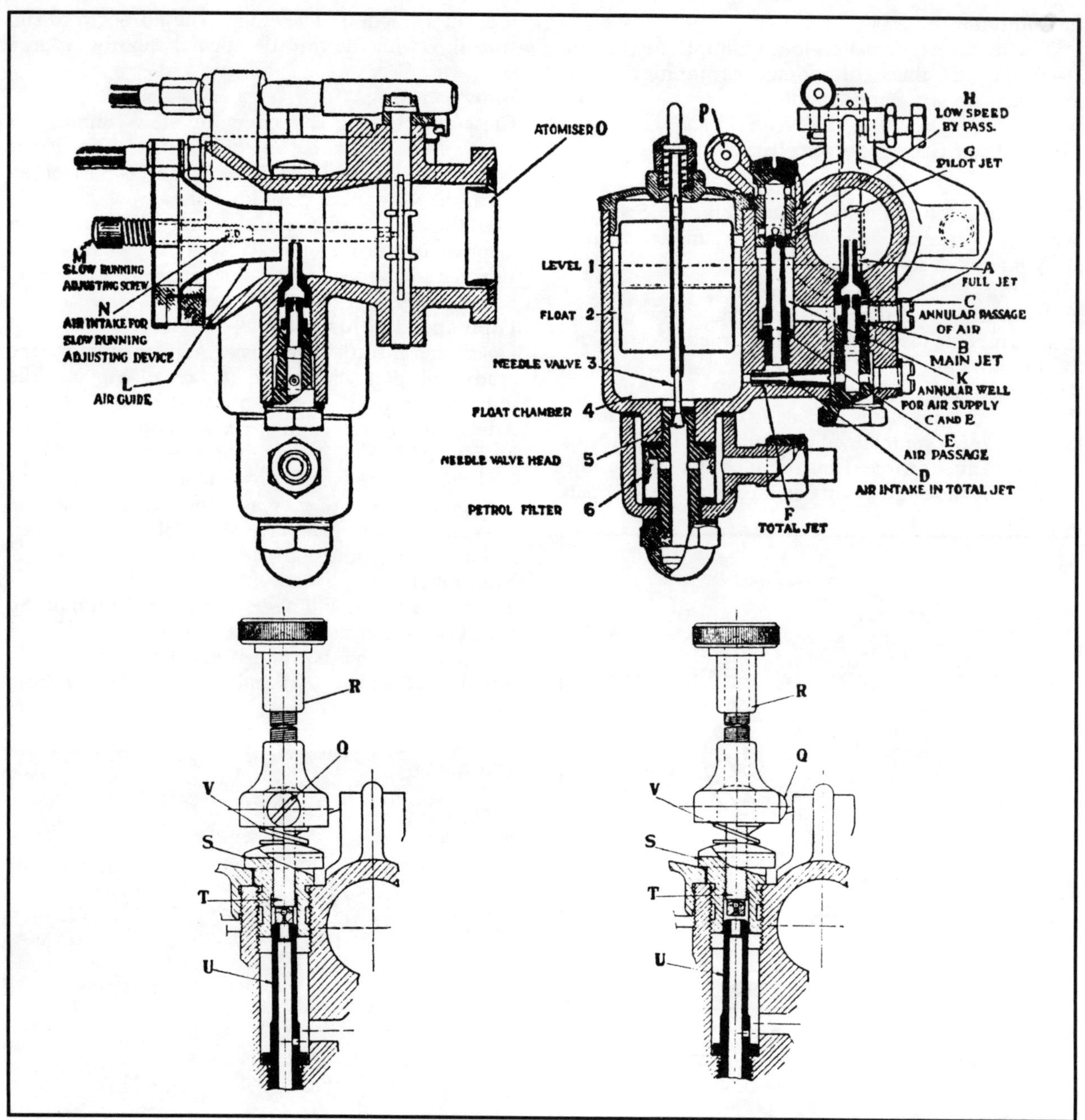

Above: Sectional views of the Bowden carburettor.

Below: Bowden carburettor (Type B) starting device. In the left-hand view, the control knob R is shown in the normal position. On the right it is set rich for starting from cold.

---

and improved fuel economy; whether some of these claims were real or a figment of the imagination is open to conjecture.

There were two basic types, the A and B; on type A the starting control is on the handlebars and on the B the adjusting knob is on the carburettor itself. The Bowden is similar in principle to car carburettors, having a butterfly valve and separate jets. There are four jets; main, pilot, total and full. The latter pair are fixed to suit the particular engine. Tuning is normally confined to adjusting the throttle stop screw and slow-running speed (M in the sectional view).

Slow-running adjustment (Type A)

To adjust for easy starting turn the adjusting screw M as far in as it will go. Open the twistgrip a fraction, not too far or there will be insufficient suction on the pilot jet. The mixture control lever should then be moved to the closed position (for cold starting), which closes the air intake P, in turn enrichening the pilot mixture.

Tickle the carburettor, start up and run the

engine for a short while to warm it up. Move the mixture control to the normal position (open) and decrease the revs to tick-over speed. Adjust the throttle stop screw if necessary.

Gradually unscrew the adjustment screw M, which weakens the mixture by opening a pilot air intake. When the engine has achieved a steady beat, cease turning the screw and readjust the throttle stop screw for a slow tick-over.

If the engine refuses to run smoothly and all the signs of a weak pilot mixture are there, even when the pilot adjusting screw is right home, it may mean a larger pilot jet is needed. Possibly the pilot jet is blocked.

Power-adjustment (Types A & B)

Give the machine a blast on a long straight road, cut the ignition and close the throttle. Check the plug colour for a weak or rich mixture. A whitish look indicates the former and if the plug nose is sooty, a rich mixture is evident. Fit the appropriate larger or smaller jet. As Bowden jets are thin on the ground these days it may be necessary to resort to a little bodgery, as outlined in the Triumph carburettor section.

Cold starting (Type B)

Open the throttle approximately 1/16 in and turn the starting device knob to the RICH position. Depress the tickler for a couple of seconds, start up, and return the knob to the NORMAL position.

Warm starting (Type B)

Do not flood the carburettor. Leave the knob in the NORMAL position and start up.

Maintenance

Float level is set and should never need altering — fortunately there are no permutations of floats, as is the case with Amac and B & B carburettors.

Flooding is usually caused by dirt trapped under the needle seating; remove the chamber lid and base, clean the seating and petrol filter. Check for a punctured float or bent needle.

Due to multifarious jet passageways there is always a strong possibility of fuel blockages within. For this reason the petrol filter in the float chamber base-union should not be left out. If blockage does occur, remove the two cheese-headed screws on the side of the mixing chamber and blow out the passageways with an airline or tyre pump.

Amal carburettors with separate float chambers and Monobloc types

As mentioned at the beginning of this chapter, potential sources of air leaks should be attended to before attempting to tune the carburettor. In the case of the common Amal zinc-alloy bodied carburettor the point about flange distortion deserves special attention.

There are two types of pre-Monobloc, one where the primary air to the main jet and pilot jet enter jointly through the main air intake (models 274, 275,

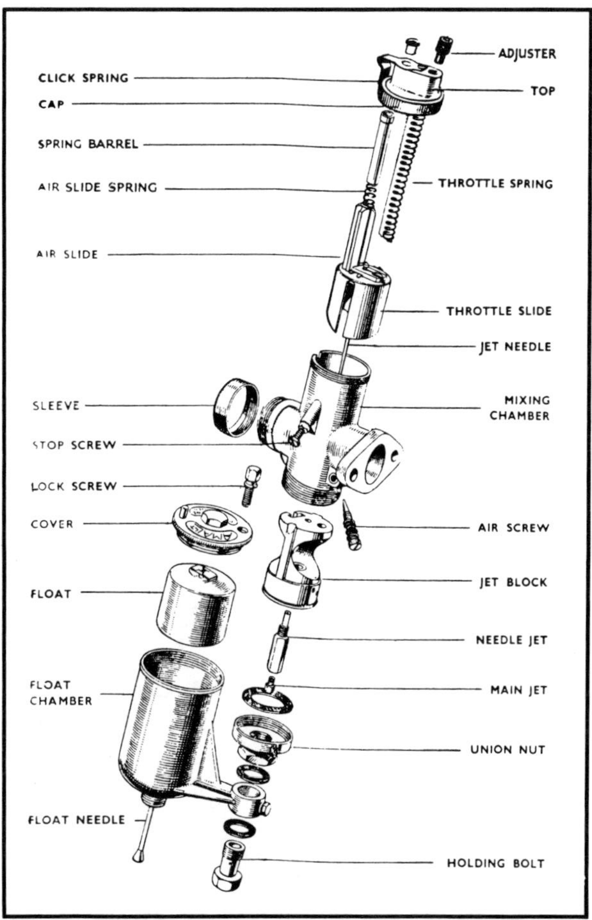

The component parts of the standard (pre-Monobloc) Amal carburettor.

276, 289) and the other where the main jet primary air comes in through four visible ports around the base of the mixing chamber, and where the air supply to the pilot jet is separate (types 74, 75, 76, 89). The pilot jet in pre-Monoblocs is embodied in the jet block whereas that in the Monobloc is separate and sealed by a cover nut.

The procedure for tuning pre-Monobloc and Monobloc carburettors is identical therefore the following notes apply to both types.

1st stage: Main jet

Test at full throttle with the bike underway. If the engine runs heavily (lumpy) at full throttle the main jet is too big. Verify by checking the sparking plug in the following manner; after a fast run de-clutch and stop the engine quickly, whip out the plug and examine the end. If sooty the mixture is too rich. Fit a smaller jet.

All main jets are numbered — the larger the number the more fuel is metered. Monobloc jets are not interchangeable with those in pre-Monobloc carburettors.

If power seems better at less than full throttle, or with the air lever slightly closed, the main jet is probably too small. A whitish appearance on the

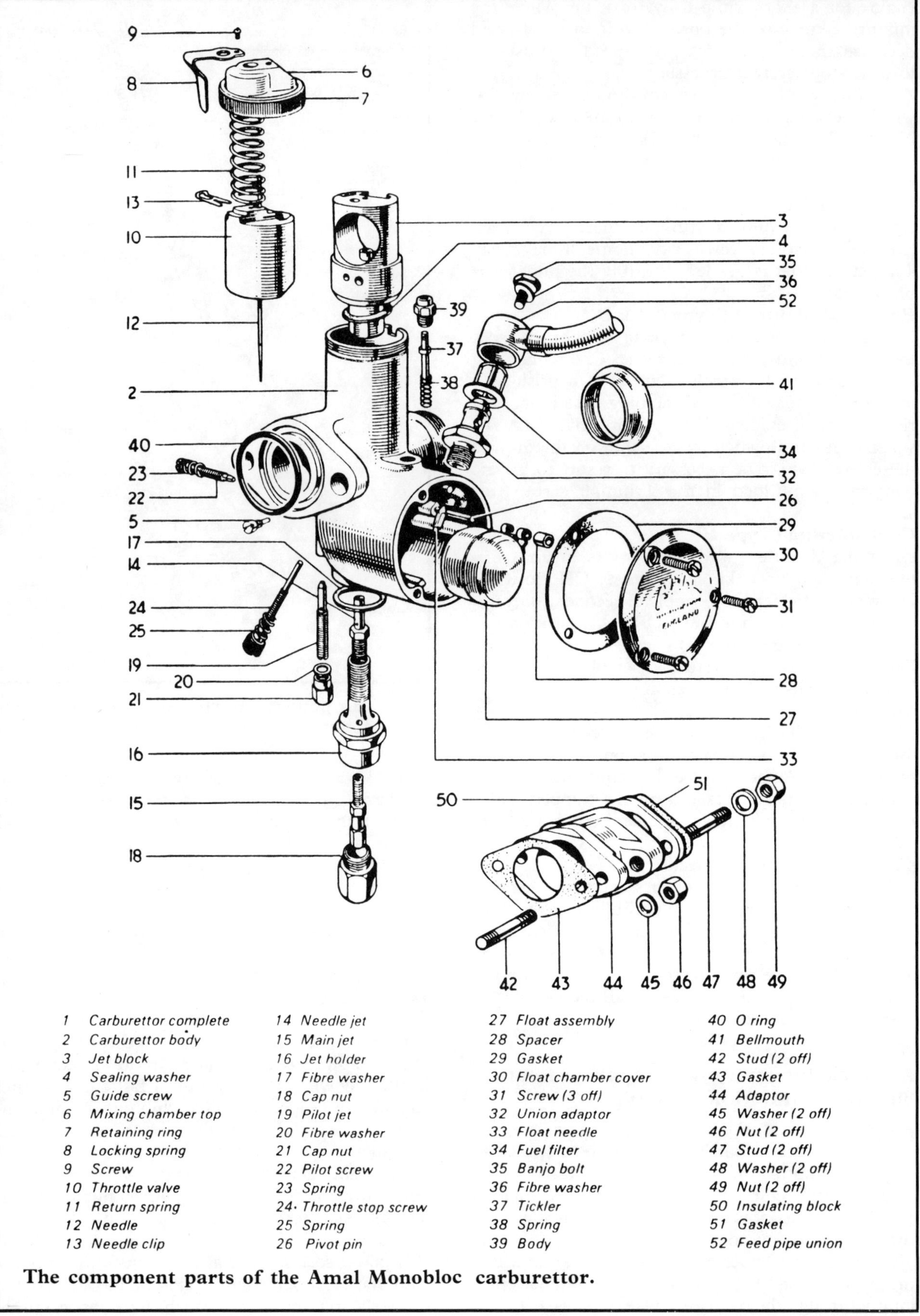

The component parts of the Amal Monobloc carburettor.

plug tip will confirm a weak mixture. Fit a larger jet.

2nd stage: Pilot jet

Set the engine idling fast with the twist grip shut off and with the slide on the throttle stop screw (ignition retarded). Loosen the stop screw nut and screw down the throttle stop until the engine runs slower and begins to falter, then screw the pilot air screw in or out to make the engine run steadily. Lower the throttle stop screw a fraction and adjust the pilot air screw once again until a steady tick-over is achieved. It may be necessary to repeat the sequence before an even beat is gained. Lock the throttle stop screw. It is difficult to give a definite ruling on how many turns open to set the pilot air screw. All engines, even two identical ones of the same make, differ in their requirements. Generally, however, the setting will be no less than 3/4 of a turn and no more than 1 1/2 out.

3rd stage: Throttle cutaway

If, as you take off from the idling position the engine spits back, try enrichening the pilot mixture by screwing in the adjuster a touch. If this does not prove effective, return it to its original position and fit a slide with a smaller cut-away.

The amount of cut-away is marked on top of the slide, thus on a pre-Monobloc slide the figure 6/3 means a number 6 slide with a number 3 cut-away. The next size larger cut-away would be a 6/4, and so on. Monobloc slides are numbered 376/3, 376/4 etc.

If the engine appears to run lumpily when the throttle slide comes into effect, it may be that a throttle slide with a larger cut-away is needed (to weaken the mixture) or the needle is set too high.

4th stage: Needle adjustment

The needle controls a wide range of throttle openings and influences the acceleration. Try the needle in as low a position as possible, ie with the clip in a groove as near the top as possible. If the acceleration is poor and with the air slide partially closed the results are better, raise the needle a couple of grooves. If this makes things better, try dropping it one groove and test the machine.

Needle jets wear over a prolonged period but needles seem to last indefinitely. A new needle jet sometimes makes an enormous difference to the petrol consumption — another ten or fifteen miles per gallon might be gained from an old carburettor.

Remember — raising the needle enrichens the mixture and lowering it weakens it.

Needles and needle jets are marked; the numbers should tally with the machine maker's specification and there is no need to deviate from this, except when changing over to alcohol fuel.

Summary

To cure richness:

1st Stage: Fit a smaller jet
2nd Stage: Screw out pilot air screw
3rd Stage: Fit a slide with a larger cut-away
4th Stage: Lower needle one or two grooves

To cure weakness:

1st Stage: Fit a larger main jet
2nd Stage: Screw in pilot air screw
3rd Stage: Fit a slide with a smaller cut-away
4th Stage: Raise needle one or two grooves

Float Problems

A carburettor which persistently floods may suffer from any of the following faults:

(a) dirt under the float needle
(b) punctured float
(c) bent float needle (pre-Monobloc models)
(d) fuel level too high (more likely with pre-Monoblocs)
(e) float chamber canted over (clip-fitting pre-Monoblocs)

Punctured floats can be repaired by soldering the affected area, although it is all too easy to make a mess of things and end up with more leaks than you started with! Use a small electric iron and *Baker's Fluid*. The repair can be tested by immersing the float in near boiling water, when bubbles will issue forth from the damaged spot if there is still a leak.

Float needles wear, developing ridges on their seatings, but it is not worth trying to rectify the damage by lapping as replacements are easily obtained (at least for the foreseeable future).

Cables

Both control cables should be adjusted with the minimum amount of backlash and there should be no signs of fraying. These points may seem obvious but it is surprising how many so-called concours machines fall down on such small details. Oil the cables occasionally and if possible fit a nylon-lined cable on the throttle control (it is sometimes possible to thread a nylon lining into the old type of fabric-covered outer to maintain originality).

If a throttle cable breaks miles away from civilisation try wiring up the air control cable to the throttle slide, using the air lever as a throttle. Although you may not achieve perfect control, at least it will get you home. Another bodge is to strip off the cable outer, loop the inner wire over your knee and tie the end to the tank cap, or some other part of the bike, and drive home with a knee-operated throttle.

Finishing the body

Amal carburettors of the zinc-based alloy type were never highly polished as we see at today's concours events. Pre-Monoblocs were usually coated with a matt creamy-silver finish on the alloy parts. This can be reproduced, to most restorers' satisfaction at any rate, by spraying with a modern car aerosol cellulose.

The carburettor should be dismantled completely and all holes blocked off with corks, wooden dowels etc; the body and float chamber are then lightly grit-blasted to help key the paint. Thoroughly clean the parts and remove all traces of grit with a

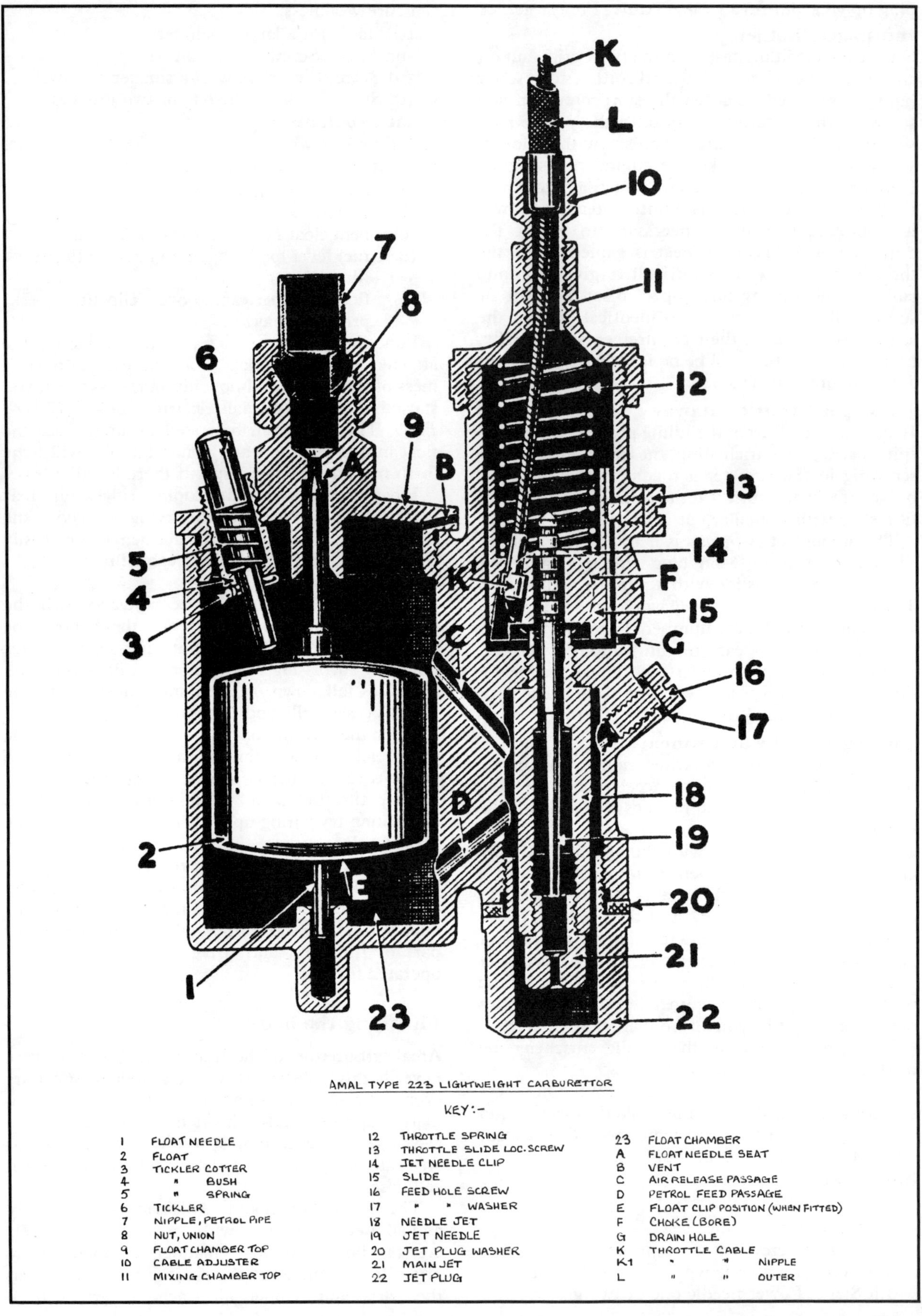

AMAL TYPE 223 LIGHTWEIGHT CARBURETTOR

high-pressure air-line. Apply a cellulose etch-primer and two coats of aerosol silver. Car makers change colour shades like they change their socks so it is difficult to specify a particular shade — however, at the time of writing a finish such as *Vauxhall Silver Starmist*, or *Silver Fox* is suitable. There are of course many other similar paints available at Halfords branches.

Will the finish stain? The answer is — yes, eventually, just as it did when the carb was made! If you want to retain an as-new finish then don't start the engine, just store the bike away as a lifeless exhibit in one of the many collections that are springing up worldwide.

The Amal lightweight carburettor (Type 223)

A single-wire device, usually with air cleaner and strangler, the Type 223 was fitted to many lightweight motorcycles of around 125 cc.

Mixture control

A normal Amal main jet is fitted (with a jet number of around 65 to 85 depending on the type of engine) which supplies full-power control. Mixture is fed through a needle jet above the main jet and a tapered needle controls strength at lower throttle openings.

The needle is adjustable for height, being clipped in normal Amal fashion to the main slide, although the spring clip shape is circular in the case of the 223.

The float chamber is combined with the mixing chamber as one zinc-based alloy casting but the internal details are quite conventional. Float needles are fairly short (top feed) and suffer from taper-seat wear. The float level is fixed. Float chamber lids differ in minor details (union thread diameters and tickler dimensions) on various machines. Some lids are fixed with two screws and others are threaded. Most Type 223s were top-feed but bottom-feed was available when requested.

There were similar lightweight carburettors in the Amal range (259, 261 etc.) but their action was identical in most respects therefore the sequence of tuning for the Type 223 will suffice for these models also.

Idling

In the idling position at very small throttle openings the mixture is controlled by means of the parallel portion of the needle. This enters the needle jet and provides a restriction.

Mid-speed range

This is controlled by the throttle valve and tapered needle, as in larger Amal models. A weak mixture in the intermediate stages between the pilot stage and main jet operation can be rectified by raising the needle a notch or two.

Needle position has a significant effect on these small carburettors and it is not advisable to run small two-stroke machines on weak mixtures for long. When running-in, a richer mixture is recommended to prevent the engine from overheating and partially seizing.

Most lightweight machines spend their lives being thrashed on three-quarters to full throttle therefore adjustment of needle position and main jet will always produce satisfactory results.

A weak mixture will result in the engine popping-back or hesitating and can be cured by raising the needle, as mentioned, or fitting a larger main jet if the trouble occurs at full throttle. A plug check will verify mixture strength (refer to pre-Monobloc/Monobloc Amal instructions).

Needleless Amals

Earlier lightweight Amals, as fitted to small capacity motorcycles (eg. Coventry-Eagle, 150 cc Royal Enfield, New Imperial etc) and many industrial machines, had no mixture needle.

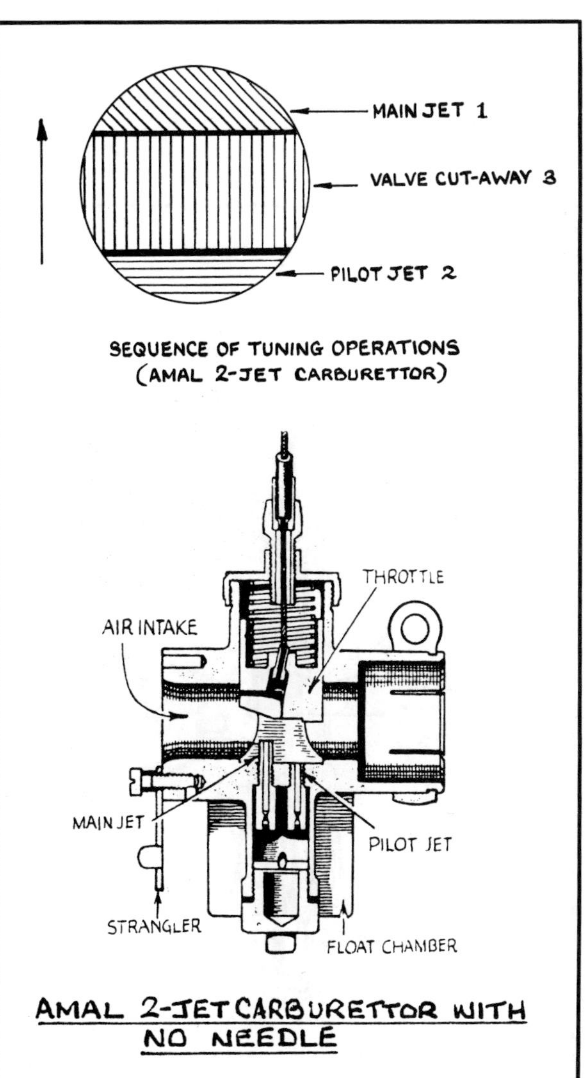

A sectioned view of the Amal lightweight carburettor.

Working on the two-jet Binks principle, a main jet and pilot jet are situated in the mixing chamber bore. Together with the throttle valve cut-away these jets control the mixture from idling to full throttle. Results are surprisingly good. Providing the jet and slide combination is correct there will be no discernible difference in the action of needleless Amal and that of a post-war needle-jet Amal.

The main jet is the tall one, situated nearest the air intake. Under touring conditions this should be correct with the air lever 1/4 closed; on a warm day the lever can be opened fully when flat-out. Most two-jet Amals were of the single-wire type with a manually-operated air strangler (in the form of a shutter) on the intake. In this case the strangler should be closed for starting and fully opened for normal running, a suitable main jet size being chosen for full throttle conditions. The smallest pilot jet consistent with good idling should be chosen but if a flat spot is experienced when opening-up from the idling position an increase in size is indicated.

Weakness at 3/8 to 5/8 throttle can be rectified by fitting a valve with less cutaway. Cutaways range from number 0 (flat-bottomed) to number 5, which has a 5/16 in chamfer.

Swapping a post-war carb. for a pre-war type

Owners of "fifteen shillings tax" utility lightweights of the 1933-35 period may be interested in the following hint.

The post-war lightweight Amal, as fitted to BSA Bantams, had similar stub-fitting dimensions to their pre-war 2-jet ancestors. The later Amal can therefore be fitted to an early machine; in order for it to resemble a 2-jet model some faking is necessary. Outwardly, the two carburettors are very similar except for the air strangler arrangement. The Bantam-type air cleaner should be removed and substituted by a small machined flange, to which a pivoting air-flap is fixed. (Copy the pre-war design).

The fake carburettor will hardly be noticed, and spares are readily obtained for the later model.

Racing carburettors, GP, RN, and TT Amal

All racing Amal carburettors have air slides contained within separate housings on the side of the main bodies. On the GP model the needle is outside of the main choke area but still within the throttle

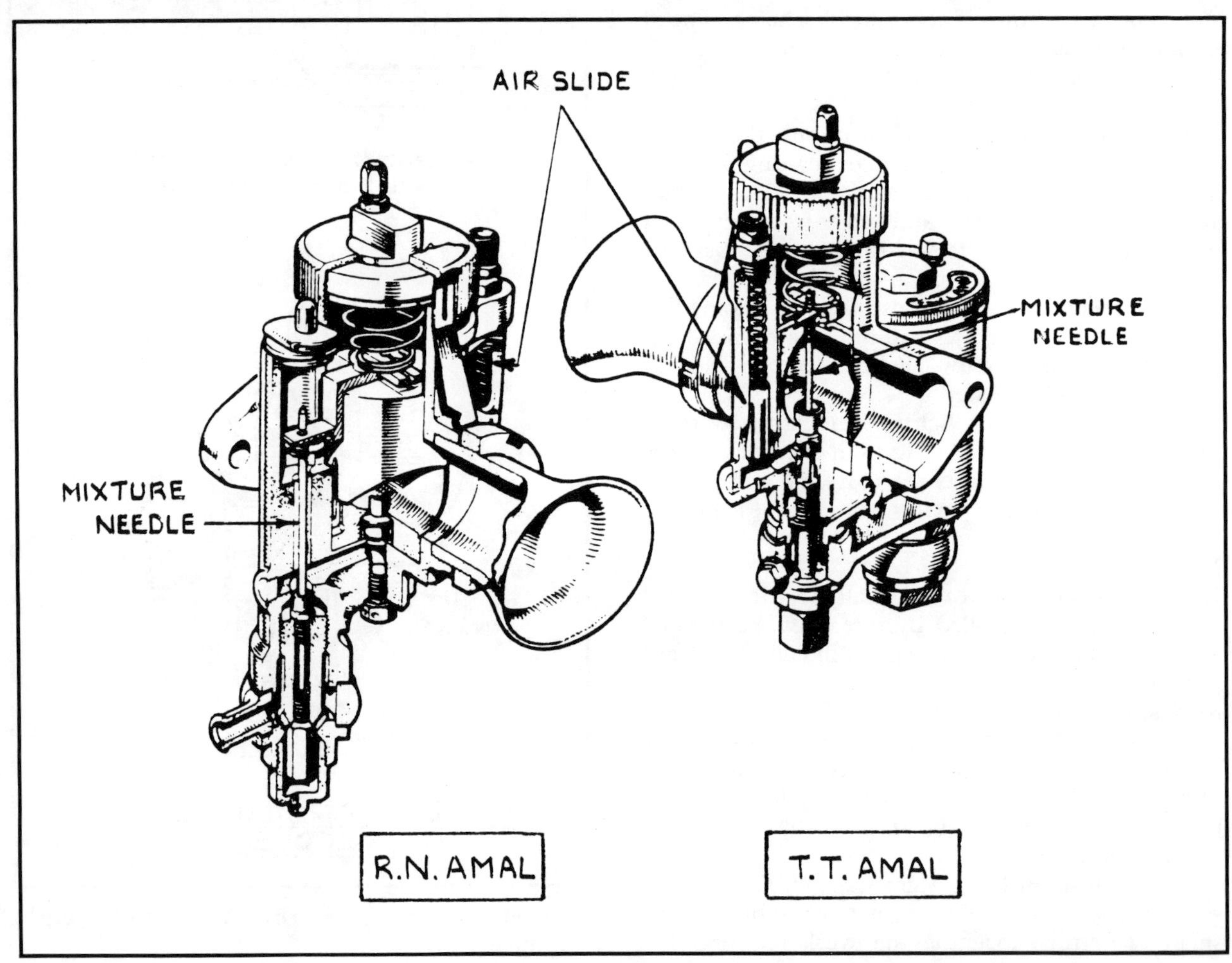

slide; the RN type features a mixture needle operating in its own housing.

As far as tuning is concerned there is no basic difference in the sequence of operation of TT, GP, and RN types. One point to bear in mind is that the pilot adjuster works the opposite way to standard Amals. The screw controls fuel, not air, therefore turning the screw outwards enrichens the mixture.

Main jet
Test the machine on a straight road at high revs, cut the engine, declutch and inspect the plug. The correct colour should resemble that of milk chocolate with a slight hint of grey on the electrode tip. A white appearance will indicate a weak mixture, and black richness.

All the racing types mentioned have the desirable feature of a remote mixture control which, because of its location, does not obstruct the carburettor bore. Thus the air lever can be used as a compensating device when experimenting with jet sizes. Closing the air valve will enrichen the mixture, so if the engine runs better with it shut it is an indication that the main jet is too small.

Pilot adjustment
Bear in mind the earlier remarks about pilot adjustment screws on racing models. Adjust until a reasonably slow rate of running is achieved. There is not much point in obtaining a steam-engine tickover with a racing engine if it spits and cuts-out as soon as the throttle is yanked open. Err on the side of richness, and make sure the initial take-off is good.

Slide cutaway
The amount of slide cut-away controls mixture strength from low openings up to around the half-throttle mark, so if there are signs of weakness fit a valve with a smaller cut-away. Cut-aways go up in 1/16 in increments, so have a number of slides to hand when tuning. Although the makers would not be happy with the idea, slides can be filed on the leading edges. It's not quite so easy to put metal back on if the experiment proves unsuccessful!

If a megaphone is substituted for a straight-through pipe, the settings will be entirely different and the whole tuning sequence must be repeated. With a megaphone the cut-away is usually reduced and the needle may need lowering a notch or two.

Needle position
As with standard Amals, raising the needle enrichens the mixture. Symptoms of excessive richness in the intermediate range (above half-throttle) are lumpy running and general flatness. To some extent cut-away and needle settings are interlinked. It is often necessary to go back to the previous stage after adjusting needle height.

Taking the DB32 Gold Star BSA as a typical example, TT carburettor settings are:- throttle slide no. 7, needle position 3 for touring purposes. When racing on petrol with a GP carburettor the settings would be: throttle slide no. 5, needle position 4.

Flooding
Flooding is invariably caused by grit under the float needle seating but a punctured float is occasionally encountered.

Remote-mounted float chambers are usually fitted to prevent frothing, a mysterious malady brought on by vibration and which can result in loss of revs, at the most inopportune moment. The chamber is usually suspended from a Silentbloc rubber-bonded mounting attached to a convenient bracket in the vicinity of the tank fixings. The flexible pipe connecting the chamber to the carburettor body should be as short as possible, and correct float level should be observed.

SU carburettors

The motorcycle type MC2 SU carburettor is of the variable-choke, variable jet orifice pattern originally evolved for cars.

Needle sizes are specified for motorcycle types and there is no need to stray from the manufacturer's recommendations. (The only deviation from this rule is when changing over to alcohol fuels). To verify the needle type, remove the suction chamber, slacken the side needle screw and withdraw the needle. Identification will be found on the flat tip or shank. If, for some reason, mixture strength is suspect then the needle alone should be changed; the jets fitted (providing the carburettor has not been got-at by a previous owner) are set by the makers for the machine in question.

The needle is fitted with the end of the parallel shoulder flush with the piston bottom face. The jet adjusting nut is for idling corrections.

Piston assembly
To detach the suction chamber and piston unit remove the oil cap. Take out the two cheese-head side screws. Lift the suction chamber slightly, insert one hand underneath to depress the piston (upwards) and carefully lift the assembly clear. Some juggling may be required if the carburettor is in situ, so be careful not to bend the needle.

When replacing the unit hold the piston up initially and then guide it into the main jet as the plunger sinks home. A slot in the smaller diameter piston engages with a nib in the body.

Tuning
Warm the engine up. Adjust the idling by means of the throttle stop screw, making fine adjustments with the jet adjustment nut. Screwing the nut up weakens the mixture. Move it one flat at a time, applying slight downward pressure on the jet lever. Three flats in either direction is normally satisfactory; any more might indicate an induction pipe leak, or possibly an ignition fault.

A rich idling mixture will result in lumpy running with black emission from the exhaust; a *Colourtune* analyser is useful in determining incorrect mixture strength at low revs.

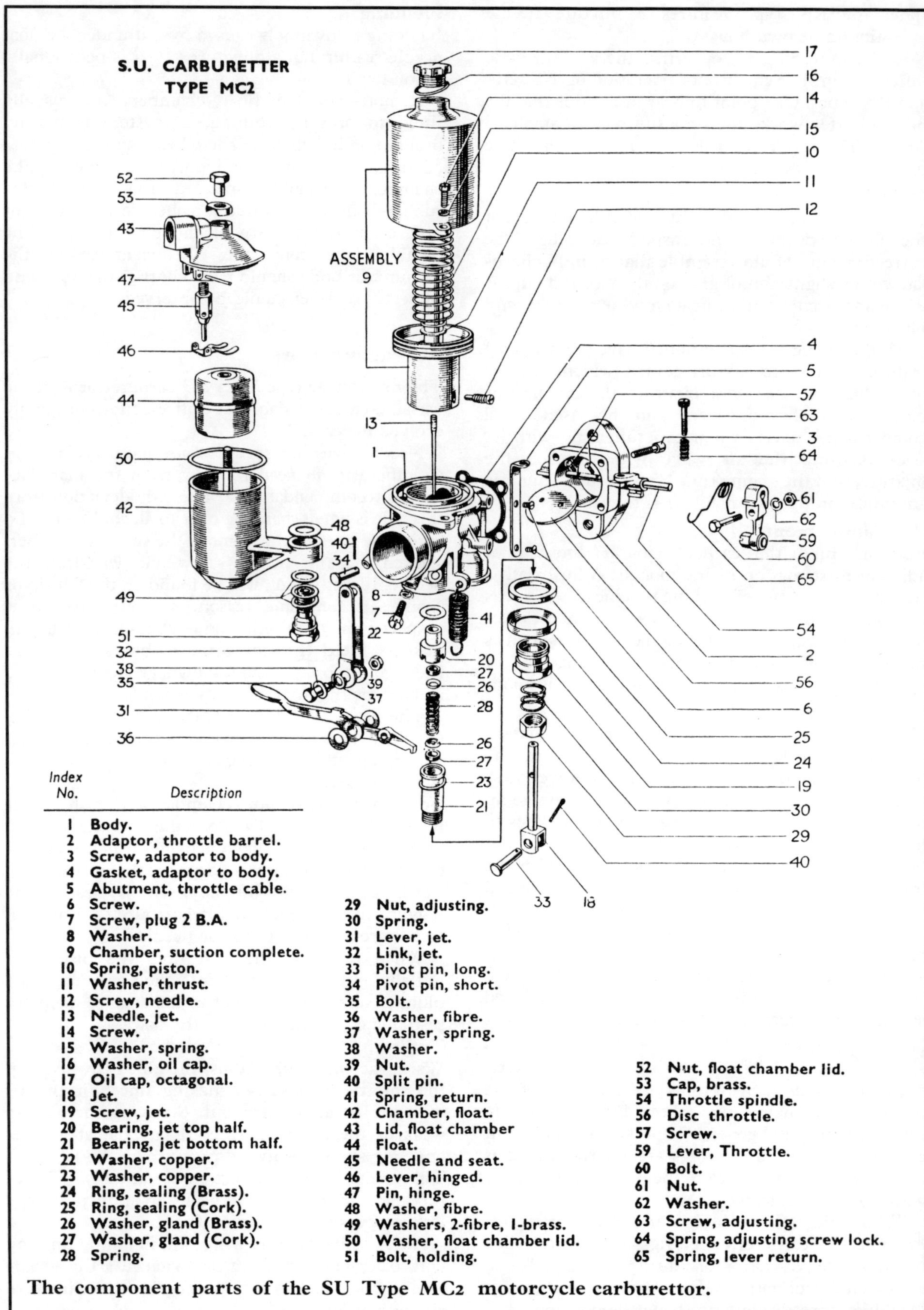

The component parts of the SU Type MC2 motorcycle carburettor.

Sticking piston

To test for a sticking piston, remove the air cleaner and poke your finger in the carburettor mouth; lift the piston slightly — it should drop with a click. If it seems to move lethargically, lower the jet by means of the lever and try again.

A sticking piston will cause poor slow running, stalling at traffic lights etc., and can also result in a lack of power and poor fuel consumption figures.

The trouble is almost certainly due to one of the following:

1 Dirt on the piston
2 Contact between piston and suction chamber
3 Sticking of piston rod in its bush
4 Needle binding on the jet

Dealing with the above points in order, a dirty piston (1) and suction chamber should be meticulously cleaned in thinners or petrol. Do **not** use emery tape! Assemble dry, with oil on the piston rod only.

If there is contact between the piston and chamber (2), slackening of the two fixing screws and moving the chamber a fraction to one side (a thou or two only) usually does the trick. If there is a pronounced high spot this can be removed with a scraper — **but go easy!**

A sticking piston rod (point 3) is invariably due to grit particles introduced into the oil. Clean it and recharge with thin machine oil. Check the oil level occasionally and ensure that the cap (with joint washer) is securely in place. A leaking cap can cause a rich mixture (strange though this may seem). The automatic piston action is impaired so giving less main air in proportion to fuel required.

Point 4 is a common occurrence in carburettors which have passed through many hands. Normally the jet needle should not contact the jet bore when all is well. If it is found that sticking is reduced or eradicated altogether when the jet is lowered, this is a sure sign that a binding needle is the culprit.

The needle may be bent — a pronounced shiny spot on one side, together with an oval jet, signifies either misalignment or an incorrectly centred main jet.

Re-centring the main jet

Firstly, try turning the jet round 180 degrees. This sometimes works if the lever has been connected up with the jet in a different position to that in which it was originally centred. If not, proceed as follows:

1 Screw the jet adjusting nut up as far as it will go, the jet head being raised to contact it so the jet is as high as possible.
2 Slacken the locking screw which releases the jet and bush assembly; these should now to able to move sideways.
3 Raise the piston and allow it to drop. Repeat. This action should move the jet centrally, the needle budging it over a fraction.

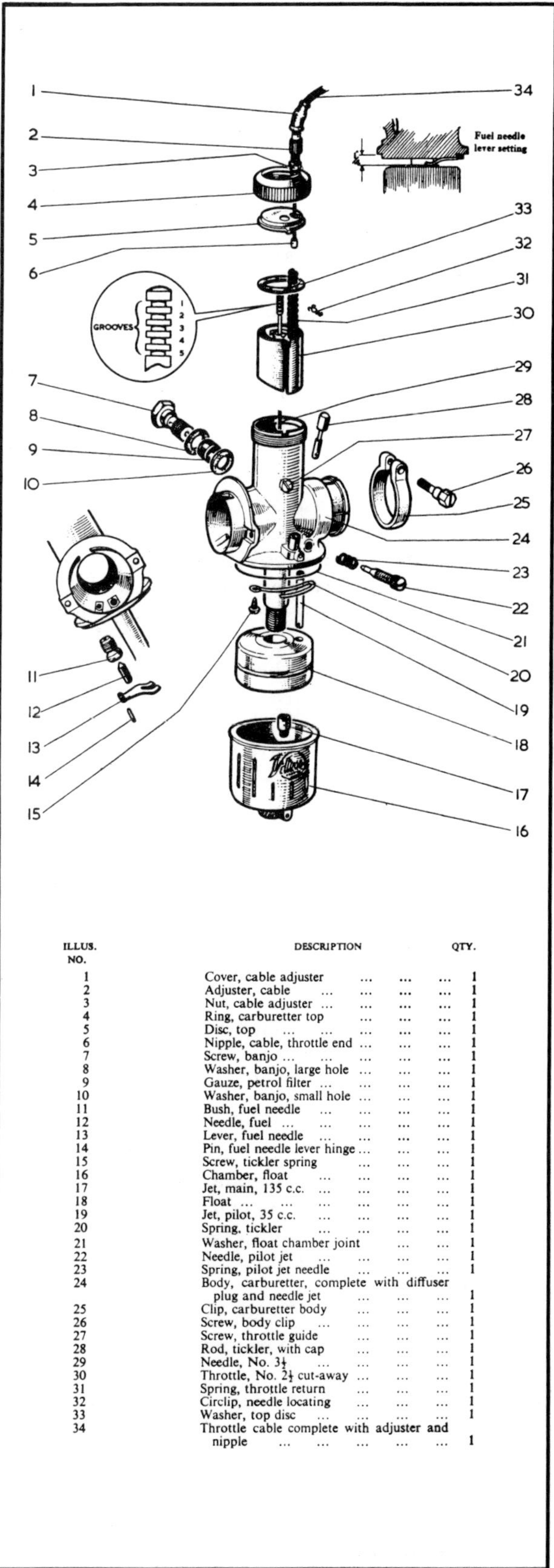

ILLUS. NO.	DESCRIPTION	QTY.
1	Cover, cable adjuster	1
2	Adjuster, cable	1
3	Nut, cable adjuster	1
4	Ring, carburetter top	1
5	Disc, top	1
6	Nipple, cable, throttle end	1
7	Screw, banjo	1
8	Washer, banjo, large hole	1
9	Gauze, petrol filter	1
10	Washer, banjo, small hole	1
11	Bush, fuel needle	1
12	Needle, fuel	1
13	Lever, fuel needle	1
14	Pin, fuel needle lever hinge	1
15	Screw, tickler spring	1
16	Chamber, float	1
17	Jet, main, 135 c.c.	1
18	Float	1
19	Jet, pilot, 35 c.c.	1
20	Spring, tickler	1
21	Washer, float chamber joint	1
22	Needle, pilot jet	1
23	Spring, pilot jet needle	1
24	Body, carburetter, complete with diffuser plug and needle jet	1
25	Clip, carburetter body	1
26	Screw, body clip	1
27	Screw, throttle guide	1
28	Rod, tickler, with cap	1
29	Needle, No. 3½	1
30	Throttle, No. 2½ cut-away	1
31	Spring, throttle return	1
32	Circlip, needle locating	1
33	Washer, top disc	1
34	Throttle cable complete with adjuster and nipple	1

The component parts of the Villiers Type S22 carburettor showing the fuel needle lever setting

4 Tighten the locking screw and return the jet to its normal position.
5 See that the piston drops with a click. If it does not, the centring procedure will have to be repeated as the final tightening of the locking screw must have displaced the jet.

Flooding
Usually due to dirt on the needle valve seating. Clean the seating and float bowl. A punctured float, rare in SUs, will also cause flooding. Replace.

Check also the setting of the hinged fork lever. The correct setting is when a 3/8 in diameter rod will slide between the curved portion and the float chamber spigot, with the needle on its seat. (refer to the cross-sectional diagram).

Leakage from around the base of the mixing chamber could be due to a faulty jet gland washer or locking screw washer. Re-centre the jet as described after renewing these parts.

General maintenance points on SUs
Check for manifold leaks by smearing with oil when the engine is running. Bubbles will isolate the leak. Fit new gaskets where necessary.

Check the action of the piston and rod occasionally. Give three drops of machine oil monthly.

Always refit the washer under the plastic cap. Omitting it may cause restricted spindle lift. Don't replace the cap with one off a car (the motorcycle type has no hole).

Don't mess about with the piston spring. Stretching it will upset carburation, so fit a new one if in doubt.

Don't stress the throttle spindle torsion spring beyond its normal travel. It may become coil-bound, restricting throttle movement. (Replace if necessary).

Don't run without the air filter for long periods. It is there for a reason.

Petrol taps

A simple hint to remember regarding Enots push-pull petrol taps can be summed up by the word hexagON. When the hexagonal end is pushed, the tap is ON — the opposite end of the plunger is round and knurled on the edges. Remember — hexag-ON!

When a machine has been standing with a dry tank for a while it is quite normal for the tap to leak slightly. With luck the leak will stop when the cork swells up. If not, a new cork is required. These are still available from specialist dealers (refer to *Classic Bike, The Classic Motor Cycle,* and *Classic Mechan-*

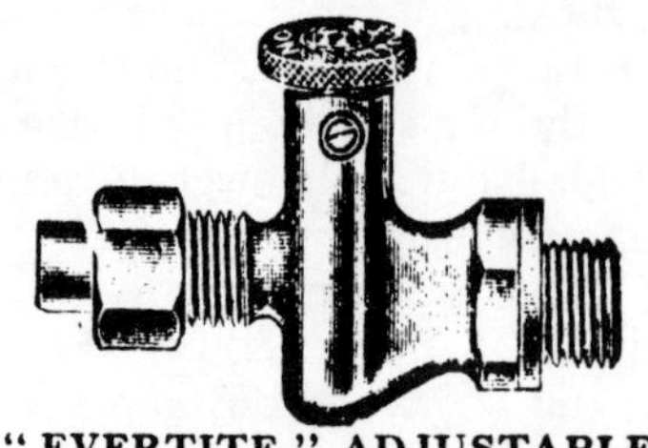

" EVERTITE " ADJUSTABLE CORK-SEATED PETROL TAP.

Screwed ⅛ × ¼ gas or ¼ × ¼ gas. Nickel-plated.
No. **T2/215/*107*** .. .. .. each **2/4**

For commercial vehicles.
Screwed ¼ × ⅜ gas or ⅜ × ⅜ gas. Brass.
No. **T2/215a/*300*** .. .. each **4/-**

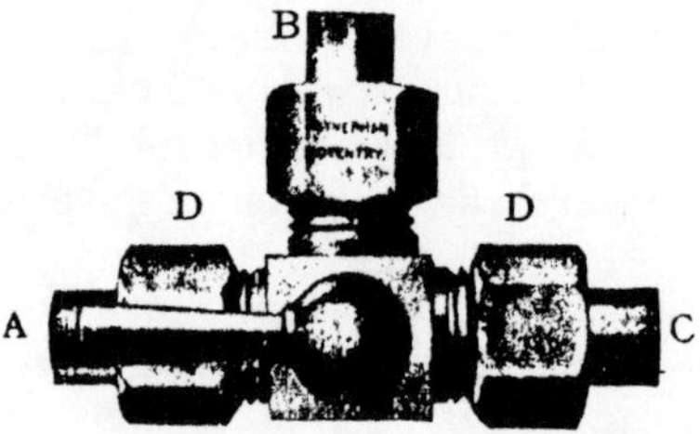

" ROTHERHAM " THREE-WAY ANGLE TAP. No. 44.

When handle is at A, tap is on to A and C from inlet. At B, tap is on C from inlet. At C, tap is on at A and C. At D, tap is shut off.

Nipple ¼ in. liner.
No. **T2/236/*203*** .. .. each **3/-**
„ **T2/236/*2403*** .. per doz. —

Nipple 3/16 in. liner.
No. **T2/237/*203*** .. .. .. each **3/-**
„ **T2/237/*2403*** .. per doz. —

" ROTHERHAM " PETROL TAP (T10).
Brass.
Heavy type, ¼ in. bore.
5/16 in. liner, ¼ in. gas.
No. **T2/225/*105*** .. .. each **1/11**
„ **T2/225/*1605*** .. . per doz. —

A selection of taps. The *Evertite* tap (above left) was familiar to motorcyclists of the post-war years, whilst the Rotheram reserve-level model (below right) dates back at least to 1924 when it was adopted by BSA for their new lightweight 250.

"ROTHERHAM" PETROL TAP (T3).

With collar for tank. Screwed ⅛ in. gas.

¼ in. liner.

No. **T2/211/*101***	.. .. each	**1/5**
„ **T2/211/*1102***	.. per doz.	—

$\frac{5}{16}$ in. liner. Brass.

No. **T2/212/*101***	.. .. each	**1/5**
„ **T2/212/*1107***	.. . per doz.	—

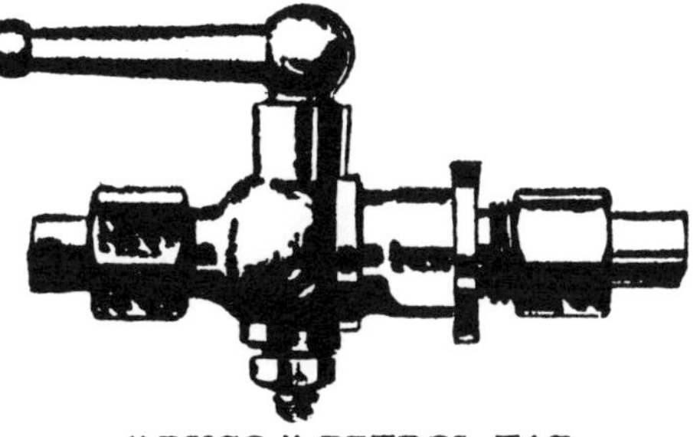

"DUCO" PETROL TAP.

Double union. Brass.

¼ in. gas. ¼ in. liner.

No. **T2/220/*104*** ..	.. .. each	**1/**
„ **T2/220/*1303***	.. per doz.	–

¼ in. gas. $\frac{5}{16}$ in. liner.

No. **T2/221/*101*** ..	.. .. each	**1/**
„ **T2/221/*1109***	.. . per doz.	–

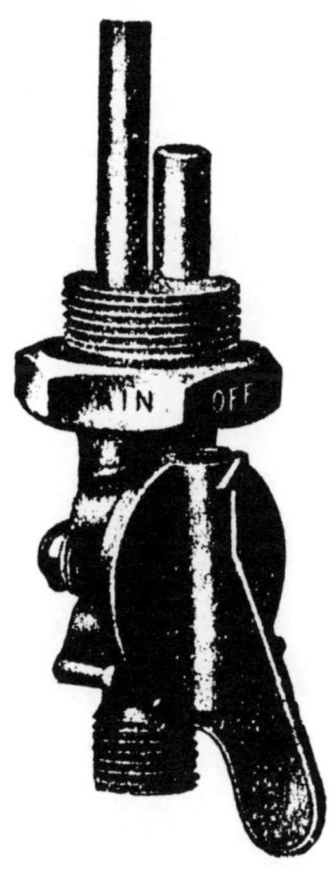

"ENOTS" CORK-SEATED TWO-LEVEL PETROL TAP.

Special Model for Morris.

No. **T2/232/*305*** ..	.. .. each	**4/6**
„ **T2/232/*3600***	.. per doz.	—

Can only be supplied in ⅞ × 20T.

"ROTHERHAM" PETROL TAP.

Two-level type. With cork seat.

Supplied in ¼ in. or ⅜ in. gas for ¼ in. or $\frac{5}{16}$ i pipe.

No. **T2/238/*208***	Brass	.. each	**3/-**
„ **T2/238/*2710***	..	.. per doz.	
„ **T2/238/*210***	N.P.	.. each	**3/6**
„ **T2/238/*3000***	..	.. per doz.	–

ics for addresses). New corks are easily made from wine bottle corks sliced up with a Stanley knife; the centre hole is best burned-in (with a red-hot rod) rather than drilled.

Taper-seat taps are prone to seepage once worn and grinding-in of the seatings is rarely successful. Nothing more abrasive than *Brasso* metal polish should be used — keep withdrawing the tapered portion every few turns to avoid scoring. Ensure that the spring pressure is still maintained after reassembly. It's worth knowing that ships' chandlers and yachting centres still sell the old pattern petrol and oil taps.

Petrol pipe finishes

There is little doubt that plating a copper petrol pipe can induce embrittlement. Regardless of this fact petrol pipes were, almost without exception, plated in some way. In the veteran and vintage period the standard finish was dull or bright (ie. polished) nickel. Later on chromium was used, although cadmium became quite common during the war.

The matter of polished copper petrol and oil pipes has been discussed at length in the motorcycling press over the years. Those for a natural finish claim greater resistance from fatigue cracks. Those against say a copper finish is not original. Both are of course correct — ultimately the choice lies with the restorer.

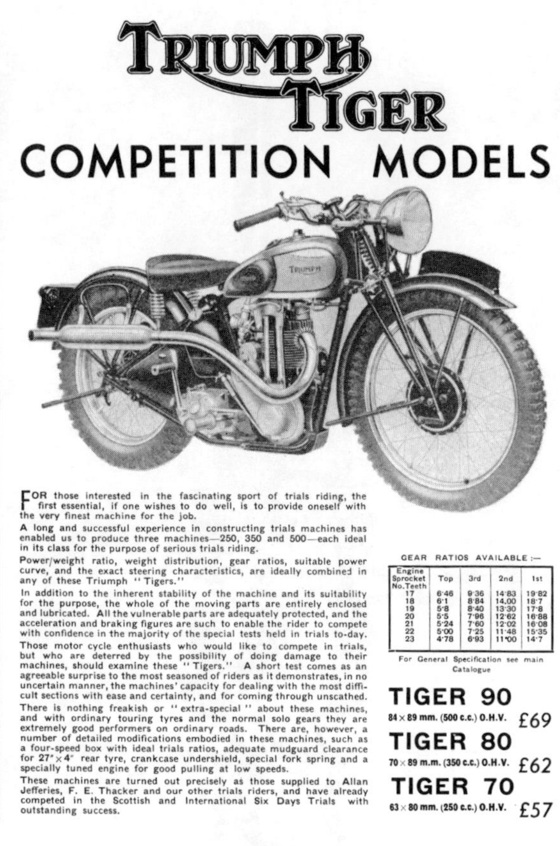

Chapter 7

Electrics

Magnetos, dynamos, magdynos, cvc units, coil ignition, alternators, lighting

Magneto problems

MANY magnetos on offer at autojumbles are of doubtful quality. Some are built up from a variety of parts, not all from the same make of magneto, whilst others are jammed solid through years of idleness. Unless the mag has been rebuilt by a specialist and can be demonstrated to emit cracking sparks it is worth very little.

The cost of a professional overhaul is quite steep as many man-hours are involved. The following notes are intended to assist the reader in carrying out his own preliminary inspection and elementary overhaul of what is usually regarded as a mystifying box of tricks. Magnetos have not changed much in seventy years so the procedure is basically similar if the instrument is a 1911 Bosch or a mid-fifties Lucas.

Rotating armature magnetos are by far the most common type in use and generally give more trouble than the stationary-coil pattern, so it is the former which will receive more attention in the following pages.

Preliminary examination

If the magneto is apparently dead-on-arrival there are a few elementary checks to be carried out as it is foolhardy to expect a machine of unknown origin to perform reliably. Sometimes a bodged mag might produce an occasional feeble spark for the vendor but there is no guarantee such encouraging signs will continue when it is bolted up to the motorcycle.

Let us assume you have bought a magneto and it doesn't spark. Don't worry unduly as the snag may be easily rectified.

A very common problem on 'built-up' magnetos — those which are doctored-up for sale — is for an 'opposite-hand' contact breaker unit to be fitted, so the first thing to check is the direction of rotation of the magneto. This must match your engine, and the contact breaker plate must belong to the magneto in question. Sounds obvious, but it's not always the case.

Somewhere on the magneto body should be an arrow denoting which way its makers intended it to revolve. The contact breaker arm should have a trailing action as the spindle is revolved in the direction of the arrow. An instrument is expressed as being clockwise or anti-clock **as viewed from the driving spindle end**.

Everyone knows that contacts should open and shut, and that the contact arm must touch the cam in order to make this happen. Nevertheless it is surprising how many times hastily-assembled autojumble magnetos do not even fulfil this elementary consideration! It is possible to encounter

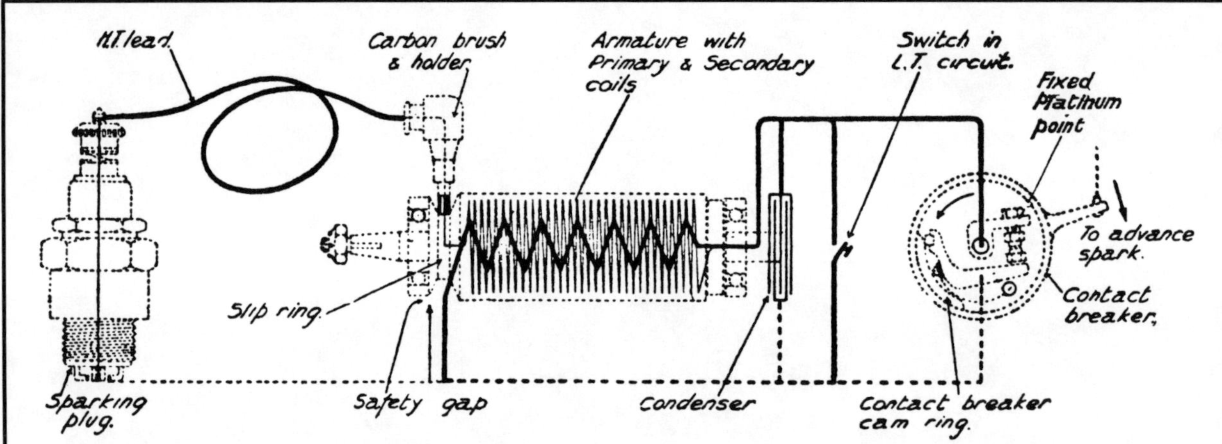

DIAGRAM OF CIRCUITS, ETC., OF A MAGNETO FOR A SINGLE-CYLINDER ENGINE. In the above diagram are shown the essential features of a magneto and the various paths along which the low and high-tension currents flow. The low-tension current is produced in the primary windings on the armature (thick lines). One connection goes to the fixed platinum point, thence across the points when in contact, returning through the metal body of the magneto (dotted lines) to the other end of the primary coil. When the platinum contacts are separated a high voltage current is induced in the secondary coil (thin lines) on the armature, passing via the brass slip-ring, carbon collecting brush, H.-T. lead to the sparking-plug central electrode, across the plug points and back to the secondary winding via the frame of the machine. The switch is not an essential fitting, but may in some cases be considered desirable.

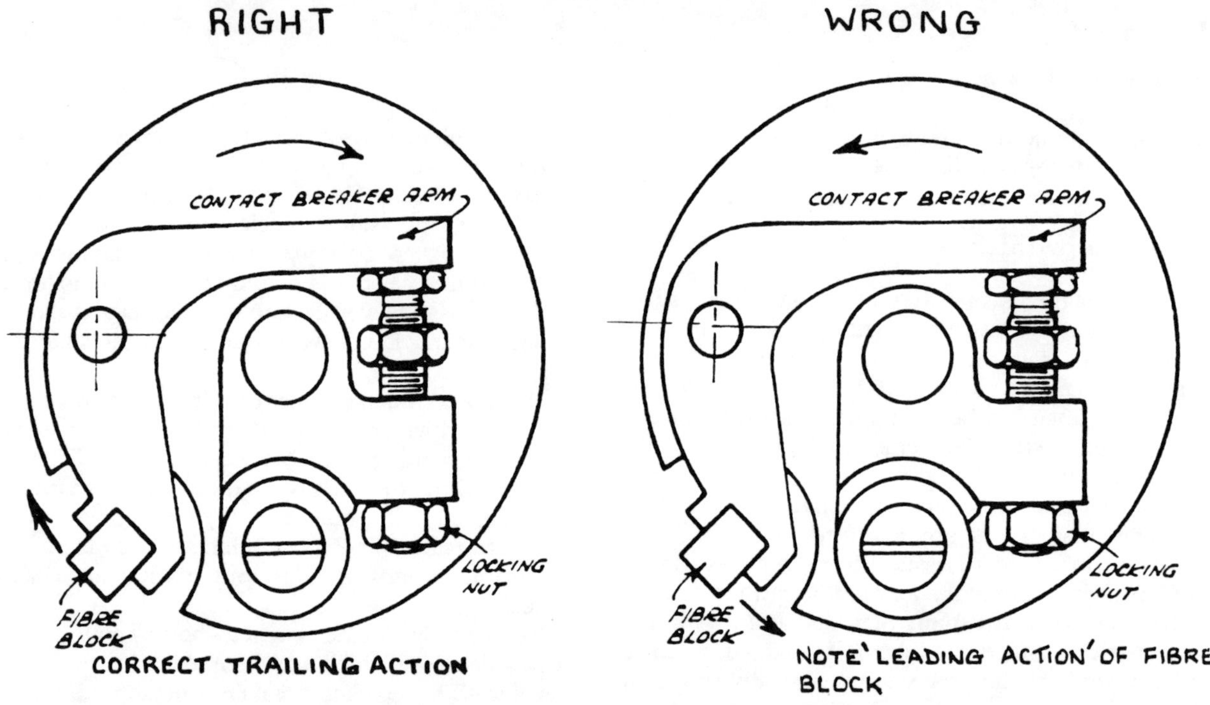

contact breakers which are hopelessly small in overall diameter in which the arm does not touch the cam ring. Obviously therefore, the right-size contact breaker must be fitted and the points should close square to each other.

Face cams

Many round ML and Lucas magnetos have face cams, a form of contact breaker which gives little trouble. Quite often they will spark in either direction without alterations, unlike the ring-cam type, but to alter permanently the mag from clock to anti-clock (or vice-versa) an opposite-hand cam plate is required. These are generally marked L and R. The points unit remains the same.

In times of emergency existing camplates can be altered by cutting new slots in them. The plates are

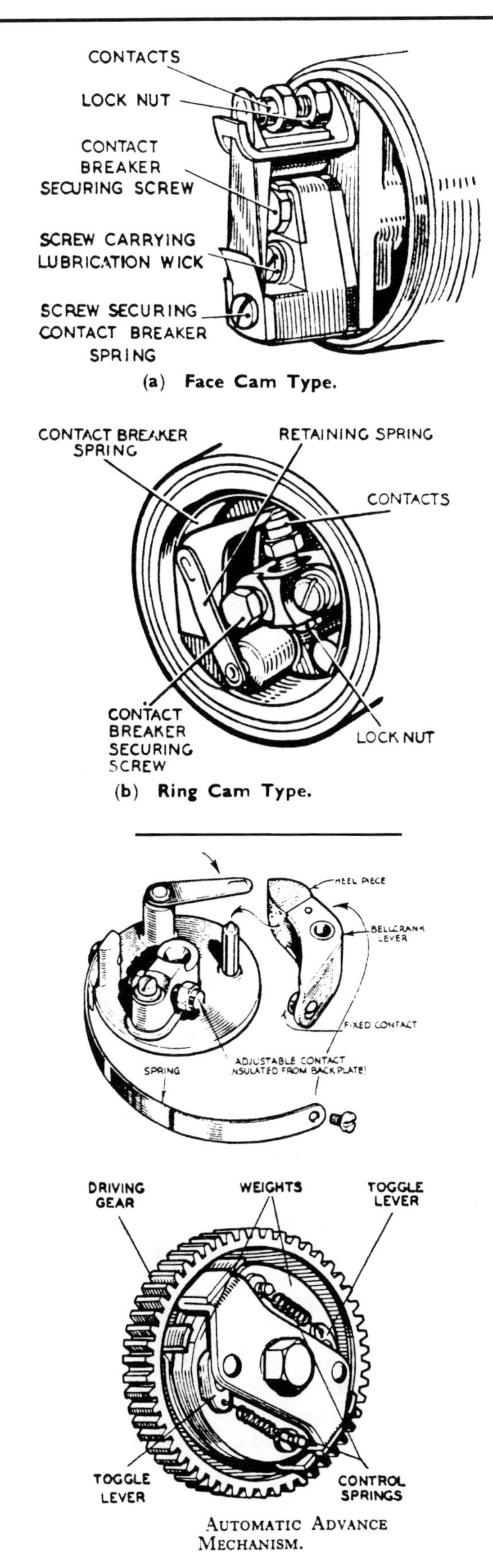

(a) Face Cam Type.

(b) Ring Cam Type.

Automatic Advance Mechanism.

hardened so the slots have to be ground in; this is easily accomplished with a thin metal-cutting abrasive disc fixed to a grinding machine spindle or electric drill.

Face cam contact breakers are easy to work on and require hardly any maintenance. Sometimes the black Bakelite pushrod (which prods the points open) can stick and needs cleaning to restore free movement. Apply a tiny drop of thin oil. During points adjustment go easy when tightening-up as the base metal is very soft and it's all too easy to strip the threaded hole. Almost without exception the points should be set at .012 in (twelve thou) on all face-cam contacts, vintage or modern. Points should be clean (dress with a dead-smooth swiss file or emery paper) and flat, and should close squarely to each other.

When replacing the contact breaker assembly make sure the body engages with the slot in the end of the armature shaft. Apply a drop of thin machine oil to the felt lubricating pad and cam-plate. One small point, often misinterpreted, is that the short spring steel blade which fits on top of the main contact blade should have the turned-up bit facing uppermost.

Internal timing of a magneto

Having checked the points, the relationship between the points-opening position and maximum armature flux must now be ascertained. Twice every revolution of the magneto spindle a maximum flux occurs, irrespective of whether it is a single, twin, or four-cylinder machine.

If the spindle is slowly turned by hand, a definite resistance should be felt when approaching maximum flux, and if you let go of the spindle it should rock backwards again. Remove the contact breaker and the flux positions can be sensed more easily. If the mag can be rotated with no resistance whatsoever this is a sure sign the magnet is tired and will need re-magnetising. The process of re-magnetising only takes a fraction of a second with the right equipment but it will entail a visit to a friendly magneto specialist.

Assuming that the points begin to part **the merest fraction** after maximum flux, on full advance, all is well and it is likely that the correct contact breaker is fitted. When the cam-ring is retarded it will be noticed that the maximum flux position is well past **before** the points begin to open as you can't have it both ways! A stronger spark is always obtained in the full advance position, although most good magnetos perform well over a considerable degree of adjustment.

Above: The two basic types of contact breaker unit.
Centre: A typical contact breaker unit showing the various parts.
Below: An automatic advance unit.

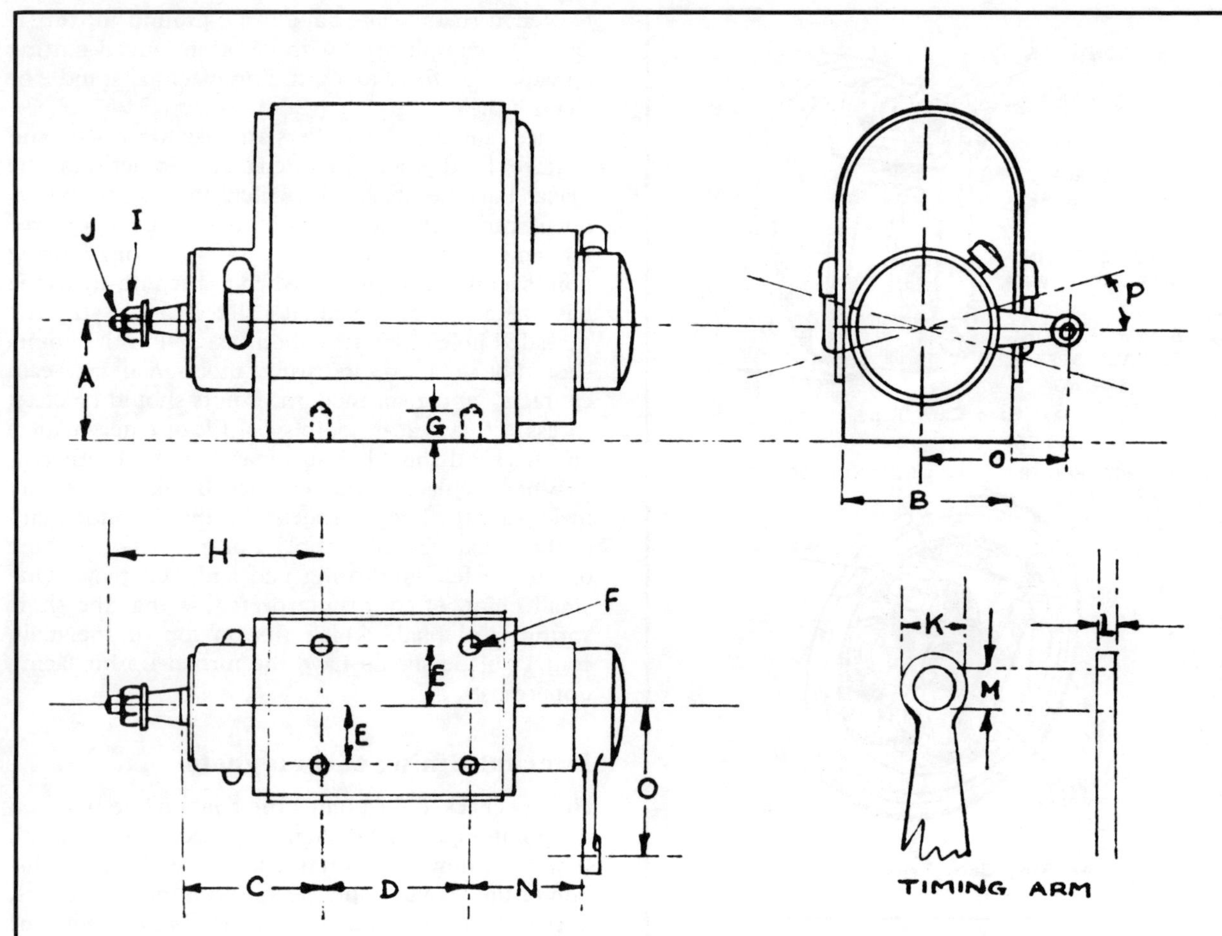

STANDARD PLAN FOR K & M MAGNETOS. (see table)

BRITISH STANDARD	GERMAN STANDARD	SPARKS PER REV.	A	B	C	D	E	F	G	H	I	J	K	L	M	N	O	P
M1	ZA1	1	35	95	59	0	41	9/32" x 19/32"	2 LUGS	67	1.B.A SCREW	1/2"	14	6	1/4"	55 or 35	50	15°
M2	ZA2	2	35	95	59	0	41	"	"	67	"	1/2"	14	6	1/4"		50	15°
Mv	ZAV	2	35	95	59	0	41	"	"	67	"	1/2"	14	6	1/4"		50	15°
K1	ZE1	1	45	75	39.5	50	25	3/16" B.S.W.	11	61.5	5/16" B.S.W.	3/4"	14	6	1/4"	55 or 35	50	15°
K2	ZE2	2	45	75	39.5	50	25		11	61.5		3/4"	14	6	1/4"		50	15°
Kv	ZEv	2	45	75	39.5	50	25		11	61.5		3/4"	14	6	1/4"		50	15°

M1— MIDGET SINGLE CYL. MAGNETOS (UP TO 2½ h.p.): M2— SMALL TWINS: MV— LIGHTWT. 'V' TWINS: K1— STANDARD SINGLE CYL. (3½ to 5 h.p.): K2— STANDARD TWIN SIZE (180°): Kv— 'V' TWINS (6 to 10 h.p.)

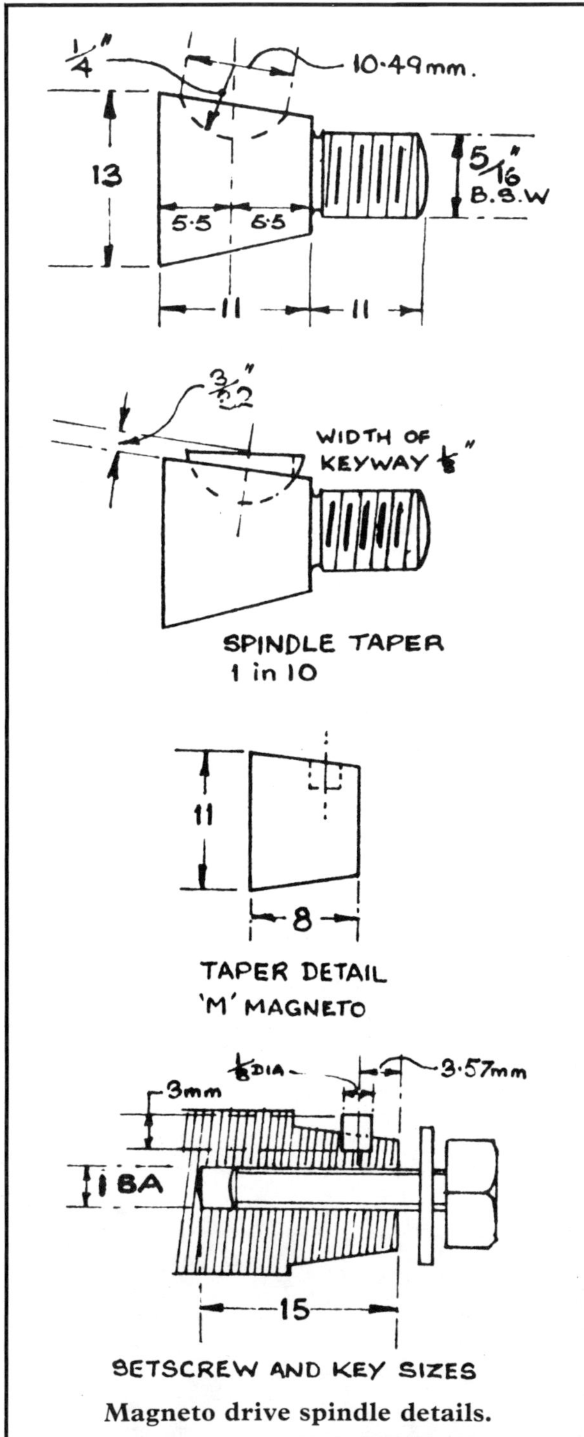

Magneto drive spindle details.

The internal timing of a magneto is very carefully determined by the makers during construction. As stated, there are two maximum flux positions. These occur 180 degrees apart; in a single cylinder machine only one max flux is utilised of course, parallel and V twins (more of which later) use both flux positions. The function of the contact breaker is to close the primary circuit for a certain period; during this period of closure the induced voltage in the primary is rising rapidly to a maximum, therefore there will be a current build-up in the closed primary circuit. When the contacts begin to open a very large voltage kick is induced into the secondary, or outer, armature winding and thus to the sparking plug. It follows that there is a definite point during the rotation of the armature in which the primary voltage is at its maximum, and where the contacts should separate. (In practise the contacts part just after the theoretical dead centre armature position.)

If the points were to open far too soon, due to "foreign" parts being fitted, the outcome would be an apparently dead magneto.

Incorrect contact breaker

Points opening, say, a quarter of a revolution out of phase could mean that someone has popped the wrong contact breaker in just to make the magneto saleable. Perhaps the breaker is an opposite-hand unit, or even one off a different make altogether.

Providing the "odd" contact breaker is a good fit on its taper and is mechanically sound, there is every chance it can be used in lieu of the correct item.

Assuming the contact breaker appears suitable in all other aspects, file off the old key from the tapered face. Reposition the unit, until by trial and error the ideal situation is found where the points start opening a touch after maximum pull is sensed. (To put it into engine terminology, this is a fraction after the armature has rocked over top dead centre.) A smear of engineers' blue on the contact breaker taper will indicate the armature key position — mark the position and solder on a new key. The key does not take any load so it will not shear off. (Note: when conducting these experiments the cam ring should be set in the advanced position.)

Wrong cam ring

The contact breaker is not always the culprit. Occasionally the cam ring is wrong, or has been rotated in its housing through someone losing the stop-screw. In the case of a four-screw-fixing magneto end-housing it is possible for the whole housing to be 90 degrees (or 180 degrees) out of position, although this should be immediately apparent (the advance and retard cable attachments will also be incorrectly situated).

V twin magnetos are a law unto themselves and particular attention must be paid to their cam rings. The author recalls a Brough Superior which caused no end of mystifying troubles until it was discovered that the previous owner had fitted a 47½ degree cam ring to its 60 degree magneto! V twins always were a curse to the unfortunate mag manufacturer as it was just not (theoretically) possible to obtain sparks of equal intensity on both cylinders, even when correct cam rings were fitted. Ingenious attempts were made to compensate for theoretical shortcomings, such as staggered pole-tips and armature cores, but as we all know V twin engines run quite happily in spite of everything.

No hard-and-fast rules can be laid down about repositioning cam rings in their housings as all mags are different. With some makes, BTH for example, it is a relatively simple job, but with others a modification might be required. Although the manufacturers would have been appalled at the idea it is sometimes necessary to grind new slots in the cam ring if all else fails. Such mods should not be carried out indescriminately; always search for the correct parts first. Generally the foregoing snags do not apply to post-war magnetos, which were more standardised than their vintage ancestors.

During the last war BTH turned out some very nice single and twin-cylinder stationary engine magnetos with fixed ignition. These crop up brand new from time to time. The lack of advance-and-retard facilities can be overcome by fitting a vintage BTH contact breaker housing, which will usually go straight on without further modification. The armatures are also interchangeable. Due attention should be given to end-clearances (adjust bearing shims to suit).

Pick-up problems

On rare occasions a magneto may be encountered

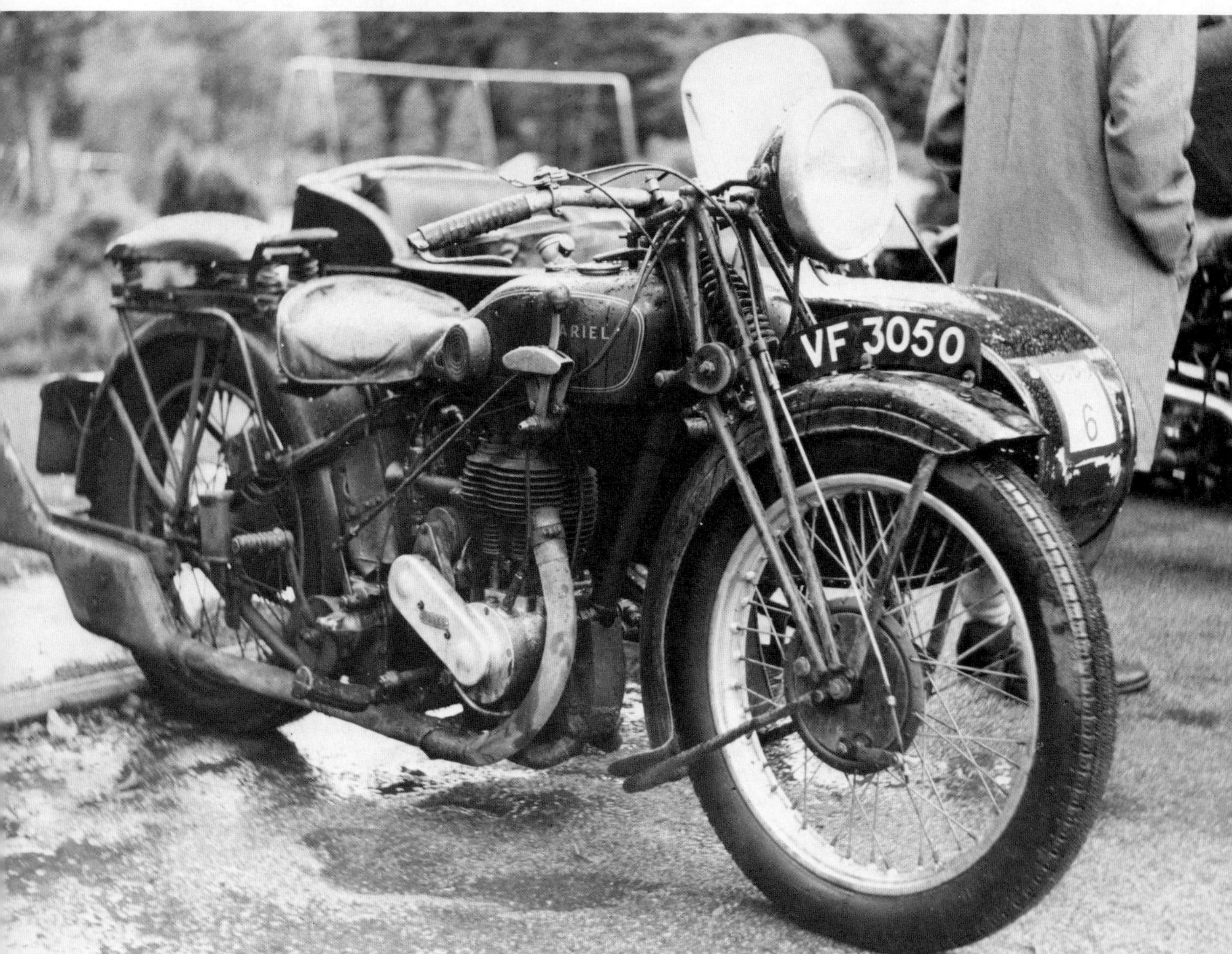

This well-used 5½hp (557cc) Ariel outfit of 1928 vintage is fitted with a post-vintage Lucas Magdyno for everyday use. Owner Phil Barton, a well-known VMCC trials rider, drives the Ariel in all weathers. It is curious that Ariels retained the tank-top oil sight feed when they introduced their up-to-the-minute saddle tank design – a mixture of old and new ideas. The cradle frame was brought out for the 1926 Show, together with a twin-port cylinder head for the 497cc ohv model.

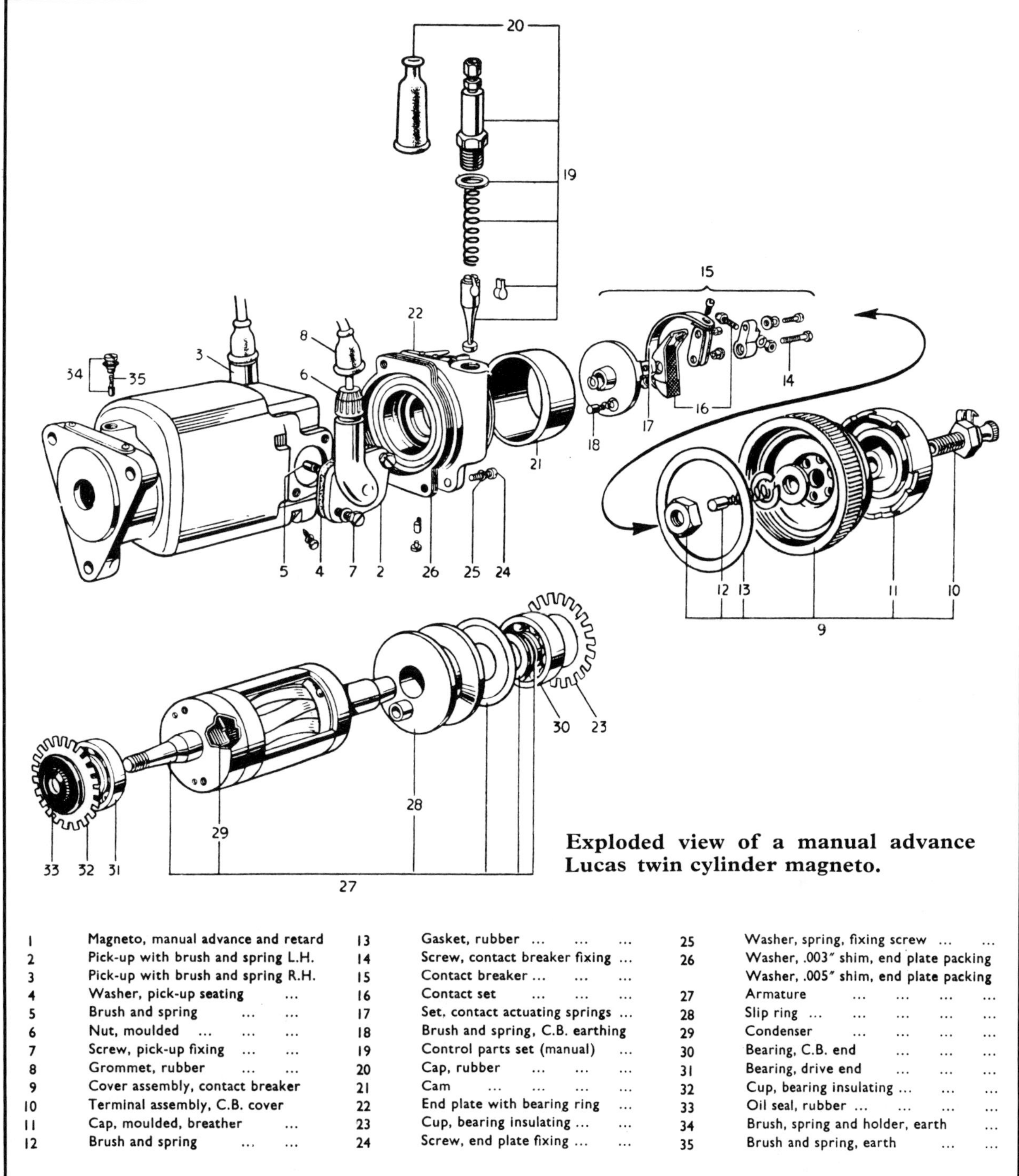

Exploded view of a manual advance Lucas twin cylinder magneto.

1	Magneto, manual advance and retard	13	Gasket, rubber	25	Washer, spring, fixing screw ... ...
2	Pick-up with brush and spring L.H.	14	Screw, contact breaker fixing ...	26	Washer, .003" shim, end plate packing
3	Pick-up with brush and spring R.H.	15	Contact breaker		Washer, .005" shim, end plate packing
4	Washer, pick-up seating ...	16	Contact set	27	Armature ... ...
5	Brush and spring	17	Set, contact actuating springs ...	28	Slip ring ... ...
6	Nut, moulded	18	Brush and spring, C.B. earthing	29	Condenser ... ...
7	Screw, pick-up fixing	19	Control parts set (manual) ...	30	Bearing, C.B. end ... ...
8	Grommet, rubber	20	Cap, rubber	31	Bearing, drive end ... ...
9	Cover assembly, contact breaker	21	Cam	32	Cup, bearing insulating ... ...
10	Terminal assembly, C.B. cover	22	End plate with bearing ring ...	33	Oil seal, rubber ... ...
11	Cap, moulded, breather ...	23	Cup, bearing insulating	34	Brush, spring and holder, earth ...
12	Brush and spring	24	Screw, end plate fixing	35	Brush and spring, earth ... ...

which **should** work but does not, even when every other factor checks out satisfactorily. Remove the Bakelite pick-up. Look for the brass slip-ring segment. If it has travelled **past** the pick-up hole when the points open then something is amiss. This strange situation means that the current has no hope of travelling out through the HT lead and could be caused through any of the following:

1 Wrong armature fitted by the previous owner
2 Incorrect slip-ring (unlikely)
3 Different contact-breaker (most probable)
4 A combination of all the above. (Mercifully, **most** unlikely!)

When the points open, the HT carbon brush must be in contact with the slip ring **in both advance and retard positions.** Again, V twin magnetos should be given special attention in this respect — it may be necessary to juggle about with the cam ring position, or limit the extent to which it moves in advance and retard directions, to prevent cutting-out on one cylinder under certain conditions (refer to V twin magneto timing).

Pick-up brushes have a tendency to jam in their holders so give the brush and spring a good clean and examine the Bakelite holder for cracks which promote tracking. It is amazing how sparks, which have a mind of their own, prefer to travel along tortuous paths in preference to a small plug gap. (I well remember a Two-Speed Scott which would cut-out under racing conditions due to sparks jumping from plug terminal to radiator bottom, a distance of almost 5/8 in! I eventually cured this annoying habit by sticking rubber patches underneath the radiator and using shorter sparking plugs.)

Dismantling

A complete magneto overhaul should not be attempted unless the restorer possesses skill, good tools, patience and clean working conditions. If all these prerequisites are available, then read on.

The bench top must be cleared. Spread a clean piece of paper or lino on the working surface before commencing operations and have a tin handy for various small screws. Magneto manufacturers were fond of using what the engineering trade calls oddball threads for which you never manage to find taps and dies.

Remove the safety spark gap screw

Neglect to observe this point will result in a smashed slip-ring when the armature is withdrawn. This small steel pointed screw is usually found underneath the magneto body, diametrically opposite to the pick-up holder.

At the other end of the mag will be found another (larger) screw **which must also be removed.** Usually of brass, flat-headed or slightly domed, extraction of same will reveal a carbon earthing brush and light spring. Just to confuse amateur restorers, Joe Lucas hides this brush underneath a serial number plate on some post-war mags.

Pick-up dodges

Mention has been made of pick-up brushes sticking in their holders. It is equally possible for the spring and brush to shoot out and roll down the nearest grid if the job is being carried out by the roadside! A couple of vintage hints might come in handy for such a misfortune. The first get-you-home dodge is to roll up a piece of silver paper (cigarette foil etc) and use this as a brush substitute. Push it up the pick-up hole so that the other end rubs on the slip-ring. Tip number two is a little messy as it involves tearing a small torch battery to pieces in order to salvage the carbon rod. Dress a piece of carbon to fit the pick-up — using the edge of a matchbox. If the pick-up is on top of the mag you can do without the spring temporarily, otherwise wedge the carbon rod in its hole so that the tip is just kissing the slip-ring.

Armature withdrawal

To return to bench dismantling, undo the contact breaker centre screw, withdraw the contact breaker and remove any screws which hold the end housing in place. Leaving the armature in situ for the time being, carefully withdraw the end-housing (don't prise it off with a screwdriver). Note if any shims are fitted.

Before withdrawing the armature it is most important to place a "keeper" across the magnet poles. Magneto manufacturers always recommended a soft iron bar but most amateurs repairers find a large steel lathe tool ideal for the purpose. If you cannot fit a bar across the poles some sort of hefty G-clamp will suffice. Leave the keeper in position all the time the armature is not at home, otherwise the magnets will be considerably weakened. Some more recent magnetos are blessed with magnets which retain their qualities almost indefinitely and do not require the use of keepers, but it is better to play safe.

Armature checks

Windings can be checked quite easily without the aid of instruments, by means of a simple test requiring only a small battery (4 to 6 volts) and some wire. Temporarily replace the contact breaker centre screw and attach a wire from this to one battery terminal. Take a piece of stiff wire, loop it round the slip-ring with the twist to secure it, and bring the other end out to within 1/8 in of the metal armature body. This forms a spark gap.

Connect a piece of insulated wire to the other battery terminal — it does not matter which way round the battery is connected — and bare the free end. Jab the armature body quickly with this wire and, with luck, you should be rewarded with a nice fat spark at the gap.

This signifies that the secondary windings are almost certainly in good order. No spark means an

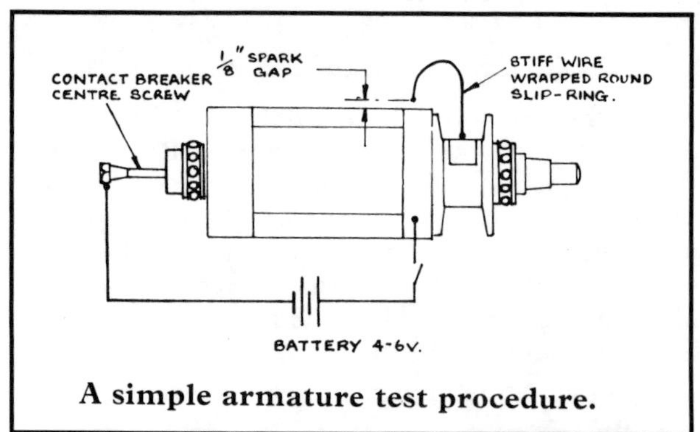

A simple armature test procedure.

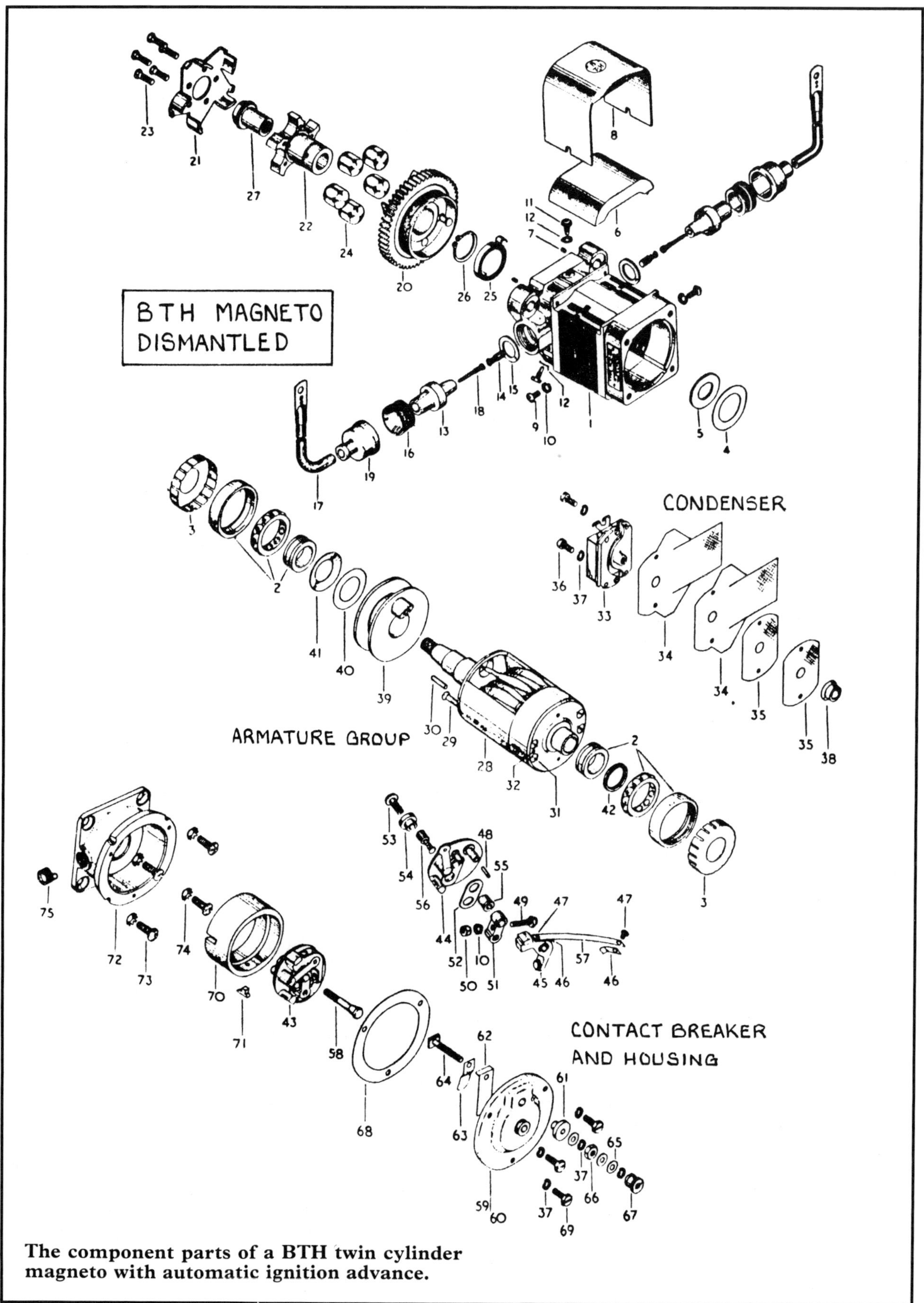

The component parts of a BTH twin cylinder magneto with automatic ignition advance.

open-circuited armature. It is most unusual for the primary winding to be faulty, being made of fairly thick wire; almost without exception the trouble will be in the outer (secondary) windings.

Duff condenser

In rare cases lack of continuity can be caused by a bad connection to the condenser — either a dry joint at the soldered end or verdigris on the tab. There is no easy way for an amateur mechanic to conduct a full condenser test without instruments. Any competent electrician can do it in minutes. A duff condenser manifests itself in bad starting, misfiring, or a complete stoppage. Blackened contacts with brilliant flashes at the points will, without doubt, confirm condenser trouble.

Magneto condensers are, of course specially made to fit within the confines of the armature end-piece. Replacements are hard to come by but enterprising individuals might like to know that a Villiers flat condenser (as used in lawn mower flywheel mags) will fit inside the armature end. Some ingenuity is required to make the necessary connections and a screwed ferrule must be made to accept the contact breaker centre screw.

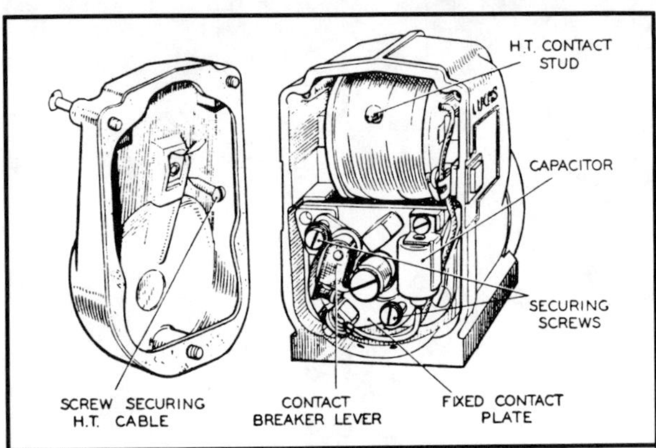

The Lucas rotating magnet magneto is generally most reliable, the only faults likely to be encountered being dirty points, a dud condenser or a broken-down coil.

Shellacitis

This debilitating disease of armature windings only occurs in early shellac-coated wire, and fortunately not in modern insulations. Over a period of many years the shellac breaks down and goes soggy. Eventually it runs and jams the armature solid in its tunnel; usually this happens on a hot day when the bike has been parked for a while. Lunging on the kickstarter can result in a fractured armature spindle, or at the very least, slipped timing.

So, if the armature is the least bit spongy, a rewind is strongly advised or trouble will strike as sure as night follows day. Placing the armature in a warm environment for a lengthy period will, strangely enough, harden the shellac again. Care must be exercised not to overheat it, gentle heat applied for a few weeks is far more effective than an hour or two in an oven (which latter course of action could result in a ruined armature). Usually the armature can be secreted away on top of, or inside, a central-heating boiler cabinet for the winter period. A magneto treated thus functioned well for a further 75,000 miles, including a Land's End — John O'Groats run, on one of the author's machines.

A get-you-home bodge for a melted armature is to remove the offending component, scrape out all traces of shellac from the armature tunnel, and paint the windings with quick-drying cellulose. A skin is formed on the windings which, hopefully, contains the melted shellac. An alternative is to scrape out all traces of shellac from the armature tunnel and dust the sticky armature windings liberally with French Chalk to absorb all the free-flowing shellac. Note that these are only temporary 'get you home' measures as inevitably the problem will re-occur if the armature is not again removed and rewound.

All rewound armatures, and those made since the late thirties, are properly coated with a seemingly indestructible resin and do not suffer from shellacitis. Generally speaking, pale yellow-coloured windings are OK.

Rewinds

In this age of disposable goods it is a sad fact that many old trades are dying out. Gone are the days when boots could be soled and heeled. Tyre gaiters are as obsolete as celluloid collars. Unfortunately trade recessions have seen off most remaining armature winders, so it may be necessary to travel far afield to find a craftsman willing to tackle a magneto armature. Reference to adverts in the classic motorcycle magazines will provide a short list.

Most rewinders prefer to receive the complete instrument so they can check bearing condition and magnetism etc. Naturally they will be reluctant to rectify amateurish attempts at magneto renovation.

On a few occasions the writer has rewound his own magnetos, employing his faithful *Adept* miniature lathe adapted for slow-speed operation. A "Heath-Robinson" traverse mechanism was rigged up and the armatures were wound with many thousands of turns of ex-WD enamelled copper wire (hardly thicker than human hair). Silk (actually remnants of exotic vintage underwear!) was used for interlayers between every few windings and the whole lot was soaked in polyurethane varnish and baked. (Originally windings were vacuum-impregnated). The experiments were successful but so time-consuming it is unlikely they will be repeated.

Reassembly

Examine the bearings and renew if necessary. Fortunately magneto bearings are still available at bearing stockists, being currently manufactured by RHP Ltd.

Removing a bearing inner ring is difficult without the proper extractor, so it is advisable to fabricate a temporary split-tubular tool to grip the bearing groove. Attempting to shift the ring by means of wedges is dodgy, often resulting in Bakelite slip-ring damage.

There must be little or no play in the armature shaft; end-play in face-cam magneto results in varying point gaps. Shims are usually added behind the bearing inner ring or removed from between the body and contact breaker housing. Lubricate the bearings with high melting point grease.

Testing

Peace of mind will be gained if the magneto is given a thorough bench test, sparking across a gap of 3/16 in when motored at approximately 950 rpm. A belt drive can be rigged up from the lathe motor or from a separate washing machine motor.

As a matter of interest, every magneto was given a

MAGNETO BEARINGS
RHP
single row separable

D d B

R.H.P. No.	d mm.	D m.m.	B m.m.	LIMITING R.P.M. (GREASE)
EN 5	5	16	5	37500
EN 6	6	21	7	31500
EN 7	7	22	7	30000
EN 8	8	24	7	28000
EN 9	9	28	8	24500
EN 10	10	28	8	24500
EN 11	11	32	7	22500
EN 12	12	32	7	22500
EN 13	13	30	7	22500
EN 14	14	35	8	19500
EN 15	15	35	8	19500
EN 16	16	38	10	18500
EN 17	17	44	11	17000
EN 18	18	40	9	18000
EN 19	19	40	9	18000
EN 20	20	47	12	15500

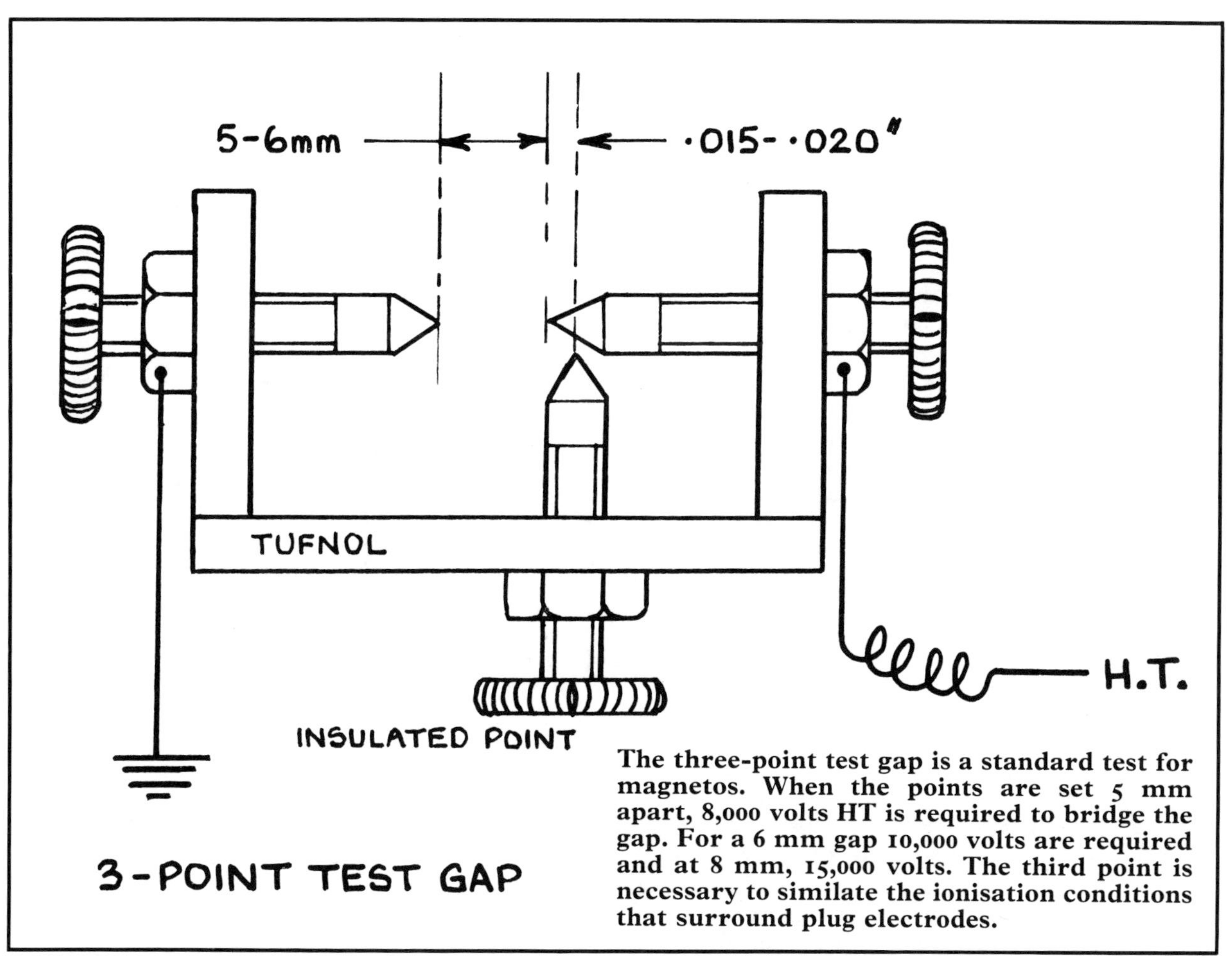

The three-point test gap is a standard test for magnetos. When the points are set 5 mm apart, 8,000 volts HT is required to bridge the gap. For a 6 mm gap 10,000 volts are required and at 8 mm, 15,000 volts. The third point is necessary to similate the ionisation conditions that surround plug electrodes.

full running test in the vintage days. In 1920 the BTH standard test was an endurance run of 12 hours duration with a spark gap of 5.5 mm. The magneto was driven at 3000 rpm. This was followed by a low-speed test in which the instrument had to perform reliably at 85 rpm with the timing lever set on full advance. The test was repeated at 200 rpm on full retard. The magneto was then dismantled, cleaned and inspected. Finally, each instrument was run for four hours and checked. No wonder magnetos were so expensive!

Slip-ring repairs

Thanks to modern epoxy resin adhesives broken slip-rings present no problem. A chipped flange can be repaired quite easily with *Araldite* if the broken bit is still available, but sometimes the restorer is confronted with a flangeless slip-ring, due to past "bodgery".

The only solution in this instance is to make a new flange from *Paxolin or Tufnol;* invariably only one flange (the outer) is damaged so the replacement can be copied from the remaining part. Mount the magneto armature in the lathe chuck and centre the projecting shaft. Machine off the damaged flange, leaving a shoulder (see sketches). Turn a disc of *Tufnol* to the appropriate outside diameter and bore it to a slip-fit on the slip-ring shoulder. Leave the disc sides parallel for the time being.

Araldite the flange in position and leave it in gentle heat for a day. When it is firmly stuck, mount the armature in the lathe again and vee the flange inner-face. A sharp tool is required for this task. Polish the flange with fine glasspaper and the slip-ring is as good as new!

"Where do I get *Tufnol* sheet?" the reader may well ask. There are two likely sources. Old-established wireless repairers generally have a few bits lying about; another possible supplier is the stockist of ex-WD equipment. Alternatively, try begging some from your local light engineering firm.

One other dodge worth remembering concerns scored slip-rings where the carbon pick-up brush has worn a deep groove. Slight scoring can be rectified by a simple turning operation, but if the groove is very deep (usually caused through excessive spring pressure or unsuitable brush material) the following measures can be taken.

Rough-up the groove with coarse sandpaper to provide a key. Build up the affected area with *Araldite* and after it has **thoroughly** cured machine the surface true. A sharp parting tool is ideal for the job. Polish with dead-smooth glasspaper, followed by metal polish. The repair will last many years.

Slip-rings should be kept clean by inserting a petrol-soaked rag through the pick-up hole. Wrap the rag round a wooden dowel — not metal, which

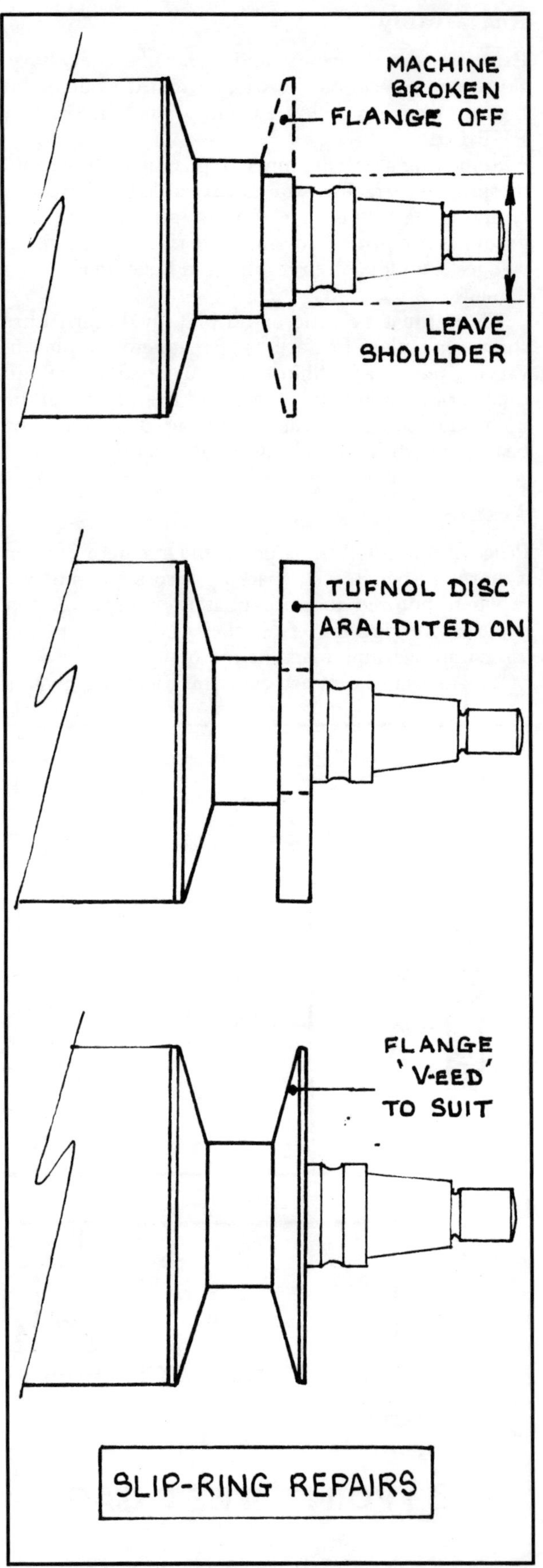

SLIP-RING REPAIRS

would give you a shock when the motor is turned over.

Periodic attention to the contact breaker points and slip-ring will make all the difference to starting and general running.

Timing

The following timing procedures will be found suitable for early vintage engines when the makers' figures are unknown. Fine adjustment may be necessary after testing.

1 **Single-cylinder two-strokes:** Set the piston on top-dead-centre, fully retard the magneto. The points should just be breaking (contact breaker arm just beginning to ride up the cam). Couple up and check again.

2 **Single-cylinder four-strokes:** Uncouple the magneto, or withdraw the drive pinion slightly off its taper. Set the timing lever on full advance. Bring the piston up to TDC (compression stroke). By means of a rod poked through the plug or compression tap hole mark this position. Rotate the engine backwards about a quarter of a turn. Make a mark on the timing probe (a pencil will serve as a probe) about 3/8 in. above the TDC mark. Slowly bring the piston up to this point; the contact breaker should just be parting. Couple up and check. Adjust after test.

A good average figure for vintage motors is an ignition advance of 35 degrees before TDC (points just opening, magneto fully advanced). This corresponds with the following measurements, in millimetres, of the piston before TDC for the given strokes:

Stroke (mm)	35° piston lead (mm)
70	7.6
72	7.8
74	8.0
76	8.2
78	8.5
80	8.7
82	9.0
84	9.1
85	9.2
86	9.4
88	9.6
90	9.8
92	10.0
94	10.2

Model / use	Piston position	Advance
BB32GS		
Touring, Trials and Scrambles	7/16 in.	(38°)
Racing (Petrol and Petrol Benzole)	15/32 in.	(39°)
Racing (Alcohol Fuel)	3/8 in.	(35°)
BB34GS		
Touring and Trials	1/2 in.	(41°)
Scrambles	7/16 in.	(38°)
Racing (Petrol and Petrol Benzole)	1/2 in.	(41°)
Racing (Alcohol Fuel)	7/16 in.	(38°)
CB32GS, DB32GS		
Touring, Scrambles and Racing (Petrol and Petrol Benzole)	15/32 in.	(39°)
CB34GS, DB34GS		
Touring (CB34GS only), Scrambles and Racing (Petrol and Petrol Benzole)	13/32 in.	(36°)
Touring (DB34GS only)	1/2 in.	(41°)
DB34GS, DBD34GS		
Clubman's *only*	15/32 in.	(39°)

BSA Gold Star timing details. Above: A magneto pinion extractor is essential. Middle: Checking the ignition timing with a degree disc. Below: Gold Star ignition timing recommendations.

96	10.5
98	10.7
100	11.0

3 **V twin engines:** Although some manufacturers seemed to disagree, it was commonly accepted that No 1 cylinder was the rear cylinder on a V twin, therefore No 1 magneto cam would be correct for this. Set the timing lever on full advance and No 1 piston the appropriate amount before TDC (firing stroke, both valves shut). To quote two examples, the settings for the 1100 cc sv JAP and 1000 cc ohv JAP are 38° and 45° respectively. The contacts should be just separating.

Cam wear in old V twin magnetos is fairly common so don't be surprised if the maker's timing figures do not tally on both cylinders. A discrepancy of two or three degrees between the settings on No 1 and No 2 cam will not make the slightest difference; minor variations in points gaps are also of little consequence — if one is .010 in and the other .013 in there is nothing to grumble about.

1920 Lucas Magdyno

Fitted to motorcycles of the early vintage period (usually large capacity sidecar machines) the original Lucas *Magdyno* featured a 3-brush E3 6 volt dynamo housed within a large horseshoe magnet. A separate switchbox mounted either on the tank side

Details of the 1920 Lucas Magdyno.

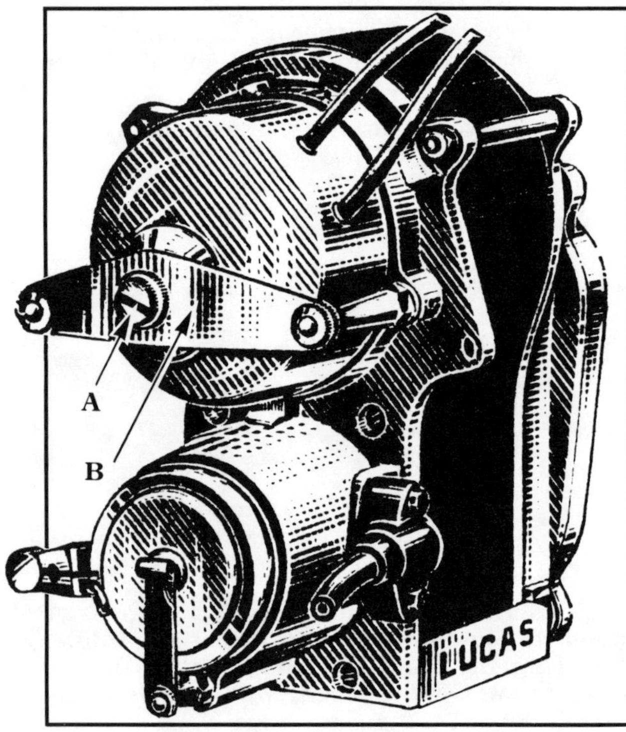

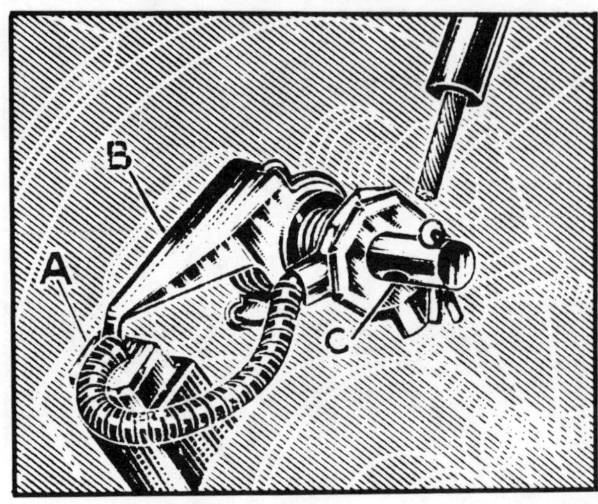

A—brush.
B—spring holding brush in position.
C—terminal hole.

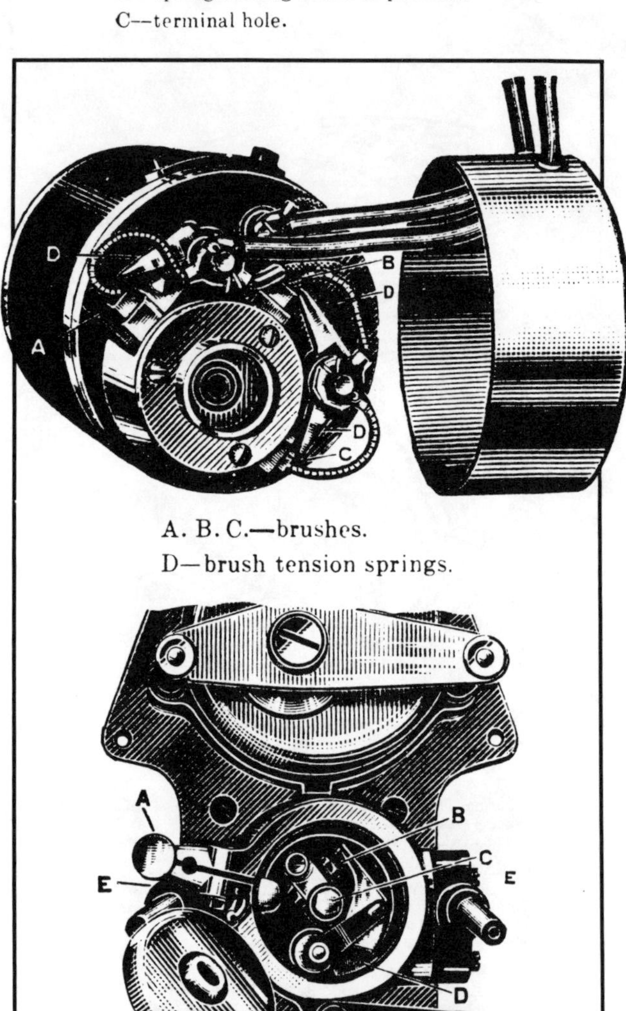

A. B. C.—brushes.
D—brush tension springs.

A—contact breaker lever.
B—contact breaker points.
C—centre screw.
D—fibre block.
E—pick-ups.

or on the motorcycle frame contained a cut-out unit.

The gear ratio between the magneto and dynamo was 3.7 : 1, which gave an effective ratio between crankshaft and dynamo of 1.8 : 1 when the *Magdyno* was driven at half engine speed. The dynamo output was 5.5 amps, with a cut-in speed of 1000 rpm. Charging current was regulated by a third brush placed mid-way between the main output brushes.

Dynamo inspection

To remove the dynamo it is only necessary to loosen screw A, then by lifting strap B, the dynamo can be extracted by pulling forward. Withdrawal of the dynamo does not interfere in any way with the ignition part of the *Magdyno*.

In order for the dynamo to function correctly the brush gear and commutator should be inspected by removing the end cover. All three brushes should slide easily in their holders and the 'pigtail' leads should be insulated (and not fouling other metal parts.) New brushes can be adapted from car dynamo brushes, filed to suit. Bed-in with strip glass-paper (refer to general instructions on dynamos).

The commutator surface must be clean and free from oil, brush dust, etc. Should any grease or oil work on to the commutator through over-lubrication it will not only cause sparking of the brushes, but in addition, clogging-up of the commutator grooves with carbon and copper dust. The grooves should be cleaned out with a thin saw blade, as mentioned later in this Chapter.

In order to connect up the terminal wires compress the springs on the terminal posts and simply push the wires through the holes provided. The outer hole is for a split pin to prevent loss of the springs and washers.

Switchbox

The switch has four positions and at the extreme position in either direction a stop is provided to prevent further rotation of the handle (the correct handle is rather like a duffle-coat toggle in shape). The positions are:

1 **Off** — Lamps off, dynamo off.
2 **Charge** — Lamps off, dynamo charging, arranged to give (by means of a shunt resistance) half its maximum output.
3 **High** — High filament of headlamp, tail (and sidelamp where fitted) switched on. Also the resistance coil in the shunt circuit is cut out allowing the dynamo to give its full output.
4 **Low** — With the exception that the low filament is on in place of the high filament the conditions are exactly as in position High.
5 **In special cases** the switchbox was altered to enable the full output of the dynamo to be obtained in the charge position.

The cut-out functions as any normal cut-out in a 3rd brush circuit, insofar as it automatically closes the generator to battery circuit as soon as the dynamo reaches a sufficient speed. It does not in any way switch off, or regulate, the dynamo output when the battery is fully charged.

Clean the cut-out points with emery paper and check that they operate when the dynamo speeds-up. Don't make the mistake of trying to set the points too close by bending down the restricting tag as the dynamo may then cut-out late (or not at all). If the cut-out fails to operate, check the windings and connections thereto. Replacement cut-outs for these early switch-boxes are non-existent but it is usually possible to fit a similar unit from a vintage car Lucas switch-panel — such items turn up regularly at autojumbles. Failing that, adapt a more modern 6V cut-out to fit, or even do away with it (as a last resort!) and rig-up a manual switch to cut the dynamo in and out when required. A good memory is needed should the latter course of action be adopted or a flat battery will be the certain outcome!

Wiring

All wiring is carried out with 5 mm insulated cable, originally termed low-tension wire, similar in outward appearance to Bowden throttle cable. An earth-return system is used and all cables must be clipped neatly in position to prevent chafing. Refer to the wiring diagram for a typical early Lucas *Magdyno* layout.

Magneto

The magneto portion of the early *Magdyno* is quite conventional, with the usual type of ring-cam contact breaker. Versions were available for singles and twins. (No 1 terminal on the magneto connects to the back cylinder on a V twin).

Points-gap should be set at .012 in.

Lamps

Tail lamp; type MT 110.
Side lamp; type R330 (bayonet-fitting rim).
Head lamp; type R40 and R510 (bayonet fitting rim).

Battery

Under normal conditions, providing the lamps are used a fair amount, the battery should be charged in the daytime for a period equal to that which the lamps are used at night time. If the motorcycle is used very little for night work, but for long runs in the daytime, it is advisable to charge for about one hour only after commencement of each journey, and then turn the switch to the off position.

The battery should **never** be disconnected when the dynamo is in circuit.

Originally, Lucas supplied sheet-metal battery

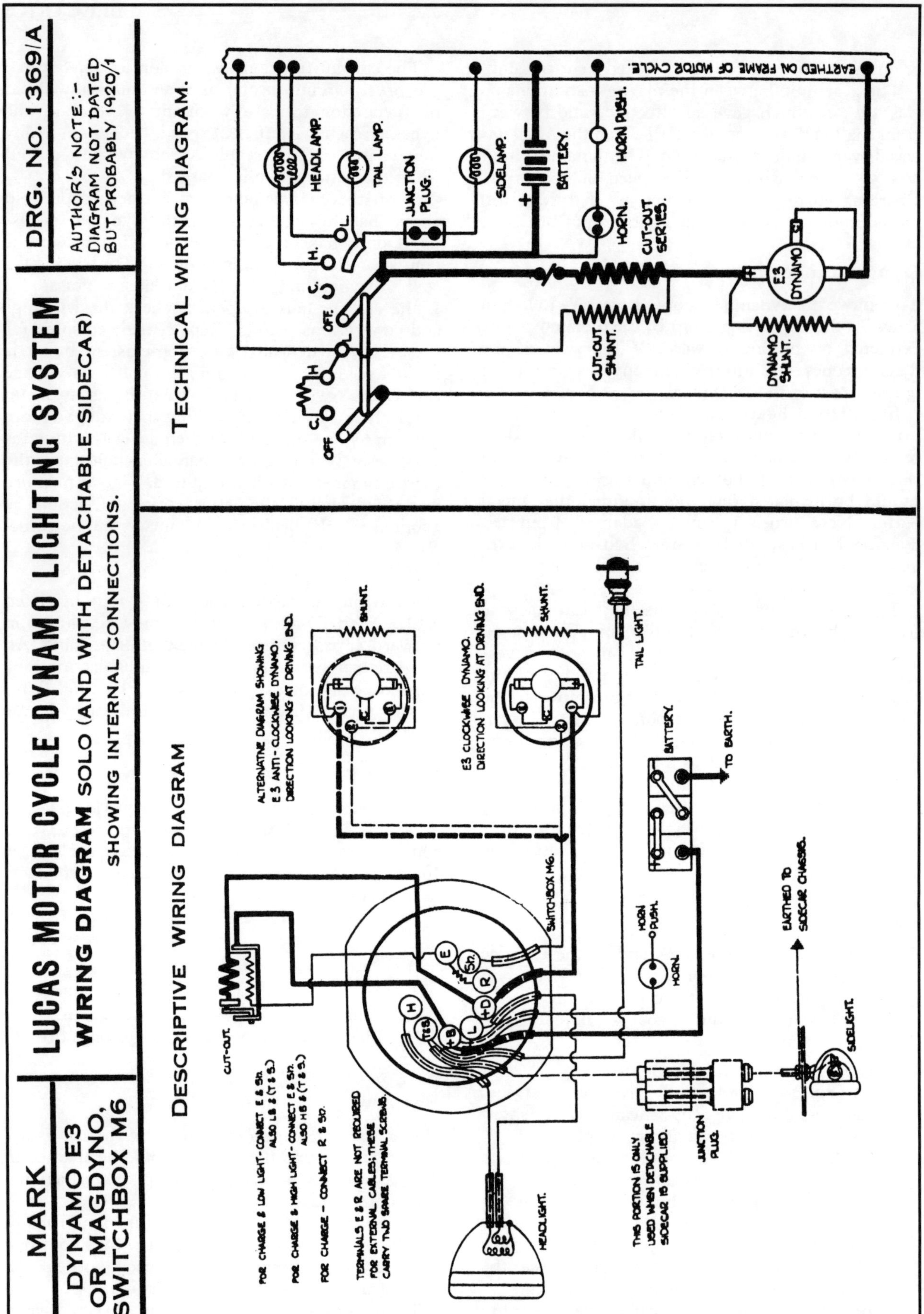

MARK

DYNAMO E3 OR MAGDYNO, SWITCHBOX M6

LUCAS MOTOR CYCLE DYNAMO LIGHTING SYSTEM

WIRING DIAGRAM SOLO (AND WITH DETACHABLE SIDECAR) SHOWING INTERNAL CONNECTIONS.

DRG. NO. 1369/A

AUTHOR'S NOTE:- DIAGRAM NOT DATED BUT PROBABLY 1920/1

TECHNICAL WIRING DIAGRAM.

EARTHED ON FRAME OF MOTOR CYCLE.
HEADLAMP.
TAIL LAMP.
JUNCTION PLUG.
SIDELAMP.
BATTERY.
HORN PUSH.
HORN.
CUT-OUT SERIES.
CUT-OUT SHUNT.
E3 DYNAMO
DYNAMO SHUNT.

DESCRIPTIVE WIRING DIAGRAM

ALTERNATIVE DIAGRAM SHOWING E3 ANTI-CLOCKWISE DYNAMO. DIRECTION LOOKING AT DRIVING END.
E3 CLOCKWISE DYNAMO. DIRECTION LOOKING AT DRIVING END.
SHUNT.
TAIL LIGHT.
BATTERY.
TO EARTH.
SWITCHBOX M6.
HORN PUSH.
HORN.
EARTHED TO SIDECAR CHASSIS.
SIDELIGHT.
CUT-OUT.
JUNCTION PLUG.
HEADLIGHT.
THIS PORTION IS ONLY USED WHEN DETACHABLE SIDECAR IS SUPPLIED.

FOR CHARGE & LOW LIGHT - CONNECT E & Sh. ALSO L & Z (T & S.)
FOR CHARGE & HIGH LIGHT - CONNECT E & Sh. ALSO H & Z (T & S.)
FOR CHARGE - CONNECT R & Sh.
TERMINALS E & R ARE NOT REQUIRED FOR EXTERNAL CABLES; THESE CARRY TWO SPARE TERMINAL SCREWS.

A typical early Lucas wiring diagram.

boxes containing a bank of very slim special batteries. Unfortunately these batteries are no longer available and modern batteries will not fit inside the container. However, it may be of interest to know that small 2V accumulators can be purchased from model shops; these will fit in with suitable packing and wired in series to produce 6V. Usually the boxes were clamped to the saddle-tube or occasionally on the chain stays.

Lucas Magdyno, late post-vintage and post-war

The standard Lucas *Magdyno* is so well known that a description of its general features would be superfluous. Reliable, well made, and long lasting, the familiar *Magdyno* (a Lucas trade name) was of course fitted to countless thousands of British motorcycles.

Routine attention

The following should be carried out every six months or so. Lubricate the magneto contact breaker. The breaker cam is lubricated by a wick contained in the c.b. base; remove the contact breaker by taking off both springs — the long one with the contact attached and the short flat blade. Remove the breaker unit complete and put a drop of oil on the felt wick and points tappet. Light oil (3 in 1) is recommended. Don't forget that the short spring blade is fitted with the bent portion facing outwards.

Service the contacts, as mentioned at the beginning of this Chapter. The correct gap is .012 in.

Clean the slip-ring occasionally by means of a petrol-dampened rag wrapped round a piece of wood. See that the HT lead is correctly fitted to the Bakelite pick-up; the lead should be bared for $^{1}/_{8}$ in approximately, pushed in the holder, then a small thin copper washer is fitted, finally the end is splayed-out. Clean inside the pick-up. A splodge of plasticine around the HT lead and screwthreads will keep out rain.

Oil the advance and retard cable and maintain correct adjustments. The cable holder, containing the advance/retard plunger and spring, should have a locking (tab) washer — cadmium plated for perfectionists — fitted under its shoulder. Also, a small rubber shroud fits over the cable stop.

Routine dynamo maintenance is limited to cleaning the commutator (more of which later) and keeping a watchful eye on brush condition.

Dismantling

Remove the drive end cover, held by four countersunk screws. This will reveal the slipping clutch mechanism — a form of shock absorbing drive which relieves peak tooth loading. The drive is taken from the gear centre A which is keyed to the magneto shaft, via friction disc C and star spring D to the dynamo gear G. The drive gear can be locked with a U shaped rod fashioned from $^{1}/_{4}$ in diameter steel. Each leg should be approximately 1 in long with a $3^{3}/_{16}$ in centre distance. One end fits in the drive wheel hole and the other locks in the top hole in the magneto body.

One of the last "pre-flywheel magneto" Villiers engines, a 269cc long stroke unit with a separate CAV magneto housed in a 1922 two-speed belt drive Ixion. Villiers engines possessed excellent pulling powers for their size – this particular machine is invariably ridden to VMCC rallies by its owner, Bill Colclough, who thinks nothing of pitting man and machine against steep Derbyshire passes.

Undo the securing nut after bending back the tab washer. The clutch spring, friction washer and drive gear are then withdrawn. Examine the fabric gear condition and replace if the teeth are worn knife-edged.

The magneto itself should then be inspected and tested (see general instructions earlier in this Chapter).

Slipping clutch assembly

Key the gear centre on to the magneto spindle,

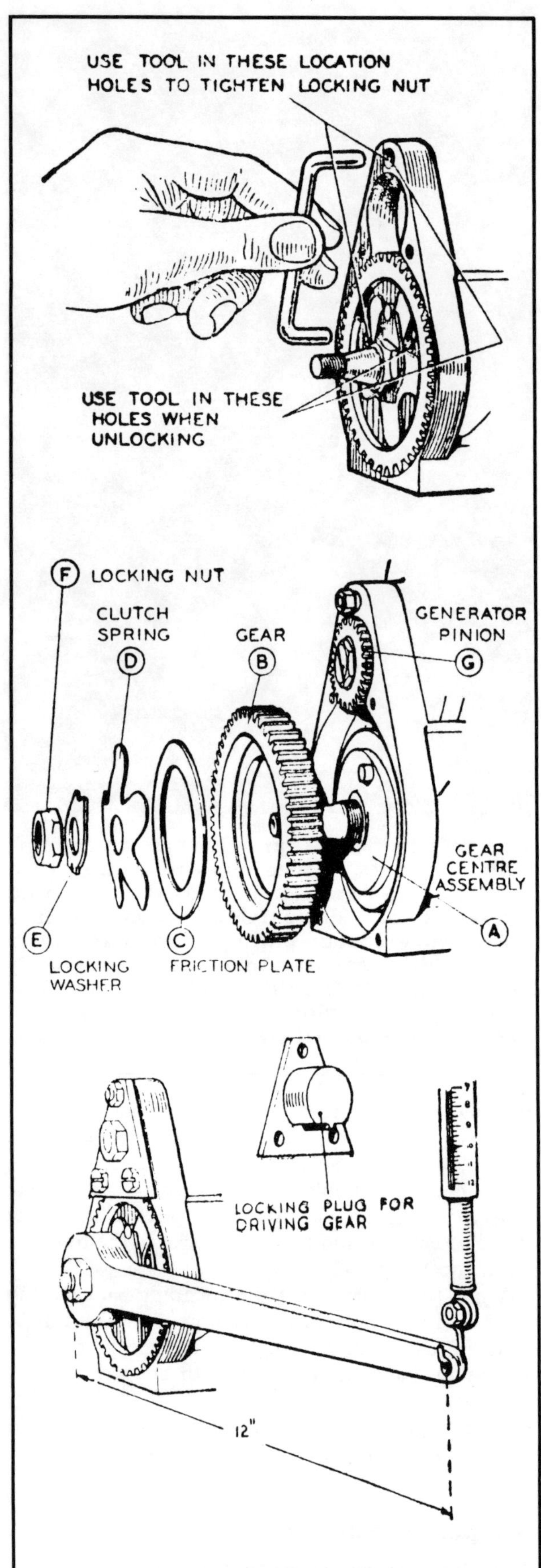

replace the friction disc, spring and locking washer. Tighten the fixing nut fully.

Providing the star spring is in good order, the amount of preload should work out automatically. This can be checked by locking the drive gear and applying a fixed loading to the driving spindle. The recommended figure is 4 to 10 ft lb, when slippage commences.

Fitting

It is most important to check gear-meshing when the *Magdyno* is bolted or clamped to its platform to ensure that the drive teeth are not bottoming. Excessive drive-side bearing wear and worn gear teeth will be the outcome if this point is not observed.

Allow a slight amount of backlash, adjusting by means of brass shims under the *Magdyno* base. Always keep the fixing strap well tightened — this has a habit of coming loose, whereupon the magneto platform frets away.

Details

Concours enthusiasts who wish to turn out their *Magdynos* 'as-new' will find the following comments of interest.

1 Dynamo steel bodies were originally plated with a thin cadmium or zinc finish which evaporated shortly after the machine left the showroom. In order to replate the shell, the field coil must be removed. Alternatively, the body can be bead-blasted and sprayed with a silver (aerosol) cellulose.
2 Brush inspection bands on E3H/M and E3L/M/N dynamos were normally black-enamelled, not chrome as sometimes seen at concours events.
3 Aluminium magneto bodies were left as-cast, not highly-polished.
4 Drive-gear end plates, being of a different aluminium composition to the bodies, were lighter in colour (usually anodised).
5 Contact breaker covers were cadmium-plated, or occasionally chrome. (On WD magdynos cadmium was standardised.)
6 Most screws were cadmium plated, this finish also being applied to the advance & retard spring housing (zinc is a good substitute). The brass earthing-brush holder was **not** plated or polished.

Dynamos, general maintenance

Every few thousand miles remove the cover band and inspect the commutator and brush-gear.

Brushes should move freely in their holders. Check the spring action. If a brush sticks, clean it with a petrol-dampened rag. It is imperative to replace a brush exactly as it came out, so mark it in

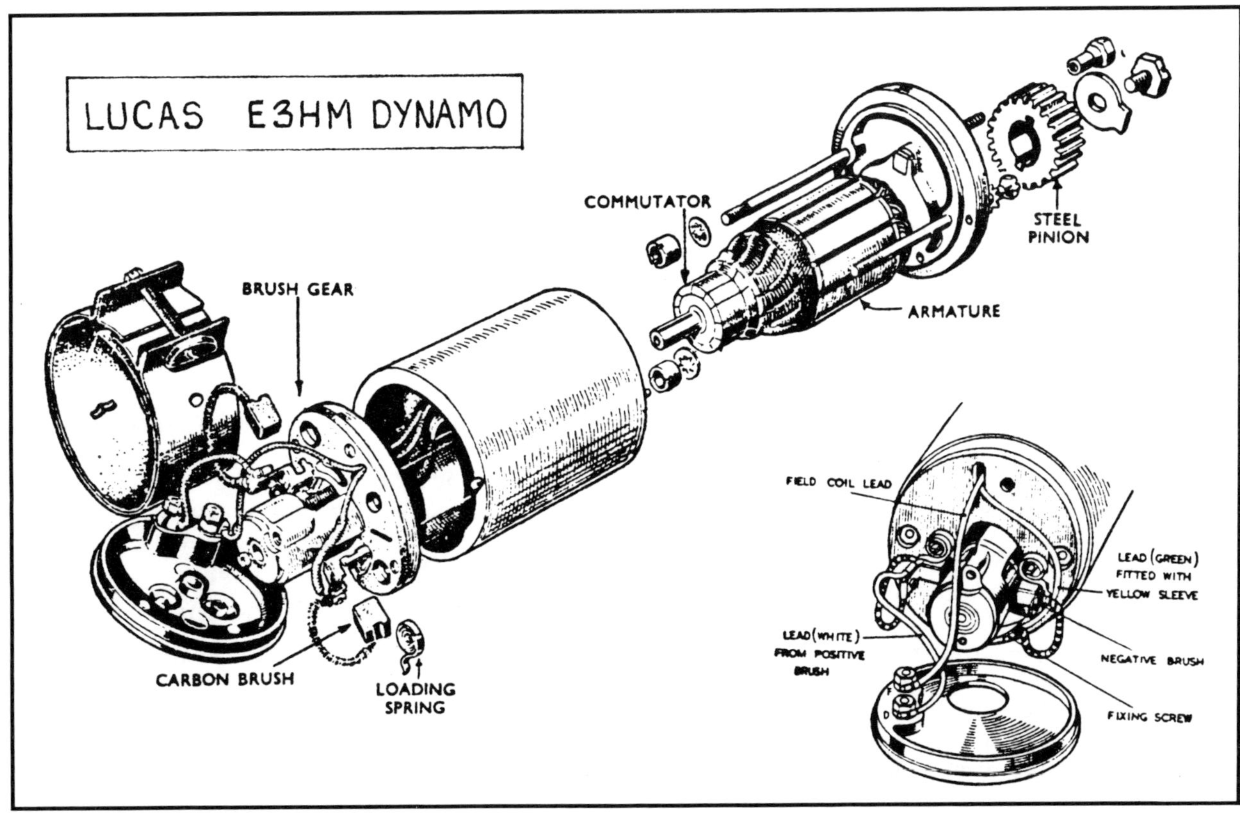

some way with a scriber. If the brush is put in the wrong way round it will not bed on the commutator and severe sparking will ensue (with little or no output).

A brush which has worn so far as to allow the hairpin spring to rest on the brush carrier should be replaced. In any event you might as well fit new brushes during a major overhaul.

In the case of Lucas E3H/E3HM dynamos (as fitted to *Magdynos*) the brush spring pressure should be in the region of 10-15 oz. Genuine Lucas brushes are pre-formed, making bedding-in unnecessary. However, with so many pattern parts coming on the market it is wise to play safe and bed-in **all** brushes. Replacement brushes for vintage dynamos are practically unobtainable therefore it is often necessary to file-down car dynamo brushes to fit.

To bed-in a brush, wrap a strip of fine glass-paper round the commutator and rock it gently in the direction of rotation, applying gentle finger pressure to the brush. Inspect the brush from time to time and carry on bedding-in until full contact is achieved. Actually, the job does not take long and can be carried out when you're sitting comfortably, watching TV! In service the brush face will develop a fine polish and the commutator a glossy brown appearance.

Commutator machining

Inspect the commutator. If it is just dirty or blackened, clean it with a petrol-moistened rag. After a prolonged mileage the commutator segments may be scored or badly worn; in this event they must be skimmed on a lathe.

Mount the armature between centres, or fix one end in a 3-jaw chuck and bring up the tailstock centre to the commutator end (armature shafts are usually centred both ends). Check that the armature is running true in all respects. The recommended machining speed is between 300 and 400 rpm, or a surface speed of 100 to 150 ft per min with carbon-steel tools and 250 ft per min for high-speed tools. For tungsten-carbide-tipped tools the speed can be much higher, approximately 500 to 700 ft per min.

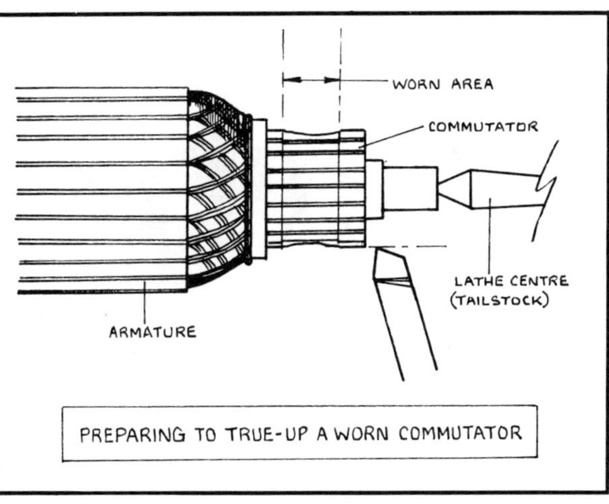

PREPARING TO TRUE-UP A WORN COMMUTATOR

The recommended tool angles are as follows; top rake 20 to 30 degrees (high-speed steel) or 13 to 16 degrees (tungsten carbide); front clearance 5 to 7 degrees; side cutting angle 20 to 25 degrees with a side clearance of 8 degrees. The tool should be accurately adjusted by height. No lubricant is required. Just in case some amateur turners are frightened by the above figures — they can rest assured that a good sharp knife tool will do the trick. Copper is very easy to turn.

The copper commutator must be finished true to the armature bearing spigot to within .005 in. A superfine finish is desirable.

Undercut the mica

After machining, the mica in between the copper segments must be slotted to a level slightly below (approximately .015 in to .020 in) that of the copper. This is accomplished with a hacksaw blade fixed in a pad-saw holder. If the teeth are too wide, they can be ground to suit.

The important point to remember is that the mica must be cut cleanly away between the segments. Don't just 'vee' the slots — they must be square in section. After slotting, bevel the edges with a smooth three-cornered swiss file.

Even if the commutator is in good fettle and does not need machining it is a sound idea to clean out the slots as described. Over a long period copper and carbon dust collects therein, destroying the efficiency of the dynamo.

Dynamo testing (Lucas 2-brush type)

A simple test with the dynamo in situ can be carried out with a 0-10v voltmeter and two pieces of insulated wire fitted with crocodile clips.

Withdraw the D and F connections to the dynamo. In their place, stick two short lengths of wire. Twist these together, so connecting the Dynamo and Field. Clip the voltmeter negative lead to earth on the Magdyno body and connect the voltmeter positive lead to the bared ends of the joined D and F wires.

Start the engine and let it tick-over. The voltmeter should show a reading of 4 to 8 volts, demonstrating that the dynamo is working. If a voltmeter is not available, a rudimentary test can be made with a 6v bulb which, of course, should light up when the motor is running slowly (it will almost certainly blow if the engine is revved).

Motoring test (2-brush dynamos)

Another simple check which any amateur mechanic can undertake is the motoring test, with the dynamo off the machine. Join up the D and F connections as before and attach a length of wire to the joint connection. Fix a clip to the other end. Attach the clip to the positive terminal of a 6v battery. Connect another piece of wire to the negative battery terminal and touch the bare end against the dynamo frame. The dynamo should then motor round willingly.

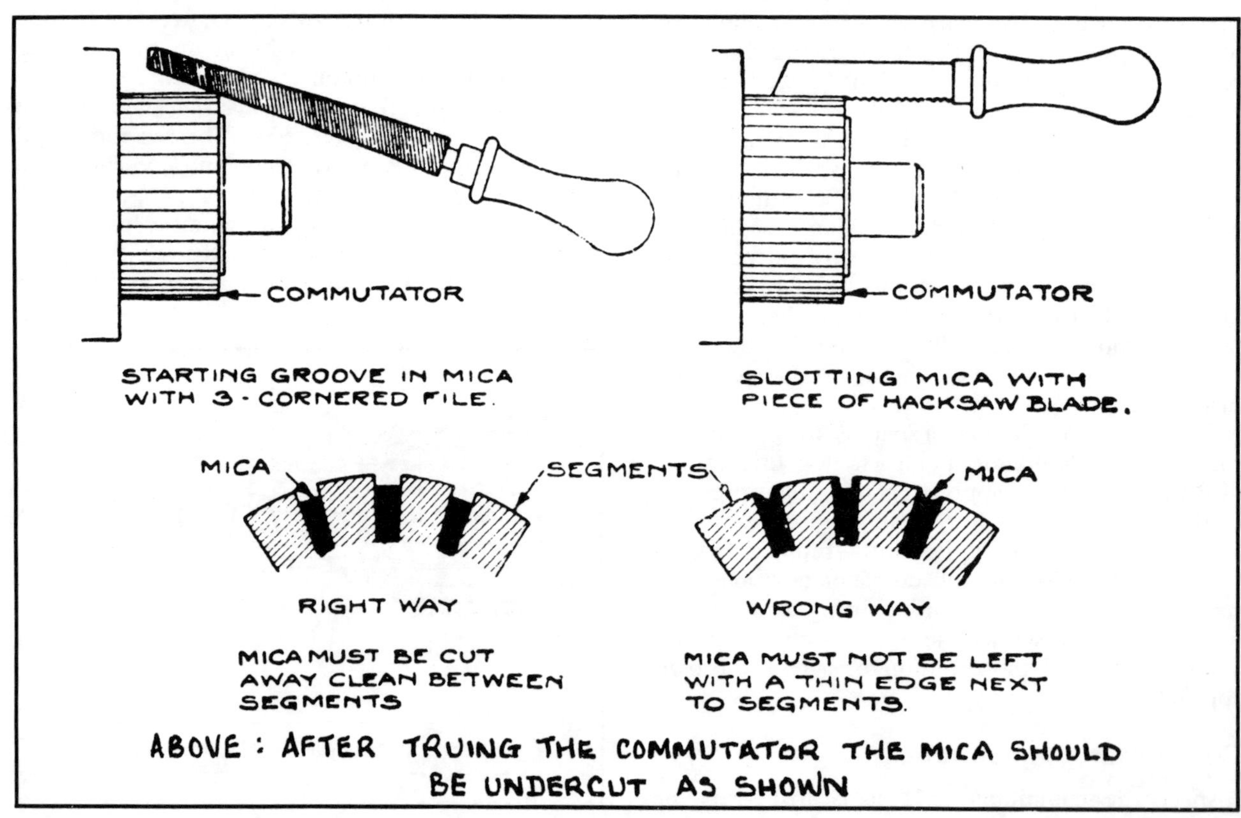

ABOVE: AFTER TRUING THE COMMUTATOR THE MICA SHOULD BE UNDERCUT AS SHOWN

The motor test is not an absolutely certain way of judging general dynamo condition. A dynamo will sometimes motor, albeit spasmodically, if there is a dry joint in one of the commutator connections but will not give full ouput in service. Nevertheless it is a useful spot-check, indicating life or otherwise. "Where there's life there's hope" goes the old saying.

Motoring test (3-brush dynamos)

Older types of 3-brush dynamos with cut-outs mounted on the dynamo frames can also be motored in a similar manner. Connect the dynamo positive to the battery positive. The battery negative is temporarily connected to the dynamo frame and the second (F1) terminal is earthed.

The dynamo should motor when the cut-out points are pressed together. This is an easy test to make, only requiring three hands!

If the dynamo does not motor, try by-passing the cut-out. Take the battery positive wire directly to the positive brush — if the armature revolves, the problem could be a faulty cut-out.

Old 3-brush dynamos often suffer from solder-flinging, a disease which afflicts commutator connections. This is caused by the output rising beyond that for which the dynamo was designed; disconnecting the battery is fatal to a 3-brush charging circuit. It must be remembered that the battery is an integral part of the system, being a resistance in the armature circuit, and if it is removed the voltage will increase to dangerous levels. The first thing that happens is the lamp bulbs will increase in brilliance — for a few fleeting moments you will be able to see the road ahead as though it were daylight — and then they will 'pop', leaving you in total darkness.

Examine the commutator soldered connections — there may be several dry joints through an absence of solder. A blackened or burnt commutator will confirm the fact that sparking has taken place due either to poor brush contact (which in itself can cause overheating) or open-circuited armature coils.

It may be possible to salvage the armature by resoldering the commutator connections, a difficult job to do neatly. Strip off some of the fabric bandage in order to get at the wires. Use a large iron and make sure you don't create more dry joints than you had before. Sometimes the armature wires break just where they enter the commutator; to repair a broken connection remove the remaining fragment from the commutator and solder in a short piece (approx 3/8 in long projection) of copper wire of appropriate gauge. Bare the armature wire for a short distance and splice the two together with thin fuse wire. Solder the join. Finish off the job by winding a few turns of thin string round the end of the armature, paint the string with polyurethane varnish and apply a layer of fabric, again varnished.

This repair should last for years if done properly. It may be regarded with horror by armature winding specialists. If it doesn't work then nothing is lost and the armature can then be forwarded to the said specialists, to cries of "I told you so". (However, the writer wishes to point out that one large 6v dynamo replaced thus lit his path for another 60,000 miles at least!)

Checking armature windings

There are various means whereby armature coils can be checked for continuity or shorting. Competent electricians will be able to apply a voltage-drop-test to each armature coil by passing a current through the windings in turn. The field coil is disconnected. The test is in accordance with Ohm's Law (C x R = E) in which each coil, when normal, possesses a certain resistance and thus there is a fall in potential when current flows through the circuit.

Little or no potential drop between adjacent segments will indicate a defective or short-circuited coil which is then investigated. A sensitive voltmeter and two probes are generally used in this test.

Another, more sophisticated, test is by means of an instrument called a growler in which the dynamo

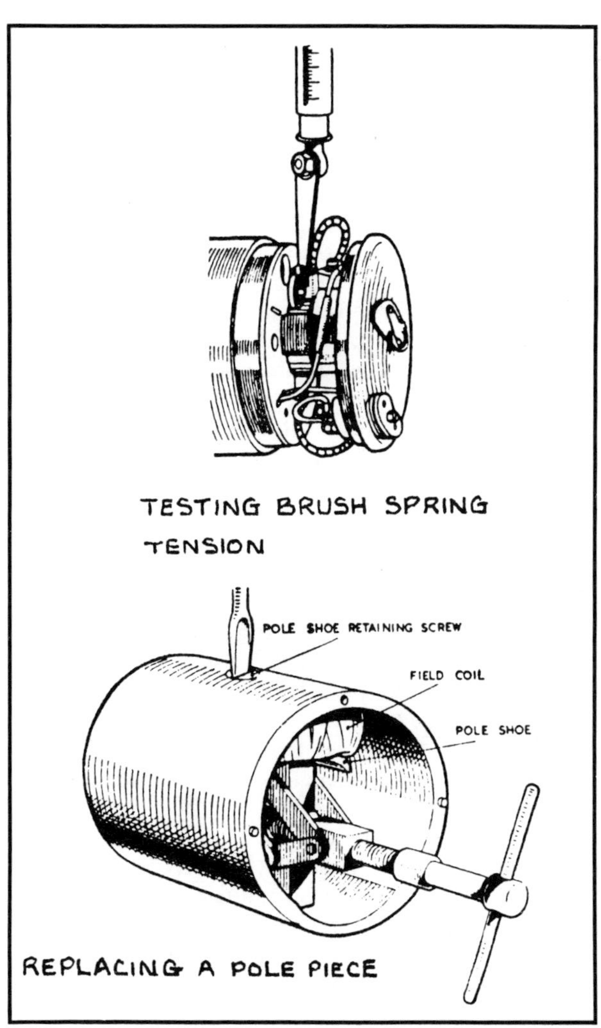

TESTING BRUSH SPRING TENSION

REPLACING A POLE PIECE

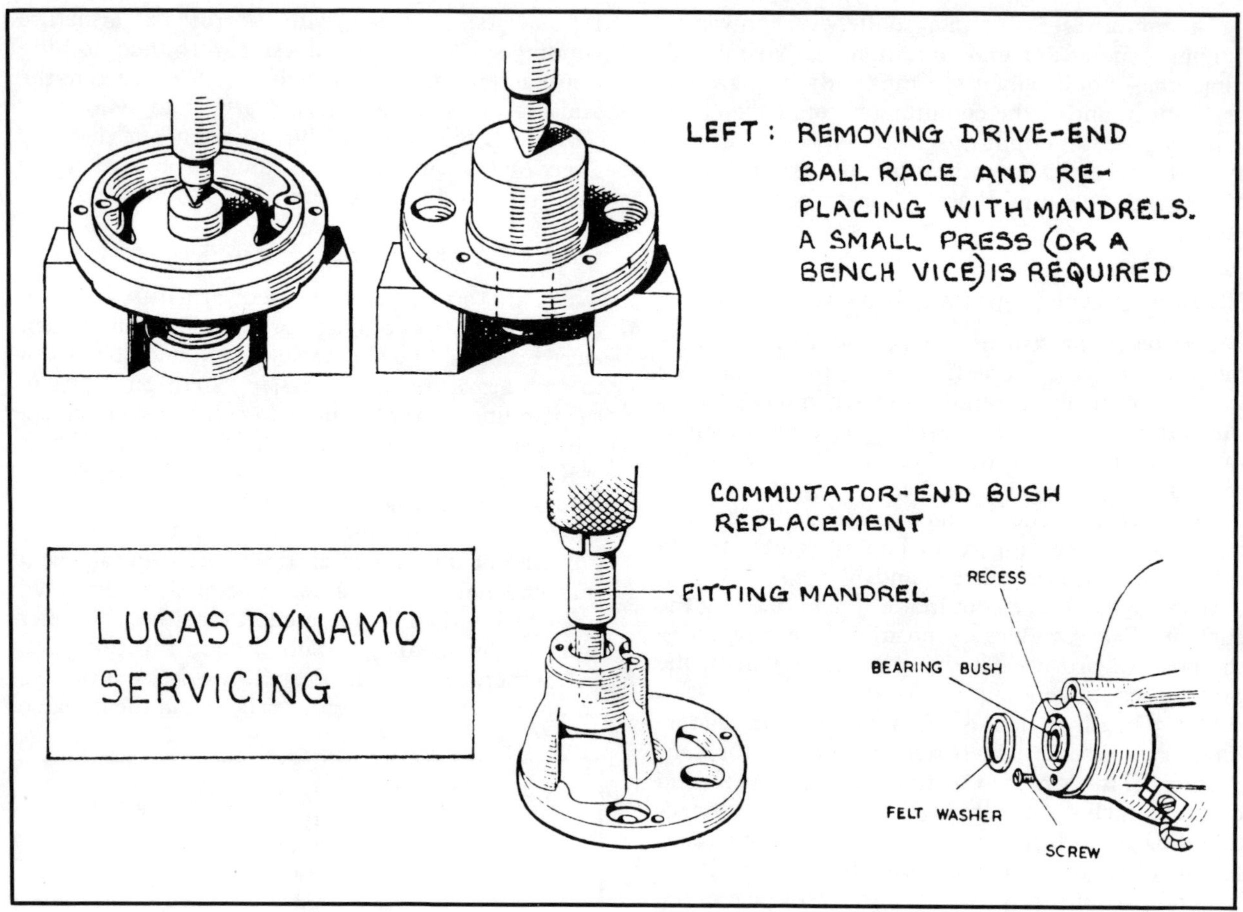

armature is slowly rotated on a V-block laminated core. Defective or short-circuited coils are quickly highlighted by varying magnetic fluxes — in essence a growler is a transformer in which the armature windings on test form the secondary coils. Various versions of these devices existed at one time and most rewinders possess one form or another.

The amateur restorer, who may possess little or no electrical knowledge, need not despair, as he can still carry out simple armature tests with a minimum of equipment.

Shorts

First of all the armature windings can be tested for shorts to earth. Normally the coils are insulated and no current should pass from them (or from the copper segments to which they are connected) to the armature core or spindle. All that is required in the way of equipment is a small battery (6v will do) and two lengths of wire. Connect the negative battery terminal up to the armature shaft. Connect one end of the other wire to the battery positive and bare the free end. Quickly jab the commutator segments with the bared end — if there is a flash it means that the commutator or windings are short-circuited to earth. It stands to reason that the test must be made quickly to avoid damaging the battery, in fact it is better to use an old battery rather than the one off the bike.

Continuity

A somewhat similar battery test can be employed when checking armature coils for continuity. Connect a length of wire to each battery terminal and bare the ends. Any battery will do, even a bicycle lamp dry battery. Touch the ends lightly on adjacent commutator bars and there should be a flash. If one bar is 'dead' it means that a winding is faulty, or the connection to the commutator is broken. Crude though it may be, this test gives a rough indication of the armature's condition. Points to remember when conducting this and the previous short-circuited test are that the leads should only contact for a fraction of a second and that an unused portion of the copper segments away from the brush path should be chosen. If a fault is suspected, the armature can then be taken to a firm of armature rewinders for further tests and, if necessary, a rewind.

Field coil

A dynamo will not work (no matter how good the armature) if the field coil is open-circuited or shorted. The field coil is the one found inside the

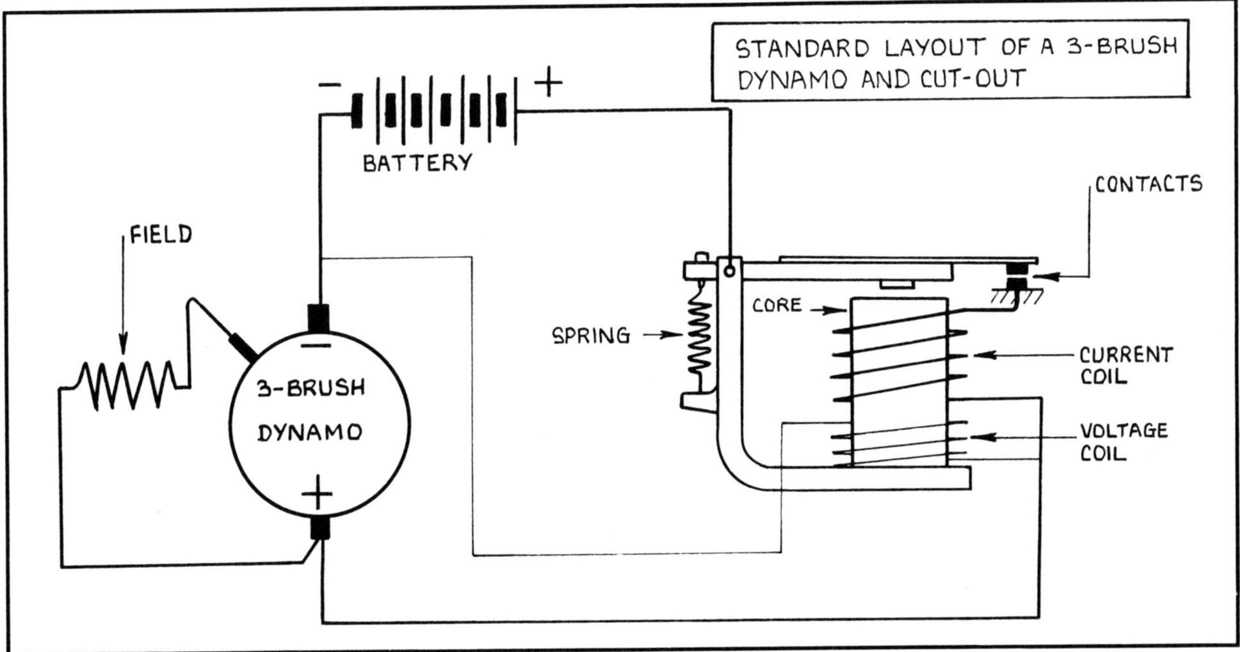

dynamo body, squashed between the pole piece and shell. The pole piece is electromagnetic and is only magnetised when the dynamo commences to revolve and a current (provided by the dynamo itself) circulates round the field coil. To check the condition of a field coil put a 6v 3 watt bulb in series with the field coil and battery. The bulb should be dim, compared with the amount of brightness when connected direct to the battery. A dull glow indicates that the field coil is continuous and providing a resistance in the test circuit. If the bulb does not light up, an open-circuit is indicated. Alternatively a brightly lit bulb signifies a possible short within the field windings.

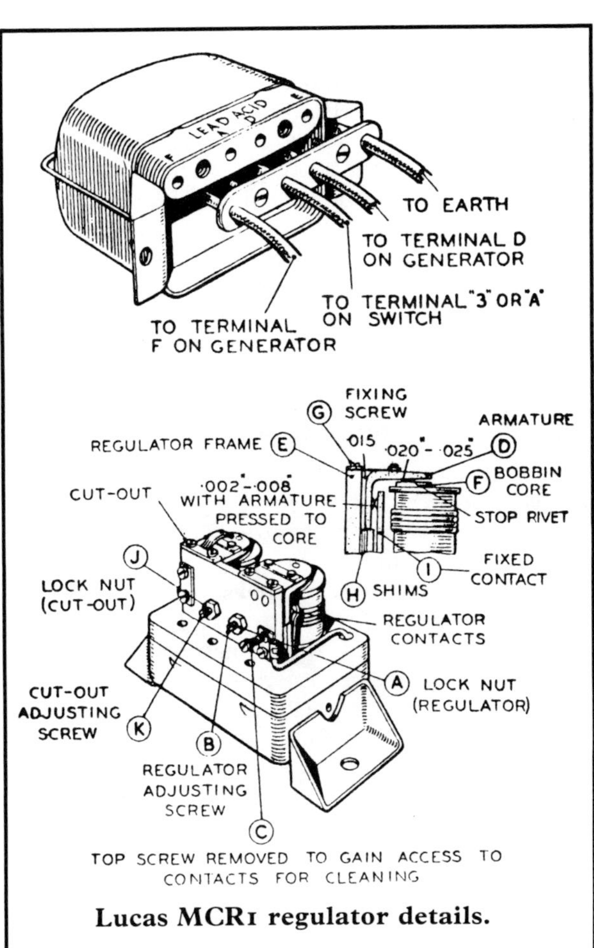

Lucas MCR1 regulator details.

Pole reseating

During dynamo assembly the pole screws were tightened well and truly home, following which metal was punched into the screw heads. To remove a field coil, the slots must be cleaned and an impact driver employed to shift the screws.

When replacing a coil, the pole-pieces must be correctly reseated, taking care not to damage coil insulation. The original reseating tool resembled a miniature car scissor jack, inserted between the pole and armature shell. These tools are almost extinct so the amateur must improvise with some form of clamping device, or force the pole-piece in position by means of nut-and-bolt jacks. As internal clearances are very small, the pole must be pressed well home and the securing screws firmly tightened.

Regulator units MCR1 and MCR2

The MCR1 cut-out and voltage regulator was introduced around 1935, which, together with a 2-brush Lucas dynamo, replaced the older and less efficient 3rd-brush regulating system . The main drawback with the latter was its propensity for boiling batteries during the summer months if the rider forgot to cut down his charging rate.

In 1949 the MCR2 was introduced, this unit being immediately recognisable by a small raised dome on the back of the outer cover. This domed pressing hid a 38 ohm carbon resistance, an improvement on the MCR1's wire-wound resistor. Apart from this feature there was very little difference between the two units — the procedure for testing remains the same.

Positive earth lighting system

Some machines have the battery positive connected to the frame instead of the negative. This does not affect regulator adjustment except that voltmeter connections should be reversed.

Regulator

The function of the regulator is to maintain a pre-determined dynamo voltage at all speeds, the field strength being controlled by the automatic introduction of a resistance in the generator field circuit. A current, or series, winding on the same core compensates this voltage figure in accordance with the output current, to ensure that the battery does not receive an excess current when discharged. Therefore the charging current depends on the differential between the controlled dynamo voltage and battery terminal voltage, and is at a maximum when the battery is discharged. It will be observed that the charging current gradually tapers off as the battery becomes charged and its voltage rises, so there is no need to worry if only a small charge is registered on the machine's ammeter after a few miles running. In addition, a form of temperature compensation ensures that the voltage characteristics of the regulator are matched to those of the battery for large variations in working temperature.

Cut-out

The cut-out is simply an automatic switch connected between dynamo and battery. A pair of contacts is held open by a spring and closed electromagnetically.

When the engine is running fast enough to cause the dynamo voltage to exceed that of the battery, the contacts close and the battery receives a charging current. When the dynamo speed is slow (or stopped) the contacts open, thus disconnecting the dynamo from the battery. If the contacts remained shut the battery would discharge rapidly through the dynamo windings.

Test data

	MCR1 Cut-out	MCR2 Cut-out
Cut-in voltage	6.2 – 6.6 volts	6.3 – 6.7 volts
Drop-off voltage	3.5 – 5.3 volts	4.5 – 5.0 volts
Reverse current	0.7 – 2.5 amps	3.0 – 5.0 amps

	Regulator (setting in open circuit)	
10°C 50°F	8.0 – 8.4 volts	7.7 – 8.1 volts
20°C 68°F	7.8 – 8.2 volts	7.6 – 8.0 volts
30°C 86°F	7.6 – 8.0 volts	7.5 – 7.9 volts
40°C 104°F	7.4 – 7.9 volts	7.4 – 7.8 volts

Locating faults

Assuming the dynamo to be in good working order, as already described, disconnect the wire from the A terminal of the regulator and connect it to the positive terminal of a voltmeter. Connect the voltmeter negative to earth on the machine. If there is no reading on the meter, examine the wiring for chafing or broken connections. On the other hand a reading will indicate that the wiring is in order and the fault lies in the regulator.

Regulator adjustment

Remove the regulator cover and insert a piece of paper between the cut-out points. Connect the positive terminal of a 0-10 volt moving-coil voltmeter to the D terminal on the regulator and the negative to earth on the machine.

Start the engine and increase the speed gradually until the voltmeter needle flicks and then steadies. The voltmeter reading should be within limits at a particular temperature. If it is not, the regulator must be adjusted as follows.

Stop the engine. Release locknut A on the regulator adjusting screw B. Turn the screw clockwise to raise the setting or anti-clockwise to lower it. Very little movement is required. Do up the locknut when the correct figure is achieved.

It is important to remember that the engine should not be raced when carrying out this test as the dynamo is on open circuit and would build up a high voltage, giving an incorrect voltmeter reading. No more than half throttle is required.

Regulator mechanical setting

First of all clean the points, by removing screw C and slackening the screw beneath to enable the fixed contact to be swung outwards. Polish the points with fine emery cloth.

Slacken the two small screws G on top of the regulator frame. Insert a .015 in feeler (MCR1) between the back of the armature D and the regulator frame E. (.020 in on the MCR2).

Press the armature back against the frame and down on top of the bobbin core, with the feeler in position, and lock the two G screws. Check the air gap between the core and flap. Adjust if necessary. In the case of MCR1 unit the air gap is .025 in, achieved by removing shims from the back of the fixed contact. The correct figure for the MCR2 is .012 in to .020 in, achieved by bending the fixed contact bracket.

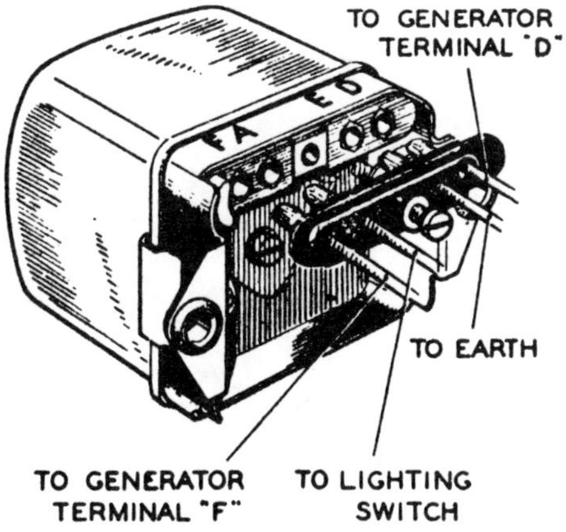

TO GENERATOR
TERMINAL "D"
TO EARTH
TO GENERATOR
TERMINAL "F"
TO LIGHTING
SWITCH

REGULATOR ADJUSTMENT
SCREW
CONTACTS
RESISTANCE
CUTOUT ADJUSTMENT
SCREW
CUTOUT FIXED
CONTACT
STOP PLATE
CUTOUT
CONTACT BLADE
MOVING CONTACT
FIXED CONTACT

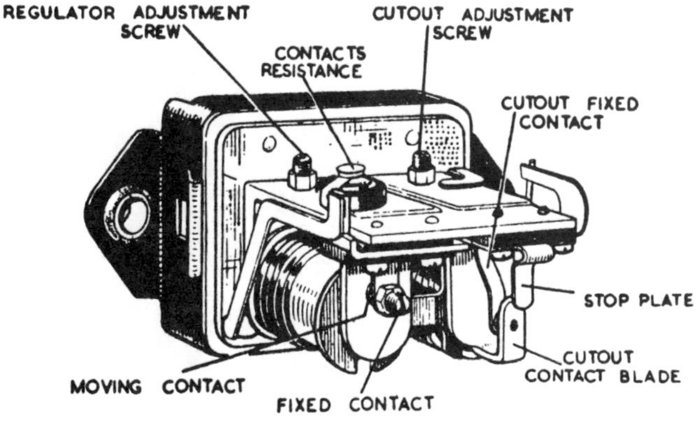

Control Box Connections and Internal Layout.

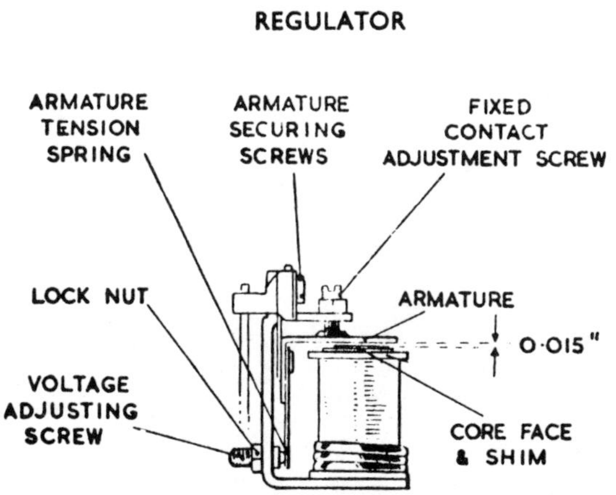

REGULATOR
ARMATURE
TENSION
SPRING
ARMATURE
SECURING
SCREWS
FIXED
CONTACT
ADJUSTMENT SCREW
LOCK NUT
ARMATURE
0·015"
VOLTAGE
ADJUSTING
SCREW
CORE FACE
& SHIM

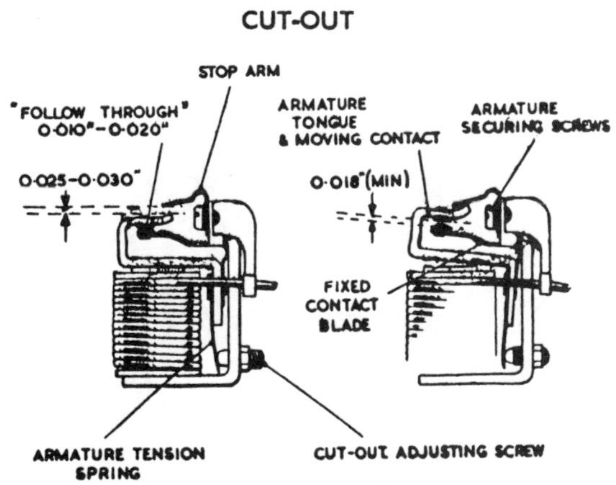

CUT-OUT
STOP ARM
"FOLLOW THROUGH"
0·010"–0·020"
ARMATURE
TONGUE
& MOVING CONTACT
ARMATURE
SECURING SCREWS
0·025–0·030"
0·018"(MIN)
FIXED
CONTACT
BLADE
ARMATURE TENSION
SPRING
CUT-OUT ADJUSTING SCREW

Regulator and Cut-Out Adjustment and Setting.

REGULATOR
CUT-OUT
REGULATOR & CUT-OUT FRAME
RESISTANCE
SHUNT
COIL
SERIES
COIL
SHUNT
COIL
SERIES
COIL
F
A
E
D

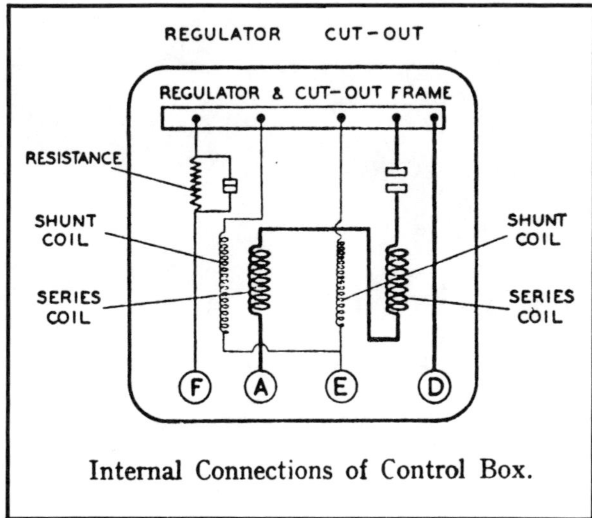

Internal Connections of Control Box.

Details of the Lucas RB107 control box.

The gap between the regulator contacts should now be .002 in to .008 in (MCR1) or .006 in to .017 in (MCR2). Reset, if necessary, the electrical adjustment after a further engine test.

Cut-out and voltage regulator unit RB107

This unit could be described as an updated version of the MCR2 unit, having many features in common with the older cvc box. The test procedure is similar and should be carried out in the following manner.

Remove the wire from terminal A and connect it to the voltmeter terminal. Connect the other voltmeter terminal to earth. A reading will indicate a sound battery circuit to terminal A, or defective cables if there is no reading. Re-connect the wire to terminal A.

Check that the wiring between dynamo terminal D and control box terminal D, and between dynamo terminal F and control box F is in good order.

An unusual subject for restoration, this 1933 pressed-steel frame Coventry-Eagle was rebuilt from a rusty wreck by the Author. It features the extremely rare semi-unit 150cc Coventry-Eagle engine (most others had Villiers power units). The renovation of the engine proved a daunting task, involving making a crank assembly and adapting a Villiers flywheel magneto to replace the missing Lucas unit. The enamel C-E badge was made from copper and enamelled with coloured resin.

COVENTRY-
EAGLE
HY-6568

Electrical setting

Connect one terminal of a moving coil voltmeter to terminal D and the other terminal to E on the control box. Remove the live battery terminal.

Start the engine and gradually increase the speed until the voltmeter needle flicks and then steadies out. Stop the engine. The reading should be within limits as shown in in the accompanying table:

Setting data RB107

Cut-out	
Cut-in voltage	6.3 – 6.7 volts
Drop-off voltage	4.8 – 5.3 volts
Reverse current	3.0 – 5.0 amps
Regulator	
10°C 50°F	7.7 – 8.1 volts
20°C 68°F	7.6 – 8.0 volts
30°C 86°F	7.5 – 7.9 volts
40°C 104°F	7.4 – 7.8 volts

Slacken the adjusting screw locknut and turn the screw clockwise to raise the setting, and anti-clockwise to lower it. When the correct setting is achieved, do up the locknut.

Adjustment should be carried out within 30 seconds to avoid overheating the shunt winding (so causing false settings to be made). Do not run the engine at more than half speed.

Mechanical regulator setting RB107

Slacken the locknut on the voltage adjusting screw and unscrew the adjuster until it is well clear of the armature tension spring. Slacken the two armature securing screws.

Insert a .015 in feeler gauge wide enough to cover completely the core face between the armature and core shim. Press the armature down and tighten up the two securing screws. With the feeler in position, screw the adjustable contact down until it just touches the armature contact.

Tighten the locknut and reset the voltage adjusting screw as previously described.

Electrical setting of cut-out RB107

Connect a voltmeter between terminals D and E on the control box. Start the engine and slowly increase the speed and note the voltmeter reading, which should be 6.3 to 6.7 volts. Adjust if necessary by turning the screw clockwise to raise the setting and anti-clock to lower it. Re-test and note the reading; if all is well do up the locknut.

As with regulator adjustment, make alterations as quickly as possible due to temperature rise effects.

If the cut-out operates but no charge is registered, check the points and clean if necessary. If the cut-out fails to work, the internal control box wiring may be open-circuited (eg. there may be a break in the cut-out coil).

The Lucas Maglita

The original thinking behind this wondrous gadget, the ML and its successor the Lucas *Maglita,* was to produce a lighting and ignition unit not much bigger than an ordinary magneto. It had been known for some time that an ordinary magneto could be modified to produce sufficient current to power a small bulb or two. This current was 'borrowed' from the primary wiring of the magneto armature, in conjunction with an induction or choke coil. The magneto would still carry on with its normal function of supplying sparks, albeit at slightly reduced intensity; Messrs FRS Lamps (who made such a conversion) recommended that the machine should be started with the lighting circuit switched off.

The *Maglita* could be considered a development of the 'something-for-nothing' scheme, consisting of a single armature wound with a low-tension winding revolving between bar magnets. Sitting on top of the magnets is an induction coil with a laminated core. The primary of this coil is connected to a contact breaker and condenser, so that when the armature rotates an alternating voltage is induced in the windings and a spark is produced via the secondary coil windings.

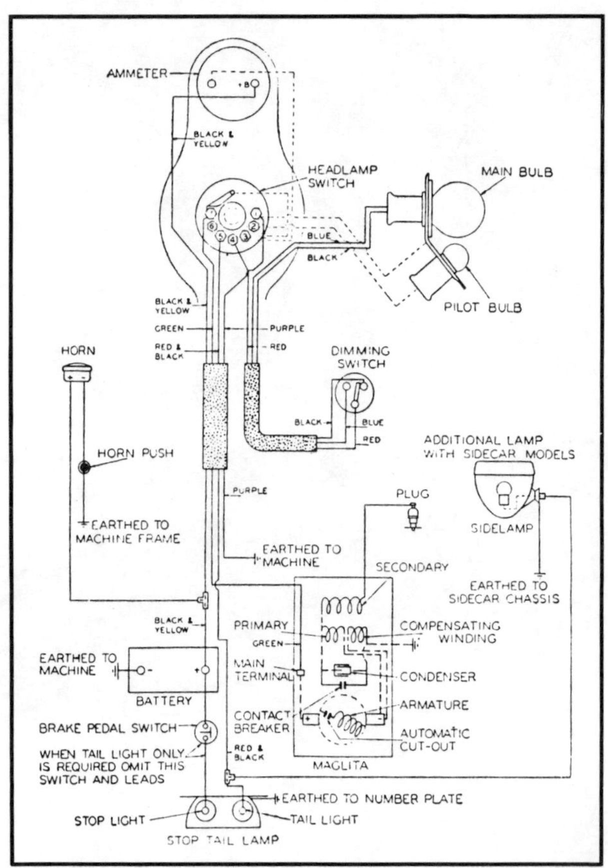

A typical wiring diagram for Lucas Maglita lighting and ignition.

The revolving armature has a commutator, from which the meagre lighting current is collected by two carbon brushes. Maintenance is restricted to commutator cleaning, in the usual way, and occasional renewal of the brushes.

The points should be cleaned and set at .012 in. Put a spot of light machine oil on the cam every 1000 miles or so. When lubricating the face cam remember the oil hole under the contact breaker and don't forget the lubricator on the spindle end.

The Lucas *Maglita* is fitted with a form of centrifugal cut-out; this should not be meddled with but if its action is suspect a simple test can be made to isolate the fault. Assuming that the ammeter does not register a charge when the engine is running (and when the switch is on "charge") temporarily by-pass the cut-out by taking a wire from the positive terminal to the collector brush, and then the brush itself.

If the lamps light, the fault is in the cut-out. Check also the wiring from the generator to the headlamp switch. In the case of the 250 cc Rudge the lead from the positive battery terminal is connected to the B ammeter terminal; do not connect the battery in a reverse direction or the magnets may become partially demagnetised. Do not remove the armature unnecessarily as this also weakens the magnets — always use a 'keeper'.

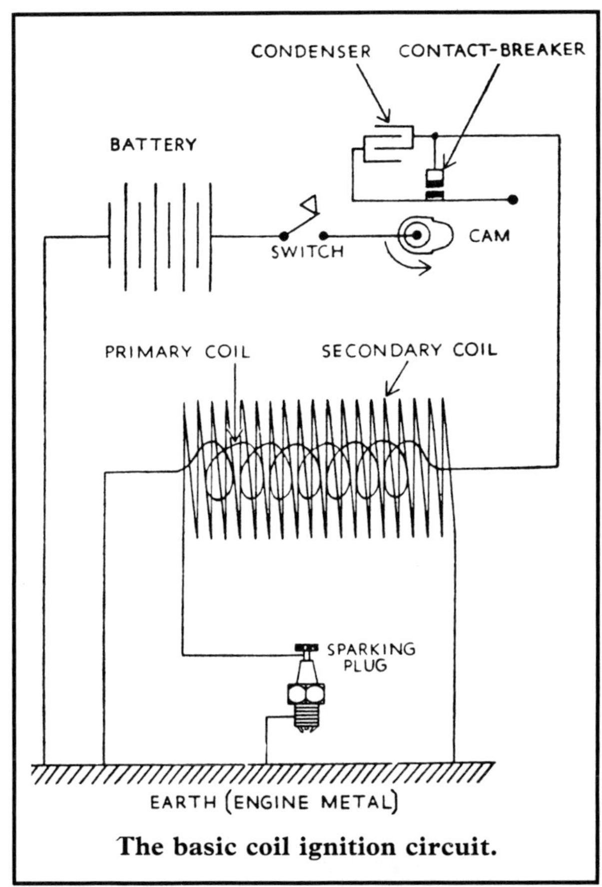

The basic coil ignition circuit.

Coil ignition

The most common causes of ignition failure on a coil-ignition system are, in order of likelihood:

1 Dirty or stuck points
2 Faulty wiring to coil or distributor terminals
3 Dud condenser
4 Faulty coil

Dealing with the above points in order, rectification of fault 1 is obvious — clean and reset the points to .015 in (or .012 in if recommended by the manufacturer). Badly pitted contacts should be replaced.

Item 2, faulty wiring, is easily checked. If there is a tiny spark when the contact breaker points are separated by hand, with the ignition switched on, this usually signifies that the wiring is sound to the contact breaker/distributor unit. Verification with a voltmeter is advised if there is any doubt. To check the input voltage to the coil place one voltmeter lead on the coil SW terminal and the other to earth. Full battery voltage should be registered — if not, suspect faulty connections or a dirty switch.

A dud condenser, item 3, usually manifests its presence by severe sparking at the contact breaker points. Bad starting, misfiring, or complete engine failure could also follow. Check by substitution, but make sure you don't replace the faulty condenser with an equally dud item or you will have endless problems!

Item 4, faulty coil, is a relatively rare snag. To check the coil primary windings connect a voltmeter to the CB terminal, after removing the wire leading to the contact breaker. The other voltmeter lead is connected to earth. When the ignition is switched on, the voltmeter should indicate almost full battery voltage. If the reading is appreciably lower, suspect a high resistance in the coil primary. No reading means a broken coil winding or faulty internal connections.

There are ways of checking secondary HT coils for continuity but the ultimate test is on the motorcycle — if no spark is forthcoming, then further text-book checks are of academic interest! (Without wishing to cast aspersions in any direction, one wonders if writers of electrical manuals have ever ridden motorcycles . . .). It is not unknown for a coil to cut-dead after a high speed blast and then decide to function as normal just when the unfortunate rider has given up hope by the roadside. Then there is the coil which will emit an anaemic spark on test but will not fire the engine . . . and the coil which gives up the ghost on hot days only.

One personal experience with a recalcitrant coil may be of interest to readers. The motorcycle, a 250 cc two-stroke, suffered from bad starting and occasional misfiring. Both coil and condenser were checked with favourable results. A new plug temporarily cured the problem, but after 100 miles the bike again had the sulks. Another new plug gave it a lease of life, again temporarily. Eventually it was decided to replace the miniscule HT coil with an enormous 6v Bosch (obtained from a scrapyard Volkswagen Beetle).

Results were, if the readers will pardon the expression, electrifying! The machine's performance was transformed; starting became a one-prod affair hot or cold and acceleration was vastly improved.

Contact breaker units

Typical of motorcycle contact breaker units, types DK and D1A2 require little in the way of maintenance.

DK type — Unscrew the two screws holding the contact breaker baseplate to the distributor and lubricate the automatic timing device thus exposed. Thin machine oil is recommended, paying particular attention to the pivots. Smear the cam lightly with thin grease or oil.

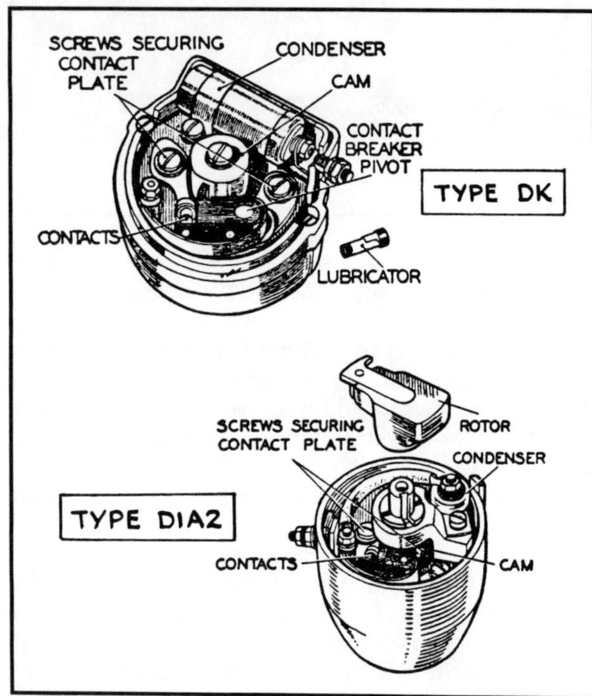

The two basic types of Lucas contact breaker unit.

D1A2 type — Take the distributor off the engine and remove the cover and rotor. Inject thin machine oil through the aperture between cam and contact breaker baseplate.

Remove the screw from inside the rotor boss and apply a few drops of thin machine oil in the tapped hole. The spindle is drilled to allow oil to reach the cam bearing. Smear the cam lightly with thin grease or oil.

On all types of contact breakers and distributors remove the bakelite lids occasionally and wipe them clean inside. A light spray with *WD40* will keep moisture at bay.

Stick rigidly to the machine manufacturer's recommended contact breaker setting figures (usually .015 in).

Wipac flywheel magnetos

The following service information, reproduced by kind permission of Wipac Ltd., covers a representative selection of Wipac flywheel magnetos.

Included are the *Geni-mag* as used on very early D1 BSA Bantams, the popular *Series 55/Mk8* flywheel ignition generator on the 125 cc RE Enfield (the same generator, in opposite-rotation guise, was also used on Bantams) and the *Bantamag,* which was used on various cyclemotors.

With regard to the *55/Mk 8 generator,* there is perhaps one further point to add. Rapid wear of the sintered bronze crankshaft outrigger bush (that's the one in the centre of the stator plate) should not be blamed on the magneto. The fault is more likely due to faulty crankshaft alignment — certainly in the case of the BSA Bantam, which has a long spindly generator-side mainshaft. It is unfair to expect the small bronze bush to contain the shaft's gyrations.

If the correct porous-bronze *Oilite* (or *Lubrook*) bush is not to hand, a new one can be made from nylon. This will last almost indefinitely (use *Nylatron GSM* if available).

Below: Twin headlamp (Miller) arrangement on big Panthers in 1936. Note the comprehensive instrument console, complete with 8-day clock. *(Photo: Panther Owners Club.)*

Opposite and following page: Service instructions for the Wipac *Genimag* as fitted to the BSA Bantam and the Series 55 Mk 8 generator as fitted to the 125cc Royal Enfield two-stroke.

SERVICE INSTRUCTIONS

FOR THE WIPAC GENIMAG

FLYWHEEL IGNITION GENERATOR

RUNNING MAINTENANCE

The magneto requires very little maintenance and if the following notes are observed the life of the machine should prove trouble free.

Check and if necessary re-adjust the contacts once every 5,000 miles. (See Service Instructions.)

Occasionally clean the contacts by inserting a dry smooth piece of paper between them and withdrawing while the contacts are in the closed position. Do not allow the engine to run with oil or petrol on the contacts or they will start to burn and blacken, and if they do, lightly polish with a piece of smooth emery cloth.

After every 5,000 miles it is necessary to re-lubricate the cam oil pad. This is done by removing the pad and squeezing and working into it a Summer grade of motor transmission grease which will very closely resemble that used at the factory. Do not use ordinary grease.

Do not run with a faulty or damaged high-tension lead and occasionally clean away mud and dirt from around the H.T. insulator.

If the magneto requires any attention beyond the replacement of contact points and condenser, it is recommended that the complete machine should be sent to us or to an authorised Wico service station. The following information is given for the benefit of those unable to do so :—

GENERAL MAINTENANCE

Checking the Magneto for spark

If the engine fails to start and there is an indication of the magneto causing trouble, the spark can be checked by holding the H.T. lead $\frac{3}{16}$" away from a point on the frame. When the engine is kicked over in the usual way, a spark should jump this gap. If no spark is visible, see that the H.T. lead is in good condition and examine the contact breaker. Make sure there are no metallic particles inside the housing and that the contacts are perfectly clean, and the gap is correct to the recommended setting. If the contacts are found to be in a burnt or badly pitted condition, a faulty condenser is indicated. If the contact breaker appears to be in order the stator plate may be removed from the engine complete with coils, and the leads of the ignition coil should be examined to ensure that there is no break in the wiring. One lead will be found to be joined to a tab which is clamped underneath one of the nuts which anchor the stator to the stator housing. If this is in order check the other end of the primary ignition coil which is connected to the back of the insulated post which projects into the contact breaker recess at the front of the magneto. The screw which locks this in position will be found underneath the lighting coil on the right-hand side looking at the inside of the stator housing when in its upright position. The condenser lead is also joined to this point. If both these are connected and the tabs are not earthing on the stator plate the ignition coil should be in working order. In the unlikely event of the H.T. insulation of the secondary coil breaking down, it should be possible to detect signs of charring either on the binding tape of the coil, the insulating gaskets or the H.T. insulator.

Replacement of Coil

To remove the coil, the H.T. insulator which is held by two screws outside the housing must be taken off. The removal of the stator is effected by unscrewing the three clamp nuts. The stator may then be gently eased off the three stator plate studs. Care must be taken not to jerk it, otherwise the lead which connects the lighting coils to the terminal on the stator may be broken. The live end of the primary ignition coil lead must then be disconnected from the contact breaker terminal post. In order to slide the coil from the iron limb, it is necessary to straighten the small brass tab which will be found on the side of the coil which faces the stator housing. If the coil is grasped firmly in one hand with the fingers under the insulator gaskets and on either side of the core, it may be quite easily pulled off. To refit the ignition coil proceed as follows :—

(a) Hold the coil in the left hand with the brass contact pointing away from the line of vision and the lead wires projecting downwards from the underside, and drop the leads through the rectangular hole in the two insulating gaskets, the extended end of which must point in the same direction as the coil tab.

(b) With the other hand push the coil core through the coil making sure that the brass locking tab riveted to the iron is on the same side as the coil contact. Drive the fibre wedge provided in between the core and the coil on the same side as the locking tab and bend over the tab.

THE WIPAC GROUP — BLETCHLEY ENGLAND
NORTHERN AREA BRANCH AND SERVICE DEPOT 7 PARK SQUARE, LEEDS

Ref. B.47.R.

SERVICE INSTRUCTIONS

FOR THE WIPAC SERIES 55 MK 8

FLYWHEEL IGNITION GENERATOR

RUNNING MAINTENANCE

The magneto requires very little maintenance and if the following notes are observed the life of the machine should prove trouble free.

Check and if necessary re-adjust the contacts once every 5,000 miles. (See Service Instructions.)

Occasionally clean the contacts by inserting a dry smooth piece of paper between them and withdrawing while the contacts are in the closed position. Do not allow the engine to run with oil or petrol on the contacts or they will start to burn and blacken, and if they do, lightly polish with a piece of smooth emery cloth.

After every 5,000 miles it is necessary to re-lubricate the cam oil pad. This is done by removing the pad and squeezing and working into it a Summer grade of motor transmission grease which will very closely resemble that used at the factory. Do not use ordinary grease.

Do not run with a faulty or damaged high-tension lead and occasionally clean away mud and dirt from around the H.T. insulator.

If the magneto requires any attention beyond the replacement of contact points and condenser, it is recommended that the complete machine should be sent to us or to an authorised Wico service station. The following information is given for the benefit of those unable to do so :—

GENERAL MAINTENANCE

Checking the Magneto for Spark

If the engine fails to start and there is an indication of the magneto causing trouble, the spark can be checked by holding the H.T. lead $\frac{3}{16}''$ away from a point on the frame. When the engine is kicked over in the usual way, a spark should jump this gap. If no spark is visible, see that the H.T. lead is in good condition and examine the contact breaker.

Make sure there are no metallic particles inside the housing, and that the contacts are perfectly clean, and the contact breaker gap is correct to the recommended setting.

If the contacts are found to be in a burnt or badly pitted condition, a faulty condenser is indicated. If the contact breaker appears to be in order, the stator plate may be removed from the engine complete with coils.

To do this, the following procedure should be adopted :—

Unscrew the two cover securing screws and remove the cover, unscrew the cam screw and withdraw the cam free of the shaft. The small cam key in some instances may leave its keyway, so care should be taken to make sure of this point when taking the cam from the shaft. Next remove the three stator plate securing screws. The stator can now be withdrawn clear of the engine.

The leads of the ignition coil should be examined to ensure that there is no break in the wiring. One lead will be found to be joined to a tab which is clamped underneath one of the nuts which anchor the stator coil assembly to the stator housing. If this is in order, check the sleeved lead of the primary ignition coil which is connected to the front of the insulated post, which also carries the condenser lead and contact breaker return spring.

The screw which locks the insulated post in position will be found underneath the low tension coil on the right-hand side looking at the inside of the stator housing when in its upright position.

There is, however, no need to remove this screw for any of the investigations recommended in these instructions. The second screw lying at a larger radius and appearing over the top of the coil is the earthing screw for the No. 2 terminal on the front of the machine.

If the leads joined to the insulated post are in order and firmly clamped and the tags not earthing in any way, the ignition coil should be in working order. Should it be necessary to completely remove the stator plate entirely, the low and high tension leads should be freed from the insulated terminal boards on the front of the unit and the plugs respectively, the former by the loosening off of the grub screws and withdrawing the low tension leads which are coloured through the rubber insulator. The stator plate assembly should then be entirely free of the engine.

In the unlikely event of the H.T. insulation of the coil breaking down, provided this is not internal, it should be possible to detect signs of charring on the binding tape of the coil. If the absence of spark is due to tracking, track burns may be visible on the insulator gasket.

Replacement of Ignition Coil

The removal of the stator coil assembly is effected by first disconnecting the ignition lead from the coil, then freeing the white, red and green low tension leads from the terminals marked 3, 1 and 4 respectively, and unscrewing the two clamp nuts. The live lead of the primary winding of the ignition coil must then be disconnected from the insulated post by removing the securing screw. The stator coil assembly may then be gently eased off the two stator plate studs.

In order to slide the ignition coil from the iron limb, it is necessary to straighten the small brass tab which will be found on the side of the coil which faces the stator housing. If the coil is grasped firmly in one hand with the fingers under the insulator gasket and on either side of the core, it may be quite easily pulled off.

THE WIPAC GROUP — BLETCHLEY ENGLAND
NORTHERN AREA BRANCH AND SERVICE DEPOT 7 PARK SQUARE, LEEDS

Ref. B.94.R.

Lucas alternators

The RM14 alternator is similar in mechanical appearance to the RM12 but employs the bridge-connected rectifier circuit as used with the RM13. It was designed for use with twin and four-cylinder machines and as such has a slightly different ignition circuit arrangement. Whereas the ignition coil primary winding and contact breaker are connected in parallel for the RM13, the RM14 primary coil winding and contact breaker are connected in series. The adoption of this more conventional practice is because twins, being fitted with distributor electrodes, are unaffected by premature sparking before the contacts separate.

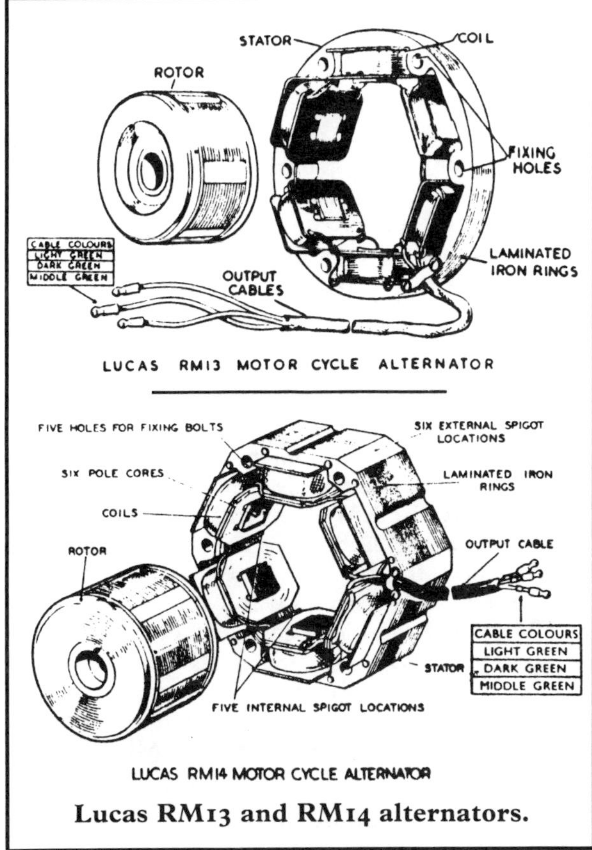

Lucas RM13 and RM14 alternators.

TEST 1

CHECKING DC CIRCUIT

CONNECT A 0-15AMP AMMETER IN SERIES WITH BATTERY

SWITCH POS.	CORRECT READING (AMPS)	
	RM 13 GENERATOR	RM 14 GENERATOR
OFF	1½-2½	2½-3½
PILOT	½-1½	1½-2½
HEAD	¼-¾	2½-3½

RUN ENGINE AT 2000 R.P.M.
IF READING IS LOW ON ONE POSITION CHECK CONNECTIONS
IF READING IS LOW, OR THERE IS NO READING, PROCEED TO TEST 2 TO CHECK ALTERNATOR.

Output control

The alternator carries three pairs of series connected coils, one pair being permanently connected across the rectifier bridge network. The purpose of this latter pair is to provide some degree of charging current for the battery whenever the engine is running.

When the ignition key is at the IGN position the connections for the basic charging circuit are as follows:

1 **Lighting switch off**
Output taken from one pair of coils — light green and dark green — the remaining coils are short-circuited. The flux set up by the current flowing in the short-circuited coils interacts with the rotor flux and regulates the alternator output to its minimum value.

2 **Lighting switch Pilot**
Output taken from one pair of coils — light green and dark green — the remaining coils are disconnected and the regulating fluxes are consequently reduced. The alternator output therefore increases and compensates for the additional parking light load.

3 **Lighting switch Head**
In this position the output from the alternator is further increased by connecting all three pairs of coils in parallel.

4 **Emergency starting**
In the EMG position the battery is not isolated from the alternator and will in fact receive a charge whilst the machine is being run with the ignition switch in this position.

This arrangement is a safeguard against continuous running in the EMG position. The back pressure of the battery will increase as it is charged, until it is sufficiently strong to affect the ignition system. Misfiring occurs, reminding the rider to switch back to normal running (IGN).

For competition purposes, without lighting equipment or battery, the machine can be run permanently in the EMG mode, providing the cable normally connected to the battery negative terminal is earthed to the machine.

Demagnetised rotors

If a current from the battery passes through the alternator windings when the engine is running, the rotor arm can become partially demagnetised. This may happen if the rectifier breaks down, or if the battery connections are reversed. Always make sure the battery positive terminal is connected to the machine frame.

Testing procedure

The following instruments are required:

Moving coil AC voltmeter 0-15v

Moving coil DC voltmeter 0-15v (or DC ammeter 0-15 amps)

1 ohm load resistance capable of carrying 8 amps without overheating.

12v battery and 6 watt bulb (rectifier test)

Engine speed for testing

For the main tests using the AC voltmeter and DC voltmeter the engine must be run at approximately 2000 rpm.

Common faults

1 Battery — No charge. Check battery condition and test the alternator
2 Battery — Insufficient charging. Test battery condition and proceed with Tests 1, 2 and 3
3 Rough running — 'IGN' Position. Check for faulty earth connection from battery, rectifier, or high resistance connection in the battery feed through the headlamp switches to the coil.
4 Rough running (or will not run) in EMG position. Check rectifier Test 3. If the rectifier appears functional examine leads and connections from ignition switch to coil and from coil to distributor. Check condition of contacts, condenser etc. If machine still refuses to start, check alternator, Test 1.

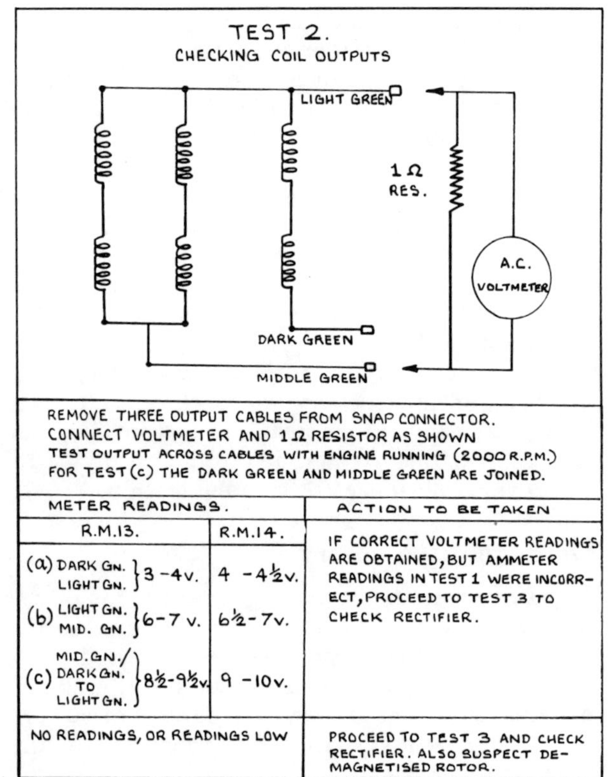

REMOVE THREE OUTPUT CABLES FROM SNAP CONNECTOR.
CONNECT VOLTMETER AND 1Ω RESISTOR AS SHOWN
TEST OUTPUT ACROSS CABLES WITH ENGINE RUNNING (2000 R.P.M.)
FOR TEST (c) THE DARK GREEN AND MIDDLE GREEN ARE JOINED.

METER READINGS.			ACTION TO BE TAKEN
	R.M.13.	R.M.14.	
(a) DARK GN. / LIGHT GN.	3 -4v.	4 -4½v.	IF CORRECT VOLTMETER READINGS ARE OBTAINED, BUT AMMETER READINGS IN TEST 1 WERE INCORRECT, PROCEED TO TEST 3 TO CHECK RECTIFIER.
(b) LIGHT GN. / MID. GN.	6-7 v.	6½-7v.	
(c) MID. GN./ DARK GN. TO LIGHT GN.	8½-9½v.	9 -10v.	
NO READINGS, OR READINGS LOW			PROCEED TO TEST 3 AND CHECK RECTIFIER. ALSO SUSPECT DE-MAGNETISED ROTOR.

Test 1

a Turn the ignition switch to the IGN position, with the lighting switch off.
b Connect a DC voltmeter between the centre connection of the rectifier — light brown lead — and frame (earth). Full battery voltage will be registered. This proves continuity from the battery through the ignition switch to the rectifier. If no reading is obtained check wiring for loose, broken or dirty connections.
c No reading should be obtained with the ignition switch in the OFF position.
d With the ignition switch in the IGN position, and the DC voltmeter connected alternately at the other two rectifier tags — dark and light green leads — a reading of approximately 1-2 volts should be registered, due to the back leakage through the rectifier.

Test 2

a With the ignition switch in the IGN position, remove the three green leads from the (rectifier side) snap connectors; the low voltage reading should still be obtained, with the voltmeter connected to the middle green cable.
b The reading at the middle green cable should be obtained with the lighting switch in the OFF and HEAD positions but not in the PILOT position. This test checks the switching of the alternator coils for all charging combinations.
c Turn the ignition key from the IGN position to the EMG position; no reading should be obtained at the middle green cable.

Testing the EMG circuit

a Replace all leads in the snap connectors. Connect the DC voltmeter between the CB terminal of the ignition coil and frame (earth), with the ignition contacts open and the ignition switch in the IGN position. Full battery voltage should be registered.
b The low voltage reading should be obtained with the ignition switch in the EMG position.

Lucas RM12 alternator (four and six lead)

It may be of interest to summarise the development of the RM12 alternator, prior to the introduction of the RM13, as fitted to Triumph 5TA motor cycles.

Phase 1 A single wound alternator, using four main leads and a double-banked rectifier, was fitted to all machines prior to engine no. 35334.

Phase 2 To provide current to give adequate battery charging under widely varying conditions and generally improve performance, a double-wound alternator, using six main leads and a single banked rectifier, was fitted to all machines from engine no. 35334 to engine no. 38988.

Phase 3 To provide for continuous running in the EMG position, the double wound alternator arrangement was modified and the new equipment

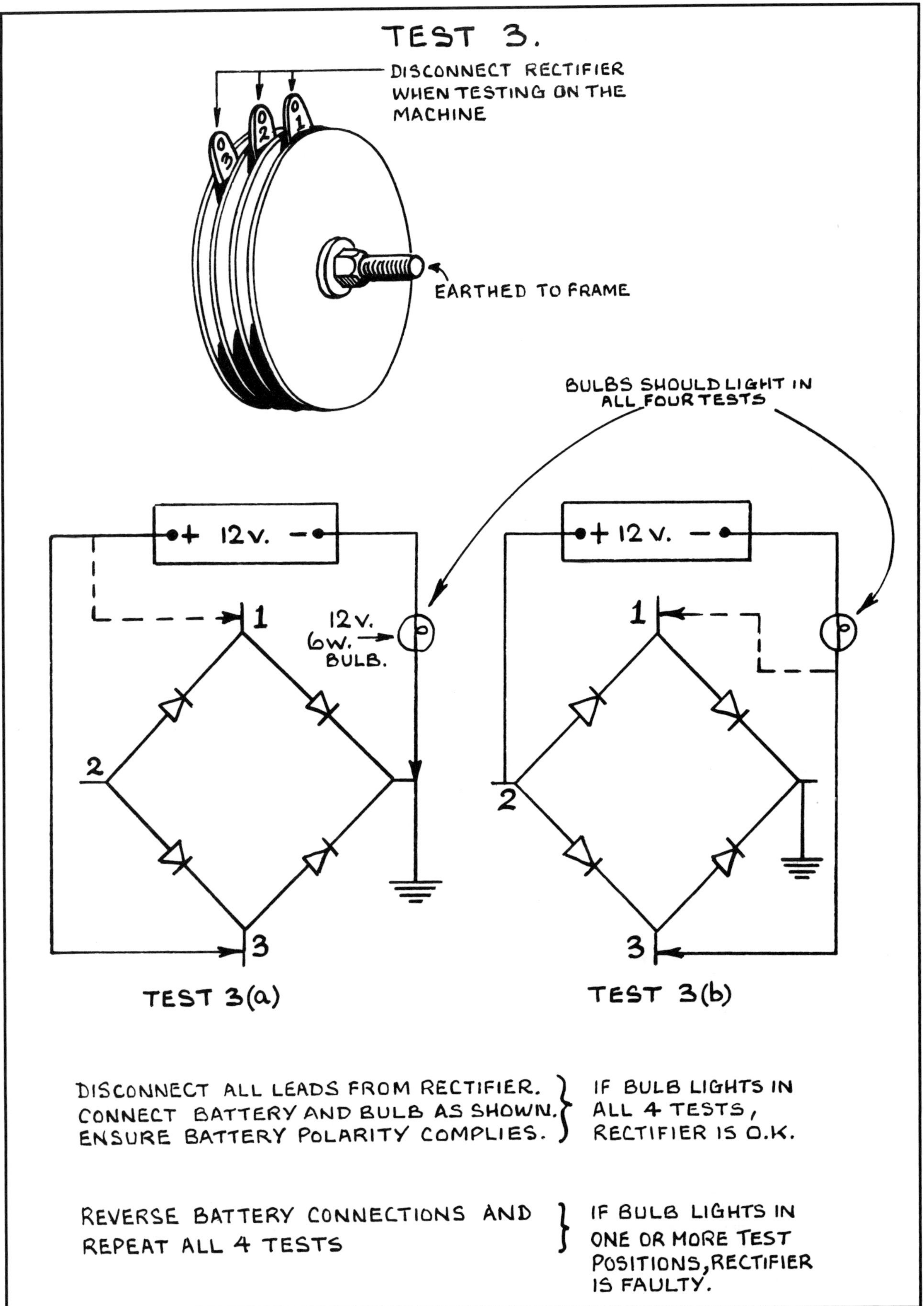
TEST 3.
DISCONNECT RECTIFIER WHEN TESTING ON THE MACHINE
3
2
1
EARTHED TO FRAME
BULBS SHOULD LIGHT IN ALL FOUR TESTS
+ 12v. -
1
12v. 6W. BULB.
2
3
TEST 3(a)
+ 12v. -
1
2
3
TEST 3(b)
DISCONNECT ALL LEADS FROM RECTIFIER. CONNECT BATTERY AND BULB AS SHOWN. ENSURE BATTERY POLARITY COMPLIES.
IF BULB LIGHTS IN ALL 4 TESTS, RECTIFIER IS O.K.
REVERSE BATTERY CONNECTIONS AND REPEAT ALL 4 TESTS
IF BULB LIGHTS IN ONE OR MORE TEST POSITIONS, RECTIFIER IS FAULTY.

fitted to all machines subsequent to engine no. 38989. Many Phase 2 machines were brought up to Phase 3 specification, which involved fitting a new rotor, resistor and bracket, resistor leads, new switches, switch harness, and a modified alternator feed cable arrangement. (The change-over was detailed in Lucas Service Bulletin SB/GN/12, May 1953).

The RM13 alternator, smaller, and with a circular stator and bridge rectifier, made its appearance around August 1953 (Lucas Service Bulletin SB/GN/6). The RM14 model was introduced in January 1954 (Lucas Service Bulletin SB/GN/15).

Villiers flywheel magnetos

The Villiers Company, during its long period of manufacture, produced over 3,000,000 two-stroke engines and about 70 different engine models. Originally titled the Villiers Cycle Co. in July 1898 (later Villiers Engineering Co.), their first engine in 1912 was — would you believe — a four-stroke! A two-stroke followed in 1913, the 269 cc model of fond memory. This had a separate conventional magneto and was logically termed the Mark I unit.

During 1915, the Mark II, prefix A series was introduced, followed by the Mark III (prefix B) in 1920, the Mark IV (prefix C) in 1921 and, significantly the Mark V (prefix D) in 1922 — significantly, because this year saw the introduction of the Villiers flywheel magneto, a feature which was to remain as part of the general motorcycle scene for so many years. Many other proprietary engine makers gave up the struggle, being unable to compete with Villiers; no longer did the small motorcycle manufacturer have to purchase separate magnetos and carburettors — the little Villiers unit came as a complete package. A man could now set-up as a motorcycle assembler in little more than a garden shed, purchasing his components from Wolverhampton and Birmingham. A cheap runabout didn't even need a gearbox. Direct belt-drive would suffice, or if the customer could afford it, Villiers made a free-engine device to bolt straight on the crankshaft.

So many versions of the Villiers flywheel magneto

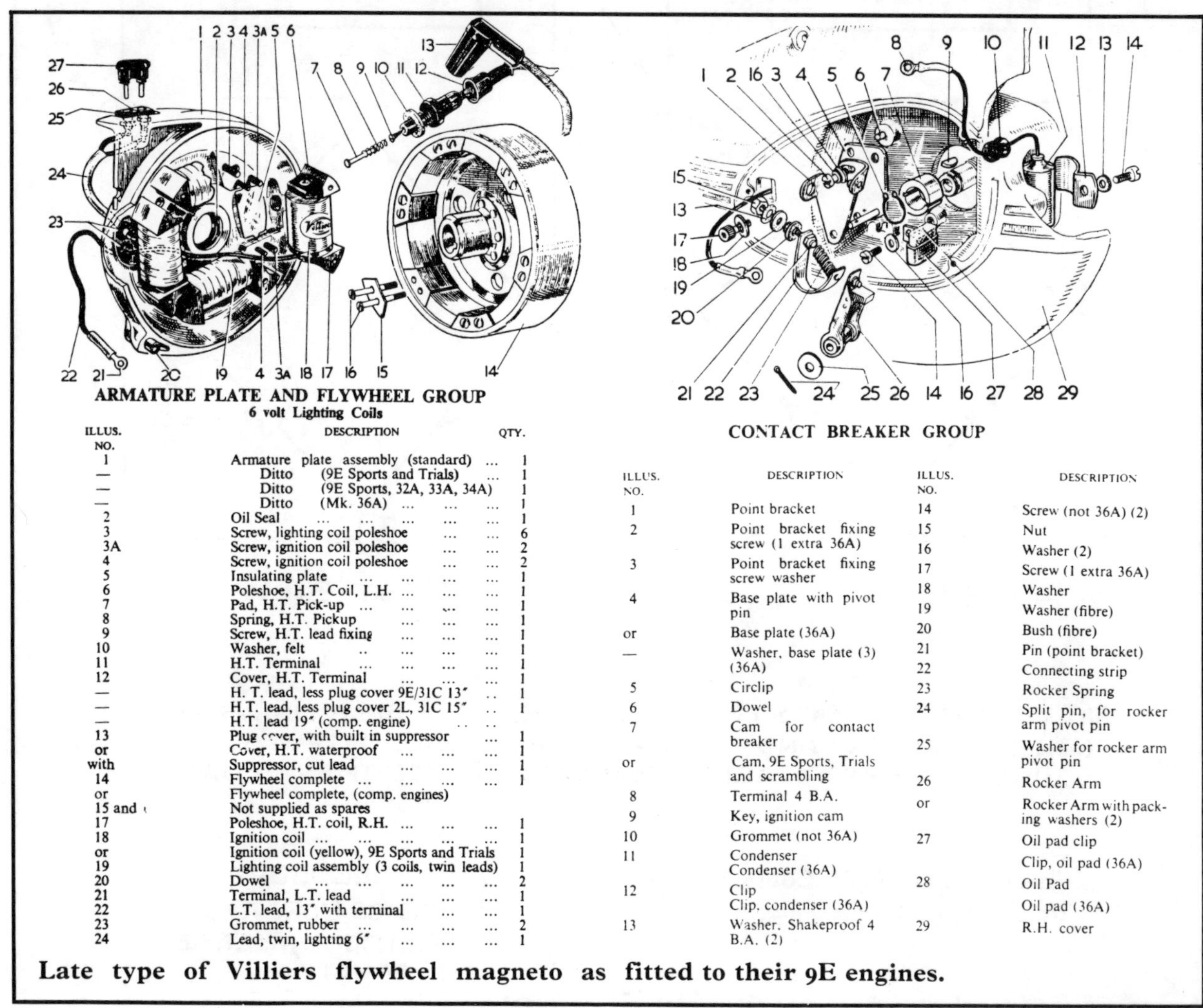

ARMATURE PLATE AND FLYWHEEL GROUP
6 volt Lighting Coils

ILLUS. NO.	DESCRIPTION	QTY.
1	Armature plate assembly (standard)	1
—	Ditto (9E Sports and Trials)	1
—	Ditto (9E Sports, 32A, 33A, 34A)	1
—	Ditto (Mk. 36A)	1
2	Oil Seal	1
3	Screw, lighting coil poleshoe	6
3A	Screw, ignition coil poleshoe	2
4	Screw, ignition coil poleshoe	2
5	Insulating plate	1
6	Poleshoe, H.T. Coil, L.H.	1
7	Pad, H.T. Pick-up	1
8	Spring, H.T. Pickup	1
9	Screw, H.T. lead fixing	1
10	Washer, felt	1
11	H.T. Terminal	1
12	Cover, H.T. Terminal	1
—	H. T. lead, less plug cover 9E/31C 13"	1
—	H.T. lead, less plug cover 2L, 31C 15"	1
—	H.T. lead 19" (comp. engine)	
13	Plug cover, with built in suppressor	1
or	Cover, H.T. waterproof	1
with	Suppressor, cut lead	1
14	Flywheel complete	1
or	Flywheel complete, (comp. engines)	
15 and	Not supplied as spares	
17	Poleshoe, H.T. coil, R.H.	1
18	Ignition coil	1
or	Ignition coil (yellow), 9E Sports and Trials	1
19	Lighting coil assembly (3 coils, twin leads)	1
20	Dowel	2
21	Terminal, L.T. lead	1
22	L.T. lead, 13" with terminal	1
23	Grommet, rubber	2
24	Lead, twin, lighting 6"	1

CONTACT BREAKER GROUP

ILLUS. NO.	DESCRIPTION	ILLUS. NO.	DESCRIPTION
1	Point bracket	14	Screw (not 36A) (2)
2	Point bracket fixing screw (1 extra 36A)	15	Nut
3	Point bracket fixing screw washer	16	Washer (2)
4	Base plate with pivot pin	17	Screw (1 extra 36A)
or	Base plate (36A)	18	Washer
—	Washer, base plate (3) (36A)	19	Washer (fibre)
5	Circlip	20	Bush (fibre)
6	Dowel	21	Pin (point bracket)
7	Cam for contact breaker	22	Connecting strip
or	Cam, 9E Sports, Trials and scrambling	23	Rocker Spring
8	Terminal 4 B.A.	24	Split pin, for rocker arm pivot pin
9	Key, ignition cam	25	Washer for rocker arm pivot pin
10	Grommet (not 36A)	26	Rocker Arm
11	Condenser Condenser (36A)	or	Rocker Arm with packing washers (2)
12	Clip Clip, condenser (36A)	27	Oil pad clip
13	Washer, Shakeproof 4 B.A. (2)		Clip, oil pad (36A)
		28	Oil Pad
			Oil pad (36A)
		29	R.H. cover

Late type of Villiers flywheel magneto as fitted to their 9E engines.

ELECTRIC LIGHTING SETS—*continued*

HEAD LAMPS

TAIL LAMP No. MT210.

LUCAS №D40

BATTERY PUW7E.

LUCAS MOTOR CYCLE C.V.C. REGULATOR AND CUT-OUT UNIT

LUCAS

BATTERY LIGHTING SET.
For Solo Machines.

Designed to meet the requirements of those riders who wish to avail themselves of the advantages of electric lighting but who cannot arrange to fit a Magdyno," " Maglita " or separate dynamo set to their present machines. Set consists of battery No. PUW7E, head lamp D40 with switch at back and girder brackets, tail lamp MT210, complete with cables, etc. Black finish.

No. CL16/35/*3300* .. .. per set £2 5 0

LUCAS C.V.C. CONVERSION SET.

Converts Lucas "Magdyno" or separate dynamo set to compensated voltage control, the system which is now fitted as standard on majority of British motor-cycles. This system keeps the battery properly charged under all conditions without attention. It ensures a steady brilliant driving light which remains undiminished at all normal speeds. Set consists of a combined voltage regulator and cut-out, dynamo, terminal eyelet.

No. **CL16/100/*1500*** .. .. complete **21/-**
,, **CL16/100/*1400*** .. .. doz. lots ,, —

State make of machine, model and year when ordering.

LUCAS

MOTOR CYCLE HEAD LAMPS.

Lucas Type D42.

Lucas Type D142.

Lucas Type DU42.

The three Lucas motor cycle head lamps shown above are usually supplied with Lucas " Magdyno," " Maglita " and separate dynamo sets. **Type D142** has a 8¼ in. front and is a bold-looking lamp with a clean, pleasing line. Free from instruments, it is intended for use where an instrument panel is used. Fitted with 24-watt gas-filled double filament Lucas Blue-Star bulb, it gives a brilliant high-power driving light with dipped non-dazzling beam controlled by switch on handlebar or instrument panel.

Type D142. Black and chromium with fork brackets.

No. CL16/50/*3706* .. .. each **50/-**

Type D42 and **Type DU42** are usually supplied with Lucas " Maglita " lighting and ignition sets. They are designed on similar lines to Lucas car head lamps. All have a 7-in. front, but DU142 and DU42 incorporates switch and ammeter in lamp, while D42 uses separate switches or instrument panels fitted to machine.

Type D42. Black and chromium with fork brackets as D 142.

No. CL16/52/*3309* .. .. each **45**

Type DU42. Black and chromium, with switches, ammeter, cables and girder brackets.

No. CL16/53/*4500* .. .. each **60** -

This page from a pre-war Brown Brothers catalogue shows period Lucas headlamps and also the 'new' cvc conversion set introduced for 1936 (top right) to enable a three-brush dynamo to be converted to two brush with cut-out and voltage regulator.

were made it would need another book to describe detail changes. However, apart from basic overall diameters (early versions were, as one writer put it, 'like dustbin lids') and permutations of ignition and lighting coils, they remained similar in principle until the end. In fact many thousands of lawn mowers (principally *Atco* models) had flywheel mags which were interchangeable with motorcycle types, except for the absence of lighting coils.

Faults

There is little to go wrong with a flywheel magneto. However, it is undeniably true that generations of motorcyclists have cursed the wretched object when plagued with starting problems.

Ignition coils have a tendency to give up the ghost without warning, although this does not always result in **total** ignition failure. Sometimes internal arcing occurs, resulting in feeble or intermittent sparks with poor starting on occasions. A fat spark should be seen and heard when the HT wire is held about 1/4 in away from the cylinder, and the engine is revolved **briskly**. The pick-up should be checked to see if the short spring, which makes contact on a stud in the coil body, is intact. A large blob of plasticine around the Bakelite holder will stop rain getting in.

Poor starting can also be the result of a broken down capacitor, which in early Villiers units is a flat tin-plated object housed inside the contact breaker box. These condensers are fairly reliable but if severe sparking at the contact breaker points is noted, a replacement should be sought. In an emergency it is possible to wire-up a car-type tubular condenser, this being mounted outside the backplate with the connecting wire taken out through a convenient hole. Indeed, if the entire flywheel mag packs up the motorcycle can be used temporarily by converting the engine to coil-ignition; a small battery is required and the normal Villiers contact breaker is wired-up accordingly.

Removing the flywheel

Flywheel magnets should be bridged with a metal "keeper" when the flywheel is removed. Although the Villiers *Hammer-tight* magneto spanner is fairly well known, there may be some novices unaware of its significance. The tool is in the form of a flat single-ended ring spanner, designed to be clouted on the thickened end with a hammer. To remove a flywheel, apply the spanner and give the end a sharp crack — this of course serves to slacken the crankshaft nut — and a further welt (same as a clout) will draw the flywheel off its taper.

It is worth rummaging through the stock of lawn-mower repairers when coils and capacitors are required (the writer bought two flywheel magnetos with engines and mowers attached for under ten pounds; one was robbed of parts for a Coventry-Eagle and the other mows his grass to this day!). Alternatively, autojumbles often have Villiers parts in profusion.

Lamps

Pre-war Lucas

Seven and eight-inch Lucas headlamps are identical in design if not in size. To adjust the focus stand the bike on level ground about 25 feet away from a light-coloured wall. Slacken the lamp securing bolts and tilt the shell until the beam height (main beam) is the same as, or just below, the glass centre height from floor level. The beam should be uniform and without a dark centre. If the bulb requires adjustment, slacken the focusing clip and move it backwards and forwards until the desired effect is achieved. Tighten the clip.

When removing the reflector and rim, it's a good idea to place a cushion on the front mudguard to stop the reflector from rolling about on its connecting wires. Do not use metal polish on the reflector as its plated surface is very delicate. A wipe over with soapy water is recommended, or if you want to take a chance try a very light polish with *Silvo* (not *Brasso*) on a soft rag. (If you shift the plating don't blame the author!)

Reflectors should by choice be silver-plated, although nickel is a tolerable substitute on a show machine. Most pre-war lamps had flat frosted-glass lenses, supplies of which have almost dwindled away. Many glaziers are able to cut new glasses out of a similar material; if not, clear glasses can be coarse sand-blasted to simulate a dimpled effect.

Pre-focus substitutes

Car pre-focus units, as fitted to many BMC models during the 'fifties and 'sixties, can often be transplanted in standard 7 in Lucas motorcycle headlamps.

It may be necessary to drill a hole in the car reflector to acept a push-in pilot bulb holder. This should be done by drilling a ring of 1/16 in diameter holes, joining them up with a Swiss file. A large drill would just tear out the thin reflector material. Pilot bulb fittings (Lucas pattern) are also available at car accessory shops.

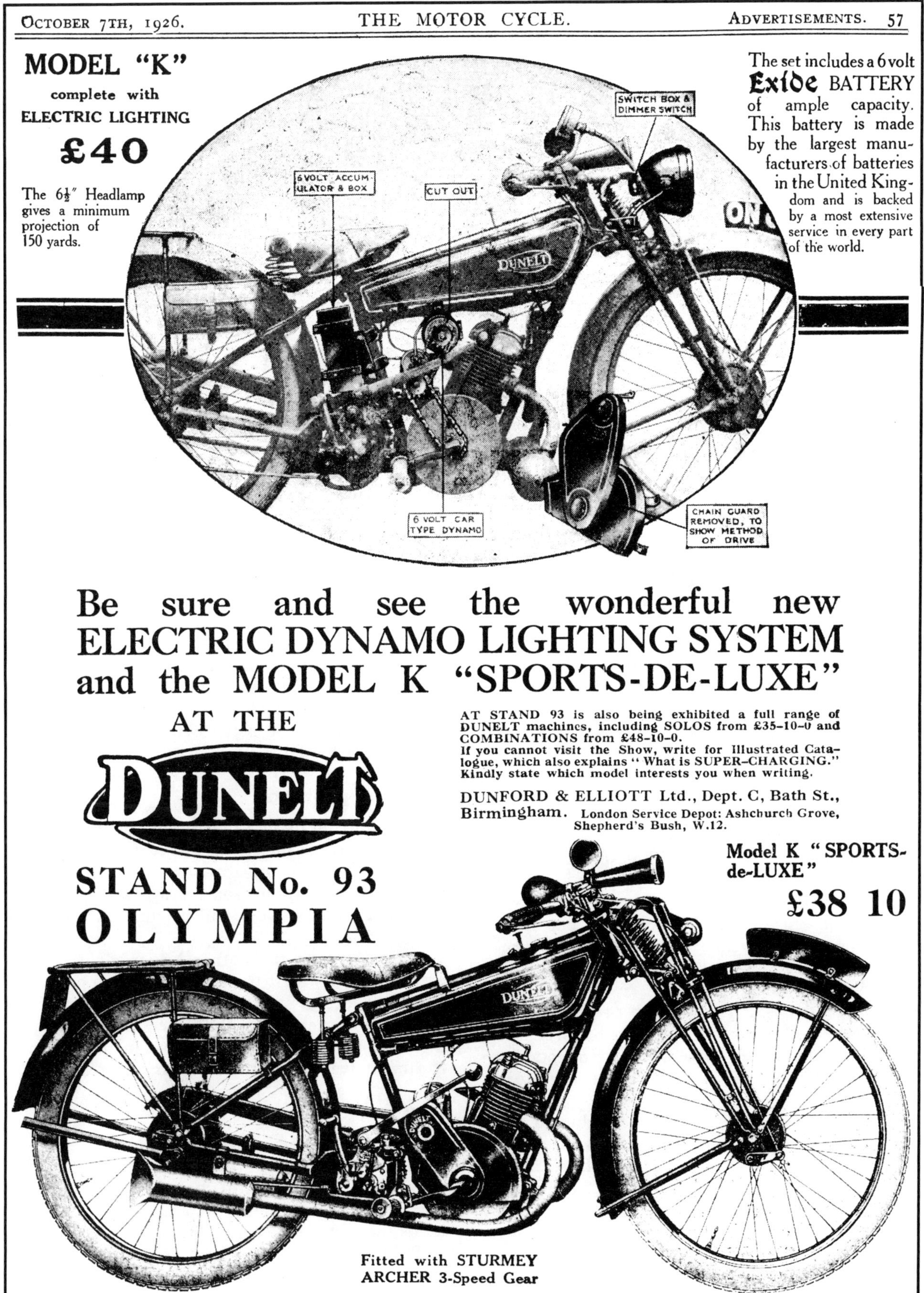
OCTOBER 7TH, 1926.
THE MOTOR CYCLE.
ADVERTISEMENTS. 57
MODEL "K"
complete with
ELECTRIC LIGHTING
£40
The 6½" Headlamp gives a minimum projection of 150 yards.
SWITCH BOX & DIMMER SWITCH
6 VOLT ACCUMULATOR & BOX
CUT OUT
6 VOLT CAR TYPE DYNAMO
CHAIN GUARD REMOVED, TO SHOW METHOD OF DRIVE
The set includes a 6 volt Exide BATTERY of ample capacity. This battery is made by the largest manufacturers of batteries in the United Kingdom and is backed by a most extensive service in every part of the world.
Be sure and see the wonderful new
ELECTRIC DYNAMO LIGHTING SYSTEM
and the MODEL K "SPORTS-DE-LUXE"
AT THE
DUNELT
STAND No. 93
OLYMPIA
AT STAND 93 is also being exhibited a full range of DUNELT machines, including SOLOS from £35-10-0 and COMBINATIONS from £48-10-0.
If you cannot visit the Show, write for illustrated Catalogue, which also explains "What is SUPER-CHARGING."
Kindly state which model interests you when writing.
DUNFORD & ELLIOTT Ltd., Dept. C, Bath St., Birmingham. London Service Depot: Ashchurch Grove, Shepherd's Bush, W.12.
Model K "SPORTS-de-LUXE"
£38 10
Fitted with STURMEY ARCHER 3-Speed Gear

Chapter 8

Paint Work

Preparation; stripping, rust removal and protection. Coachpainting, masking, hand-lining, spraying hints.

Stripping off the old paint

STRIPPING paint is a messy job. By far the easiest way to tackle the problem is to take all the parts to a shot-blasting specialist who will blast the lot off for you.

If professional help is not available in your locality the only alternative is to use one of the proprietary paint removers such as *Nitromors*. Several applications may be necessary on stove-enamelled finishes, followed by much wire-brushing and washing-down with turps substitute. The water-washable variety of paint remover is not to be recommended unless it is intended to shot-blast the parts soon after drying. Rust forms very quickly indeed.

When using *Nitromors* it is advisable to wear rubber gloves and a pair of goggles as the stuff is quite powerful — wash it off bare skin immediately. Remove every scrap of paint with the aid of a scraper or wire brush. Cheap plastic pan-scrubbers can be used on mudguards and frame tubes, or wire wool for delicate parts.

The old blowlamp method is not very satisfactory on motorcycle parts, even though it was widely recommended in the vintage years. Burning paint off takes a long time and is jolly hard work. There is also a danger of damaging soldered components (vintage flat tanks for instance) if the flame is held in one spot for too long.

The rust problem

The most daunting task in any renovation project is how to overcome the ravages of rust. This dreaded disease of the metal must be removed completely or treated chemically in some way, otherwise any further restoration work will be ruined in the long term.

Over the years the author has tried just about every method of rust treatment known to mankind. Some concoctions worked admirably whilst others caused more headaches than the rust itself! Here then is a short survey of the various methods of rust treatment available to the amateur restorer.

Blasting

The only 100% successful, absolutely certain, way of conquering the rust problem is to remove the rust by physical means until bright metal remains. Having got that profound statement out of the way let us therefore discuss the pitfalls of grit-blasting.

There are two main problems. One is that generally, the amateur restorer cannot do the blasting himself. (Some firms hire out their equip-

ment but this is of academic interest if you live out in the wilds of Scotland or Canada!) The second and more serious problem concerns those garages with no experience of vintage motor cycle parts who can cause an awful lot of damage to delicate bits by the incorrect use of a grit blaster.

So be warned. A powerful blaster in unskilled hands, with the wrong kind of grit in the machine, can wreak havoc with thin toolboxes and chainguards. Early veteran valanced mudguards have been known to come back warped and looking like Nottingham lace. Make sure that the firm concerned know their stuff when it comes to choosing the correct grade of grit or bead for your irreplaceable parts. Personal recommendations from fellow-enthusiasts will help here.

There are those cautious individuals who will not entertain grit-blasting at any cost. They say that the removal of rust by blasting weakens frail

Acquisition of a small polishing head will make many jobs so much easier. Wire brushes such as these remove rust in no time. ***(Photo: Dendix-Gem Brushes Ltd.)***

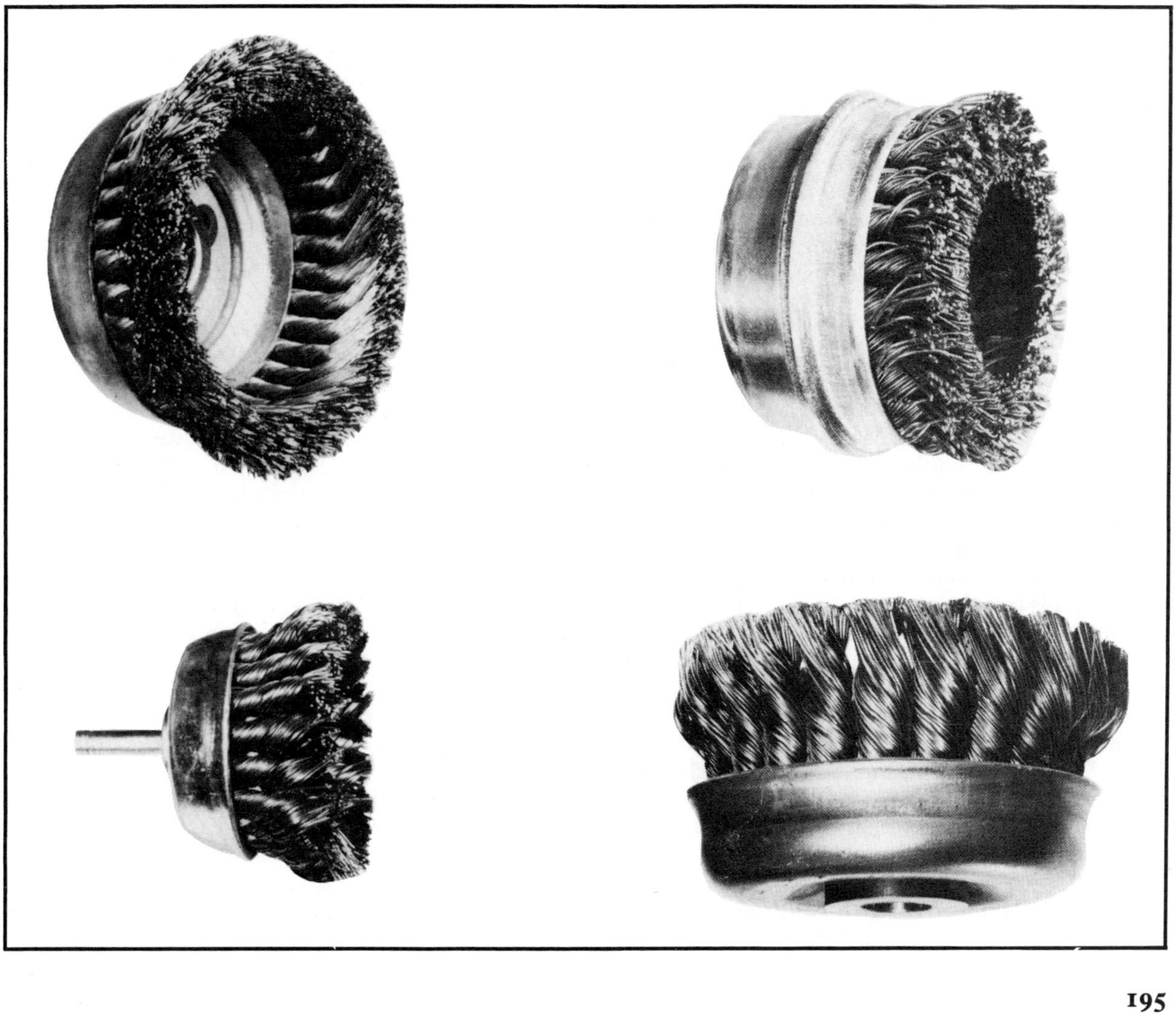

structural members. This axiom is true of already badly-pitted components, such items as early Druid forks having little metal to spare for any kind of vigorous treatment. It is as well therefore to use glass beads or very fine grit whenever possible and most parts will survive.

All threads must be masked off with layers of masking tape. Wooden bungs can be inserted into threaded holes, or old bolts will serve the same purpose. Do not expect the stove-enameller to dismantle swinging arms, headstocks and forks. Headstock bearing cups can be left in situ but they **must** be protected with wooden plates, or washers, clamped in place with a length of stud-iron.

Wheels can be enamelled in the assembled state but bearings and spindles must be removed. The hubs can be blanked off the same way as headstock tubes.

Engine components requiring blasting need special attention. Oil passageways should be blocked-off with wooden bungs — even so, thorough cleaning out with a powerful airline is vital after blasting. Fine glass beads will not destroy mating surfaces or threaded components. A blasting specialist will advise in critical applications.

It is important to list all the parts before parcelling them up for attention. Unfortunately, valuable parts do go missing either in transit or in a busy bead-blasting shop. It has been known for another customer to inadvertently walk off with components not belonging to him! The minute the parts are collected from the grit-blaster give them a quick coat of etch-primer. Don't leave bare metal untreated overnight, and remember that sweaty fingers will promote rapid rusting. Aluminium can be sprayed with WD40 for the time being.

Chemical rust-stoppers

The alternative to physical removal of rust is to render it inert by means of one of the many rust-killers on the market. Most are phosphoric-acid based and give off unpleasant fumes. Make sure the treatment is carried out in a well-ventilated room, and don't smoke while you are working.

The procedure with almost every chemical converter is to brush on the liquid and leave it for a day or so. Rust is transformed into an inert layer (usually blue-black).

Unfortunately there is one big snag with ninety per cent of such remedies, something that the makers do not mention in their literature. A rash can appear on the paint surface weeks or even months later. This appears to be due to a delayed chemical reaction and nothing can be done about it. Undoubtedly the rust is neutralised, as the makers claim, but a concours finish may eventually suffer.

Useful products are David's *Bondaprimer* and Finnigans *Brown Velvet*. Both are primers claimed to possess rust-inhibiting qualities. Widely used by restorers for lashing over grit-blasted surfaces, such primers flow easily and dry quickly. Although the makers say they can be painted directly over rust it is advisable to remove the rust altogether to be certain of a lasting finish.

Galvafroid and Holt's *Zinc Coat* are zinc-rich primers which help to keep rust at bay. Being very thick, brushmarks are difficult to avoid but this will not matter too much on cyclecar chassis or under mudguards.

If it is intended to have the parts stove enamelled, leave the priming stages to the painter. Brushed-on DIY primers and fillers will not usually stand up to stoving temperatures or to an epoxy resin coating process.

Stove enamel

Without doubt the best and most durable finish for vintage machinery is that obtained by the stove enamelling process. A depth of gloss, together with a hard scratch-resistant surface, is imparted into the finish and most quality machines were finished thus in the vintage period. It is fairly true to say that in the early days of the Vintage Motor Cycle Club concours judges would not entertain anything less than stove enamel on cycle parts.

As its title suggests, stove enamel is a baked-on finish so it is wise to check whether a component is fabricated from soft-soldered tin-plate. Pioneer motorcycle petrol tanks, veteran and early vintage chaincases and toolboxes were often examples of the tinsmith's art, therefore it's best to play safe and hand-finish such components. In fact many petrol tanks around 1900/1905 were finished in an air-drying silver (eg. Pheonix, Quadrant, Excelsior etc) for this reason alone.

Unless they are given clear instructions to the contrary, some stove enamellers will not bother filling-in pit marks. Naturally such time-consuming work is very expensive and most firms will come to an agreement with the customer over preparation. Occasionally, enamellers will allow the amateur to do the filling-in and flatting-down in between coats (even loaning materials in special cases) although it usually takes years to develop such a degree of co-operation!

If the stove enameller recommends a certain type of filler, then abide by his recommendation. Stoving fillers must be bakeproof and most ordinary body fillers are simply not good enough. Usually an etch primer coat is applied first to key into the metal, followed by a heat-resistant high bake filler. To achieve a really good finish at least three coats should be applied over the primer/undercoat, each being flatted-down by hand.

A good wax polish is all that's needed after stoving; cutting back is neither necessary nor desirable. Washing and leathering down with a soft chamois leather every so often will help to maintain

A useful set of wire brushes for the restorer. Note the long valve guide cleaners. *(Photo: Dendix-GEM Brushes Ltd.)*

the appearance of a stove enamel finish. Furniture polish or *Pledge* aerosol wax is usually preferable to car polishes, some of which are quite abrasive.

Powder coating

It is open to question whether powder coating gives a comparable finish to either stove enamel or hand-painted coach enamel but there is no doubt about its durability or resistance to damage. New powders are being formulated all the time and in the not-too-distant future it may be possible to match the results of stove enamelling, to the satisfaction of concours enthusiasts.

Powder coating is a dry process and has the advantages of speed and economy in materials. Usually only one coat is applied over the bare metal; unfortunately severe pit-marks will still be evident after coating as there are no fillers available to withstand the high temperatures involved.

Thermosetting polyester or epoxy resins are used for motorcycle components, and polyurethane for domestic applications. Parts receive an even, scratch-resistant coating, and the system is ideal for irregular-shaped objects which would be difficult to paint by conventional methods. Due to an electrostatic charge being passed through the workpiece the powder, which is sprayed from a special nozzle, clings to the entire surface with a regular thickness throughout. After coating, the parts pass through a high temperature oven whereupon the powder flows and bakes into a hard shiny mass.

Soft-soldered tanks and toolboxes would be damaged in the baking oven so these parts will have to be finished with air-drying paints the old-fashioned way.

Although not of general interest to vintagents it is worth mentioning another type of powder coating, the thermoplastic version, encompassing such materials as nylon, polyethylene PVC and PTFE. Commonly referred to as plastic coatings, the finish imparted by nylon and its close relatives would be quite unacceptable to concours aspirants, but trials enthusiasts would be more interested in the knock-resistant properties of these coatings. PVC or black nylon coatings are useful alternatives to the old celluloid sheathing which was applied to Rudge handlebars and Bluemels steering wheels.

Epoxy "Two-pack" paints

Some professionals swear by two-pack epoxy paints such as the Berger *Epilux* range, which can be brushed or sprayed in the conventional manner.

A good depth of finish can be achieved and the surface is very tough and durable. There are drawbacks however. The amateur painter should bear in mind that once the two constituent parts are mixed he must use up the paint as soon as possible. So, once the job is started he must see it through to the end.

In cold weather two-pack epoxy paints display a marked reluctance to harden — in colloquial terms — to 'go off'. **All** painting should be carried out in a dry, warm, and well-ventilated atmosphere; in the case of two-pack epoxies this advice is vital, paying particular attention to ventilation and health precautions. Some epoxies give off toxic fumes when mixed and the correct breathing apparatus **must** be employed. Paint manufacturers will generally advise.

Cellulose

Brushing cellulose was quite popular at one time but is now going out of favour with restorers due to difficulties in covering large areas (wide mudguards are almost impossible to paint without getting brushmarks). On the other hand spraying cellulose is widely used by professionals and amateurs alike and excellent results can be achieved with the simplest of equipment.

In the author's opinion, cheap "airless' electric sprayguns are not worth considering for motorcycle restoration work. It is a simple task to construct a small portable compressor, using a secondhand Hoover fridge motor/compressor coupled to a redundant oxygen cylinder as a reservoir. A blow-off (safety valve) must be fitted and it is advisable to incorporate a filter-regulator on the air outlet.

Cellulose should not be applied over oil-based paint (domestic gloss or coach enamel) as it will lift or wrinkle the base material.

Acrylics

Acrylic paints are now widely used by professional car refinishers because of their good covering powers. Constituent components are mainly a plasticising medium and a derivative of Perspex. Drying time is short. High-build versions are available for increased covering power. Many amateur restorers report good results.

Synthetic enamel

Obtainable in spraying quality, synthetic enamel can be applied over cellulose or acrylic (but not vice-versa). Considered to be more resistant to chipping than cellulose. Many car aerosol finishes consist of synthetic enamel, which is fairly quick-drying.

Aerosols

There is no reason why a complete motorcycle should not be finished with aerosol paints (cellulose or synthetics) apart from the question of expense. Indeed, many restorers of Japanese motorcycles (brave fellows) find this the most satisfactory method from the point of view of colour-matching.

It will generally be found more economical to complete all the preliminary stages by hand, with brushing etch primers and stoppers before applying numerous coats of spray-on undercoat. Each undercoat should be rubbed-down, as described in the section on coach-painting. (The beginner should also pay particular attention to points 1 and 5 under Spraying Hints).

Many petrol tanks were finished in matt silver or odd shades of polychromatic colour in the 'classic' period. In almost every case an exact match can be found amongst the plethora of car aerosols available.

Spraying hints

1 Always work in a warm dry atmosphere. Dampness causes blooming.
2 Thin the paint to the correct viscosity. Most beginners try to put too much on at once.
3 Set the spray gun to give a good spray pattern. An oval pattern is best. A figure of eight shape could mean the air pressure is too high or the spray setting too wide. Adjust pressure (which could be anything from 30 to 65 psi) and the paint flow needle.
4 Hold the gun at right angles to the job, maintaining a uniform distance of eight to twelve inches (depending on the type of gun).
5 Always actuate the trigger before sweeping across the workpiece and follow through afterwards. Don't be afraid of wasting a little paint.
6 Holding the gun too far away results in a rough, dull, finish. Too near, and the paint may run.

The restorers' art is well evident in these shots of an immaculate four pipe Ariel Square Four spotted at an Oulton Park meeting.

Don't expect to become an expert in half an hour. Skilled vehicle refinishers serve a five year apprenticeship learning their trade — the quickest way to successful results is to get an expert to show you the ropes.

Touching-up damaged areas is best accomplished with a small *Humbrol* or *Badger* air-brush. These outfits consist of a midget spraygun operated by a separate aerosol canister, together with a glass paint container and the necessary plastic tubing. The advantage of an air-brush lies in its ability to cover small areas; an adjustment is provided by means of which the spray pattern can be set to encompass a chipped area the size of a penny, or to cover a complete tank panel. Indeed, complete petrol tanks can be sprayed with an air-brush, using a synthetic enamel or cellulose paint.

So far, the matter of working environment has hardly received mention. This, and the subject of preparation, are the two most important aspects of amateur paintwork. The various stages in achieving a concours finish, ie etch-priming, filling, rubbing-down and undercoating, are just the same for brushed or sprayed paintwork. The spray-painter will therefore benefit from the advice contained within the following pages.

Coach painting

The world's premier concours event for vintage motorcycles is probably that held in conjunction with *The Vintage Motor Cycle Club's* annual *Banbury Run*. For many years Banbury class winners have set the standard for others to follow; it may be argued by some experts that restored machines are now far better than they were ever turned out by their makers. There is probably some truth in this belief but it cannot be denied that the results achieved by some dedicated amateurs are quite remarkable and a credit to the vintage movement.

Beginners to restoration work can take heart from the fact that many a Banbury winning machine has been brush-painted in a ramshackle garden shed or garage. There is no reason why a coach-painted finish cannot equal, or indeed surpass, a sprayed finish. As in any other form of restoration work much patience and elbow grease are needed. In Victorian times coach-painters would reckon on about thirty days to prepare and paint a carriage body; one writer of the period noted that owners of the new-fangled horseless carriages were impatient to have their vehicles finished and took them out on the road as soon as the paint had dried. Grave suspicion was levelled at our transatlantic cousins who were rumoured to be painting their carriages quickly by means of compressed air!

One hundred years ago a coach painter was a highly-skilled craftsman, often mixing his own paints from ground pigment, linseed oil, turps and various other jealously guarded secret ingredients. The tradition has continued to this day, although modern coach paints and materials have made the craftsman's life so much easier. Coachpainting was always carried out in special dust-free rooms; before painting commenced, floors and walls would be wetted to lay the dust and the door was kept securely locked until work finished for the day. Nobody would dare to enter until the paint was dry, then it would be flatted-down and the whole process would start all over again, special care being taken in the final varnishing stage. Up to fifteen coats in all would be applied; as a testimony to the skill of bygone craftsmen many carriages built in the last century still display their original finish.

No longer is it necessary to mix one's own stoppers — modern body fillers are far superior to anything our grandfathers used. Modern gloss

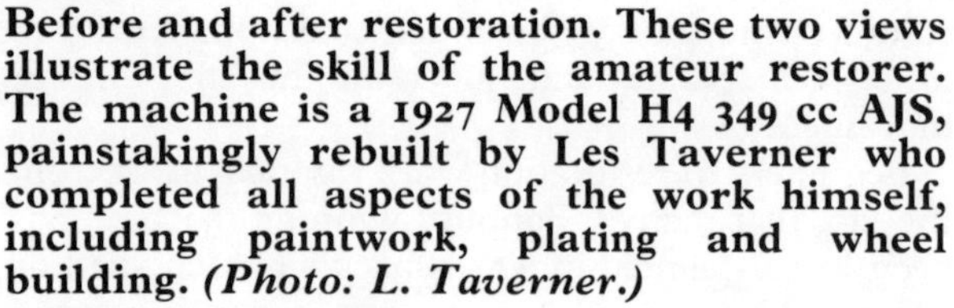
Before and after restoration. These two views illustrate the skill of the amateur restorer. The machine is a 1927 Model H4 349 cc AJS, painstakingly rebuilt by Les Taverner who completed all aspects of the work himself, including paintwork, plating and wheel building. *(Photo: L. Taverner.)*

paints are probably much better than the coach enamels of only thirty years ago; at one time it was almost impossible to eradicate brush-marks and the enamel would take days to dry!

To coach-paint motorcycle parts requires little in the way of materials. Good brushes are essential no matter whether coach enamel or ordinary paints are used.

Priming coat

Let us assume that your cycle parts have been stripped, de-rusted and thoroughly cleaned with turpentine substitute (white spirit).

Apply one coat of etch-primer as soon as possible after grit-blasting. It is no use at all painting over rust, hoping that if enough coats are put on the rust will not come through. Etch-primers, as their name suggests, eat into the metal and provide a good bond for further coats. Most paint manufacturers list an etch-primer in their range. *Bondaprimer* is useful as a first coat and many restorers like its free-flowing properties. Any cheap brush will do at this stage, but keep it to one side for priming only.

Stopping

I have never yet restored a machine that hasn't been riddled with rust pits. These can be filled quite easily with a knifing stopper. When filling pit-marks in round tubing, a scrap of card or celluloid folded to the tube contour will help.

Large dents in petrol tanks can be filled at this stage with a body-filler such as *Isopon* or *Plastic Padding*. It's as well to leave it to harden-off for much longer than the makers recommend – a week is usually sufficient. After drying-out, the stopper can be rubbed down smooth until you are left with a blemish-free surface. Fill-in any pinholes left.

Make sure you don't go through the primer when rubbing down; if you do, another priming coat should be applied over the area affected. At one time I used wet-and-dry emery with water for rubbing down fillers until I was advised to try something called production paper. This stuff looks like sandpaper but does not readily clog. Car accessory shops often stock it. Production paper is used dry, which means that there is less chance of causing rust to appear again if you go through to bare metal.

Glass-fibre stopping paste is to a certain extent porous, therefore it is better to be cautious and rub this down dry also. Experience has shown that some stoppers harbour moisture for a considerable period, the trouble only manifesting itself at some future date when the paintwork is completed. Tiny blisters appearing on the surface could indicate moisture trapped in the filler; minute pin-pricks elsewhere might mean more serious trouble in the form of a still-active phosphoric acid based rust killer, or possibly non-compatible materials (eg. cellulose over oil-based paint).

This stage of stopping and rubbing down is very important and is the key to success in your repaint. Patience is a virtue and any rushed work is sure to show through the finished surface.

Environment

The workshop, or shed, where the painting is done must be warm, dry and dust-free. Unfortunately most garages and outhouses have none of these desirable qualities so the amateur must make the best of what he's got. Some enthusiasts use the bathroom for paintwork projects but this scheme is fraught with problems, not least of which is the matter of preserving marital harmony!

It is easy enough to provide temporary heating in the garage but how to get rid of dust is the amateur painter's biggest headache. Painting outside is not satisfactory as there are flies, soot and birds to contend with. All my painting is done in an ordinary garage-cum-workshop; even so I manage to avoid dust by adopting a few simple rules. Follow my plan and you won't go far wrong.

1 **Choose the right kind of day** for the final coat. The best conditions are when it has been raining (this lays the dust outside) and when there is no wind. A still, warm atmosphere is ideal.

2 **Do not admit visitors** when you are painting. Lock the doors from the inside. Admittedly you have the dilemma of losing friends or getting a good finish; the choice is a hard one.

3 **Wear the right clothing** No woolly pullovers or other fluffy dust-laden garments. If you are very keen and not easily embarassed, wear a hair-net as it's surprising how much dust flies out of even clean hair.

4 **Throw water all over the floor** before painting, and if possible spray the walls also. A damp dust-sheet stretched across the ceiling also helps.

5 **Don't make sudden movements** while painting is in progress, like opening out a handkerchief with a flourish. For that matter try not to sneeze all over the job.

6 **Hang up the parts wire wire, not string.** Whenever possible, hang parts upside down (petrol tanks for instance). Even when you have taken this precaution it's amazing how often a midge or "daddy-longlegs" will decide to commit suicide on the most conspicuous portion of the workpiece. That's life.

7 **Always use a tack-rag** and use it often. To those unfamiliar with the terminology, tack-rags, or tacky-cloths as they are sometimes called, are sticky squares of cheesecloth purpose-made for removing dust prior to painting. All you do is wipe the rag over the surface and it will attract dust like flies to a flypaper. Tack-rags are obtainable at good motor factors and decorator's supply shops; they come in packets of ten or twelve. Ordinary rags or handkerchiefs are quite useless for the purpose, leaving more dust and lint than they are meant to remove.

Undercoating

It is seldom that one can get away with less than three undercoats on vintage frames. Sometimes mudguards need up to six thick undercoats to cover up blemishes or remaining pit-marks. That's the bad news, now for the good. You need not be too particular about dust at this stage as you will be rubbing-down between coats anyway.

Buy a medium-priced brush, or brushes, for undercoating and keep them for this purpose only. *Harris's* domestic paint brushes are good enough at this stage, so purchase a 3/4 in, one-and-a-half inch, and two inch brush. They should last years if looked after.

Only experience will tell you how much paint to put on to avoid runs. There is not much written advice that can be given, except to make long sweeping strokes and not short jabs with the brush. Remember you are not stippling, you are **distributing** paint over the surface with a **flowing** motion.

See that the undercoat is well-mixed with a **clean**

It is hard to imagine that the rusty wreck (left) was transformed into the immaculate machine depicted on the right. Another Les Taverner restoration, a 1926 225cc Royal Enfield two-stroke. *(Photos: Les Taverner.)*

screwdriver before use. (I'll bet if you instructed a committee to design a tool for mixing paint they would end up with a thing exactly like a screwdriver!)

Use the recommended undercoat always. *Tekaloid* coach enamel, the restorers' favourite, has its own high-build undercoat as do most other brands of coach paint. Ordinary domestic gloss paint such as *Berger* and *Crown* are quite satisfactory for general restoration work and will stand up to arduous use; *Crown* undercoat (grey) is thick and covers well.

The brush must be kept clean and supple, always, between coats. Never stand it for any length of time on its bristles in a jar of turps, as the said bristles may be permanently distorted. (More about brushes later.)

Rubbing down

After each coat of undercoat the surface must be flatted-down with wet and dry emery, grade 320. Fill a bucket with cold water, add a squirt or two of washing-up liquid to avoid clogging, and away you go. If possible, do your rubbing-down in sunlight so you can see how much paint is coming off.

A very old coachpainter's tip worth mentioning is to add a spot of colour to each undercoat — the dregs of an old paint tin will do — so when you rub down you can see just how far to go before striking bare metal. Each layer will show up as a different shade, just like contours on a map.

Proceed with the undercoating, allowing about two days or more between coats until a good smooth surface free of pitmarks and indentations is evident. Large flat surfaces such as veteran petrol tanks and sidecar bodies are best flatted-down with emery paper wrapped round a cork pad (rubbing-down pads are sold in do-it-yourself shops). The last undercoat layer should be rubbed-down with well-used fine paper.

When you are satisfied with the results, the next stage — top or colour coats — can be tackled. Swill down the working area to damp down paint dust and start painting when the floor is still wet.

Gloss coats

Depending on how particular you are, up to six brushed-on top coats are needed. It is not really necessary to varnish over the last coat, except on lined petrol tanks. Bear in mind that varnish will darken a light-coloured petrol tank, which may cause problems if the machine is all one colour — in this event a slightly lighter gloss can be mixed for the tank.

When tanks or cycle parts are subsequently lined the last coat should be flatted with very fine emery paper. Lining takes better on a matt surface, as we shall see later.

Above: How to find them! This very original 1927 277 cc Triumph was stored for most of its life in the manchester area, winning an award for the most original machine at the annual Belle Vue Classic Bike Show. Price when new was £37.10s.

Paint

So, what sort of paint do you need? To some extent it depends on what you want to use the bike for when it's finished. Many a club concours event has been won with a brushed-on oil paint obtained from the local D-I-Y supermarket. Really superb results can be achieved with ordinary *Berger* domestic gloss, to mention just one brand; almost all modern gloss paints have reached a stage of perfection where they are quite good enough for our purposes. If you want to ride in the odd trial, or ride your vintage machine to work every day it is well worth considering ordinary gloss as an alternative to coach enamel.

Most expert restorers use *Tekaloid* coach enamel (a Croda product), although it should be remembered that several paint manufacturers offer a similar coach paint, albeit to special order. *Tekaloid* covers well and brush-marks flow-out easily; however it would be wrong to assume that this, or any other coach enamel for that matter, can achieve magical results. **There is no substitute for good preparation.**

For the average motorcycle you will need about half a litre of metal primer, a litre of grey undercoat, and a litre of black gloss. Plus of course a tin of paint for the tank if it is a different colour.

Regarding petrol tank colours, ask for a *Tekaloid* colour chart and if there's nothing suitable on that, try perusing a *Berger* trade British Standard Colour Chart. Most paint manufacturers issue similar charts and there is a good chance you will find something near enough; almost every colour can be matched (even that diabolically difficult vintage Triumph grey-green) with clever mixing. Sometimes only the smallest measure of colour will make all the difference.

Bear in mind when mixing colours that paint darkens considerably on drying. Try to match the colour to an unfaded portion of the machine — behind the tank knee-pads for instance. Do a few test samples and wait until the paint has thoroughly hardened before making the final decision. A sample which is apparently too light and new looking might be the correct shade after a couple of weeks.

Perfectionists always filter their paint through a piece of nylon stocking before use. Even **new** paint should be filtered and it is best to use a new, clean, receptable every time (*Pot-Noodle* food containers are excellent for the job). Pour just enough paint out for the job in hand and throw away the container after use. Don't dip the brush in the paint tin as it's surprising how much foreign matter finds its way in there.

Brushes

It cannot be stressed too highly the importance of purchasing only the best brushes at this stage. It is worth going to some trouble and expense to obtain Hamilton's *Perfection Plus* brushes; in the author's experience there are none better and it will repay you to look after them like gold.

So, what's special about *Perfection Plus* brushes? Nothing out of the ordinary; they are just well made, have a good long bristle, and what matters most is that the bristles don't come out (well, *hardly ever*, as W.S. Gilbert would have put it). Keep the bristles scrupulously clean by washing in white spirit, followed by paintbrush cleaning solution, then lukewarm soapy water and finally rinse under the tap.

When the bristles are dry, wrap them in kitchen foil or cling-film to keep the dust out and to retain the shape. Don't listen to people who tell you to leave brushes standing in water. Brushes should **not** be left standing on their bristles in old paint or turps, or flung on the bench to collect swarf.

One method of ensuring brush cleanliness between coats is to fill a clean white container (small enamel basin) with white spirit and dip the brush into it. Specks of dirt and old paint will be observed to float out of the bristles. Shake off the white spirit by striking the brush handle smartly on the edge of the bench and dip the bristles into a second

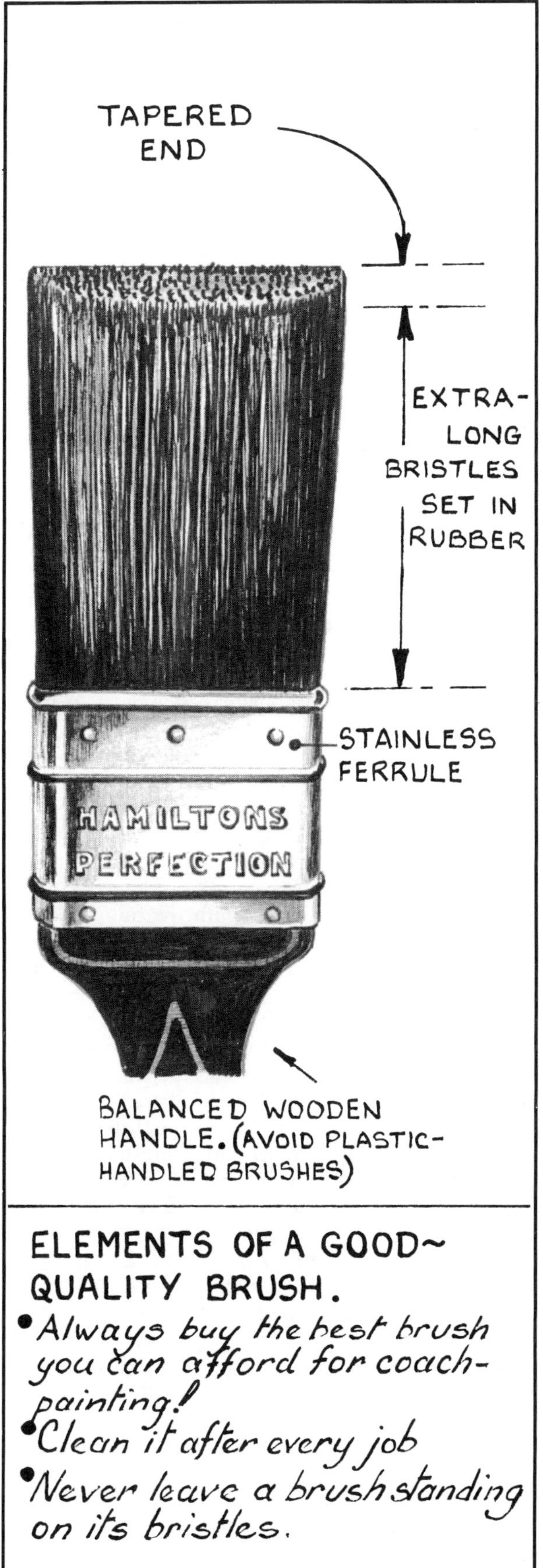

ELEMENTS OF A GOOD-QUALITY BRUSH.

- Always buy the best brush you can afford for coach-painting!
- Clean it after every job
- Never leave a brush standing on its bristles.

container holding clean turps. Repeat again, for a third time, until no more dust specks or other floating bodies emerge. This is an old coach-painters method which has stood the test of time, still being practised today by expert restorers.

Old brushes have well-tapered bristles, which is why some old craftsmen used to "run-in" their new brushes by rubbing them dry over a rough brick. Cheap brushes are not worth buying; although it may be a generalisation, beware of those with plastic handles and mild-steel ferrules. Bristles which open out like daffodils after the first application are all too common in supermarket brushes. Good coach-painting brushes will last twenty or more years if looked after.

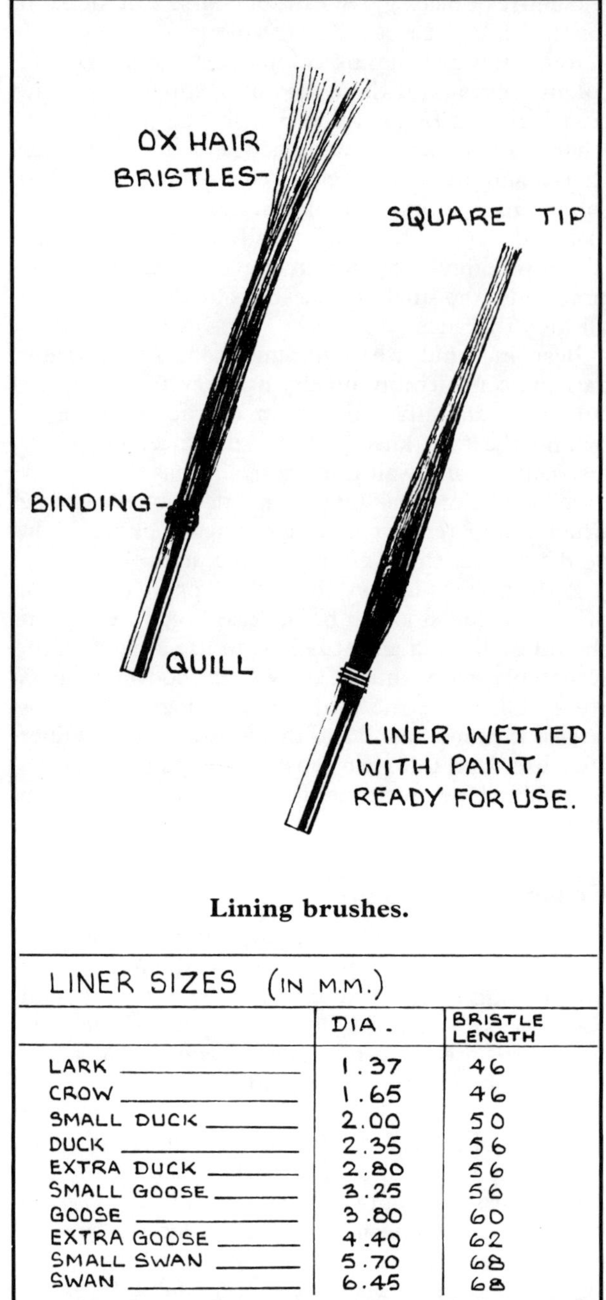

Lining brushes.

LINER SIZES (IN M.M.)

	DIA.	BRISTLE LENGTH
LARK	1.37	46
CROW	1.65	46
SMALL DUCK	2.00	50
DUCK	2.35	56
EXTRA DUCK	2.80	56
SMALL GOOSE	3.25	56
GOOSE	3.80	60
EXTRA GOOSE	4.40	62
SMALL SWAN	5.70	68
SWAN	6.45	68

Painting

The painting can proceed, choosing the widest brush practicable for the component in hand. A two-inch brush may be necessary for mudguards, whilst a half-inch or 3/4 in will do for smaller cycle parts. Bear in mind environmental considerations — in other words take every precaution possible to eliminate dust, as discussed earlier.

Again experience will dictate how much, or how little, paint to apply without making a mess. Wipe a tack-rag (the painter's best friend) over the surface to pick up dust flecks.

Dip the brush fully into the paint. This may seem obvious, but many nervous individuals just jab it in half an inch and don't charge the bristles properly. Remove excess paint on the container rim.

Apply a long stroke lengthways on the workpiece, then another one in line with it but about a brush-width away. Blend in the two with cross strokes, brushing-out to distribute the paint. Then gently, in an un-hurried manner, do some more lengthways strokes without recharging the brush.

Some amateur painters use their brushes as though they were pasting wallpaper, brushing backwards and forwards with gay abandon. For the last strokes the brush can be held lightly between thumb and forefinger, thumb uppermost, letting the brush weight itself provide the fine pressure. Too much paint will, of course, cause runs. Once a run develops in oil-based enamel it may take weeks to harden sufficiently to be rubbed out. Economy of medium is the keynote to success. In the old days coachpainters took a pride in their brushwork. It was considered good practice to do the strokes up and down on vertical panels (as on the sides of bodywork) and lengthways on mudguards. The strokes would be neat, unbroken and in line. Even though modern paint flows-out much better it is still a good idea to follow this code, if only to give runs less chance of forming.

Each coat should be rubbed-down very carefully, the penultimate coat receiving the merest degree of etching with well-worn wet-and-dry emery. Two pieces of ultra-fine emery rubbed together will take the cutting edge off, so avoiding deep scratches in the finished surface.

Hang the parts up with wire (old plastic-covered cable is ideal) and leave the workshop immediately the last coat is applied. Don't be tempted to carry on with some bench fitting while the paint dries. It will be safe to re-enter after six hours or so, but try to resist the urge to fiddle with the parts in case anything drops off its wire.

Leave the painted components for as long as possible (two to three weeks) and swill them in cold water to harden the surface. Even after this, the

A nice example of hand lining on this 1929 Norton tank. Poor lining can spoil an otherwise well-restored machine. For long-lasting results the lining should be applied over a matt surface and varnished over afterwards. If hand-applied, polyurethane yacht varnish provides a durable finish.

parts should be handled with care.

It is not necessary to cut back the finished coat with abrasive polish, as with cellulose. Finish off with a good wax polish and you should have a depth of colour indistinguishable from stove enamel. Maintain the appearance with regular washing and drying-off with a chamois leather.

Hand lining

Sometimes called pinstriping across the Atlantic, lining is an ancient art owing its origins to heraldic design in mediaeval days. The only written work I have ever seen on the subject was in a Victorian penny magazine, *Work*. It is interesting to reflect that life in the 1880s was hard for the amateur painter, who often had to grind his own pigments and mix stoppers— indeed, one article in the same magazine described how emery paper could be made!

At one time every coachworks and motor bicycle factory employed at least one lining craftsman. Today they are an extinct species, although their terminology is still with us. Take for instance the peculiar names given to brushes, or ox hair liners in quill, to give them their full name.

The thinnest brush is a Lark which has bristles 1.37 mm diameter by 46 mm. long. The next size up is a Crow, followed by Small Duck, Duck and Extra Duck. The larger sizes of liners start at Small Goose with bristles 3.25 mm. diameter by 56 mm. long and end with a Swan (6.45 mm. diameter by 68 mm. long).

All these liners are of course set in quills, hence their quaint ornithological titles. Bristle quality is superb, a fact which is reflected in the relatively high prices of these hand-made tools. The ratio of bristle-to-quill is about two parts bristle to one part quill and generally they are used without handles; this means you have a very slender brush which is held between thumb and forefinger.

The long bristle is essential for holding a reserve of paint and for guiding the tip when painting a straight line. An ordinary artists' watercolour brush would be quite useless for lining as it would wander from side to side making a wobbly line, so familiar in beginners' work. Anyone who has attempted lining with a paint-box brush is bound to be disappointed. Use of the proper tool will alter his outlook entirely.

I have always purchased my liners from Hamiltons but it has to be said they are not easy to obtain unless you live in a big city with a very good decorators' supplier. Obviously the sale of liners (catalogue no. 463 in Hamiltons' list) is limited so you cannot expect your local paint shop to have them in stock. If, however, your dealer has ordinary Hamiltons' brushes on his display board, ask him to send off for a list of liners, pencils and writers, and order what you want from that. Most dealers will oblige.

In times of emergency I have made my own lining brushes from human hair set in quills. The hair must be long and straight; for some odd reason natural blonde female hair seems to be ideal for the job. (How you go about procuring a sample is another matter!) Cut a straight lock of hair about three inches long; without allowing the hairs to separate, dip the cut ends in *Araldite* and insert the lock into a quill for a depth of approximately half an inch. Leave the brush to harden-off for twenty four hours before use. Make a number of lining brushes of different diameters and you're in business. Home-made brushes are not generally as successful as commercially-made examples but it is well worth experimenting on these lines if you live in some remote part of the globe. Try various animal hairs — horse hair may be satisfactory if not too coarse.

Lining technique

The surface must be thoroughly prepared and flatted-down. There must be no pit-marks or sundry indentations to cause the brush to skip or deviate from its true path.

Special lining paints are available (eg *Dagger-Lac* in the USA and *Keeps Signwriters' Enamel* in the UK) but a *slow-drying* domestic gloss will suffice. Under no circumstances should cellulose be used as this dries far too quickly.

Drop a blob of paint in the middle of a palette, which can be an old dinner plate or an offcut of clean plastic. Roll the liner in it to charge the bristles. Draw the bristles an inch or two along the palette to remove excess paint and to straighten out the bristles.

Experiment on an old mudguard and try the smallest size of liner first. Hold it lightly between thumb and forefinger with the thumb uppermost (see sketch). The second or third finger is used as a guide along, say, the edge of a mudguard or petrol tank.

To commence a line lay the bristles down almost horizontally without dithering. Draw the brush towards you, making a line of even width as you go. At first this is not easy. What usually happens is that the line starts off too thick due to excess paint and eventually peters-out just when you don't want it to. It will be a long time before success is achieved, so do not expect to become proficient in half an hour.

It may be necessary to experiment with paint viscosity, so have some turpentine or white spirits handy to mix on the palette. The tiniest drop of turps will make a lot of difference. Some synthetic enamel paints sold in model shops tend to dry too quickly so if you find your liner not responding as it should, wash it out and start afresh with new paint.

Corners are tricky at first until you learn how to adopt a flourishing, almost flamboyant, sweep of the wrist. Joining-up a corner with a straight line often

A sketch from the Author's notebook detailing the layout and lining of a 1923 Triumph Gloria sidecar prior to renovation. It is essential to record such details before the paint is stripped off. This applies equally to motorcycle petrol tanks — usually the original colour and lining width can be discerned under the kneegrips.

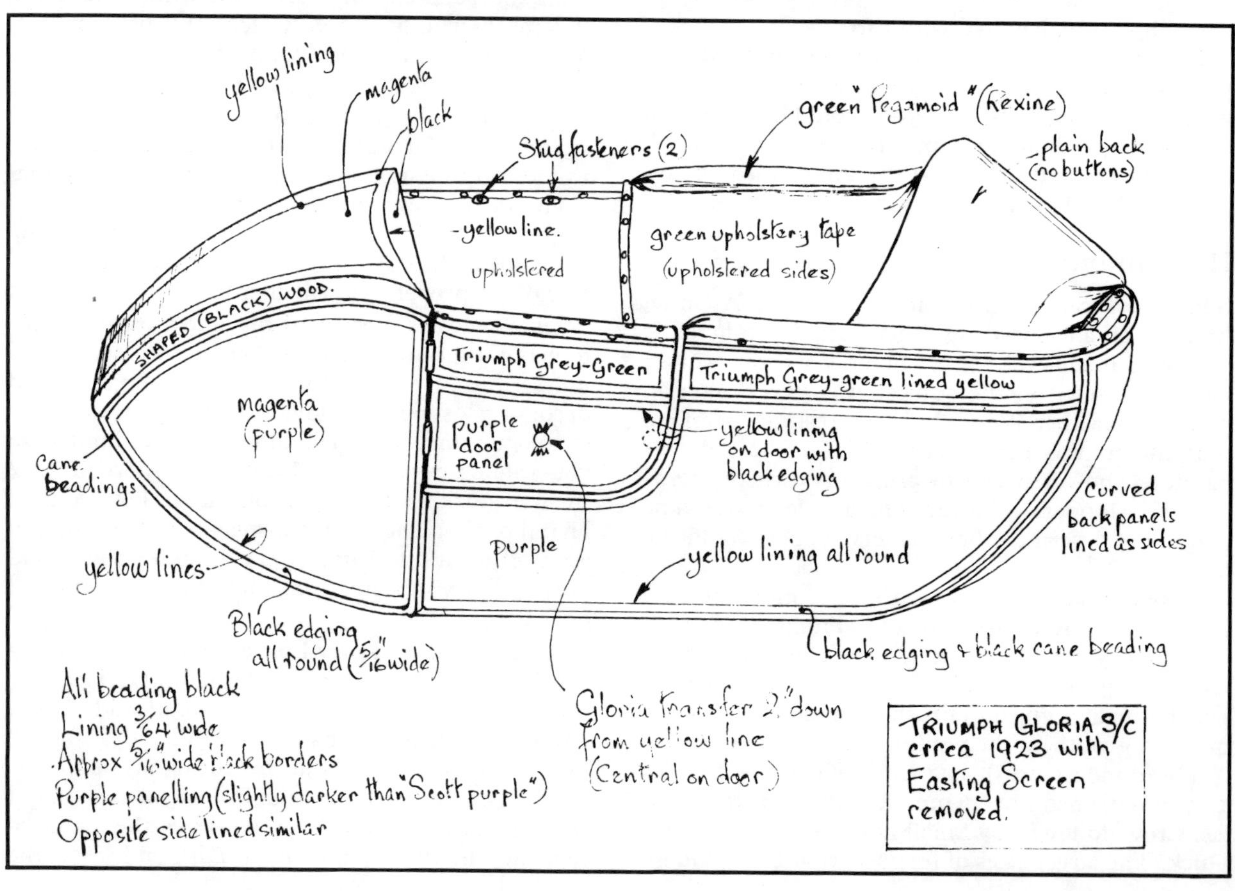

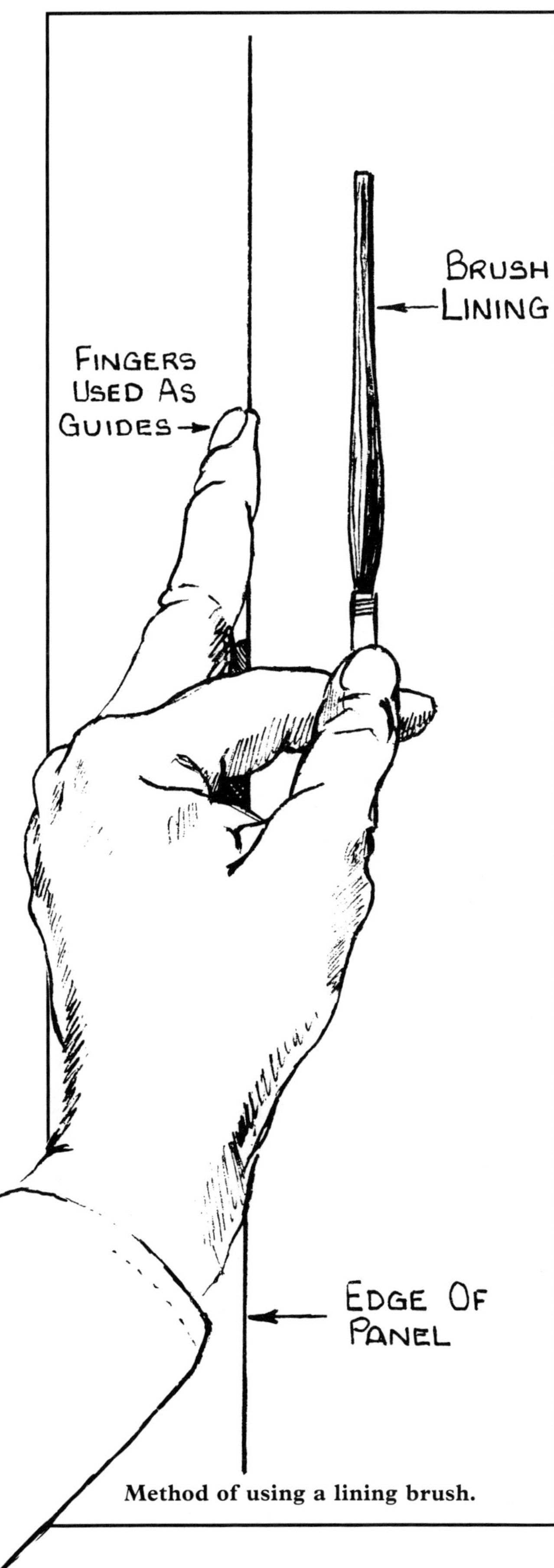

Method of using a lining brush.

results in a slight mismatch of line-widths but such flaws can usually be rectified by touching-in with the base colour after the line has dried.

Gold lines are the worst to contend with as most gold paints sold in model shops and general stores are worse than useless for our purposes. Many restorers have found to their cost that some gold paints dissolve in the final varnishing stage, leaving an unholy mess. Others disperse in petrol, washing away your gold lining when the tank overflows. The traditional materials for gold lining consist of bronze powder mixed in bronzing medium or gold size, the latter being used also for fixing transfers. Bronze powder is obtainable in pale or dark shades, the former being generally acceptable for motorcycle lining. Ask for *Ardenbrite,* a Robinson & Neal product.

A few motorcycle petrol tanks in the vintage period were lined with genuine gold leaf. Applying gold leaf is a very skilled process indeed which takes many years to learn, therefore the amateur is not advised to attempt this art-form. There are few craftsmen left capable of gold-leafing, and not many suppliers of the necessary materials. Briefly the process involves making the line to be leafed in gold size; when the size is almost dry the gold leaf is very carefully placed in position, pressed down and left to harden-off. Excess gold is dusted off, a line of the appropriate width remaining.

Gold leaf comes in book form, the small leaves (microscopically thin) being interspersed with paper. Transferring the gold leaf from the book to the workpiece is an art in itself; usually a leaf is lifted by gently blowing edge-on to the book whereupon a sort of palette knife is inserted underneath the leaf. The gold itself is so thin and fragile it would powder-away at a touch, hence the great skill required!

The Beugler Striper

There is on the market a simple lining tool which is a godsend to amateur restorers. Made in America by Beugler Stripers, Mail Order Dept., P.O. Box 29068, Los Angeles, Ca 90020, the *Beugler Striper* consists of a tubular paint reservoir with a metering wheel at one end and a plunger knob at the other.

The plunger, which has the appearance of a small Best and Lloyd hand oil pump knob, has no other function than to expel residual air after the paint barrel is filled.

Two kits are available, the De Luxe and the Professional. Both kits contain identical lining tools but the Professional version has seven different widths of wheelhead compared with the De Luxe kit's three. Wheelheads have knurled wheels for drawing a line and are obtainable singly; in fact Beuglers can supply double wheelheads which do two lines side-by-side, and Jumbo wheelheads for wide lines. The standard range in the Professional

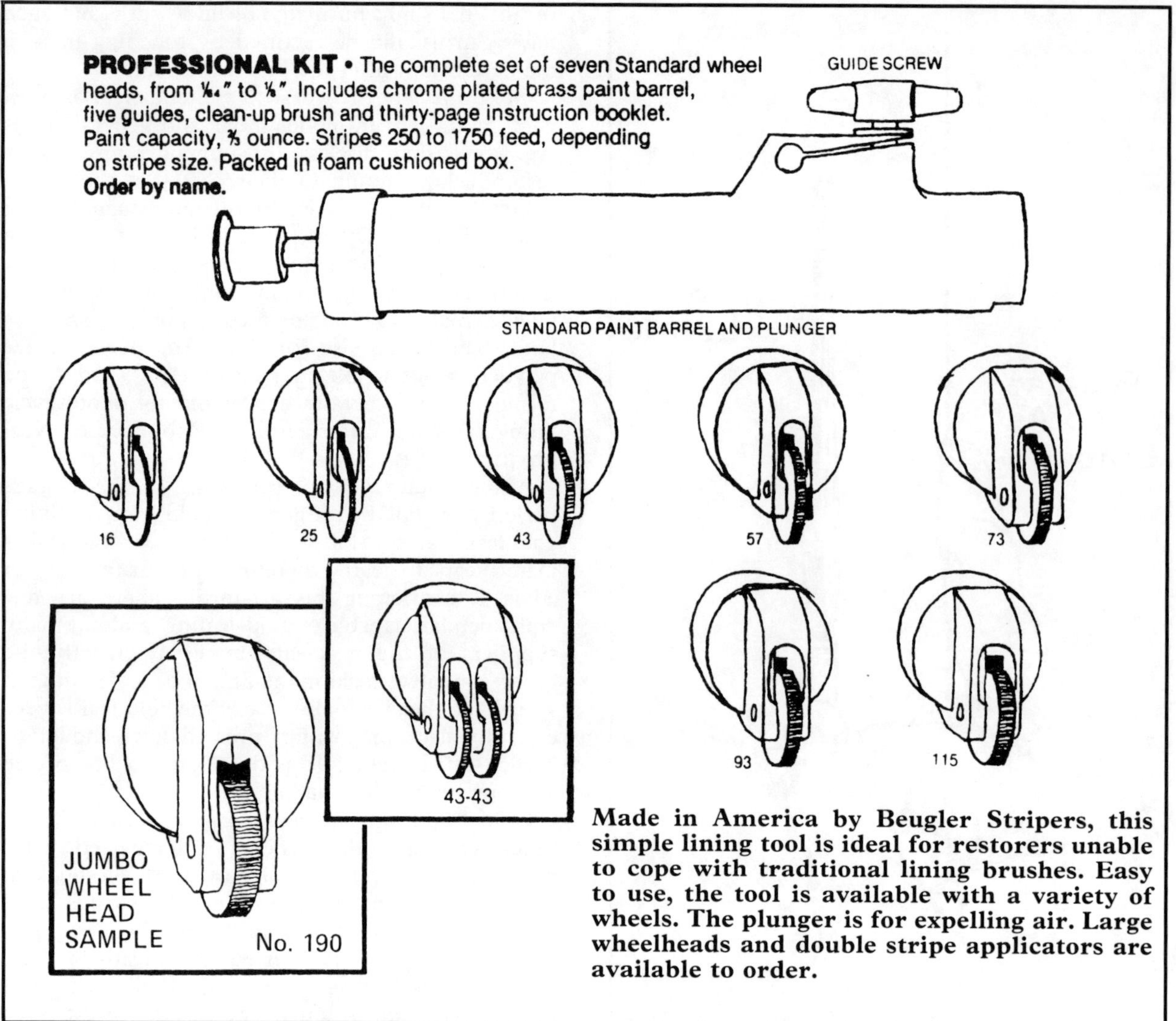

Made in America by Beugler Stripers, this simple lining tool is ideal for restorers unable to cope with traditional lining brushes. Easy to use, the tool is available with a variety of wheels. The plunger is for expelling air. Large wheelheads and double stripe applicators are available to order.

kit covers line widths from 1/64 in to 1/8 in. Jumbo heads start at one eighth and go up to almost 1/2 in (not that you are likely to need such a wide line on motorcycle parts).

According to their publicity leaflet, Beuglers have been selling their stripers, as they call them, since 1934. A similar but much cruder tool used to be advertised in motor magazines in the 1950s; the author recalls this British-made lining tool as being little more than a toy, one which must have disappointed many a purchaser. The *Beugler Striper* is a different kettle of fish, being a precision instrument nicely finished in chrome, and what's more it works.

Paint is metered by the knurled wheel which runs in a trough. There is no wick or ball-valve to go wrong. Regulation of the paint flow is by means of the closely-toleranced orifice, so paint viscosity is of some importance. Beuglers recommend *Dagger Lac* or *Keeps Signwriters' Enamel*, although a thick oil-based paint will suffice.

Metal guide fingers are included with each kit; these clamp in the toolpost so that the line can be guided by a mudguard edge or body moulding. Magnetic guide strips are also available.

Comprehensive instructions are included with each striping tool so that even the rawest novice can make perfect lines with a few minutes' practise. To charge the striper the wheelhead is lifted off and the paint barrel is filled; the makers say that a line of 100 to 500 feet in length (according to the stripe width) can be made from one filling. The applicator head is replaced and residual air is expelled by carefully pressing the plunger as the tool is held vertically. When a small drop of paint appears at the base of the wheel the striper is ready.

There's not much that can go wrong. If there is a break in the line after commencement it means the paint has rapidly dried on the wheel. To avoid this, the tool must be primed before applying a stripe simply by running the wheel on a test surface and then immediately placing it in position on the workpiece. The instructions state "it is important that you do not wait between priming and appli-

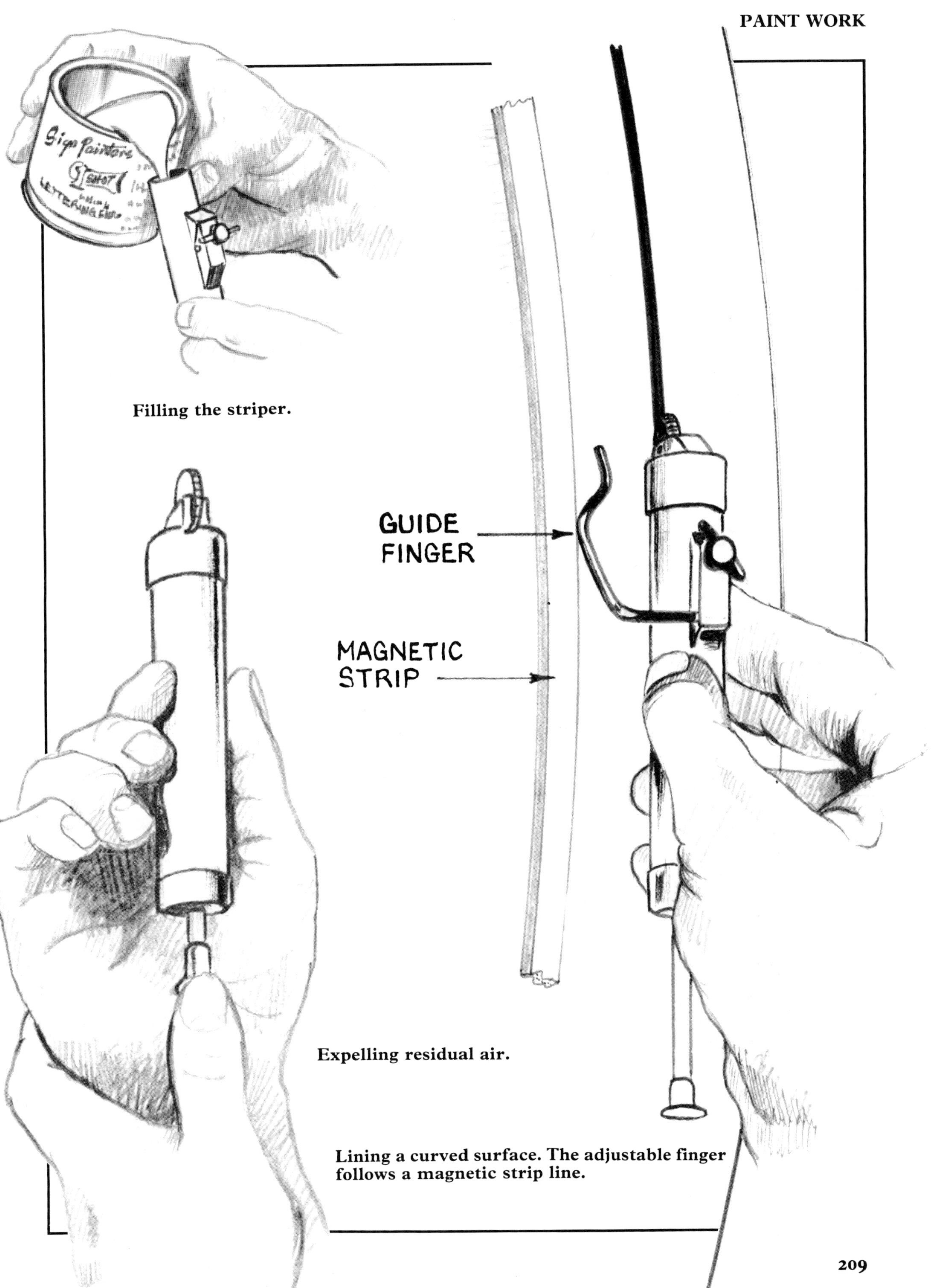

Filling the striper.

Expelling residual air.

Lining a curved surface. The adjustable finger follows a magnetic strip line.

A 1929 500cc ohv Radco "Ace", made by E.A. Radnall & Co., of Dartmouth Street, Birmingham – a company better known for their lightweight two-strokes.

cation of the stripe, as the paint will again skin over." By beginning and ending on a piece of masking tape any such skips are easily avoided.

Beautifully uniform, straight lines can be made and it's just as easy to go round corners. In fact, lines made by the *Beugler* tool are more even in width than those made by traditional methods. The drawbacks? Well, being a precision instrument the Striper is not cheap, but then it will last a lifetime. (Footnote:- at the time of writing the European agent is:- S. Gerber, Beugler Stripers, Postbus 122, 3971LE, Driebergen, Holland).

Fixing transfers

Newcomers to restoration work may well be perplexed by the various types of transfers on the market today; those readers who have been restoring bikes for many years tend to forget that at one time they had to ask how to apply a tank transfer, or for that matter how to mend a puncture or fix a spring-link. There are young men coming into the game now who have never heard of such things as Castol XXL, Easting Screens, tyre gaiters, belt punches or Pratts Petrol!

For the benefit of younger readers undergoing their first attempts at renovation the following notes on transfers will be of interest.

Gold-size transfers

Probably the most common transfers in the vintage period. Very durable. Can usually be recognised by the imprinted outline of the emblem on the reverse side (the colours can only be seen by holding the transfer up to a strong light). Apply as follows:-

1 Carefully peel off the backing paper (separate it with the thumb nail).
2 Apply a thin coat of gold-size to the emblem, or lettering, making sure every part is coated. Note: only a **thin** coat is necessary. Clear varnish will do just as well as gold size but don't try to hasten the drying time by holding it by a fire as the transfer may crack.
3 Leave the varnish to go tacky — almost dry.
4 Apply the transfer to the tank, making absolutely certain it is correctly aligned as there is no second chance.
5 Carefully press the transfer and smooth it out, working from the middle outwards to remove bubbles.
6 Leave it for an hour or so.
7 Dab the backing tissue with water and carefully peel it off. Wipe over the transfer with a damp rag to remove excess gum.
8 After two days, varnish over the transfer with clear polyurethane varnish.

Spirit transfers

Similar in appearance to gold-size transfers, these are the type usually stocked by the *VMCC Transfer Scheme*. Instead of applying gold-size the back of the transfer is wiped over with a mixture of 75% meths and 25% water and applied within a minute or so.

Otherwise all the stages are the same, ie separate backing paper, wipe emblem with diluted meths, apply, remove tissue with a damp rag. After drying,

A wartime shot of a Norton "Big Four" outfit with sidecar wheel drive. Note the fitting of a tank-top air filter. WD machines were finished in olive drab, khaki, or a mixture of both on occasions!

the transfer should be varnished.

Waterslide type

A cheaper transfer, easily recognised by the design being visible in full colour. Very easy to apply but watch for air bubbles.

The transfer is placed in a saucer of water, face up. When loose, the emblem is slid off onto the tank or whatever. Press out air bubbles and varnish when dry.

Just a word about authenticity. With few exceptions waterslide transfers are not as accurate as could be desired. Check the design in comparison with an original insignia if possible — you may find the colours are all wrong. Cheap reproduction BSA transfers are notable culprits, with "piled arms" motifs bearing little resemblance to the original design. For that matter waterslide Bantam cockerels look more like Mallard ducks in colour and form! Some marques fare rather better than others (Matchless for example) but the Norton trademark is often abused.

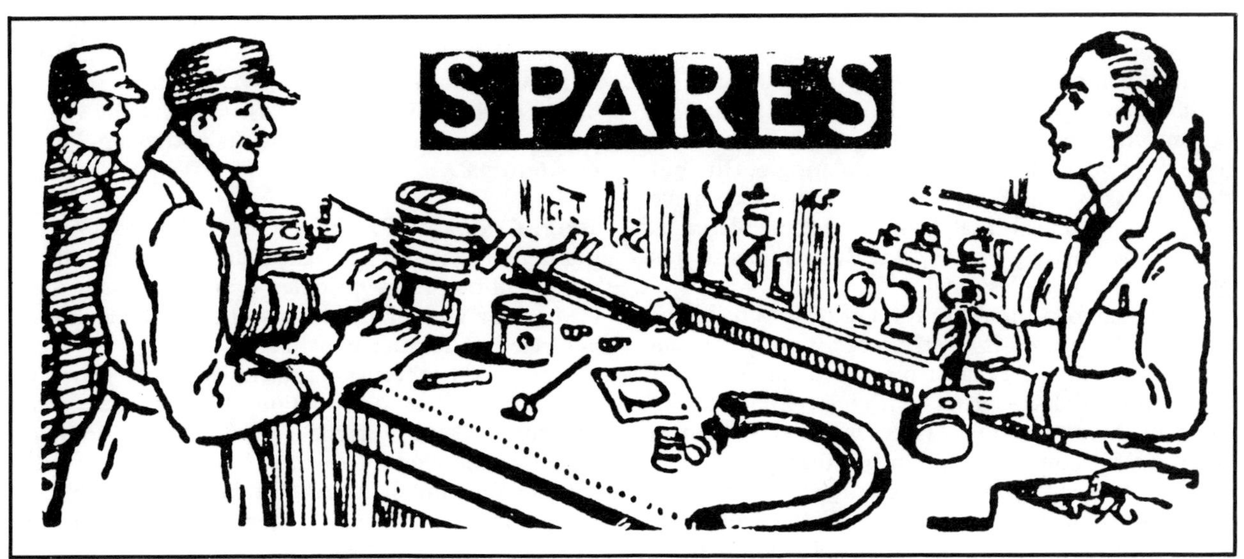

Chapter 9

Electroplating at Home

Preparation. Nickel plating. Aluminium refinishing.

Electroplating processes

A brief resumé of the various plating processes commercially available will be of interest to the reader, who may well be perplexed by the whole subject of electroplating. It is not proposed to delve into the mysteries of chemistry — indeed, the beginner requires no special knowledge to be able to set up and operate a small nickel plating plant in his workshop.

Most commercial processes involve the use of toxic liquids, such as cyanide, and are therefore beyond the scope of the amateur. A few enthusiasts have built small-scale chromium plating outfits but the process is highly complex, requiring expensive equipment and health safeguards. Chrome plating is closely governed by Factory Act Regulations so it is best left to the professionals.

To the layman the restoration of his bright bits is simple. All he does is to strip off his rusty control levers, handlebars, exhaust pipes and cart them off to the nearest electroplaters with instructions to dip them in the plating tank. He then expects them to emerge all bright and shiny in five minutes.

Unfortunately there is much more to the whole procedure than he may imagine! First of all every scrap of old plating has to be removed and the parts then undergo a time-consuming polishing procedure to eradicate all pit-marks and blemishes, This is the expensive element in the process. When all the parts are highly polished it is only then that the various stages of electroplating can commence.

Dull Nickel. This is the original plating finish as used in the early days. It is based upon a solution of nickel sulphate and ammonium sulphate, sometimes called a double nickel solution. Canning's *Albo* is an improved version of a double salt solution, and this is what is used in the popular *Dynic* home plating outfits. Parts have to be lightly polished after plating but the result is a beautiful silvery sheen.

Albo, when used warm, was mixed at the rate of 32 ozs. per gallon of water, maintained to a pH value of 5.6 to 5.8.

Bright Nickel. Extensively used by commercial plating concerns. The chances are that your vintage parts will be bright-nickelled if you have sent them off to the platers. Parts come out of the tank shining and need no further polishing.

The first bright nickel finishes appeared generally in 1937 with the introduction of Canning's *Lumax* solution. Other bright solutions are *BQ840, Gleamax* and *Super Gleamax*. Maintenance of these solutions is much more difficult than with dull nickel; impurities such as copper, zinc, lead, and iron can play havoc with the deposit, causing ugly

Two views of a veteran Scott. Note the superb nickel plating — Scott radiators should be entrusted only to a specialist electroplater with experience in this kind of work.

stains, cracking, or non-adhesion. Such contamination can easily occur when articles are dropped into the plating tank (accidents can happen . . .) Not recommended for the amateur plater.

Black Nickel produces a jet-black appearance and is a good finish for electrical components, name-plates and instrument parts. A matt-black finish is achieved by bead blasting the parts; vintage nuts and bolts such as those found on AJS and Sunbeam machines could be finished thus as an alternative to chemical black.

Chromium Plating was first used commercially around 1925 but did not make its appearance on motorcycles until the very end of the vintage period (1929/30). Thus its use is not encouraged on earlier machinery.

Nickel is usually plated onto the base metal to form a protective layer for the microscopically thin flash of chrome (as little as 0.00002 in. thick in some cases). If chrome was deposited direct on steel, atmospheric impurities would soon force it off again by galvanic action.

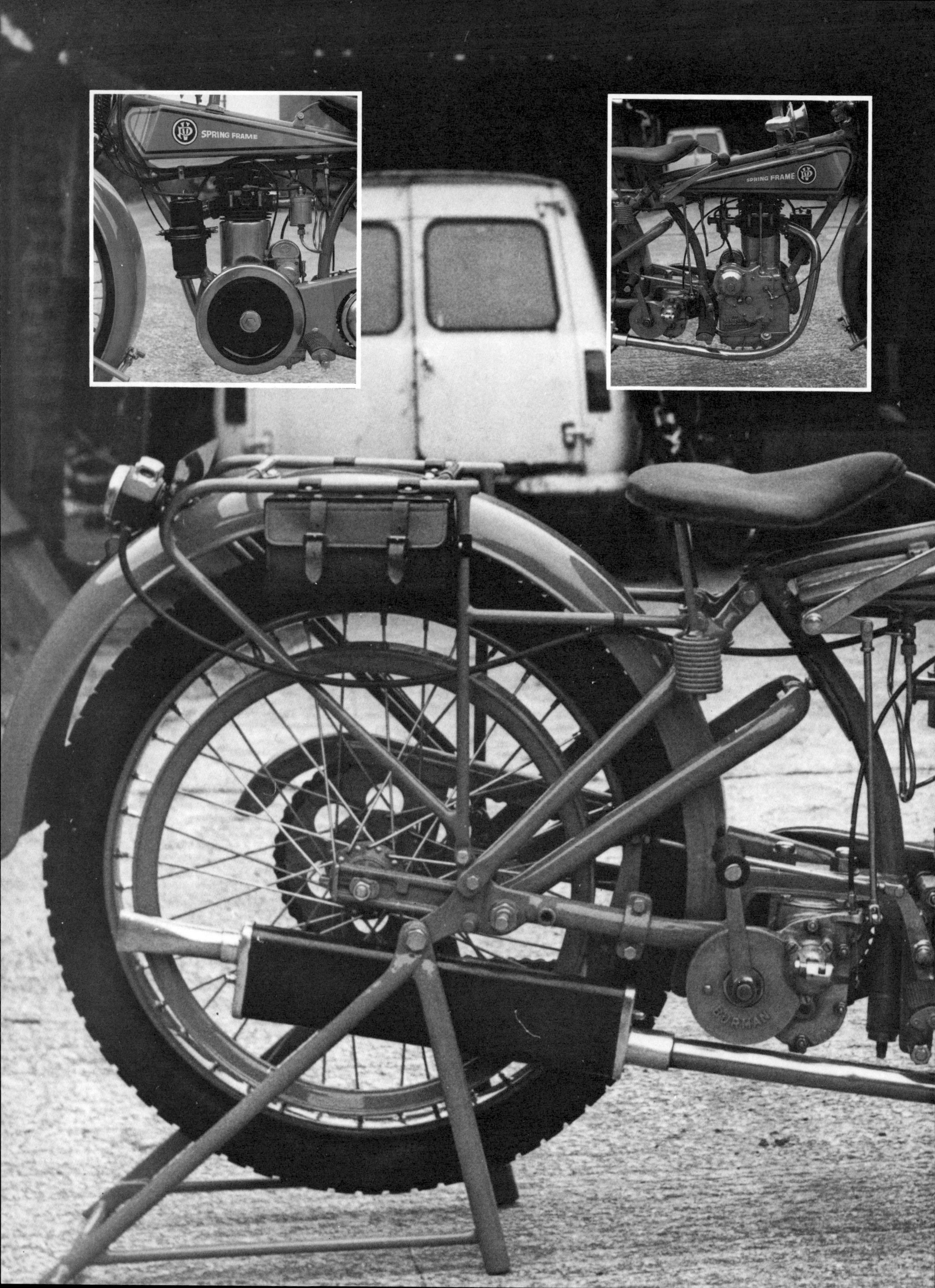
SPRING FRAME
SPRING FRAME
BURMAN

TA 9291
SPRING FRAME

Photos on previous pages: Manufactured in 1924, the Perry Vale (PV for short) is equipped with a Bradshaw "oil boiler" engine of 350cc capacity, BTH magneto and Binks carburettor. Bradshaw engines were fitted to dozens of "lesser" makes including DOT, one of which survives in the hands of Bob (Sherlock Holmes) Currie.

The PV-Bradshaw restored by Richard Lancaster is a perfect example of an amateur restoration. Every aspect of the work including paintwork, plating and pipe bending was undertaken in Richard's home workshop. His attention to detail has resulted in major concours awards for the PV, including class wins at Banbury, Belle Vue and the Isle of Man.

As far as the restorer is concerned, the end-result will depend entirely on the amount of elbow grease spent in polishing. Chrome will not hide pit marks. Preparation is very expensive so the restorer is advised to do most of the polishing at home!

Hard Chrome is used industrially for coating parts subject to wear (hydraulic rams etc). Quite different from cosmetic chrome plate, a thick layer is built up and then ground to size. Expensive but useful for reclaiming worn telescopic fork legs.

Copper plate is also useful for building up worn surfaces.

Cadmium. A typical solution contains from 2½ to 3 oz. per gallon of sodium cyanide, therefore is also beyond the amateur's resources. Used for protecting nuts and bolts.

Zinc is widely used in the engineering industry as a substitute for cadmium. Easy to plate, bright in appearance. Large quantities of nuts, bolts and other small components can be barrel-plated quite cheaply.

Tin-Nickel resembles bright nickel but does not readily tarnish. Useful for the everyday rider of vintage machines although a little too bright for concours fanatics.

Anodising is not strictly speaking an electroplating process as it does not involve the deposition of metal. A thin film of aluminium oxide or hydroxide is formed on the surface of an aluminium casting or pressing, so preventing further corrosion. A relatively simple and cheap process.

Aluminium parts can be coloured by the addition of a dye, thus crankcases are sometimes anodised grey (model aeroplane enthusiasts will be familiar with red or blue cooling fins on small diesel engines!)

Setting-up a home plating outfit

Reliable electroplaters are few and far between, as any restorer knows to his cost. Even if a trustworthy craftsman is found, there is always the chance of an irreplaceable part going missing. Things can disappear indefinitely in the bowels of a plating vat and it is of little consolation to be offered financial compensation for the loss of a veteran Scott carburettor body!

So, why not nickel plate the parts yourself? Apart from having everything under your control there are other advantages — the cost factor being the most significant. For a minimal outlay (let's say the cost of a new tyre) a complete plating plant can be set up in the home, big enough to deal with everything except an exhaust pipe.

No great skill is required. There are no dangerous chemicals to contend with. The whole apparatus can be assembled on a kitchen worktop.

The Dynic kit

Dynic Sales, of 1 Bell View Cottages, Banbury Road, Ladbroke, Leamington Spa, Warwickshire CV33 ODA (telephone Southam 4313), market a

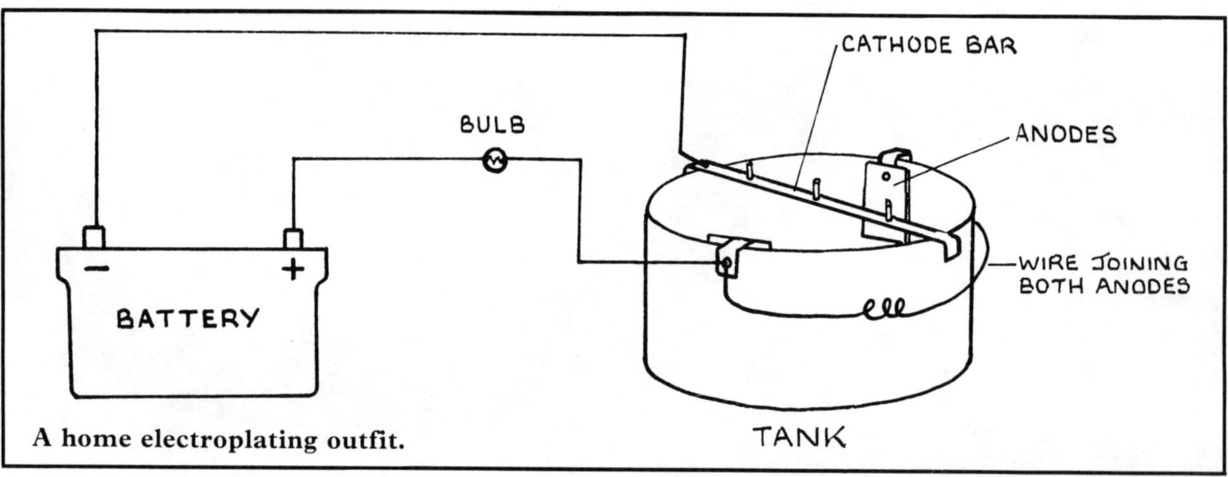

A home electroplating outfit.

An instruction booklet is included with every Dynic kit.

Below: Details of the anode bar assembly.

small nickel plating kit especially for the amateur. Two versions of the lot are available, the *Standard* and the *Major*. With both outfits all the necessary chemicals are included, together with nickel anodes and copper wire, enabling the amateur to nickel plate such items as carburettor bodies, lamp rims, screws, and any other part which will fit in an eight-pint enamel pan *(Standard Kit)* or large enamel bucket *(Major Kit)*. (Dynic do not handle chrome plating chemicals, recognising that the process is not possible in home workshops).

The Dynic kits do not employ new-fangled gimmicry, like some processes advertised in the motoring press a few years ago. On the contrary; the Dynic process is nothing more or less than a scaled-down commercial nickel-plating plant, exactly the same as employed by motorcycle manufacturers in the vintage era.

An old six or twelve volt battery provides the power source and the only other items the restorer must provide are the heater, thermometer and tank.

The plating tank

The container should be enamelled (ie vitreous enamel). Hardward stores are likely sources for large saucepans or enamelled buckets; quite often "seconds" with a few chips around the rim, can be bought cheaply.

Galvanised buckets are totally unacceptable as the plating solution would attack the zinc coating. The

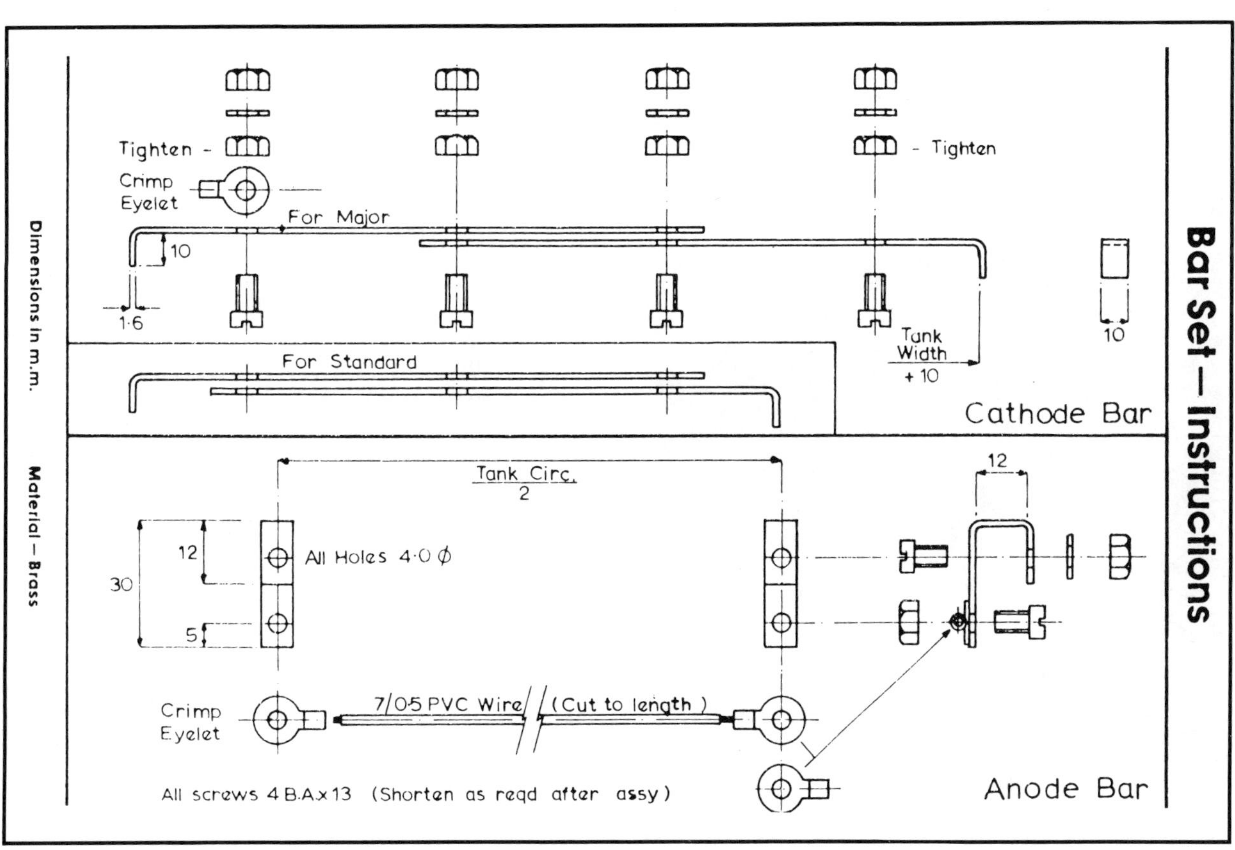

No, it's not new – this 1955 598cc Panther with Watsonian Albion sidecar is the result of four year's hard labour. Owner John Eaves restored the outfit – it's a lot smarter than those we used to see plodding their way to the seaside at weekends, loaded with kids and jam butties!

A close-up of the engine unit of John Eaves' machine.

tank must be able to withstand direct heat, in the form of a primus stove or gas ring. Stainless steel is not satisfactory as, again, solution contamination would result.

Glass, earthenware, or plastic can be considered, providing the tank is placed in a separate (outer) vessel containing hot water, this water jacket being warmed by means of an immersion heater. (Solution contamination could occur if the immersion heater was placed directly in the plating tank). Commercial platers use rubber-lined, lead-lined or plastic tanks with special non-reacting immersion heaters.

Having purchased the tank, the next step is to make a cathode bar. This is simply a strip of brass or stainless steel which serves two functions, to hang the parts from and to carry the current to the said parts. The cathode bar is placed across the top of the container and, when operations commence, is connected to the negative battery terminal.

Two nickel anodes — flat plates of pure nickel — are supplied and brackets must be made to hang them on either side of the tank. Fabricate brackets from brass or stainless steel (they do not come into contact with the liquid) and attach terminals to them as shown in the sketch. The anodes are connected to the positive wire from the battery. Plastic insulated wire as used for motorcycle wiring is ideal for all connections.

It is recommended that the anodes are wrapped in mesh bags (muslin or old nylon stocking) during the plating process to prevent particles of solid nickel from breaking away and floating about the tank. Bandages will suffice for this purpose although many amateurs seem to manage without them.

Heating source

The plating solution must be maintained at a temperature of 90/100°F, so a small thermostatically-controlled hotplate, gas ring or old camping stove is needed to stand the tank on. My own heater is a rusty old paraffin camping stove, bought for a few coppers in a junk shop, but it has served its purpose for many years.

Buy a small glass thermometer from Boots so that you can check the temperature from time to time — low temperature can lead to dull deposits and excessive heat gives rise to brownish-coloured plating which takes a devil of a lot of polishing. It will be found that once the recommended temperature has been reached, and this is not terribly critical, very little heat is required to maintain it. In fact for small parts the heater can be switched off once the temperature is reached and plating commences — generally the container will conserve its heat long enough for the plating process to finish.

If much plating is envisaged, a permanent platen can be made up using an electric ring element from a cooker, together with its Simmerstat control.

Energy source

A discarded car or motorcycle battery, providing it has some life left in it, can be used to supply the plating current. It does not have to be a good battery. Used in conjunction with a charger it should last for years as current demand is minimal (one amp per 15 sq ins of parts undergoing plating).

A bulb (tail-lamp or headlamp bulb) is connected up in the positive line between the battery positive and anode connections. This enables the current density (ie., the amperage) to be adjusted to suit the size of parts to be plated. Larger parts need a larger current and a larger wattage bulb in circuit. That's a rule to remember.

A current density of lamp per 15 square inches is required which will result in a nickel deposit of .001 in. (one thou) per hour. Too high a current will cause the deposit to become rough and dull. Too low a current will simply mean that it will take longer to plate a reasonable thickness. If in doubt, choose the smaller size of bulb, in accordance with the following table:

Sq. in	Sq. cms	Bulb (watts) (12 volt supply)	Amps
5 – 5	30 – 100	5	1/2
15 – 35	100 – 200	21	1 1/2
35 – 50	200 – 300	36	3
Over 50	Over 300	60	5

Plating solution

Measured amounts of *Albo* nickel salts are provided with each kit; all that needs to be done is to mix the crystals with hot water (100°F maximum). Proportions are equivalent to 2 lbs per gallon (200 g per litre).

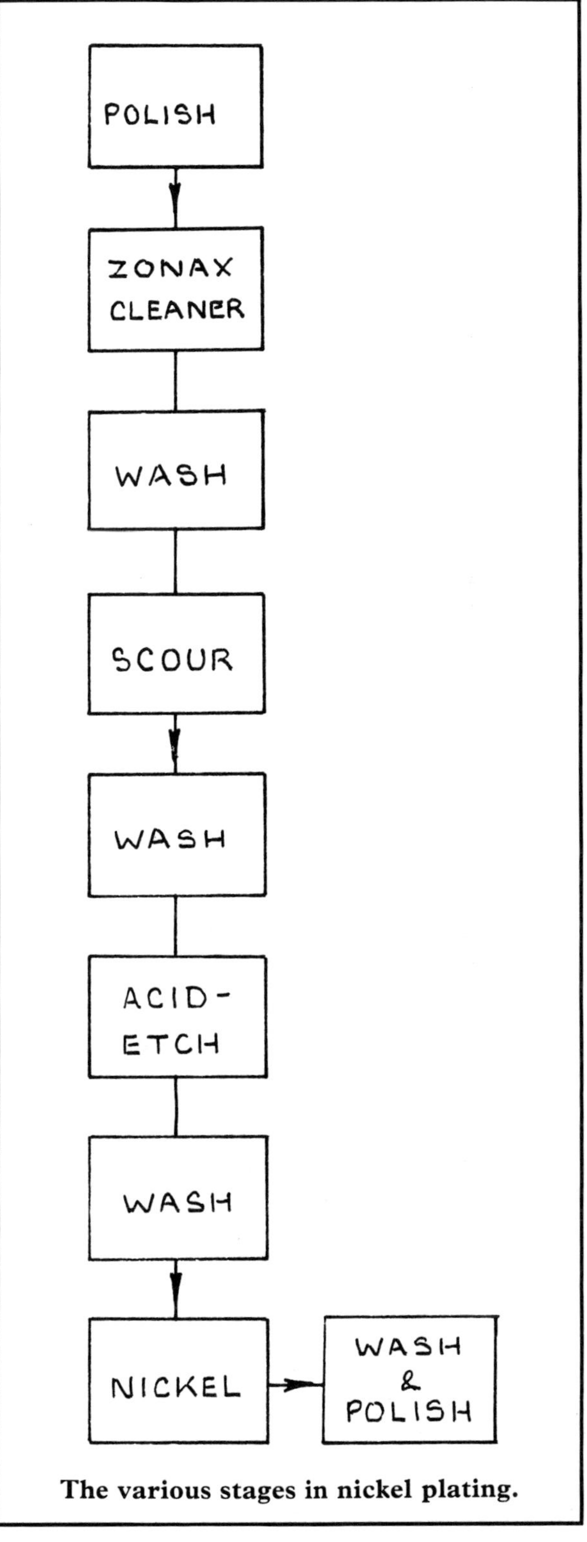

The various stages in nickel plating.

The *Standard* kit takes 5 pints of water and the *Major* 15 pints. It will take a little while for the crystals to dissolve thoroughly. Solution density should be 1110 SG (an ordinary battery hydrometer can be used to check this). SG is the specific gravity of a liquid — in other words the concentration. If the SG is too low, add nickel salts; if too high add cold water. Allow it to settle for an hour or two and tip it into the plating tank. Any muck (dead flies etc) can be removed if the solution is filtered through an old nylon stocking. Solution cleanliness is very important at all times.

The pH value (the amount of acid present) should be checked with Comparator Test Papers — remember litmus papers at school? A small book of test papers is included, and to test for the correct pH value (5.6 to 5.8) dip a piece in the solution.

If the test paper turns purple, add a few drops of clean battery acid (dilute sulphuric, which can be obtained from chemists to the required concentration). Check again with another paper. The correct colour should be a brown to dull yellow.

Check the liquid from time to time (before each plating session) and adjust the acidity as mentioned above. If the test paper turns bright yellow, too much acid has been added and a small amount of nickel carbonate will have to be introduced to redress the balance. This is rarely necessary however.

Once mixed correctly, the nickel solution will remain stable for ages and can be used over and over again. Only when it becomes badly contaminated should it be necessary to mix a new batch. (My last batch has lasted for about five years, having plated the parts from five bikes and one cyclecar). You should now have the plating tank filled and wired-up, but don't as yet connect up the battery terminals. Leave the last connection until ready to plate.

Preparing the parts

Good preparation is absolutely essential in order to obtain a perfect plated finish. Every pit mark and scratch must be polished-out or they will show up clearly in the finished product. Nickel plate will **not** fill in pitting, it will only make it more obvious.

The stripping of plated deposits can be accomplished in the following manner:-

Nickel: electrolytically in a sulphuric acid solution (3 parts acid, 2 parts water). A lead-lined tank is employed in which the parts to be stripped form the anode and the lead lining the cathode. Nickel can also be stripped without electricity, the parts being immersed in a solution of nitric acid (1 part), sulphuric acid (2 parts), and water (1 part). A stone or glass jar can be used as a tank. Keep a careful watch on the parts or they might get eaten away.

Nickel can, of course, be removed physically with files and emery cloth. It is also possible to plate over a part-nickelled surface providing that the nickel is sound and not flaking.

Chrome can be stripped from brass or bronze quite easily by immersing the parts in dilute hydrochloric acid (2 parts acid to 1 part water).

Electrolytic stripping is preferable for steel parts as these are affected by hydrochloric acid. A solution of caustic soda is used (1 lb per gallon) and the part to be stripped becomes the anode; if a steel tank is used this becomes the cathode with a 6 volt pressure.

Cadmium and zinc can both be stripped in dilute hydrochloric acid (3 parts acid to 1 part water) in a stone jar. Again, a close watch should be kept to avoid etching the underlying metal.

Some proprietary rust-removers will also strip cadmium over a short period.

IMPORTANT WARNING
When handling acids, please take great care and if possible enlist help from a chemist in preparing solutions.

Always add acid to water — never vice versa. Store chemicals in a safe place. Wear rubber gloves and glasses.

Rusty bits

Rust-pitted steel parts should have every scrap of rust removed by soaking in *Jenolite* or some other phosphoric acid-based rust remover.

Earthenware or plastic containers will do for the purpose. Immerse the parts for an hour or two and shift the rust with a wire brush, followed by a good wash in water. If the parts are not to be plated the same day, spray them in WD40 to prevent rust from reappearing.

Some rust removers give off nasty fumes, so open all the windows and wear rubber gloves. There is a danger of rust removers eating into steel parts (particularly threaded items) if they are left too long in the solution so watch their progress carefully.

There is no easy way to polish out rust pits. Much patience is required. A single control lever can take up to two hours to prepare for plating if it's badly rusted. The work can be done by hand with a variety of files, emery tape and metal polish but some form of rotary polishing head is strongly advised.

Emery discs mounted in an electric drill are a big help; the drill should be bench-mounted to leave both hands free. Commercial polishers use huge floor-mounted buffing machines of 5 hp or so, running at 2,900 rpm, but the amateur will be happy with a home-made polishing head utilising an old fridge motor and a *Picador* spindle. Buffing mops are obtainable from tool merchants; at least two should be acquired, one heavy-duty stitched mop for rough work and a finishing mop made from white calico fabric.

Felt bobs are, as their name suggests, discs of hard felt. A dressing of emery powder is applied to the periphery by means of a special glue, the dressing being renewed when worn down. Few amateurs will have access to these so the next best thing is a linishing disc held in an electric drill.

Safety precautions

Polishing is a hazardous operation at the best of times. A mop can grab the workpiece with such ferocity that, before the operator is conscious of it, the component has hit the workshop roof and gone out through the window. More seriously, a jam-up can result in a broken wrist or damaged eyesight (always wear goggles). It is best not to wear a tie when polishing, for obvious reasons.

Surfacing

A stick of polishing compound will be required. Various grades are available for commercial work (Cannings' *Lustre, Crown, Diamond* etc) but for most amateur usage a plain brown compound is satisfactory.

Initial surfacing is best done by hand with files, working down from medium-cut to dead smooth, after which linishing can commence. In the absence of machinery this can be accomplished with emery tape (not emery paper, which disintegrates rapidly).

When all pit-marks and scratches are removed, the surfaces are then buffed to a high polish. Prior to plating, the component must be mirror-finished. (Hexagon nuts are best dealt with four or six at a time, threaded on a rod or bolt. All the flats can be polished together).

Will it go in the tank?

Long objects, such as gear operating rods and handlebars, can be plated one half at a time. After plating one end, the part is removed and chemically cleaned etc. and then reversed. Surprisingly you can't see the join! Exhaust pipes are generally too big for the amateur's plating tank but there is no reason why all the preparatory work should not be carried out before taking them to a commerical plater.

Wheel rims, even if they can be dealt with in the workshop, are seldom worth replating. It is very difficult polishing around spoke dimples, and rim beads can harbour a considerable amount of rust which mess-up the tank. Not many professional platers will touch old wheel rims so it is advisable to seek replacements.

The amateur will be able to plate nickel directly over steel, brass and copper with ease. Nickel will also take on silver-solder and will adhere to a soft-soldered joint. As mentioned previously, it will also plate over a nickelled surface providing the part is thoroughly cleaned and etched etc. Cast-iron is sometimes difficult to plate due to porosity; if possible the pores should be filled with silver solder or braze prior to polishing.

Chemical cleaning

Stage 1
The first stage in electroplating is to thoroughly degrease the components in a chemical cleaner. *Zonax* metal cleaner (supplied by Dynic) is mixed in the ratio of 6 oz per gallon of hot water. Any metal container can be used for the cleaning tank.

Wire up each part with copper wire (about 22 swg), twisting the wire firm so the parts don't drop off. This wire stays in place right throughout the various plating stages and from now on the parts are not touched by hand.

Bring the metal cleaner to near boiling point and suspend the parts in it. Two to five minutes will suffice.

Stage 2
Wash each part by swishing it round in a bucket of cold water — don't remove anything from the water until ready for the next stage.

Stage 3
Scrub thoroughly every square inch of the parts with pumice powder — *Ajax* powder seems to work as well — again taking care not to handle the components directly. A piece of *Formica* makes an admirable scrubbing board and a toothbrush is useful for small parts.

This stage is quite important, and if omitted could lead to the plating not sticking. Parts examined under an eyeglass after scouring will show minute scratches on the surface. These scratches help to key the deposit.

Stage 4
Wash the parts again to remove any traces of powder.

Stage 5
Acid etch. Purchase from a chemist one gallon of battery acid (sulphuric), or a 20% solution of hydrochloric. The etching tank can be a plastic bucket, clearly labelled **ACID** (and kept well away from children). Suspend the parts for one minute or so, during which time they will fizz merrily.

Stage 6
Wash, yet again. I find it best to have two or three wash tanks so the water does not get contaminated too quickly. Change the water frequently. All parts should be left completely immersed until the plating tank is ready to accept them.

Stage 7
Nickel plate. This is the interesting stage. Heat up the solution, having checked the pH and density values as mentioned earlier.

Connect the anodes (nickel plates) to the battery positive and the cathode bar to the negative.

Wire-up the parts to the cathode bar and gently

A highly-polished crankcase may look nice but it is hardly a standard finish. This Sunbeam also features a non-original carburettor, magneto and Allen screws around the timing chest. One exhaust port is blanked off — some owners reckoned this modification resulted in greater performance.

lower them in the tank. The bulb should light up immediately — if it doesn't you have a bad connection somewhere.

To your delight you will note that nickel will flash all over the parts almost immediately they are immersed. About one hour is sufficient to obtain a reasonable deposit but you can give it longer if you wish. If you have got your sums right in calculating the surface area (not forgetting that, for example, a headlamp rim has an inside as well as an outside surface) the correct bulb size will give a deposit of .001 in per hour.

Do not lift the parts out of the solution during plating to see how things are getting on. This breaks the circuit and allows an oxidising film to flash over. Every few minutes the cathode bar should be agitated to break down air bubbles, which if left undisturbed can cause pitting.

Stage 8
Wash again.
Stage 9
Polish the parts when dry. *Solvol Autosol* is ideal, bringing up a silver sheen which looks more authentic than commercial bright nickel. Steel parts not for immediate use should be sprayed with WD40 or wrapped in cling film.

Building-up worn parts

It is worth remembering that loose press-fits can be restored by plating the worn surfaces with nickel. Bearing outer rings, taper-fits, slack threads etc. can all be treated in the plating tank. Surfaces should be shot-blasted or roughened with emery prior to plating.

Although nickel is much too soft to reclaim worn bearing tracks, slack crankpin tapers can be restored to size with a deposit of approximately .005 in. The bearing tracks must be stopped-off with tape or polyurethane varnish. After plating, the tapers are then ground between-centres and lapped into the flywheels. There should be no problems with embrittlement on a touring engine.

Aluminium refinishing

Very few engines were turned out with buffed crankcases. Such work was very expensive. It would be quite wrong to polish major castings on a cheap 'thirties lightweight when every penny counted to its original makers. Show machines were occasionally finished thus, original photos of which tend to mislead restorers.

Crankcase and gearbox castings can be boiled in household detergent to give an as-new appearance. A mop bucket makes a good boiler, mounted over an old primus stove. About half a packet of detergent to one bucket produces a strong solution, which should be brought to the boil and then left to simmer for an hour or two. Scrub the parts with a stiff brush and rinse in cold water. This method is cheap and leaves all the original casting fettling marks in the surface.

Timing covers and gearbox ends are best prepared and polished by hand. Machine buffing may save time but there is a great danger of rounding off edges and elongating screw holes. All deep scratches must be filed out by hand, after which the casting is then attacked with medium grade wet-and-dry emery dipped in paraffin. This is a filthy, time-consuming job, but there is no better way. Work through two or three grades of emery, finishing off with the finest. Use plenty of paraffin. Crevices can be dealt with by means of riffler filers, scrapers and strip emery wrapped around a slotted rod.

Finish off with *Solvol Autosol* and lots of elbow grease. You should be left with a shine every bit as good as that produced by a buffing machine.

Chapter 10

The Final Touches

Saddlery, gas lamp maintenance, horns, speedos, miscellaneous workshop jobs.

Saddlery

NOT many amateur restorers re-cover their leather pan saddles in spite of the fact that this aspect of the renovation is relatively simple. It's a case of knowing how to go about it, which puzzled me for a long time until I hit upon a system.

Perhaps I should point out that I've never actually watched a professional saddler at work and my method is one devised over a period of years. Some will say it's not the right way to tackle the job, but it works. The Radco system was published in a 1983 copy of the *Vintage Motor Cycle Club Journal* and is reproduced here in full; friends and fellow members of the VMCC who have tried the modus operandii report successful results, so why not have a go?

Materials required

1 Piece of leather
2 Padding (see notes)
3 Darning needles and strong thread
4 A home-made stretching frame
5 Miscellaneous items, ie ball of string, two dozen bifurcated rivets (3/16 in x 1/2 in), one yard brown leather strap (5/8 in wide x 1/8 in thick)

Selecting the leather

If a remnant of the original top is available, this will, of course, serve as an example of the required grade of leather. Most saddles were covered in good-quality plain brown leather of about 14 swg or 16 swg thickness (excuse the engineering terminology!) In my experience saddlers are happy to advise on the right kind of material once the project has been explained to them, and they don't seem to mind giving away trade secrets.

Quite often shoe repairers have the odd piece of material, but if you have a few bikes to restore, it pays to acquire a large piece from a leather supplier. I think I'm right in saying leather is classified in skins and half-skins as far as sizes are concerned.

Before purchasing the leather examine it carefully for imperfections such as holes or deep scratches. The original skin owner might have damaged itself on barbed wire or fence nails! I always buy what I term chrome leather which is shiny brown on one side and tough on the other.

Soaking

You can work wonders with leather once it is thoroughly wet. Leaving a generous allowance of about two inches all round, cut out a sufficiently large piece to cover the saddle top and immerse the piece in a bowl of cold water. Weight it down with a clean stone (don't use a lump of metal like I once did

— this left a nasty stain in the leather) and leave it to soak for a week.

Needles and thread

Plain round needles are difficult to push through two thicknesses and most special leatherwork needles in craft shops are either too big or too small. As a result of experiments I have found that ordinary large darning needles (approx. 2 in long) ground to a triangular section are the answer. No doubt such needles have existed for generations; if so, my apologies to the original inventor.

It only takes a few minutes to grind up two or three needles on a fine rotary stone. The blunt end is stuck in a cork or pin-vice and the tapered portion is then ground to a neat triangular section on the side of the stone. Final sharpening is done by hand on a slip-stone. It should be mentioned that eye-protection is absolutely vital whilst performing the grinding; the prospect of a darning needle whizzing through the air is a daunting one!

Strong brown thread, about three times the diameter of cotton, should be procured from a saddler or needlework shop. I believe old craftsmen rubbed the thread through a block of beeswax, but not having this readily to hand I use a wax furniture polish which does the trick. Waxed thread is easier to pull through leather and does not rot. Brown nylon thread is also available and may well be superior to waxed-cotton but I have not tried it.

One other needle will be needed, a large curved sailmakers' needle, which looks like a scimitar — I'll come to this later.

The stretching frame

Lay the saddle pan on a 1 in piece of wood or blockboard and draw round it. Cut the shape out with a fretsaw. Screw three metal brackets (pressed-steel shelf brackets will do) to the base as shown in the sketch. The height of the brackets is not important; four to six inches is about right. Position them so that the saddle pan will be in line with the wooden base in plan view.

Knock a large number of nails around the edge of the base-board approximately 3/4 in apart. For once, neatness is not necessary at this stage, unless

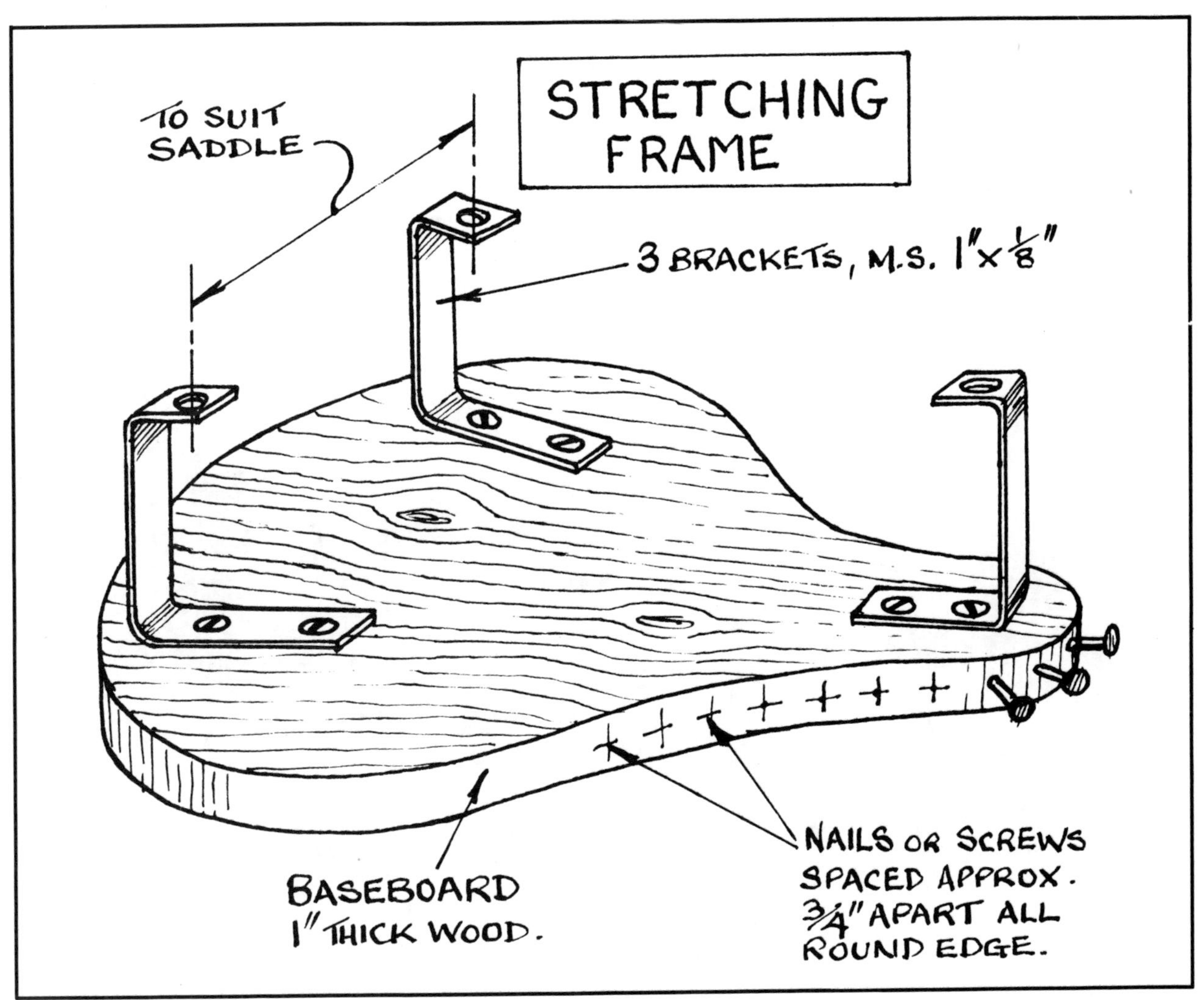

you intend to keep the jig for years. Screw a short piece of angle iron or a block of wood underneath the base so that it can be fixed in the vice.

Strapping

Most saddle tops were stitched to a leather strap fixed around the underneath edge of the metal pan. Some of the more expensive examples were covered in leather on the bottoms also, but this is rather difficult to do. Unless you are an absolute purist for authenticity I would recommend the strap-fixing method as it is much simpler to reproduce.

Purchase a length of leather strap 5/8 in wide by 1/8 in thick — some dog leads are ideal — and two dozen nickel-plated 3/16 in x 1/2 in bifurcated rivets. If the metal pan is not already drilled, mark out and drill a series of 3/16 in diameter holes 1 1/4 in apart around the edge (extra holes will be required round the nose).

The general idea is to fix the strap so that about 1/4 in projects all round the edge. The domed heads should be on the strap side (ie underneath the saddle) and it is just as well to make a neat job of the riveting as everyone will want to peer underneath the saddle when it's finished. Originally rivets were clenched over on the strap side but my method is neater and there is no likelihood of the clenched ends rusting away, as used to happen.

Padding

There appears to have existed in the vintage years a particularly virile species of termite whose sole diet consisted of motorbike saddles *(Brookus Vulgaris?)* They laid their eggs in horsehair or felt padding and chomped their way through many a saddle top. Happily, the bug seems to be extinct, probably seen off by Messrs Terry and Feridax respectively, but it would be wise to guard against its reappearance by renewing the old felt padding. Armstrong *Armaflex* is a dense black foam rubber favoured by the upholstery trade and appears to be ideal for saddles. This material is 1/2 in thick, springy to the touch, and can be stuck to the saddle pan with contact adhesive.

When the adhesive is fully cured, shape the edges of the padding with a sharp blade and finish off with coarse sandpaper. Round off the corners nicely as any bumps could show through afterwards.

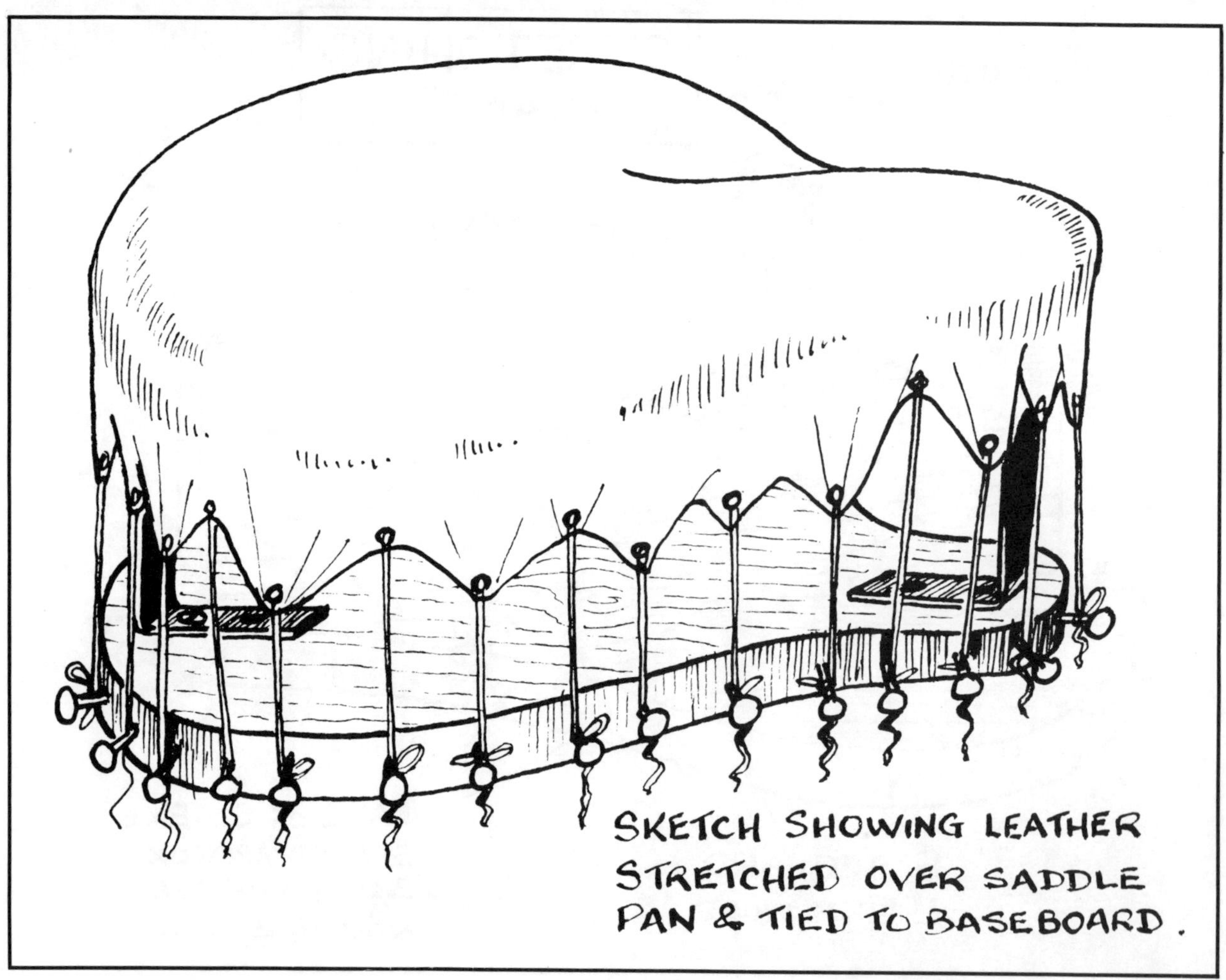
SKETCH SHOWING LEATHER STRETCHED OVER SADDLE PAN & TIED TO BASEBOARD.

Moulding the top

Remember that it is much better to err on the large side when cutting out the new top — leave plenty round the edges; it can be trimmed off later. As mentioned earlier, the leather must be really soggy before it can be moulded to shape.

Pierce a number of holes all round the edges and tie a ten-inch length of stout string through each hole. This is where the sailmakers' needle comes in handy, for making holes and threading string through.

Fix the stretching frame securely in the vice and bolt the saddle base to it by means of the three fixing bolts. Lay the wet leather top in position and fasten three or four strings at the back of the saddle to the stretcher nails. Pull the leather quite firmly forwards and tie a couple of strings at the front end. Stretch the leather sideways, from the middle outwards, and fix a few more strings on either side.

The stretching process requires a fair amount of strength and a lot of patience to avoid creases. Work round the saddle, pulling out any wrinkles and tying the strings in turn. Firmly manipulate the top to shape with the palms of your hands and re-tension the strings from time to time. Keep the leather wet all the time with a sponge and it will eventually mould itself to shape.

The whole exercise is rather difficult to explain so it is hoped the sketches will make sense. When the last string is tightened the leather should be left for a week or so to dry out naturally (with all the strings in position). Do not attempt to hasten the drying-out process by sticking it in the oven or in front of the fire.

Stitching

Don't be put off by the thought of wielding a needle. The correct stitch to use is the saddle stitch, accomplished with two needles, as outlined in the sketch. Alternatively one needle can be used, taking two steps forward and one step back as it were.

I prefer to stitch the new top in position whilst all the tensioning strings are in place, although I can't help thinking there must be an easier way. I once tried cutting all the strings away prior to stitching but the leather tended to slacken off. So, using triangular needles and waxed thread, commence stitching half-way along one edge. It will not be necessary to pre-drill any holes as the needles should pull through easily if they have been sharpened correctly. Start the needle on its way with a metal thimble and help it through with a small pair of pliers. Each stitch should be neat and dead in line with its neighbour. Cut away the tensioning strings as you work round to facilitate access to the underside.

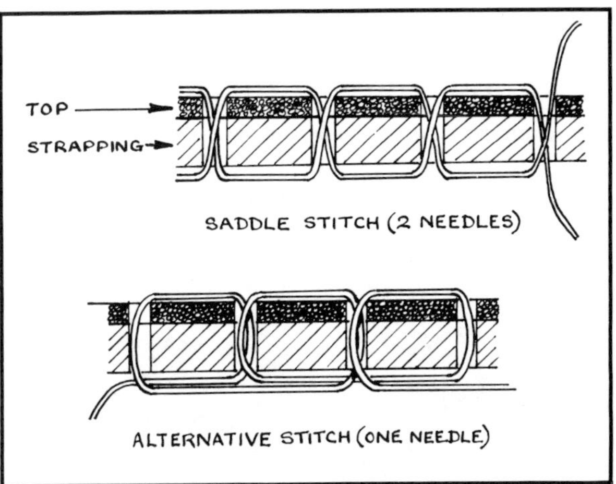

When the new top is securely stitched to the leather strapping cut off all surplus material with a sharp Stanley knife, taking care not to slice into the strapping.

Finishing off

Smooth-off the cut edge with a hot spoon handle and run brown boot polish along it. This will tone the edges, giving a professional finish to the job. Finally, give the top a good polish with saddle soap, followed by boot polish if you like. Keep it in good trim, especially after wet rides, with saddle soap.

A toolmaker or engraver might like to make himself a Brooks, Lycett, or The Leatheries stamp to impress into the nose flanks to impart an air of authenticity.

The finished job. Covered and stitched by the "Radco method". Total cost approximately £5.

Sprung saddles

Motorcycle restoration work gets easier as the years go by, thanks to those concerns now making replica parts. Sprung saddles of the Terry type were at one time almost impossible to find, most people having slung them away in the mid-1950s, with the general introduction of dualseats.

Various firms make fine replicas of single-seats, together with mounting springs and new saddle tops in leathercloth. As the latter are so reasonably priced it is hardly worth going to the trouble of making your own.

Whether or not it is decided to cut-out and stitch a new top in the home workshop (a task which does not present any problems if the old cover is to hand) do remember to salvage the original maker's nameplace. This can be riveted to the new top with nickel-plated bifurcated rivets. Lycett elastics are impossible to obtain but the enterprising mechanic can make himself a set from lugggage aero-elastics using the old end-fittings. If the latter are missing, a new batch will have to be fabricated from mild steel sheet, a fiddling job at the best of times. An original fitting is required as a pattern; draw out the developed shape on thin tinplate and use this as a template. If necessary, have a dummy run, making a trial example out of tin to see how things work out. Cut out the shapes from sheet steel, using an *Abrafile,* and bend-up the end-fittings hot. As stated, it's an awkward job but there is no easy solution.

To fix a cord in its metal fitting, first of all open-out the tubular portion a little and coat the inside with Dunlop *Thixofix* adhesive. Apply some to the fabric outer of the cord and push it through the fitting, leaving a small amount projecting through the hook end. Clench the tubular portion over the cord. Finally rivet-up. (Original rivets bore a close resemblance to common-or-garden nails).

Luggage elastic is not quite as good as the original Lycett material, but a seat repaired thus will last a reasonable period. A piece of rubber interposed between elastics and saddle cover will help to stiffen up the assembly. Elastic cords invariably broke where the round wire hooks cut into them, so it's a good idea to wrap a few turns of electrician's' tape around these parts.

Dualseats

There is really little to be said about reproduction dualseats and covers except to issue a dire warning. The quality of some is simply dreadful so, to avoid disappointment, do consult fellow marque enthusiasts before spending money and examine the product if possible.

Try to reclaim original seat bases no matter how rusty or cracked they may be. At least you can be

Patent spring seat pillar on a 1922 Ariel.

A home-made "flapper bracket" (pillion seat) and toolboxes on a 7hp AJS.

A home-made dualseat does nothing to improve the looks of this late vintage Sunbeam. Many owners of early machinery perpetrated such foul deeds in the 1950s in an effort to bring their bikes up to date. This picture was taken at an early VMCC Rally — nobody noticed or cared about minor deviations in those days as long as the bike performed well.

---

assured they will fit, which is more than can be said about certain repros. A shot-blasting session will improve matters, followed by welding and strengthening with sheet metal or layers of glass fibre.

It used to be the custom to produce reproduction seat bases in glass fibre but concours enthusiasts, being what they are, now demand metal bases. Quality varies enormously, but please spare a thought for the repro manufacturer; the demand for certain dualseats is rather small so he can hardly be expected to invest in very expensive press-tool machinery. Shortcuts are made, hence complaints about authenticity and quality.

Nevertheless there **are** good reproduction seats and covers available for most popular models. It's just a case of shopping around for the best examples.

Horns

Bulb horns suffer from two snags, one being small boys and the other grit. For some reason bulb horns have held a fatal fascination for youngsters ever since the pioneer period and there is no reason to surmise that the position will change in the next sixty years.

Fortunately bulbs are still made, being supplied by such specialist concerns as *The Complete Automobilist,* and it is worth remembering that Far Eastern countries churn out cheap reproduction antique horns which can be robbed of their bulbs.

If a horn ceases to function, or produces an asthmatic cough instead of a loud toot, the problem is probably due to a minute particle of grit in the reed. A slip of paper passed through the reed will usually clear the snag, but avoid bending the brass tongue. If this is distorted or dislodged it will be almost impossible to reset correctly.

Electric horns

Lucas *Altette* horns were fitted to many thousands of British motorcycles of the pre- and post-war periods. Generally reliable, minor adjustments may be required after a long period of use. If the horn

401

HORNS—*continued* HUBS, KNEE GRIPS

STADIUM HIGH FREQUENCY HORN.

Gives a sharp, penetrating note with a long range. With switch and wire. 4 or 6 volt. Chromium-plated finish.

No. **CH6/212/*905*** .. .. each **12/6**

LUCAS ALTETTE HORN.

No. H.F.**934.** M/C.

A high frequency horn with attractive front. The mechanism is totally enclosed so that weather will not affect its performance. High-pitched note; musical and penetrating. Chromium-plated and black, with push but less cable. 6 volt.

No. **CH6/214/*1611*** .. .. each **22/6**
,, **CH6/214/*1500*** .. doz. lots ,, —

MOSELEY PILLION KNEE GRIPS.

Filled with sponge rubber, covered black leather cloth, with clips for attaching to motor cycle saddle.

No. **CK1/10/*208*** .. .. per pair **3/6**

KLAXON "KIFONET" HORN.

Type H.F.X.

Flat front, with push, terminals and wire.

Black Enamelled.

No. **CH6/224/*711*** .. .. each **10/6**

Chromium front.

No. **CH6/224a/*905*** .. .. each **12/6**

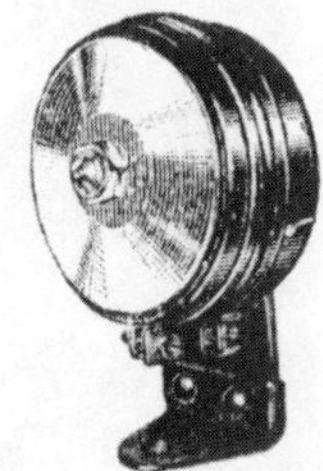

LUCAS Nº HF 1140

LUCAS ELECTRIC HORN.

No. H.F.1140.

Similar construction to the Altette. Pleasing, penetrating note, but not so powerful as the Altette. With push and cable. 6 volt. Ebony black with polished tone disc.

No. **CH6/215/*1103*** .. .. each **15/-**
,, **CH6/215/*1000*** .. doz. lots ,, —

LUCAS HORN BULBS.

With socket.

No. **CH9/27/*307*** 60 and 32 .. each **4/9**

LUCAS HORN REEDS.

No. **CH9/60e/7** .. 40 .. each **-/9**

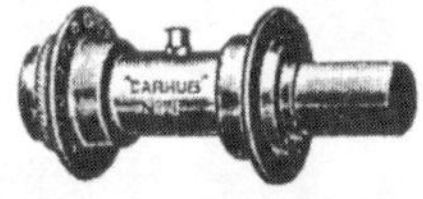

SIDE CAR HUB No. 1.

Drilled for 32 spokes by 14 gauge. Spindle end ⅞ in. diam. Width over flanges 2⅞ ins.

No. **CH16/6/*600*** .. .. each **8/-**

"Q" ELECTRIC HORN.

Complete with cable, switch and universal fitment. 4 ins. diam. chromium-plated dome. Weight approx. 1¼ lbs. 4 or 6 volt.

No. **CH6/213a/*905*** each **12/6**

"JOHN BULL" KNEE GRIPS.

No. 11.

Concave in shape to receive and retain the knee. As used in TT races. Screw or strap fitting.

No. **CK1/8a/*604*** .. .. per pair **9/6**

"JOHN BULL" KNEE GRIPS.

No. 3.

Oval Wedge Pattern.

Size 4¾ ins. × 3¾ ins.

No. **CK1/8b/*304*** .. .. per pair **5/-**

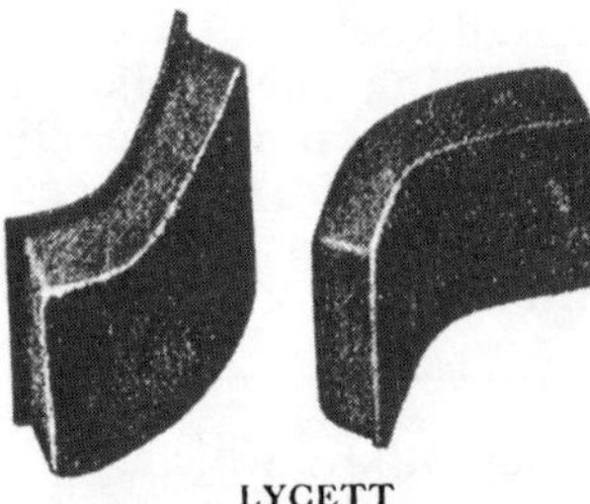

LYCETT PILLION KNEE GRIPS.

Ensure comfortable riding position for pillion passenger. Sponge rubber pads, covered black leather cloth. Bolt securely to saddle.

No. **CK1/9/*306*** .. .. per pair **4/9**

This page from Brown Brothers 1936 catalogue shows a variety of fittings. Both types of Lucas horn illustrated were popular fittings on pre-war and early post-war bikes. It is interesting to note that John Bull knee grips (George Dance pattern) were catalogued as late as this, belonging to much earlier period.

Head Offices and Warehouses. Wholesale only:

GREAT EASTERN STREET, LONDON, E.C.2

126 GEORGE STREET, EDINBURGH, 2

Branches:
Aberdeen, Acton, Belfast
Birmingham, Bournemouth
Bristol, Cardiff, Carlisle
Croydon, Dublin, Dundee
Eastbourne, Edinburgh
Glasgow, Inverness

Branches:
Hull, Leeds, Liverpool
London, W.1
Manchester, Newcastle
Nottingham, Southampton
Stoke-on-Trent
Wolverhampton

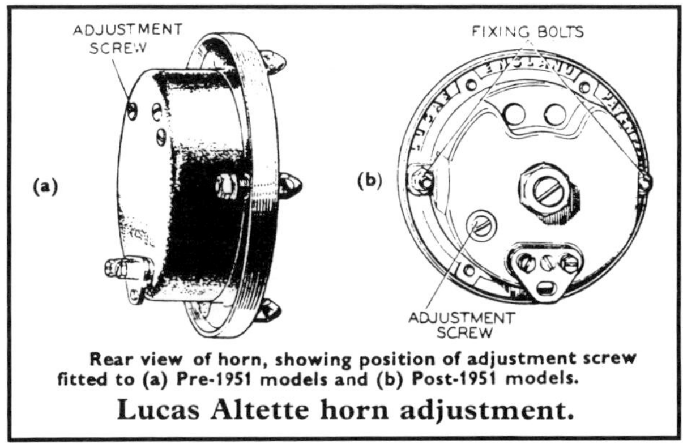

Rear view of horn, showing position of adjustment screw fitted to (a) Pre-1951 models and (b) Post-1951 models.

Lucas Altette horn adjustment.

becomes uncertain in action or does not sound a continuous note, it does not follow that the horn has broken down. A burnt-out coil is, in fact, very rarely encountered. The performance of the horn may be upset by the fixing bolt working loose, or by the vibration of some adjacent part. To check this, remove the horn and do a bench test. It may be found that the trouble is due to faulty wiring, bad connections, or a dirty horn-push.

Adjustments

The adjustment of a horn does not alter the note characteristics but merely takes up wear of vibrating parts. If the horn is used repeatedly when badly out of adjustment it may become damaged due to excessive current consumption. If, when the button is pushed, the horn does not take any current (with an ammeter connected in series with the horn) it is possible that the horn has been adjusted so that its internal contact breaker is permanently open.

After adjusting, note the current consumption, which must not exceed 3-4 amps. A horn may give a good note, yet be out of adjustment and using excessive current. The adjustment is made by turning the rear slotted screw (usually in a clockwise direction.)

The underside of the screw is serrated, and the screw must not be turned for more than two or three notches before re-testing. If the adjustment screw is turned too far in a clockwise direction, a point will occur at which the armature pulls in but does not separate the contacts.

Some models have no adjustment screw at the back of the horn. Adjustment is carried out by means of the grub screw and locking collar behind the large domed centre nut. Take care that the large nut securing the sound disc is not disturbed. The locking collar needs a special pronged tool, made from an old screwdriver with the middle portion ground away.

Renovation of an *Altette,* or similar, horn amounts to removing the rim, tone disc, and steel diaphragm to get at the innards. Keep all the special acorn nuts as these are almost impossible to replace. When removing the diaphragm it will be necessary to juggle it about from side to side before it can be lifted out — don't try and prise it — as the underneath part is restrained by its slotted armature.

Usually the inside will be full of dust and maybe the odd insect or two. Clean it out without disturbing the coil or wiring. Lightly clean the contacts with emery paper. Apply a light coat of *Bondaprimer* or similar rust-proofing primer to the inside. Finish the tone disc (this is the flat circular plate on the outside) with a black wrinkle aerosol paint for authenticity. The rim and acorn nuts should be chrome plated (on WD models nuts were cadmium and the rims painted in olive-drab). Bodies were in black gloss on civilian models.

New gaskets can be cut from brown paper and smeared lightly with gasket cement. Test the horn and adjust as described. All horn wiring connections should be sound as quite a high current is involved (horns are never wired directly through the motorcycle's ammeter). Make sure the horn button body makes good contact with the handlebars and that there is a good earth path from the bars to the machine frame.

Smiths speedometers

These popular Chronometric instruments were fitted to almost every make of British bike at one time so there must be many requiring servicing by now. In my youth I rebuilt thousands of Smiths instruments (and eventually got sick of the sight of them!) but the experience stood me in good stead for future restoration work. The following notes are therefore more in the nature of a collection of hints and tips for the amateur restorer as it is understood that he will not have the facilities for a complete overhaul of a Chronometric movement.

Removing a tight bezel

The first snag in stripping a Smiths speedometer, for inspection or renovation, is how to get the bezel off. The brass rims have fine RH threads which are more often than not seized. There's nothing to get hold of and many bodgers resort to the hammer and chisel method. On no account must the rim or body be gripped in a vice as this would distort the whole case and probably crack the glass. So how do you shift a stubborn rim?

In the writer's small instrument shop there were three simple tools for dealing with obstinate speedometer bezels; a strap wrench for easy rims, a large pair of nutcracker-type clamps (home-made) and a fixture to hold the speedometer bodies. The strap wrench principle will be familiar to everyone, consisting of a loop of leather belting bolted to a piece of flat mild steel bar. Some car oil filter removers are similar.

The tight-bezel persuader was an enormous pair

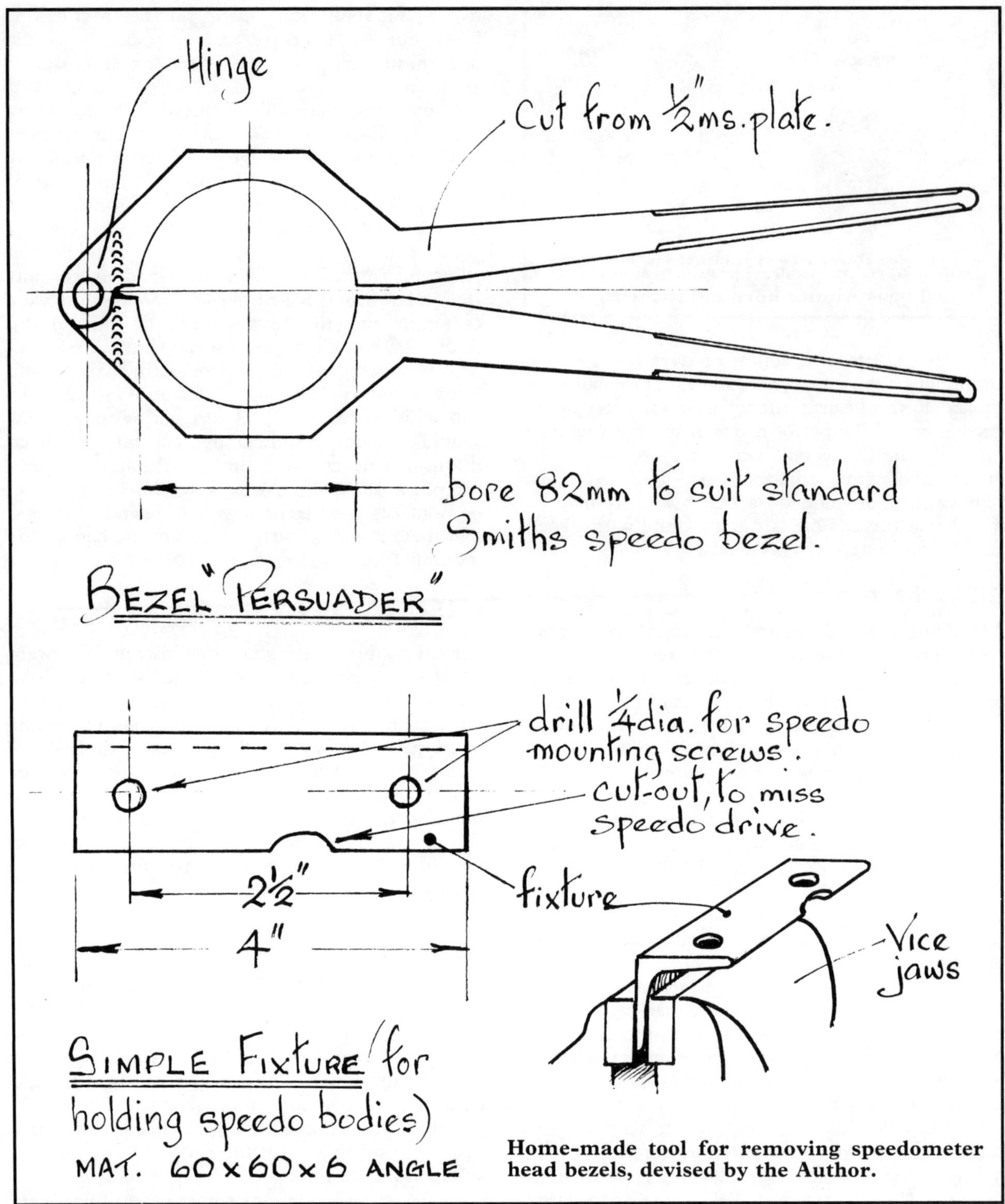

Home-made tool for removing speedometer head bezels, devised by the Author.

of pliers, cut from ½ in steel plate, with a hinge at one end and handles at the other (see sketch). The inside diameter, that portion which clamps the bezel, was bored out smooth to the exact rim diameter before splitting. On our Mk I. Persuader we knurled the bore but found this marked brass bezels and was quite unnecessary. A de-luxe version with fibre-lined jaws could be made by the perfectionist, but our all-steel version did everything that was asked of it.

Ninety nine per cent of tight bezels could be shifted with relative ease — how about the one per cent you may ask? Well, the bad news is — they had to be cut off! The instrument shop mentioned handled mainly WD speedometers and many of these had seen wartime service overseas. Some

Where there's a will, there's a way. Spotted on a Moto Guzzi, a wooden toolbox. Perhaps the owner is a cabinet maker.

Lucas lamp and horn on the Author's ohv AJS. Acetylene lighting sets were rarely polished nickel throughout, nine out of ten being finished as shown. Black Japan and nickel is what the makers called it. All the paintwork on this machine was brushed-on domestic gloss.

instruments were full to the brim with evil-smelling water and only the bodies could be salvaged; in such cases the bezels would be slit with a junior hacksaw. At least one firm is now manufacturing new bezels in stainless steel.

Extracting the movement

A complete strip-down of the works will be beyond most restorers, unless they happen to be watchmakers, but routine maintenance is easily carried out. Usually cosmetic work on the case is needed. So the innards will have to be extracted. Removal of two cheese-headed screws and shakeproof washers from the base will allow the complete works, with dial in situ, to be withdrawn.

Speedometer needles (ie hands) are extremely fragile. They are press-fitted so great care should be exercised when prising them off. If the movement is in excellent condition it is best to leave the needle and dial in position and let well alone. Once the needle is removed, the dial can be lifted off, together with the thin paper gasket underneath.

Dials should be handled by the edges only. An oily thumb-print will be almost impossible to obliterate. **Never** attempt to clean dials in petrol or paraffin or you will smear the lettering, which is soluble in such fluids. A light swill in soapy water will suffice. With skill and patience a dial can be touched up with white paint *(Humbrol* enamel) using a very fine sable-haired water colour brush.

New dials

A recent development by D. McMahon (Supplies) of 1-3. Northey Rd., Foleshill, Coventry, CV6 5NF, is the manufacture of Smiths speedometer and 8-day clock dials. These are very accurately printed on thin, yet very strong, plastic sheet. (Replica Miller ammeter dials are also obtainable and reproduction Triumph and Vincent dials are in hand).

A simple way of reproducing non-standard, or early speedometer dials is by the photographic method. Any competent amateur photographer should be capable of making his own dials providing he owns a good camera, that is, one with a sharp lens. First of all the dial is drawn two or three times full size, either white on black or vice versa. *Letraset* rub-on numerals are ideal if he does not possess artistic ability.

The dial is then photographed. Those amateurs with access to an ancient plate camera are in a fortunate position as the dial can be measured (actual size) directly on the ground-glass viewing screen. In the case of 35 mm equipment the dial is measured in the enlargement stage, using a pair of dividers on the enlarger base-board. An actual-size print of the dial is thus achieved; it will be observed that irregularities in lettering or layout which were noticeable in the drawing are proportionally reduced, giving a neat appearance to the dial.

The printed dial is then stuck on top of the old one, or on a thin disc of tin, with a suitable adhesive. Thinly-applied *Evostick* is as good as anything. Avoid bumps or creases which would ruin the effect. Does the dial fade? Well, it will eventually (as will any other photographic print) but you should get at least five years use out of it — anyway, you can always stick another one on if you were smart enough to make half a dozen in the first place!

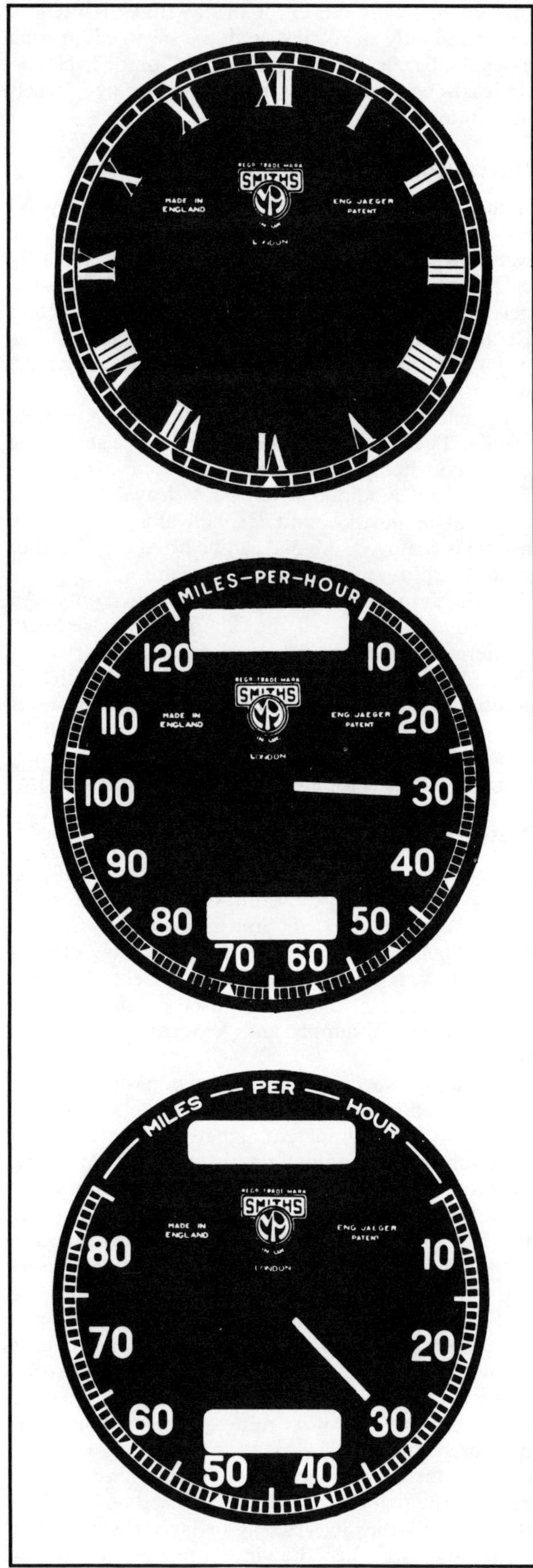

Above and top of opposite page: A selection of instrument dials reproduced photographically from originals.

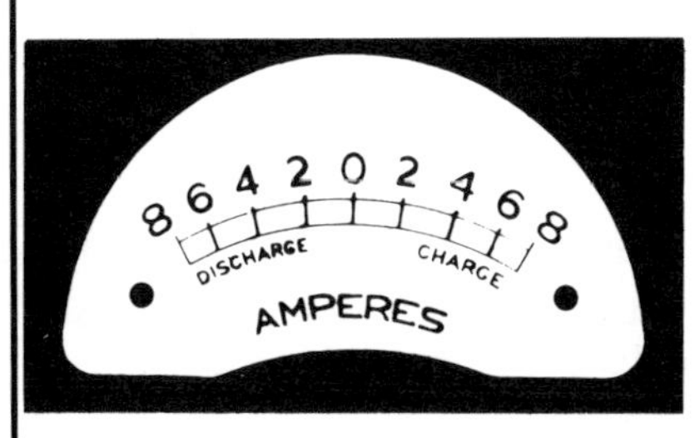

Movement calibration

The easiest way out, if any bits are required, is to pick up a spare speedometer at an autojumble and build up one instrument out of the two. Speedos with poor dials and damaged glasses can be obtained very cheaply.

Almost all Smiths chronometric movements are interchangeable, but watch out for different gear ratios (fortunately the choice is limited) or opposite-hand rotation.

Wash the movement in benzene or petrol, or get a watchmaker to run it through his ultrasonic cleaner for you. Take care not to damage the hairspring or small detent leaf springs. Leave the works to dry and then lubricate all pivots with clock oil or *3-in-one* oil. Movements very rarely give trouble and seem to last almost indefinitely; it is almost unknown for bearings to wear out or ratchet wheels to strip. The most common snag encountered is a seized main spindle or stripped main drive gear. Main spindles run in plain bearings in the zinc-alloy frames so they need lubricating occasionally. Unless you know what you are doing, don't attempt to strip the movement itself — even skilled watchmakers think twice before tackling the job — if it's faulty rob another old speedometer for the clockwork bit.

Do not try to dismantle the mileometer drum and

A superbly-restored 1925 344cc JAP-engined Royal Enfield owned by Royal Enfield expert Ivor Mutton. Note the well-engineered exhaust system.

its ratchet drive mechanism unless you have plenty of time to spare, or you could be left with a myriad assortment of wheels, ratchets, and tiny springs on your hands.

Mileage recorders can be damaged beyond repair by attempting to turn back the mileage; rotating the drum the opposite way will bend the leaf springs. With care, the job **can** be done on the bench providing each leaf is gingerly lifted with a small screwdriver whilst the corresponding wheel is rotated. On no account must force be used.

Most War Department speedometers had their rims secured so DRs could not fiddle the mileage. If you find a Smiths 0-80 mph speedo with a small semi-circular cut-out in the lower edge of the rim and a rivet which engages in this cut-out, the chances are it's ex-WD. An unplated or dull-cadmium bezel will confirm the fact.

A rudimentary check for speedometer accuracy can be made in the amateur's workshop providing a lathe is at hand. Whilst the following method is not ideal, it is usually better than comparing the instrument with another one, which could be even less accurate.

Make up a dummy drive spindle to fit in the lathe chuck or collet. A piece of 3/16 in or 1/4 in diameter steel rod about 1 1/2 to 2 in long is filed to a square at one end to fit the speedometer spindle. Holding the speedometer in one hand, run the lathe at a low speed to correspond with a reading of about 30 or 40 mph. As lathes have fixed ratios it will not be possible to select a precise speed. No matter, so long as you don't exceed the capabilities of the speedometer mechanism at the outset.

With the aid of a stopwatch observe how long it takes for the mileage recorder to trip over one mile. With a bit of practice you will begin to note how the ratchet mechanism works, when the drum begins to revolve, and when it stops. If, for example, the mileage drum takes one minute to register one mile the dial should of course indicate sixty miles per hour. Two minutes and the needle should show 30 mph. The all-important point is to time the mileometer as accurately as possible and then by simple mathematics (what would we do without calculators?) convert this into speed. These tests are best carried out with the instrument out of its case so that adjustments can be made.

The speedometer needle might be reading too fast or too slow. The instrument can be calibrated by removing or adding bob-weights on the escapement spindle. This shaft is easily recognized, being the one which jiggles back and forth in a demented fashion. Usually two or three disc weights will be found. More can be made from sheet metal, if necessary. Keep checking the speed after adjustments and eventually it should be possible to get the speedometer to within two mph of its theoretically correct speed.

Bezels and boxes

A word of warning about replating bezels. Make sure the plating company masks off the fine thread before plating otherwise it will not fit. Speedometer cases were finished in what could best be described as a satin-gloss black.

If the speedometer works well on test and doesn't work at all on the bike, this could be due to one of two possible snags. The obvious one is a broken cable or stripped drive-box gear. The other can be quite mystifying — if the bike is newly renovated you could have fitted an opposite hand speedometer drive-box. This particularly applies to those flat pancake-shaped boxes driven from the bike wheel; some machines have the drive on the nearside and other on the offside, thus there are two types in use. Fortunately, if the wrong one is fitted and the bike ridden, the speedometer will be unharmed. A fault with this type of drive-box is worn-out drive pegs; the drive plate can be removed by chipping away the securing rivets, after which the pegs can be built up with weld.

Finally, it should be mentioned that there are now several instrument repairers willing to tackle old speedometers and rev-counters. Reference to the classic magazine adverts will provide the necessary addresses.

Acetylene lamp maintenance

This book would not be complete without a brief mention of acetylene lamps and their problems. In the vintage period the principle and operation of carbide, or gas, lamps was common knowledge — so much so that it was not often thought necessary to include reference to them in instruction books.

The generator

For the sake of appearance all dents should be removed; it is quite easy to take a water chamber to pieces to get at the inside, being a soft-soldered unit.

The bottom container, or carbide cup, must be closely examined for hairline cracks which would allow the gas to escape. Brass age-hardens and acetylene gas appears to accelerate the process (probably due to the copper content). Whatever the reason, cracks occur in all old containers and they must be silver-soldered to effect a sound repair.

A new rubber washer should be made to fit between the water container and the carbide cup. This seal is a potential source of leaks. Hardware stores often have a selection of rubber rings for food preserving jars and some of these fit certain generators. Filter pads (when fitted) are to be found under water containers, generally secured in position with cupped discs and nuts. These should be cleaned or replaced but most generators work well without them.

All that remains is to check that the water tap is

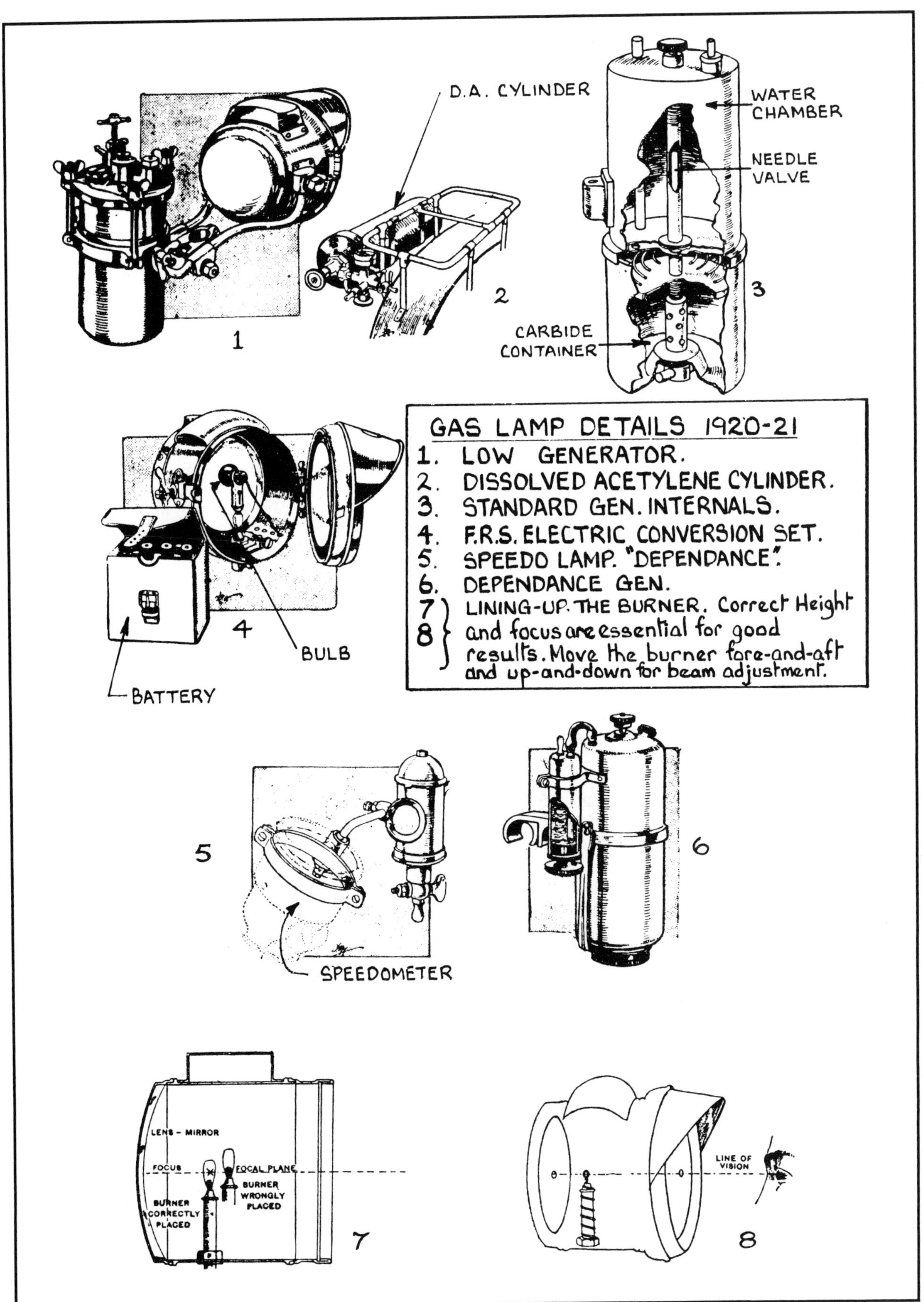
D.A. CYLINDER
WATER CHAMBER
NEEDLE VALVE
CARBIDE CONTAINER
1
2
3
GAS LAMP DETAILS 1920-21
1. LOW GENERATOR.
2. DISSOLVED ACETYLENE CYLINDER.
3. STANDARD GEN. INTERNALS.
4. F.R.S. ELECTRIC CONVERSION SET.
5. SPEEDO LAMP. "DEPENDANCE".
6. DEPENDANCE GEN.
7, 8 LINING-UP. THE BURNER. Correct Height and focus are essential for good results. Move the burner fore-and-aft and up-and-down for beam adjustment.
4
BULB
BATTERY
5
SPEEDOMETER
6
LENS - MIRROR
FOCUS
FOCAL PLANE
BURNER CORRECTLY PLACED
BURNER WRONGLY PLACED
7
LINE OF VISION
8

working. No hard-and-fast rule can be given regarding the number of drips per minute as all generators (and burners) vary in their requirements. If the reader is inexperienced with gas lighting he would do well to observe the following points:-

1 Check that the water is dripping at a steady rate (try about one drip every two or three seconds as a starting point) but avoid flooding the generator.
2 Always open both lamps whilst making initial adjustments to avoid a build-up of gas inside.
3 Wait until there is a distinct smell of acetylene gas before lighting-up. Be patient and wait for at least four or five minutes.
4 Always blow-out the flame at the end of a run — don't leave it to die out, which could choke the burners with carbon.
5 Check all rubber tubing frequently. Never use copper pipe, which reacts with acetylene gas (an explosion could occur).
6 Clean out the carbide cup immediately after use. Don' t tip the remains down the sink.

Headlamps

Although there may be those who disagree, the best lamps, as far as workmanship is concerned, were made by Miller. Not far behind were products of the other members of the big three lamp manufacturers, Powell and Hanmer, and Lucas. Some of the large accessory houses sold cheap lighting sets which gradually disintegrated over rough roads of the period. Head and tail lamps are subject to frightful vibration on rigid machines therefore all rivets, wing nuts and screw-tops must be tight. (It is a sound idea to wire-up generator wing nuts to prevent loss).

It is sometimes forgotten that an acetylene headlamp is a computed optical system with a light source, reflector and lens. All three components must be in good condition, and for the system to be optically correct the front lens and reflector should be compatible. If the lamp is original, all will be well, but don't expect perfect results from a made-up autojumble lamp.

Most burners are adjustable for height and focus, so stand the bike on the garden path at night and move the burner up and down and fore-and-aft until the best results are achieved. Burners are calibrated in flow rate but this is of academic interest if you only have one at your disposal! Headlamp burners have two converging jets which produce a spade-shaped flame. These tiny jets soon get blocked but they can be cleaned with very fine wire or bristle. Originally a jet-cleaner would have been clipped inside the headlamp shell just to one side of the burner.

When experimenting with different types of burners don't go rash and fit one much too powerful for your lamp as this could result in a cracked reflector. Large motor cars were equipped with enormous lighting sets fed from running-board generators, so you could mistakenly fit a large jet from one of these.

Rubber tubing should be neatly clipped out of harm's way, avoiding hot exhaust pipes and girder fork springs. Home-brew shops sell suitable rubber tubing.

Rear lamps

There is nothing much that can be done to improve the performance of a standard tail lamp, except to fit a separate generator. Most impecunious motor-cyclists ran both lamps off one generator but better results can be obtained from a separate unit for each lamp, the tail lamp generator being clipped to the carrier leg or seat stay tube. Rear lamp burners have a single jet which blocks easily, so remember the advice to blow out the flame. Do not fit a double-burner in an attempt to improve illumination as this will crack the glass.

As mentioned earlier, rear lamps suffer on rigid-framed bikes. When the lamp is not in use, secure hinged lenses with locking wire to avoid losing them. Some smaller tail lamps have a habit of blowing out in gusty conditions so make regular checks to see if the flame is still there.

Carbide

Calcium carbide for acetylene lamps is still available at some cycle shops and through specialists advertising in the vintage press. It may also be available in areas frequented by pot-holers, who use it in their lamps. Always store it in well-sealed tins in dry conditions.

The author recalls visiting a carbide packaging works many years ago to watch those beautifully-designed tins, which old riders will remember so well, being filled by a hopper device. The worker responsible for despatch remarked that most of their production was destined for Africa, where gas lamps were still in use as recently as the 1950s. Four different colours were used in the container art-work; red, yellow, blue and green. Woe betide the despatch department if they sent a crate of green tins to an area which normally had red! The customers would refuse to accept the unfamiliar tins and one hardware merchant in an isolated outpost was obliged to return an entire consignment, with instructions for the factory to send the correct coloured tins next time!

Gas lamps and the law

Fortunately for vintage motorcyclists certain concessions were made in the MOT Test requirements regarding the fitment of acetylene lighting sets.

Strictly speaking, such equipment is regarded as "of decorative value only" and should therefore be rendered inoperative for the purposes of the Test. If

In contrast, this 1929 Ariel is rather spoilt by the odd-shaped exhaust pipe – perhaps a temporary measure fitted just before the Banbury Run where this photograph was taken.

the writer recalls correctly, an opaque disc should be fitted behind the lamp glass, or the tubing removed. A rear reflector is obligatory. If in doubt, the lighting set can be removed entirely for the MOT Test, in which case the examiner will be obliged to pass the machine providing all other features comply. (It is doubtful if acetylene lamps are legal after lighting-up time, although so far as is known no test case has been brought against a rider thus equipped. A responsible vintage motorcyclist will, of course, exercise due caution at all times.)

Miscellaneous jobs in the workshop

There may be a few younger readers of this work about to embark on their first restoration project, so for their benefit some simple tasks will be described. The fascination of rebuilding old motorcycles lies in the fact that the restorer must indeed be a Jack of all Trades.

Soft soldering

Sooner or later the beginner will find something which needs soldering, or a control cable to make up, so this is one skill he **must** acquire. Incidentally, the expression *sweating* is sometimes used by old hands to describe the joining of two pieces of metal together with soft solder. Tinning simply means the coating of a surface (or soldering iron) with molten solder.

If the novice experiences difficulty in soldering he can take heart from the fact that some motorcyclists with thirty years riding to their credit have similar problems. A few never learn to make a sound joint.

For solder to take the joint must be scrupulously clean and at the right temperature. Too cold and the solder will not flow. Too hot, the surface quickly oxidises and the solder sizzles off in little balls. In the latter condition no amount of flux will help matters as it burns into a hard black crust.

The most common job to be encountered is the making-up and soldering of control cables so this operation will serve as an example of the art.

Equipment needed

The basic essential is a soldering iron — either a large electric model or the old-fashioned copper bit variety. If the latter is preferred, a camping gas-stove gives a clean flame for warming the iron. As for the solder, use either tinmans' in sticks, or cored solder. If you use the former, you will also need flux in paste form.

An old file will come in handy, and have a couple of rags to hand. For shortening the cable inner you will need a flat cold chisel and an anvil (a solid block of metal will do — **not** the top of the vice jaws!) A sharp pair of side-cutters may be required if the outer needs shortening.

Making a cable

1 Bowden inner wire comes in coils. Unravel a length and judge how much is required for the job in hand, by offering it to the machine and tying it up where necessary. Allow for generous sweeps. Make a mark with chalk or pencil where it is to be cut.

2 Tin the area for about 1/2 in either side of the cut mark. This is to stop the wire strands from flying apart when the wire is cut.

Warm-up the iron (if it's the old type, wait until it starts to give off a greenish tinge in the flame) and quickly clean-up the tip with a file. Apply solder and flux and deftly wipe the solder over the copper bit until it is well coated (this is where the old rag comes in). The iron is now tinned — unless a goodly area of the bit is well covered you will never have much success in soldering.

Smear some flux on the Bowden cable. Apply more solder to the iron and tin the cable thoroughly, until the solder is seen to permeate into the strands. At first, most beginners tend to cake the solder on in layers; actually, very little solder is required providing the temperature is right.

3 When you are satisfied that the wire is thoroughly tinned it can be cut. A sharp blow with the cold chisel will sever the wire cleanly.

4 Solder a nipple on one end. In most cases it is better to deal with the handlebar control end last. For example, when making a throttle or air control cable, the first nipple to be soldered on is the tiny parallel one which fits inside the throttle or air slide. Let us assume the nipple is pear-shaped, with a counterbore in one end. Tin the wire as described. Push the nipple on with a light smear of flux. Hold the hot iron on the nipple until it has firmly stuck. Now comes the all-important bit.

The wire strands must now be belled-out (splayed) inside the nipple counterbore by means of a centre-punch or small ball-peine hammer. It is this feature which gives the cable strength. Holding the cable with the nipple downwards apply the iron and run more solder down the wire until the nipple counterbore is completely filled. It is now virtually impossible for the nipple to pull-of.

5 So now you have a length of inner wire with one nipple attached. Measure off a length of outer to suit, leaving room for adjustment (the inner should stick out further than is really necessary, being trimmed to length in the next stage).

Fit end ferrules and cable adjuster (if required). Ferrules should be a good push-on fit. A light tap with a blunt centre-punch on the outside of the ferrule will stop it sliding off (ferrules were originally crimped with a special tool). Feed the inner into the outer, smearing graphited oil on the wire as you go.

6 Temporarily fit the cable. Assuming for a moment it is a clutch control; fit the pear-shaped nipple in the clutch withdrawal arm, screw the cable adjuster home and hold the withdrawal arm in place with an elastic band.

Fix the outer in the handlebar lever and mark off where the barrel nipple should go. Remove the cable, slide the barrel nipple on, tin the wire and cut it to length as previously described. The nipple can now be soldered in position, swaging-out the wire end as outlined in stage 4. Clean-up the nipple with an old file, making sure it is free to swivel in the lever.

Try the control action and make adjustments where necessary. A Bowden outer can be shortened in the following manner (without unsoldering a nipple). Pull the end ferrule off and remove a little of the outer fabric covering; using a pair of side-cutters open out the last metal coil a little and pull endways, then unwind a few turns of outer sheath. Snip off the surplus (watch out for the inner wire — you don't want this severed in the bargain). Replace the ferrule. This method is handy when up to a 1/4 in has to be removed.

Silver soldering

Silver soldering, sometimes referred to as hard soldering, is employed when a much stronger joint is required than could be achieved by ordinary soft-soldering. It is ideal for repairing brass carburettor parts, permanently securing nipples on copper oil or petrol pipes, or when fabricating small steel items.

The beginner will find a low-melting point silver solder easier to handle as there is less chance of melting the parent metal. A very low-melting point material would flow at around 296 to 300 degrees C; still in the low-melting point category a solder such as *Stubs No. 3* melts at 595/630 degrees C and gives a tensile strength of 22 tons/sq in. Generally speaking, the higher the melting point, the greater the tensile strength. *Easy-Flo* is a moderately strong silver solder having a tensile strength of 30 tons/sq in and a melting point of 630°C.

Silver solder consists of silver and copper in various proportions, together with the addition of zinc and cadmium for certain purposes. It is

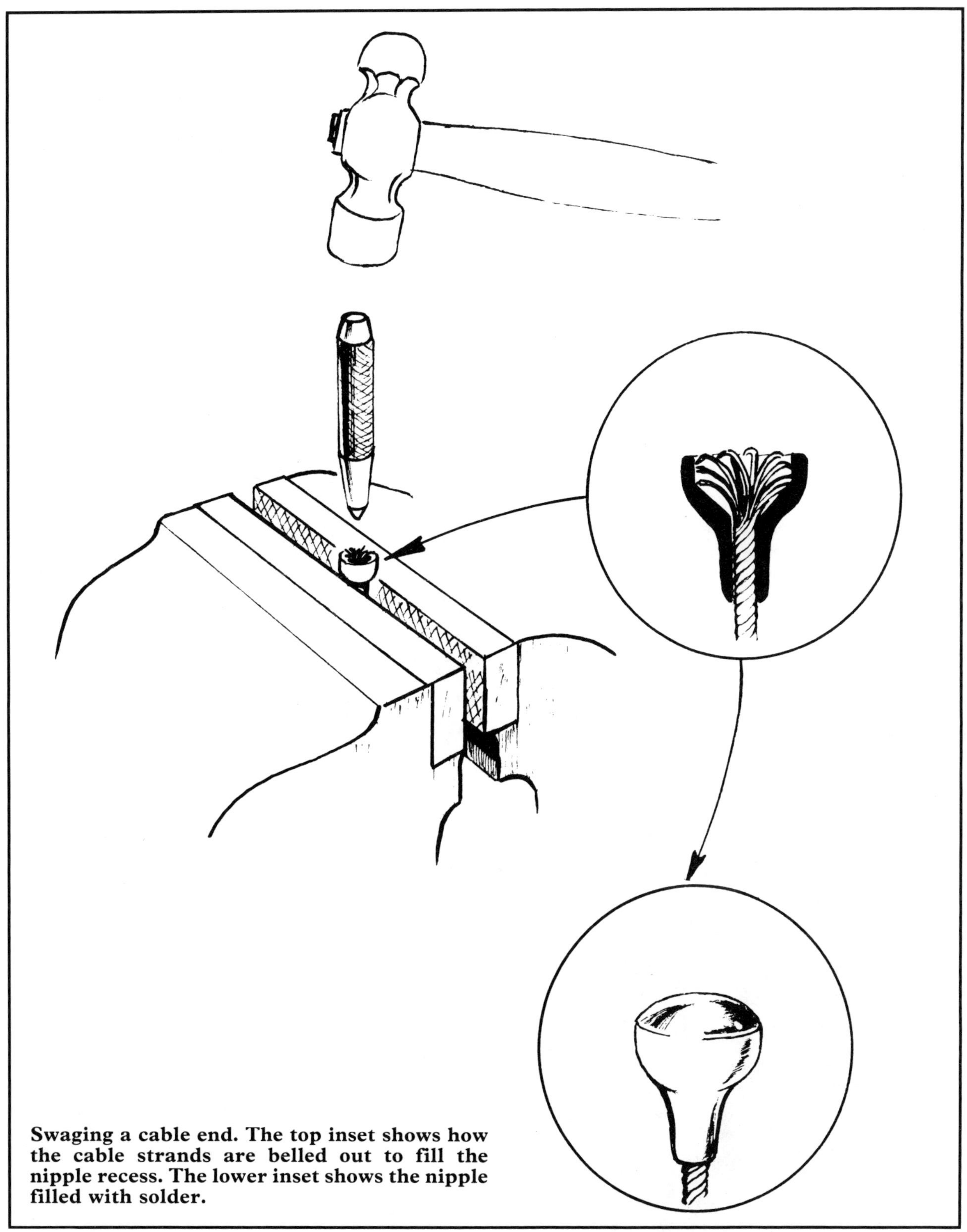

Swaging a cable end. The top inset shows how the cable strands are belled out to fill the nipple recess. The lower inset shows the nipple filled with solder.

available in strip or wire form, and occasionally in small sheets (for instrument makers etc). It also happens to be frightfully expensive, but on the bonus side only minute quantities are needed. Engineers' merchants stock various grades and will usually advise on their suitability for special applications.

As silver solder melts at a far higher temperature than soft solder a soldering iron cannot be used. Small jobs can be handled with a Ronson blowtorch,

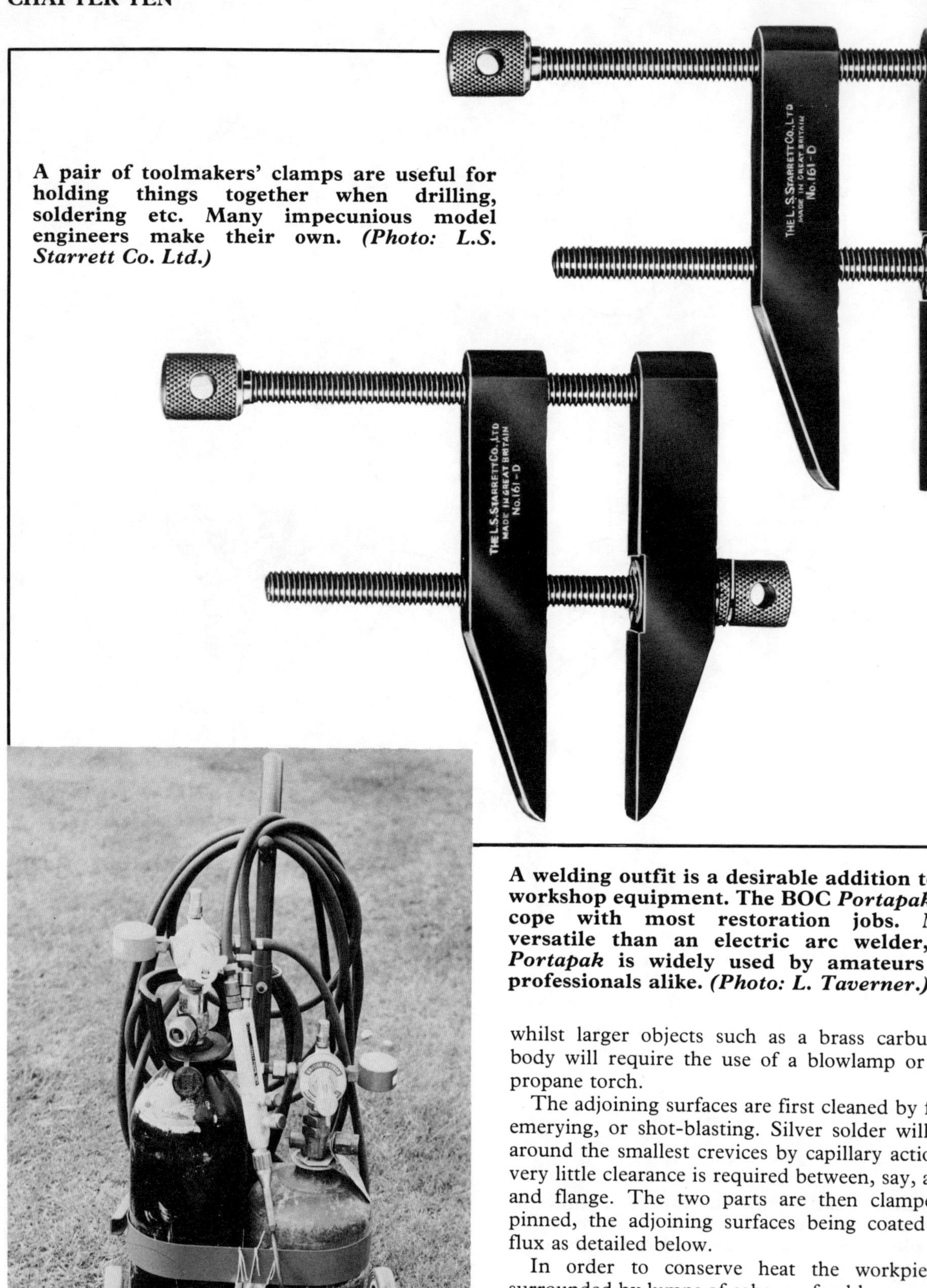

A pair of toolmakers' clamps are useful for holding things together when drilling, soldering etc. Many impecunious model engineers make their own. *(Photo: L.S. Starrett Co. Ltd.)*

A welding outfit is a desirable addition to the workshop equipment. The BOC *Portapak* will cope with most restoration jobs. More versatile than an electric arc welder, the *Portapak* is widely used by amateurs and professionals alike. *(Photo: L. Taverner.)*

whilst larger objects such as a brass carburettor body will require the use of a blowlamp or large propane torch.

The adjoining surfaces are first cleaned by filing, emerying, or shot-blasting. Silver solder will flow around the smallest crevices by capillary action, so very little clearance is required between, say, a pipe and flange. The two parts are then clamped or pinned, the adjoining surfaces being coated with flux as detailed below.

In order to conserve heat the workpiece is surrounded by lumps of coke, preferably on top of a few fire-bricks. (A small hearth can be built up temporarily.) A clean flame is needed for good results; other requisites are a tin of borax and a spatula for applying it. The spatula can be a 6 in length of wire of about 12 swg thickness hammered flat at one end.

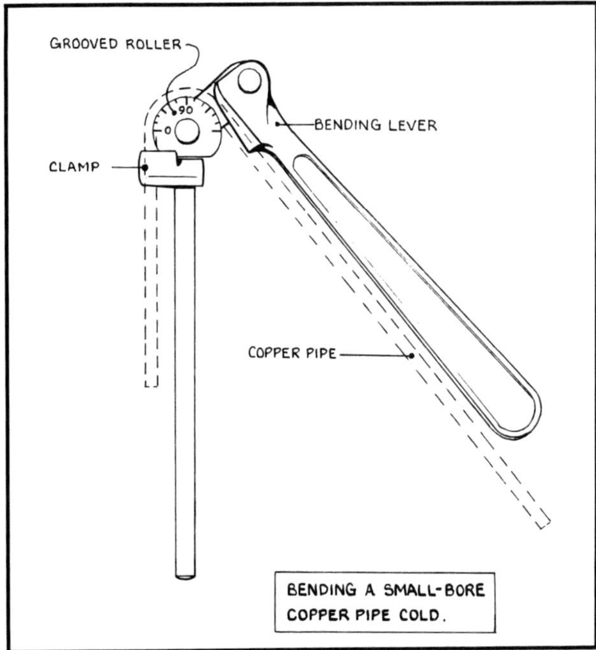

BENDING A SMALL-BORE COPPER PIPE COLD.

Borax flux is in the form of white powder, not unlike common salt in appearance. The best method of application is to mix a little with water in a tin lid and smear the paste on the joint surfaces. Heat up the workpiece gently until the borax is seen to fuse and then bring the torch a little closer and continue heating up to bright red. There are two methods of applying silver solder; the first, directly, with the solder held in a pair of tongs. Some prefer the alternative of snipping off a short piece of silver solder and depositing this on the joint face prior to heating. Very little is required to make a sound joint. Most beginners apply far too much, consequently having to file half of it away afterwards.

As the workpiece is heating up it often helps to apply a little more borax paste, wiping it round the joint line with the spatula. When the correct temperature is reached, the silver solder will suddenly flash around the joint, fully penetrating every crevice. For this to occur, it follows that both parts of the job must attain an equal temperature, so the flame must be played equally on the two components. An obvious point perhaps, but a common pitfall, is to have one bit too cold whilst the other dissolves in a molten heap.

If the job has been done properly, with the minimum of silver solder, the joint should display a neat fillet and no further cleaning-up should be necessary. If the novice finds with chagrin that he has also managed to silver solder the clamping arrangement to the job — not to worry, it happens to the best of us!

Brazing and welding

The process of brazing is very similar to that of silver soldering except that a higher temperature is generally required. Fluxes vary with the type of rods used and temperatures involved (around 600° to 750°C).

The heat source can be bottled gas, for which a large variety of torches and nozzles are available. Purchase the largest size of bottle your pocket will allow.

In the long run a set of oxy-acetylene equipment such as the BOC *Porta-Pak* is the best bet as this can also be used for welding. The *Porta-Pak* features approximately 1/3rd size bottles mounted on a stand, together with torch and gauges etc. If possible, all welding and brazing should be carried out in a separate enclosure, well away from the bikes — for obvious reasons.

Electric arc welding sets are now very popular and can be obtained at modest prices. A set with an operating capacity of at least 140 amps is advisable — anything smaller will limit the thickness of metals which can be joined. Suitable sets are advertised weekly in *Exchange & Mart*.

Almost any metal can be welded these days, although it takes an expert to deal with certain aluminium alloys, magnesium, and fancy tool steels. New rods appear almost weekly, so what was an impossible task a few years ago is now commonplace in professional welding shops.

It is unfortunately not possible to give the reader a crash course in welding within these pages. Indeed, it would require another book of this size to describe the process adequately. There are many publications on the subject of welding, most of them available in public libraries. However, there is no substitute for practical experience. One lesson from a competent welder is worth 10,000 written words on the subject. The beginner should therefore seek the practical aid of a time-served welder or enrol for a night school session.

Pipe bending

Possession of an oxy-acetylene or propane gas outfit will mean that the amateur can extend his horizons into pipe manipulation. New handlebars and exhausts can be formed with the skilful application of heat, whilst smaller tubes are usually bent by means of a proprietary hand tool (available in sizes from 3/16 in up to 3/8 in diameter).

Hot bends

In order to avoid distortion the tube is filled with sand; ordinary sea-shore sand will do providing it is thoroughly dried. The matter of drying is very important to avoid gas pockets when heat is applied.

Plug one end of the pipe with a wooden bung and pour in the sand. As it is being poured, tap the pipe frequently to settle the sand, which must be free from lumps. When the pipe is almost full to the brim, and well compacted, insert another plug. This can be wooden, although some people use rags or wedges of paper.

Make a template of the required curvature from thick wire. It does not really matter whether the template follows the inside or outside radius, or the tube centre-line, so long as you know what you are doing. One end of the tube must be secured in some way, or if it is a simple curve a wooden former can be made. Mark the tube where it is to be bent. The tubing should be longer than is actually required, surplus being cut off afterwards.

Two pairs of hands are better than one when it comes to the bending operation — a helper can wield the torch while you do the bending. A large flame is required and the entire portion to be bent must be thoroughly heated (and this includes the sand inside, which takes a while to warm up). Try to bend the pipe in one smooth action. If you don't quite make it in one go the pipe must be brought up to temperature again. When heating, keep the flame on the move and avoid cold spots.

Thick-walled tube is easier to bend as it is less likely to kink or flatten. Exhaust pipes, which are generally around 18 swg require a modicum of skill in handling so it is advisable to buy enough material for two or three attempts! Handlebars are easily bent due to their comparatively thick-wall section, gradual curves being formed cold and tight joggles hot by the method described, employing special jigs and fixtures.

Precautionary measures

Many of the processes mentioned in this final chapter involve the use of naked flames. A complete conflagration of the workshop and its precious contents is always a distinct possibility unless a few precautionary measures are taken.

Don't store petrol in the workshop and always wheel completed bikes outside when brazing or welding. Have all wiring and electrical appliances checked by a competent electrician. Most importantly, mount a fire extinguisher of approved pattern (local Fire Officers will be happy to advise) in a prominent position. Newly-restored machines have been known to backfire and self-ignite.

One other way of losing your completed masterpiece is to have it stolen. Burglary is, regrettably, on the increase — so always keep the workshop well secure and you should enjoy the fruits of your labour for many years to come.

Happy Riding!

Index